Internet Business: Commerce and Tax

Second Edition

Internet Business: Commerce and Tax

Second Edition

Julian JB Hickey LLB (Hons), LLM (Tax), PhD
Solicitor, Partner, Bird & Bird LLP

With contributions from:

Shiv Mahalingham, Managing Director, Transfer Pricing, Alvarez & Marsal Tax and UK LLP

Colin Kendon, Head of Employee Incentives & Benefits Team, Bird & Bird LLP

JORDANS

Published by
Jordan Publishing Limited
21 St Thomas Street
Bristol BS1 6JS

Whilst the publishers and the author have taken every care in preparing the material included in this work, any statements made as to the legal or other implications of particular transactions are made in good faith purely for general guidance and cannot be regarded as a substitute for professional advice. Consequently, no liability can be accepted for loss or expense incurred as a result of relying in particular circumstances on statements made in this work.

Images created by Gary Bristow, www.garybristow.com.

'The Internet', front cover image: Patent(s) Pending & Copyright © Lumeta Corporation 2000–2011. All Rights Reserved. LUMETA, LUMETA Logo, IPSONAR and the IPSONAR logo are the trademarks and service marks of Lumeta Corporation.

Just-Eat Case Study reproduced by kind permission of the Just-Eat team, www.just-eat.com.

OECD (2001), Attribution of Profit to a Permanent Establishment Involved in Electronic Commerce Transactions; A Discussion Paper from the Technical Advisory Group on Monitoring the Application of Existing Treaty Norms for the Taxation of Business Profits, February 2001, Draft for Public Comment, http://www.oecd.org/ctp/tt.

OECD (2001), Tax Treaty Characterisation Issues Arising from E-Commerce Report to Working Party No. 1 of the OECD Committee on Fiscal Affairs, 1 February 2001, http://www.oecd.org/ctp/tt.

British Library Cataloguing-in-Publication Data

A catalogue record for this book is available from the British Library.

ISBN 978 1 84661 304 3

Typeset by Letterpart Ltd, Reigate, Surrey

Printed in Great Britain by CPI Antony Rowe, Chippenham and Eastbourne

For my family

PREFACE

Over ten years have passed since the first edition, and tax remains a constant issue to be considered for all internet-based businesses and e-commerce transactions. This book examines the corporation tax and VAT issues relevant to the important areas of internet business. It also considers potential tax issues for shareholders in an internet-based company. The first edition coincided with the dot.com bubble bursting in a spectacular fashion in 2000, but we are now witnessing an equally spectacular resurgence in internet-related business activity: for example, in 2011 the Russian search engine Yandex raised over US$1.3 billion from its initial public offering (IPO)[1] and the business networking site LinkedIn was valued at over US$4 billion from its IPO.[2] Ebay announced that mobile commerce is likely to generate almost $5 billion in merchandise volume in 2011 for the company.[3] Facebook has also launched the process for its IPO, which will raise $5bn, giving the company a value of $80bn.[4]

Since the first edition we have also witnessed an explosion of internet-based business and social networking opportunities (such as Facebook, LinkedIn and Twitter), which have marked a radical transformation in how our society communicates and interacts (eg Facebook has some 845m monthly active users).[5] All of this has been achieved with considerable leaps in the development of technology, such as smartphones, which provide access to telecommunications and the internet and so enable us to download digital content from anywhere in the world. All of this facilitates most forms of commerce via the use of information technology.

The internet has marked a dramatic shift in consumer behaviour, specifically a move away from high street shopping to one-click internet shopping from the comfort of our home and workplace. Retailers have had to adapt to the opportunities and challenges of the marketplace by creating and protecting a presence on the global network, and by meeting

---

[1] See www.bloomberg.com ('Yandex jumps on first day in biggest 2011 Tech IPO', 25 May 2011).

[2] See www.reuters.com ('LinkedIn ups IPO range, stokes social media frenzy', 17 May 2011).

[3] Ebay Inc: see www.ebayinc.com/news#20111019006903 (19 October 2011).

[4] *The Financial Times*, 1 February 2012.

[5] As at 31 December 2011. See *The Financial Times*, 1 February 2012.

the demands of supplying goods and services within an international market. The internet provides an electronic portal to both domestic and international markets, which depending on the nature of the supply may represent the provision of services electronically (eg by the downloading of electronic content relating to books, films and games) or the provision of goods by delivery through the retailer or a commercial intermediary.

HMRC is launching a campaign, which is planned to begin in Spring 2012, to encourage traders using e-marketplaces to pay the taxes owed on their activities in circumstances where they are currently delinquent. The necessity to launch a campaign targeting e-traders illustrates the extent to which the e-marketplace has exploded in growth, with the consequential risk to the Treasury of lost revenues where traders fail to pay their taxes.

One reviewer of the first edition commented that, 'this is a useful book; it is a practical guide to the problems of electronic commerce and centres around taxation'. Another commented: 'On the whole, this guide takes a practical approach to the subject and provides practitioners with a good overview of the main tax issues that have evolved.' I hope that the second edition has at least met this benchmark, and that it will provide a first point of reference to matters on taxation of internet business, so that it aids those new to the whole area, whilst also acting as a point of reference for more experienced advisers. The second edition has involved writing new chapters, and considerable updating and reworking of existing chapters to reflect changes in law and the evolution in e-commerce activities, and the sophistication of the issues involved.

The current edition of this book is divided into the following principal parts:

- Part I. This part provides a general overview of the nature of internet business and e-commerce activities. It also provides a summary of the components of the information technology world that underpin the commercial activities of e-commerce.
- Part II. This part provides an overview of the main business structures used to carry on the activities referred to in Part I. It also examines the types of commercial intermediary used to carry out activities in a supply chain. A summary is also provided on contract formation and governing law for commercial contracts.
- Part III. This part provides an examination of the principal direct tax issues that arise for internet business and e-commerce transactions where carried on by a company (which will tend to be the main business form).
- Part IV. This part provides an overview of share-based employee incentives for private technology companies, and the tax issues arising for employee and director shareholders.
- Part V. This part provides an examination of the principal VAT issues that arise for internet business and e-commerce transactions.

- Part VI. This part provides a case study in relation to how an actual internet business is carried on using IT. The case study relates to Just-Eat.co.uk and illustrates the supply chain from IT and commercial perspectives.

We do not cover issues relating to UK customs and excise duty, which are beyond the scope of this edition.

I am grateful for the support of my colleagues at Bird & Bird LLP, in particular the comments of Mathew Oliver and Adam Singer (on direct tax issues), and Caroline Brown (on VAT issues) on the draft of this edition. I am grateful for the contribution of my colleague, Colin Kendon (assisted by Fleur Benns), without whom Part IV would not have existed. Chapter 9 on transfer pricing has been materially enhanced by Shiv Mahalingham agreeing to update it with the benefit of his immeasurable experience. Many thanks to my colleague David Gent, who reviewed Chapter 2 on structures for internet business; and to Adam Gillert who kindly provided comments on Chapter 4; and thanks to Felicity Passmore for help with proof-reading. I would also like to thank the Just-Eat team for contributing the case study at Part VI, and, in particular, Mike Wroe and Marcus Jennings for their time in discussing the Just-Eat business model.

I would like to acknowledge the help of my publishers in preparing this edition, in particular, thanks to Kate Hather for deciding to commission it.

Finally, I would like to thank my wife, Katherine, for her support and encouragement during the long period it has taken to write this edition.

Needless to say, responsibility for any errors and omissions is mine. While all reasonable care has been taken in the preparation of this publication, this book should not be relied upon as a substitute for legal or other professional advice (such as valuation advice) which should be obtained before implementing any new transaction and business structure. Please note especially that tax law and practice can change rapidly and the application of tax law to any particular situation may not be straightforward. The authors would be happy to assist in these situations.

Julian JB Hickey

January 2012

PREFACE TO THE FIRST EDITION

The purpose of this book is to provide a guide from a UK perspective on the business and tax law framework which applies to information technology and e-commerce. This book is the product of a variety of articles and conferences in which I have been involved. It is intended to be of use to both the domestic and international multi-disciplinary practitioner, and for this reason a number of general areas are included.

The book is not intended to be a tax planning manual. Instead, it is designed to ease the non e-commerce specialist into the framework of business and tax law which will apply to their chosen method of e-commerce business. Inevitably, it is impossible to give definitive guidance on an area which is being developed in a piecemeal and somewhat unsatisfactory way. However, it is possible to deal with the basic framework which will apply to e-commerce.

As a starting point for dealing with clients' problems the book is as succinct and as user-friendly as possible. It is hoped that both multi-disciplinary and specialist practitioners will find it of interest in guiding them into this interesting new world.

I would like to thank several people for their assistance in the writing of this book. Foremost, I am grateful to Stephen Honey of Jordan Publishing Ltd for his commitment to publication of this work. My thanks go to Dr David Southern (University of London) for providing useful suggestions, and also for the assistance provided by Gary Mills and Gareth Green (Ernst & Young) who commented on the transfer pricing chapter. I am also indebted to Robin Mathew QC and Dr Christopher Rose for agreeing to contribute their respective chapters.

No doubt, despite the considerable endeavours which have been made in ensuring accuracy, some errors will remain. Any suggestions for improvement in the material are welcomed, and should be addressed care of my publishers.

Finally, a special thank you to my mother for her support and encouragement during the writing of this book.

Julian JB Hickey, Barrister

The Intellectual Property Institute
London
November 1999

CONTENTS

Part II
Internet Business: Legal and Commercial

TABLE OF CASES

References are to paragraph numbers.

TABLE OF STATUTES

References are to paragraph numbers.

TABLE OF STATUTORY INSTRUMENTS

References are to paragraph numbers.

TABLE OF EC MATERIALS

References are to paragraph numbers.

TABLE OF OTHER MATERIALS

References are to paragraph numbers.

LIST OF ABBREVIATIONS

AIA	annual investment allowance
AMV	actual market value
APA	advance pricing agreement
ASCII	American Standard Code of Information Interchange
B2B	business to business
B2C	business to consumer
BIT	binary digit
Brussels Regulation	Council Regulation 44/2001/EC of 22 December 2000 on jurisdiction and the recognition and enforcement of judgments in civil and commercial matters, OJ L 012, 16/01/2001 pp 1–23 (Brussels I)
CA 2006	Companies Act 2006
CAA 2001	Capital Allowances Act 2001
ccTLD	country code top level domain
CDPA 1988	Copyright, Designs and Patents Act 1988
CD-ROM	compact disc read-only memory
CEMA 1979	Customs and Excise Management Act 1979
CGT	capital gains tax
CoJ	Court of Justice of the European Union
CPC	contingent purchase contract
CPR	Civil Procedure Rules 1998, SI 1998/3132
CSOP	company share option plan
CTA 2009	Corporation Tax Act 2009
CTA 2010	Corporation Tax Act 2010
CUP	comparable uncontrolled price
DNS	domain names system
DTA	double taxation agreement
DVD	digital video drive or digital versatile disc
EBT	employee benefit trust
ECJ	Court of Justice of the European Union (also referred to as CoJ)

e-commerce	electronic commerce
EDI	electronic data interchange
EEA	European Economic Area
EEC	European Economic Community
EIS	Enterprise Investment Scheme
e-mail	electronic mail
EMI	enterprise management incentive
ER	entrepreneurs' relief
ESOP	employee share ownership plan
EU	European Union
EU Implementing Regulation	Council Implementing Regulation 282/2011/EU laying down implementing measures for Directive 2006/112/EC on the common system of value added tax (recast), OJ L77/1, 15/03/2011 pp 1–22
FA 2011	Finance Act 2011
FRS 10	Financial Reporting Standard 10, *Goodwill and Intangible Assets* (December 1997, as amended) (Accounting Standards Board)
GAAP	generally accepted accounting practice
gTLD	generic top level domain
HTML	hypertext markup language
ICANN	Internet Corporation for Assigned Names and Numbers
ICTA 1988	Income and Corporation Taxes Act 1988
IE	Internet Explorer (Microsoft)
FY	financial year
IHT	inheritance tax
IHTA 1984	Inheritance Tax Act 1984
Institutions, the	Collective institutions of the European Union: the Commission, the Parliament, the Council and the Court of Justice
Intelsat	International Telecommunications Satellite Organisation
IP	Internet Protocol
IPO	initial public offering
ISP	internet service provider
IT	information technology
ITA 2007	Income Tax Act 2007
ITEPA 2003	Income Tax (Earnings and Pensions) Act 2003

ITTOIA 2005	Income Tax (Trading and Other Income) Act 2005
JSOP	joint share ownership plan
JV	joint venture
LAN	local area network
LLP	limited liability partnership
LLPA 2000	Limited Liability Partnerships Act 2000
MAP	mutual agreement procedure
NIC	National Insurance contribution
NPV	net present value
OECD	Organisation for Economic Co-operation and Development
OECD Model Convention	Model Tax Convention on Income and on Capital (OECD), as it reads on 22 July 2010 (also referred to as 'Model Convention')
OS	operating system
PE ratio	price:earnings ratio
plc	public limited company
QCB	qualifying corporate bond
QuESOP	qualifying employee share ownership plan
R&D	research and development
RAM	random access memory
RCA	readily convertible asset
Rome I	Regulation 593/2008/EC of the European Parliament and of the Council of 17 June 2008 on the law applicable to contractual obligations (Rome I), OJ L 177, 04/07/2008 pp 6–16
SAD	Single Administrative Document
SCCR 2001	Social Security (Contributions) Regulations 2001, SI 2001/1004
SLD	second level domain
SMEs	small and medium-sized enterprises
SOHO	Small Office Home Office
SPA	sale and purchase agreement
SPM	secure payments mechanism
SRA	scientific research association
SSAP 13	Statement of Standard Accounting Practice 13
SSCBA 1992	Social Security Contributions and Benefits Act 1992
T&C	terms and conditions

TCGA 1992	Taxation of Chargeable Gains Act 1992
TCP	Transmission Control Protocol
TEU	Treaty on European Union (Maastricht Treaty) (Maastricht, 7 February 1992, Cm 1934)
TFEU	Treaty on the Functioning of the European Union
TIOPA 2010	Taxation (International and Other Provisions) Act 2010
TOMS	Tour Operators Margin Scheme
UMV	unrestricted market value
URL	uniform resource locator
VAT	value added tax
VATA 1994	Value Added Tax Act 1994
VAT Directive	Council Directive 2006/112/EC on the common system of value added tax, OJ L 347, 28/11/2006 p 1
VC	venture capital
VCT	venture capital trust
VIES	VAT Information Exchange System
WAN	wide area network
WDA	Writing down allowance
WPIIS	Working Party on Indicators for the Information Society (OECD)

PART I

INTRODUCTION

CHAPTER 1

INTERNET BUSINESS

1.1 E-COMMERCE

1.1.1 Introduction

E-commerce markets offer significant rewards for both entrepreneurs and tax authorities throughout the world due to the revenues which can be created in those markets. Investment on a worldwide basis in information technology (IT) for 2011 is forecast to be US$3.6 trillion.[1] Recent research estimates that the global e-commerce market will be worth about €675 billion in 2011.[2] For 2012, it is estimated that total e-retail sales will be worth £77 billion.[3] Focusing on the UK, it is estimated that as a nation we spent £68 billion shopping online in 2011.[4] Another recent report suggests that 42.6% of us are shopping online at least once a week, and that the average individual is spending £71 per month on goods purchased online.[5] A survey carried out by the UK Office for National Statistics shows that in 2009 the value of e-commerce sales by non-financial businesses was £408.3 billion, sales achieved by businesses over a website were valued at £115 billion, e-commerce non-website sales (eg via electronic data interchange (EDI)) were valued at £293.3 billion, and 76% of businesses had a website.[6]

The purpose of this chapter is to examine the nature of the structure and terminology of the e-commerce, IT, e-infrastructure and internet world. Subsequent chapters consider the tax issues associated with setting up an e-commerce business, and the particular tax points that are capable of arising in respect of transactions carried on in the e-commerce and e-infrastructure world. The interaction of tax with IT and the early application of IT by businesses, especially in the context of e-commerce

---

[1] Gartner, available at www.gartner.com: 2011 Press Releases.
[2] See www.imrg.org ('European Online Shoppers to Spend €52 bn in Run-up to Christmas', 17 November 2011).
[3] See www.imrg.org. (Strong finish to 2011 for online sales.)
[4] See www.imrg.org. (Strong finish to 2011 for online sales.)
[5] www.ecommera.com/news/press-releases: *Trading Intelligence Report* (9 August 2010).
[6] *E-commerce and ICT Activity* 2009 (26 November 2010), available at www.statistics.gov.uk/pdfdir/ecom1110.pdf.

transactions, sparked considerable commercial, academic and professional interest.[7] No specific scheme of taxation exists in respect of
internet business transactions. As a result, the setting up and the
day-to-day operation of internet businesses and e-commerce transactions
must be slotted into the general framework of tax law. In 1999 the then
Government adopted the position that no major changes would be made
to existing tax legislation and that no new taxes would be introduced in
respect of e-commerce, whilst reserving its position to adopt changes
where necessary to deal with technological developments.[8] To date there
have been no specific taxes introduced specifically to apply to e-commerce
transactions, but the nature of the technology has resulted in changes to
the value added tax (VAT) rules relating to the place of supply of
services.[9]

Tax issues arise in the context of particular e-commerce and
e-infrastructure activities. For example, what are the circumstances in
which a non-UK e-retailer can be taxed in the UK? In what circumstances
could a UK e-retailer be taxed overseas because of orders received from,
and deliveries made to, another country? Can an internet service provider,
or the operator of a host electronic shopping site via a computer server be
held accountable, as agents, for the tax on profits generated by businesses
using their services? If software is available as a free download what are
the tax consequences of such activities, specifically is the customer liable
to any sales taxes? What are the VAT consequences when a UK customer
accesses a website via a smart phone whilst travelling abroad, and orders
the supply of goods and/or services which are delivered in the UK?

The tax treatment of e-commerce and e-infrastructure is potentially a
complex area. From the outset a distinction must be made between:

(1)   the persons who develop, manufacture and operate IT (ie the
e-infrastructure world); and

(2)   the application of IT for the purposes of carrying on e-commerce
activities on either a business-to-business (B2B) or business-to-
consumer (B2C) basis.

---

[7]   *Intertax* devoted a specific issue to the area dealing with 'International Tax Issues in
Cyberspace' (Vol 25, April 1997) with contributions for the UK, Japan, US, Canada,
Germany and France. Also see *Bulletin for International Fiscal Documentation* Vol 50
(1996), which contains articles in respect of tax and the internet. See Frances M Horner
and Jeffrey Owens 'Tax and the web: new technology, old problems' *Bulletin for
International Fiscal Documentation* Vol 50 (1996) at 516 and David R Tillinghast 'The
impact of the internet on the taxation of international transactions' *Bulletin for
International Fiscal Documentation* Vol 50 (1996) at 524. Another article on the internet
is to be found: M Loten 'Doing business on the internet' *Bulletin for International Fiscal
Documentation* Vol 50 (1996) at 361.

[8]   *Electronic Commerce: The UK's Taxation Agenda* (26 November 1999), para 2.10.

[9]   See Part V, Chapter 22 for more details.

The tax rules that arise in respect of activities referred to in (1) above will be those that are common to many types of business activity. For example, the circumstances in which a company will be taxed by a country, the extent to which relief is given for expenditure on technology used in business and the amalgamation of businesses through mergers and acquisition activity are all issues that arise on a day-to-day basis within the tax system. This book examines the general UK tax framework in the context of internet business, covering matters such as taxes on internet business (Chapter 5), the charge to corporation tax on companies carrying on business in the UK, including reliefs for expenditure on intellectual property rights (Chapter 7), VAT on business supplies (Chapter 17), and specific issues relating to taxation of computer software (Chapters 10 (corporation tax) and 21 (VAT)).

The tax issues that arise in respect of activities referred to in (2) above, in other words, from the application of IT (such as e-commerce), is an area that represents difficulties far removed from traditional tax issues for businesses. Issues include the circumstances in which a tax authority can tax inbound and outbound e-commerce activities, and the circumstances in which VAT applies to internet business transactions. Parts III and V of this book examine specific UK tax rules in the context of internet business activities, covering matters such as taxes on inbound and outbound e-commerce (Chapters 6 and 8), the VAT consequences of supplies of goods and/or services within Europe (Chapters 17 to 20) and the VAT aspects relating to electronically supplied services (Chapter 22).

1.1.2 What is e-commerce?

Any goods or services that are capable of being supplied either digitally or by physical delivery because a contract is entered into via the internet between parties on a B2B or B2C basis represents a form of e-commerce. For these purposes, e-commerce includes the provision of digital content via premium rate telephone numbers (which can be accessed via a personal computer, smartphone, mobile device or interactive digital TV). The UK Government in *Electronic Commerce: The UK's Taxation Agenda* described e-commerce as:[10]

> '... doing business electronically, whether communicating by PC, interactive television, console gaming machine or through high street kiosks. It includes Electronic Data Interchange (EDI), the exchange of documents in structured or coded form between business computers ...'

In the Government's Performance and Innovation Unit report *e-commerce@its.best.co.uk* the following was proposed as a working definition of e-commerce:[11]

---

[10] *Electronic Commerce: The UK's Taxation Agenda* (26 November 1999) para 1.4.
[11] September 1999, para 3.4. The same definition is referred to at para 1.3 of *Electronic Commerce: The UK's Taxation Agenda* (26 November 1999).

'... using an electronic network to simplify and speed up all stages of the business process, from design and making to buying, selling and delivery e-commerce is the exchange of information across electronic networks, at any stage in the supply chain, whether within an organisation between businesses and consumers, or between the public and private sectors, whether paid or unpaid.'

In April 2000 the Organisation for Economic Co-operation and Development (OECD) approved two definitions of e-commerce based on a narrower and broader definition of the communications infrastructure, and these were supplemented by proposed guidelines.[12] The definitions are of use in illustrating the breadth of what comprises e-commerce from both a domestic and cross-border perspective:[13]

'Narrow definition

An Internet transaction is the sale or purchase of goods or services, whether between businesses, households, individuals, governments, and other public or private organisations, conducted over the Internet. The goods and services are ordered over the Internet, but the payment and the ultimate delivery of the good or service may be conducted on or off-line.

Guidelines for the Interpretation of the Definitions (WPIIS proposal April 2001)

Include: orders received or placed on any online application used in automated transactions such as Internet applications, EDI, Minitel or interactive telephone systems

Broad definition

An electronic transaction is the sale or purchase of goods or services, whether between businesses, households, individuals, governments, and other public or private organisations, conducted over computer-mediated networks. The goods and services are ordered over those networks, but the payment and the ultimate delivery of the good or service may be conducted on or off-line.

Guidelines for the Interpretation of the Definitions (WPIIS proposal April 2001)

Include: orders received or placed on any Internet application used in automated transactions such as Web pages, Extranets and other applications that run over the Internet, such as EDI over the Internet, Minitel over the Internet, or over any other Web enabled application regardless of how the Web is accessed (eg, through a mobile or a TV set, etc.)

---

[12] The definitions were developed by the OECD Working Party on Indicators for the Information Society (WPIIS): see *The Statistics Newsletter*, OECD, Issue 2, June 2001, and *ICT Use by Businesses: Revised OECD Model Survey* (DSTI/ICCP/IIS(2005)2/ FINAL), at p 14.

[13] The definitions were developed by the WPIIS. See *The Statistics Newsletter*, OECD, Issue 2, June 2001.

Exclude: orders received or placed by telephone, facsimile, or conventional e-mail.'

The US has defined the term 'electronic commerce' for the purposes of the Internet Tax Freedom Act in the following way:[14]

'... any transaction conducted over the Internet or through Internet access, comprising the sale, lease, license, offer, or delivery of property, goods, services, or information, whether or not for consideration, and includes the provision of Internet access.'

E-commerce represents the application of IT for the purposes of carrying on an economic activity either within a country or on a cross-border basis. As illustrated in Figure 1.1, e-commerce takes many different forms and these depend on e-infrastructure businesses, all of which are dependant on the building blocks of IT.

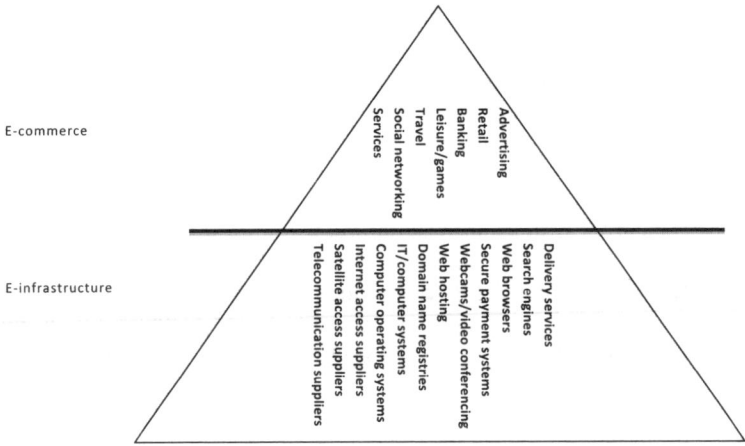

Figure 1.1: E-commerce and e-infrastructure

The essential feature of e-commerce is the supply of services by digital delivery (such as via a website), or the supply of goods under a contract being executed by digital means (such as e-mail (electronic mail) or a website). E-commerce is dependant on e-infrastructure as shown in Figure 1.1, such as telecommunications. The typical characteristics of e-commerce for supplies of digital and physical goods are illustrated below (although each will be specific to the relevant supply chain for a particular business).

---

[14]   7 USC § 151 (1998), HR 4328 at Section 1104(3).

Example 1.1: Digital supplies

Retailer Ltd operates a website through which it markets digital content. The website features several thousand films and music content that can be supplied to customers via digital download directly to computers, smartphones and other portable devices. Customers access the website via their preferred choice, such as smartphone etc (the service of which will be provided independently of Retailer Ltd).

Retailer Ltd's terms and conditions of contract with customers include the following matters relating to the service:

- Retailer Ltd provides an online digital service for the sale and supply of films and music to consumers for non-commercial use;

- Retailer Ltd's services are provided via its website;

- Retailer Ltd uses its website service to provide customers with information concerning the price and availability of digital content;

- to use the website a customer must register an account with Retailer Ltd, with details of a valid bank card to enable payment to be made for services ordered over the website;

- Retailer Ltd provides its customer with a licence to use the digital content for non-commercial purposes;

- Retailer Ltd provides its customers with links to third party websites as a convenience to its own customers, and Retailer Ltd is not responsible in any way for the content or services provided by those third party websites;

- the display of content on Retailer Ltd's website is an invitation to the customer to offer to buy content, and the submission of an order by a customer is an offer to buy content from Retailer Ltd (ie submitting an order is subject to Retailer Ltd's acceptance of the offer);

- Retailer Ltd will be treated as accepting an offer from a customer when notice of acceptance (from Retailer Ltd) is received by the customer via their e-mail account. Once this has occurred a contract has been formed for the supply and payment of the digital content;

- by clicking on the 'check out' button or by ticking a box stating 'I accept the terms and conditions' at the end of the order process the customer consents to be bound by the terms and conditions specified on the website.

The supply chain for Retailer Ltd's website may look like this:

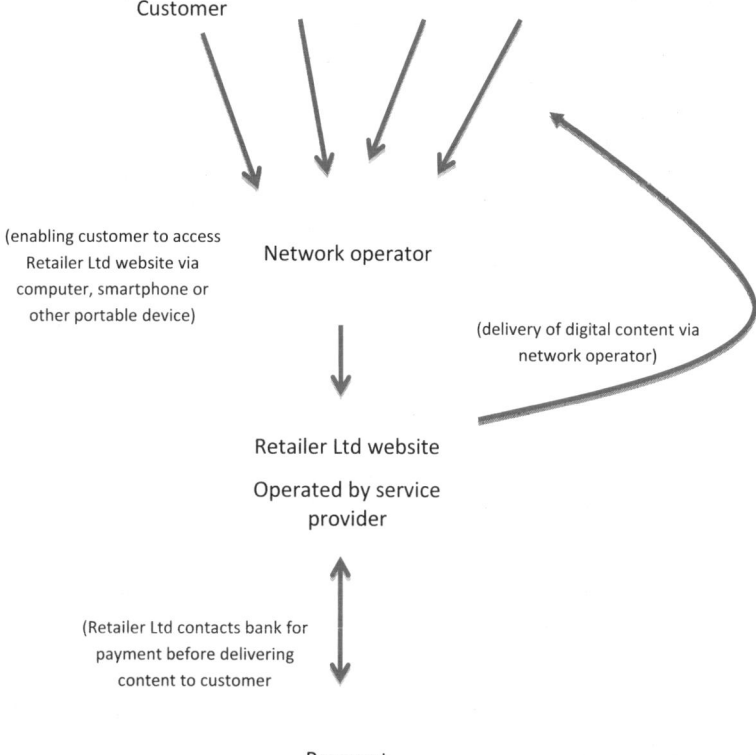

The nature of the supply chain will alter if Retailer Ltd acts as an agent for a third party. If Retailer Ltd supplies digital books to customers, it may do this on behalf of publishers that own the copyright in the books. In these circumstances, the terms and conditions of sale may indicate that Retailer Ltd acts solely as agent on behalf of the publisher; and that a licence is sold by the retailer, as agent, which creates a binding agreement between the customer and the publisher as to the terms of use of the digital book.

It is possible that a supplier may provide internet services that enable the user to store personal content on external storage devices, with the aim of enabling the user to access and synchronise the content with multiple devices (such as computers, smartphones and other portable devices). The terms and conditions of such services will be the subject of a legal agreement between the supplier and user. These services may be made available either for free or on a subscription basis (either initially or once usage reaches a specific level).

Example 1.2: Physical goods

If Retailer Ltd supplies goods to customers the e-commerce aspects of the supply will be very similar to supplies of digital content. Both types of supply will use e-infrastructure to enable customers to access the website, and the same type of payment mechanisms will be used. However, the delivery process will be different, by the very nature of the content being supplied. Digital products will be delivered via the internet as a direct download to a customer's device, whilst physical goods will be delivered by the postal system or specialist courier services. Retailer Ltd's conditions of contract with customers in these circumstances are likely to include the following additional matters:

- all goods shown on the website are available for delivery within specific locations (eg the UK, Channel Islands, Europe, North America);

- all goods are subject to availability;

- Retailer Ltd reserves the right to substitute any goods with goods of equivalent value and quality without any notice to the customer;

- the method of creating a binding contract between the retailer and customer may be specified as taking place only on acceptance of the order, which is treated as taking place only on despatch to the customer of the goods that have been ordered;

- goods are delivered as specified in the order unless a specific date is chosen by the customer;

- prices advertised on the website exclude delivery charges, which are payable in addition;

- title to any goods will only pass to the customer on delivery provided that the retailer has received payment in full for the goods;

- details of specific delivery arrangements and price charges (eg same day delivery, before or after 1 pm deliveries etc);

- deliveries are not made on Sundays or public holidays, and orders will be delivered on the next working day;

- delivery is subject to Retailer Ltd's reasonable endeavours and other specific issues relating to when third party courier services are used, when courier unable to make delivery etc.

Contracts will be subject to other terms and conditions which are required by law (this is considered further in Chapter 4). The characteristics of contracts for the supply of services/goods, shown above, are a general overview only and it is not intended to be a full analysis of all relevant provisions in such agreements.[15]

Example 1.3: Telecommunication services

E-commerce is dependant on e-infrastructure, such as telecommunications. Each person in the supply chain, whether business or customer, will have a contract with one of the participants in the e-infrastructure world. Customers will have some form of arrangement with a telecoms company, whether rental of a fixed land line or a mobile phone. The terms and conditions of the contract will cover a wide range of matters, such as the nature of services supplied, access to the network, user guides, changes to the service, call prices (with VAT to be added to charges), termination, etc. The contract with a provider will also usually deal with premium-rated calls (see **1.1.3**), text messaging services and multi-media messaging services. Where a mobile phone is provided to a customer because they have agreed to enter into a telecom services agreement for a minimum period then the phone is typically provided for no charge or for a charge (reflecting a material discount on its normal price). However, if the agreement is cancelled then the phone will typically be returned to the supplier.

1.1.3 Telecom premium rate services

Telecommunication suppliers provide special number services to businesses. One example of this is the '0800' prefix, which indicates that a free phone service is offered. A person who dials this number is not charged. Instead the call is charged to the business organisation using the 0800 number. Some phone numbers designated by a telecom provider represent a premium rate service. These services are charged to the user via their landline account or mobile phone account. Premium rate numbers are indicated, typically, by an '09', '118', '0871', '0872' or '0873' prefix in the UK.[16] Premium rate number services are capable of being used by telephone, computer (internet or bulletin board), mobile phone (SMS) or interactive digital TV.

Calls made by a person to these numbers are at premium rate to cover the costs of the company providing the service. A percentage of the call charge will be paid to the telecom provider, which enables the business using the premium rate number to be funded through use of that number. The content provided is typically access to a live conversation forum, to an advice line, to financial information or to customer support services. The call charge is at a high rate to cover the costs of providing the service, and the costs of the telecom provider in ensuring that the facilities to run these special services are in place (eg 24/7 availability). Agreements exist

---

[15] This is not intended as a substitute for obtaining legal advice on the matters set out in this chapter and Chapter 4.

[16] Numbers beginning 0871, 0872 and 0873 (where the price paid per minute is 5 pence or more) are regulated by PhonepayPlus (see www.phonepayplus.org.uk).

between the telecom provider and the service company. These agreements will have their own tax implications, such as VAT on fees for services (see Part V, which examines VAT).

The scope of services that are capable of being provided through premium rate telecom numbers is extensive. The regulator of the numbers with the prefix '0871', '0872' or '0873' lists the following as an illustration of the services, which are capable of being provided:[17]

Live Psychic/Tarot and Horoscope Services	Pay-per-page or Image Services
Live Chat Services	Consumer Credit Services
Live Entertainment Services	Virtual Chat Services
Subscription Services	Childrens Services
Competition Services	Betting Tipster Services
Customer Support Services	Advice Services
Data Capture Services	Directory Enquiry Services
Interactive Broadcast Services	Pay for Product Services
Technical Support/Information Services	International Call Routing Services
Sexual Entertainment Services	Contact and Dating Services
Professional Advice Services Counselling Services	Fundraising and Charitable Promotion Services
Remote Gambling Services	Anonymous SMS Services

The provision of these services will have tax implications for the supplier, such as the circumstances of when VAT should be charged on supplies to domestic and international users (see Part V which examines VAT). The supply chain for the provision of premium rate services to a user will typically be as shown in Figure 1.2.

Within the supply chain shown in Figure 1.2 the network operator will receive the fees relating to the premium rate number. The user will pay the fees via either a landline account or a mobile account. The network operator will share a percentage of the revenues generated by the telephone number with the service provider. A service provider would generally expect to receive a percentage of the fees generated each time the premium rate number is called, based on the duration of the call. The service provider may either deliver the content directly to the user or it may subcontract the provision of the content to a third party. Where a third party, under a sub-contract, provides the content the user will generally only perceive a seamless service being provided by the service provider (and not from the third party). The service provider will generate business through advertising the premium rate number via e-mail, internet search engine browsers, adverts in newspapers and on TV.

---

[17]   See PhonepayPlus at www.phonepayplus.org.uk/For-Business/New-to-PhonepayPlus/ Service-Types.aspx (June 2011).

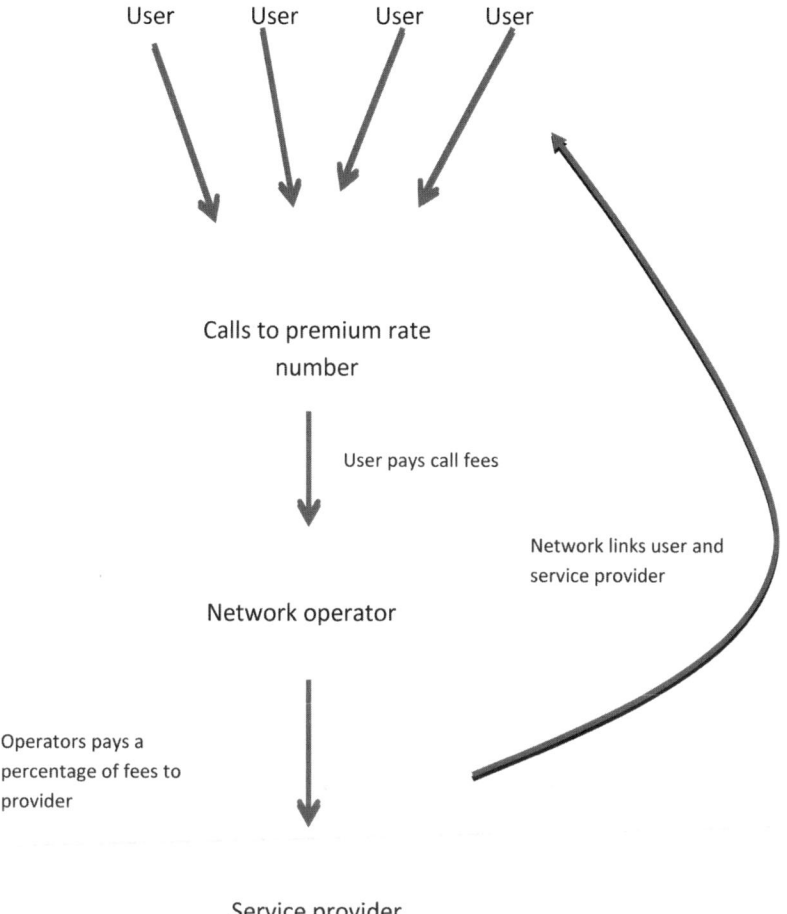

Figure 1.2: Typical supply chain for the provision of premium rate services to a user

A network operator will probably deal with some service providers on a direct basis because of the likely volume of calls (and therefore profits) that those clients will generate. However, smaller service providers which generate lower call volumes are likely to be dealt with by a reseller acting on behalf of the network operator. The reseller will have an agreement with the network operator whereby the smaller clients are dealt with by them in terms of providing premium rate numbers, and in consideration of which the network operator receives a percentage of the revenues which are generated using the premium rate number.

1.2 INFORMATION TECHNOLOGY

1.2.1 IT: the e-infrastructure bedrock

IT is the bedrock of the e-infrastructure world; without IT there would be no e-commerce capable of being carried on either within the UK or on a cross-border basis. IT enables information of varying types, such as sound, images and raw data, to be transferred across long distances in the twinkling of an eye. There can be no doubt that IT has also revolutionised the workplace. The rapid evolution of SOHO[18] as a result of the development of mobile computing and mobile telecommunication technology has transformed the way people work, with many now in a position to work outside the office (sometimes referred to as 'telecommuting' or 'web commuting'). This raises the possibility of people working outside the UK where employed by a person in the UK. In this regard, an individual may be subject to taxes in the UK and also in the country in which they live and work.

IT has received statutory recognition in UK law. For example, one interpretation is provided by the Carriage of Goods by Sea Act 1992, which provides in s 5 that:

> '"information technology" includes any computer or other technology by means of which information or other matter may be recorded or communicated without being reduced to documentary form.'

The same definition is adopted in s 57 of the Police Act 1996. For the purposes of the Local Government Act 1988, the term had the following meaning prior to that Act's repeal by the Local Government Act 1999:[19]

> '"information technology" means any computer, telecommunications or other technology the principal use of which is the recording, processing and communication of information by electronic means.'[20]

1.2.2 Components of IT: how does a computer work?

IT is the technology we use to maintain and process information. This technology comprises hardware, which is represented by the physical plastic boxes, wires, keyboards and screens, with which we are familiar in using at home and at work. Everything we see when a computer is turned off is hardware. When the computer is turned on, like many other pieces of equipment, it follows a series of instructions. These instructions are called programs, which enable the computer to perform a wide variety of tasks (such as word processing, sending e-mails, performing mathematical calculations, gaming, editing digital photographs – the possibilities are

---

[18] Small Office Home Office.
[19] With effect from 2 January 2000.
[20] Sch 1, para 14.

almost limitless). Usually, programs are not created by the individual user of the computer, but either come pre-installed or are purchased separately and installed (copied from a device, such as DVD, or transferred by electronic download) onto the computer's hard drive at a later date. Software can be bought on the high street, by mail order and by 'downloading' (copying) from the internet. Computer programs can contain thousands, sometimes several millions, of separate instructions.

A detailed review of how a computer and the internet work is beyond the scope of this book, but a general overview is provided in the following sections.[21]

When a programmer writes a line of a basic program, it will look something like:

    if item:stocklevel<100, then reorder(item)

It may not be easily intelligible to a layman, but, to us, it does have recognisable words and, sometimes, an understandable sequence of logic. A computer, however, cannot understand instructions in this form. The instruction has first to be converted (using a special piece of software called a compiler or interpreter) into a form that the computer can process. This form is binary notation and it is used for storing computer programs and data.

Binary notation uses only two digits, 0 and 1, compared with the ten digits in decimal notation. However, these two digits can be combined to form infinite variations of numbers, or codes, which are used to transfer messages to the computer's microprocessor (the 'brain' of the computer).

Computers are powered by electromagnetism. Regardless of the voltage, an electrical current within the computer, or a section of computer disk or DVD, is either ON or OFF, or magnetised or not magnetised, or up or down, etc. Computers can 'read' the on/off messages of binary codes.

In decimal notation, we recognise the value of the number 215, almost without thinking. The last digit, 5, denotes the number of single units, the middle digit, 1, the number of tens and the first digit, 2, the number of hundreds. More digits to the left indicate ten times the value of the digit to the right: thousands, tens of thousands, etc.

In binary notation, the far right digit, as with decimals, denotes the number of single units. The next digit from the right denotes the number

---

[21] See books such as A Clements *Principles of Computer Hardware* (Oxford University Press, 2006) and R White, *How Computers Work* (QUE, 1999) for a detailed examination.

of twos, the next the number of fours, eights, 16s, 32s, 64s, 128s, and so on. So, the decimal number 215 would be expressed, in binary notation, as:

1 1 0 1 0 1 1 1

Reading from the left, there is one 128, one 64, no 32, one 16, no 8, one 4, one 2 and one 1.

128+64+16+4+2+1=215.

A computer needs many programs to function. When it is switched on an operating system (OS) is initiated. This takes care of the nuts and bolts of the computer: how to respond to key presses and mouse clicks, how to read the media such as hard drives and USB ports, whether a CD-ROM[22] or DVD[23] drive is present, how to allocate document and data files to disk space, and so on. Popular operating systems are the all-conquering MS Windows in its various versions (XP, Vista, Windows 7) and the Apple Mac OS Lion.

When the OS has done its initial start-up work, the computer user can select, from an onscreen menu or by clicking a desktop icon, an application system to run 'on top of' the OS. This could be an accounts system, word-processing, stock control, video-conferencing program or any of thousands of other downloadable systems.

As information is entered into a computer, a combination of the application system (e g word processing) that is currently being used and the OS will convert the key-presses into binary code and allocate resources for the data to be processed (in 'RAM' (random access memory)) then permanently stored, if necessary, on the computer's hard drive, either inside the computer or somewhere (such as via an external storage server, like the iCloud) else via a fixed or wireless network connection.

The software will have been programmed to recognise what type of data is being inputted by its human user, and to what real-world entity it relates. A stock-control system, for example, will store the number of an item in stock, number on order, delivery times, etc as purely numeric binary values. A stock item description is stored as a series of binary codes representing letters and other characters. There are various universal coding systems for this, the most well-known being ASCII (the American Standard Code of Information Interchange) in which capital A is represented by 65, B by 66, etc. There are other codes for lower-case letters and characters such as punctuation. In a word-processing system, almost all input will be stored this way. Other types of data are

---

[22] Compact disc read-only memory.
[23] Digital video drive.

programmed to hold dates (usually as an internal numeric value, which is then interpreted and displayed as a date), logical values (simply Yes or No which can be represented by one binary digit, or 'BIT'), images and sound will be treated in a similar way. Each of these separate pieces of data is stored in a 'field'.

A collection of fields, holding information about, say, one stock item, is called a 'record'; many records holding information about all stock items are held in a file.

People familiar with spreadsheets tend to view records as 'rows' and fields as 'columns'. Often, several files storing related data are called a 'relational database'. This would include files for stock movements, suppliers, orders placed, usage, sales, etc, which are linked together to enable the user to view information from various viewpoints.

Software is written by developers, who may be individuals or corporates such as Microsoft, and is distributed via CD-ROM, DVD or the internet. The latter forms of media are either inserted or downloaded to the computer, which then copies and installs the program onto the hard drive of the computer, or network of connected computers. These physical information carriers raise specific tax issues.

The sale of a CD-ROM or DVD does not represent a sale of the right to commercially exploit the software on it. The software is primarily protected by a range of intellectual property rights, the most important of which is copyright. Inherent within any transaction involving the purchase of software incorporated on a physical media is the distinction between the sale of the physical carrier, such as the DVD, a coated piece of plastic, and the software, the use of which is licensed. Where software is acquired directly onto the computer via a download over the internet there will only be a licence of the software that is entered into by the end user.

The following is a typical licensing clause, which might be incorporated into the software user contract where the software is delivered using physical media:

> Ownership of software: As licensee, you own the media upon which the software is fixed, but the owner retains title and ownership of the software recorded on the original media and all subsequent copies of the software regardless of the form or media in which or on which the original and other copies may exist. This licence is not a sale of the software or any copy.

For tax purposes the drafting of such a clause is important because many tax jurisdictions make a distinction between a licence for intellectual property rights, such as copyright, and a sale or lease of physical property (ie the media upon which the software is delivered). In some situations, the person paying for the use of a licence, ie the licensee, must deduct tax at source (called withholding tax) on the payment for the use of the right.²⁴ In some cases, the hardware, such as a replacement microprocessor (the central processing unit of a computer) is sold outright, whilst the software permanently encoded on it will be licensed.²⁵ In this situation, it is arguable that 'withholding tax' should not be applied in respect of the payment, which can be attributed to the right to use the software, which forms part of the physical microprocessor. However, in recent years, some tax authorities have shown a keen interest in deconstructing 'package prices'. A package price is an inclusive price for the use of the physical goods and the intangible property such as a licence to use computer software. Tax administrations that disaggregate package prices are usually those which impose withholding taxes on payments for the use of intangible property.

Example 1.4

X Ltd, incorporated in Country A, sells 100,000 hardware components to Y Inc, an associated company incorporated and trading in Country B. The hardware components contain a software element, which is the subject of intellectual property protection (owned by X Ltd). The sale price of £1million for the hardware components is a package price that includes an amount for a licence to use the software element. The tax authority of Country B disaggregates the package price and requires the purchaser (as licensee of the copyright) to apply 20% withholding tax (£200,000) to the amount attributable to the software licence.

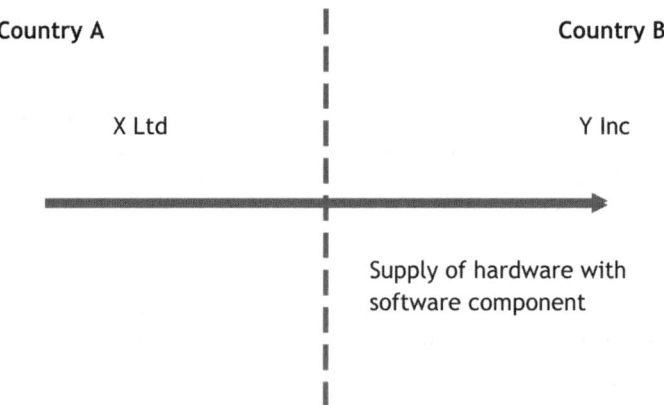

1.2.3   Interaction of hardware and software

It is important to remember that the software recorded on a CD-ROM, DVD, USB key or the hard drive within a computer is nothing more than

---

²⁴ See Chapters 6 (Inbound UK E-Commerce: Scope of Charge to Tax) and 8 (Outbound UK and International E-Commerce: Scope of Charge to Tax).

²⁵ See generally C Reed and J Angel (eds) *Computer Law* (Oxford University Press, 6th edn, 2007) for an analysis of the rights and obligations arising in respect of information technology and its exploitation.

a series of binary codes, which are read into the computer's microprocessor (which is in essence the brain of the computer). This microprocessor distributes instructions to the computer's hardware components so that they may perform the tasks required to accomplish the purposes of the specific program. For example, the microprocessor may direct the computer's monitor to show a group of icons linking to other specific programs (eg e-mail, search engines etc) when it is turned on.

1.2.4   Computer networks: linking IT together

E-commerce depends upon the ability of each computer user being able to communicate with each other through the medium of their actual hardware (whether it be a computer located at home/work or a mobile device). In this regard, e-commerce specifically depends upon a computer being able to be part of a network of other computers. Each computer attached to a network contains the necessary connection circuitry and software, which enables them to talk with each other. Computers communicate with each other across different networks through a special language called the Transmission Control Protocol (TCP). Each computer that forms part of a network will have TCP installed on it. The effect of TCP is that it breaks information down into separate 'packets' of data.

A computer user who sends an e-mail with an attachment will see a single e-mail containing the information that is intended for the recipient. However, the sending computer will use TCP to break that e-mail into multiple packets of data, which are then transmitted across to the recipient network. The recipient computer then uses TCP to reassemble the packets of data to reflect the format in which the information was sent. The method by which the packets of data find their way to the intended recipient computer is known as the Internet Protocol (IP).[26]

Often the computers within a network are connected to a central store called a 'server', which serves the computers in the network with available software and data. This allows each computer to have access to the same software and to the same data, as necessary. A network of computers may be connected directly by cable or wireless. In addition, the network allows communication between individual computers within a business organisation via e-mail.

In a computer network, most processing is carried out locally (a specific computer) and the results of the processing are returned to the server for storage. Larger mini or mainframe computers carry out all their processing centrally, and communicate with users via 'dumb' terminals. If any computer attached to a network fails, the network normally continues

---

[26]   For further details on how the TCP/IP protocols operate to transfer data across the internet see **1.3**.

to function, and, as most data and programs are 'backed up'[27] automatically on the server, the failed computer can be replaced.

A local area network (LAN) normally covers a single site within a business organisation. A wide area network (WAN) covers several geographical sites, but usually with dedicated cable connections, often using existing telephone lines. A LAN, or WAN, is an effective and efficient method of updating and sharing information between organisations for business purposes. The cost of installing a LAN network can often qualify for tax relief as an expense of carrying on a trade.[28]

A network may be formed as an 'intranet' within a business so that only specific computers in that organisation can access common information. Access to the intranet will be 'firewalled' so that other external computers cannot access its information. If computers outside the network are permitted access, then the network is commonly referred to as an 'extranet'.

1.2.5   Fixed networks

The network through which information passes may be fixed, in other words there are permanent links between the computers (such as within an office environment): typical of a LAN; or flexible, as where a mixture of internal 'hard-wired' and external connections are used, such as a WAN. Prior to the advent of the internet, networks had to use common operating systems to be able to access information stored in a way specific to their type of computer attached to the network. However, internet technology (eg TCP/IP), enables information to be shared between a wide diversity of hardware and software technologies.

1.2.6   Flexible networks

In a flexible network, the passage of information from sender to recipient will not always follow the same route; such a network is referred to as a 'packet-switching' network and at the heart of such networks are 'routers'. Each message and request for access to particular information, initiated using a computer, carries an address or locator. The routers built into a flexible network will find a route for the message or request, in theory the fastest, to its destination. A router is akin to a dynamic car satellite navigation system, which directs the car towards its intended destination by the quickest and most efficient route, avoiding any traffic jams on the network. Within a packet-switching network it is possible that a stream of information, which is split into packets, will arrive at their

---

[27]   Back-up: copy of software and data, which can be re-loaded in the event of a technology failure.

[28]   See Chapter 7.

destination in a different order from which they were sent. However, the recipient computer will then reassemble the information into the appropriate format. In other words, data that is sent across the internet, such as web pages, e-mail and files is divided into 'packages'. Each package contains details relating to the sender, recipient and where that 'package' belongs within the overall data stream. If any piece of IT within the network fails or is the subject of a material delay then a router can redirect the package via the quickest alternative route.

1.3   THE INTERNET

1.3.1   Introduction

An examination of the history of the internet is beyond the scope of this book. Many valuable works are available that explore its evolution.[29] *The Road Ahead* by Bill Gates describes the internet and its historical background in the following terms:[30]

> 'The internet is a loose collection of interconnecting commercial and non-commercial computer networks. The constituent networks are tied by telecommunications lines and by their shared reliance on standard communication protocols (rules). This decentralized structure makes sense when you consider the origin of the internet.
>
> The internet is an outgrowth of a government network called the ARPANET, which was created in 1969 by the Defense Department so that defense contractors and researchers could continue to communicate even after a nuclear attack. Rather than try to harden the network against nuclear weapons, ARPANET's designers decided to make it resilient by distributing its resources in a completely decentralized way – so that destruction of any part of the network, or even most of it, wouldn't stop the overall flow of information. The network quickly found favour among computer scientists and engineers in industry and universities and it became a vital communication link among far-flung collaborators.'

The internet is, in simple terms, a vast flexible network of networks that are connected by routers using varied communication highways (such as fixed data lines, satellites and wireless connectivity). This is possible because of the development of software that is not 'platform dependent'; in other words, computers of differing architectures and operating systems are able to communicate and understand each other.

---

[29]   J Ryan *A History of the Internet and the Digital Future* (Reaktion Books, 2010); J Naughton *Brief History of the Future: Origins of the Internet* (Phoenix, 2nd revised edn, 2000).

[30]   Penguin, 1996, at pp 110 and 111.

The US has provided a legal definition of the internet for the purposes of the Internet Tax Freedom Act.[31] Under s 155(6) the Act defines the term 'internet' as meaning:

> '... the combination of computer facilities and electromagnetic transmission media, and related equipment and software comprising the interconnected worldwide network of computer networks that employ the Transmission Control Protocol/Internet Protocol, or any predecessor or successor protocol, to transmit information.'

The UK Government's Performance and Innovation Unit report *e-commerce@its.best.uk* defines 'internet' as 'an "open" network allowing anyone to exchange data – as opposed to a "closed" system such as an Extranet'.[32] The term 'Extranet' is defined as: 'A "closed" network, accessible only to certain organisation or individuals, that operates using Internet technology.'[33]

1.3.2   Internet structure

A basic illustration of the internet is shown in Figure 1.3 below.

1.3.3   Telecom infrastructures: cables

The internet is dependent upon domestic and international telecommunication infrastructures incorporating copper cables, fibre-optic cables, radio and satellite communication. Internet data is transferred throughout a country's telecommunication network; but cross-border data has to be transferred between country networks via high speed submarine cables and satellites. The worldwide submarine network has several advantages, such as reliability and security. In addition it is usually more cost-effective than satellite communication.[34] This form of infrastructure facilitates e-commerce in all of its guises (ie retail shopping, video-conferencing, e-mail, etc). However, it seems likely that the future of worldwide communication with remote areas lies with geo-stationary satellite communication, which requires no physical transmission medium over most of its course.

The first commercially viable transatlantic cable, known as 'TAT-1', was laid between Scotland and Newfoundland in 1956. Many more of these cables have since been laid across the North Atlantic and Pacific Oceans, and digital technology has enabled far more separate 'messages' to be conveyed over one cable. For example, the transatlantic cable called 'TAT-14' is the fourteenth such cable to have been commissioned to

---

[31]   HR 4105. See US Code, Title 4, Chapter 6 – Moratorium on certain taxes, ss 151–155.
[32]   September 1999, p 125.
[33]   September 1999, p 125.
[34]   For further details see the International Cable Protection Committee website at www.iscpc.org (2011).

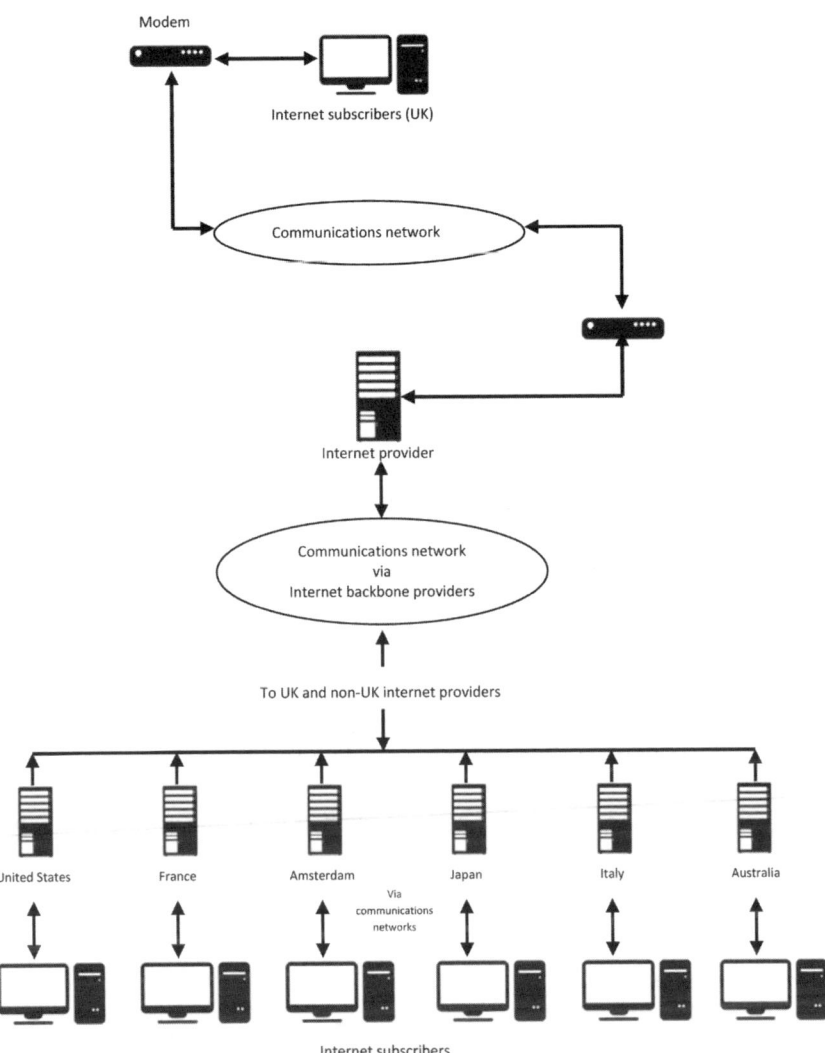

Figure 1.3: Basic structure of the internet

convey telephone data between the US and Europe (with landing points in the UK, Denmark, France, Germany and The Netherlands).[35] The cable, known as 'SEA-ME-WE 4' (approximately 20,000 km long), links three continents and has landing points in 14 countries (including France, Egypt, Saudi Arabia, Pakistan, India, Malaysia and Singapore). These cables have landing points in specific countries, and are operated by cable

---

[35] For details of the worldwide infrastructure relating to these submarine cables see www.underseacable.net (2011).

stations located at the landing points. The cables are usually of fibre-optic construction with armoured protection to maximise their economic life under the oceans.

Telecommunication suppliers make profits by offering their networks as a conduit for the transfer of data, or for carrying voice signals or images. Revenues are generated from fees paid by businesses and individuals for use of the telecommunication network; and from leasing permanent lines, with the capacity to carry large data traffic, to internet service providers (ISPs).[36] Telecommunication suppliers will also source revenues from fees paid by third parties for using cable ducts and telegraph poles for the purpose of enabling those third parties to lay their own fibre-optic cables. In a domestic context agreements will exist between telecommunication providers and other business entities, such as ISPs, for the permanent use of specific lines on the network.

1.3.4   Telecom infrastructure: satellites

Satellites are able to transmit data representing images and sound by using radio and microwaves. Given the curvature of the planet and the fact that radio and microwares only travel in straight lines it is necessary for a geo-stationary satellite to be used for the transfer of data streams around the world. The effect of a geo-stationary satellite is that it can 'see' over the horizon, with the result that such a device can receive data and almost simultaneously re-transmit the data to another part of the world.

Such a satellite is controlled and maintained in a constant position above the earth by a control centre. The satellite and its control centre once tended to be owned by intergovernmental organisations, such as Intelsat[37] (International Telecommunications Satellite Organisation) or government bodies, whereas the sending and receiving stations are typically owned by telecommunication companies within each country. However, Intelsat's operations are now owned by a non-government company located in Luxembourg, which operates the world's largest fixed satellite services business.[38]

An illustration of the nature of services that can be delivered using satellite technology in the context of e-commerce are provided by the business of Intelsat. The company provides satellite communications services worldwide, supplying video, data and voice connectivity across the world.[39] A company like Intelsat earns revenue by selling satellite

---

[36]   Individuals and all but the largest companies do not maintain their own internet network. Instead they use an ISP, which allows a specific computer to become, usually via a telephone line, connected to a large network. ISPs include BT, AOL, Virgin and Sky.

[37]   See www.intelsat.com (2011).

[38]   See www.intelsat.com (2011).

[39]   See www.intelsat.com (2011).

transponder capacity to its clients, whilst also creating revenue through the sale of end-to-end managed communications services.[40]

Satellite operators will provide a wide range of services to customers. These include providing long-distance telephone and data services to telecommunications operators throughout the world. Additionally, broadcasters will require the services of satellite communications in order to transmit news, sports and entertainment programmes, and financial institutions will need access to their services in order to achieve rapid credit verification and authorisation for some transactions. Multinationals operating throughout different sectors will also require such communication services to facilitate their global operations. ISPs use satellite technology to enable their customers to gain access to internet sites in other countries where it is most cost-efficient.

1.3.5 Routers

Computer networks interconnect with other networks throughout Europe and the world. In this way, information can be transferred across continents. The points of connection between the networks are linked by what are known as 'routers'. A router is a computer with a single purpose: to seek out the fastest route by which to send information/data. Often this information is broken down into small 'packets' which may themselves be sent via different routes, reassembling themselves into a coherent whole at the recipient's end. In essence the function of a router is to prevent data being transferred to the wrong destination. A router is programmed with a specific set of rules, which tell it in what direction a 'packet' of data should be sent with a particular address attached to it. The following example illustrates the interconnectivity provided by routers within a flexible network.

Example 1.5

Alpha Ltd has an internet account with Internet Service Provider (ISP1) which is based in Country A and ISP1 uses Network 1. Alpha Ltd sends an e-mail, including a file attachment, to a client in Australia, who has an internet account with ISP2, which uses Network 4 (based in Australia).

Each network is located in different countries. There is no fixed network between Network 1 and 4. Once the e-mail and attachment is sent from the computer at Alpha Ltd, the computer will use its TCP/IP language to divide the data into separate packages (each containing information as to where it belongs within the data stream, the identity of the sender and recipient). The routers operating within Network 1 will scan the packages and will recognise the address of the sender and recipient (by reference to a table of instructions recorded on the router). The routers operating within Network 1 will determine the quickest route for the data packages to Network 4. Depending on the capacity of the different networks this may involve the

---

[40] See www.intelsat.com (2011).

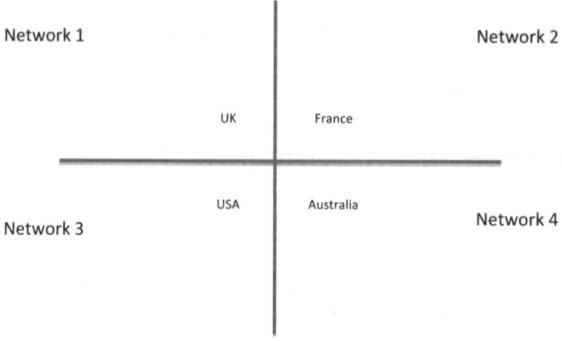

packages being sent through a combination of Networks 2 and 3 in order to reach Network 4. It is also possible that the data packages will arrive at Network 4 in a different order than they were sent by Network 1. Each router within the different networks will forward the packages towards Network 4, and a router within that network will then send them to the recipient's computer (via ISP2). The recipient's computer will use TCP/IP to reassemble the packages into the e-mail and attachment, as sent by Alpha Ltd.

1.3.6   Domain names

The domain names system (DNS) is the key to enabling a computer to find another computer on the internet. The DNS is regulated by a non-profit-making organisation called the Internet Corporation for Assigned Names and Numbers (ICANN).[41] The function of ICANN is to manage the internet's domain name system and the allocation of IP addresses. The organisation supervises the operation of root servers (name servers) which contain the IP addresses of all the domain registries around the world.

The DNS converts a web address, such as www.jordanpublishing.co.uk, into an IP address which identifies where the computer is located on the internet. The IP address for www.jordanpublishing.co.uk is 213.123.35.131 (such a translation is sometimes referred to as 'resolving the domain name'). A domain name is typically made up of three distinct elements, as shown in Figure 1.4.

1.	2.	3.
www.	Name of domain	country, or entity designation, such as 'co.uk' or '.com', etc.
eg www.	jordanpublishing	.co.uk

Figure 1.4: Elements of a domain name address

---

[41]   See www.icann.org (2011).

Many domain names indicate the country with which an entrepreneur has registered a name. For example, the extension '.uk' indicates that the name is registered in the UK, whilst '.ch' shows that the name has been registered in Switzerland. Such extensions are known as country code top level domains (ccTLDs). There are also second level domains (SLDs) which represent the division of a country code such as '.uk' into subcategories. For instance, the .uk extension has been divided into 'co.uk', 'ac.uk' and 'org.uk', each respectively intended for commercial organisations, academic institutions and not-for-profit organisations.

'Root name servers' have a record of alphanumeric domain names, ie those we see used for advertising, and which a user will input to an internet browser in order to access a website; but which are translated by those servers into a numeric IP address so that a computer and router can identify where a web page can be accessed or to where an e-mail should be delivered.

As can be seen above, a domain name is a unique address in alphanumeric format corresponding to a 12-digit numeric address for a particular computer server on a specific network in a country which is connected to the internet. Internet users are able to access any information and e-commerce sites which are associated with a domain name by specifying either the domain name or the 12-digit numeric address in the address section of an 'internet browser'.

Each IP address is unique. The information held on these name servers is copied by other servers, owned by ISPs, whose function it is to resolve domain names. The effect of this is that since computer servers attached to a network know the IP address for specific registries (copied from the name server), a request by a user for a specified domain name will be forwarded to the appropriate computer to enable access of the desired website.

The use of alphanumeric domain names instead of the numeric addresses has enabled business and non-business organisations to achieve prominence in domestic and international markets. The commercial value of domain names can be immense because of the recognition value which they have for internet users. By specifying a domain name seen in advertising, internet users are able to find and interact with the e-commerce site of their choice.

The country in which a domain name is registered will not necessarily indicate the physical location of the organisation or individual which registered the name. A French or Swiss company can register a '.uk' domain name as easily as a company incorporated in England. Similarly, a business may register a domain name in each jurisdiction in which it wishes, whether or not it trades in that country. For example, anyone accessing 'www.hickey.co.uk' might assume that they are interacting with an entity located in the UK. This need not be the case since the domain name can merely be a façade or 'shop front' so that in reality the computer server operating the e-commerce site associated with that domain name is located in another country on the other side of the world. However, to register some addresses it may be necessary to establish a connection with the relevant country, so, for example, to register a '.mc' address it is necessary to prove a connection with Monaco. Appendix A sets out a list of domain name registries and whether there are any residency requirements that must be met in order to obtain a registration (these requirements may have tax implications, which are discussed in Chapters 6 and 8).

It is possible for an organisation to acquire what is known as a generic top level domain (gTLD), such as '.com', '.net' and '.org'. A name ending with the extension '.com' typically, but not necessarily, indicates that the website is operated by a commercial organisation, whilst '.org' is intended for non-profit making organisations and '.net' for network operators.

Each and every domain name is authorised and registered by a relevant naming authority that covers a particular country or geographic area. In the UK the naming authority is called 'Nominet'.[42] Most countries throughout the world have established naming authorities for domains. Domain names can be acquired for many low-tax countries, such as Liechtenstein (.li), Jersey (.je), Guernsey (.gg), Bermuda (.bm) and the Bahamas (.bs) by a business operating anywhere. This will be helpful where economic activities can be carried on from these jurisdictions, so as to assist in creating value for these businesses.

Once a domain name is registered, it is stored on the naming authority database, and then replicated at key points within the internet. Anyone, located anywhere in the world, who knows the domain name of a particular business or organisation can then access the website which is associated with that name. For instance, the domain name extension for Anguilla is '.ai' and domain names registered in Anguilla are not only accessible by consumers in Anguilla but can also be accessed by consumers anywhere in the world. A domain name may also be detected and incorporated into the databases of various search engines, such as Google, Yahoo, Bing and Lycos; the effect of this is to greatly increase consumer access to e-commerce sites through the operation of sponsored links and other forms of advertising direct to a user's desktop or mobile device.[43]

---

[42]   See www.nominet.org.uk (2011).
[43]   The number of search engines in operation is considerable: see www.thesearchenginelist. com (2011).

1.3.7   Internet search engines

The internet enables a user to have access to a wealth of information and e-commerce services, whether available in the user's country of residence or in another country located on the other side of the world. The opportunities created by the internet also pose a problem in that it has become difficult for users to locate and identify relevant information and services due to the scale of the internet. This is also a problem for any business seeking to obtain orders from users of the internet. Our ability to find a book in a random selection on a bookshelf is easy, but locating one in a library with no indexes or references could take a considerable amount of time! The function of 'search engines' within the structure of the internet is to provide an index of subjects available. All web pages have a description embedded into them of the general nature of the page and certain key words. An e-commerce retailer of computers in London would probably include the words: *computer, laptop computer, information technology, IT, software, games, word-processing, london, tottenham court road, england, uk, retailer, repairer, company, distributor* on their web page. These words are registered with the search engine provider and anyone searching for COMPUTERS in TOTTENHAM COURT ROAD LONDON would be presented with this site (amongst several!). A search for: COMPUTERS or for UK COMPANY, would still find the site, but it would form part of a list of several hundreds, or thousands, of others, too.

One of the main revenues available to the operators of internet search engines is advertising (including sponsored links) of websites operated by other businesses carrying on e-commerce activities. In other words, sponsored links appear at the top of or in a prominent position on a search engine's results page. Revenues are also derived from sponsored links which occur where a business has an agreement with the search engine provider to show a link to that business's domain name along side the search engine results for the entry which has been submitted. Revenues may also be created from a computer user clicking on a link which is displayed on the search engine website (ie pay-per-click); and these are websites which are displayed where contextually relevant to the search request submitted by the computer user.

It is also possible for a search engine to generate revenues from the licensing of mirror sites. In other words, someone else acquires the right to use the search engine database and acts as the host in another country. The advantage of this is that the search engine site is local to a particular country offering quicker performance times. The advertisement banners will also reflect the market of that country. The licensing of the search engine site will involve tax-related issues in respect of intellectual property. Copyright may exist in a database and it is possible that any payment made for the use of the search engine database by a licensed party could represent payment of a royalty on which a withholding tax may be applied. In addition to payments for copyright, the licence agreement will involve issues relating to trade mark use and goodwill. The terms of the licence payment may either be based on a royalty or lump sum. Payments such as these will have both domestic and international tax implications.[44]

An additional source of income for internet search engine providers is likely to be through 'value added links'. This is where a search engine provider pays for every link made by it to another internet provider's site.

An e-commerce retailer may also pay a search engine supplier to show its domain name when certain types of request are submitted to a search engine. For instance, the retailer can specify the type of search terms that will produce its domain name in the search results. Thus a yoga instructor practising in London could pay for 'yoga instructor London' to be associated with her website.

1.3.8   Web-browsers

'Browser technology' is the basis of the success of the internet. A browser is the software which enables an individual user to access information held on the internet. Some of the most well-known browsers are Microsoft's Internet Explorer (IE) and Apple Mac's Safari. These programs enable the user to type in a domain name address (or uniform resource locator, 'URL') such as www.bbc.co.uk, which is then located and displayed on a computer monitor or mobile device. Web pages are written using HTML,[45] which encrypts the document with information about how it should be displayed, and with information about links to other pages elsewhere on the internet.

1.3.9   Internet service providers ('ISPs')

The gateway to the internet for most individuals and for many companies is via one of a range of ISPs. In exchange for the facility offered by ISPs (such as content and general access to the internet), subscribers pay a monthly fee. Examples of commercial providers are BT, AOL, Sky, Virgin Media and Tesco. ISPs provide access to a network, which is linked to networks operated by other ISPs, usually via network backbones.

ISPs come in many forms. Some simply provide access to the internet. Others, such as AOL, have a range of facilities and information accessible only to their subscribers. Some represent a joint venture company between domestic internet providers who are developing an international internet service and others may simply be a single business established for

---

[44]   See Chapter 6 for details.
[45]   Hypertext markup language.

providing access to a particular market. These smaller operators will normally lease line capacity from larger internet service providers.

Introduction

PART II

INTERNET BUSINESS: LEGAL AND COMMERCIAL

CHAPTER 2

STRUCTURES FOR INTERNET BUSINESS

2.1 INTRODUCTION

A wide and diverse range of structures can be used for carrying on e-commerce and e-infrastructure businesses in the UK. A summary of the key types of structure is set out in Table 2.1.

At its simplest, a trading business can be operated as a sole trader, without the use of any 'business wrapper', but also without the benefit of a separate legal entity insulating the liability of the trader. To achieve this limited liability status, a privately financed economic activity will typically be structured in one of the following three ways:

(1)   as a company limited by shares incorporated in a part of the UK;

(2)   as a UK establishment of an overseas enterprise, where the overseas enterprise is registered to do business in the UK without having a separate legal entity operating in the UK; or

(3)   as a limited liability partnership incorporated in a part of the UK.

In addition, a company, a limited liability partnership, a limited partnership with a general partner and a European Economic Interest Grouping[1] may be used as the vehicle for a joint venture undertaking by two or more participants.

The purpose of this chapter is to consider the nature of the main types of business structure for carrying on an e-commerce and e-infrastructure related business. This chapter then goes on to consider the tax-based incentives which may be available, in limited circumstances, to encourage external investment by individuals and corporations in some business entities (principally via the Enterprise Investment Scheme).

Internet Business:
Legal and Commercial

---

[1]   Details of which are beyond the scope of this chapter.

Table 2.1: Summary of UK business structures

Business Structure	Formation	Nature of economic activity	Type(s) of business structure available	Members' liability	Owner of business property	Type of members' interest
Registered company	Under the Companies Act (CA) 2006.	Any form of economic activity.	PUBLIC	PUBLIC	Company and not the members.[2]	A company limited by shares may divide its capital into different classifications, eg:
			Public company (limited by shares).[3]	Limited by shares.	Company possesses separate legal personality.[4]	1. Ordinary shares providing the right to dividend and capital.
			Share capital must not be less than £50k or the prescribed Euro equivalent.[5]			2. Preference shares providing the right to dividend and capital in priority to holders of ordinary shares.
			PRIVATE	PRIVATE		
			No minimum share capital.	Limited by share capital or by guarantee or unlimited.		
				Unlimited companies can be registered with or without the capital divided into shares.		

---

2   *Maccaura v Northern Assurance Co Ltd* [1925] AC 619.

3   CA 2006, s 4(2).

4   *Saloman v Saloman and Co Ltd* [1897] AC 22.

5   CA 2006, ss 761 and 763.

Business Structure	Formation	Nature of economic activity	Type(s) of business structure available	Members' liability	Owner of business property	Type of members' interest
UK establishment (permanent establishment) or a non-resident corporation	A fixed place of business through which the business of an overseas enterprise is wholly or partly carried on.[6]	Any form of economic activity.	No legal personality separate from the overseas enterprise.	Depends upon the law applicable to the overseas enterprise.	Overseas enterprise by which the UK establishment is created.	Depends upon the law applicable to the overseas enterprise.
Limited liability partnership (LLP)	Under the Limited Liability Partnerships Act 2000, as amended.	Any form of economic activity.	Separate legal personality.[7] Requires at least two members.[8]	Limited to the amount contributed by the member to the LLP.[9]	LLP and not its members.	As provided in the LLP agreement, or in the absence of an agreement the members are deemed to share equally in the capital and profits of the LLP.[10]

6   See Art 5 of OECD Model Tax Convention.
7   Limited Liability Partnerships Act 2000, s 1(2).
8   Subject to the exceptions outlined in **2.4.1**.
9   Unless agreed otherwise by the members and save for certain rights of recovery of a liquidator under the Insolvency Act 1986.
10 Limited Liability Partnerships Regulations 2001, SI 2001/1090, reg 7(1).

Business Structure	Formation	Nature of economic activity	Type(s) of business structure available	Members' liability	Owner of business property	Type of members' interest
General partnership[11]	Two or more persons (incorporated or individuals).	Any form of economic activity.	Single partnership or member of a limited partnership (see below).	All partners are jointly and severally liable for all debts and obligations incurred by the firm while the partner is a member.[12]	Property is held and applied by the partners for the purposes of the partnership and property must be applied in accordance with the partnership agreement.[13]	According to percentage or interest in partnership profits as provided in the partnership agreement or in the absence of an agreement the partners are deemed to share equally in the capital and profits of the partnership.[14] There is no interest capable of assignment.[15]
	Regulated by the Partnership Act 1890.	Persons who carry on a business in common with a view to profit[16]		A company may be a partner so having a partnership with partners which are all limited companies will create a liability 'shield'.	An English partnership does not have separate legal personality.	

The use of a general partner/limited partner structure for an e-commerce and e-infrastructure business has become less popular since the Limited Liability Partnerships Act 2000 enabled the establishment of LLPs with many of the equivalent tax benefits but without risk to the members' limited liability status if they participate in the management of the LLP. As a result, this chapter does not discuss the general partner/limited partner structure in further detail.

11 Partnership Act 1890, s 9.
12 Partnership Act 1890, s 20.
13 Partnership Act 1890, s 24.
14 *Hadlee v Commissioner of Inland Revenue* [1993] STC 294, PC.
15 Partnership Act 1890, s 1.

Business Structure	Formation	Nature of economic activity	Type(s) of business structure available	Members' liability	Owner of business property	Type of members' interest
Limited partnership 'Silent partner'	Two or more persons (incorporated or individuals).	Any form of economic activity.	Partnership Act 1890	GENERAL PARTNER	As for general partnerships.	As for general partnerships.
	One or more of the persons must be a general partner(s) and one or more must be limited partner(s).[17]		Limited Partnerships Act 1907	Liable for all the debts and obligations of the firm.[18]		A limited partner does not have power to bind the firm and cannot take part in the management of the partnership business.
			Group partnership with general and limited partners.	LIMITED PARTNER		A limited partner who participates in the management of the firm will become liable for all debts and obligations of the firm incurred while it takes part in the management.[19]
				Liability is limited to the amount contributed to the partnership.[20]		
				A limited company may be a limited partner.[21]		

17 Limited Partnerships Act 1907, s 4(2).
18 Limited Partnerships Act 1907, s 4(2).
19 Limited Partnerships Act 1907, s 6(1).
20 Limited Partnerships Act 1907, s 4(2).
21 Limited Partnerships Act 1907, s 4(4).

It is beyond the scope of this chapter to provide a detailed commentary on the formation procedures for business structures. Further practical guidance can be obtained from works such as *International Corporate Procedures.*[22]

2.2   COMPANY INCORPORATION IN THE UK

A company is for all purposes a separate legal person.[23] A company can enter into contracts, borrow money, rent buildings and carry on any economic trade or activity. A company can buy another company. The property of a company, such as intellectual property in computer software, is owned by the company and not by its shareholders.[24] A company can lose money and go into insolvency.

A company is normally financed by the contribution of cash or payments in kind (such as the transfer of a business or other assets) in exchange for shares, which makes the contributors members of the company. Future members can be admitted by the allotment of new shares or the transfer of shares by an existing member. Each share in the company will carry rights under the articles of association and CA 2006, such as the right to receive notice of meetings and vote and the right to receive a dividend from distributable profits. The advantages of using a company to establish a business are examined later in this chapter (see **2.5**). First let us consider the nature of a company within the UK.

A company can be formed by registration in accordance with CA 2006.[25] CA 2006 allows various types of company to be formed, which are a company limited by shares,[26] a company limited by guarantee[27] or an unlimited company.[28] The formation of a company creates a number of obligations on the persons who are responsible for managing the company.[29] For example, a company is required to produce annual accounts, and the directors are required to produce a report each year[30]

---

[22]   See   www.jordanpublishing.co.uk/publications/commercial/international-corporate-procedures.

[23]   CA 2006, s 16; *Salomon v Salomon & Co Ltd* [1897] AC 22, HL.

[24]   *Macaura v Northern Assurance Co Ltd* [1925] AC 619.

[25]   A company may also be formed in other ways, such as by Royal Charter. However, incorporation by registration under CA 2006 is the normal way in which a company is formed.

[26]   The liability of such a company's members is limited to the amount, if any, which is unpaid on the shares issued to the members (CA 2006, s 3(2)).

[27]   The liability of such a company's members is limited to such amount as the members undertake to contribute to the assets of the company in the event of it being wound up (CA 2006, s 3(3)).

[28]   The liability of such a company's members is not limited (CA 2006, s 3(4)).

[29]   For more detailed analysis regarding the formation of a company the reader is referred to *International Corporate Procedures*: see www.jordanpublishing.co.uk/publications/commercial/international-corporate-procedures.

[30]   CA 2006, s 415.

which must be sent to the Registrar of Companies.[31] A registered company must always have a registered office to which all communications and notices can be sent.[32]

Pre-formed companies can be acquired 'off-the-shelf' from formation agents, such as Jordans Limited, or a company can be incorporated on the same day of submission of the formation documentation to the Registrar of Companies. A checklist for the formation of a company using the Jordans formation service is provided at Appendix B.

2.2.1 Public and private companies

CA 2006 distinguishes between a public and private company.

A company is a public company if it is stated to be such in its certificate of incorporation.[33] Only a company limited by shares or a company limited by guarantee and having a share capital can qualify as a public company.[34] In addition, it is also necessary for such a company to obtain a trading certificate before it can commence trading.[35] The name of any public company ends with the words 'public limited company' or the abbreviation 'plc'.[36] Certain provisions of CA 2006 only apply to public companies, including a number of restrictions relevant to maintenance of share capital and the issue of new shares. One advantage of using a public company is in order to make it easier to raise finance for the company. This is because a private company is prohibited from offering shares to the public.[37] A public limited company is required:

(1) to have an authorised minimum nominal share capital of £50,000 or the prescribed equivalent in Euros;[38] and

(2) to have at least one-quarter of the nominal value of the share capital be paid up plus any premium.[39] A public company with a share capital of £50,000 may therefore only require £12,500 to be paid up by its members, leaving £37,500 of share capital to be called up.

A company which is not a public company is deemed to be a private company.[40] The name of any private company must end with the word

---

[31] CA 2006, s 441 (but note that different requirements apply to small companies, medium-sized companies, unquoted companies and quoted companies).

[32] CA 2006, s 86.

[33] CA 2006, s 4.

[34] CA 2006, s 4.

[35] CA 2006, s 761.

[36] CA 2006, s 58

[37] CA 2006 s 755.

[38] CA 2006, ss 761 and 763.

[39] CA 2006, s 586.

[40] CA 2006, s 4.

'limited' or the abbreviation 'Ltd'.[41] Amongst the many advantages of using a private company are that there are no minimum nominal share capital requirements and there are fewer restrictions on the maintenance of capital and on the issue of new shares. Persons wishing to set up a company to carry on a business usually start with a private company and then convert the company into a public company if they wish to offer shares to the public or list the company's shares on a public market.

CA 2006 does not impose conditions on the type of person who can form a company. Thus, a natural or legal person, UK national or foreign national, can form a UK registered company. Upon registration of the company's memorandum, the registrar issues a certificate to the effect that the company is incorporated which specifies whether it is a public or private limited company.[42]

2.2.2   Management

CA 2006 provides model articles of association, which are to be used in default of other articles being adopted by the company, or insofar as not excluded.[43] Whichever articles of association are adopted by the company, they are binding upon the company and its members.[44] The articles usually establish the rights attaching to the shares and set out the arrangements for the management of the company including, for example, the procedures for holding meetings of shareholders and directors and how the directors are to be appointed.

Every company must have at least one director who is a natural person.[45] A private company can operate with only one director but a public company must have at least two directors and a company secretary.[46]

2.2.3   Corporate personality and membership liability for corporate obligations

A company has separate legal personality distinct from its members.[47] This means that a company can enter into contracts, for example, for the hire of plant or machinery, or for the rental of telecommunication lines from permanent internet backbone networks.[48]

---

[41]   CA 2006, s 59.
[42]   CA 2006, s 15.
[43]   CA 2006, ss 18 and 20. See the Companies (Model Articles) Regulations 2008, SI 2008/3229.
[44]   CA 2006, s 33.
[45]   CA 2006, s 155.
[46]   CA 2006, ss 154 and 271.
[47]   *Salomon v Salomon & Company* [1897] AC 22.
[48]   See Chapter 1 for details on the nature of the e-infrastructure network.

The concept of separate legal personality is pierced 'where special circumstances exist indicating that the company is a mere façade concealing the true facts'.[49] This may happen where a company is used for the purposes of carrying on fraudulent activity. Otherwise the assets, debts and obligations are those of the company and not the members.[50] Creditors do not generally have a claim against the assets of the company's members.

The liability of a company's members is determined by reference to their shareholding. Shares are issued by a company in exchange for cash or for assets transferred to the company. Where a company is limited by shares, the members are liable only for the amount (if any) unpaid on the shares.[51] However, the concept of limited liability may only be of notional value where the business is small and has borrowed to finance its operations. In these circumstances, it is common for a bank to obtain personal guarantees from the directors and/or shareholders in respect of the finance granted to the company. The members would then be liable in their capacity as guarantors.

> *Example 2.1*
>
> A Ltd is a retail business selling products via the internet. Fred and George are the directors and shareholders of the company. Fred's shares in the company are fully paid, whilst George still owes £10,000 for his shares. A Ltd purchases its products from suppliers and then sells them on to customers in the UK and abroad via its website. As a result of trading difficulties, the company passes into insolvency owing £50,000 to its suppliers and having received £20,000 of advance payments from customers for its products. In this example, the liquidator can require George to contribute the balance owing on his shares to the company. However, the individual customers and the suppliers will generally only have a claim against the company and will have no right to claim against Fred and George.[52]

2.2.4   Shareholder rights

The rights that attach to shares can vary. A company is usually permitted to create different classes of shares carrying various rights or restrictions under its articles of association.[53] For example, a company may issue

---

[49]   *Woolfson v Strathclyde Regional Council* (1978) SLT 159, at 161, per Lord Keith.

[50]   *Macaura v Northern Assurance Co Ltd* [1925] AC 619.

[51]   Insolvency Act 1986, s 74(2)(d) and the Companies (Model Articles) Regulations 2008, SI 2008/3229, Sch 1, reg 2.

[52]   In certain circumstances there will be an obligation on directors to contribute to the assets of a company on an insolvent liquidation where there is evidence of wrongful trading. This is usually where reasonable steps to minimise a loss to creditors were not taken when the directors knew or should have known that that there was no reasonable prospect of avoiding insolvent liquidation. Such a liability can also arise where there is an intention to defraud creditors. See generally the Insolvency Act 1986, ss 213 and 214.

[53]   See the Companies (Model Articles) Regulations 2008, SI 2008/3229, Sch 1, reg 22.

preference shares that give the holders a right to dividends or capital in priority to holders of ordinary shares in the company. Shares are personal property of the member.[54] As such, shares can be transferred by sale, or under a will. Shares normally carry the right to vote at shareholders' meetings, for example, for the purposes of appointing directors or issuing new shares. In addition, a share normally carries the right to a proportion of the remaining proceeds of the company when it is wound up.

2.2.5   Minimum share capital requirements and raising corporate equity finance

A registered public company must meet minimum share capital requirements, otherwise it will not be granted a trading certificate. The authorised minimum capital is currently £50,000 (2011) or the prescribed equivalent in Euros.[55] The capital of a public company can be raised from public or private sources. The principal markets for raising capital from the public in the UK are the Main Market and Alternative Investment Market of the London Stock Exchange plc.[56]

2.2.6   Transferability of company shares

Shares in a company are freely transferable unless restrictions on transfer are incorporated into the articles of association of the company.[57]

It is not uncommon to find restrictions in the articles of a private company that enable the directors to refuse to register a transfer in their absolute discretion or upon specified grounds. For example, the model articles provided for by CA 2006 allow the directors to refuse to register a transfer of shares.[58] A public company cannot impose restrictions on the transfer of fully paid-up shares if it wishes to have its shares listed on the London Stock Exchange.[59]

Shares in a company can be held by any person irrespective of nationality. Partnerships may hold shares in the name of the firm.

2.2.7   Register of members

Every company is required to maintain a register of its members.[60] The particulars to be registered by the company include the name and address of each member, the date of registration and cessation of membership

---

[54]   CA 2006, s 541.
[55]   CA 2006, ss 763 and 765.
[56]   For further details see generally: www.londonstockexchange.com and www.businesslink.gov.uk (2011).
[57]   CA 2006, s 544.
[58]   See Companies (Model Articles) Regulations 2008, SI 2008/3229, Sch 1, reg 26.
[59]   Listing Rule LR 2.2.4R and AIM Rules for Companies (February 2010) Rule 32.
[60]   CA 2006, s 113.

and the number of shares held. Failure to comply with these requirements exposes the company and each officer of the company who is in default to a fine.[61] The register must be kept at its registered office or at an alternate inspection location.[62] All members of a company are entitled to inspect the register free of charge. CA 2006 does not recognise the existence of bearer shares in respect of a company.

2.2.8 Shareholder control

CA 2006 requires shareholder approval for a company to take certain actions, such as the issue of new shares. Some of the requirements are for 'special resolutions' (at least 75% of those voting at a meeting or 75% of voting rights for a written resolution) and some are for 'ordinary resolutions' (at least 50% of those voting at a meeting or 50% of voting rights for a written resolution). English law permits shareholders to enter into agreements between themselves which determine how voting rights will be exercised by each of them. For example, shareholders may contract with each other to exercise their votes to prevent an alteration of their company's share capital unless each of the shareholders consents to the alteration.[63] The shareholders' agreement could also require the consent of shareholders for certain actions of the board of directors of the company.

2.2.9 Tax treatment

An overview of the tax treatment of a UK company in setting up and carrying on a business is provided in Chapter 7.

2.3 UK ESTABLISHMENT

Registration of a UK establishment is where an overseas enterprise is registered to do business in the UK without having a separate legal entity operating in the UK. As a result, the matters discussed above in relation to public and private companies will depend upon the requirements of the state of incorporation of the overseas enterprise.

The decision as to whether to use a business structure that has an actual legal presence in a trading jurisdiction must be balanced against the benefits offered by e-commerce. The nature of the IT market means that it may be necessary only for certain types of business to establish a physical location in one country where profits are to be remitted from other countries and nowhere else.

---

[61] CA 2006, s 113(7).

[62] CA 2006, s 114(1) and Companies (Company Records) Regulations 2008, SI 2008/3006.

[63] *Russell v Northern Bank Development Corporation* [1992] 3 All ER 294.

2.3.1 Filing requirements

Once a UK establishment is registered, it will need to make certain filings with the UK Registrar of Companies, including details of certain changes affecting the overseas enterprise (such as any change of name, constitution or officers) and the following accounts filings:

(1) if the overseas enterprise is incorporated in a European Economic Area (EEA) state, it must file the accounts it is required to produce by that state;

(2) if the overseas enterprise is incorporated in a state outside the EEA which requires it to produce audited accounts, it must file those accounts; and

(3) if the overseas enterprise is incorporated in a state outside the EEA where it has no requirement to produce accounts, it must produce and file accounts consistent with CA 2006 or the International Financial Reporting Standards.[64]

2.3.2 Tax treatment

An overview of the tax treatment of a non-UK company in setting up and carrying on a business is provided in Chapter 6.

2.4 LIMITED LIABILITY PARTNERSHIP (LLP)

An LLP is a body corporate with separate legal personality, the members of which have limited liability upon registration of the LLP.[65]

2.4.1 Basis of establishment

An LLP is formed by registration under the Limited Liability Partnerships Act 2000 (LLPA 2000). An LLP, like a company, can own property, employ people and enter into contracts on its own account. Many of the legal provisions applicable to companies also apply to LLPs.[66] In many ways it can be treated as a variety of company, with the management flexibility of a partnership combined with the features of a body corporate.

An LLP is formed where two or more persons associated for carrying on a lawful business with a view to profit subscribe their names to an incorporation document.[67] Unless the members have agreed otherwise,[68]

---

[64] Overseas Companies Regulations 2009, SI 2009/1801, Pts 5 and 6.
[65] Limited Liability Partnerships Act 2000, s 1.
[66] LLPA 2000, s 15.
[67] LLPA 2000, s 2(1).

the liability of members is limited to the amount that they have contributed to the LLP. This is subject to the following exceptions:

(1) amounts withdrawn by a member in the 2 years before the commencement of a winding-up can be clawed back if the member making the withdrawal knew or ought to have concluded that, after the withdrawal and any withdrawals in contemplation at that time, there was no reasonable prospect of the LLP being able to avoid an insolvent liquidation;[69]

(2) there are provisions equivalent to those which apply to companies that require a contribution to the assets on an insolvent liquidation where there is evidence of fraudulent or wrongful trading by members (see further, note 52 above);[70] and

(3) if the membership of the LLP falls below two, and the business of the LLP is continued, then after 6 months the benefit of limited liability status is lost and the remaining member becomes jointly and severally liable with the LLP for debts incurred.[71]

The mutual rights and duties of the members are governed by agreement between the members, or between the LLP and its members.[72] If no agreement exists between the members then certain default provisions will apply by virtue of the Limited Liability Partnerships Regulations 2001, which provide, amongst other things, that every member is entitled to share equally in the capital and profits of the LLP, every member may take part in the management of the LLP, no person may be introduced as a member or voluntarily assign an interest in an LLP without the unanimity of all members and that ordinary matters may be decided by a majority of the members, but no change in the nature of the business of the LLP can be made without the unanimity of all members.[73]

Every member is an agent of the LLP.[74] However, an LLP is not bound by a member's dealings with third parties if the member has no authority to act for the LLP and the third party knew that the member had no authority or did not know or believe the person to be a member of the LLP.[75]

---

[68] Insolvency Act 1986, s 74 (as modified by the Limited Liability Partnerships Regulations 2001, SI 2001/1090).

[69] Insolvency Act 1986, s 214A (as inserted by the Limited Liability Partnerships Regulations 2001).

[70] See Insolvency Act 1986, ss 213 and 214 (as modified by the Limited Liability Partnerships Regulations 2001).

[71] LLPA 2000, s 4A.

[72] LLPA 2000, s 5.

[73] Limited Liability Partnerships Regulations 2001, reg 7.

[74] LLPA 2000, s 6(1).

[75] LLPA 2000, s 6(2).

Certain 'Designated' members are responsible for, amongst other things, appointing an auditor (if required), signing accounts on behalf of members, delivering accounts to the Registrar of Companies, delivering any notification to the Registrar (such as a change in members or registered office) and preparing, signing and delivering an annual return.[76]

2.4.2　Tax treatment

Generally an LLP is treated as tax transparent (in the same way as partnerships). Accordingly, the profits of an LLP will be taxable in the hands of each partner. Unlike limited companies, an LLP is not generally liable for corporation tax. A detailed review of LLPs is beyond the scope of this book.

2.5　ADVANTAGES OF TYPICAL BUSINESS STRUCTURES ON ESTABLISHMENT OF A UK BUSINESS

Table 2.2 sets out some of the key advantages associated with the most likely choices of business structure for an e-commerce and e-infrastructure business.

Table 2.2: Advantages of typical business structures on establishment of a UK business

Private company limited by shares[77]	Registration of a UK establishment of an overseas enterprise	Limited liability partnership
Limited liability.[78]	Subject to overseas enterprise status (overseas enterprise retains direct liability for UK establishment).	Limited liability.[79]
Separate legal entity.	No separate legal entity from the overseas enterprise.	Separate legal entity.
Same day incorporation.	Slower registration process but can operate for a month before registering.	Same day incorporation.

---

[76] LLPA 2000, Limited Liability Partnerships (Application of the Companies Act 2006) Regulations 2009, SI 2009/1804 and the Limited Liability Partnerships Regulations 2001.

[77] The most likely form of UK company to be used when establishing a UK business.

[78] Subject to the exceptions outlined in note 52 above.

[79] Subject to the exceptions outlined in **2.4.1**.

Private company limited by shares[77]	Registration of a UK establishment of an overseas enterprise	Limited liability partnership
Requires at least one director who is a natural person.	No need for UK directors.	Requires at least two members.[80]
Directors do not need to be UK nationals.	No need for UK directors.	Members do not need to be UK nationals.
Can be formed with nominal share capital which can be unpaid.	No capital requirements.	Can be formed with nominal capital investment.
UK company accounts to be prepared and may need to be audited.	Overseas enterprise accounts may need to be prepared and filed.	UK LLP accounts to be prepared and may need to be audited.
Corporation tax on worldwide profits and gains (between 20% and 26% (2011), with the main rate reducing to 25% from 1 April 2012).	Corporation tax on UK establishment's profits and gains (at full rate (26%) subject to a tax treaty), with the main rate reducing to 25% from 1 April 2012.	Transparent.

2.6 JOINT VENTURES

2.6.1 Basis for establishment

Where it is commercially desirable to collaborate with other people in an e-commerce or e-infrastructure business this can be achieved in several ways. Such collaboration can be achieved by creating a company or LLP in which both collaborators hold a specific proportion of the shareholding or membership interest (eg 50:50 or 60:40). The amount of shares/membership interest held usually reflects the extent of that party's economic contribution to the collaboration. The concept of 'joint venture' is not a person, although the business structure through which the collaboration is carried on may possess separate legal personality. It is equally possible that the joint venture could be carried on through a partnership,[81] or on a cross-border basis via a European Economic Interest Grouping.[82] Participation in a joint venture will have tax consequences on formation, ongoing operations, and on termination.

---

[80] The LLP can still operate with one member but see **2.4.1** for the implications of doing so.
[81] See Table 2.1.
[82] Details of which are beyond the scope of this chapter.

Example 2.2

Internet Technologies Ltd (IT Ltd) and Internet Access Provider Ltd (IAP Ltd) decide that they wish to develop technology to meet a specific problem experienced in the transfer of information between internet access providers. IT Ltd is to provide the use of technologies developed in-house, while IAP Ltd is to contribute the use of personnel, technologies and facilities for the purposes of the collaborative project. The parties agree that the joint venture should be carried on through the medium of a company to be called 'Joint Venture Technologies Ltd'. The parties transfer their respective contributions to the joint venture company in exchange for the issue of shares, which are held in equal numbers. The parties enter into a shareholders' agreement, which defines how the parties are to vote on specific issues in controlling the company, such as appointment of management. Additionally, the shareholders' agreement specifies that the venture is to terminate after 6 years unless agreement to the contrary is reached. The termination is to be effected by seeking voluntary liquidation.

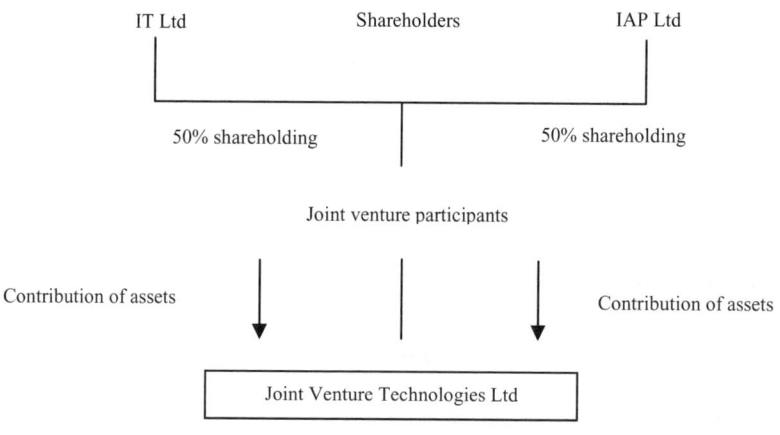

Joint Venture Vehicle

2.7   TAX-BASED INCENTIVES

The UK provides a range of tax-based incentives to attract investment directly into the shares of companies carrying on certain types of qualifying activities. The incentives are achieved through schemes such as the Enterprise Investment Scheme (EIS) and venture capital trusts (VCTs).[83]

---

[83]   A detailed examination of these tax-based incentives is beyond the scope of this chapter. The reader is referred to HMRC's website at: www.hmrc.gov.uk for further information, or alternatively consult with an appropriate professional adviser.

2.7.1 Enterprise Investment Scheme

Introduction

Incentives for persons to invest in an e-commerce or e-infrastructure business can be achieved through the use of the EIS. The EIS can also be used for the purposes of financing research and development activities related to such business activities.[84]

Benefits to an EIS investor

The advantage of organising a business through the EIS is that it offers a tax-based reward to individuals who invest in such a company.[85] The relief is in the form of a set-off against an individual's income tax liability; the amount of relief is calculated by reference to the amount subscribed for shares in an EIS company.[86] The minimum amount qualifying for relief in any tax year is £500, and the maximum is £500,000 (increasing to £1 million in respect of investments made on or after 6 April 2012).[87] The relief is the amount that corresponds to 30% of the amount subscribed for in the company.[88]

> *Example 2.3*
>
> A person subscribes for shares worth £40,000 in an EIS company, which specialises in e-commerce retailing. The individual is entitled to income tax relief of £12,000.[89]

The relief operates to reduce an individual's tax liability on total income for the tax year in which the shares are subscribed.[90] However, for an individual there is a time-based cost to the investment since the shares in an EIS company must be retained for at least 3 years otherwise the income tax relief will be withdrawn.[91]

---

[84] Note that the Government announced in the Autumn Statement 2011 that it will introduce a new Seed Enterprise Investment Scheme which will provide income tax relief of 50% for individuals on investments of no more than £100,000 in qualifying companies, which will be able to raise up to £150,000 under this scheme. The relief will provide an exemption from CGT on gains on shares within the scope of the new relief. It will apply to shares issued on or after 6 April 2012 and will be available to individual investors with a stake of less than 30% in the company.

[85] The provisions governing the EIS are provided by ITA 2007, Part 5, ss 156–257 and the Taxation of Chargeable Gains Act 1992 (TCGA 1992), ss 150A–150C. For more information see HMRC's website at: www.hmrc.gov.uk/eis.

[86] ITA 2007, s 158.

[87] The legislation will be included in the Finance Bill 2012.

[88] 30% (2011/12): ITA 2007, s 158(2A) in respect of investments made on or after 6 April 2011: FA 2011, s 42.

[89] Ie 30% of £40,000.

[90] ITA 2007, s 158. The deduction is made in priority to other reliefs (see generally ITA 2007, s 27(5)).

[91] ITA 2007, s 158(4).

No claim for tax relief is available to the individual investor unless the company has carried on a qualifying business activity, or a research and development activity, for a period of 4 months.[92] It is also important to ensure that any e-commerce or e-infrastructure business that is established to use the EIS as a source of investment is set up on a bona fide commercial basis. This is because no relief is available unless the shares were subscribed and issued for bona fide commercial purposes, and not as part of an arrangement the main purpose of which is tax avoidance.[93] An individual is eligible for relief in respect of a company which is an active company that exists wholly for the purpose of carrying on one or more qualifying trades, or that so exists apart from purposes capable of having no significant effect (other than in relation to incidental matters) on the extent of the company's activities.[94]

On disposal of shares in an EIS company no capital gains tax liability arises if the shares are held for the relevant period.[95] If a loss arises on disposal of the EIS shares it is possible for the individual to obtain relief for the capital loss against income tax.[96] This is an alternative to the usual set-off of a capital loss against chargeable gains arising in the same tax year, or carrying forward the capital loss. It is also possible to have some or all of the amount subscribed for shares in an EIS company set against any chargeable gain.[97] The effect of this is that an amount of the chargeable gain that is matched with the expenditure on EIS shares is deferred until a chargeable event occurs (ie sale of the shares), so that the deferred gain will only arise at the time of the chargeable event.

An individual cannot qualify for EIS relief if that person is connected with the company, except in certain prescribed circumstances.[98] An individual is connected with the company if he or she is an employee, partner or director of the issuing company or any subsidiary.[99] It is also possible for a director to qualify for relief in limited circumstances.[100]

How to qualify as an EIS company

To enable an investor to qualify for income and capital gains tax relief, the investee company must be a qualifying EIS company.[101] It is a fundamental requirement that the investee company is a qualifying

---

[92]   ITA 2007, s 176.
[93]   ITA 2007, s 176(4)(b).
[94]   ITA 2007, s 137(1)(a), (7).
[95]   TCGA 1992, s 150A(2). The relevant period is 3 years from the issue of the shares (in respect of shares issued after 5 April 2000): see ITA 2007, s 159(2).
[96]   ITA 2007, s 131.
[97]   TCGA 1992, s 150C, Sch 5B.
[98]   ITA 2007, ss 162, 163, 169.
[99]   ITA 2007, s 167.
[100] ITA 2007, s 168(1).
[101] ITA 2007, s 157.

company carrying on a qualifying trade as required under the EIS rules.[102] As is the case in respect of a venture capital trust, the gross asset limits for an EIS company are £7 million immediately before the issue and £8 million immediately after the issue of its shares.[103] A company can qualify under the EIS umbrella even though it is not incorporated in the UK.[104] To qualify a company must: (a) exist wholly for the purpose of carrying on a trade in the UK;[105] (b) be an unquoted company;[106] and (c) not at any time, subject to certain exceptions, be the subsidiary of another company or control another company.[107]

Most categories of trade with an e-commerce or e-infrastructure focus (excluding financing and certain services) should be capable of qualifying for the EIS (but see below for further discussion on excluded activities). For a company to qualify as an EIS company and hence enable a person to claim relief for the purposes of research and development, such an activity must actually be carried on at the time the shares are issued, or be started immediately afterwards.[108] A trade will not qualify if one or more excluded activities together amount to a substantial part of the trade. The categories of excluded activities include: dealing in land, financial activities and receiving royalties or licence fees (save as where relating to the exploitation of relevant intangible assets). HMRC regards excluded activities as a substantial part of a company's trade where they amount to more than 20% of the trade.[109] Specifically the term 'excluded activities' is exclusively defined as comprising:[110]

(1) dealing in land, in commodities or futures or in shares, securities or other financial instruments;

(2) dealing in goods *otherwise than* in the course of an ordinary trade of wholesale or retail distribution; points to note are:

---

[102] HMRC provides guidance on this matter in *Enterprise Investment Scheme – Qualifying Trades Tax Bulletin* Issue 54, August 2001.

[103] ITA 2007, s 186; the Chancellor announced in the 2011 Budget that the gross assets test will be increased to £15 million immediately before the investment. This change will be enacted in the Finance Act 2012 and will take effect for shares issued on or after 6 April 2012.

[104] ITA 2007, s 180.

[105] The company cannot be the parent company of a trading group: ITA 2007, s 137(1).

[106] ITA 2007, s 143. An unquoted company is one that does not market its shares to the general public. As an EIS company is unquoted, there are additional tax-based advantages to a person who invests in such a company. A capital loss incurred in the disposal of such shares may be set off against income and so reduce tax liability for that tax year: see ITA 2007, s 131.

[107] ITA 2007, s 139.

[108] ITA 2007, s 179.

[109] See the 'trading activities' section of the HMRC guidance on Enterprise Investment Schemes (at www.hmrc.gov.uk/eis), para 2.4.

[110] ITA 2007, s 192.

    (a) a trade of wholesale distribution is one in which goods are offered for sale and sold to persons for resale by them, or for processing and resale by them, to members of the general public for their use or consumption;[111]

    (b) a trade of retail distribution is one in which goods are offered or exposed for sale and sold to members of the general public for their use or consumption;[112]

(3) banking, insurance, money-lending, debt-factoring, hire-purchase financing or other financial activities;

(4) leasing (including letting ships on charter or other assets on hire);

(5) receiving royalties or licence fees;

(6) providing legal or accountancy services;

(7) property development;

(8) farming or market gardening;

(9) holding, managing or occupying woodlands, any other forestry activities or timber production;

(10) ship building;

(11) producing coal;

(12) producing steel;

(13) operating or managing hotels or comparable establishments or managing property used as an hotel or comparable establishment;

(14) operating or managing nursing homes or residential care homes or managing property used as a nursing home or residential care home;

(15) providing services or facilities for a business carried on by another person if the business consists wholly or as to a substantial part of activities falling within (1) to (14), and a controlling interest in the business is held by a person who also has a controlling interest in the business carried on by the provider of the services or facilities.[113]

There is also a requirement that research and development activities that are intended to result in a qualifying trade that will be carried on mainly

---

[111] ITA 2007, s 193(3).

[112] ITA 2007, s 193(4).

[113] ITA 2007, s 199; but there is an exception for a qualifying subsidiary.

in the UK.[114] The research and development must be carried on in the UK for the relevant period.[115] 'Research and development' for the purposes of EIS relief is defined as 'activities that fall to be treated as research and development in accordance with generally accepted accounting practice'.[116] To obtain EIS status the company must be carrying on a qualifying trade, which is essentially any activity except for those specified in the Income Tax Act 2007 (ITA 2007), s 192 (see above list). The rules require that the trade of the company must not at any time in the relevant period consist of one or more specified activities if that activity amounts to a substantial part of the trade of the company. The excluded activity of relevance in the context of research and development and information technology-based activities is the receipt of royalties or licence fees.[117] However, ITA 2007 provides a safe harbour in respect of a trade that consists, to a substantial extent, of the receipt of royalties and licence fees, if the royalties and licence fees (or all but for a part that is not a substantial part in terms of value) are attributable to the exploitation of relevant intangible assets.[118] An intangible asset is a 'relevant intangible asset' if the whole or greater part (in terms of value) of it has been created: (a) by the issuing company; or (b) by a company which was a qualifying subsidiary of the issuing company throughout the period during which it created the whole or greater part (in terms of value) of the intangible asset.[119]

2.7.2 Venture capital trust

Introduction

A VCT is an authorised investment trust whose shares are listed on the Stock Exchange and which broadly invests in small higher-risk trading companies whose shares and securities are not listed on a recognised stock exchange.[120] A detailed examination of the VCT is beyond the scope of this chapter. A VCT must be approved by HMRC, and meet various qualifying conditions.[121]

---

[114] ITA 2007, s 179.

[115] Namely, a period of at least 3 years, starting from the issue of the shares: see ITA 2007, s 173.

[116] ITA 2007, ss 257 and 1006.

[117] ITA 2007, s 192(1)(e).

[118] ITA 2007, s 195. An 'intangible asset' means any asset that falls to be treated as an intangible asset in accordance with normal UK accounting practice: ITA 2007, s 195(6).

[119] ITA 2007, s 195(4). References to the creation by a company of an asset that is intellectual property are to its creation in circumstances in which the right to exploit the asset vests in the company (whether alone or jointly with others): ITA 2007, s 195(5). For these purposes 'intellectual property' is defined as meaning: (a) any patent, trade mark, registered design, copyright, design right, performer's right or plant breeder's right; and (b) any rights under the law of a country or territory outside the UK which correspond or are similar to those falling within (a): ITA 2007, s 195(6).

[120] See ITA 2007, Part 6. See generally the HMRC guidance on its website: www.hmrc.gov.uk.

[121] ITA 2007, Part 6.

Benefits for an investor

A material tax advantage of investing in a VCT is that investors are entitled to tax relief on the amount subscribed for on new shares in the venture capital trust.[122] The maximum amount of subscription eligible for relief in any year is £200,000 (2011/12).[123] The relief operates by permitting an amount equal to 30% (2011/12) of the total subscription as a deduction against the individual's income tax liability.[124] The amount is capable of reducing or extinguishing the individual's tax liability.[125] The shares must be held for at least 5 years to qualify for income tax relief.[126] A further tax advantage of holding venture capital trust shares is that a distribution by such a company, ie a dividend, is exempt from income tax.[127] Relief is limited to subscriptions of no more than £200,000 (2011/12).[128] Where an individual disposes of VCT shares, there is no chargeable gain for the purposes of capital gains tax provided that the shares were acquired within the permitted maximum of £200,000 in the tax year in question.[129] However, the shares must be held in a company that is still a VCT at the time of disposal.[130]

---

[122] ITA 2007, ss 261–263.
[123] ITA 2007, s 262(3).
[124] ITA 2007, s 263.
[125] ITA 2007, s 23.
[126] ITA 2007, s 266.
[127] ITTOIA 2005, s 709.
[128] ITTOIA 2005, s 709.
[129] TCGA 1992, s 151A(1).
[130] TCGA 1992, s 151A.

CHAPTER 3

COMMERCIAL INTERMEDIARIES

3.1 INTRODUCTION

Any person carrying on an e-commerce or e-infrastructure business may wish to consider appointing a commercial intermediary. A business considering operating in an overseas market may wish to consider establishing some form of actual presence in that non-UK market. One of the issues which will need to be considered is whether costs should be incurred in creating an 'own brand' presence with a physical presence in the overseas market, or whether a commercial intermediary should be appointed. The appointment of a commercial intermediary in an overseas market for the purposes of carrying on an e-commerce or e-infrastructure business is an option available to anyone, subject to the requirements of local law. A key commercial advantage is that it should avoid the significant costs associated with establishing a business structure within the target market. Obviously, the appointment of a commercial intermediary may also occur in a supplier's domestic market in order to benefit from the intermediary's business activities, for example, a courier/distribution network. For a discussion of the general benefits that are likely to arise from appointing an intermediary see **3.3**.

A further advantage of appointing a commercial intermediary in an international market is that in certain circumstances it can be used for tax-effective purposes in minimising tax on profits attributable to providing goods and/or services in another country (this aspect is considered later in this chapter: see **3.8**). The services of an introduction agent in an overseas country can legitimately be used to minimise profits, which will be attributable (and therefore taxable) in that overseas country.[1] This objective should be achieved because the economic function of an introduction agent is generally minimal compared with the functions and risks undertaken by fully fledged agents. For this reason more revenues can potentially be allocated to another country, which will normally be the country in which the principal, appointing the agent, is a resident. The extent to which revenues can successfully be allocated

---

[1]   The extent to which this form of tax planning can achieve tax savings in a particular overseas country will need to be considered in conjunction with advice being obtained from professional advisers. See also Chapter 9 (Transfer Pricing).

between connected persons will depend on the transfer pricing treatment of the relevant transactions: this topic is considered in Chapter 9.

In appointing a commercial intermediary to act in an overseas market it is important to ensure that no tax liabilities are accidentally created for the principal by virtue of the agent's activities: this topic is considered in Chapters 6 (inbound e-commerce) and 8 (outbound e-commerce). If an intermediary is appointed to act as a distributor in an overseas country it is less likely that the person will create a tax liability in that country for the appointing party since a distributor will usually act on an independent basis without being regarded as the agent of another person. Where an agent acts for a principal on either a disclosed or undisclosed basis it is also necessary to consider the VAT consequences for both parties (these are considered in Chapter 17).

There are many forms of commercial intermediary that can be used in a supply chain for the provision of goods or services, and these are considered in this chapter.

Example 3.1

Alpha US Inc appoints Beta UK Ltd, an unconnected person, as its introduction agent for the purposes of soliciting and identifying orders for goods made by Alpha US Inc. The agent fulfils this function by operating an internet trading site within the UK. The agent is paid a commission for each order accepted by Alpha US Inc. Beta UK Ltd effectively operates an advertising window or 'shop front' for Alpha US Inc within the UK. Orders are placed by UK consumers with Beta UK Ltd, but these are transferred to a computer server owned by Alpha US Inc. It is via the US company that the order is processed, accepted and delivered. The economic function performed by the introduction agent is minimal: it is solely responsible for hosting a website in the UK, and part of this involves providing the necessary advertising for attracting potential customers. The agent will be entitled to a commission on arm's length terms. It is anticipated that the amount of the commission should be a small proportion of overall sales receipts, which should substantially be allocated to the US company (due to the economic functions performed by it). In other words, the processing, acceptance and delivery of the goods (including being responsible for any defect in the goods) should justify higher profits being allocated to the US company on each and every transaction. The same analysis should also be the case even if Beta UK Ltd were connected with Alpha US Inc.

Example 3.2

Based on the facts of the example above, alternatively, a commercial intermediary might be appointed to act in its own name (ie without the existence of the principal being disclosed) and to conclude contracts with third parties via the medium of e-commerce trading sites. The effect of this is that arrangements will typically exist under which the agent passes on to the principal (eg Alpha US Inc) orders which are then delivered in accordance with a scheme laid down by the principal. If, as in the above example, Alpha US Inc delivers the products, bears all risks as to loss of the goods in transit to the customer and the risk of any default by a customer in payment, then these risks should justify a higher profit margin being retained by Alpha US Inc. Although the UK company in this scenario has power to conclude contracts with customers upon which it will be liable, it is nonetheless possible to minimise the profits which are to be attributed to the UK company. If the US company is to compensate the UK company for any liability it incurs as a result of the contracts, this should also minimise the profit margin of the UK company. This should be the case where the US company bears the risks of delivery, and retains title to the goods until delivery to the UK customers. Alternatively, it may be the case that the agent is granted power to consign goods once it has concluded contracts with third parties. Possession of physical goods for onward transmission carries risk which should be reflected in the commission rate of the agent.

3.2 LEGAL CONTROL OF COMMERCIAL INTERMEDIARIES

The relationship between commercial intermediaries and their appointing parties is generally governed by a written contract (see Chapter 4 for how contracts are formed under the laws of England). Additionally, local jurisdictions may have specific legislation that regulates the operation of particular commercial intermediaries. Within the EU, regulations may also exist which deal with particular commercial relationships. For example, the Commercial Agents (Council Directive) Regulations 1993 provide for rules governing the form and content of agreements in respect of commercial agents.[2]

Generally, the main source of rules in the UK governing the relationship between a commercial intermediary and the appointing party is the written contract (the terms of which will be construed in accordance with UK law where governed by the laws of England). It is of paramount importance that any such commercial arrangement is carefully planned and drafted with precision; and that where appropriate professional advice is taken.

3.3 BENEFITS OF APPOINTING A COMMERCIAL INTERMEDIARY

The benefits of appointing a commercial intermediary should include the following, although the nature of the benefits in any particular situation will depend on carrying out appropriate due diligence on the intermediary, and properly structuring the appointment of the intermediary by taking legal and tax advice relevant to the circumstances:

---

[2]   SI 1993/3053.

(1)   An intermediary will typically have an extensive knowledge of the target market, and accordingly should be in a position to operate efficiently in identifying local market opportunities. For example, such an intermediary could be appointed to host a 'mirror' website in the target country, which would be tailored by the intermediary to reflect the local market. In other words, an intermediary should be in a position to use its knowledge of the target market and implement appropriate advertising.

(2)   An intermediary will usually be in close geographic proximity to the target market. This is important in the context of e-commerce and e-infrastructure activities because it should facilitate quicker and more efficient access times for customers to internet trading sites.

(3)   Appointment of an intermediary in a target market should result in faster and more efficient delivery of goods and/or services (eg where the principal is located on a different continent or in another country).

(4)   An intermediary can generally be used to create a permanent presence within a country to create brand awareness of goods or services. Title to a brand or trade mark will typically be held by the principal, which generally means that the creation of brand awareness by the intermediary is for the benefit of the principal. However, the creation of a permanent presence in an overseas country may create a tax presence in that country: this aspect is considered in Chapters 6 (UK inbound e-commerce) and 8 (UK outbound e-commerce).

(5)   A commercial intermediary bears the burden of start-up costs and generally the appointing party will only need to pay for the services of the intermediary and/or supply of the goods.

(6)   If the commercial intermediary is a connected person, it may have tax advantages for the appointing party. For example, if the intermediary is a subsidiary and located in a low tax jurisdiction, the relationship can be attributed with sufficient risk and obligation of such a nature that it should be capable of justifying retention by that intermediary of a larger proportion of the receipts attributable to its economic activities. In this way, more of the receipts in respect of transactions can be retained in a lower tax jurisdiction (the concepts relating to transfer pricing are considered in Chapter 9).

(7)   A commercial intermediary, who is not connected with the appointing party, may assume the risks of everyday business in carrying on that activity in the target market.

(8) Appointment of an entity local to a particular target market is sometimes the first step towards takeover, and thus acquisition by the appointing party of an economic interest in that market.

(9) Appointment of a commercial intermediary may also be effective because it may undertake responsibility/liability to the third party within the jurisdiction for the goods/services, or alternatively the intermediary may limit the risk of the foreign exporter by guaranteeing the performance by the third party of its obligations such as payment of the price.

The extent to which any of the foregoing advantages can be achieved must be carefully considered in the context of identifying an appropriate commercial intermediary in the target market, and carrying out all necessary enquiries into the reputation and financial solvency of that person. Where appropriate advice should also be sought as to whether the commercial arrangement is appropriately documented for the purposes of the relevant law governing the relationship.

3.4 THE FAMILY OF COMMERCIAL INTERMEDIARIES

Many types of commercial intermediary exist from the perspective of UK law. Table 3.1 highlights the principal types of intermediary that may be chosen for the purposes of carrying on an overseas activity outside the UK, or a trade in the UK by an overseas trader. Some commercial entities are, as a matter of law, only able to do certain things or incur specific responsibilities and liabilities because of the characteristics that are attributed to that person acting in a certain capacity. Because of either the inherent limitation on function, or undertakings assumed by a commercial intermediary, a 'sliding scale' operates in respect of the payments a commercial intermediary should be entitled to expect. However, in each case it is necessary to take appropriate professional advice as to whether the relationship that is being created achieves the desired financial, legal and tax objectives of the parties involved.

Table 3.1: Commercial intermediaries

Intermediary	Description
Representation agent (also known as an 'introduction agent')	Such an agent has authority to solicit orders from third parties, but does not have the power to conclude contracts. Any prospective orders are communicated to the principal (whether located in the same country or elsewhere). The principal then determines whether or not to accept the order, and will usually make arrangements for delivery of goods/services to the third party. Orders solicited by A and passed to P for approval P ◄————————► A ◄————————► C Orders processed, accepted and delivered by P
Agent acting for disclosed principal	This is an agent who discloses that it is working on behalf of another person. Generally, the work of such an agent results in the formation of a contract directly between the principal and third party. The way in which the agent is to conduct business, for example, in terms of the scope for accepting orders placed via internet trading sites, will be governed by the contract between principal and agent. Orders solicited by A P ◄————————► A ◄————————► C Orders processed, accepted and delivered by A in accordance with rules provided for by P
Agent acting for undisclosed principal	This type of agent deals with the outside world apparently for its own account. The UK undisclosed principal is potentially liable on the contacts entered into by the agent. This is because once the third party discovers that the agent is operating for an undisclosed principal it can elect to sue the principal. Under this type of arrangement the agent would appear to be, for example, a sole internet trader concluding contracts directly with customers. Orders solicited by A P ◄————► A ◄————► C Orders processed, accepted and delivered by A in accordance with rules provided for by P On discovery that A is agent for P, C may elect to sue P for any default on the contract, e.g., product quality

Intermediary	Description
Del credere agent	Under this form of arrangement the agent undertakes to indemnify its principal in circumstances where a buyer fails to pay the price of the goods. Since this type of agent accepts the risk of bearing the cost of the goods the agent is entitled to what is known as the del credere commission.[3]
Broker	A broker generally operates as a negotiator, and has no possession of any goods. For example, a broker may negotiate a price for goods not in its possession via the use of e-commerce.
Mercantile agent	Under this arrangement the agent has possession of goods owned by the principal. The agent consigns products to third parties on the direction of the principal, or alternatively is given authority to supply third parties directly with goods from stock held by it. A mercantile agent usually has authority to conclude contracts directly with third parties on behalf of its principal. Since a mercantile agent assumes more risk than, say, an introduction agent it should be entitled to a higher commission. This is because the agent has possession of the goods and will generally be responsible for their safety in the absence of specific agreement. The Factors Act 1889 defines in s 1(1) a mercantile agent as an agent who in the customary course of business has authority to sell goods, or to consign goods for sale, or to buy goods or to raise money on the security of goods. In the context of internet trade an agent of this type might be appointed to sell goods via the medium of an internet trading site, with power to consign goods from stock held by it once orders have been accepted.
Distribution arrangement	A distributor is a person appointed by a supplier to sell products within a specific territory. The distributor buys goods at wholesale prices from the manufacturer/supplier. The distributor is in business on its own account and sells the goods to third parties at a resale price. The difference between the resale price and wholesale price generally represents the profit of the distributor on each transaction.
Franchise arrangement	A franchise is the grant of a right to exploit a business format. A franchisee is a person in business for their own account who pays money to make use of the business format idea. A franchise could be granted in respect of a business format idea for the operation of an e-commerce business site.

Internet Business: Legal and Commercial

---

[3] For an illustration of this practice see *Gabem Management Ltd v Commissioners for Revenue and Customs* [2007] STC (SCD) 247.

Intermediary	Description
	Under a franchise arrangement the franchisee pays for the right to use the commercial know-how, registered trade marks and other associated copyright that relate to how a business in a particular sector is operated.[4] A franchise agreement may also include a number of other mixed elements, such as the grant of a commercial lease to property from which to run the business format. Additionally, the franchise could provide for the provision of goods to the franchisee for use in the business.

As can be seen from Table 3.1 there is a variation in the risks, rights and responsibilities attaching to the commercial intermediaries. For instance, the responsibilities and risks of an introduction agent are significantly less than the risks of a del credere agent. Thus, if an associated intermediary is appointed as an introduction agent it should only be entitled to a limited commission on the customers it introduces to its principal. Such an arrangement could be utilised between connected parties where the introduction agent is located in a high tax jurisdiction, and works on behalf of a principal in a low tax jurisdiction. The limited risk of an introduction agent should justify higher payments of receipts to the principal. It must be emphasised that the use of the specific intermediaries with limited legal risks, etc is no substitute for having in existence economic transactions that support the choice of intermediary. In other words, what actually happens at 'ground level' must be reflected in the choice of business structure implemented for transactions.

3.5   AGENCY

Agency is based on the relationship of three persons. These are the principal, agent and third party. In *Customs and Excise Commissioners v Johnson*,[5] Woolf J cited with approval the definition of agency in *Bowstead on Agency*,[6] which states:

> 'Agency is the relationship between two persons, one of whom expressly or impliedly consents that the other should represent him or act on his behalf and the other of whom similarly consents to represent the former or so to act.'

It is important to realise that agency is generally the result of a contractual agreement. The parties to the agreement can decide precisely how the agency is to operate, for example, the extent of the powers available to the agent in concluding contracts with third parties on behalf

---

4   The payment for use of intellectual property may be subject to withholding tax (see Chapters 6 and 8).

5   [1980] STC 624, at 629.

6   Sweet & Maxwell, 15th edn, 1986, at p 1.

of the principal. In *Garnac Grain Co Inc v H M F Faure & Fairclough and Bunge Corporation*[7] the court commented on the nature of the agency relationship as follows:[8]

> 'The relationship of principal and agent can only be established by the consent of the principal and the agent. They will be held to have consented if they have agreed to what amounts in law to such a relationship, even if they do not recognise it themselves and even if they have professed to disclaim it … The consent must, however, have been given by each of them, either expressly or by implication from their words and conduct. Primarily one looks to what they said and did at the time of the alleged creation of the agency. Earlier words and conduct may afford evidence of a course of dealing in existence at that time and may be taken into account more generally as historical background. Later words and conduct may have some bearing, though likely to be less important. As to the content of the relationship, the question to be asked is: "what is it that the supposed agent is alleged to have done on behalf of the supposed principal?"'

A commercial agent is defined under the Commercial Agents (Council Directive) Regulations 1993 as:[9]

> '… a self-employed intermediary who has continuing authority to negotiate the sale or purchase of goods on behalf of another person (the "principal"), or to negotiate and conclude the sale or purchase of goods on behalf of and in the name of that principal.'

An agent is appointed to represent the commercial interests of the appointing party, known as the principal. An agent is sometimes provided with authority to contractually bind its principal to transactions with a third party. As the connectors in Figure 3.1 show, it is possible for rights and duties to exist between all three parties. The nature of these rights and duties varies according to the type of agency agreement that exists. As the figure illustrates, for the purposes of e-commerce, a commercial intermediary such as an agent can be appointed to solicit orders, or accept orders.

The scope of the authority of an agent in representing its principal will comprise 'actual authority', which is the authority to represent the principal as determined by the contract appointing the agent; and also 'apparent authority', which is the authority to be attributed to the agent in consequence of the conduct of the parties and the circumstances of the case.[10]

---

[7]   [1967] 2 All ER 353, HL.
[8]   [1967] 2 All ER 353, at 358, HL.
[9]   SI 1993/3053, reg 2(1), as amended by SI 1998/2868.
[10] *In Freeman & Lockyer (a firm) v Buckhurst Park Properties (Mangal) Ltd* [1964] 2 QB 480, at 503, Diplock LJ said: 'An "apparent" or "ostensible" authority, on the other hand, is a legal relationship between the principal and the contractor created by a representation, made by the principal to the contractor, intended to be and in fact acted on by the contractor, that the agent has authority to enter on behalf of the principal into

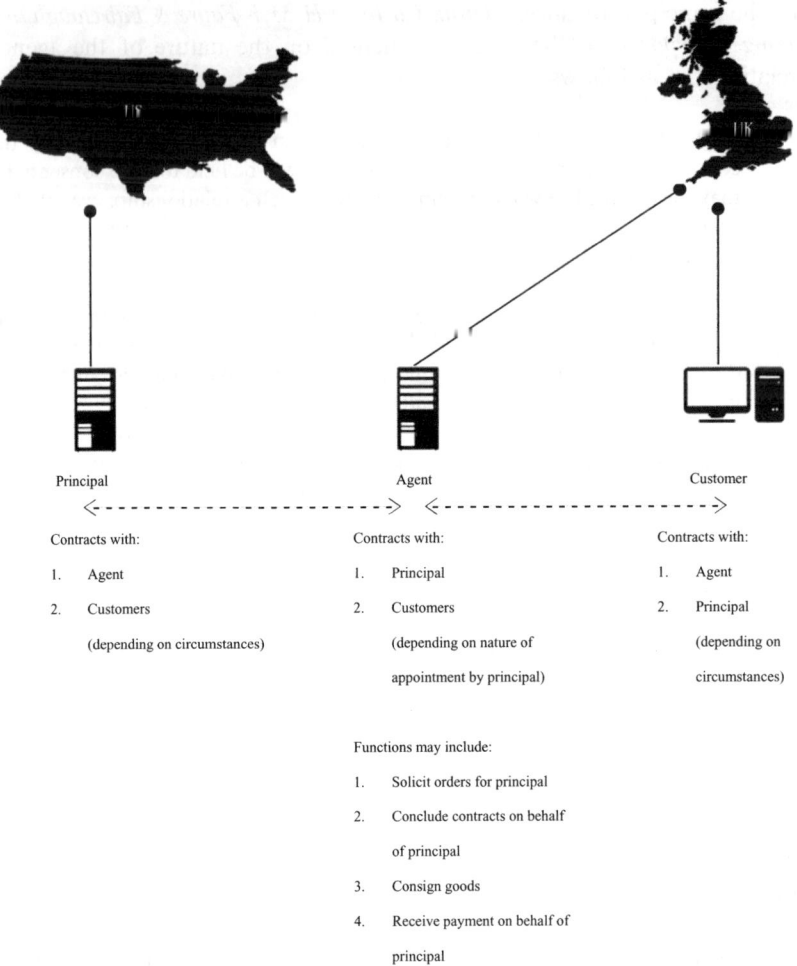

Figure 3.1: Relationships arising under agency

3.5.1   Agency classification

Broadly, agency falls into two categories. Agents act for either disclosed or undisclosed principals. The nature of the relationship differs significantly for legal purposes. For example, an agent acting for an undisclosed principal generally incurs more risk as a result of the legal rule that the agent is liable on the contract concluded with third parties. This is because the contract is formed between the agent and third party since as far as the outside world is concerned the agent appears to be the principal.[11] Due to the variations in the type of risks that are attributed to different agency arrangements it is possible to choose a relationship which will

a contract of a kind within the scope of the "apparent" authority, so as to render the principal liable to perform any obligations imposed on him by such contract.'

[11]   *Oystertec plc v Barker* [2003] RPC 29.

support the chosen pricing arrangements between connected persons. For example, if the parties want to limit the commission of an agent, and maximise the returns to a principal located in a low tax jurisdiction, it is desirable to establish an agency arrangement under which the agent incurs minimal legal and therefore economic risk. An arrangement that could meet this objective is the use of a disclosed agency whereby any contract concluded with a third party is with the principal and not the agent. Alternatively, the parties may use a simple introduction agent arrangement. The benefit is that these agents generally assume minimal risk.

Table 3.2 summarises the nature of the distinction between a disclosed and an undisclosed agent. However, it is important to take appropriate legal and tax advice as to the nature of the rights and obligations which arise under these relationships.

Table 3.2: Agency categories

Type	Nature of relationship
Disclosed agency	Principal liable on contracts entered into with third parties by agent. Actions of agent create contractual responsibilities between principal and third party. Agent not generally liable on contract concluded on behalf of principal with consumers.[12] Agent may undertake personal liability on contract.[13]
Undisclosed agency	The agent initially becomes liable to the third party on the contract that has been concluded between the two parties (ie the agent incurs contractual responsibilities and liabilities).[14]

---

[12] *Phonogram v Lane* [1982] 3 CMLR 615, at para 23: Lord Denning MR commented: 'The general principle is, of course, that a person who makes a contract ostensibly as an agent cannot afterwards sue or be sued upon it.'

[13] See *Montgomerie v United Kingdom Mutual Steamship Association* [1891] 1 QB 370 and *Foxtons Ltd v Thesleff* [2005] EWCA Civ 514, [2005] 2 EGLR 29.

[14] As to the nature of the liabilities created in an undisclosed agency, in *Oystertec plc v Barker* [2003] RPC 29, at para 5, Jacob J stated: 'Whenever any agent acts for an undisclosed principal he is, to the outside world, the principal. The outside world treats him as a principal and is entitled to treat him as a principal. Whether he has a private arrangement with someone else is no business of the outside world as far as its dealings with him are concerned.'

Internet Business: Legal and Commercial

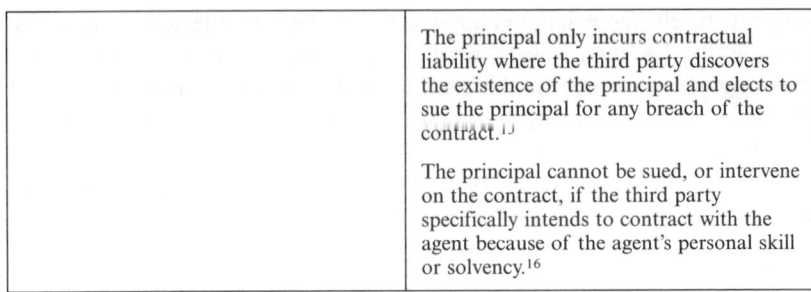

	The principal only incurs contractual liability where the third party discovers the existence of the principal and elects to sue the principal for any breach of the contract.[15]
	The principal cannot be sued, or intervene on the contract, if the third party specifically intends to contract with the agent because of the agent's personal skill or solvency.[16]

It is important to appreciate that because of the consensual nature of agency, it is possible to inject risk into the arrangement over and above that which the law would otherwise imply into the agency relationship. For example, in the case of a disclosed agency arrangement the agent is not generally liable on the concluded contract with the third party. Instead, a binding legal contract exists between the principal and third party. However, the risks of the agent can be increased, and accordingly the expectation of a higher commission can be justified by the agent entering into what are known as 'collateral warranties' with the third party.[17] For example, the agent might undertake that the goods supplied under the contract are of satisfactory quality, or perhaps that the consignment of goods will comply with their description, or that the goods are fit for their intended purpose.

3.5.2   Commission

The UK has no specific non-tax legal rules on the actual rate and amount of commission that an agent should receive, since this is something to be negotiated by the parties. However, there is some guidance as to how the remuneration of a commercial agent should be determined (as to which see below). The issue of remuneration is of critical importance where the appointment of a commercial intermediary is made by a connected person on a cross-jurisdiction basis. Such pricing issues need clarification by the assistance of transfer pricing advisors: the topic of transfer pricing is considered in Chapter 9.

It has been recognised by the courts that the work of an agent is precarious and subject to risk. Any commission should reflect the commercial risk of an agent's business activities. In *Alpha Trading Ltd v Dunnshaw-Patten Ltd*,[18] Lawton LJ commented:

> 'The life of an agent in commerce is a precarious one. He is like the groom who takes a horse to the water-trough. He may get his principal to the negotiating table but when he gets him there he can do nothing to make him

---

[15]   See *Thomson v Davenport* (1829) B & C 78; *Muldoon v Wood* [1998] EWCA Civ 588.
[16]   See *Siu Yin Kwan v Eastern Insurance Co Ltd, The Osrey* [1994] 1 All ER 213.
[17]   See *Teheran-Europe Co Ltd v ST Belton (Tractors) Ltd* [1968] 2 QB 53.
[18]   [1981] QB 290, at 308.

sign, any more than the groom can make a horse drink ... Once the signing has been done, the agent is in a different position altogether, because by that time the principal has accepted the benefit of the agent's work. In those circumstances, he ought not to be allowed to resile from his obligations to the agent once the agent has done his work and the principal has accepted the benefit of it.'

The Commercial Agents (Council Directive) Regulations 1993[19] provide that if an agreement between principal and agent is silent on commission, then a commission is to be paid on the following basis, and by reference to the following considerations:[20]

'In the absence of any agreement as to remuneration between the parties, a commercial agent shall be entitled to the remuneration that commercial agents appointed for the goods forming the subject of his agency contract are customarily allowed in the place where he carries on his activities and, if there is no such customary practice, a commercial agent shall be entitled to reasonable remuneration taking into account all the aspects of the transaction ...

A commercial agent shall be entitled to commission on commercial transactions concluded during the period covered by the agency contract –
(a)   where the transaction has been concluded as a result of his action; or
(b)   where the transaction is concluded with a third party whom he has previously acquired as a customer for transactions of the same kind.

A commercial agent shall also be entitled to commission on transactions concluded during the period covered by the agency contract where he has an exclusive right to a specific geographical area or to a specific group of customers and where the transaction has been entered into with a customer belonging to that area or group.'

These Regulations apply to commercial agents: see **3.5**.

3.5.3   Agency, distribution and franchise arrangements

A distributor is generally classified as a reseller of goods and is normally entitled to anticipate making a reseller's profit on sales. A distributor does not usually act on behalf of another person and is not accountable to another person, as an agent is to its principal. A distributor has no power to bind the supplier of the goods to a contract with third parties due to the fact that it has no agency function.

A franchisee, like a distributor, is in business for its own account with no power to bind the franchisor, ie the person permitting exploitation of the business format idea. A franchisee is like a distributor in that it operates rather like a reseller, but is also an exploiter of a business format idea.

---

[19]   SI 1993/3053.
[20]   Regs 6 and 7.

By contrast, a simple commission agent is generally entitled only to a percentage of the value of each transaction it concludes between its principal and a third party. This is because an agent is not an independent reseller.

Any documentation appointing a commercial intermediary should be structured so as to ensure that the risks, duties and obligations that justify an arrangement being treated as either a specific type of agency, distribution or franchise agreement are in place. However, such documentation is no substitute for real, substantial economic transactions. In all of these circumstances it is important to take appropriate legal and tax advice.

3.6   IDENTIFYING AND CLASSIFYING COMMERCIAL INTERMEDIARIES

The UK has no form of legislation that precisely identifies the material characteristics of each and every type of commercial intermediary. Sometimes this distinction is of importance for tax and transfer pricing[21] purposes. The distinction is sometimes necessary to determine because many arrangements between connected persons are not the subject of proper legal documentation. It is possible to draw a number of conclusions as to the nature of a commercial intermediary by what that party is required to do. For example, the following points are useful indicators:

- The fact that an agreement permits a person to sell goods to third parties at any price it chooses, with payment of a fixed amount for the goods to a supplier points to a resale arrangement (ie the person is acting as a distributor/reseller).

- The fact that a person is required to provide details of customers and accounts of moneys received and paid out is a clear pointer that the person is selling as an agent. A person who pays wholesale prices, as opposed to being required to account for the whole proceeds of a sale received from a third party, to another is likely to be classified as a reseller (distributor).

3.7   LEGAL DOCUMENTATION

One of the problems with the use of the word 'agency' is that it has become used in a number of circumstances to describe situations that are not proper agency relationships. A contract which merely places

---

[21]   This is the examination of pricing structures adopted between connected persons for the supply of either goods and/or services. The function of transfer pricing is to ensure as far as practicable that an arm's length price is paid for transactions between connected parties: this topic is considered in further detail in Chapter 9.

'principal' and 'agent' tags on parties to an agreement will not succeed in automatically creating an agency relationship. The labels used in agreements cannot be relied upon as creating the relationship desired to be brought into existence.[22] The courts have held on several occasions that the description of a relationship as being one of agency has in fact been as a matter of commercial reality a relationship of manufacturer and reseller.[23] By contrast, the courts have equally held an agency relationship to exist despite the fact that the contract between the parties excluded such a possibility.

The important point to remember is that the legal documentation creating arrangements must reflect the risks and obligations which are common to that specific relationship. The mere use of labels does not necessarily create a relationship of that type. Legal documentation for any arrangement should reflect the economic role performed by the participants.

3.8   ADVANTAGES OF AGENCY CATEGORIES FOR TRANSFER PRICING PURPOSES

Agency takes many different forms, which attract a range of risks to the role of principal and agent. This range of differences can be used to support the pricing structure chosen by parties. For example, an agent working as a representative for a disclosed principal does not incur the same risks as an agent working for an undisclosed principal. An agent working for an undisclosed principal enters directly into contractual relations with the third party, ie the consumer. A third party in this context has the choice of suing the agent or alternatively electing to sue the principal. In this scenario the agent would justifiably be entitled to a higher fee for the provision of its services.

Example 3.3

Alpha Inc appoints Beta UK Ltd to sell goods manufactured by it within the UK. Both companies are associated. Alpha Inc holds the majority of the shares in Beta UK Ltd. The appointment is solely for the sale of goods through the use of internet trading sites. Beta UK Ltd is appointed to act as an undisclosed agent. In other words, this means that consumers in the UK will believe that they are contracting for the provision of goods from a UK company. The presence of a US company in the transaction will not be indicated in any way through the activities of the UK company. Because the UK company acts as an undisclosed agent it is initially liable on the contract for supply of the goods. This means that the consumer will in the first instance have the right to sue the UK company. The use of this type of agent justifies a higher commission to it than, say, a mere introduction agent. Such

---

22   See *Fenston v Johnstone* (1940) 23 TC 29.
23   See eg *WT Lamb & Sons v Goring Brick Co Ltd* [1932] 1 KB 710; or *International Harvester Co of Australia Pty Ltd v Currigans Hazeldene Pastoral* (1958) 100 CLR 644.

choice of commercial intermediary can be used to support the pricing structure chosen between the associated parties.

Other types of agent may incur more risks because of the additional services they provide to their principal. The allocation of risk to a person is one factor for justifying a higher payment to that person. For example, a del credere agent guarantees that the third party will pay for the goods it purchases. The del credere agent incurs an additional risk over and above that of a normal agent, which justifies a higher commission on transactions. The creation and use of a del credere agent would be of value where a principal is located in a high tax jurisdiction. The risks undertaken by the del credere, ie responsibility for discharge of the buyer's contractual obligations to the seller, would justify the attraction of higher commission rates.

Example 3.4

US Internet Trading Inc appoints UK Intermediary Ltd as a del credere agent for the purposes of selling products manufactured by the US company. The point of sale will be via internet trading sites. The UK company is appointed to market the products to two distinct categories of client: businesses and the general public. The UK company is appointed on the basis that it will guarantee the payment of the purchase price for products by each and every buyer.

An order for £30,000-worth of goods is placed via the internet trading site by an authorised business entitled to access and place orders via the business section of the trading site. Under the terms of access the business buyer is entitled to delivery of the goods on order, and for payment within 60 days to be made to UK Intermediary Ltd. No payment is made within the 60-day period. Because the agent is a del credere, it is obliged to pay the £30,000 to US Internet Trading Inc. The intermediary will then be left to pursue a claim for payment against the business buyer itself. For the increase in responsibility the del credere should be entitled to a higher commission.

Alternatively, the use of an introduction agent may have several advantages. From a transfer pricing perspective a disclosed introduction agent is not liable on any contract between principal and third party, ie the consumer. Neither is the agent responsible for concluding the contract. The legal risks associated with the activities of such an agent are limited. This means that the introduction agent should be limited to a lower rate of return. An introduction agent is a person appointed to solicit customers, for example, through the use of internet trading sites, and who acts as a go-between for the principal and third party. The introduction agent has no power to conclude contracts between the principal and third party. The solicited orders are submitted to the principal, who decides whether or not to accept the order. An introduction agent represents the interests of a person in the sense that such an agent is eager to acquire business, because he or she is rewarded by a commission for each order accepted.

Any foreign trader must, however, be careful in appointing an agent. The arrangement should be structured so that it cannot be used as the basis for the UK tax authority claiming that a trade is being carried on in the UK through that agent for the purposes of applying a corporation tax charge, or that a trade is being exercised within the UK so that an income tax charge can be applied.

3.9 TAXATION OF UK REPRESENTATIVES OF NON-RESIDENTS TRADING IN THE UK

3.9.1 Definition of a UK representative

In certain circumstances, it is possible for the UK tax authority to assess a non-resident through its UK representative (known as a 'permanent establishment'). The legislation governing the collection machinery where the non-resident is a company is contained in Chapter 6 Part 22 of the Corporation Tax Act 2010 (CTA 2010); and where the non-resident is an individual the collection machinery is contained in Chapter 2B of Part 14 of the Income Tax Act 2007 (ITA 2007).[24]

Broadly, in connection with a non-resident company, the effect of the legislation is to impose obligations and liabilities in relation to corporation tax on the UK permanent establishment (such as a physical branch or agent located in the UK) through which that non-resident carries on a trade.[25] A branch or agency is only a UK representative if the non-resident carries on a trade through a permanent establishment.[26] A permanent establishment is defined as meaning either (a) a fixed place of business in the UK through which the business of the non-resident company is wholly or partly carried on, or (b) an agent acting on behalf of the non-resident company that has and habitually exercises in the UK authority to do business on behalf of the non-resident company.[27] The circumstances in which a permanent establishment comes into existence are considered in further detail in Chapter 6.

A UK representative could be the person who operates a computer server in the UK for a non-resident company. Of course a branch or agency would need to exist which was used as a centre of economic operations to produce profits for the non-resident: see Chapters 6 and 8.

If the non-resident company does not carry on a trade through a permanent establishment in the UK, then there can be no UK

---

[24] ITA 2007, s 835C(2). Similar provisions apply for the purposes of tax on capital gains: Taxation of Chargeable Gains Act 1992, Part 7A.
[25] CTA 2010, s 969.
[26] CTA 2010, s 969. See CTA 2010, s 1141.
[27] CTA 2010, s 1141(1).

representative. In these circumstances the non-resident is responsible for complying with its UK tax obligations in respect of any UK source trade.

Example 3.5

X Inc sets up a branch in the UK through which it operates an e-commerce business. The profits for 2011/12 are £1 million. The branch will constitute a UK representative of X Inc. Accordingly, the branch will be responsible for the assessment and payment of the UK tax attributable to the profits of the branch.

Example 3.6

Z SA, based in Spain, operates a computer server in the UK. The server acts as a conduit for relaying customer orders placed via an e-commerce website hosted by the UK computer server. A computer server in Spain then processes the order, interrogates the UK computer server for further information concerning the customer, processes the payment details and issues the delivery order. Delivery is made from Spain. In these circumstances there is no permanent establishment in the UK through which a trade is carried on. Accordingly, there is no UK representative. Any income tax liability which might arise because a trade is being carried on in the UK would be the responsibility of Z SA. It is unlikely that a trade would be carried on in the UK because the operations from which the profits arise are not in the UK, and the terms of the double taxation agreement with Spain should ensure that there is no liability to tax since there would need to be a permanent establishment in the UK.

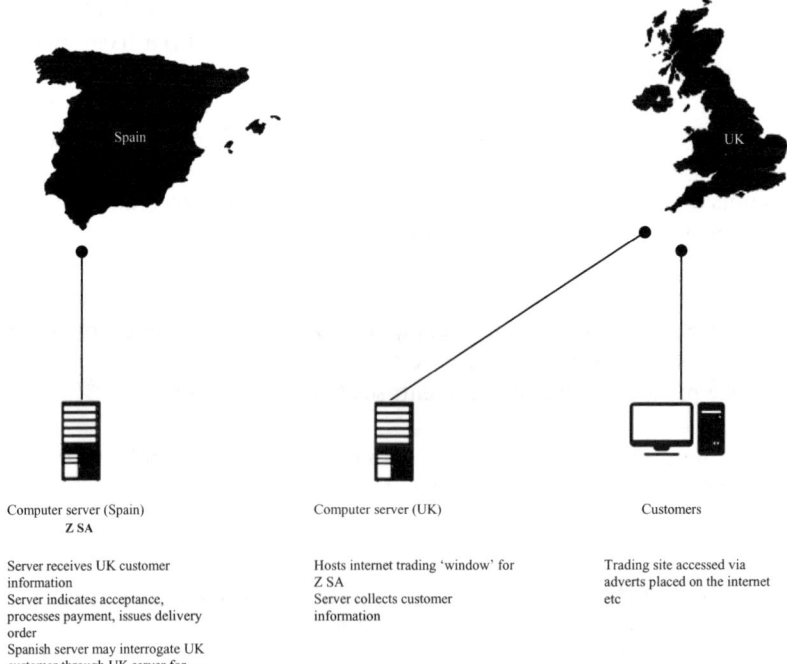

Computer server (Spain) **Z SA**	Computer server (UK)	Customers
Server receives UK customer information Server indicates acceptance, processes payment, issues delivery order Spanish server may interrogate UK customer through UK server for further information	Hosts internet trading 'window' for Z SA Server collects customer information	Trading site accessed via adverts placed on the internet etc

3.9.2 Obligations of a UK representative

The obligations and liabilities of a non-UK resident company are treated as if they were the obligations and liabilities of the UK representative.[28] Generally, the UK representative is jointly responsible with the non-resident for all the tax obligations arising from the trade carried on through the permanent establishment.[29] The permanent establishment is treated as the UK representative of the non-resident company in respect of chargeable profits attributable to the establishment, and it will continue to be so treated in respect of such profits even after ceasing to be a permanent establishment of the non-resident.[30]

The non-resident company is bound by any acts or omissions of its UK representative in the discharge of the obligations and liabilities imposed on the UK representative.[31]

---

[28] CTA 2010, s 970.
[29] CTA 2010, s 970(3). There are certain exceptions in CTA 2010, s 971.
[30] CTA 2010, s 969(3).
[31] CTA 2010, s 970(4). There are certain exceptions in CTA 2010, s 971.

CHAPTER 4

CONTRACTS: FORMATION AND LEGAL REQUIREMENTS

4.1 INTRODUCTION

This chapter focuses on the contract law of England and Wales (laws differ in other parts of the UK such as Scotland). Contract law is an important element of the supply of goods and/or services which are made either business to business (B2B) or business to non-business consumer (B2C). Many of the basic common law contract principles apply irrespective of whether the supply is made via the internet, mail order, telephone or pay TV; and express and implied terms will determine the rights and obligations of the seller and purchaser in respect of matters such as the quantity, price, time and place of delivery and quality of the goods and/or services that are supplied. If goods and/or services are supplied on a cross-border basis the governing law for that supply will be determined by the rules of either an international convention or the principles of law provided by the courts.

The law of contract is important for tax purposes since it assists in identifying whether a person is carrying on a trade in the UK for the purposes of income tax and corporation tax (this is dealt with in Chapter 6). For VAT purposes it is always important to identify the nature of the supply which is being made in order to determine the correct VAT treatment. Often, a written contract will determine all the rights and obligations that arise between the parties in relation to a supply of goods and/or services.[1] However, it is also possible that the nature of the rights and obligations between the parties will be determined by their conduct (ie by what is done and said) to the extent that the written contract does not cover all the supplies made between the parties.[2] In this regard, it is always important to ensure that any form of supply is properly and comprehensively referred to in the contract in order to create certainty of VAT treatment. It is necessary to consider the nature of what has been agreed in the contract between the supplier and customer to identify the supply. The VAT treatment of e-commerce transactions is examined in Part V.

---

[1]   *A1 Lofts Ltd v HMRC (and related appeal)* [2010] UKFTT 581 (TC), [2009] EWHC 2694 (Ch).

[2]   *A1 Lofts Ltd v HMRC (and related appeal)* [2010] UKFTT 581 (TC), [2009] EWHC 2694 (Ch).

The purpose of this chapter is to explain the essence of the rules relating to contract formation relating to supplies of goods and/or services via e-commerce. It is beyond the scope of this book to provide a detailed commentary on such issues, and professional advice should be taken on all matters referred to in this chapter.[3]

4.2   CONTRACT FORMATION: E-COMMERCE

4.2.1   Introduction

A contract creates binding obligations between two or more persons for the supply of either goods or services. The traditional view is that a contract comes into existence when an unconditional offer (made by Person A) is unequivocally accepted (by Person B). Each contracting party must also give consideration for the other party's undertakings, otherwise there will be no contract unless it is by way of a deed. The contracting parties must also have capacity to enter into the contract, otherwise it will potentially be unenforceable. It is also worth noting that a contract will not be formed if there is no intention to create legal relations and terms will not form part of a contract unless they are properly incorporated. The following commentary identifies the nature of the main constituent elements of a contract, and how a contract is formed in the context of e-commerce transactions. The timing as to when a contract is formed is significant since it will be important in deciding when a supply is made for the purposes of VAT, and issues such as whether a non-resident company is trading in the UK.[4] A detailed review of these non-tax matters is beyond the scope of this chapter, and professional advice should be taken appropriate to the circumstances. As noted, contract and other laws vary in different parts of the UK and the following focuses on the position under English and Welsh law.

4.2.2   Offer distinguished from an invitation to treat

An offer by Party A must be distinguished from an invitation to treat by Party A since such an invitation, of itself, is not capable of forming a binding contact. An invitation to treat is often a preliminary stage in the process towards the conclusion of a contract. An invitation to treat is regarded as an invitation to another person to make an offer, which is then capable of being accepted. For example, does a seller who advertises goods on a website make an offer for the sale of those goods to anyone who sees the 'offer' and purports to accept it? If that were the case an acceptance, in these circumstances, from every person would create a

---

[3]   For detailed consideration of these matters, see Morris *The Conflict of Laws* (Sweet & Maxwell, 17th edn, 2009) and Dicey, Morris and Collins *The Conflict of Laws* (Sweet & Maxwell, 14th edn, 2006).

[4]   These aspects are considered in Chapter 6.

binding contract requiring the seller to supply the goods (irrespective of whether the seller had sufficient amounts of the goods in stock).

The general rule is that there is an invitation to treat where goods are displayed in a shop; and it is the customer who makes an offer to buy when the goods are presented at the checkout for payment.[5]

Generally, an offer must be communicated to the offeree and the terms of the offer must be clear and made with the intention that it should be binding if accepted. An offer is only capable of being accepted, if the offer has not lapsed, for example, after expiry of a time-limit.

> *Example 4.1: the Argos experience*[6]
>
> Argos is a catalogue retailer, and in September 1999 its internet trading site advertised television sets for £2.99 each, subject to availability, which should have been priced at £299.99. The pricing was a mistake, and Argos commented that none of the orders placed by prospective customers had been confirmed. By the time the company discovered its mistake several hundred orders had been placed using its internet site. Argos decided to refuse to meet any of the orders placed for the television sets. Did the advert constitute an offer, capable of a simple acceptance, or an invitation to treat? This illustrates the importance of the 'invitation to treat'/'offer' distinction in the context of e-commerce.

It is always advisable to ensure that there is as much certainty as possible over the circumstances in which an offer is made, and when the offer will be treated as being accepted. For example, by ensuring terms dealing with such matters are incorporated into a binding contract with the customer (ie so it is clear that only an invitation to treat is made) and by avoiding automatic messages on receipt of orders that might be construed as an acceptance (see below).

4.2.3 Acceptance

For an offer to be accepted, it must usually be an acceptance that is unqualified (ie no new terms are made since any 'counter-offer' on different terms cancels the original offer and itself becomes an offer capable of acceptance in the usual way). In some instances the courts have been prepared to find the existence of a contract even where the offer and acceptance were at variance. The neat distinction traditionally drawn has not prevented the courts finding there are contracts where parties seek to impose their terms on each other in a so-called 'battle of forms'.[7] The form of the acceptance can vary: for example, it may be in the form of writing or conduct, such as the supply of goods, or provision of services

---

[5] *Pharmaceutical Society of Great Britain v Boots Cash Chemists Ltd* [1953] 1 QB 401.

[6] For details of the story see http://news.bbc.co.uk/1/hi/business/441740.stm.

[7] *Butler Machine Tool Co Ltd v Ex-Cell-O Corporation (England) Ltd* [1979] 1 WLR 401.

in response to an offer.[8] Since conduct can amount to acceptance, there is a long line of cases that illustrate the dangers and uncertainties which can result from a failure to agree on clear written terms before commencing supply.[9]

It is generally necessary for the acceptance to be communicated to the person making the offer (sometimes referred to as the 'offeror')[10] and the general rule is that acceptance has no effect until communicated. Silence by the party to whom the offer is made is usually not indicative of acceptance of that offer.[11] However, there is a general principle that a postal acceptance of an offer is effective once posted (even though the acceptance will not have come to the notice of the offeror until it is received).[12] A postal acceptance is only effective if it is reasonable to use the post and/or the terms of the offer permit acceptance using the postal system.

If instantaneous forms of communication are used an acceptance is only effective if communicated to the offeror.[13] Instantaneous methods of communication would include telex, telephone and, by extension, video conferencing. The reason this follows the general rule (ie rather than the postal acceptance exception) is that the sender of the acceptance will usually know whether or not the message has been received successfully; and if not received that they will need to try again. The question of when acceptance is received can be problematic if a person uses a less-instantaneous method of communication (such as a telex message sent out of business hours) since messages may be delayed, sent out of working hours or never reach their intended recipient. The question may arise as to if or when acceptance by such means occurred. The courts have indicated this must be resolved by reference to the intention of the parties, by sound business practice and in some cases by a judgment where the risk should lie (eg a telex sent outside business hours may only be treated as effective during business hours).[14]

There is little precedent expressly addressing the treatment of newer forms of communication such as e-mail and there has been academic debate as to whether e-mail in particular should be treated as a form of

---

8   *Re Charge Card Services* [1989] Ch 497.
9   *RTS Flexible Systems Ltd (Respondent) v Molkerei Alois Muller Gmbh & Co KG (UK Production) (Appellant)* [2010] UKSC 14.
10 *Entores Ltd v Miles Far East Corp* [1955] 2 QB 327; *Brinkibon Ltd v Stahag Stahl und Stahlwarenhandelsgesellschaft mbH* [1983] 2 AC 34.
11 *Felthouse v Bindley* (1862) 142 ER 1037. See also *The Leonidas D* [1985] 1 WLR 925.
12 *Adams v Lindsell* (1818) 1 B & Ald 681; *Henthorn v Fraser* [1892] 2 Ch 27.
13 *Entores Ltd v Miles Far East Corp* [1955] 2 QB 327; *Brinkibon Ltd v Stahag Stahl und Stahlwarenhandelsgesellschaft mbH* [1983] 2 AC 34.
14 See *Brinkibon Ltd v Stahag Stahl und Stahlwarenhandelsgesellschaft mbH* [1983] 2 AC 34, at 42, where Lord Wilberforce comments that in relation to modern communications: 'No universal rule can cover all such cases; they must be resolved by reference to the intention of the parties, by sound business practice and in some cases by a judgment where the risk should lie.'

instantaneous communication (like telex) or if the postal rule should apply. The limited judicial consideration that has been given would tend to indicate the courts may be disinclined to apply the postal rule (at least on certain facts) and may treat e-mail as an instantaneous form of communication in line with the general principles above.[15] Best practice is for the offer to be as precise as possible as to the means of acceptance and the circumstances (e g hours) in which it will be effective.

The offeror can control the means of acceptance by specifying that only certain forms of acceptance will be binding.[16] It is often especially important in an e-commerce context to ensure that the terms of an offer make it clear as to the circumstances in which an offer will (or will not) be treated as being accepted via e-mail, twitter, instant messaging or orders placed over an internet site.

Example 4.2

A Ltd, a company trading in England, sells language translation software for the UK and international markets. The software is marketed through advertisements in computer journals and websites. Rosa, a resident of Birmingham, submits an order via A Ltd's website for software that will translate English and French text into Italian. The order is submitted, and payment made via the A Ltd website. The price is £400. Upon delivery Rosa discovers that one item of computer software is missing. The remaining software is successfully installed but converts French text into Ukrainian.

Assuming display of software on A Ltd's website is an invitation to treat, submission of the order by Rosa is an offer to buy the software and acceptance occurs (and a binding contract is formed) when notice of acceptance is deemed communicated to Rosa.

Where the contract is deemed made can be important for tax and so the circumstances of acceptance can be significant for tax practitioners (see Chapter 6). For example, if a contract is concluded by letter the contract is deemed made where the offer is accepted, i e where the letter is posted,[17] whilst in relation to instantaneous methods of communication such as telephone the contract is made at the place where the acceptance is received.[18]

---

[15] The timing of acceptance by email was considered in *Thomas and another v BPE Solicitors (a firm)* [2010] EWHC 306 (Ch), although the case was decided on other grounds and the comments should be treated as interesting rather than definitive.

[16] *Financings Ltd v Stimson* [1962] 1 WLR 1184.

[17] *Cowan v O'Connor* (1888) 20 QBD 640.

[18] *Entores v Miles Far East Corp* [1955] 2 QB 327.

4.2.4   Consideration

The undertakings given by each contracting party must be supported by consideration.[19] In other words, a benefit must be given to the promisor (eg a person promising to supply goods will usually receive payment for the goods), or a detriment incurred by the promisee (in this example, payment of the price or a promise made by the promisee in return).[20] The consideration must come from the person seeking to rely on the promise, ie the promisee (in the foregoing example, this might be the person making payment for the goods).[21] The consideration must have value, but can be nominal, and need not be adequate.[22] For example, a payment of £1 for a valuable promise would be sufficient consideration to create a binding contract for performance of that promise. However, as a general rule, performing an act which is already a pre-existing obligation is not sufficient consideration.[23]

4.2.5   Contract formalities

Generally, there are no formalities for the creation of a valid contract, such as a requirement that the contract be made in writing, or evidenced in writing, although there are a number of statutory exceptions, which are beyond the scope of this book. English and Welsh law generally imposes no specific written formalities for contracts which are concluded by e-mail, although contracts must comply with regulations applicable to e-commerce and local legal advice would need to be sought in the context of other jurisdictions.

4.2.6   Terms of the contract

Express terms

Generally, terms will not be effective unless they are made known and agreed as part of the acceptance. Agreeing express terms allows greater certainty for both parties and may be required by regulations (eg see **4.5**). Sometimes the terms will be included in another document, which is referred to in the offer, for example, a contract which is made subject to the standard terms settled by a representative body, such as a trade association. Online suppliers often seek expressly to incorporate terms by

---

19   Unless the promises are made in a deed. An instrument is a deed if it is clear on its face that it is intended to take effect as a deed, and is executed as a deed. An instrument is executed as a deed if it is signed by the individual making it, witnessed and delivered (essentially 'delivery' means an act indicating that the deed is binding on the person making it): see Law of Property (Miscellaneous Provisions) Act 1989, s 1.

20   *O'Sullivan v Management Agency & Music Ltd* [1985] QB 428.

21   *Thomas v Thomas* (1842) 2 QB 851; *Pollway Ltd v Abdullah* [1974] 1 WLR 493; *Tweddle v Atkinson* (1861) 121 ER 762.

22   *Wild v Tucker* [1914] 3 KB 36; *Thomas v Thomas* (1842) 2 QB 851.

23   *Stilk v Myrick* (1809) 2 Camp 317.

requiring the customer who is using a website to view the terms and click an 'I Accept' button (that is accompanied by incorporation language indicating that by clicking they accept that those terms will govern the contract) before being allowed to proceed with the transaction. Incorporation is important and professional advice should be taken on this issue. To the extent any terms are incompatible with any rule of law they will generally be excluded.[24]

Implied terms

A term may be incorporated in a contract such as where either (a) the parties are deemed to have intended to include such a term, (b) the law deems such a term to be incorporated in the contract or (c) the term is implied by custom.

For example, a term might be implied where a reasonable bystander would regard the term to be incorporated in the contract[25] or for the purposes of giving 'business efficacy' to a transaction, ie where a term is necessary to make the agreement work,[26] although the courts are wary of excessive intervention and do not have discretion to write a new contract. The approach taken by the courts has often varied in different cases and on different facts and the resulting uncertainty demonstrates the advantage of a clear, comprehensible, documented agreement.

In certain circumstances terms are implied by virtue of the operation of legislation. For example, terms relating to the sale of goods are implied by the Sale of Goods Act 1979;[27] and terms relating to the provision of services are implied by the Supply of Goods and Services Act 1982.

4.3   COUNTRY JURISDICTION: E-COMMERCE SUPPLIES

Any supply of goods and/or services made between persons who are resident within the UK is generally governed by the laws of the UK, and any breach of contract will be subject to enforcement in the courts of the UK. Where a contract exists between persons located in different countries then specific rules of multilateral international conventions may determine in which jurisdiction the contract can be enforced and the

---

[24]   See eg the Unfair Contract Terms Act 1977 and the Unfair Terms in Consumer Contracts Regulations 1999, SI 1999/2083.

[25]   In *Shirlaw v Southern Foundries Ltd* [1939] 2 KB 206, at 227, MacKinnon LJ commented: 'Prima facie that which in any contract is left to be implied and need not be expressed is something so obvious that it goes without saying; so that, if while the parties were making their bargain, an officious bystander were to suggest some express provision for it in the agreement, they would testily suppress him with a common "Oh, of course!"' (affirmed [1940] AC 701).

[26]   *Luxor (Eastbourne) Ltd v Cooper* [1941] AC 108. See also *The Moorcock* (1889) 14 PD 64.

[27]   See ss 12–15. The Act was amended by the Sale and Supply of Goods Act 1994.

governing law of the contract. However, if no convention applies then jurisdiction and governing law will be determined by the rules of English domestic law.[28]

4.3.1 Brussels Regulation

The Brussels Regulation on jurisdiction and the recognition and enforcement of judgments in civil and commercial matters (Brussels Regulation, also known as 'Brussels I')[29] governs the jurisdiction of courts of each Member State of the European Union (EU) in relation to civil and commercial matters.[30] The Regulation will generally only apply to contractual disputes between persons domiciled in EU Member States. For example, a claim for breach of contract by a consumer domiciled in England against a supplier domiciled in New York will not be subject to the jurisdiction of the Regulation. In such circumstances, the general common law of England will need to be considered.[31] The Brussels Regulation does not apply to revenue, customs or administrative matters.[32] A more detailed examination of the Regulation is beyond the scope of this chapter.

4.3.2 Lugano Convention

The Lugano Convention applies to relations between Member States of the European Community and Iceland, Norway and Switzerland for the purposes of determining jurisdiction over civil and commercial disputes.[33] The Convention is enacted in UK law by the Civil Jurisdiction and Judgments Act 1982.[34] The Convention is substantially similar to the Brussels Regulation.[35]

---

[28] See **4.3.3** and *Spiliada Maritime Corp v Cansulex* [1987] AC 460, which states that the test of jurisdiction is whether England is the more appropriate forum than any other foreign forum available or that justice requires the case be heard in England.

[29] Council Regulation 44/2001/EC of 22 December 2000 on jurisdiction and the recognition and enforcement of judgments in civil and commercial matters, OJ L 12/2, 16/01/2001 pp 1–23. The text can be accessed at: http://europa.eu.int/eur-lex/en.

[30] The Brussels Regulation is applied in UK law by the Civil Jurisdiction and Judgments Act 1982 (see also Civil Jurisdiction Order 2001, SI 2001/3929).

[31] See **4.3.3**.

[32] Art 1.1.

[33] For details refer to the European Commission Treaties Office database: http://ec.europa. eu/world/agreements/prepareCreateTreatiesWorkspace/treatiesGeneralData.do?step= 0&redirect=true&treatyId=7481 (2011).

[34] A copy of the text can be accessed at www.legislation.gov.uk. The Civil Jurisdiction and Judgments Act 1991 was amended by the Civil Jurisdiction and Judgments Regulations 2009, SI 2009/3131 to accommodate the Lugano Convention, which was agreed by the European Community, Iceland, Norway, Switzerland and Norway on 30 October 2007.

[35] For specific details refer to the Convention.

4.3.3 Non-convention countries

In the absence of an applicable convention the English courts will assume jurisdiction over a dispute where a claim form has been served on a defendant who, if an individual, is physically within England or, if a corporation, is present in England.[36] Further, the English courts will have jurisdiction where a defendant voluntarily submits to the jurisdiction of the English courts.[37]

In limited circumstances it is possible to obtain permission to serve a claim form outside of England and Wales.[38] The court must be satisfied that England and Wales is the proper jurisdiction to bring the claim.[39] A claim form may be served outside the jurisdiction with the permission of the court in relation to a contract where certain grounds exist.[40] The grounds are where the contract (a) was made within England and Wales (which may depend on the circumstances of acceptance), (b) was made by or through an agent trading or residing within the jurisdiction, (c) is governed by English law or (d) contains a term to the effect that an English court shall have jurisdiction to determine any claim in respect of the contract.[41] Another ground is where a claim is made in respect of a breach of contract committed within the jurisdiction of England and Wales.[42]

4.4   GOVERNING LAW: E-COMMERCE

4.4.1   Rome I Regulation[43]

Scope

The parties to a transaction for the supply of goods and/or services are entitled to choose the applicable law which will govern their contractual obligations. In connection with the law applicable to contracts, the purpose of the Rome I Regulation (Rome I) is to apply a uniform set of rules for the purposes of determining the applicable law that will govern a contractual relationship. Rome I applies to contracts that have been

---

[36]   Civil Procedure Rules 1998 (CPR), SI 1998/3132, Section A, Part 6, r 6.5.

[37]   CPR: e g where a counterclaim can be made under Part 20, and r 11(5) gives the court jurisdiction where a defendant files an acknowledgment of service but then fails to make an application disputing the court's jurisdiction.

[38]   CPR, Section A, Part 6, r 6.36.

[39]   CPR, Section A, Part 6, r 6.37(3).

[40]   CPR PD 6B (Service out of the jurisdiction), para 3.1(6).

[41]   CPR PD 6B (Service out of the jurisdiction), para 3.1(6).

[42]   CPR PD 6B (Service out of the jurisdiction), para 3.1(7).

[43]   Regulation 593/2008/EC of the European Parliament and of the Council of 17 June 2008 on the law applicable to contractual obligations (Rome I), OJ L 177/6, 04/07/2008 pp 6–16.

concluded after 17 December 2009.[44] Member States of the EU are subject to the Regulation.[45] The laws which may be applied to a contract under the Regulation are not limited to the laws of Member States; it is entirely possible that any law in the world could be applied as identified by Rome I (eg the laws of the US to e-commerce transactions entered into with purchasers based in any Member State).[46]

Rome I applies to situations involving a conflict of laws, to contractual obligations in civil and commercial matters.[47] However, it has no application to matters of a revenue, customs or administrative nature.[48] The Regulation does not apply to a number of situations, and these include: obligations arising under bills of exchange, cheques, promissory notes and other negotiable instruments; questions governed by the law of companies; issues such as whether an agent is able to bind a principal; and insurance contracts.[49] Rome I will apply if a dispute is to be heard in the courts of an EU Member State.

The law applicable under the Regulation will determine, in particular, the following matters in relation to a contract:[50]

- interpretation;

- performance;

- the consequences of a total or partial breach of obligations, including the assessment of damages;

- the ways of extinguishing obligations, prescription and limitation of actions; and

- the consequences of nullity of the contract.

On matters relating to the manner of performance of the contract (eg when delivery is to occur) and the steps to be taken where there is defective performance, Rome I requires regard to be had to the law of the country in which performance takes place.[51]

---

[44] Contracts entered into before this date are subject to the provisions of the Rome Convention of 1980. The Convention of 1980 is enacted in UK law by the Contracts (Applicable Law) Act 1990.

[45] Rome I, Art 29.

[46] Rome I, Art 2.

[47] Rome I, Art 1.

[48] Rome I, Art 1.

[49] Rome I, Art 1.2. The matters to which the Regulation does not apply are listed in Arts 1.2 and 1.3.

[50] Rome I, Art 12.1.

[51] Rome I, Art 12.2.

Rome I provides that the existence and validity of a contract, or of any term of a contract, will be determined by the law which would govern it under the Regulation.[52] If a contract is concluded between persons who, or whose agents, are in the same country the contract is regarded as formally valid if it satisfies the formal requirements of the law that governs it under the Regulation, or of the law of the country where it is concluded.[53] If the contract is concluded between persons who, or whose agents, are in different countries the contract is formally valid if it satisfies the formal requirements of the law which governs it under the Regulation, or of the law of the country where the contract is concluded.[54] A detailed review of Rome I is beyond the scope of this chapter.

4.5 EUROPEAN REGULATIONS

The supply of goods and/or services is subject to specific rules, many of which have developed in consequence of the UK's membership of the European Community. A number of the important developments are discussed in the following sections, although other regulations may also be applicable, especially in the context of transactions with consumers. In addition to UK laws, online suppliers also need to be aware of laws applicable in other relevant jurisdictions. A detailed review of these matters is beyond the scope of this chapter, and professional advice should be taken appropriate to the circumstances.

4.5.1 Consumer Protection (Distance Selling) Regulations 2000

The Consumer Protection (Distance Selling) Regulations 2000[55] provide for protection of consumers in respect of distance contracts. The Regulations implement EU law, which is designed to create a minimum level of protection for consumers throughout the EU. The Regulations apply to 'distance contracts' other than excluded contracts.[56] The

---

[52] Rome I, Art 10.1.
[53] Rome I, Art 11.1.
[54] Rome I, Art 11.2.
[55] SI 2000/2334.
[56] Reg 4. Excluded contracts are contracts: (a) for the disposal of an interest in land, except for a rental agreement, (b) for the construction of a building where the contract also provides for a disposal of an interest in land on which the building is constructed, except for a rental agreement, (c) relating to financial services, (d) concluded by means of an automated vending machine or automated commercial premises, (e) concluded with a telecommunications operator through the use of a public pay-phone, (f) concluded at an auction (reg 5(1)). Further, the Regulations only apply in part (so that regs 7–19(1) do not apply) to contracts for the supply of food or other goods intended for everyday consumption supplied to the consumer's residence or to his workplace by regular roundsmen; or contracts for the provision of accommodation, transport, catering or leisure services, where the supplier undertakes, when the contract is concluded, to provide the services on a specific date or within a specific period (reg 6(2)).

Internet Business:
Legal and Commercial

Regulations are limited to contracts made by a supplier with a consumer,[57] and apply to a contract made exclusively by means of distance communication.

A 'distance contract' is defined as meaning:[58]

> '... any contract concerning goods or services concluded between a supplier and a consumer under an organised distance sales or service provision scheme run by the supplier who, for the purpose of the contract, makes exclusive use of one or more means of distance communication up to and including the moment at which the contract is concluded.'

The term 'means of distance communication' is defined as meaning 'any means which, without the simultaneous physical presence of the supplier and the consumer, may be used for the conclusion of a contract between those parties'.[59] A non-exhaustive list of such means is contained in Sch 1 to the Regulations, which includes: telephone with human intervention,[60] telephone without human intervention (automatic calling machine, audiotext),[61] videophone (telephone with screen),[62] videotext (microcomputer and television screen) with keyboard or touch screen,[63] e-mail[64] and television (teleshopping).[65]

Some of the main implications of the Regulation are that supplier's dealing with consumers must:

• provide certain information in good time prior to the conclusion of the contract;

• provide confirmation of key information in a durable medium with certain deadlines;

• perform the contract within 30 days from the date of the consumer's order (unless otherwise agreed); and

• allow the consumer a 'cooling-off' period in which to end the contract (this cooling-off period will be extended if certain key information has not been provided).

---

[57] A 'supplier' is defined as 'any person who, in contracts to which these Regulations apply, is acting in his commercial or professional capacity'; and 'consumer' is defined as meaning 'any natural person who, in contracts to which these Regulations apply, is acting for purposes which are outside his business' (reg 3(1)).

[58] Reg 3(1).

[59] Reg 3(1).

[60] Item 6, Sch 1.

[61] Item 7, Sch 1.

[62] Item 9, Sch 1.

[63] Item 10, Sch 1.

[64] Item 11, Sch 1.

[65] Item 13, Sch 1.

The obligations imposed under the Regulations upon a supplier, which must be discharged in good time, and prior to the conclusion of the contract are as follows:

(a) provide the consumer with the following information:[66]

- identity of the supplier, and if payment in advance is required, the supplier's address;
- a description of the main characteristics of the goods or services;
- the price of the goods or services including all taxes;
- delivery costs where appropriate;
- arrangements for payment, delivery or performance;
- the existence of a right of cancellation, except where there is an exception to the right to cancellation under the Regulations;
- the cost of using the means of distance communication where it is calculated other than at the basic rate;
- the period for which the offer or the price remains valid; and
- the minimum duration of the contract, in the case of contacts for the supply of goods or services to be performed permanently or recurrently;

(b) inform the consumer if he proposes, in the event of the goods or services ordered by the consumer being unavailable, to provide substitute goods or services of equivalent quality and price;[67] and

(c) inform the consumer that the cost of returning any such substitute goods to the supplier in the event of cancellation by the consumer would be met by the supplier.[68]

The supplier is required to provide much[69] of the information referred to in (a) to the consumer in writing, or another durable medium, either prior to the conclusion of the contract or in good time and in any event during the performance of the contact (where services are supplied), or at the latest time of delivery where goods not for delivery to third parties are concerned.[70] Durable medium will, for example, include e-mail but not websites, since the supplier can change that information. The information to be so provided in durable medium also includes:

- certain information about the conditions and procedures for exercising the right to cancel;

---

[66] Reg 7(1)(a).

[67] Reg 7(1)(b).

[68] Reg 7(1)(c).

[69] Reg 8(2). The information required by reg 8 is not required to be provided where the contract for the supply of services which is performed through the use of a means of distance communication, where those services are supplied on only one occasion and are invoiced by the operator of the means of distance communication (reg 9(1)).

[70] Reg 8(1)(b).

- the address of the supplier's place of business to which the consumer may address any complaints;

- information about any after-sales services and guarantees; and

- the conditions for exercising any contractual right to cancel the contract, where the contract exceeds one year, or is for an unspecified duration.

The Regulations confer on a consumer the right to cancel the distance contract by issuing a notice of cancellation within a specified 'cooling-off' period; the cooling-off period will be substantially extended[71] if the consumer has not been provided with the necessary information in durable form.[72] In general terms, the effect of the cancellation is that the contract is treated as if it had not been made.[73] A 'notice of cancellation' is a notice in writing or in another durable medium which, however expressed, indicates the intention of the consumer to cancel the contract.[74] Upon cancellation the supplier must within 30 days of the notice being given reimburse any sum paid by or on behalf of the consumer under or in relation to the contract free of any charge.[75] The cancellation of any distance contract also has the effect of cancelling any related credit agreement.[76] On cancellation of such a contract the consumer is required to restore the goods to the supplier, and during the period prior to restoring the goods, retain possession of the goods and take reasonable care of them.[77] Unless the parties to a distance contract otherwise agree the supplier is required to perform the contract within a maximum of 30 days from the day after the consumer submits his order to the supplier.[78]

---

[71]   Regs 11 and 12, eg, provide that in the case of goods the cancellation period ends on the expiry of the period of seven working days beginning with the day after the day on which the consumer receives the goods if reg 8 has been complied with, but if reg 8 is not complied with the cancellation period may extend to 3 months and 7 working days beginning with the day after the day on which the consumer receives the goods. Regs 11 and 12 also provide for a 'cooling-off period' in the case of services and provisions addressing situations where the required information is delivered late during the 3-month period.

[72]   Reg 10(1). The period for cancellation of a contract for the supply of goods is governed by reg 11, and a contract for the supply of services is governed by reg 12. The right of cancellation is subject to various exceptions specified in reg 13, such as contracts for the supply of audio or video recordings or computer software if they are unsealed by the consumer.

[73]   Reg 10(2).

[74]   Reg 10(3).

[75]   Reg 14. The supplier is entitled, subject to certain conditions, to make a charge not exceeding the direct costs of recovering any goods supplied under the contract where a term of the contract provides that the consumer must return the goods upon cancellation, and the consumer does not do so or returns the goods at the expense of the supplier (reg 14(5)). There are certain exceptions to this: see reg 14(6) and (7).

[76]   Reg 15(1).

[77]   Reg 17(3).

[78]   Reg 19(1). Subject to exceptions, if the supplier is unable to perform the contract within

The EU Regulations upon which these Regulations are based will be repealed and replaced by the recent Consumer Rights Directive,[79] which must be implemented by EU Member States by the deadline of 13 June 2014. The Consumer Rights Directive will differ in a number of significant ways. At the time of writing the UK Government also proposes consulting on revoking the Regulations (and certain similar legislation) in order to replace them with a single consolidated Consumer Rights Bill.[80]

4.5.2 Electronic Commerce (EC Directive) Regulations 2002

The Electronic Commerce (EC Directive) Regulations 2002[81] implement an EC Directive on certain legal aspects of information society services, and specifically in connection with e-commerce.[82] The Regulations have no application in the field of taxation.[83] However, they apply to several areas, including activities of information society service providers, commercial communications and unsolicited commercial communications.

The Regulations also make provision for contracts concluded by electronic means.[84] They require, except when otherwise agreed by persons who are not consumers, that where a contract is to be concluded by electronic means, a minimum type of information will be given by a service provider prior to an order being placed by the recipient of the service.[85] The information which must be given in a 'clear, comprehensible and unambiguous manner' is as follows:[86]

- the different technical steps to follow to conclude the contract;

- whether or not the concluded contract will be filed by the service provider and whether it will be accessible;

- the technical means for identifying and correcting input errors prior to the placing of the order; and

- languages offered for the conclusion of the contract.

---

30 days because the goods or services ordered are not available the supplier is required to inform the consumer, and reimburse any sum paid by or on behalf of the consumer (reg 19(2)).

[79] OJ 2011 L 304/64.
[80] http://nds.coi.gov.uk/content/detail.aspx?NewsAreaId=2&ReleaseID=
421254&SubjectId=2.
[81] SI 2002/2013.
[82] The directive is Directive 2000/31/EC.
[83] Reg 3(1).
[84] Reg 9.
[85] Reg 9.
[86] Reg 9(1).

There are also obligations on the service provider to indicate which codes of conduct he subscribed to and information on how those codes can be consulted electronically (except when otherwise agreed by persons who are not consumers).[87]

There is no obligation to provide the foregoing information in respect of contracts concluded exclusively by exchange of e-mail or by equivalent individual communications.[88] A service provider is required to ensure that the contract terms and general conditions provided to the recipient must be capable of being stored and reproduced by the recipient.[89]

Under the Regulations, unless parties who are not consumers have agreed otherwise, where the recipient of the services places his order through technological means, a service provider is required to:[90]

- acknowledge the receipt of the recipient's order without undue delay and by electronic means; and

- make available to the recipient appropriate, effective and accessible technical means allowing him to identify and correct input errors prior to the placing of the order.

For the foregoing purposes, a 'service provider' is defined as 'any person providing an information society service',[91] and 'recipient of the service' is defined as 'any person who, for professional ends or otherwise, uses an information society service, in particular for the purposes of seeking information or making it accessible'.[92] The term 'information society services' is defined as 'services within the meaning of Art 1(2) of Directive 98/34/EC ... as amended by Directive 98/48/EC ...',[93] which provides as follows:

> '"Service": any Information Society service, that is to say, any service normally provided for remuneration, at a distance, by electronic means and at the individual request of a recipient of services.
>
> For the purposes of this definition:
> – "at a distance": means that the service is provided without the parties being simultaneously present,
> – "by electronic means": means that the service is sent initially and received at its destination by means of electronic equipment for the processing (including digital compression) and storage of data, and

---

[87] Reg 9(2).
[88] Reg 9(4).
[89] Reg 9(3).
[90] Reg 11(1). These requirements do not apply to contracts concluded exclusively by exchange of electronic mail or equivalent individual communications: reg 11(3).
[91] Reg 2(1).
[92] Reg 2(1).
[93] Reg 2(1).

entirely transmitted, conveyed and received by wire, by radio, by optical means or by other electromagnetic means,
– "at the individual request of a recipient of services": means that the service is provided through the transmission of data on individual request.

An indicative list of services not covered by this definition is set out in Annex V.

This Directive shall not apply to:
– radio broadcasting services,
– television broadcasting services covered by point (a) of Article 1 of Directive 89/552/EEC.'

The indicative list of services set out in Annex V is as follows:

'1. Services not provided "at a distance"

Services provided in the physical presence of the provider and the recipient, even if they involve the use of electronic devices:

(a) medical examinations or treatment at a doctor's surgery using electronic equipment where the patient is physically present;
(b) consultation of an electronic catalogue in a shop with the customer on site;
(c) plane ticket reservation at a travel agency in the physical presence of the customer by means of a network of computers;
(d) electronic games made available in a video-arcade where the customer is physically present.

2. Services not provided "by electronic means"
– Services having material content even though provided via electronic devices:
(a) automatic cash or ticket dispensing machines (banknotes, rail tickets);
(b) access to road networks, car parks, etc., charging for use, even if there are electronic devices at the entrance/exit controlling access and/or ensuring correct payment is made.
– Off-line services: distribution of CD roms or software on diskettes.
– Services which are not provided via electronic processing/inventory systems:
(a) voice telephony services;
(b) telefax/telex services;
(c) services provided via voice telephony or fax;
(d) telephone/telefax consultation of a doctor;
(e) telephone/telefax consultation of a lawyer;
(f) telephone/telefax direct marketing.

3. Services not supplied "at the individual request of a recipient of services"

Services provided by transmitting data without individual demand for simultaneous reception by an unlimited number of individual receivers (point to multipoint transmission):

> (a) television broadcasting services (including near-video on-demand services), covered by point (a)of Article 1 of Directive 89/552/EEC;
> (b) radio broadcasting services;
> (c) (televised) teletext.'

4.6 TERMS AND CONDITIONS: WEBSITES

Each business that uses a website should include the terms and conditions (T&C) of use of the site by people accessing it, including the T&C for any supplies of goods and/or services made through the website. Ideally users would be required to view and expressly click to agree the T&C for websites (see **4.2.6**) before being allowed to use it, but few operators regard this as acceptable and so (despite the 'incorporation' risk) the most common approach is to put a prominent link to the T&C on each page of the site (in case the user accesses a particular page directly) with a title indicating that the link is to important legal terms. Where goods and services are provided or there are other particular risks a much more robust approach to incorporation is necessary (see **4.2.6**).

The T&C will usually cover a range of matters, such as data protection, privacy, security (e g user's obligations as to passwords), intellectual property right ownership, limitation of liabilities, links to third party sites, contract formation and governing law in the event of any dispute.

The T&C for a website should normally include terms dealing with the following matters, amongst others (this is an illustrative list of some of the areas often covered and does not address matters relevant to the sale of goods or services, and its scope will depend on the nature of the business):

General

- The identity of the person who owns and operates the website (including reference to the registered address and contact details and its VAT registration number and other matters required by regulations).[94]

- A statement that use of the website by a person means that such person accepts to be bound by the T&C in consideration of the access provided to the website.

---

[94] Including e g Electronic Commerce (EC Directive) Regulations 2002, SI 2002/2013, reg 6 and (if relevant) the amendments to legislation made by the Companies (Trading Disclosures) Regulations 2008, SI 2008/495.

- If the person accessing the site does not agree to the T&C then that person is not permitted to use the website and agrees not to access it.

- T&C should specifically indentify the website (domain name) to which they apply.

- T&C should state the standards of conduct the user must comply with (eg not use the site to engage in civil or criminal wrongs) and the actions the site provider may take as a result (eg co-operation with law enforcement).

- The data protection and privacy statements and information (required by regulation or good practice) are usually addressed in another 'click-wrapped' separate privacy policy document, prominently linked on each web page. Following a change in the UK law in May 2011[95] (implementing changes in EU law), the use of cookies and the like (to which consent requirements now often apply) has become more problematic for providers.

Intellectual property rights

- T&C should state that material, the appearance and layout of the website and any software are subject to intellectual property right protection, where appropriate (eg trade marks, copyright).

- T&C should not permit the user to copy, modify or alter, broadcast, distribute, sell or license any material on the website unless expressly authorised to do so.

Alterations to the website

- T&C should specify that the provider of the website is entitled to modify the T&C, and that use of the website is acceptance of any modifications.

Third party websites

- T&C should state that access (via links) is at the user's own risk.

- T&C commonly seek to limit rights to link to the site (eg to minimise the risk that third parties use the site to indicate endorsement of their own, abuse trade marks or misrepresent their relationship with the provider).

---

[95] Pursuant to the Privacy and Electronic Communications (EC Directive) (Amendment) Regulations 2011, SI 2011/1208.

Other matters

- T&C should be drafted such that no liability is accepted for any loss or damage arising from use of the website to the extent permitted by law (eg the website is provided 'as is' and may be out of date).

- The user agrees to indemnify the provider of the website for any liability, loss or damage arising from their use of the website.

- T&C should explain the governing law applicable to use of the website, and which apply to the T&C.

- T&C should usually allow the provider to change the website or withdraw the services/site at any time.

- T&C should state whether the service is only limited to users in a particular country or continent, such as the UK, Europe, the US, etc.

Websites will also need specific terms addressing any supply of goods or services, which will include many legal and commercial matters, by way of a few examples, including:

- Specifications of what is (and is not) being purchased.

- The mechanisms of offer/acceptance.

- Delivery terms (eg time of supply and passage of risk and title to goods).

- Dealing with matters relating to the sale of goods and services, consumer protection and compliance with legal requirements.

- Ownership and licences of intellectual property rights (eg in software supply there will commonly be an intellectual property licence which will include limitations on the use of the software).

- Charges and payment (including whether supply includes or excludes VAT).

- Termination/cancellation rights.

- Limitations of liability.

- Governing law and jurisdiction.

The lists provided above are merely illustrative of some of the matters that will need to be dealt with by a business.

The website and privacy T&C, and the T&C governing the supply of goods and services will each need to be drafted and formed to provide a comprehensive framework for the relevant business, and professional advice should always be taken to ensure that the terms are compliant with relevant laws.

PART III

UNITED KINGDOM TAXATION: GENERAL

CHAPTER 5

TAXES ON INTERNET BUSINESS

5.1 WHAT IS TAX, AND HOW IS IT CHARGED?

Tax is a compulsory obligation to pay money to the government.[1] The *Oxford English Dictionary* defines 'Tax' as:[2]

> 'a. A compulsory contribution to the support of government, levied on persons, property, income, commodities, transactions, etc., now at fixed rates, mostly proportional to the amount on which the contribution is levied.'

The method by which a tax payment is calculated varies according to the type of tax. In some cases the amount of tax to be paid is fixed as a specific percentage of profits from a designated source such as an e-commerce trade; and the tax liability is often imposed upon the person who creates the profits from that source.[3] This is known as direct taxation (see **5.2**).

In contrast, VAT is imposed on the use or consumption of various forms of supply, such as a telecommunication or electronic service. The person paying for use of the service is required to pay tax calculated by reference to the value of that service.[4] However, the person paying the tax is not necessarily the person who accounts for the tax to the government. This is known as indirect taxation (see **5.3**).

Tax can arise at a variety of points in the supply chain for an internet business, and any associated e-commerce transactions. Figure 5.1 provides an illustration of where tax can arise in the supply chain on these activities.

United Kingdom
Taxation: General

---

[1] For a historical introduction to UK tax law see the excellent book by JA Kay and MA King *The British Tax System* (Oxford University Press, 5th edn, 1990).

[2] *The Oxford English Dictionary*, 2nd edn, 1989; online version June 2011. www.oed.com/view/Entry/198260, accessed 23 June 2011.

[3] For corporation tax see Corporation Tax Act 2009 (CTA 2009), Part 3; and for income tax see Income Tax (Trading and Other Income) Act 2005 (ITTOIA 2005), Part 2.

[4] For value added tax see Value Added Tax Act 1994 (VATA 1994), s 1.

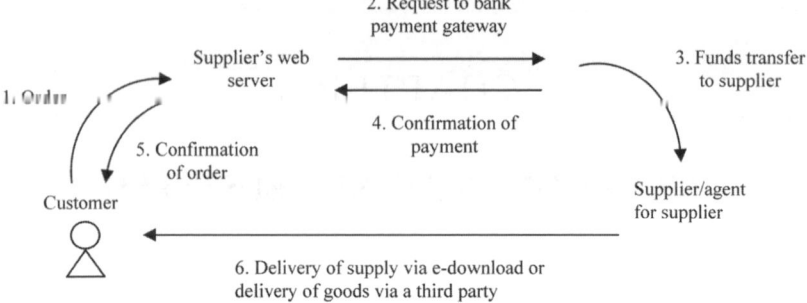

Figure 5.1: Tax arising in the supply chain for an internet business

5.1.1   Tax issues

The potential tax issues which arise include:

(1)   How is the supplier taxed? Is it subject to corporation tax or income tax? Is the supplier required to charge VAT on its supplies to the customer? Is the supplier's web server capable of creating a taxable presence in the UK or another country?

(2)   How is the customer taxed? Is the customer taxable, and is the cost of the supply subject to any tax relief in calculating the customer's taxable profits? Is the customer liable to pay VAT on the supply? If so, can the customer recover the VAT costs attributable to that supply?

(3)   If a commercial intermediary (eg an agent) is used in the supply chain, does this person create a taxable presence for the supplier in the agent's country of residence (if in separate countries)? What are the VAT consequences if the supply chain is across several countries in the EU? Is the VAT analysis any different if supplies are made to the EU or supplies are made out of the EU?

The nature of the taxes referred to above are summarised in this chapter.

Before considering the application of specific tax charges to internet business activities it is appropriate to recognise the fact that there is no constitutional limitation on the right of the UK to impose a tax charge on profits derived from the economic activities of a person, wherever that person is in the world. However, the tax charges that are imposed in the UK have their own territorial limits, since under their terms direct taxes (ie corporation tax and income tax) are chargeable only on a resident in the UK or on a non-resident in respect of certain specified activities carried on in the UK. The scope of these tax charges is discussed in this chapter.[5] Where a company incorporated abroad is controlled by a UK taxpayer, profits of the company may be taxable in the UK.[6] The circumstances in which overseas income from e-commerce is taxed in the UK are examined in Chapters 6 and 8.

The tax legislation does not provide any specific definition of the 'United Kingdom' (UK) other than to stipulate that the territorial sea of the UK is treated for the purposes of the corporation tax legislation as part of the UK.[7] The same approach is applied for the purposes of income tax.[8] However, the general rules of interpretation apply and provide that the UK means 'Great Britain and Northern Ireland'.[9] Great Britain comprises England, Wales and Scotland.[10] The Channel Islands (namely, the Bailiwicks of Jersey and Guernsey) do not form part of the UK since these are the residual vestiges of the Crown's claim to the Dukedom of Normandy.[11] Neither is the Isle of Man part of the UK since the Crown's claim derives from its rights as the Lord of Man.[12]

5.2 DIRECT TAXATION

5.2.1 Corporation tax

Corporation tax is imposed at the rates shown in Table 5.1 (2011/12) on a company's chargeable profits (comprising income and chargeable capital gains) for a financial year (commencing on 1 April).[13]

While companies pay tax on their chargeable profits,[14] the 'rate' of corporation tax to be applied is determined by comparing the bands against the company's 'augmented profits'.[15] 'Augmented profits' are, very

---

[5] See the comments as to territorial limit made by Lord Herschell in *Colquhoun (Surveyor of Taxes) v Brooks* (1889)14 App Cas 493, at 503, where he said: 'The Income Tax Acts, however, themselves impose a territorial limit; either that from which the taxable income is derived must be situate in the United Kingdom or the person whose income is to be taxed must be resident there': approved in *National Bank of Greece SA v Westminster Bank Exor and Trustee Co (Channel Islands) Ltd* [1971] AC 945, at 964; and *Clark v Oceanic Contractors Inc* [1983] STC 35, at 41, per Lord Scarman.

[6] For the attribution of profits to a corporation see Income and Corporation Taxes Act 1988 (ICTA 1988), s 747 (controlled foreign companies); for the attribution of income to individuals see Income Tax Act 2007 (ITA 2007), s 714 (transfer of assets abroad).

[7] CTA 2010, s 1170.

[8] ITA 2007, s 1013.

[9] Interpretation Act 1978, s 1 and Sch 1.

[10] See the Union with Scotland Act 1706, preamble, art 1.

[11] For the historical background see:
www.royal.gov.uk/MonarchUK/QueenandCrowndependencies.

[12] For the historical background see:
www.royal.gov.uk/MonarchUK/QueenandCrowndependencies.

[13] CTA 2009, s 2.

[14] Referred to as 'taxable total profits' in CTA 2010, s 4.

[15] CTA 2010, s 32.

broadly, a company's chargeable profits plus certain exempt dividends (grossed-up) that it has received from non-group companies, including from non-UK companies (as of 1 July 2009). These dividends are known as 'franked investment income'.

Table 5.1: Corporation tax rates (2011/12)

Tax rate	Bands (£)
Small profits rate: 20%	Up to £300,000
Effective marginal rate: 27.5%	£300,000 to £1.5 million
Main rate: 26% (reducing to 25% for 2012/13)	£1,500,001 or more

The small profits and marginal rates do not apply to a 'close investment holding company' (eg a closely held company that does not trade), so such companies will be taxed at the main rate regardless of the level of their profits, but this is unlikely to be of relevance to a company carrying on an e-commerce activity.[16] The impact of the effective marginal rate is to gradually increase the rate of tax paid on profits as they move from the small profits rate to the main rate. The effective marginal rate is normally applied to a company's chargeable profits falling between the bands by first taxing the profits at the main rate (26%), and then deducting 'marginal relief'. This relief is calculated based on a formula with reference to a company's augmented profits. If, however, the company has not received any franked investment income (ie the company's chargeable profits and 'augmented profits' are the same figure falling between the bands), the marginal rate can be applied to such company's profits via an alternative calculation, by applying the small profits rate up to £300,000, and then applying the marginal rate to the rest of its profits.

The tax calculation will, however, be affected if a company has 'associated companies', as then the bands above (ie £300,000 and £1,500,000) are reduced pro rata by the number of associated companies.[17] A company is an associated company of another if it has control of the other or if both are under the control of the same person or persons.[18] Computations are also further complicated if, for example, a company's period of account is more or less than 12 months, or if the period spans two financial years which have different tax rates. The corporation tax regime applies to profits that comprise income and chargeable capital gains made from the disposal of assets.[19] The profits of a company are principally calculated by reference to CTA 2009, CTA 2010 and the Taxation (International and

---

[16] CTA 2010, s 18.
[17] CTA 2010, s 24.
[18] CTA 2010, s 25(4).
[19] CTA 2010, s 2(2).

Other Provisions) Act 2010 (TIOPA 2010). Chargeable gains are calculated by reference to the Taxation of Chargeable Gains Act 1992 (TCGA 1992).[20]

The label 'corporation tax' is slightly misleading to the non-tax lawyer, because it applies to business structures that would not usually be regarded as companies for the purposes of the Companies Act 2006 (CA 2006).[21] For the purposes of corporation tax, a 'company' means 'any body corporate[22] or unincorporated association but does not include a partnership, a local authority or a local authority association'.[23] Thus, clubs which operate e-commerce sites for membership subscriptions or sale of club merchandise are potentially liable to corporation tax.[24]

As Table 5.2 (see **5.2.6**) illustrates, a company is subject to corporation tax if it is resident in the UK. Where this is the case the profits that may be subject to tax in the UK include those accruing to it on a worldwide basis.[25] A non-resident company will be subject to UK corporation tax where it carries on a trade in the UK through a permanent establishment.[26] One issue in this context is the extent to which an item of information technology, such as a computer server used to carry on an e-commerce trade or a satellite earth station, can constitute a permanent establishment for the purposes of corporation tax. In essence the piece of machinery should not, of itself, be capable of causing a taxable connection with the UK: this aspect is considered in Chapter 6. A non-resident company will be subject to UK corporation tax on its worldwide profits if it becomes centrally managed and controlled from the UK. Guidance for non-resident companies on how to prevent this is provided in Chapter 6, and Appendix H provides an illustrative protocol of management guidelines for a non-UK company to follow where it has management representatives in the UK.

Detailed consideration of corporation tax rules is beyond the scope of this book, and the reader should take appropriate professional advice

United Kingdom
Taxation: General

---

[20] TCGA 1992, s 8.

[21] CA 2006 defines a company as 'a company formed and registered under this Act ...' (s 1(1)). The essential characteristic of a company, which distinguishes it from other business structures, is that a company has a separate legal personality from those of its members (see *Salomon v Salomon & Co* [1897] AC 22): see generally Chapter 2. By contrast, a trust, partnership (unless a Scottish partnership) and an EEIG (unless registered in the UK) do not have separate legal personality: see generally Chapter 2.

[22] CA 2006, s 1173 defines a 'body corporate' as including: 'a body incorporated outside the United Kingdom, but [does] not include – (a) a corporation sole, or (b) a partnership that, whether or not a legal person, is not regarded as a body corporate under the law by which it is governed.'

[23] CTA 2010, s 1121.

[24] See *Conservative and Unionist Central Office v Burrel* [1982] STC 335.

[25] CTA 2009, ss 1, 5(1).

[26] CTA 2009, s 5(2).

where necessary. An overview of the key aspects of corporation tax for carrying on a business in the e-commerce and/or e-infrastructure arena is provided in Chapter 7.

5.2.2 Income tax

Individuals, and generally not companies,[27] are subject to income tax ranging from 20% up to 50% (2011/12)[28] in respect of income and profits derived from specific sources. The rules governing the application of this tax are provided by ITTOIA 2005 (trading and other non-employment income), the Income Tax (Earnings and Pensions) Act 2003 (ITEPA 2003) (employment income) and ITA 2007. In determining the rates that apply, each individual is entitled to a personal allowance, which effectively provides an amount of tax-free income (for 2011/12 this is £7,475 for an individual aged under 65).[29] However, for an individual whose net income exceeds £100,000 the allowance is reduced by one-half of the excess.[30]

An individual is subject to income tax if either resident or ordinarily resident in the UK.[31] The chargeable gains of an individual are subject to capital gains tax (unlike a company, where chargeable gains are subject to corporation tax).[32]

As Table 5.2 (see **5.2.6**) illustrates, a company is generally not subject to income tax, but it will nevertheless be subject to this tax (rather than corporation tax) where it is non-resident and carries on a trade within the UK otherwise than through a permanent establishment.[33] In this context, it is possible, in some circumstances, for a company using IT to trade via the internet to be subject to an income tax charge in the UK.

A detailed consideration of the income tax rules is beyond the scope of this book, and the reader should take appropriate professional advice where necessary.

5.2.3 Capital gains tax

Capital gains tax (CGT) is a tax on chargeable gains accruing from the disposal of assets. CGT is applied to individuals and the circumstances in

---

[27] CTA 2009, s 3(1), unless the company is non-UK resident and not subject to corporation tax because it carries on a trade through a permanent establishment. If the trade is not carried on through a permanent establishment then the non-resident company is potentially within the charge to income tax under ITTOIA 2005.

[28] A basic rate of 20% applies to income up to £35,000 (ITA 2007, s 10)). A higher rate of 40% applies to income up to £150,000 (ITA 2007, s 10(5A)) and an additional rate of 50% applies to income in excess of £150,001 (Finance Act 2011 (FA 2011), s 1).

[29] ITA 2007, s 35.

[30] ITA 2007, s 35(2).

[31] ITA 2007, s 829.

[32] TCGA 1992, s 2.

[33] ITTOIA 2005, s 5.

which it is imposed are determined by TCGA 1992.[34] Subject to specific exceptions, the tax rate on capital gains is 18% (2011/12).[35] If an individual is subject to higher rate income tax then the capital gains over the relevant threshold will be taxed at a rate of 28% (2011/12).[36] Each individual is entitled to an annual exemption for CGT purposes in respect of a specified amount (for 2011/12 this is £10,600).[37] A rate of 10% (2011/12) applies to gains qualifying for entrepreneurs' relief (the relief is subject to a maximum lifetime limit of £10 million).[38]

A tax charge will be imposed on gains derived from the disposal of assets situated in the UK by a UK resident or a person ordinarily resident in the UK.[39] A non-resident individual will be subject to tax where he disposes of an asset situated in the UK and which is used for the purposes of a trade carried on in the UK through a branch or agency.[40]

A detailed consideration of the CGT rules is beyond the scope of this book, and the reader should take appropriate professional advice where necessary.

5.2.4 Double taxation agreements

Double taxation agreements (DTAs) are arrangements entered into between the UK and another country. Broadly, the purpose of a DTA is to eliminate or limit the extent to which profits, royalties, interest or chargeable gains that are received by a resident of another country (such as the US) can be taxed by the country in which the profit, income or chargeable gain arises (such as the UK). In other words, the purpose of a DTA is to eliminate or limit double taxation. Double taxation agreements have effect in UK law as part of the tax legislation as a result of TIOPA 2010.[41] Many of the agreements are based upon the principles of the OECD[42] Model Tax Convention on Income and Capital (the 'Model Convention').[43]

The Model Convention uses the term 'permanent establishment' as the key to determining the rights of respective countries in their ability to tax business profits. Article 7(1) of the Model Convention illustrates how the term is used for the purposes of determining the taxing rights of a country:

United Kingdom
Taxation: General

---

[34] TCGA 1992, s 2(1).
[35] TCGA 1992, s 4(2).
[36] TCGA 1992, s 4(4).
[37] TCGA 1992, s 3.
[38] TCGA 1992, ss 169H–169S.
[39] TCGA 1992, s 2(1).
[40] TCGA 1992, s 10.
[41] TIOPA 2010, s 2(1).
[42] Organisation for Economic Co-operation and Development: see www.oecd.org.
[43] The current version was issued in July 2010: see www.oecdbookshop.org/ (June 2011).

'1. Profits of an enterprise of a Contracting State shall be taxable only in that State unless the enterprise carries on business in the other Contracting State through a permanent establishment situated therein. If the enterprise carries on business as aforesaid, the profits that are attributable to the permanent establishment ... may be taxed in that other State.'

Example 5.1

An Italian company receives income from a trade carried on through an office in the UK. The UK/Italian double taxation agreement is based on Art 7 of the Model Convention, and accordingly the Italian company will only be taxed by the UK on profits *attributable to a permanent establishment* in the UK. The taxable profits are those derived from the UK office (see Art 7 of the UK–Italy DTA).

Careful attention should be given to double taxation agreements since they can be of significant help in eliminating source taxation on royalties (eg arising from the exploitation of copyright and other forms of intellectual property); and in preventing information technology from creating a taxable presence in a country if there is an appropriate permanent establishment article (see Chapter 8 at **8.5**).

5.2.5 Taxation of worldwide income and chargeable gains

The UK tax regime applies in many cases to income and chargeable gains that are derived from activities carried on by a person throughout the world. The globalisation of the marketplace available to persons carrying on e-commerce makes it imperative for them to know the circumstances in which they will be taxed on income and gains accruing from outside the UK. It is equally important that overseas traders are aware of the precise circumstances in which they will be taxed in jurisdictions with which they are trading, such as the UK.

Table 5.2 (see **5.2.6**) summarises the circumstances in which a person will be taxed on worldwide income, or merely upon income and gains accruing within the UK. The circumstances in which a non-resident will be taxed in the UK are also identified.

5.2.6 Summary of UK tax rules

The UK tax rules are summarised in Table 5.2.

Table 5.2: Scope of UK tax rules

Person	Worldwide income/gains taxed	Only UK income/gains taxed
Company		
Resident in UK	✔ Within charge to corporation tax 'all profits wherever arising': CTA 2009, s 5(1). 'profits' include income and chargeable gains: CTA 2009, s 2(2). Plus any income/gains attributed to a UK resident under the controlled foreign company rules: ICTA 1988, s 747(1); TCGA 1992, s 13.	x
Non-resident in UK	x	✔ Within charge to corporation tax (a) trading income directly or indirectly arising through or from a permanent establishment in the UK used to carry on a trade in the UK; and (b) any income from property used/held by or for the permanent establishment (referred to in (a)); and (c) any chargeable gains arising from the disposal of assets situated in the UK used for the purposes of the trade carried on through the permanent establishment (referred to in (a)); and

Person	Worldwide income/gains taxed	Only UK income/gains taxed
		(d) any chargeable gains arising from the disposal of assets situated in the UK which were used or held for the purposes of the permanent establishment (referred to in (a)): CTA 2009, ss 5, 19 TCGA 1992, s 10B.
		✔ Within charge to income tax to the extent there is no corporation tax liability but usually only where a trade is carried on in the UK and there is no double taxation agreement requiring the existence of a permanent establishment.
Individuals		
Income		
Resident in UK	✔ Within the charge to income tax (a) taxed on profits or gains accruing from any type of property whether situated in the UK or elsewhere; (b) taxed on profits or gains accruing from any trade, profession or vocation whether carried on in the UK or elsewhere. Plus any income attributed under the transfer of asset rules: ITA 2007, s 714.	x
Non-resident in UK	x	✔ Within the charge to income tax (a) taxed on any profits or gains from any property situated in the UK;

Person	Worldwide income/gains taxed	Only UK income/gains taxed
		(b) taxed on any profits or gains from any trade, profession or vocation exercised within the UK. Specific rules apply to an individual who is non-domiciled.
Gains		
Non-resident in UK	x	✓ Within the charge to income tax. Where a non-resident is carrying on a trade in the UK through a branch or agency, it is taxed on chargeable gains accruing from the disposal of assets situated in the UK: (a) used for the purposes of a trade carried on through a branch or agency in the UK; or (b) used or held for the purposes of the branch or agency: TCGA 1992, s 10(1). Specific rules apply to an individual who is non-domiciled.
Resident or ordinarily resident in UK	✓ Within the charge to income tax. Taxed on all chargeable gains which accrue: TCGA 1992, s 2(1). Plus any gains attributed under the controlled foreign company legislation: TCGA 1992, s 13.	x

5.3   INDIRECT TAXATION

5.3.1   Value added tax

Tax is imposed in the UK, and throughout the EU, on supplies of goods and/or services through the system of value added tax (VAT). The scheme of VAT is governed in the UK by an EU VAT Directive,[44] which is implemented in domestic UK law by the Value Added Tax Act 1994 (VATA 1994).

VAT is charged on taxable supplies made in the UK by a taxable person in the course or furtherance of business.[45] In appropriate circumstances, it is possible for a supplier to claim credit for VAT incurred in the course of its business (known as 'input VAT') against VAT which is received from customers on supplies made by it (known as 'output VAT') (thus enabling the supplier to eliminate the cost of VAT from its costs of carrying on business).[46] VAT is an EU tax, and it accordingly applies to intra-EU trade, and to trade with other countries outside of the EU (in respect of inbound EU supplies). The scope of these charges is examined in later chapters: see Part V.

The rate of VAT depends upon how the transaction, known as a 'supply', is classified. Transactions can be classified in one of three ways. Supplies which are designated as standard-rated are subject to a tax of 20% (2011)[47] of the value of the supply. Some supplies are classified as exempt[48] or zero-rated,[49] which are discussed in Part V, Chapter 17. This effectively means that the rate of VAT is nil from the perspective of the ultimate consumer; but if the supply is classified as exempt the supplier will not be able to recover its own VAT costs incurred in making the supply; whereas if a supply is zero-rated, the supplier will be able to recover its own VAT costs incurred in making the supply. Key questions in this area are the extent to which the supply of computer software via the internet can be classified as the supply of goods and/or services; the extent to which digital supplies of books qualify for zero-rating; the extent to which a computer server can constitute a connection for VAT purposes; and how supplies of electronic services are to be classified. These questions are examined in Part V.

---

[44]   Council Directive 2006/112/EC on the common system of value added tax, OJ L 347, 28/11/2006 p 1 (VAT Directive).

[45]   VATA 1994, s 4.

[46]   VATA 1994, s 24.

[47]   VATA 1994, s 2.

[48]   VATA 1994, s 31 and Sch 9.

[49]   VATA 1994, s 30 and Sch 8.

Example 5.2

> If a computer manufacturer purchases 100,000 microchips for installation in hardware at a price of £500,000 (expressed to be exclusive of VAT) it would pay an additional £100,000 in VAT.

The liability to account for UK VAT is imposed upon any person who is required to be registered as a taxable person under VATA 1994.[50] In broad terms, the requirement to register depends upon a person having a turnover in excess of £73,000 (2011).[51]

Normally, a service is treated as supplied in the UK if the supplier belongs in the UK, unless the person to whom the supply is made is a 'relevant business person' (ie for B2B supplies), in which case the service is supplied in the country in which the recipient belongs.[52]

Whether a supplier belongs in the UK is determined under VATA 1994, as construed by the VAT Directive.[53] A supplier is based in the UK if it has its usual place of residence in the UK; and this means where the supplier is a company, the place where it is legally constituted (ie the country where it is incorporated).[54]

If a non-UK recipient of services is a relevant business person, then the UK will not be regarded as the place of supply, and instead the services will be supplied where the recipient belongs (unless overriding place of supply rules apply in Sch 4A to VATA 1994) (these are summarised in Chapter 17 at **17.10.2**).[55] A person is treated as a 'relevant business person' if that person:[56]

(1) is a taxable person within the meaning of Art 9 of the VAT Directive (broadly a person carrying on an economic activity);

(4) is registered under VATA 1994;

(3) is identified as a taxable person under the law of another Member State; or

(4) is registered under an Act of Tynwald (the laws of the Isle of Man) for the purposes of any tax imposed under that Act which corresponds to VAT,

United Kingdom Taxation: General

---

[50] VATA 1994, s 3(1).
[51] VATA 1994, s 3 and Schs 1–3A.
[52] VATA 1994, s 7.
[53] VATA 1994, s 9.
[54] VATA 1994, s 9.
[55] VATA 1994, s 7A(5). See Part V.
[56] VATA 1994, s 7A(4). See Chapter 17 (at **17.11**) for further details.

and the services are received by the person otherwise than wholly for private purposes.

For the purposes of the place of supply rules for services, a 'relevant business person' is treated as belonging in a 'relevant country', which means (a) if the person has a business establishment, or some other fixed place of establishment, in a country (and none in any other country), that country; or (b) if the person has a business establishment, or some other fixed establishment or establishments, in more than one country, the country in which the relevant establishment[57] is located, or (c) if none of the foregoing apply, the country in which the person's usual place of residence is located.[58] These aspects are examined in Part V.

Example 5.3

Retailer plc places an order for 10,000 toasters from Manufacturer in the UK at a cost of £200,000 plus VAT. The order is placed by electronic data interchange (EDI). Manufacturer uses EDI to tell its warehouse operation to ship the products to the Retailer.

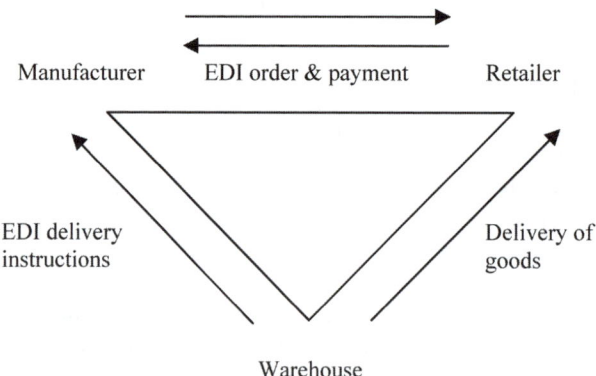

Both Manufacturer and Retailer are located in the UK, and are VAT registered. Manufacturer issues a VAT invoice for £200,000 plus VAT at the standard rate. Retailer in carrying on its business is making taxable supplies with the consequence that it has the right to recover the VAT costs incurred by it on the order received from Manufacturer.

In some circumstances, supplies are deemed to take place in the UK due to the fact that they are a supply of services received by a relevant business person who belongs in the UK.[59] The types of supplies which are within this category include telecommunication services and electronically-supplied services.[60]

---

[57]　This means whichever of the person's establishments is most directly concerned with the supply: VATA 1994, s 9(4).
[58]　VATA 1994, s 9(3).
[59]　VATA 1994, s 8(2).
[60]　VATA 1994, s 8(2) and Sch 4A. See Chapter 17 at **17.11** for more details.

In addition, from 1 January 2015,[61] Council Directive 2008/8/EC[62] provides that VAT on telecommunications, radio, television broadcasting and electronic services supplied by a supplier established within the EU to non-taxable customers also established within the EU (ie intra-EU B2C supplies) will be charged in the Member State where that customer belongs/is established.[63]

A grey area for the purposes of VAT is the extent to which a piece of IT can constitute a fixed establishment where it is supported by necessary human resources for its operation. The possibility exists for a person to use IT, such as a computer server, as a fixed establishment, with the result that it is possible to locate a supply outside the charge to UK VAT. This aspect is considered in Part V.

VAT may also apply to transactions involving the supply of goods in pursuance of an order placed via a website. The obligations imposed upon traders within Europe are complex. Traders are required to monitor the place of supply of goods, and the type of person receiving the supply (namely whether the customer is a business or non-business recipient). For example, in some instances, a UK trader must apply UK VAT to the supply of goods to another Member State of the EU, while in some circumstances a UK trader is required to apply VAT of the Member State to which the supply is made (the place of supply turns on the identity of the recipient, namely whether a business or non-business recipient). In some circumstances, VAT must be accounted for on the acquisition of goods from other Member States of the EU where the recipient is VAT registered. These aspects are considered in Chapters 17 to 20.

United Kingdom
Taxation: General

---

[61]   See Chapter 22 for further details.

[62]   12 February 2008, amending Directive 2006/112/EC, as regards the place of supply of services.

[63]   See further at http://ec.europa.eu/taxation_customs/taxation/vat/how_vat_works/e-services/index_en.htm (see also Council Regulation 143/2008/EC of 12 February 2008 concerning the inclusion of these services in the 'one stop shop'/special registration scheme).

CHAPTER 6

INBOUND UK E-COMMERCE: SCOPE OF CHARGE TO TAX

6.1 INTRODUCTION

Most commercially operated e-commerce and e-infrastructure activities will be carried on by a company.[1] Non-UK resident corporate traders with genuine economic presence in their country of incorporation should effectively be able to avoid other national tax regimes, whilst carrying on pan-European business activities from their own tax jurisdiction by ensuring that they only pay internet service providers (ISPs) for web hosting services (who act no more than as independent agents acting in the ordinary course of their business). Generally, the type of service provided by an ISP (ie acting as a portal for a non-resident's website) should not be sufficient to create a presence in a country so as to attract a tax charge for the non-resident. However, the Organisation for Economic Co-operation and Development (OECD) has commented that the existence of a website on a computer server that is operated by a non-resident in another country is capable of constituting a permanent establishment, in respect of which the business profits of that establishment would be capable of being taxed.[2] The OECD position is considered further in Chapter 8 since HMRC practice is that a website, either alone or operating on a computer server, cannot constitute a permanent establishment.[3]

This chapter examines the connecting factors that must exist for tax purposes before a company (whether incorporated in or outside the UK) is subject to either UK corporation tax or income tax (see **6.2–6.4**). The role of double taxation agreements (DTAs) is also examined since such agreements operate to limit the UK's domestic tax charge (see **6.5–6.8**). This chapter also considers the views of the OECD on the application of DTAs to e-commerce (see **6.9**) since many of the UK's DTAs mirror the fundamental principles reflected in the OECD Model Tax Convention. Many of the aspects examined in **6.9** will be relevant to outbound UK

---

[1] For an overview of the non-tax issues relating to the operation of a company see Chapter 2.

[2] See the OECD Commentary on the Model Taxation Convention, para 42.3 on Art 5; and para 45.5 (UK's Observation on the Commentary).

[3] See the OECD Commentary on the Model Taxation Convention, para 42.3 on Art 5; and para 45.5 (UK's Observation on the Commentary).

internet business activity (ie the provision of goods and/or services) to another country since most DTAs will been influenced by the OECD Model Tax Convention.

The taxation of intellectual property rights licensed to a UK person by a non-resident are also considered in this chapter (see **6.11**). For example, where software is licensed under copyright and royalties are paid to a non-resident then withholding tax must be applied to the royalties.

The corporation tax issues relating to setting up and operating an internet business are considered in Chapter 7.

The VAT aspects relating to inbound and outbound e-commerce activities are dealt with in Part V.

The flowchart at the end of **6.10** (see Figure 6.1) provides a summary of the scope of UK direct charges on a company.

6.2   RESIDENT AND NON-RESIDENT CORPORATIONS

Unless an internet business activity is within a specific charge to corporation tax or income tax, there is no right for the UK tax authorities to impose direct tax on the economic activity.[4] A company, irrespective of where it is incorporated, is subject to corporation tax if it is a resident of the UK, and this connection can be achieved in one of two ways. A company is a UK resident if either (a) it is incorporated in the UK[5] or (b) it has its central management and control in the UK.[6] A UK resident company is subject to corporation tax on all of its profits (both income and chargeable gains) irrespective of where they arise. Whether the first test (point (a)) applies is easily satisfied by reference to the register of incorporated companies maintained at Companies House.[7] However, the second test (point (b)) is formulated by the case-law and it is not

---

[4]   Tax can only be charged on a taxpayer if the charging statute clearly and unambiguously applies. Otherwise HMRC has no right to charge tax. This is a fundamental principle of UK tax law: see *Partington v Attorney-General* (1869) LR 4 100, at 122, HL, where the judge (Lord Cairns) made the following points, which are applicable in the UK today: 'If the person sought to be taxed comes within the letter of the law he must be taxed, however great the hardship may appear to the judicial mind to be. On the other hand, if the Crown, seeking to recover the tax, cannot bring the subject within the letter of the law, the subject is free, however apparently within the spirit of the law the case might otherwise appear to be.'

[5]   CTA 2009, s 14(1).

[6]   *De Beers Consolidated Mines Ltd v Howe* 5 TC 198, at 213. In that case the judge (Lord Loreburn LC) said: 'a company resides, for the purposes of income tax, where its real business is carried on ... I regard that as the true rule; and the real business is carried on where the central management and control actually abides.' See also *Unit Construction Co Ltd v Bullock (Inspector of Taxes)* [1959] All ER 831, at 836, HL, and *American Thread Co v Joyce* 6 TC 163, at 165.

[7]   The Registrar is under a duty to retain all information required to be delivered to the Registrar under the Companies Acts. See ss 1080 and 1085 of the Companies Act 2006.

straightforward to apply. The test is a question of fact, the answer to which is influenced by physical factors, such as the location of where directors' meetings are held. Where a non-resident company is not incorporated in the UK it is important to ensure that it is not centrally managed and controlled in the UK, otherwise its worldwide profits will be subject to corporation tax.[8]

However, a non-UK-resident company is also subject to corporation tax if it carries on a trade through a permanent establishment in the UK; but the charge is limited to the UK profits attributable to that establishment.[9] The chargeable profits of a permanent establishment will comprise trading income, any non-trading income from property or rights used by, or held by or for the permanent establishment (such as interest or income derived from patent rights) and capital gains arising from assets held for the purposes of the trade of the permanent establishment.[10]

If there are no connecting factors (eg no permanent establishment) to attract a charge to corporation tax it is nonetheless possible for a non-resident company to be subject to income tax (although only at the basic rate of income tax) if it is carrying on a trade in the UK.[11] However, an income tax charge does not arise where the relevant double taxation agreement provides that profits of a trade are not taxable in the UK unless they are carried on in the UK through a permanent establishment.[12]

Example 6.1

If a microchip manufacturer is incorporated in or managed and controlled in the UK it will be required to pay corporation tax on profits derived from that trade. If a non-UK resident company manufactures computers in the US and then sells those through a permanent establishment (eg a branch) based in the UK it will also be required to pay corporation tax on profits attributable to the branch activities. By contrast a non-resident company which locates an e-commerce shopping program on computer servers based in the UK, which accepts orders and then relays these to the non-resident, who in turn gives delivery instructions to a distributor in the UK, may be subject to income tax, rather than corporation tax on the basis that it is exercising a trade within the UK. Whether a person is trading within the UK is partly determined by reference to where the contract is formed: see **6.4.8**.

---

[8]   See **6.3** for further details.
[9]   CTA 2009, s 5(2).
[10]   CTA 2009, s 19(2), (3).
[11]   ITTOIA 2005, s 6.
[12]   CTA 2009 s 21(1). The wording is based on Art 7(2) of the OECD Model Tax Convention on Income and on Capital.

6.3 CENTRAL MANAGEMENT AND CONTROL

6.3.1 Introduction

In relation to a non-UK incorporated company, and the application of the central management and control test, it is first necessary to identify the individuals at the company (e.g. directors, employees or shareholders) who decide upon strategic matters, ie matters of general policy relating to its business. Secondly, it is then necessary to determine who exercises control management and control and from where such control is exercised. The quest for determining the place of residence on this basis is a question of fact.[13] HMRC has issued a Statement of Practice[14] which is its view of the factors relevant to determining residence under the common law test. Appendix H provides an illustrative management guideline protocol which identifies the material issues that must be considered in order to preserve the non-residence of a company. The nature of the protocol will have to be tailored to a company's particular circumstances. However, it identifies the material issues which must be considered by a company's management.

Board meetings that take general policy decisions on the conduct of the non-resident's business will normally be regarded as the relevant authority for answering the question of where central management and control is exercised; and the location of such meetings will normally determine the location of the company for the purposes of UK tax residence. Other factors indicating who has central management and control include the ability of a person to control the finances of the company,[15] power to approve accounts, acquisition and disposal of assets of the business. A company (acting through its directors) that merely 'rubber stamps' the decisions of its parent shareholder or another controlling company will be likely to be centrally managed and controlled by that company, and accordingly be treated as resident in the jurisdiction of the parent/controlling company.[16] Under the articles of association of a company the source of legal authority to conduct its business will normally be vested in the board of directors. Accordingly, there is a presumption, unless the facts demonstrate otherwise, that the non-resident company is centrally controlled by the board of directors.

The articles of association of a company should ideally provide that the board of directors:

---

[13] *De Beers Consolidated Mines Ltd v Howe* 5 TC 198 at 213, where the judge (Lord Loreburn LC) commented: 'This is a pure question of fact, to be determined, not according to the construction of this or that regulation or bye-law, but upon scrutiny of the course of business and trading.'

[14] SP1/90 (9 January 1990).

[15] See *American Thread Co v Joyce* 6 TC 163.

[16] SP1/90 (9 January 1990), paras 16 and 17.

- have the power and duty to decide the ultimate direction of the company, and have the sole obligation to make all decisions concerning the effective management of the company, which shall only take place in the company's country of incorporation;

- if they establish any committees of the board of directors, that all such committees will be governed in such manner as to ensure that the place of effective management of the company is in its country of incorporation;

- if they appoint any form of advisory board, that such a board only has an advisory function, and that it will not be permitted to make any decisions concerning the effective management of the company, such decisions reserved exclusively to the board of directors; and

- shall be required to hold any strategic meetings in the country of incorporation of the company.

In the context of a non-UK incorporated company, examples of strategic decisions that, if made in the UK, could indicate UK residence would be: authorising the company entering into major contracts, formulating dividend policy, making finance decisions (such as entering into loans from a bank), deciding on major investment issues (such as buying property) and approval of capital budgets prior to submission to the shareholders. These strategic decisions can be contrasted with the operational decisions required in the day-to-day management of an organisation, for example, managing legal and tax issues, dealing with employees and managing customer relationships. The case of *Wood and another v Holden*[17] is helpful in this respect as the Court of Appeal held that an overseas incorporated company managed by an overseas trust company which received advice and recommendations from professional advisors in the UK, could not be considered to be UK resident for tax purposes purely because the trust company acted on the recommendations of the professional advisors. This case emphasises that there must be specific evidence that the central management and control of a non-UK incorporated company is governed by its overseas resident directors. In this context the authority of the directors must not be usurped by anybody in the UK (such as directors or other advisers).

To ensure that a company is not UK tax resident it will be of crucial important that all strategic decisions (eg setting and revising the parameters for investment, choice of investments) are conducted outside the UK by the board of directors. The fact that a company resident in the UK may be appointed to provide advice in its capacity as investment adviser to the board of directors of the non-resident company should not prejudice the position, provided that it is the board of directors that has the final say in every case.

---

[17] [2006] STC 443, CA.

To protect against a challenge that a company is centrally managed and controlled in the UK it is highly desirable that the following principles are adhered to in the management of a non-UK company:[18]

- the majority of directors should be tax resident outside the UK, and at least one director should be resident in the jurisdiction of incorporation of the company;

- effective management, namely day-to-day management decisions (e.g. customer relationships), should be carried out by a local resident director;

- all meetings of the board of directors will be held outside the UK;

- the board of directors must take all decisions affecting strategic matters relating to policy or management of the company's business;

- the board of directors should not 'rubber-stamp' decisions or any advice received from the UK concerning the strategic management of the business;

- no member of the board should act in matters regarding the strategic management and control of the company's business when in the UK;

- no person located in the UK should participate in telephone conferences (or any form of instantaneous communication) for the purposes of reaching decisions on strategic matters relating to the company; and

- decisions taken by the board of directors should be properly informed decisions based on a full understanding of the relevant facts (backed by a review of all relevant underlying legal, financial or other data).

In HMRC's Statement of Practice SP1/90, HMRC draws attention to some of the factors which have been regarded as relevant in the case-law.[19] Relevant factors include the location of directors' meetings, the location of where the controlling individual of a company, such as a managing director, exercises powers conferred upon him by the company and the location of the directors who actively carry on the running of the business. It is to be observed that these factors depend upon a physical location of the directors. Where the residence of a company cannot be established under the common law test in the UK, tax cannot be charged

---

[18] Appendix H sets out a management guideline protocol which identifies the material issues that must be considered in order to preserve the non-residence of a company.

[19] See also HMRC's *International Tax Manual* at INTM120210 for detailed consideration of the factors which the tax authority considers relevant.

on worldwide profits. In these circumstances, tax will be limited to the profits of a trade carried on through a permanent establishment in the UK. In the absence of a permanent establishment, income tax may be charged on profits if the company is trading within the UK.[20]

Example 6.2

> Internet Consultancy (Website) Services Inc, based in the US, establishes an office in London. The office is used to operate a website design service for UK companies. The profits of the main business in the US are the sterling equivalent of £25 million, whilst the profits of the London branch are only £500,000. The right to charge corporation tax in the UK is limited to the profits of the branch (£500,000).

Problems in the application of the central management and control test will be particularly severe where a business can be actively controlled from other countries by the use of instantaneous methods of communication and video conferencing. This problem is recognised in HMRC's Statement of Practice, which describes it in the following terms:[21]

> 'The case-law test examined in this Statement is not always easy to apply. The courts have recognised that there may be difficulties where it is not possible to identify one country as the seat of central management and control. The principles to apply in those circumstances have not been fully developed in case law. In addition, the last relevant case was decided almost 30 years ago, and there have been many developments in communications since then, which in particular may enable a company to be controlled from a place far distant from where the day-to-day management is carried on.'

Under the UK's common law test, it is possible for a company to have more than one place of residence.[22] Such a company is known as a 'dual resident' company. A company may be regarded as resident in country X because it is incorporated in that state, but it may also be regarded as a resident of the UK because its real place of business, ie its central management and control, is based in the UK. HMRC holds the view that the residence of a company can be established in the UK if a dominant person within a company, for example, a managing director, exercises powers bestowed upon that person in the UK, or if an influential shareholder exercises voting rights in the UK.[23] In this context the efficiencies represented by IT must be watched, as the example below illustrates. The effect of IT is to facilitate the diversification of management control of businesses, but this may have a material impact

---

[20]   The nature of a permanent establishment and the concept of trading within the UK are examined at **6.4**.

[21]   HMRC Statement of Practice SP1/90, para 19 (9 January 1990).

[22]   See *Swedish Central Ry Co Ltd v Thompson* (1925) 9 TC 342, at 352, per Rowlatt; and *Unit Construction Co Ltd v Bullock (Inspector of Taxes)* [1959] All ER 831, at 833, HL, per Viscount Simonds.

[23]   Inland Revenue Statement of Practice, SP1/90, para 13 (9 January 1990).

on the tax residence of a company, unless appropriate protocols are observed to protect the residency of the company.[24]

Example 6.3

Zoltan Associates SA, a family business, is incorporated in Country X, and the majority shareholder, Mr Zoltan, is a resident of the UK. The business of Zoltan Associates SA is guided by Mr Zoltan, the family patriarch. He controls the financial strings of the business and appoints its directors. Mr Zoltan 'attends' the general meeting of the company, at which crucial decisions are usually made, through the medium of a video-conferencing facility. Mr Zoltan also guides the operation of the business by sending instructions to his co-directors via e-mail. Is Zoltan Associates SA resident in the UK for the purposes of corporation tax?

In this type of scenario, the ultimate control of the company is within the UK, and on the basis of the principles described in HMRC's Statement of Practice, it is likely that the view would be taken that profits of the company were assessable to UK tax. However, if the facts are changed slightly it would be possible to ensure that the company is only tax resident in Country X.

The facts are as above, except that the business is owned by Mr Zoltan in equal shares with his two brothers. No member of the family has influence over the others in respect of how the business is conducted. The business is operated in Country X by the employees. However, the three brothers live in three different jurisdictions, the US, France and the UK. All directors' meetings take place via video-conferencing facilities. Each director has an equal voice in the company, as one-third shareholders. In this situation, the factual circumstances are such that it is not possible to say that the company is centrally managed and controlled in the UK, due to the genuine fragmentation of the decision-making process in relation to the company's affairs, ie no single person has control.

6.3.2 Dual resident companies: tie-breaker provisions

If a company is regarded as dual resident (ie tax resident in two different countries) it is possible that a double taxation agreement will contain a 'tie-breaker' rule which determines in which contracting state the company will be resident for tax purposes. Many DTAs are based on the OECD Model Taxation Convention, and Art 4 of the Model deals with the circumstances in which a person is regarded as a resident of a Contracting State. Article 4.1 provides:

---

[24] In *Electronic Commerce: The UK's Taxation Agenda* (November 1999) the following point was made on the potential impact of remote communication: 'Technological advances mean that it may become more common for central management and control to be exercised in more than one country. Businesses may increasingly have a presence in many different locations. The Board of Directors and other key managers may hold virtual rather than physical meetings (by video conference links or e-mail/discussion groups). The issue here is that this could lead to double taxation': Chapter 8, para 8.5.

'For the purposes of this Convention, the term "resident of a Contracting State" means any person who, under the laws of that State, is liable to tax therein by reason of his domicile, residence, place of management or any other criterion of a similar nature, and also includes that State and any political subdivision or local authority thereof. This term, however, does not include any person who is liable to tax in that State in respect only of income from sources in that State or capital situated therein.'

The tie-breaker rule in the OECD Model in respect of a company provides, at Art 4.3:

'Where by reason of the provisions of paragraph 1 a person other than an individual is a resident of both Contracting States, then it shall be deemed to be a resident only of the State in which its place of effective management is situated.'

The Commentary to the OECD Model Convention states that the place of effective management is 'the place where key management and commercial decisions that are necessary for the conduct of the entity's business as a whole are in substance made'.[25] Further, the Commentary indicates that the place of effective management will generally be where the senior person or group of senior persons (ie the directors) make their decisions in respect of the company, or the place where the actions to be taken by the entity as a whole are determined.[26] However, no guiding principle can be given, and emphasis must be placed on ascertaining all the facts and circumstances in order to identify the place of effective management. In the context of e-commerce and e-infrastructure activities, the OECD has published a discussion paper, *The Impact of the Communications Revolution on the Application of 'Place of Effective Management' as a Tie-breaker Rule*.[27] The concept of place of effective management is discussed in the paper, and it is commented that it is generally located:[28]

'... where key management and commercial decisions necessary for the conduct of a business are in substance made and given. This will ordinarily be where the directors meet to make decisions relating to the management of the company ...'

The OECD paper indicates that the following are the key factors in determining place of effective management:[29]

- where the centre of top level management is located;

---

[25] OECD Commentary on Art 4, para 24.
[26] OECD Commentary on Art 4, para 24.
[27] *The Impact of the Communications Revolution on the Application of 'Place of Effective Management' as a Tie-breaker Rule*, OECD, February 2001.
[28] *The Impact of the Communications Revolution on the Application of 'Place of Effective Management' as a Tie-breaker Rule*, OECD, February 2001, at para 31.
[29] *The Impact of the Communications Revolution on the Application of 'Place of Effective Management' as a Tie-breaker Rule*, OECD, February 2001, at para 31.

- where the business operations are actually conducted;

- legal factors such as the place of incorporation, location of the registered office;

- where the controlling shareholders make key management and commercial decisions in relation to the company; and

- where the directors reside.

Historically, it has been rare for a company to be resident in more than one country. However, the growth in communication technologies has radically increased the chances of a company being regarded as dual resident. The OECD discussion paper makes the following point:[30]

> 'However, the communications and technological revolution is fundamentally changing the way people run their business. Due to sophisticated telecommunication technology and fast, efficient and relatively cheap transportation it is no longer necessary for a person or a group of persons to be physically located or meet in any one particular place to run a business. This increased mobility and functional decentralisation may have a significant impact on the incidence of dual resident companies, and the operation of the place of effective management tie-breaker rules.'

The problem caused by communication technology is that it enables people in many different countries to control a business. Accordingly, the factors which tended to indicate the place of effective management and control may be blurred by the efficiencies offered by technology.[31] The following illustration is given in the OECD discussion paper:[32]

> 'If senior managers adopt conferencing through the Internet, for example, as a key medium for making management and commercial decision and those managers are located throughout the world, it may be difficult to determine a place of effective management. In such cases, a place of management might be regarded as existing in each jurisdiction where a manager is located at the time of making decisions, but it may be difficult (if not impossible) to point to any particular location as being the place of effective management.'

It is also suggested in the discussion paper that further problems may be caused by technology. For example, a company could be treated as a resident for tax purposes in two contracting states to a double taxation agreement but, as a result of the use of technology, the place of effective

---

[30] *The Impact of the Communications Revolution on the Application of 'Place of Effective Management' as a Tie-breaker Rule*, OECD, February 2001, at para 34.
[31] *The Impact of the Communications Revolution on the Application of 'Place of Effective Management' as a Tie-breaker Rule*, OECD, February 2001, at paras 35 and 36.
[32] *The Impact of the Communications Revolution on the Application of 'Place of Effective Management' as a Tie-breaker Rule*, OECD, February 2001, at para 38.

management could be located in a third state.[33] The discussion paper considers a number of potential options to resolve the limitations posed by the technology revolution, such as replacing the effective management concept, redefining the test, establishing a hierarchy of tests or denying dual resident companies the benefit of double taxation agreements.[34] The latter option operates as a deterrent against exploitation of double taxation agreements, and thus encourages the controllers of a business to ensure that it is a resident of one country.[35] For example, the US-UK DTA has adopted the denial of treaty benefit route.[36]

6.4 PERMANENT ESTABLISHMENT OF A NON-RESIDENT COMPANY

6.4.1 Introduction

A non UK-resident company is subject to corporation tax if it carries on a trade through a permanent establishment in the UK.[37] The chargeable profits of a permanent establishment will comprise trading income, any non-trading income from property or rights used by or held by or for the permanent establishment (such as interest or income derived from patent rights, copyright, trade marks) and capital gains arising from assets (such as real estate) held for the purposes of the trade of the permanent establishment.

Example 6.4

> Retailer Inc, a US incorporated company, has an agent in the UK which sells goods to UK customers. The agent solely represents Retailer Inc. The agent sells goods solely via an internet business operated exclusively from the UK, with all goods dispatched from a warehouse in the UK. The profits of Retailer Inc's worldwide activities are the sterling equivalent of £15 million. The profits attributable to the activities of the UK agent are £5 million. The UK profits will be subject to corporation tax. Any UK tax should be allowed as a tax credit against US taxes payable by Retailer Inc in connection with the UK profits.

The amount of profits attributable to a permanent establishment for corporation tax purposes is the quantum of profits it would have made if it were a distinct and separate enterprise, engaged in the same or similar

---

[33]   *The Impact of the Communications Revolution on the Application of 'Place of Effective Management' as a Tie-breaker Rule*, OECD, February 2001, at para 45.

[34]   *The Impact of the Communications Revolution on the Application of 'Place of Effective Management' as a Tie-breaker Rule*, OECD, February 2001, at para 48.

[35]   *The Impact of the Communications Revolution on the Application of 'Place of Effective Management' as a Tie-breaker Rule*, OECD, February 2001, at paras 48–78.

[36]   Art 4(5) of the US/UK Double Taxation Agreement, 24 July 2001.

[37]   CTA 2009, s 5(2).

activities under the same or similar conditions, dealing wholly independently with the non-resident company (this is considered further at **6.10**).[38]

In the absence of sufficient connecting factors to attract a charge to corporation tax it is also possible for a non-resident company to be subject to income tax (although only at the basic rate of income tax) if it is carrying on a trade in the UK.[39]

6.4.2 What is a permanent establishment?

The tax legislation defines a 'permanent establishment' as comprising one of two things, namely either (a) a fixed place of business in the UK through which the business of the non-resident company is wholly or partly carried on, or (b) an agent acting on behalf of a non-resident company which has and habitually exercises in the UK authority to do business on behalf of the non-resident company.[40] For this purpose, the concept of 'fixed place of business' includes a place of management, a branch, an office, a factory and a workshop.[41] These key words either refer to a physical presence in the UK (eg a branch) or an agent, which is a legal relationship that can arise through contractual agreements,[42] or by operation of law.[43] The concept of permanent establishment is one way in which the UK tax authority may successfully impose tax on an internet business activity, even though the company carrying on the trade is otherwise a non-resident.

> *Example 6.5*
>
> Alpha Technologies Inc, based in the US, is the developer and manufacturer of a secure payments mechanism (SPM) for e-commerce. A UK-based company called Spectrum Technologies Ltd is appointed the sole agent of Alpha Technologies Inc. The UK company, on receiving an order for a SPM, relays the order to Alpha Technologies Inc. Upon confirmation from the UK company, Alpha Technologies Inc supplies the SPM to the customer. In the first year Alpha Technologies Inc earns £5 million for supplying the SPM in the UK. These profits can potentially be assessed to corporation tax if the non-resident carries on a trade in the UK via its agency with Spectrum Technologies Ltd.

---

[38] CTA 2009, s 21(1). The wording is based on Art 7(2) of the OECD Model Tax Convention on Income and on Capital.
[39] ITTOIA 2005, s 6.
[40] CTA 2010, s 1141(1).
[41] CTA 2010, s 1141(2).
[42] See Chapter 3.
[43] See Chapter 3.

6.4.3   Agency

Even the simplest commercial agency arrangement could potentially bring an internet business activity within the charge to UK corporation tax. A non-resident who sells goods and/or services via e-commerce may need to enter into arrangements for the supply of those goods and/or services to the consumer in the country concerned. This may be achieved by the appointment of an agent or distributor (as to the range of commercial intermediaries, this was discussed in Chapter 3). Such an appointment may operate to attract a tax charge on the non-resident provided the agent has sufficient economic substance to create a permanent establishment. A non-resident company should ensure that the terms upon which it appoints an agent will not constitute a permanent establishment.

Careful tax planning is needed to ensure that agency relationships do not attract UK tax charges for a non-resident. This can be achieved by ensuring that the agent who is appointed is an 'agent of independent status acting in the ordinary course of an agent's business'; this is because such an agent does not create a UK permanent establishment.[44] There is no general definition of what constitutes an agent of independent status for the purposes of UK tax law. However, HMRC has issued guidance as to how the term will be construed, and the following is a summary:[45]

- Whether an agent is of independent status is tested by the legal, financial and commercial characteristics of the business relationship between the non-resident and the agent.

- If the relationship between principal and agent is the same as a relationship between independent businesses, dealing with each other at arm's length, then the agent will be 'an independent agent'.

- Dependent or independent status does not turn on the shareholding relationship between principal and agent. The fact that an agent is a subsidiary company does not make it a dependent agent.

- Whether an agent acts in the ordinary course of its own business is something that should be considered by reference to the facts. Matters relevant include the number of unrelated principals that the agent acted for and the extent of the business activities customarily carried out by independent agents in the specific business sector concerned.

- Assuming the agent acts in the ordinary course of its own business, in general, an agent would be independent and would not constitute an agency permanent establishment of the foreign enterprise for

United Kingdom Taxation: General

---

[44]   CTA 2010, s 1142.
[45]   See HMRC's *International Tax Manual* at INTM264080 (Non-residents trading in the UK: domestic law permanent establishment/branch or agency).

which it acts where it is independent of the principal enterprise both legally and economically. The perspective of application of this test is with relevance to the business conducted by the agent for the principal rather than, for example, any shareholding relationship between the principal and agent. Other relevant factors of independence may include: (i) the extent of the obligations which the agent has vis-à-vis the non-resident; (ii) whether the agent is subject to detailed instructions or comprehensive control; (iii) whether the agent bears the entrepreneurial risk for the business that the agent carries out for the non-resident; (iv) the degree of reliance on the agent's special skill and knowledge by the principal in the business done; and (v) whether there is reference by the agent to the principal for approval of the manner in which the business is to be conducted.

When a non-resident uses an agent restrictions should be imposed on the authority of the agent to represent the company. In particular, the scope of an agent's operating activities should be limited to assist in ensuring that the appointment of an agent does not result in the creation of a permanent establishment. For example, the agent should not be permitted to conclude contracts on behalf of the non-resident where it is a dependant agent.

By contrast to the concept of 'agent', the terms 'fixed place of business' and 'branch' are a reference to a physical presence, such as the existence of offices rather than to a legal relationship.[46] There is no definition of what is required for a place of business to be regarded as 'fixed'. However, there must be a degree of permanence between the physical location and the business that is being carried on by the non-resident company. There are no other specific requirements concerning the existence of a 'fixed place of business' and so the circumstances in which a fixed place of business can come into existence are broad. Accordingly, a fixed place of business can either be owned, rented or otherwise at the disposal of the non-resident company, and it can be used either wholly or partly for the purposes of the business. The illustrations given in the statutory provisions are not exhaustive, and so it is possible for other things to constitute a fixed place of business.

Example 6.6

Platform Ltd provides third party e-commerce vendors with access to its website so that they can sell goods to customers in the UK. Platform Ltd represents many non-resident and resident companies on this basis as an independent agent. Alpha Inc (based in the US) operates an independent retail business from the US in relation to the supply of various goods.

---

[46] For example, in *Hughes (HM Inspector of Taxes) v Bank of New Zealand* [1938]1 All ER 778, the bank was subject to tax in the UK due to the fact that it derived profits from offices (ie, a branch) opened in London.

Alpha Inc uses the e-commerce platform of Platform Ltd to sell its goods to customers in the UK. Platform Ltd's terms and conditions of sale provide, among other things, that:

- Platform Ltd acts as disclosed agent of Alpha Inc;

- any order placed for goods via Platform Ltd's e-commerce platform results in an e-mail being sent by Platform Ltd on behalf of Alpha Inc to customers confirming receipt of the order (including details of the order);

- an order placed over the e-commerce platform represents an offer by the customer to purchase goods from Alpha Inc;

- an order is accepted by Alpha Inc when the company sends the customer an e-mail confirming that the goods have been dispatched to the customer;

- goods are dispatched from the US to the customer;

- delivery rates for goods are as shown on Platform Ltd's e-commerce website;

- all ownership, title and risk relating to the goods passes to the customer at the time when the goods are dispatched from Platform Ltd's premises;

- where the delivery address for the goods is outside the US the customer (as addressee) will be the importer of the goods into their country; and

- the importer must comply with all laws of the country to which the goods are delivered, including paying any import duties and taxes (import VAT) relating to the goods.

Non-business customers place orders via the e-commerce website of Platform Ltd, which acts as agent for Alpha Inc. The order placed with Alpha Inc relates to the purchase of goods which are dispatched from the US. Individual customers receive e-mail confirmation of the orders and notice of dispatch of the goods in accordance with the terms and conditions referred to above. Alpha Inc should not be subject to UK corporation tax or income tax. This is because whilst Platform Ltd acts as agent of Alpha Inc, it acts as an agent of independent status acting in the ordinary course of its business. Such an agent does not create a permanent establishment for Alpha Inc.

6.4.4 Preparatory or auxiliary activities

There are some exclusions that can apply to a non-resident company when considering whether a permanent establishment exists. A company will not have a permanent establishment in the UK if the activities of the fixed

United Kingdom
Taxation: General

place of business or of the agent of the non-resident are of only a preparatory or auxiliary character.[47] Activities that are regarded as having a preparatory or auxiliary nature include:[48]

- the use of facilities for the purpose of storage, display or delivery of goods or merchandise belonging to the non-resident company;

- the maintenance of a stock of goods or merchandise belonging to the non-resident company for the purpose of storage, display or delivery;

- the maintenance of a stock of goods or merchandise belonging to the non-resident company for the purpose of processing by another person;

- purchasing goods or merchandise, or collecting information, for the non-resident company.

The examples provided above are not exhaustive, so it is possible that other things may constitute preparatory or auxiliary activities.

Example 6.7

Nile Sàrl, based in Luxembourg, is an internet retailer. Its only presence in the UK is through a number of warehouses containing stock. Customers place orders with Nile Sàrl over the internet. Instructions are sent by Nile Sàrl to the warehouses in the UK to deliver the stock to customers. These warehouses, of themselves, should not constitute a permanent establishment of Nile Sàrl in the UK.

6.4.5 Is a website capable of being a permanent establishment?

Although no reference is made in the statutory definition of permanent establishment to websites and computer servers it is the published view of HMRC that such forms of technology are not capable of constituting a permanent establishment. The HMRC press release on this matter provides:[49]

'In the UK, we take the view that a web site of itself is not a permanent establishment. And we take the view that a server is insufficient of itself to constitute a permanent establishment of a business that is conducting

---

[47] CTA 2010, s 1143(2).
[48] CTA 2010, s 1143(3).
[49] 'Electronic Commerce: Tax Status of Web Sites and Servers' (11 April 2000), 84/2000 (reproduced at Appendix C). In contrast the position of the OECD is that a computer sever can constitute a permanent establishment in appropriate circumstances: see 'Clarification on the application of the permanent establishment definition in e-commerce: changes to the commentary on the model tax convention on article 5' (OECD, December 2000).

e-commerce through a web site on the server. We take that view regardless of whether the server is owned, rented or otherwise at the disposal of the business.'

This announcement by HMRC creates certainty in the approach of the UK tax authorities. However, it is necessary for any e-commerce business structure operating in the UK markets to examine whether any element of its business has any feature in addition to a server and website in the UK which would cause a permanent establishment to exist. It must also be recognised that whilst the existence of a permanent establishment is necessary to create a charge to corporation tax for a non-resident, a residual charge to income tax remains in connection with any profits derived from a trade carried on in the UK. Only a DTA which requires the existence of a permanent establishment for the taxation of business profits will operate to prevent the income tax charge arising.

Example 6.8

Alpha Inc, based in the US, operates an independent retail business from the US in relation to the supply of various goods. Alpha Inc sells goods to customers in the UK via its website, which is maintained on computer servers located in both the US and the UK. Non-business customers place orders via the e-commerce website. Alpha Inc is not subject to UK corporation tax or income tax because the existence of the website and computer server in the UK does not create a permanent establishment.

Will appointing employees in the UK give rise to a permanent establishment for a non-resident company?

If a UK employee is concluding contracts in the UK, he will constitute a permanent establishment. Assuming this is not the case, and that there is no fixed place of business that the employing company operates from (whether its own or in another entity's offices), then it may be possible for there to be no permanent establishment where an internet company has employees present locally.

However, the employee's home office could itself constitute a fixed place of business of his employer. For this to be the case, the home in the UK would have to be 'at the disposal' of the employer.[50] There is no English case-law directly on this point. However, there is some Canadian case-law in the context of agency workers indicating that, for a home to be at an overseas company's disposal, factors such as the overseas company paying the expenses of the home and stipulating what facilities it contains and the company's employees being able to visit unannounced expecting the worker to be present are relevant.[51]

---

[50] OECD Commentary on Art 5(1) of the Model Tax Convention.

[51] *American Income Life Insurance Company v The Queen* (2008) DTC 3631 (Tax Court of Canada) and *Knights of Columbus v The Queen* (2008) DTC 3648 (Tax Court of Canada).

It is worth noting that HMRC has stated, in the context of the PAYE and National Insurance contributions rules, the following:[52]

> 'Generally an employer can be said to have a place of business in the UK if:
> - they have a fixed address or occupy premises where they are, or are present with the consent of the lawful owner or tenant, and
> - an activity takes place which need not necessarily be remunerative in itself, but is in furtherance of the purposes of the business. The business does not need to be of a trading or commercial nature.
>
> Some pointers to look for when considering if you have a place of business include:
> - a name plate displayed on the door or premises
> - headed letter paper
> - a listing in a phone directory
> - a lease or rent agreement or some sort of financial transaction for the use of the premises
> - a registered office
> - registration as a company incorporated outside the UK but with a place of business here for the purpose of the Companies Act 1985
> - other premises in the UK.'

While this guidance is not necessarily binding for the 'fixed establishment' test, that test nevertheless requires there to be a fixed 'place of business', so if the above factors are not present and there is no place of business, there is unlikely to be a permanent establishment on this limb of the test.

On 12 October 2011, the OECD Committee on Fiscal Affairs released for public comment a discussion draft of proposed changes to the commentary to Art 5 of OECD Model Tax Convention. The discussion points include the meaning of 'at the disposal', whether a home office can constitute a permanent establishment and the effect of the presence of a foreign enterprise's personnel in the host country.

6.4.6 Is a trade being carried on in the UK through a permanent establishment?

It should not be overlooked that a second condition must be satisfied for a permanent establishment to create a tax charge for a non-resident company. This is that the permanent establishment (meeting the conditions discussed above) is in the UK, and such an establishment must be used to carry on a trade in the UK.[53] The term 'trade' is defined in the tax legislation to include 'any venture in the nature of trade'.[54] As discussed in Chapter 7, this definition has been interpreted in UK case-law, and a number of objective factors must be taken into account in determining whether a particular activity constitutes a 'trade'. Much of

---

[52] See HMRC *Employer Further Guide to PAYE and NICs* CWG2 (2011), at p 77.
[53] CTA 2009, s 19.
[54] CTA 2010, s 1119.

the case-law in this area has focused on the so called 'badges of trade'.[55] The case-law provides an indication of the attributes that an activity must possess in order to qualify as a trade (see **6.6.1**). In this respect, a distinction must be drawn between trading with the UK and exercising a trade in the UK (see **6.4.7**).[56]

6.4.7   Non-resident company and charge to income tax

Although a non-resident company may have no 'permanent establishment', it may nonetheless be possible to impose income tax where the company receives profits from a trade carried on in the UK.[57] However, where a DTA is in place between the UK and the non-resident's country and the DTA is based on the principles of the OECD Model Tax Convention, the UK will only be entitled to tax the business profits of a non-resident where profits are derived from a permanent establishment. It is clear that many types of internet trade will not be subject to UK taxation where a DTA exists, which, based on OECD principles, would limit the application of tax to situations where there is a permanent establishment located in the UK. With e-commerce activities carried on by a non-resident there is usually no form of presence in foreign markets that are capable of amounting to a permanent establishment. However, this assumes that there are no agents or delivery centres participating in the supply chain in those foreign markets. As soon as a third party is used it is necessary to examine whether a taxable connection is being created in the foreign market.

The income tax charge may be particularly important, as the example below illustrates, to HMRC as a means of capturing e-commerce across the internet.

Example 6.9

USA Shopping Mall Inc operates an e-commerce site for its clothing merchandise, which can be accessed solely by wholesale distributors authorised by the company. The wholesalers purchase the merchandise by accessing the website, through which orders are placed, and payment can be made by credit card. A UK wholesaler places an order for merchandise worth £200,000. Is USA Shopping Mall Inc assessable to UK tax? It is likely that the US company would not be subject to any form of UK tax. However, everything will turn upon the precise facts of each case, and an identification

---

[55]   The Radcliffe Committee *Final Report of the Royal Commission on the Taxation of Profits and Income*, Cmd 9474 (1955). The 'badges of trade', as identified in the report and in subsequent cases, are: profit seeking motive; the number of transactions; the nature of the asset; existence of similar trading transactions or interests; whether the asset is repaired, modified or improved to make it more easily saleable or saleable at a greater profit; the way the sale was carried out; the source of finance; interval of time between purchase and sale; and method of acquisition.

[56]   See *Grainger v Gough* [1896] Ac 325, at 335, per Lord Herschell.

[57]   ITTOIA 2005, s 6(2).

of where the contract is entered into with the UK consumer and location of the operations which create the profits for USA Shopping Mall Inc.

In HMRC's *Electronic Commerce: The UK's Taxation Agenda* the following comment was made on e-commerce sales by non-residents, confirming that contracts entered into using instantaneous communication will typically be formed in the country in which the buyer is located (see also the discussion at **6.4.10** on internet contracts):[58]

'Whether Internet sales to the UK by non-residents constitute trading in the UK depends on the place of contract, which in turn will depend on the stages involved in its completion. Where acceptance is communicated instantaneously, the place of contract is generally in the territory to which the acceptance is communicated: that is to say, in the straightforward case of a simple offer to buy by the purchaser and acceptance by the seller, the territory of the buyer.'

The role of where the contract is formed in deciding whether a non-resident is trading in or with the UK is considered below. However, it is important to note that the circumstances in which the contract is formed is only one aspect in deciding the issue (the location of formation of the contract was the approach adopted by the courts in the nineteenth century). However, it is also necessary to consider where the economic substance of the business is located, and how the goods and/or services are supplied to the customer (this is likely to be the focus of the courts going forward, although there can be no guarantee the nineteenth-century approach will not have a material influence).

6.4.8   Trade in the UK: location of contract formation

In the case of *Grainger & Son v William Lane Gough*[59] it was emphasised that it is a question of fact whether or not a person is exercising a trade within the UK.[60] What are the elements that constitute a trade within the UK? The judge considered that, 'there is a broad distinction between trading *with* a country and carrying on a trade *within* a country'.[61] It was considered that the export of goods to the UK does not in itself amount to a trade within the UK, and that soliciting orders does not amount to a trade, whether by agent, circulars or advertisements.[62] In another case, *Werle & Co v Colquhoun*,[63] the court said that the following circumstances may be material in considering whether or not a trade is carried on in the UK (the list is a generalisation of the circumstances put forward by the court):

---

[58]   Chapter 8, para 8.13.
[59]   [1896] AC 325.
[60]   [1896] AC 325, at 335.
[61]   [1896] AC 325.
[62]   [1896] AC 325, at 336.
[63]   (1888) 20 QBD 753, 1 TC 402.

- Where is payment made by the purchasers, for example, to an agent in the UK?

- Are the receipts given in the UK?

- Where are the goods delivered? Who is the carrying agent selected by the purchaser in the UK or the seller in the foreign country?

- Did the non-resident corporation use agents who issued advertisements or circulars in the UK for the purpose of causing contracts to be entered into in the UK?

In the course of giving judgment, one judge said:[64]

> '... in each case, when you come to consider is there a trade carried on in England, it is a question of fact. It is a question of fact which is now divided into two. Is there a trade carried on and, if so, is that trade carried on in England? It is a question of fact in each case.'

The judge went on to say that 'a trade may be carried on in England without having an establishment at all';[65] and that it is not essential that profits be received in the UK, or that there be an establishment in the UK. The essential factor is whether the contracts are made in the UK. If so then the trade is carried on in the UK. This is because the making of contracts is the very substance and essence of a trade.[66]

However, the courts have emphasised on several occasions that the location of where the contracts are formed is one of the principal factors in determining whether a trade is carried on in the UK. In *Maclaine v Eccott*[67] the following summary of the law was given by the judge issuing the principal opinion of the court:[68]

> 'The question whether a trade is exercised in the UK is a question of fact, and it is undesirable to attempt to lay down any exhaustive test of what constitutes such an exercise of trade; but I think it must now be taken as established that in the case of a merchant's business, the primary object of which is to sell goods at a profit, the trade is (speaking generally) exercised or carried on (I do not myself see much difference between the two expressions) at the place where the contracts are made. No doubt reference has sometimes been made to the place where payment is made for the goods sold or to the place where the goods are delivered, and it may be that in certain circumstances these are material considerations; but the most important, and indeed the crucial, question is, where are the contracts of sale made? Statements to this effect by Lord Justice Brett and Lord Justice Cotton in *Erichsen v Last* ((1881) 8 QBD 414) were quoted with approval in

---

[64]   *Werle & Co v Colquhoun* (1888) 20 QBD 753, 1 TC 402, at 408.
[65]   (1888) 1 TC 402, at 411.
[66]   (1888) 1 TC 411, at 411–412.
[67]   (1926) 10 TC 481, 131 LT 601.
[68]   (1926) 10 TC 481, at 574–575, per Viscount Cave LC.

this House in the case of *Grainger v Gough* ([1896] AC 325); and the same principle was the basis of the decisions in *Werle v Colquhoun* ((1888) 20 QBD 753), *Lovell and Christmas v Commissioners of Taxes* ([1908] AC 46), *Greenwood v Smidth* ([1922] 1 AC 417), and *Wilcock v Pinto* ([1925] 1 KB 30).'

6.4.9   Trade in the UK: substance of the trade

Despite a focus in the earlier case-law with where the contract is formed, it must be recognised that the place where the contract is formed is not wholly conclusive in deciding whether a trade is carried on in the UK. In the case of *Firestone Tyre Co Ltd v Lewellin*,[69] the judge made the following observations:[70]

> '... the place of sale will not be the determining fact if there are other circumstances present that outweigh its importance, or unless there are no other circumstances that can. Since the courts have not attempted to lay down that those other circumstances are or may be, singly or in combination, and it would be, I believe, neither right nor possible to try to do so, I think it is true to say that, within wide limits which determine what is a permissible conclusion, the question whether a trade is exercised within the UK remains, as it began, a question of fact for the Special Commissioners.'

The judge then went on to quote with approval the observations in *FL Smidth & Co v Greenwood*, where the judge said:[71]

> 'The contracts in this case were made abroad. But I am not prepared to hold that this test is decisive. I can imagine cases where the contract of resale is made abroad, and yet the manufacture of the goods, some negotiation of the terms, and complete execution of the contract take place here such circumstances that the trade was in truth exercised here. I think that the question is, where do the operations take place from which the profits in substance arise?'

The central principle to be identified from this line of case-law is that the location of the contract is not wholly determinative. It is necessary to look at the nature of the transactions between the parties. For instance, the location of the place of manufacture or appropriation of stock, the place of delivery and receipt of payment are all relevant considerations. Although in some cases of e-commerce the contract will be formed abroad, there will be situations where other factors will tend to show that the centre of operations from which profits arise is in the UK. In these circumstances the e-commerce trader will be trading in the UK. It is doubtful that the existence of a website operating on a computer server in the UK would be sufficient of itself to attract an income tax charge on

---

[69]   [1957] 1 All ER 561, HL.
[70]   [1957] 1 All ER 561, at 568, HL, per Lord Radcliffe.
[71]   (1922) 8 TC 193, at 203, per Atkins LJ.

profits of a non-resident (even in the absence of the protection of a DTA requiring the existence of a permanent establishment). Whilst the issue will always be a question of fact as to whether a business structure has the necessary elements to be regarded as trading in the UK, a computer server can usually be set up in a country as a passive piece of IT machinery, so that it performs functions as a mere conduit for passing information back to the non-resident's country in which the true economics and machinery of the business are situated. Ideally, a structure will be adopted by a non-resident that uses IT outside of the UK to process orders, trigger payment, issue delivery orders for goods and/or services.

Example 6.10

Ecommerce Ltd, a UK company, provides third party e-commerce vendors access to its website so that they can sell goods to customers in the UK (which is described as a 'facilitation' service). Ecommerce Ltd allows access to its website to many non-resident and resident companies on this basis. Alpha Inc (based in the US) operates an independent retail business from the US in relation to the supply of various goods. Alpha Inc uses the e-commerce platform of Ecommerce Ltd to sell its goods to customers in the UK. Ecommerce Ltd's terms and conditions of sale provide, among other things, that:

- Ecommerce Ltd is not the agent of any seller;

- Ecommerce Ltd is authorised by a buyer to act as its limited representative to conclude on its behalf contracts directly between it and sellers for sales of goods via the service offered by Ecommerce Ltd;

- any contract formed is between the seller and the buyer; and

- goods are dispatched by sellers directly to the buyers.

Non-business customers place orders via the e-commerce website of Ecommerce Ltd, which are concluded on the terms mentioned above. Ecommerce Ltd concludes the contract with the Sellers (based on the limited representative basis of the buyer referred to in the contract). Alpha Inc should not be subject to UK corporation tax or income tax. This is because Ecommerce Ltd does not act as agent of Alpha Inc. Furthermore, Alpha Inc does not carry on a trade through Ecommerce Ltd because it enters into the contract from the US, and dispatches the goods from the US. In any event the terms of the US–UK DTA would require a permanent establishment to exist in the UK.

6.4.10 Internet contracts

The method of formation of contracts via the internet is not the subject of specific legislation. The formation of a contract is determined by the rules of contract law (see Chapter 4, which examines how contracts are formed, and which country will have jurisdiction over disputes). Generally, where communications are made over the internet it is instantaneous. On this basis the rules relating to contracts made over the telephone or fax should apply. Where a prospective buyer responds to an 'invitation to treat' from an e-commerce site, a contract will generally be formed when the notification of acceptance is received by the prospective buyer (ie the consumer). The country where the internet contract is formed is likely to be the country where the notification of acceptance is received by the buyer.[72]

> *Example 6.11*
>
> Z Inc carries on business as an e-commerce trader in DVDs. The e-commerce equipment and the trader are based in New York. The website is accessed by consumers in the UK. Goods are selected, billing information is completed and the consumer transmits an offer to purchase the selection of goods to the trader's computer via the internet site. The computer based in the US automatically sends notification of acceptance and that the DVDs will be delivered within 3 weeks. In these circumstances a contract should be formed in the UK. The extent to which the profits from such an activity can be taxed depends upon whether a permanent establishment exists in the UK (since the provisions of the US–UK DTA require a permanent establishment to exist in the UK before a tax charge on business profits can be imposed on a US company).

The observations about DTAs must be borne in mind. Where a DTA does not exist, a non-resident e-commerce trader may be subject to income tax where, as in the above example, the contract is formed in the UK, and if the UK is the place where the profits in substance arise. In the absence of a DTA there is no additional requirement for a permanent establishment to exist and accordingly HMRC's power of taxation will not be restricted.

The parties to a contract can stipulate the mode of contract formation. With the appropriate structure in place, it should be possible to ensure that a contract is not made in the UK.

HMRC has provided guidance on the circumstances in which it considers a contract is formed in the context of e-commerce transactions.[73] The guidance provides as follows:

> **'E-commerce**
>
> A website proffering goods for sale amounts to an "invitation to treat" in relation to those goods.

---

[72] *Entores v Miles Far East Corporation* (1955) 2 QB 327; *Brinkibon Ltd v Stahag Stahl GmbH* [1983] 2 AC 34.

[73] HMRC Guidance Manual INTM263060 *Non-residents Trading in the UK: Making of Contract.*

When a customer places an order for a particular item on the website, this will constitute an "offer" to purchase the item.

The question is how, when and where the acceptance of the customer's offer is to be regarded as having crystallised.

1. In *JSC Zestafoni Nikoladze Ferroalloy Plant v Ronly Holdings Ltd* [2004] Colman J held that an acceptance by fax constituted an "instantaneous communication". The fax took effect on receipt as the sender's machine would generally indicate whether the message had been received "effectively" (as opposed to having been received only in part). Accordingly it would seem that an e-mail acceptance should also be regarded as an instantaneous communication.

2. There are therefore two potential times when acceptance crystallises:
   a. the more likely option is that it occurs once the customer makes payment online and is presented with an order acknowledgment page; and
   b. alternatively the latest stage when it might occur is when the order confirmation email is sent out.

   In either case, there is a good argument that the place of contract is the UK.

3. An offer can be accepted not only by a written acceptance, but also by conduct … Ordinarily, accepting payment for goods is a classic example of acceptance of an offer to purchase the goods.

4. The order acknowledgment web-page would seem to be a communication of the vendor's acceptance of the customer's offer to purchase. The contract is probably, therefore, concluded in the UK once the customer there sees this web-page.

5. The very latest time when the contract can be concluded is when the vendor issues an e-mail confirming the order. An e-mail acceptance should be regarded as an instantaneous communication, in the same way that a fax communication is regarded as instantaneous, ie, it is effective upon receipt by the offeror.

6. In effect the sale is concluded when the payment is accepted, when the order is acknowledged on-screen, or when the purchaser receives the order confirmation e-mail. The contract is concluded in the UK at that time, and the postal rule does not apply.

7. This is not affected by any terms on the vendor's web-site reserving the right to refuse to supply for any reason. Such terms are not binding until a binding contract is formed between the parties. The right to refuse to supply (insofar as it is reasonable) and the right to cancel only make sense if the vendor is under an obligation to deliver. If there is no contract and the vendor is under no obligation to deliver, there is nothing to cancel and no useful purpose to the right to refuse to deliver.'

6.5 DOUBLE TAXATION AGREEMENTS

In considering how UK tax will be applied to internet business activities carried on by a non-resident, it is necessary to refer to the principles of the OECD Model Double Taxation Convention. Many of the UK's DTAs are based upon the concepts of the Model. Among other things, a

DTA limits the extent to which UK tax can be applied on the activities of a non-resident. The scope of that relief will depend upon the nature of the terms of the relevant DTA. To date, the UK is signatory to over one hundred DTAs. If a DTA does not exist, it will be easier for HMRC to tax an internet business carried on by a non-resident. This is because the UK tax charge will not be limited by the requirement for a permanent establishment to exist. In the absence of a DTA, all corporation tax will be imposed in similar circumstances to that anticipated by the business profits article of a DTA, namely a non-resident must carry on a trade in the UK through a permanent establishment situated in the UK. In the absence of a corporation tax charge, all income tax charge can be imposed on the profits of a trade that is carried on in the UK.

Where a DTA exists, it is necessary to consider the operation of the agreement because it may relieve tax where there would otherwise be a charge under the normal principles of UK domestic tax law. However, DTAs cannot operate to impose a wider tax charge than that which exists under domestic legislation.

For a general overview on the nature of the OECD Model Convention see Chapter 8 at **8.5**.

6.6   BUSINESS PROFITS

DTAs impose important limitations upon the ability of a country (such as the UK) to tax a non-resident. For example, Article 7(1) of the Model Convention deals with business profits (e.g. trading profits) and only permits a non-resident to be taxed by the country of source (ie the location where profits are created/arise) on profits arising from a permanent establishment. The business profits Article will limit the right of the UK to tax a non-resident where there is not a permanent establishment. For example, the right to impose income tax where a non-resident is exercising a trade in the UK will be extinguished by a DTA unless a permanent establishment does exist. The OECD conference held in Turku, Finland, recognised that a computer server was in fact capable of constituting a permanent establishment.[74] However, in contrast, HMRC considers that a website operating on a server is not capable of being a permanent establishment.[75]

Example 6.12

> X Inc is an internet trader which has a computer server located in the UK. In the 2011/12 tax year profits of £200,000 are derived from a trade of selling computer software to people in the UK who access the UK computer server. Orders and payment are processed by a US computer server. Delivery

---

[74]   OECD, 'Electronic Commerce: The Challenges to Tax Authorities and Taxpayers' (1997), at paras 93–102.
[75]   See **6.4.5**.

is initiated by the US server, but the actual transfer (ie the download) is from the UK server. X Inc asks for your advice as to whether HMRC can impose corporation tax or income tax on these profits on the basis that the UK server is a permanent establishment. An illustration of the method of business is shown below.

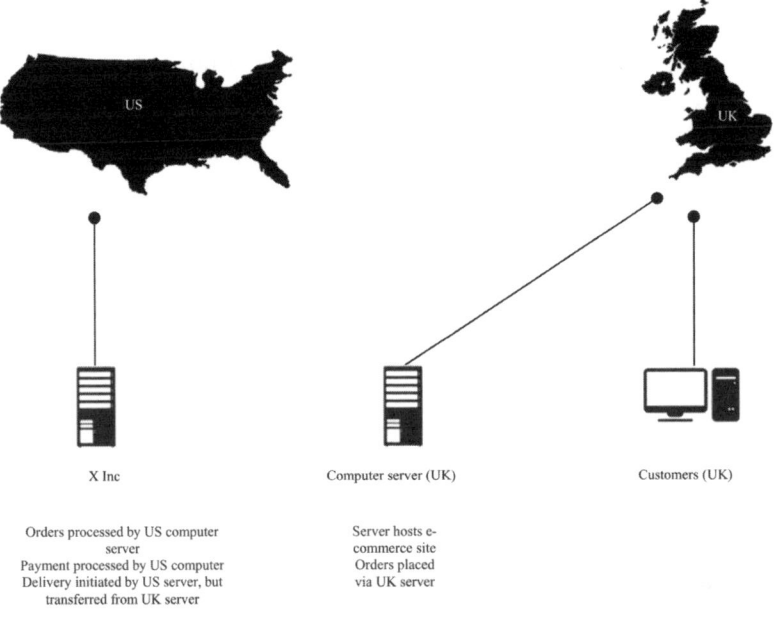

| X Inc | Computer server (UK) | Customers (UK) |

Orders processed by US computer server
Payment processed by US computer
Delivery initiated by US server, but transferred from UK server

Server hosts e-commerce site
Orders placed via UK server

The answer to this question of tax liability depends upon whether the computer server (ie automated machinery) can constitute a permanent establishment for the purposes of corporation tax. If a DTA is in place between the US and the UK, reference must be made to the rights the UK has to tax a resident of the US. Under the UK–US DTA, Art 7(1), the right to tax a US resident is limited to profits which are solely attributable to a permanent establishment. There must be a permanent establishment for a corporation tax charge to arise. In this example, there is nothing to constitute a UK permanent establishment. If corporation tax cannot be imposed on this basis, could income tax be charged on the basis that the e-commerce trade is exercised in the UK? The DTA only permits taxation of a non-resident's profits where these are derived from a permanent establishment. Can it be said that a trade is exercised through a permanent establishment where there is only a computer server located in the UK? The answer to this based on current HMRC practice is no. Clearly, in this example, as the economic function of the servers minimal there can be no income tax charge.

6.7 WHAT IS A PERMANENT ESTABLISHMENT?

It must be remembered that a DTA operates to limit the domestic tax charge, and it is always necessary to consider the terms of a DTA carefully to see if they apply in any given situation. The OECD Model Tax Convention is a helpful guide to the contents of many DTAs. The definition of a permanent establishment is cast in wide terms; Art 5(1) of the OECD Model Tax Convention provides:

> '1. For the purposes of this Convention, the term "permanent establishment" means a fixed place of business through which the business of an enterprise is wholly or partly carried on.'

The Model Convention goes on to define the type of subject matter that is included within the concept of permanent establishment. Article 5(2) provides:

> '2. The term "permanent establishment" includes especially:
> a) a place of management;
> b) a branch;
> c) an office;
> d) a factory;
> e) a workshop; and
> f) a mine, an oil or gas well, a quarry or any other place of extraction of natural resources.'

The OECD Model Convention envisages that a contracting state is only entitled to tax the profits of a non-resident that are attributable to a permanent establishment. For example, Art 7(1) of the UK–Italy DTA,[76] which is based upon the Model Convention provides:

> 'The profits of an enterprise of a Contracting State shall be taxable only in that State unless the enterprise carried on business in the other Contracting State through a permanent establishment situated therein. If the enterprise carries on business as aforesaid, the profits of the enterprise may be taxed in the other State but only so much of them as is attributable to that permanent establishment.'

Clearly the DTA envisages the possibility of taxing anything which comes within the concept of permanent establishment through which a business is carried on by a company. Assistance in the interpretation of permanent establishment can be obtained from the Commentaries to the Model Convention (see **14.6**). The use to which these Commentaries can be put in determining the tax position of a non-resident is therefore of significance.

6.8 AGENCY

As previously discussed in this chapter, the concept of agency is important in bringing a non-resident into the charge to corporation tax (see **6.4**). Where a DTA exists, based upon the principles of the OECD

---

[76] Double Taxation Relief (Taxation on Income) (Italy) Order 1990, SI 1990/2590.

Model Tax Convention, no agency can be used as a tax charge unless it is a permanent establishment within the meaning of the Convention. The rules relating to the taxation of agents is important in the context of internet business, because arrangements will usually be in place in countries for the delivery of goods and/or services ordered via the internet.

A dependent agent usually creates a taxable presence. Article 5(5) of the OECD Model Tax Convention (2010) provides that a person other than an agent of an independent status, who acts on behalf of an enterprise and:

> '... habitually exercises, in a Contracting State an authority to conclude contracts in the name of the enterprise, that enterprise shall be deemed to have a permanent establishment in that State in respect of any activities which that person undertakes for the enterprise, unless the activities of such person are limited to those mentioned in paragraph 4 [reproduced at **6.9**] which, if exercised through a fixed place of business, would not make this a fixed place of business a permanent establishment under the provisions of that paragraph.'

6.9 EXCLUSIONS FROM DEFINITION OF PERMANENT ESTABLISHMENT

Many of the UK's DTAs define a permanent establishment, based on Article 5(4) of the OECD Model Tax Convention which excludes the following matters from the concept of permanent establishment:

> '... the term "permanent establishment" shall be deemed not to include:
> (a) the use of facilities solely for the purposes of storage, display or delivery of goods or merchandise belonging to the enterprise;
> (b) the maintenance of a stock of goods or merchandise belonging to the enterprise solely for the purpose of storage, display of delivery;
> (c) the maintenance of a stock of goods or merchandise belonging to the enterprise solely for the purpose of processing by another enterprise;
> (d) the maintenance of a fixed place of business solely for the purpose of purchasing goods or merchandise or of collecting information, for the enterprise;
> (e) the maintenance of a fixed place of business solely for the purpose of carrying on, for the enterprise, any other activity of a preparatory or auxiliary character;
> (f) the maintenance of a fixed place of business solely for any combination of activities mentioned in sub-paragraphs a) to e) provided that the overall activity of the fixed place of business resulting from this combination is of a preparatory or auxiliary character.'

It is clear that where these principles are included in a DTA, and a non-resident person carries on an e-commerce activity, enters into a contract with a UK consumer and dispatches delivery orders to a person

United Kingdom
Taxation: General

in the UK (who holds stock for the foreign company), the UK holder of goods will not constitute a permanent establishment of the non-resident.

Do these principles apply where a server is used within a particular jurisdiction for the delivery of computer software? Can it be said that such servers are facilities for the delivery of goods? Traditional concepts of taxation such as these are based in an era where transactions only occurred in respect of tangible and not digital items. It is unnecessary to consider these points for UK purposes since, as highlighted earlier, HMRC practice is that a website and computer server are not capable of constituting a permanent establishment.

Example 6.13

X Inc carries on an internet trade from the US with consumers who are based in the UK. All the automated machinery of the US company through which payments are made is located in the US. Delivery of ordered merchandise is achieved by sending delivery instructions to a UK company, which holds stock on behalf of the US internet trader. The nature of the trade can be shown diagrammatically as:

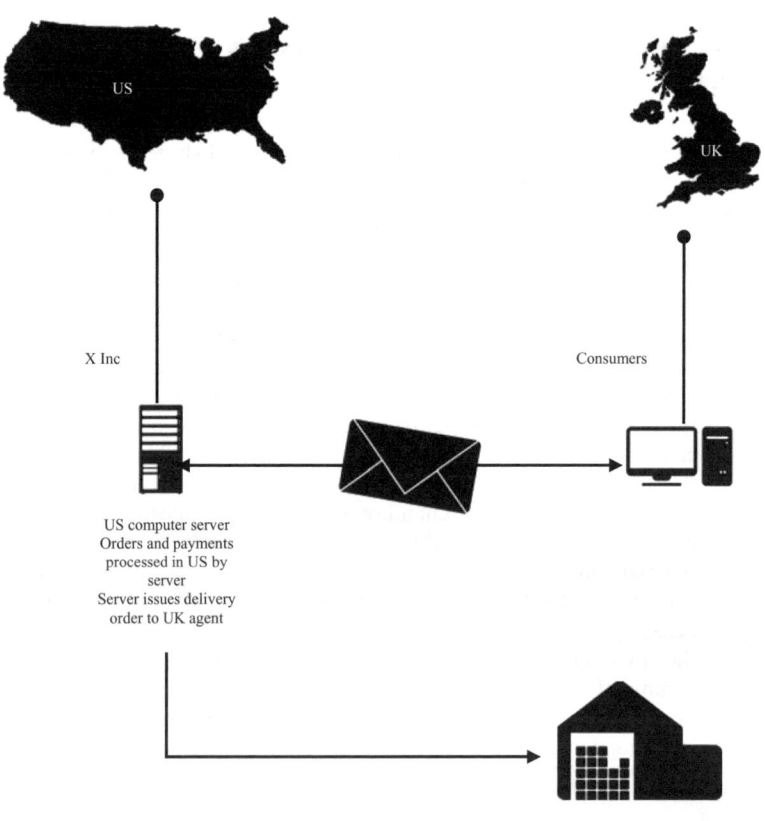

US

UK

X Inc   Consumers

US computer server
Orders and payments
processed in US by
server
Server issues delivery
order to UK agent

UK agent holds goods for delivery
on behalf of X Inc

In this example, the US company has no presence in the UK which is capable of forming the basis of a tax charge. There is no permanent establishment for the purposes of corporation tax, and the UK company which delivers merchandise for the US company is not, assuming OECD principles are contained in the DTA, capable of being an agency sufficient to constitute a permanent establishment. It is only where a permanent establishment exists that the UK tax authority will be entitled to impose a charge (this is the nature of the tax relief given to non-residents through a DTA).

It is also important to bear in mind the wording of Art 5(6) of the OECD Model, which states that an enterprise shall not be treated as having a permanent establishment solely for the reason that it carries on business in a country through a broker, general commission agent or any other agent of an independent status.

For this rule to apply the person must be acting in the ordinary course of business. The OECD Commentaries make it clear that a person will come within the scope of this part of the Article, if the person is independent of the enterprise both legally and economically and he acts in the ordinary course of business when acting on behalf of the enterprise (Commentary on Art 5, para 37).

6.10   ATTRIBUTION OF PROFITS TO A PERMANENT ESTABLISHMENT

6.10.1   UK law

Under UK tax law the amount of profits attributed to a permanent establishment for corporation tax purposes is the quantum of profits it would have made if it were a distinct and separate enterprise, engaged in the same or similar activities under the same or similar conditions, dealing wholly independently with the non-resident company.[77] The wording is based on Art 7(2) of the OECD Model Tax Convention.

Transactions between the permanent establishment and any other part of the non-resident company must be treated as taking place on such terms as would have been agreed between parties dealing at arm's length.[78]

In calculating the profits of the UK permanent establishment no deduction can be made for royalties[79] paid, including other similar payments, by the permanent establishment to any other part of the non-resident company in respect of the use of intangible assets held by

---

[77]   CTA 2009, s 21(1).

[78]   CTA 2009, s 22.

[79]   See CTA 2009, s 31. There is no definition of 'royalties'. However, the term 'royalty' is defined in CTA 2009, s 714 for the purposes of Part 8 (which is discussed in Chapter 7) as 'a royalty in respect of the enjoyment or exercise of rights that constitute an

the company.[80] However, any contribution made by a permanent establishment to the costs of creation of an intangible asset (e.g. patents, copyright etc) is a permitted tax deduction.[81]

The amount of profits subject to corporation tax is limited to those attributable to the permanent establishment.[82] It is possible to obtain certainty on the level of profits to be attributed to a permanent establishment by entering into an advance pricing agreement with HMRC (this is considered in Chapter 9 at **9.3.4**).

6.10.2   OECD Model Tax Convention and Commentary

The profits to be attributed to a permanent establishment of a non-resident company will generally be determined in accordance with the provisions of a DTA. The problem with profit attribution is that the permanent establishment is part of a far larger company, and it has no legal personality that is separate and distinct from the overall company of which it forms a part.

The OECD Model provides that the profits to be attributed to a permanent establishment are those which it might be expected to make if it were a separate and independent enterprise engaged in the same or similar activities under the same or similar conditions, taking into account the functions performed, assets used and risks assumed by the enterprise through the permanent establishment and through the other parts of the enterprise.[83]

The Commentary to the OECD Model makes the point that this principle corresponds to the 'arm's length principle' applicable to Art 9 of the OECD Model in respect of transactions between associated enterprises.[84]

---

intangible asset'; and in ITA 2007, s 913 as including a payment received as consideration for the use of, or the right to use, any copyright, patent, trade mark, design, process or information.

[80]   CTA 2009, s 31. For this purpose 'intangible asset' has the meaning it has for accounting purposes in Financial Reporting Standard 10, and specifically includes any intellectual property as defined in s 712(3) of CTA 2009 (namely (a) any patent, trade mark, registered design, copyright or design right, plant breeders' rights or rights under the Plant Varieties Act 1997, s 7; (b) any right under the law of a country or territory outside the UK corresponding to, or similar to, a right within (a); (c) any information or technique not protected by a right within (a) or (b) but having industrial, commercial or other economic value; or (d) any licence or other right in respect of anything within (a), (b) or (c)). This definition and the Part 8 CTA 2009 regime applicable to intangible fixed assets is discussed in Chapter 7.

[81]   CTA 2009, s 31(2).

[82]   CTA 2009, s 20.

[83]   OECD Model Tax Convention, Art 6.2.

[84]   OECD Commentary (para 16) on Art 7(2) of the Model Convention.

The OECD Commentary explains a two-step approach that should be taken for determining the profits of a permanent establishment, which is as follows:[85]

> 'Under the first step, a functional and factual analysis is undertaken which will lead to:
> - the attribution to the permanent establishment, as appropriate, of the rights and obligations arising out of transactions between the enterprise of which the permanent establishment is a part and separate enterprises;
> - the identification of significant people functions relevant to the attribution of economic ownership of assets, and the attribution of economic ownership of assets to the permanent establishment;
> - the identification of significant people functions relevant to the assumption of risks, and the attribution of risks to the permanent establishment;
> - the identification of other functions of the permanent establishment;
> - the recognition and determination of the nature of those dealings between the permanent establishment and other parts of the same enterprise that can appropriately be recognised ..., and
> - the attribution of capital based on the assets and risks attributed to the permanent establishment.
>
> Under the second step, any transactions with associated enterprises attributed to the permanent establishment are priced in accordance with the guidance of the OECD Transfer Pricing Guidelines and these Guidelines are applied by analogy to dealings between the permanent establishment and the other parts of the enterprise of which it is a part. The process involves the pricing on an arm's length basis of these recognised dealings through:
> - the determination of comparability between the dealings and uncontrolled transactions, established by applying the Guidelines' comparability factors directly (characteristics of property or services, economic circumstances and business strategies) or by analogy (functional analysis, contractual terms) in light of the particular factual circumstances of the permanent establishment; and
> - the application by analogy of one of the Guidelines' methods to arrive at an arm's length compensation for the dealings between the permanent establishment and the other parts of the enterprise, taking into account the functions performed by and the assets and risks attributed to the permanent establishment and the other parts of the enterprise.'

United Kingdom
Taxation: General

---

[85]   OECD Commentary (paras 21–22) on Art 7(2) of the Model Convention.

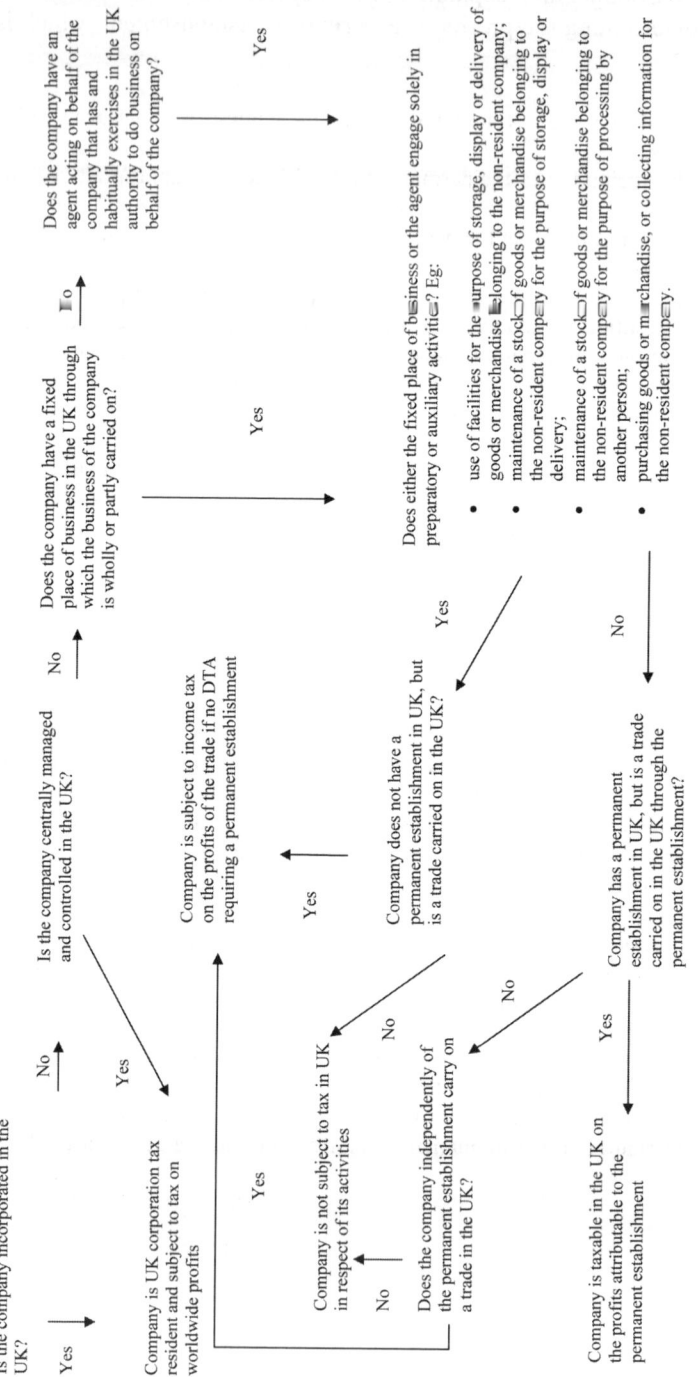

Figure 6.1: Summary of the scope of UK direct charges on a company

6.11   INBOUND INTELLECTUAL PROPERTY LICENSING

6.11.1   Introduction

The payment of royalties or licence fees for the use of intellectual property (eg copyright, know-how, patent rights) by a licensee to a licensor may be subject to deduction of tax at source, with the obligation on the licensee (ie, in the UK) to make the deduction.

In broad terms, the UK's withholding obligations are set out below:

(1)   an individual licensee who pays certain annual payments (as discussed below) which are made for genuine commercial reasons in connection with the individual's trade, profession or vocation is required to deduct tax at source at the basic rate of income tax from such payments;[86]

(2)   any corporate licensee that pays certain annual payments (as discussed below) must deduct tax at source from such payments, at the basic rate of income tax;[87]

(3)   any licensee (whether an individual or corporation) who pays royalties for the use of patent rights must deduct tax at source, at the basic rate of income tax;[88] and

(4)   any payment of royalties/periodic sums in respect of copyright (e.g. copyright in a computer programme) or right in a design to an owner whose usual place of abode is outside the UK must be made under deduction of income tax at the basic rate.[89]

Where a deduction at source is made as referred to above, the amount of income tax that is deducted from the payment is treated as income tax paid by the recipient (ie, the licensor).[90] The amount of the income tax that is treated as paid by the recipient is taken into account in determining the income tax or corporation tax payable by, or repayable to, the recipient.[91] A DTA may permit the deduction of tax at a lower rate than the basic rate of tax, or the DTA may even reduce the withholding to nil.

The characterisation of royalty payment in relation to e-commerce transactions is considered in Chapter 8.

United Kingdom
Taxation: General

---

[86]   See ITA 2007, s 900.
[87]   See ITA 2007, s 901.
[88]   See ITA 2007, s 903.
[89]   See ITA 2007, s 906.
[90]   ITA 2007, s 848(1).
[91]   ITA 2007, s 848(2).

6.11.2 Annual payments

An individual licensee who makes a qualifying annual payment (eg royalties for use of a trade mark, which is a pure income profit for the recipient because a trade is not being carried on) which is made for genuine commercial reasons in connection with that individual's trade or profession is required to deduct tax at source at the basic rate of income tax (currently 20%) from such payment.[92] Furthermore, any corporate licensee who makes a qualifying annual payment must deduct tax at source from such payment.[93] For this purpose a 'qualifying annual payment' means an annual payment that meets the following conditions:[94]

(1)   the payment must arise in the UK,

(2)   if the recipient is a person other than a company, the payment must be a payment charged to income tax under, inter alia, s 579 of ITTOIA 2005 (royalties etc from intellectual property which has a UK source), or Chapter 7 of Part 5 of ITTOIA 2005 (annual payments not otherwise charged);

(3)   if the recipient is a company, the payment must be a payment charged to income tax (as referred to in the previous point), or the payment must be from a source in the UK and chargeable to corporation tax under Part 10, Chapter 7 of CTA 2009 (annual payments not otherwise charged); and

(4)   the payment must not fall within specified prohibitions, such as being a payment of interest or annual payments for non-taxable consideration.[95]

6.11.3 Patent rights

Any licensee (whether an individual or corporation) who pays royalties for the use of patent rights must deduct tax at source at the basic rate of income tax from such payments.[96] For the withholding obligation to arise the following conditions must be met:[97]

(1)   the payment must not be a qualifying annual payment (as defined by ITA 2007, s 899), or an annual payment for non-taxable consideration;[98]

---

[92]   ITA 2007, s 900.
[93]   ITA 2007, s 901.
[94]   ITA 2007, s 899.
[95]   ITA 2007, s 899(5). See also ITA 2007, s 904.
[96]   ITA 2007, s 903.
[97]   ITA 2007, s 903(1)–(4).
[98]   ITA 2007, ss 899, 904.

(2)   the payment must have its source in the UK; and

(3)   the payment must be one that is charged to income tax or corporation tax.

It is possible that the obligation to deduct will either be reduced or extinguished by a DTA between the UK and country of residence of the recipient of the payment.

6.11.4   Copyright, right in a design and related rights

Any payment of royalties and/or periodic sums in respect of copyright[99] (e.g. copyright in computer software) or right in a design[100] (referred to in the tax legislation as the 'relevant intellectual property right') to an owner whose usual place of abode is outside the UK must be made under deduction of tax at the basic rate of income tax;[101] except where that licensor has the benefit of a DTA between the country of its residence and the UK (whereby the rate of such withholding tax is reduced, or the obligation to deduct is removed altogether).

The obligation to withhold will only arise in connection with a payment where the following conditions are met:[102]

(1)   it is a payment of any royalties, or sums payable periodically, in respect of a relevant intellectual property right;

(2)   that payment is one that is charged to income tax or corporation tax, and either:

   (a)   the usual place of abode of the owner of the right is outside the UK; or
   (b)   a person ('the seller') has assigned the intellectual property right to another person, the usual place of abode of the seller is outside the UK, the seller is entitled to periodical payments in respect of the right, and the payments are in respect of that entitlement.

No withholding obligation is imposed where the payment is made in respect of copies of works or articles that have been exported from the UK for distribution outside the UK.[103]

---

[99]   For this purpose the term 'copyright' is defined as excluding any copyright in: (a) a cinematographic film or video recording or (b) the sound-track of a cinematographic film or video recording, except so far as it is separately exploited: ITA 2007, s 907(2).

[100]   For this purpose the term 'right in a design' means design right in a design, or the right in a registered design: ITA 2007, s 907(2).

[101]   ITA 2007, s 906(5).

[102]   ITA 2007, s 906(1)–(3).

[103]   ITA 2007, s 906(4).

United Kingdom
Taxation: General

In the absence of any specific provisions relating to registered trade marks, there is no obligation to deduct tax from payments for use of such rights unless they constitute 'qualifying annual payments' (as discussed above). It should also be noted in connection with payments of royalties of relevant intellectual property (within the meaning given by ITA 2007) to a non-UK resident owner that are made through an agent resident in the UK with regard to which the agent is entitled as against the owner of the right to deduct any sum by way of commission in respect of services rendered, the amount of the payment from which the tax must be deducted is that payment less the commission.[104] However, if the person by or through whom the payment is made does not know the commission is payable, or does not know its amount, the sum representing income tax required to be deducted must be calculated on the total amount of the payment.[105] Any agreement to make the payment for the relevant intellectual property without deduction for income tax is void.[106]

Example 6.14

Search Engine Ltd, based in a low tax country, licenses the use of software to run a search engine site in the UK to MirrorSite Ltd, a company that is UK tax resident. MirrorSite Ltd agrees to pay a periodic sum of 5% of any royalties created from sublicensing the software to companies operating in the EU. The fees are payable each year for a 5-year period. In the first year, MirrorSite Ltd pays £150,000 to Search Engine Ltd. The payment is for use of copyright and a withholding tax at the basic rate of income tax (20%, 2011/12) must be deducted from the payment.

6.11.5   Inter-company royalty payments

There is no obligation to deduct income tax at source on qualifying annual payments, royalties and other sums paid for the use of patent rights and copyright under ITA 2007 (for details see preceding sections) where the payment is made by a company which reasonably believes at the time the payment is made that, among other requirements, one of the following conditions is satisfied:[107]

(1)   the person beneficially entitled to the income in respect of which the payment is made is a company resident in the UK;[108]

(2)   the person beneficially entitled to the income in respect of which the payment is made is a company not resident in the UK which carries on a trade in the UK through a permanent establishment, and the

---

[104]   ITA 2007, s 908(1).
[105]   ITA 2007, s 908(2).
[106]   ITA 2007, s 909(2).
[107]   ITA 2007 s 930. There are other qualifying recipients but these are beyond the scope of this chapter.
[108]   ITA 2007, s 933.

payment is taken into account in computing the chargeable profits of the permanent establishment;[109] or

(3) the person beneficially entitled to the income is a partnership, each member of which is a company resident in the UK, or a permanent establishment of a non-resident company whose profits are subject to UK corporation tax.[110]

6.11.6   Double taxation agreements and royalties

Royalties paid by a UK resident to a non-UK resident person are often exempt from withholding taxes as a result of the operation of a royalty article of a DTA. Most of the UK's DTA network is modelled on the OECD Model Tax Convention.[111] If the royalty Article of a DTA does not extinguish the withholding tax liability it will normally impose a restriction on the amount that can be deducted.

Relief for UK source taxation under a DTA is not automatic. A non-resident licensor must make an application, subject to the statutory exception discussed below, to HMRC and obtain authorisation so that payments can be made without deduction for tax, or at a reduced rate of tax under the DTA. Where an application is successful HMRC will direct the payer to make future payments at the rate qualifying for relief under the relevant DTA. If UK tax has already been deducted from payments prior to the application then HMRC will make a repayment of the tax deducted. There are forms for each country with which the UK has a DTA.[112] The application form may require supporting documentation, such as the licence agreement. Additionally the form will need to be certified by the taxation authority of the overseas licensor's country of residence to confirm that it is a resident of that country.

Under ITA 2007,[113] a UK company that makes a payment of royalties subject to deduction of tax under either Part 15, Chapter 6 (deduction from annual payments) or Chapter 7 (patent royalties) of that Act may, if it thinks fit, calculate the sum of income tax to be deducted under those provisions by reference to the rate applicable under a relevant DTA, and make the payment on that basis. However, the company must reasonably believe that, at the time the payment is made, the payee is entitled to relief in respect of the payment under a relevant DTA.[114] For these purposes a 'payee' means the person beneficially entitled to the income in respect of which the payment is made.[115] If the payee is not entitled to such relief the

United Kingdom Taxation: General

---

[109] ITA 2007, s 934.
[110] ITA 2007, s 936.
[111] See www.oecd.org (2011).
[112] See www.hmrc.gov.uk.
[113] ITA 2007, s 911.
[114] ITA 2007, s 911(1)(c).
[115] ITA 2007, s 913(2).

payer will be chargeable with income tax at the applicable rate in respect of the payment, together with interest. Additionally, where a payment is made without the payer having a reasonable belief that the agreement relief was due then penalties will be imposed.

Many DTAs within the UK network contain an Article to the effect that where a royalty is paid as a result of a 'special relationship' then the provisions of the DTA will not apply to the excess amount that would not have been paid in the absence of such a relationship; and accordingly there is an obligation to withhold tax on the excess. The tax rules provide an indication of the circumstances where the 'special relationship' Articles, which appear in most UK DTAs, are likely to apply. The factors to be taken into account by the taxpayer and HMRC in construing a 'special relationship' article include:[116]

(1)   whether the agreement (ie, the licence) under which the royalties are paid would have been made at all in the absence of the special relationship; and

(2)   the rate or amounts of royalties and other terms which would have been agreed in the absence of the special relationship which is in point.

The UK's domestic rules on the interpretation of the special relationship article do not apply where the special relationship provision contained in the DTA expressly requires regard to be had to the use, right or information for which the royalties are paid in determining the excess royalties.[117] The reason for this is because the DTA limits the factors to be taken into account. Further additional factors are also required to be taken into account where the asset in respect of which the royalties are paid, or any asset which that represents or from which it is derived, has previously been in the beneficial ownership of certain persons.[118]

UK law imposes an obligation on the taxpayer to show the absence of any special relationship, or the rate or amount of royalties that would have been payable in the absence of the relationship.[119]

6.11.7   Royalty characterisation and e-commerce activities

The characterisation of payments associated with e-commerce has been considered by the OECD in a report called *Treaty Characterisation of E-Commerce Payments*.[120] The way in which payments made on a

---

[116]   TIOPA 2010, s 132(3).

[117]   TIOPA 2010, s 132(6).

[118]   See generally TIOPA 2010, s 132.

[119]   TIOPA 2010, s 133(1).

[120]   February 2001 (reproduced at Appendix D).

cross-border basis are characterised will determine whether they are subject to the royalties or business profits article of a DTA. The report is considered in Chapter 8.

6.11.8   EU associated companies: royalties

There is no withholding tax on royalty payments made between associated EU companies, as a result of Council Directive 2003/49/EC on a common system of taxation applicable to interest and royalty payments made between associated companies of different Member States. The exemption applies to cross-border royalty payments between the following persons:

(1)   companies incorporated in different EU Member States;

(2)   a permanent establishment of an EU incorporated company and another EU incorporated company; and

(3)   permanent establishments of different EU incorporated companies.

For a transitional 8-year period Greece, Portugal, Latvia and Poland are permitted to impose a withholding tax on royalty payments; and Spain and the Czech Republic are permitted for a 6-year period to impose a withholding tax on royalty payments.[121] The Directive does not apply to a permanent establishment situated in a third non-EU country.

The companies must be associated, and this condition is met where either one company ('A') directly holding 25% of the capital or voting rights of the other company ('B'); or by a third company ('C') directly holding 25% of the capital or voting rights of the other companies (ie companies A and B). Crucially, the companies must be tax resident in the relevant Member State, and subject to a prescribed tax, for example, corporation tax in the UK.

The UK rules that implement the European Directive provide that royalty payments are exempt from source taxation in the UK where the following conditions are satisfied:[122]

Condition A   The royalties must be paid by a UK company, or a UK situated permanent establishment of an EU company (e.g. a company resident in The Netherlands).[123]

United Kingdom Taxation: General

---

[121] Other new entrant countries have the benefit of transitional rules. For further information see the European Commission website: http://ec.europa.eu/taxation_customs/taxation/company_tax/interests_royalties/index_en.htm (2011). Details relating to the commencement of the transitional period are provided on the website.

[122] ITTOIA 2005, s 758.

[123] ITTOIA 2005, s 758(2).

Condition B   The person beneficially entitled to the royalties is an EU company outside the UK (but not a UK permanent establishment or a non-EU permanent establishment).

Condition C   The UK company and the recipient EU company must be 25% associates.[124] Two companies will only be treated as associates if:

- one holds directly:
  - 25% or more of the capital in the other; or
  - 25% or more of the voting rights in the other; or
- a third company holds directly:
  - 25% or more of the capital in each of them;; or
  - 25% or more of the voting rights in each of them.[125]

Various anti-avoidance provisions apply, which are beyond the scope of this chapter.

---

[124] ITTOIA 2005, s 758(2).
[125] ITTOIA 2005, s 761.

CHAPTER 7

CORPORATION TAX: SETTING UP AND OPERATION OF AN INTERNET BUSINESS

7.1 INTRODUCTION

Most commercially operated internet business/e-commerce and e-infrastructure activities will be carried on by a company. This is typically because shareholders in a company have the benefit of limited liability. A corporate structure has a number of non-tax benefits, such as legal personality, the ability to raise finance through an issue of shares, either as a private placement or a listing on a recognised stock exchange (such as the Alternative Investment Market): these aspects are discussed in Chapter 2.

In summary, the key tax consequences of carrying on a business using a company are as follows:

For the company:

- As a separate legal person, the company is subject to tax on its profits. This is independent of the liability of its shareholders on any dividends paid out of distributable profits (for shareholders see below).

- The rates of corporation tax on specific profit bands are shown below. A company's chargeable profits (comprising income and chargeable gains) are taxed by reference to a financial year (the 12-month period commencing on 1 April):[1]

Tax rate	Bands (£)
Small profits rate: 20%	Up to £300,000
Effective marginal rate: 27.5%	£300,000 to £1.5million
Main rate: 26%	£1,500,001 or more
(reducing to 25% for 2012/13)	

---

[1] CTA 2009, s 2.

While companies pay tax on their chargeable profits,[2] the 'rate' of corporation tax to be applied is determined by comparing the bands against the company's 'augmented profits'.[3] 'Augmented profits' are, very broadly, a company's chargeable profits plus certain exempt dividends (grossed-up) that it has received from non-group companies, including from non-UK companies (as of 1 July 2009). These dividends are known as 'franked investment income'.

- The small profits and marginal rates do not apply to a 'close investment holding company' (eg a closely held company that does not trade), so such companies will be taxed at the main rate regardless of the level of their profits, but this is unlikely to be of relevance to a company carrying on an e-commerce activity.[4] The impact of the effective marginal rate is to gradually increase the rate of tax paid on profits as they move from the small profits rate to the main rate. The effective marginal rate is normally applied to a company's chargeable profits falling between the bands by first taxing the profits at the main rate (26%), and then deducting 'marginal relief'. This relief is calculated based on a formula with reference to a company's augmented profits. If, however, the company has not received any franked investment income (ie the company's chargeable profits and 'augmented profits' are the same figure falling between the bands), the marginal rate can be applied to such company's profits via an alternative calculation, by applying the small profits rate up to £300,000, and then applying the marginal rate to the rest of its profits. The tax calculation will, however, be affected if a company has 'associated companies', as then the bands above (ie £300,000 and £1,500,000) are reduced pro rata by the number of associated companies.[5] A company is an associated company of another if it has control of the other or if both are under the control of the same person or persons.[6] Computations are also further complicated if, for example, a company's period of account is more or less than 12 months, or if the period spans two financial years which have different tax rates.

---

[2] Referred to as 'taxable total profits' in CTA 2010, s 4.

[3] CTA 2010, s 32.

[4] CTA 2010, s 18.

[5] CTA 2010, s 24. The thresholds to which the effective marginal rate applies are decreased in proportion to the number of associated companies. A company is an associated company of another if it has control of the other or if both are under the control of the same person: CTA 2010, s 25(4).

[6] CTA 2010, s 25(4).

- Within 3 months of the beginning of the company's first accounting period, information must be given to HMRC on various matters, including when the company's accounting period began; the company's registered office; the nature of the business being carried on by the company; the date to which the company intends to prepare accounts; and the full name and home address of each of the directors of the company.[7]

- On formation, Companies House will inform HMRC that the company has been incorporated. HMRC will then send an information pack to the company (including corporation tax forms and explanatory notes, Form CT41G (New Company Details)). Form CT41G will need to be completed and returned to a specific tax office. The information that is produced is used by HMRC to determine the company's corporation tax paying and filing deadlines (which will be confirmed by HMRC sending Form CT610 (Corporation Tax Important Dates)).

- An accounting period of a company begins when it comes within the charge to corporation tax,[8] and it is treated as coming within the charge when it starts to carry on business (if the company is not otherwise within the charge to tax).[9]

- The time for payment of corporation tax depends on the amount of a company's taxable profits. If the company's taxable profits are up to £1.5 million the normal due date is 9 months after the end of it corporation tax accounting period (eg if a company's accounting period ends on 31 March the due date is on or before 1 January). If a company's profits for an accounting period are more than £1.5 million then tax is paid in instalments.[10]

- The filing date for a tax return is usually 12 months following the end of the period for which the return is made.[11]

For the shareholder:

- A corporate shareholder is subject to corporation tax on dividends unless the dividend is exempt.[12] A dividend can be subject to various exempt classes, such as distributions from: controlled companies; non-redeemable ordinary shares; portfolio holdings of less than 10% in the paying company; and transactions not designed to reduce tax.

---

[7] FA 2004, s 55; Corporation Tax (Notice of Coming within Charge – Information) Regulations 2004, SI 2004/2502.

[8] CTA 2009, s 9(1).

[9] CTA 2009, s 9(2).

[10] Corporation Tax (Installment Payments) Regulations 1998, SI 1998/3175.

[11] FA 1998, Sch 18, para 14(1).

[12] CTA 2009, Part 9A.

- An individual shareholder is subject to income tax on dividends of a UK resident company, and these are taxed as savings and investment income.[13] Dividends are taxed at income tax rates, known as the dividend ordinary (10%), upper (32.5%) and additional (42.5%) rates (2011/12).[14] A dividend from a UK resident company carries a 10% tax credit, which is a credit against the income tax liability on the dividend, and is not repayable.[15]

- An individual shareholder's disposal of shares is subject to capital gains tax if the shares are held on an investment basis. The rate of tax is either 18% or 28% (2011/12), depending on the circumstances of the individual.[16] A rate of 10% (2011/12) applies to gains of an individual qualifying for entrepreneurs' relief (the relief is subject to a maximum lifetime limit of £10 million).[17] A company is subject to corporation tax on any chargeable gain at the rates outlined above, which apply to a company.

- A transfer of shares in a company is an exempt supply for VAT[18] so no VAT will be incurred.

- A transfer of shares in a company incorporated in the UK is subject to stamp duty and stamp duty reserve tax, which is charged at 0.5% (2011/12) of the consideration paid for the shares.[19]

7.2 ROLE OF ACCOUNTING

7.2.1 Accounting rules

The purpose of accounting rules is to accurately measure economic value. In other words, the profit and loss accounts of a company are concerned with reflecting accurately its economic performance. CA 2006 imposes upon directors the obligation to ensure that the balance sheet and the profit and loss accounts give a 'true and fair' view of the company for that financial year.[20] In ascertaining profits of a company for tax purposes, many statutory provisions require the starting point to be the accounts of the company. For example, the profits of a company's trade are calculated in accordance with generally accepted accounting practice (GAAP), subject to any adjustment required by corporation tax rules.[21]

---

[13] ITTOIA 2005, s 383.
[14] ITA 2007, s 13. The ordinary rate applies to income that would otherwise be chargeable to income tax at the basic rate, the upper rate to income that would otherwise be charged to income tax at the higher rate, and the additional rate to income that would otherwise be charged to income tax at the additional rate. See Chapter 5.
[15] ITTOIA 2005, s 397.
[16] For an overview on the nature of capital gains tax see Chapter 5.
[17] TCGA 1992, ss 169H–169S.
[18] VATA 1994, Sch 9.
[19] Stamp Act 1891; Finance Act 1999; Finance Act 1986.
[20] CA 2006, ss 393 and 396.
[21] CTA 2009, ss 35 and 46.

7.2.2   Tax and accounting rules

Accountancy practice forms the bedrock of information relating to the economic performance of a company. This source of financial information is drawn upon to determine the taxable trading profits and losses of a company.[22] Subject to any express or implied rule to the contrary in a tax statute, profits are ascertained by applying the rules of GAAP.[23] In *Gallagher v Jones*, the Court of Appeal commented:[24]

> '... the reason why the courts rightly attach such importance to accepted principles of commercial accounting in this context is, of course, that these principles will normally afford the surest means of ascertaining the *true* profits or losses of a trader as the case may be.'

Trading profits are calculated by reference to the accounting period of the company.[25] The computation process is achieved by reference to GAAP.[26] A detailed examination of UK GAAP policies can be obtained elsewhere.[27] Essentially, profits are the excess of revenue receipts over expenditure incurred in earning those receipts. The approach to the computation of profits for tax purposes has been outlined by the courts.[28] In *Odeon Associated Theatres*[29] the judge stated that the profits of a company must first be calculated by reference to GAAP. These profits must then be adjusted in light of any prohibited deduction of expenditure under the tax legislation;[30] or adjusted for any specific allowance (eg capital allowances on plant or machinery relating to computer software).[31]

---

[22] CTA 2009, s 47.

[23] CTA 2009, s 46.

[24] *Gallagher v Jones (Inspector of Taxes)* [1993] STC 537, at 561 (emphasis in original).

[25] CTA 2009, s 8.

[26] See *Odeon Associated Theatres v Jones* (1971) 48 TC 257. In *Gallagher v Jones (Inspector of Taxes)* [1993] STC 537, at 560, Nolan LJ said: 'the law does not enable or require us to ascertain profits of a trade on a basis divorced from the principles of commercial accountancy.'

[27] Accounting standards can be accessed from the website of The Institute of Chartered Accounts in England & Wales: www.icaew.com/en/library/subject-gateways/accounting-standards (2011).

[28] See particularly *Odeon Associated Theatres v Jones* (1971) 48 TC 257, at 273, per Sir John Pennycuick V-C; *Gallagher v Jones (Inspector of Taxes)* [1993] STC 537 (judgment of Sir Thomas Bingham MR); *Johnston (Inspector of Taxes) v Britannia Airways Ltd* [1994] STC 763; *R v Inland Revenue Commissioners ex parte S G Warburg & Co Ltd* [1994] STC 518.

[29] (1971) 48 TC 257.

[30] *Odeon Associated Theatres v Jones* (1971) 48 TC 257, at 272–273, [1971] 1 WLR 442, at 453–454, per Sir John Pennycuick V-C.

[31] Capital Allowances Act 2001 (CAA 2001).

7.3   GAAP: THE BASIS OF COMPUTING TRADING PROFITS

The tax year of a company runs from 1 April to 31 March the following year. To the extent necessary a company's accounting period must be apportioned within the time frame of the tax year.[32]

Revenue receipts derived from an economic activity usually include any income which arises from the day-to-day activity of an enterprise, such as sales and royalties from the licensing of copyright or patent rights. The concept of revenue is referred to in Financial Reporting Standard No 5 Application Note G as being recognised by a seller 'under an exchange transaction with a customer, when, and to the extent that, it obtains the right to consideration in exchange for its performance'.[33] Revenue will be recognised in accordance with the substance and not the form of any particular transaction (e g the contractual provisions will provide evidence of the intention of the parties).[34] By contrast, revenue expenditure is the cost of earning revenue receipts, for example, the costs of employing staff, the cost of buying goods and/or services to sell on to customers via internet trading sites etc.

The time at which revenue receipts or expenditure is to be recognised in the accounts depends upon GAAP, as adjusted by any requirement of the tax legislation. For example, although a person may pay a lump sum for the right to use technology (such as copyright in computer software or an invention used for the purposes of providing a telecommunications service), it does not necessarily follow that the receipt of the lump sum by the licensor will be brought into account at the time it is paid by the licensee. One firmly established principle of accountancy is that revenue is recognised in accounts when it is earned (ie when performance of the contract occurs).[35] Correspondingly, expenditure is recognised when it is incurred, which is not necessarily when the expenditure is paid.

7.4   SOURCE OF RECEIPTS AND RESIDENCE

Corporation tax is calculated according to the source of the receipts created by a company (the basis on which profits are calculated for tax purposes are subject to a variety of rules depending on the nature of the source).[36] The scheme of taxation relevant to e-commerce and e-infrastructure activities will usually be the trading income rules (which are considered in this chapter).[37]

---

[32]   CTA 2009, s 8(5).
[33]   At para G4.
[34]   See Application Note G to FRS 5.
[35]   FRS 5, para 65.
[36]   See **7.5** for further details.
[37]   See generally CTA 2009, Part 3.

7.5 RESIDENT AND NON-RESIDENT CORPORATIONS

Unless an internet business activity is within a specific charge to corporation tax or income, there is no right for the UK tax authorities to impose tax on the economic activity.[38] A company, irrespective of where it is incorporated, is subject to corporation tax if it is a resident of the UK. A company is a UK resident if either (a) it is incorporated in the UK;[39] or (b) it has its central management and control in the UK.[40] A UK resident company is subject to corporation tax on all of its profits (both income and chargeable gains) irrespective of where they arise. The first test (point (a)) is easily satisfied by reference to the register of incorporated companies maintained at Companies House.[41] However, the second test is a creature of case-law. The test is influenced by physical considerations, such as the location where directors' meetings are held. Where a non-resident company is not incorporated in the UK it is important to ensure that it is not centrally managed and controlled in the UK, otherwise its worldwide profits will be subject to corporation tax. It is of critical importance to ensure that such a company's management is subject to strict protocols (see Appendix H for illustrative guidance on the topic).

A non UK-resident company is subject to corporation tax if it carries on a trade through a permanent establishment in the UK.[42] The chargeable profits of a permanent establishment will comprise trading income, any non-trading income from property or rights used by or held by or for the permanent establishment (such as interest or income derived from patent rights) and capital gains arising from assets held for the purposes of the trade of the permanent establishment.[43]

In the absence of sufficient connecting factors to attract a charge to corporation tax it is also possible for a non-resident company to be subject to income tax (although only at the basic rate of income tax) if it

---

[38] Tax can only be charged on a taxpayer if the charging statute clearly and unambiguously applies. Otherwise HMRC has no right to charge tax. This is a fundamental principle of UK tax law: see *Partington v Attorney-General* (1869) LR 4 100 at 122.

[39] CTA 2009, s 14(1). This is the case even if a different place of residence is given by a rule of law elsewhere.

[40] *De Beers Consolidated Mines Ltd v Howe* 5 TC 198, at 213, per Lord Loreburn LC. In that case Lord Loreburn LC said: 'a company resides, for the purposes of income tax, where its real business is carried on … I regard that as the true rule; and the real business is carried on where the central management and control actually abides.' In *Unit Construction Co Ltd v Bullock (Inspector of Taxes)* [1959] All ER 831, at 836, HL, Lord Radcliffe said that this principle was firmly enshrined into the tax law. See also *American Thread Co v Joyce* 6 TC 163 at 165.

[41] The Registrar is under a duty to retain all information required to be delivered to the Registrar under the Companies Acts. See ss 1080 and 1085 of CA 2006.

[42] CTA 2009, s 5(2).

[43] CTA 2009, s 19(2), (3).

is carrying on a trade in the UK.[44] An income tax charge does not arise where the relevant DTA provides that profits of a trade are not taxable in the UK. But a DTA, which follows OECD practice, will normally provide that the profits of such a trade will be taxable if carried on in the UK through a permanent establishment.[45]

Example 7.1

If a microchip manufacturer is resident in the UK it will be required to pay corporation tax on profits derived from that trade. If a non-resident company manufactures computers in the US and then sells those through a permanent establishment (eg a branch) based in the UK it will also be required to pay corporation tax on profits attributable to the branch. By contrast a non-resident company which locates an e-commerce shopping program on computers based in the UK, which accepts orders and then relays these to the non-resident, who in turn gives delivery instructions to a distributor in the UK, may be subject to income tax, rather than corporation tax on the basis that it is exercising a trade within the UK. Whether a person is trading within the UK is partly determined by reference to where the contract is formed.[46]

The nature of these charges to tax on a non-resident and the exceptions to the charges are examined in Chapter 6 (Inbound UK E-Commerce: Scope of Charge to Tax).

7.6 HEADS OF CHARGE TO TAX

7.6.1 Introduction

Corporation tax may be charged on either profits or pure investment income, and the extent to which expenditure is deductible in determining taxable profits is determined by reference to the source of the receipts. The relevant heads of charge to corporation tax that are likely to be encountered in the context of internet business activities are as follows:[47]

Trading profits: income receipts from a trade carried on in the UK or elsewhere (including receipts derived from intangible fixed assets held for the purposes of a trade).

Non-trading profits: income receipts derived from intangible fixed assets held on a non-trading basis.

---

[44] ITTOIA 2005, s 6.
[45] CTA 2009, s 21(1). The wording is based on Art 7(2) of the OECD Model Tax Convention on Income and on Capital.
[46] This point is analysed in Chapter 6, which deals with inbound UK e-commerce.
[47] See generally CTA 2009, s 35 (trade profits, including trading receipts from intangible fixed assets (s 747)), s 752 (non-trading gains on intangible fixed assets), Part 5 (corporate loans), s 977 (annual payments not otherwise charged), s 979 (other income), Part 9A (corporation tax treatment of company distributions).

Corporate loans:	interest on corporate loans (trading and non-trading).
Annual payments:	income receipts of an annual nature from a source not otherwise charged to tax.
Dividends:	dividends received.
Other income:	income receipts not otherwise within the application of the charge to corporation tax.

These charging provisions determine how profits and losses derived from a specific source are to be calculated for the purposes of corporation tax. However, it should be noted that once chargeable income has been ascertained it may then be possible to make elections to reduce chargeable income, for example, by the use of past trading losses.[48]

The following sections of this chapter will focus on the particular heads of charge to tax in the computation of chargeable profits.

7.6.2   Chargeable income

The sources of chargeable income for the purposes of e-commerce and e-infrastructure business activity are likely to be those derived from a trade (either UK or cross-border), an investment or royalties from licensing. A trader can deduct all appropriate expenditure of a revenue nature incurred in earning revenue receipts arising from that trade (this is considered at **7.8**). A person who carries on a trade is entitled to a number of tax reliefs (known as capital allowances), which are not always available in respect of income derived from other sources, such as investment income.

The trading profits of a company are initially calculated by reference to GAAP: see **7.2**. These principles will determine when revenue expenditure or receipts are to be recognised in the taxpayer's accounts. The time of recognition may not necessarily be when a payment is received or expenditure incurred. Once this calculation has been undertaken, adjustments must then be made for any expenditure that is prohibited from being deducted, or that is otherwise permitted as a deduction by the tax legislation. This sum will then represent the income profits of the business. In certain circumstances, it may be possible for a company that has incurred a loss to offset this against the taxable profits.[49]

The tax legislation permits, under difference circumstances, revenue and capital expenditure to be deducted: these aspects are considered at **7.8**. Revenue expenditure is that which has a recurrent quality and represents the day-to-day costs of carrying on a trade, such as the salary of employees, the rent of office accommodation or the acquisition of raw

United Kingdom
Taxation: General

---

48   For example, under CTA 2010, s 45 (carry forward of trading losses).
49   See CTA 2010, Part 4 (loss relief), and **7.10.1**.

materials to manufacture goods that the trader sells. Capital expenditure may also be deducted from receipts derived from a trade where it qualifies for relief under what is known as the capital allowances system governed by CAA 2001 (see **7.8**).

7.6.3   Chargeable gains

Once chargeable income has been computed, it is also necessary for any chargeable gains to be determined.[50] The aggregation of a company's chargeable gains and chargeable income produces the company's chargeable profits.[51] Chargeable gains for corporation tax purposes are normally calculated in accordance with capital gains tax principles.[52] Corporation tax is imposed on chargeable gains arising from the disposal of assets. The gain is calculated by deducting the expenditure incurred in acquiring the asset[53] (as increased by indexation) from the disposal proceeds.[54] The gain may be reduced by the carry forward of capital losses from previous accounting periods, or by the set-off of losses in the current period.[55] Any proceeds from the disposal of an intangible fixed asset acquired on or after 1 April 2002 will be taxed as income and not capital in accordance with the CTA 2009 regime.[56] This means that it is not possible to use capital losses against receipts derived from the disposal of intangible fixed assets acquired on or after 1 April 2002.

7.7   TAXATION OF A TRADE

7.7.1   What is a trade?

The existence of a trade is significant for tax purposes since the existence of a trade entitles the trader to a wide range of tax reliefs, such as:

(1)   the right to deduct revenue expenditure;

(2)   the right to claim capital allowances on plant and machinery; and

(3)   the right to carry forward trading losses against future trading profits.

Despite the importance of this concept to the tax legislation, it is defined in ambiguous terms as 'including any venture in the nature of trade'.[57]

---

[50]   TCGA 1992, s 8.
[51]   CTA 2009, s 2(2).
[52]   TCGA 1992, s 8(3).
[53]   TCGA 1992, s 38(1).
[54]   TCGA 1992, s 53(1).
[55]   TCGA 1992, s 2(2).
[56]   See CTA 2009, Part 8.
[57]   CTA 2010, s 1119(1). The preceding legislation referred to a trade as including 'every trade, manufacture, adventure or concern in the nature of trade': ICTA 1988, s 832(1).

The 'characteristics of a trade' is a question of law, which is determined by the courts. Whether a trade exists is a question of fact.[58] A trade has been described as a commercial transaction whereby a person supplies goods or services for reward to another person.[59] For a trade to exist there must be a bilateral transaction with another person. It is not possible to carry on a trade with oneself.[60] There is no requirement of continuity for a trade to exist. The legislation specifically provides that a trade includes 'any venture in the nature of a trade'.[61] A trade can also exist even though the activity is unlawful.[62] If a person sold prohibited handguns via the internet in the UK, this would not prevent the activity being classified as a trade, and HMRC would be entitled to raise an assessment to tax.

The question of whether a trade is carried on by a taxpayer is approached by looking at certain types of objective factors. However, where there is ambiguity in connection with these objective factors, then the subjective purpose or motive of the taxpayer is relevant. In *Clarke (Inspector of Taxes) v British Telecom Pension Scheme* the judge explained in the following terms the principles for approaching the question of what constitutes a trade:[63]

> 'If the legal or commercial characteristics of a transaction point unequivocally to trading, the trader's subjective purpose or motive cannot change the character of the transaction. But the character of the transaction may be ambiguous until resolved by reference to purpose or motivation.'

The case-law establishes that it is necessary to approach the issue of whether a trade is being carried on by determining the extent to which the indicia of a trading activity exist. In *Marson (Inspector of Taxes) v Morton*[64] the taxpayer was assessed to tax on the basis of an adventure in the nature of a trade in relation to the sale of land. Prior to the acquisition and disposal of land the taxpayer had not dealt in land, and had entered into various transactions upon the advice of a third party, with a view to making a medium- to long-term investment in land. Reliance was placed on the third party as to when to sell. The court held the transactions were entered into on an investment basis. The judgment of the court discusses the badges of a trade in the context of determining whether an activity is an adventure in the nature of a trade. The following

United Kingdom
Taxation: General

---

58   *Edwards v Bairstow and Harrison* [1956] AC 14, [1955] 3 All ER 48, HL.
59   See *Ransom v Higgs* [1974] 3 All ER 949, HL.
60   See *Ransom v Higgs* [1974] 3 All ER 949, at 955, HL.
61   CTA 2010, s 1119(1). The preceding legislation referred to a trade as including 'every trade, manufacture, adventure or concern in the nature of trade': ICTA, s 832(1).
62   *IRC v Aken* [1988] STC 69, affirmed [1990] STC 497.
63   *Clarke (Inspector of Taxes) v British Telecom Pension Scheme* [2000] STC 222, at 232, CA (see the judgment of Robert Walker LJ who delivered the unanimous opinion of the court).
64   [1986] STC 463, 59 TC 381, at 391–392.

passage from the judgment illustrates the relevant principles applicable in determining whether an activity qualifies as a trade. The judge stated:[65]

'The matters which are apparently treated as a badge of trading are as follows:

(1) That the transaction in question was a one-off transaction. Although a one-off transaction is in law capable of being an adventure in the nature of trade, obviously the lack of repetition is a pointer which indicates there might not here be trade but something else.

(2) Is the transaction in question in some way related to the trade which the taxpayer otherwise carries on? For example, a one-off purchase of silver cutlery by a general dealer is much more likely to be a trade transaction than such a purchase by a retired colonel.

(3) The nature of the subject matter may be a valuable pointer. Was the transaction in a commodity of a kind which is normally the subject matter of trade and which can only be turned to advantage by realisation ...? For example, a large bulk of whisky or toilet paper is essentially a subject matter of trade, not of enjoyment.

(4) In some cases attention has been paid to the way in which the transaction was carried through: was it carried through in a way typical of the trade in a commodity of that nature?

(5) What was the source of finance of the transaction? If the money was borrowed that is some pointer towards an intention to buy the item with a view to its resale in the short term; a fair pointer towards trade.

(6) Was the item which was purchased resold as it stood or was work done on it or relating to it for the purposes of resale? For example, the purchase of second-hand machinery which was repaired or improved before resale. If there was such work done, that is again a pointer towards the transaction being in the nature of trade.

(7) Was the item purchased resold in one lot as it was bought, or was it broken down into saleable lots? If it was broken down it is again some indication that it was a trading transaction, the purchase being with a view to resale at profit by doing something in relation to the object bought.

(8) What were the purchasers' intentions as to resale at the time of purchase? If there was an intention to hold the object indefinitely, albeit with an intention to make a capital profit at the end of the day, that is a pointer towards a pure investment as opposed to a trading deal ... Similarly, an intention to resell in the short term rather than the long term is some indication against concluding that the transaction was by way of investment rather than by way of a deal ...

(9) Did the item purchased provide enjoyment for the purchaser (for example, a picture), or pride of possession, or produce income pending resale? If it did, then that may indicate an intention to buy either for personal satisfaction or to invest for income yield, rather than do a deal purely for the purpose of making a profit on the turn ...'

If an asset is income yielding, that of itself will not always be determinative of whether it is held on an investment basis, but it will

---

[65] [1986] STC 463, at 470–471 (per Sir Nicolas Browne-Wilkinson).

usually be a relevant factor. Similarly if an asset is not income yielding it does not follow that the asset is not acquired on an investment basis.[66] Where there is a prolonged period between the purchase and sale of an asset, such a factor may indicate that the asset is held on an investment basis by the taxpayer. In *Eames (Inspector of Taxes) v Stepnell Properties Ltd* the judge said:[67]

> '... for one element at least of investment must be that the acquirer of the investment intends to hold it, at any rate for some time, with a view to obtaining either some benefit in the way of income in the meantime or obtaining some profit, but not an immediate profit by resale.'

Against the context of the foregoing, if a company bought and sold domain names with the intention of making a profit then the proceeds of the transactions would be characterised as trading income.

7.7.2   Basic rules

The measure of trading profits that will be taxed for a particular financial year is determined by reference to the accounting period for the relevant tax year.[68] The profits of a trade are required to be calculated in accordance with GAAP, but subject to any adjustment required or authorised by law.[69] The classification of a receipt or an item of expenditure will ultimately be a question of law. It should be noted that subject to any rule to the contrary, trading losses will be calculated on the same basis as trading profits.[70]

In calculating the profits of a trade it is necessary to bring into account any amounts treated as receipts of a trade, and any allowances treated as expenses of a trade for the purposes of CAA 2001 (the Act which provides tax relief for certain types of capital expenditure).[71] Receipts of a capital nature are not brought into account in calculating the profits of a trade, unless there is a specific rule to the contrary.[72] The type of expenditure which can be deducted from trading receipts is discussed at **7.8**.

United Kingdom
Taxation: General

---

[66]   [1986] 59 TC 381, at 393 (per Buckley J.).
[67]   [1967] 43 TC 678, at 692.
[68]   CTA 2009, s 8.
[69]   CTA 2009, s 46(1).
[70]   CTA 2009, s 47.
[71]   CTA 2009, s 49.
[72]   CTA 2009, s 53.

7.8   TAX RELIEF FOR EXPENDITURE

7.8.1   Introduction

Many of the tax rules apply to 'profits' from a particular source, such as the profits of a trade. This section examines expenditure in the context of determining taxable trading profits. The concept of income implies the deduction of expenditure from receipts, and the time at which revenues and expenditure are recognised will determine the income in any particular accounting period.

The tax legislation generally matches revenue expenditure against revenues, but capital expenditure is not allowed as a deduction,[73] but may be afforded some relief under the capital allowances code.[74] The following sections consider the tax reliefs available in relation to R&D expenditure (see **7.8.2**), revenue expenditure (**7.8.3**), capital expenditure (**7.8.4**) and intellectual property expenditure (**7.9**).

The rate and timing at which reliefs are given affect the tax liability of a company in that earlier reliefs in the life of a trading activity (eg relief given when expenditure is incurred) are more valuable than later reliefs (eg relief given for expenditure when an asset is sold). Whether expenditure is treated as capital expenditure, and the rate at which relief is given for capital expenditure, is an instrument of government policy that can be used to encourage a particular type of economic activity.

The distinction between revenue and capital expenditure is not a particularly easy area of tax law, and the case law on characterisation of expenditure must be carefully considered, where appropriate. The classification of expenditure is of critical importance because the timing of relief differs. Revenue expenditure is usually relieved immediately whilst capital expenditure is relieved over a number of tax years. In *British Insulated and Helsby Cables v Atherton*, capital expenditure was described in the following terms:[75]

> 'When an expenditure is made, not only once and for all, but with a view to bringing into existence an asset or an advantage for the enduring benefit of a trade, I think that there is a very good reason ... for treating such an expenditure as properly attributable not to revenue but to capital.'

The classification of expenditure is concerned not only with that on tangible goods, but also with intangible property such as contracts which establish rights within a market. For example, contracts establishing the scope of a distributor's market for the sale of computers. Problems may

---

[73]   CTA 2009, s 53.
[74]   See **7.8.4** for further details.
[75]   [1926] AC 205, at 213–214.

be experienced in applying this distinction where the technology acquired by an IT or internet business has a short economic life.

Example 7.2

Chip Computers Ltd is a manufacturer of microprocessors. The company manufactures the chip under licence from the developer, and incurs expenditure in the acquisition of a master computer program, which is used to guide the robotic arms that etch the circuit (enabling the operation of the processor). The company would not be able to manufacture the processors without the computer program, and in every sense the business is dependant on this master program. The processors are developed very quickly with the result that expenditure of £500,000 is incurred every quarter on new computer programs. How is this expenditure to be classified?

The distinction between revenue and capital expenditure is diminishing to a vanishing point in the area of IT. This is because the rate of technology growth is exceptionally high, with the result that expenditure, although of an enduring benefit to many trades, is being incurred at regular intervals. The regularity of these transactions is a characteristic which is usually associated with revenue expenditure.

7.8.2   Research and development expenditure

There are several forms of tax relief for research and development (R&D) expenditure. The nature of the reliefs for expenditure (whether revenue or capital) are considered below. A detailed discussion of R&D tax reliefs, allowances and credits is beyond the scope of this chapter, and the reader should obtain specialist tax advice for their particular circumstances.

Revenue expenditure on R&D

A revenue expense incurred by a person carrying on a trade for the purposes of R&D related to that trade, and directly undertaken by or on behalf of the company, can be deducted as an expense in computing the profits of the trade.[76] The relief is equal to 100% of the expenditure incurred by the company, and the relief is given in the year in which it is incurred. For the purposes of these provisions, expenditure incurred on R&D does not include expenses incurred in the acquisition of rights in, or arising out of, R&D, but it does include all expenses incurred in carrying out, or providing facilities for carrying out, R&D.[77]

The concept of R&D means activities that fall to be treated as R&D in accordance with GAAP.[78] This means the accounting practice of the UK as stated in Statement of Standard Accounting Practice 13 (SSAP 13).[79]

---

[76]   CTA 2009, s 87.
[77]   CTA 2009, s 87(2).
[78]   CTA 2009, s 87; CTA 2010, s 1138(2).
[79]   CTA 2010, s 1138(2). For details of SSAP 13, see www.frc.org.uk/asb/technical/

The definition of R&D is not limited to R&D carried on solely in the UK. However, the tax definition is not completely aligned with the accounting definition contained in SSAP 13.

Certain activities, as a matter of law, are deemed to be treated as, or to be outside the concept of, R&D.[80] The activities that fall either side of the definition are provided in the Department of Trade and Industry's *The Guidelines on the Meaning of Research and Development*.[81]

The Guidance provides that[82]

> 'R&D for tax purposes takes place when a project[83] seeks to achieve an advance in science or technology. The activities which directly contribute to achieving this advance in science or technology through the resolution of scientific or technological uncertainty are R&D. Certain qualifying indirect activities related to the project are also R&D. Activities other than qualifying indirect activities which do not contribute to the resolution of the project's scientific or technological uncertainty are not R&D.'

The Guidance provides that an 'advance in science or technology' means:[84]

> '... an advance in overall knowledge or capability in a field of science or technology (not a company's own state of knowledge or capability alone). This includes the adaptation of knowledge or capability from another field of science or technology in order to make such an advance where this adaptation was not readily deducible.
>
> An advance in science or technology may have tangible consequences (such as a new or more efficient cleaning product, or a process which generates less waste) or more intangible outcomes (new knowledge or cost improvements, for example).
>
> A process, material, device, product, service or source of knowledge does not become an advance in science or technology simply because science or technology is used in its creation. Work which uses science or technology but which does not advance scientific or technological capability as a whole is not an advance in science or technology.
>
> A project which seeks to, for example –

---

standards/pub0396.html. Unless otherwise expressly provided the definition does not include oil and gas exploration and appraisal (CTA 2010, s 1138(5)).

80   CTA 2009, s 87; CTA 2010, s 1138(3).

81   These guidelines have the force of law: see Research and Development (Prescribed Activities) Regulations 2004, SI 2004/712.

82   Department of Trade and Industry *Guidelines on the Meaning of Research and Development for Tax Purposes* (5 March 2004), paras 3–5.

83   The guidelines define (at para 19) a 'project' as consisting of 'a number of activities conducted to a method or plan in order to achieve an advance in science or technology'.

84   See paras 6–12 of the guidelines.

(a)   extend overall knowledge or capability in a field of science or technology; or

(b)   create a process, material, device, product or service which incorporates or represents an increase in overall knowledge or capability in a field of science or technology; or

(c)   make an appreciable improvement to an existing process, material, device, product or service through scientific or technological changes; or

(d)   use science or technology to duplicate the effect of an existing process, material, device, product or service in a new or appreciably improved way (eg a product which has exactly the same performance characteristics as existing models, but is built in a fundamentally different manner) will therefore be R&D.

Even if the advance in science or technology sought by a project is not achieved or not fully realised, R&D still takes place.

If a particular advance in science or technology has already been made or attempted but details are not readily available (for example, if it is a trade secret), work to achieve such an advance can still be an advance in science or technology.

However, the routine analysis, copying or adaptation of an existing product, process, service or material, will not be an advance in science or technology.'

Payments to research associations, universities and similar institutions

Where a sum is paid, by a person carrying on a trade, to a scientific research association (SRA), or pays a sum to a university, research institute or similar institution, that sum may be deducted as an expense of the profits of the trade.[85] The deduction is permitted in the accounting period in which the payment is made.[86] The SRA, university or similar institution must have as its object the undertaking of scientific research that is related to the class of trade carried on by the person making the payment.[87] The SRA, universities etc must be approved by the Secretary of State for the purposes of CTA 2009.[88]

Capital expenditure incurred on R&D

Under CAA 2001 where a person while carrying on a trade incurs capital expenditure on R&D related to that trade, and the R&D is directly undertaken by the person or on that person's behalf, the expenditure is allowed as a deduction in computing the profits of that trade.[89] The allowance is equal to 100% of the expenditure incurred by the trader. If

---

[85]   CTA 2009, s 88.
[86]   CTA 2009, s 88(2).
[87]   CTA 2009, s 88(1).
[88]   CTA 2009, s 88(4).
[89]   CAA 2001, s 437.

capital expenditure is incurred on R&D and a trade is subsequently set up and commenced which is connected with that research, a deduction is allowed in respect of 100% of the expenditure in taxing the profits of that trade.[90]

Example 7.3

> Alpha Enterprises Ltd incurs expenditure of £2 million on research relating to various technologies associated with video-conferencing, which is related to its trade. The taxpayer carries on a trade in the sale of video-conferencing equipment, and in the tax year 2011/12 it receives trading income of £10 million. After use of the allowance, taxable profits are £8 million.

An allowance is only available in respect of capital expenditure incurred for carrying out R&D or providing facilities for carrying out R&D.[91] In addition to these general limitations, no relief is given for expenditure incurred in the acquisition of (a) rights in R&D or (b) rights arising out of R&D.[92] No relief is permitted for expenditure on the provision of a dwelling; but this limitation does not apply if part of a building consists of a dwelling and the rest of the building is used for R&D and no more than 25% of the capital expenditure referable to the construction or acquisition of the whole building is referable to the construction of acquisition of the dwelling.[93]

Relief for SME

R&D tax relief[94] is available for small and medium-sized enterprises (SMEs).[95] The effect of the R&D tax relief is to increase R&D expenditure by an additional 100% of the amount actually incurred.[96] Accordingly, for every £100 of expenditure, a deduction of £200 will be available. Thus a total deduction of 200% is permitted. Alternatively, it is possible to claim an R&D tax credit.[97]

In the budget for 2011, the Government announced that legislation would be introduced in the Finance Bill 2012 to increase the additional deduction by a further 25%, giving a total deduction of 225% (from 1 April 2012).

---

[90]   CAA 2001, s 441.
[91]   CAA 2001, s 438(1).
[92]   CAA 2001, s 438(2).
[93]   CAA 2001, s 438(3), (4).
[94]   The conditions for entitlement to R&D tax relief are set out in CTA 2009, Part 13, Chapter 2.
[95]   CTA 2009, Part 13, Chapter 2. For details of what is currently an SME refer to HMRC's website at www.hmrc.gov.uk/forms_rates/randd.htm (2011).
[96]   CTA 2009, s 1044(8).
[97]   CTA 2009, s 1054.

R&D subcontracted to SME

Tax relief is available for R&D expenditure incurred by an SME in respect of work subcontracted to such a company.[98] Where the company qualifies under the regime it is entitled to an additional deduction in computing its trading profits equal to 30% of the expenditure.[99] Accordingly, for every £100 of expenditure, a deduction of £130 will be available.

Relief for SME: subsidised and capped R&D expenditure

Tax relief is available at the rate of an additional deduction of 30% in respect of subsidised qualifying expenditure on both in-house direct R&D and contracted out R&D.[100]

Relief for large companies

Tax relief is available for R&D expenditure incurred by large companies.[101] Where the company qualifies under the regime it is entitled to an additional deduction in computing its trading profits equal to 30% of the expenditure.[102] Accordingly, for every £100 of expenditure, a deduction of £130 will be available.

In the Autumn Statement (2011) the Government announced its intention to introduce an 'above the line' R&D tax credit (calculated as a percentage of a company's R&D spend). This will be consulted on in Budget 2012, and will be effective from April 2013.

7.8.3   Revenue expenditure

Pre-trade expenditure

The tax legislation allows revenue expenditure incurred prior to a trade to be deducted from revenue receipts derived from that trade once it has commenced.[103] This relief is available where expenditure is incurred no more than 7 years before the trade is started.[104] However, a deduction is permitted only if it would be allowed for the purposes of computing profits from a trade.[105]

United Kingdom: Taxation: General

---

[98]   CTA 2009, Part 13, Chapter 3.
[99]   CTA 2009, s 1063(7).
[100] CTA 2009, Part 13, Chapter 4.
[101] CTA 2009, Part 13, Chapter 5.
[102] CTA 2009, s 1074(7).
[103] CTA 2009, s 61(1).
[104] CTA 2009, s 61(1).
[105] CTA 2009, s 61(2).

Trade-related expenditure

Revenue expenditure that is brought into account on the basis of GAAP must be adjusted for any expenditure prohibited by the tax legislation. Of principal importance is the rule that no deduction can be made unless the expenditure is incurred wholly and exclusively for the purposes of a trade, or losses not connected with or arising out of the trade.[106] Expenditure would not, for example, be deductible where a company carrying on a trade solely of manufacturing computers pays rent for separate office space that is occupied by its distribution and marketing companies (who are carrying on separate trades).

Revenue expenditure on interest payments incurred on loans is a deductible expense.[107] For the purposes of the tax rules, a corporate borrower is referred to as a 'debtor' under a 'loan relationship' (referring to the loan), and any interest obligations are referred to as debits.[108] A company has a loan relationship if it stands in the position of a debtor as respects any money debt and the debt arises from a transaction for the lending of money.[109] The general principle is that the amounts to be brought into account by a company as debits (ie interest) for any period are those that are recognised in determining the company's profit or loss for the period in accordance with GAAP.[110] Finance expenditure incurred prior to trading is deductible as a pre-trading expense. Where this occurs the expenditure is brought into account as a trade expense in the period in which the company begins to trade.[111]

Specific relief is provided in respect of expenditure incurred on acquiring the registration of a trade mark and registered design, the extension of a registered design and the renewal of a registered trade mark.[112] Furthermore, a deduction is permitted in calculating the profits of a trade for expenses incurred in obtaining, for the purposes of a trade, the grant of a patent, an extension of the patent term or expenses incurred in connection with a rejected or abandoned application for a patent made for the purposes of the trade.[113] It should be noted that the relief for expenses on trade marks and patents applies on the basis of expenses incurred. The result of this is that it is not necessary for the fees actually to be paid before a deduction can be made.

---

[106] CTA 2009, s 54(1). See also *Mallalieu v Drummond* [1983] STC 665. If an expense is incurred for more than one purpose the expense is not prohibited if any identifiable part or identifiable proportion of the expense is incurred wholly and exclusively for the purposes of the company's trade: CTA 2009, s 54(2).

[107] The conditions for relief are set out in CTA 2009, Part 5.

[108] CTA 2009, s 302.

[109] CTA 2009, s 302(1).

[110] CTA 2009, s 307(2).

[111] CTA 2009, s 330.

[112] CTA 2009, s 90.

[113] CTA 2009, s 89.

There are many more detailed rules in the tax legislation dealing with prohibited revenue deductions, which are beyond the scope of this chapter.[114] Where necessary appropriate advice should be obtained from a professional tax adviser.

7.8.4   Capital expenditure

Relief for 'plant and machinery'[115]

Scope of relief

The typical head of relief for an e-commerce and e-infrastructure business will be in respect of 'plant or machinery'.[116] A company is entitled to claim capital allowances at the rate of 18%[117] (2012/13) per annum on a reducing balance basis for capital expenditure incurred on plant and machinery,[118] provided that the following conditions are satisfied:[119]

(a)   the person must be carrying on a trade;[120]

(b)   the person must incur capital expenditure;[121]

(c)   the expenditure must be incurred on the provision of machinery or plant wholly or partly for the purposes of the trade;[122] and

(d)   the person incurring the expenditure must own the plant or machinery in consequence of incurring the expenditure.[123]

The allowance of 18%[124] of the capital expenditure, which is applied on a reducing balance basis, is treated as an expense of the taxpayer's trade.[125] This is set against income receipts arising from the trade in the same period.[126] In certain circumstances the expenditure against which the relief is allowed must be reduced before the allowance is given; this is

---

[114]   See generally CTA 2009, Part 3, Chapter 4 (calculating trading income), Part 5, Chapter 15 (loan relationships: unallowable purpose).

[115]   This section highlights some of the principal allowances available in respect of capital expenditure. However, it does not cover first year allowances (e g relating to expenditure on environmentally beneficial plant or machinery: see CAA 2001, s 39).

[116]   Relief under this head is given by s 11 of CAA 2001.

[117]   The main rate of 20% is reduced to 18% for new and unrelieved expenditure from 1 April 2012 (FA 2011, s 10(2)).

[118]   CAA 2001, s 56.

[119]   CAA 2001, s 11.

[120]   CAA 2001, ss 11(1) and 15; or another type of qualifying activity.

[121]   CAA 2001, s 11(4).

[122]   CAA 2001, s 11(4)(a).

[123]   CAA 2001, s 11(4)(b).

[124]   The main rate of 20% is reduced to 18% for new and unrelieved expenditure from 1 April 2012 (FA 2011, s 10(2)).

[125]   CAA 2001, s 247.

[126]   CAA 2001, s 2.

because a disposal event has occurred which requires the expenditure to be reduced. The deduction that is made to take the event into account is referred to as the 'disposal value'.[127] Such a disposal value must be brought into account where, for example, the plant ceases to belong to the trader.[128] The rules provide for different values depending on the nature of the event, for example, a sale of plant or machinery will require a disposal value to be brought into account equal to the net proceeds of sale, together with any insurance money received in respect of the asset and any other compensation received of a capital nature.[129]

Example 7.4

Alpha Associates Ltd, acquire plant and machinery of an e-commerce business for £100,000. The taxpayer qualifies for relief under CAA 2001. The way in which the expenditure is off-set against the receipts of the trade is shown below:

		2011/12
	£	£
Plant expenditure	100,000	
less writing down allowance (WDA) @ 20%		(20,000)
WDA c/f		80,000
Trading income		100,000
Taxable profits		80,000
		2012/13
	£	£
Plant expenditure		
WDA pool c/f	80,000	
WDA @ 18%		(14,400)
WDA c/f		65,600
Trading income		250,000
Taxable profits etc		235,600

If the taxpayer had disposed of some of the business assets in the 2012/13 tax year for £50,000 this would represent disposal value which is deducted against the pool of expenditure. In this case the qualifying expenditure pool

---

[127] CAA 2001, s 61.
[128] CAA 2001, s 60.
[129] CAA 2001, s 61.

would be reduced to £30,000. Note that the allowance is weighted towards giving large amounts of relief in the earlier years than the later years.

Meaning of 'plant'

The term plant was described in *Yarmouth v France*[130] as follows:

'... in its ordinary sense ... [it] ... includes whatever apparatus is used by a business man for carrying on his business – not his stock-in-trade which he buys or makes for sale; but all goods and chattels, fixed or moveable, live or dead, which he keeps for permanent employment in his business.'

It is clear from this definition of plant that a number of preconditions exist in order for something to qualify as 'plant'.[131] These are that:

(1)   it must not be stock-in-trade;

(2)   it does not include items which are not used for carrying on a business;

(3)   excluded are things which are not 'apparatus ... goods and chattels'.

Premises do not qualify as plant; but, it is possible for apparatus to be either plant or premises depending upon the circumstances of each case.[132] In distinguishing what category apparatus falls into, the central question will be whether it is the means by which the business activity is carried on, or whether it is the place from which the activity is carried on.[133] Apparatus within the former classification is plant and that within the latter is premises. An interesting problem may arise in the context of e-commerce, as the example below illustrates.

In some situations, a taxpayer will have apparatus specifically designed in order to meet the purposes of a trade. A telecommunications operator may have specialist substations which house junctions and contain specialist equipment. In these situations, it does not automatically follow that what is created will be treated as plant. HMRC is entitled to examine the apparatus for which relief is claimed and disallow expenditure in respect of specific parts, because some qualify as plant and others as premises.[134] In each case, it is necessary to examine what the function of the apparatus is within the context of the taxpayer's business.[135]

---

[130]   (1887) 19 QBD 647, at 658.

[131]   See *Wimpey International Ltd v Warland (Inspector of Taxes)* [1988] STC 149, at 170–171, per Hoffmann J, and cited with approval by the Court of Appeal [1989] STC 273, at 275.

[132]   In *IRC v Barclay, Curle & Co Ltd* [1969] 4 STC 221 it was held that a dry dock was plant.

[133]   *Gray (Inspector of Taxes) v Seymour Garden Centre (Horticulture) (a firm)* [1995] STC 706.

[134]   *Bradley v London Electricity plc* [1996] STC 1054.

[135]   *IRC v Barclay, Curle & Co Ltd* [1969] 4 STC 221, per Lord Reid.

United Kingdom Taxation: General

The fact that certain items are attached to land does not prevent them from being classified as plant. In *Schofield (Inspector of Taxes) v R & H Hall Ltd*,[136] the Court of Appeal, upholding the decision of the Commissioners, held that a concrete grain silo erected at a dockside was plant because it was necessary to the way in which the taxpayer's trade of grain importing was carried on. The silo was designed to ensure efficient unloading and distribution thus facilitating bulk unloading of grain. The silo was an important part in the reception and distribution of grain. This case is potentially of relevance in supporting claims for technology, such as satellite receivers which distribute information. In other words, sending stations built on land or within buildings should be an integral instrument of a satellite communication business.

Example 7.5

Intranet Telecommunication Services plc establishes a substation for the purposes of carrying communications between its corporate users. The station operates as a central hub for the reception and distribution of information passing between its users. The structure of the substation and the equipment it houses were designed together. It is argued by HMRC that the structure is to be treated as a building from which the taxpayer's trade is carried on and the equipment housed within it is to be treated as plant. In situations such as this, it is arguable that an apportionment should be made between expenditure incurred on plant and premises.

Relief for computer software

The relief available in respect of plant or machinery expressly extends to capital expenditure incurred by a trader on the right to use or otherwise deal with computer software.[137] The term 'computer software' is not defined in the legislation. Computer software and the right to use it is treated as plant (whether or not it would constitute plant) where a trader incurs capital expenditure, for the purposes of a trade, on the acquisition of a right to use or otherwise deal with computer software.[138] The taxpayer must be entitled to the right to use the software otherwise the taxpayer will not be treated as owning the plant (ie the software).[139]

Some guidance on the application of the plant allowance is contained in HMRC's manuals of interpretation. The *Capital Allowances* manual states that all computer programs and data of any type should be treated as computer software.[140] The manual also states that where software is

[136] [1975] STC 353.
[137] CAA 2001, s 71.
[138] CAA 2001, s 71(2).
[139] CAA 2001, s 71(2).
[140] HMRC Guidance Manual CA23410 – *PMA: Computer Software*: www.hmrc.gov.uk/manuals/camanual/CA23410.htm.

transferred by 'electronic means' (eg by digital download over the internet) in circumstances where there is no physical asset, the legislation will nonetheless apply.[141]

HMRC's *Business Income Manual* provides guidance on how expenditure should be classified in the context of the revenue and capital divide (the text is reproduced in Appendix D).[142] Where software is acquired under a licence, regular payments akin to a rental are treated as revenue expenditure. The deduction of such payments is governed by accounting practice. In respect of a lump sum payment, the first issue in determining tax treatment is to identify whether the licence is a capital asset. In general terms a licence is a capital asset if it has a 'sufficiently enduring nature'. Where the software has a useful economic life of less than 2 years HMRC will accept that the expenditure is revenue.

The HMRC manual also deals with equipment acquired as a package and software owned outright. In this regard, where IT hardware and the licence to use software are purchased as a package for a single payment the expenditure has to be apportioned between the IT hardware and software.[143] Capital allowances under the general plant and machinery rules will be applied to the IT hardware expenditure, and how the balance of the expenditure attributable to the software licence is treated will depend on whether it is classified as revenue or capital. However, HMRC acknowledges that where the hardware and software are acquired on capital account and the expenditure is all within the general machinery and plant 'pool', no apportionment will be necessary in practice.[144]

The tax treatment of computer software is considered in further detail in Chapter 10.

Disposal events and values

In various prescribed circumstances a taxpayer is required to deduct disposal value of an asset from qualifying expenditure incurred in acquiring that asset. The disposal value that must be brought into account is summarised in Table 7.1, for both general plant or machinery and computer software.

Disposal value must be brought into account when one of the events shown in Table 7.1 occurs.[145] The amount of the disposal value that must be brought into account is also shown.

---

[141] HMRC Guidance Manual CA23410 – *PMA: Computer Software*: www.hmrc.gov.uk/ manuals/camanual/CA23410.htm.

[142] HMRC's *Business Income Manual*, at para BIM35810: www.hmrc.gov.uk/manuals/ bimmanual/BIM35810.htm.

[143] Ibid, at para BIM35810.

[144] Ibid, at para BIM35810.

[145] The respective statutory provisions are CAA 2001, s 61 (plant or machinery) and s 72 (software).

Table 7.1: Amount of disposal value on a disposal event

	General plant or machinery		Computer software	
	Prescribed event	*Disposal value*	*Prescribed event*	*Disposal value*
(a)	Sale.	Net proceeds of the sale + insurance received because of any event affecting the sale price + any other capital sum in respect of compensation of any description.	Grant of software right for a consideration not consisting entirely of money.	Market value of the right granted at the time of the grant.
(b)	Sale at a price below the market value, there is no charge to tax under ITEPA 2003 (employment income), the buyer is not entitled to relief under Part 2 (plant) or Part 6 (R&D) of CAA 2001 and is a dual resident investing company which is connected with the seller.	Market value of the plant or machinery at the time of the sale.	Grant is made below the market value, there is no charge to tax under ITEPA 2003 (employment income), the grantee is not entitled to relief under Part 2 (plant) or Part 6 (R&D) of CAA 2001 and is a dual resident investing company which is connected with the grantor.	Market value of the right granted at the time of the grant.
(c)	Demolition or destruction of the plant or machinery.	Net proceeds received by the person for the remains of the plant + any insurance money received in respect of the demolition + capital sums received as compensation.	Grant is made in circumstances other than those given in (a) and (b) above.	The net consideration in money received for the grant, together with (i) any insurance money received in respect of the software as a result of an event affecting the consideration obtainable on the grant and (ii) any other compensation of any description so received, so far as it consists of a capital sum.

	General plant or machinery		Computer software	
	Prescribed event	*Disposal value*	*Prescribed event*	*Disposal value*
(d)	Permanent loss of the plant or machinery.	Insurance money received for the loss + capital sums received as compensation.	N/A	N/A
(e)	Commencement of a long funding finance lease of the plant or machinery.	The greater of (i) the market value of the asset at the commencement of the term of the lease, and (ii) the qualifying lease payments.	N/A	N/A
(f)	Commencement of a long funding operating lease of the plant or machinery.	An amount equal to the market value of the plant or machinery at the commencement of the term of the lease.	N/A	N/A
(g)	Permanent discontinuance of the trade followed by the occurrence of any event within items (a)–(f).	The disposal value of the item in question.	N/A	N/A
(h)	Any event not falling within any of the foregoing items.	The market value of the plant or machinery at the time of the event.	N/A	N/A

The disposal value brought into account is not permitted to exceed the capital expenditure incurred by the taxpayer.[146] Thus, if a computer software company incurred capital expenditure of £50,000 in the acquisition of a computer server, which is subsequently destroyed in a fire, and receives insurance money of £60,000 to buy a replacement, the taxpayer is not required to bring into account disposal value in excess of £50,000. The reliefs relating to R&D also impose disposal event and disposal value provisions.[147]

Short-life assets

The depreciation allowance of 18%[148] on a reducing balance basis can cause problems where the economic life of the plant or machinery is less than the time it takes for the value to be written off in the taxpayer's accounts. In order to ameliorate this problem, relief is available that accelerates the rate of depreciation on what are known as 'short-life' assets (namely, assets with a life of less than 8 years).[149] To qualify for relief, an election must be made to HMRC.[150] An election will be beneficial for a taxpayer if the asset depreciates faster than the rate at which capital allowances are given and it is sold before the cut-off date. The cut-off point is 8 years from the end of the chargeable period when the expenditure on the asset is incurred.

The election must be within 2 years from the end of the relevant chargeable period (meaning the chargeable period in which the expenditure is incurred).[151] Although strictly the company should specifically mention *each* type of asset in respect of which an election is claimed, this is not adhered to by HMRC.[152] Relief is available only where

---

[146] CAA 2001, ss 62 and 73. Connected party transactions are subject to special rules governing the amount of the limit on disposal value: CAA 2001, s 62(2).

[147] See CAA 2001, s 443.

[148] The main rate of 20% is reduced to 18% for new and unrelieved expenditure from 1 April 2012 (FA 2011, s 10(2)).

[149] CAA 2001, s 86.

[150] CAA 2001, s 85.

[151] CAA 2001, s 85.

[152] HMRC practice (referred to at the *Capital Allowances Manual* CA23640: www.hmrc.gov.uk/manuals/camanual/CA23640.htm) states: 'If separate identification of the SLAs acquired in a chargeable period is impossible or impracticable, then you should accept an election that gives information about the assets by reference to batches of acquisitions, with their costs aggregated and shown in one amount provided that you are satisfied that:
– the assets are not specifically excluded, and
– the election gives enough information for it to be clear what is and what is not covered by it.
Strictly, each SLA should go into its own separate pool and so that the allowances on it are calculated separately. This may not be practicable where assets are held in large numbers. In cases like that capital allowance computations that give the correct statutory result, and do not abuse the SLA provisions, should be accepted even if there is not a separate computation for each asset.'

a trader has incurred capital expenditure upon plant or machinery, which is not excluded from the short-life asset relief.[153]

Example 7.6

A telecommunication provider incurs expenditure on microprocessors for incorporation in various exchanges within its network. In the 2011/12 tax year, it purchases 500,000 processors at a cost of £25 million. The microprocessors have an economic life of 4 years. The assets are scrapped at the end of this period and nothing is received at that time.

	2011/12	**2012/13**	**2013/14**	**2014/15**
Short-life pool	£25m	£20m	£16.4m	Nil
WDA @ 20%/18%	£5m	£3.6m	£2.952m	£13.448m
WDA c/f	£20m	£16.4m	£13.448m	

The relief is given by treating the short-life asset as part of a different writing down allowance pool from the general pool that exists for plant or machinery.[154] The relief must be used within 8 years of the expenditure being incurred, otherwise the asset is placed back in the general plant or machinery expenditure pool.[155]

Long-life assets

Where capital expenditure is incurred for the purposes of a trade or other qualifying activity, and it is expenditure on plant or machinery with a useful economic life of 25 years or more, then it will be treated as a long-life asset.[156] The effect of this scheme is to limit the rate of depreciation to 8%[157] rather than 18%[158] (2012/13).[159] Certain assets are not subject to the long-life asset provisions, for example, expenditure on a motor car.[160] None of the exclusions apply to IT or e-commerce activities. However, the long-life asset provisions do not apply unless the expenditure incurred within a chargeable period is in excess of £100,000.[161]

---

[153] CAA 2001, s 84. Assets excluded include various types of leased plant or machinery.
[154] CAA 2001, s 86.
[155] CAA 2001, s 86.
[156] CAA 2001, s 91.
[157] The special rate of 10% is reduced to 8% for new and unrelieved expenditure from 1 April 2012 (FA 2011, s 10).
[158] The main rate of 20% is reduced to 18% for new and unrelieved expenditure from 1 April 2012 (FA 2011, s 10(2)).
[159] CAA 2001, s 104D.
[160] CAA 2001, s 96.
[161] CAA 2001, s 99.

Where the scheme applies, the expenditure on long-life assets is placed in a pool separate from the general plant and machinery pool.[162] The allowance that is permitted in respect of a long-life asset is given against the trading receipts of the trade carried on by the taxpayer.[163]

Example 7.7

A cable television/internet access provider incurs expenditure of £10 million on the acquisition of a cable network in the 2011/12 tax year. The network has a useful economic life of 28 years.

	2011/12	2012/13	2014/15	2015/16	
Long-life pool	£10m	£9m	£8.28m	£7.29m	
WDA @ 10%/8%	£1m	£720,000	£622,400	£609,408	
WDA c/f	£9m	£8.28m	£7,617,600	£7,008,192	etc

Annual investment allowance

An annual investment allowance (AIA) of £25,000[164] (2012/13) per annum is available to all businesses in respect of qualifying expenditure.[165] It is necessary that the person owns the plant and machinery at some time during the chargeable period to qualify for the relief.[166] Expenditure covered by the £25,000 qualifies for full tax relief. Broadly, all expenditure should qualify where incurred by a company, but the relief is not available in connection with expenditure on cars, expenditure incurred in the period in which the qualifying activity is permanently discontinued or in circumstances where expenditure is incurred where the obtaining of the AIA is a main benefit.[167]

Expenditure exceeding the AIA is entered into the main or special rate pool, and writing down allowances are then given in the usual way (subject to meeting the relevant qualifying conditions for relief). Where a company is a member of a group of companies the AIA is shared between them, and can be allocated to qualifying expenditure as they think fit.[168]

---

[162] CAA 2001, Part 2, Chapter 10A.
[163] CAA 2001, s 2(1).
[164] The amount of the entitlement to AIA is reduced from £100,000 to £25,000 for expenditure incurred on or after 1 April 2012: FA 2011, s 11.
[165] CAA 2001, ss 38A, 51A–51N. The AIA is made only in the chargeable period in which the qualifying expenditure is incurred with the consequence that it cannot be deferred to a later period.
[166] CAA 2001, s 51A(1).
[167] CAA 2001, s 38B. For other restrictions see CAA 2001, s 38B: General exclusion 5.
[168] CAA 2001, s 51C.

7.9 INTELLECTUAL PROPERTY RIGHTS

7.9.1 Scope of relief

The taxation of a company's exploitation of intellectual property rights (referred to in the tax rules as 'intangible fixed assets'), and the expenditure and/or receipts relating to such exploitation, is based on the accounting treatment of such assets, as adjusted by the tax rules provided in Part 8 of CTA 2009. Part 8 applies to intangible fixed assets created by a company on or after 1 April 2002, or acquired by a company on or after 1 April 2002 from a non-related party, or acquired by a company on or after 1 April 2002 from a related party in specified circumstances.[169]

The effect of Part 8 of CTA 2009 is to permit all sums written off in a company's accounts in respect of intangible fixed assets to be deducted for corporation tax purposes, and for all receipts arising from such assets to be treated as revenue items, except to the extent adjustments are required by specific rules.[170] The effect of Part 8 is to make no distinction between income and capital receipts. Reinvestment relief is available where the proceeds arising from the sale of intangible fixed assets are reinvested in similar assets.[171]

7.9.2 Meaning of intangible fixed asset and intellectual property

The concept of 'intangible fixed asset' owned by a company is defined as meaning 'an intangible asset acquired or created by the company for use on a continuing basis in the course of the company's activities'.[172] An 'intangible asset' is given the same meaning as it has for UK accounting purposes.[173] The Accounting Standards Board's Financial Reporting Standard 10, *Goodwill and Intangible Assets* (FRS 10) defines intangible assets as 'non-financial assets that do not have physical substance but are identifiable and are controlled by the entity through custody or legal

United Kingdom
Taxation: General

---

[169] CTA 2009, s 882(1). Various anti-avoidance rules apply to ensure that 'existing assets' (ie those created or acquired before 1 April 2002) do not obtain relief under the Part 8 (see CTA 2009, ss 893 and 895).

[170] A detailed review of these rules is beyond the scope of this chapter. Various reliefs are available under Part 8 for intra-group transfers of intangible fixed assets and the transfer of trades and businesses which include such assets. Anti-avoidance rules may also apply to the realisation of intangible fixed assets, or to deny a deduction for expenditure on intangible fixed assets. Professional tax advice relevant to the particular circumstances should be sought where appropriate.

[171] CTA 2009, Part 8, Chapter 7.

[172] CTA 2009, s 713(1). Intangible assets which are held as trading stock are outside this definition.

[173] CTA 2009, s 712(1). See the Accounting Standards Board's Financial Reporting Standard 10, *Goodwill and Intangible Assets* (December 1997, as amended), available at www.frc.org.uk. However, some intangible assets are specifically excluded from the definition such as oil licences, financial assets and rights in companies or trusts (see CTA 2009, Part 8, Chapter 10).

rights'.[174] An intangible asset does not need to be included on the company's balance sheet for it to be regarded as a fixed asset.[175] The rules provide that the definition of an 'intangible asset' shall include any 'intellectual property', which is defined as:[176]

'(a)   any patent, trade mark, registered design, copyright or design right, plant breeders' rights or rights under section 7 of the Plant Varieties Act 1997,

(b)   any right under the law of a country or territory outside the United Kingdom corresponding or similar to a right within paragraph (a),

(c)   any information or technique not protected by a right within paragraph (a) or (b) but having industrial, commercial or other economic value, or

(d)   any licence or other right in respect of anything within paragraph (a), (b) or (c).'

Goodwill is included within this regime.[177] For these purposes, 'goodwill' is given the same meaning it has for accounting purposes.[178] For accounting purposes, goodwill represents the difference between the price at which a business is sold and the total value of the separate assets of the business after deducting the value of the liabilities assumed. The Part 8 regime does not apply to an intangible asset to the extent such an asset is held either: (a) for a purpose that is not a business or other commercial purpose of the company; or (b) for the purpose of activities in respect of which the company is not within the charge to UK corporation tax.[179]

7.9.3   Accounting and intellectual property

For accounting purposes, the amortisation of intangible fixed assets is determined in accordance with FRS 10. 'Amortisation' is the writing down of the value of an asset over a period of time. The accounting standard is the basis of giving tax relief for expenditure on intangible fixed assets. In addition, the accounting treatment of these rights also forms the basis for determining when income receipts will be brought into account. The amounts to be taken into account in computing a company's corporation tax liability are referred to as 'credits' and 'debits'; and these are derived from the gains and losses referred to in the company's accounts.

FRS 10 provides that there is a rebuttable presumption that the useful economic life of intangible assets is less than 20 years.[180] On this basis, the

---

[174] FRS 10, para 2.
[175] CTA 2009, s 713(3).
[176] CTA 2009, s 712(3). However, the definition is subject to the list of excluded assets: see Part 8, Chapter 10.
[177] CTA 2009, s 715(1).
[178] CTA 2009, s 715(3).
[179] CTA 2009, s 803.
[180] FRS 10, para 19.

value of such assets should be amortised in the profit and loss account of a company on a systematic basis over their useful economic lives.[181]

Intangible assets purchased separately from a business should be capitalised at cost.[182] If acquired as part of a business the accounting standard provides it should be capitalised separately from goodwill at its fair market value.[183] If an intangible asset is developed internally it can only be capitalised if it has a readily ascertainable market value;[184] otherwise the costs of developing such an asset must be written off as incurred. Any intangible assets having an indefinite useful economic life should not be amortised.[185]

FRS 10 provides that positive purchased goodwill should be capitalised as an asset,[186] whilst internally generated goodwill should not be capitalised.[187] Purchased goodwill is shown as an asset on a company's balance sheet. It is the difference between the cost of an acquired entity and the aggregate of the fair values of that entity's identifiable assets and liabilities. If goodwill has a limited useful economic life the goodwill must be amortised on a systematic basis over its life.[188]

Goodwill that is regarded as having an indefinite useful economic life is not amortised.[189] The Standard provides that a straight line method of amortisation should be used unless another method is shown to be appropriate. There is a rebuttable presumption that the useful economic life of purchased goodwill is limited to a period of 20 years or less.[190] It is necessary to obtain the advice of an accountant to determine the appropriate treatment for the assets in a company's accounts.

7.9.4 Intangible fixed assets: credits and debits

The tax treatment of credits (ie receipts) and debits (ie expenditure) in respect of intangible fixed assets is determined by the basis on which such assets are held by the company.[191] Where royalties are recognised for accounting purposes on or after 1 April 2002 the CTA 2009, Part 8 regime will apply.[192] However, Part 8 only applies to royalties and not to an

United Kingdom
Taxation: General

---

[181] FRS 10, para 15.
[182] FRS 10, para 9.
[183] FRS 10, para 10.
[184] FRS 10, para 14.
[185] FRS 10, para 17.
[186] FRS 10, para 7.
[187] FRS 10, para 8.
[188] FRS 10, para 15.
[189] FRS 10, para 17.
[190] FRS 10, para 19.
[191] CTA 2009, s 745.
[192] CTA 2009, s 896.

amount to be brought into account in connection with the realisation of a pre-1 April 2002 asset (the receipts of which will be characterised as capital).[193]

In the case of a trade, the deductible debits and taxable credits which are brought into account under the regime are regarded as receipts and expenses of the company's trade.[194] This means that the usual corporation tax rules (see generally 7.6) will then apply to the amounts that are brought into account as part of the taxpayer's trading activities.

A summary of the position is shown in Tables 7.2 and 7.3, together with the basis for how non-trading credits and debits are treated.

Table 7.2: Tax treatment of intangible fixed asset credits

Intangible fixed asset credits	Tax treatment
(1) Credits brought into account in any accounting period in respect of an asset held for the purposes of a trade carried on by a company.	Treated as receipts of the trade.[195]
(2) Credits brought into account in any accounting period in respect of an asset held for the purposes of a property business carried on by the company.	Treated as receipts of the business.[196]
(3) Credits which do not fall within the preceding categories are known as 'non-trading credits'.	Matched against non-trading debits for the purposes of computing a company's aggregate non-trading gain or loss on intangible fixed assets.[197] There is a non-trading gain if: (a) there are only non-trading credits; or (b) non-trading credits exceed the amount of non-trading debits.[198] The amount of the non-trading gain is in each of the foregoing circumstances either the aggregate amount of the credits, or the amount of the excess.[199]

---

[193] CTA 2009, s 896(3).
[194] CTA 2009, s 747.
[195] CTA 2009, s 747.
[196] CTA 2009, s 748.
[197] CTA 2009, s 751.
[198] CTA 2009, s 751(2).
[199] CTA 2009, s 751(3), (4).

Table 7.3: Tax treatment of intangible fixed asset debits

Intangible fixed asset debits	Tax treatment
(1) Debits brought into account in any accounting period in respect of an asset held for the purposes of a trade carried on by the company.	Treated as expenses of the trade.[200]
(2) Debits brought into account in any accounting period in respect of an asset held for the purposes of a property business carried on by the company.	Treated as expenses of the business.[201]
(3) Debits which do not fall within the above categories are known as 'non-trading debits'.	Non-trading debits are matched against non-trading credits for the purposes of computing a company's aggregate non-trading gain or loss on intangible fixed assets.[202] If there is a non-trading loss because either: (a) there are only non-trading debits; or (b) there is an excess of non-trading debits over non-trading credits, then the taxpayer is entitled to deduct the non-trading loss against total profits.[203] Where there is a non-trading loss the company is entitled to claim to have the whole or part of the loss set off against the company's total profits for the relevant accounting period.[204] Alternatively the loss can be surrendered by way of group relief under Part 5 of CTA 2010 to other companies within the same group as the taxpayer.[205] If a loss is not utilised in one of the foregoing ways it is carried forward to the next accounting period of the company.[206]

7.9.5   Intangible fixed assets: accounting basis or fixed rate relief

Part 8 provides for tax relief where a loss is recognised in a company's profit and loss account in connection with capitalised expenditure[207] on

---

[200] CTA 2009, s 747(3).
[201] CTA 2009, s 748(3).
[202] CTA 2009, s 751(5).
[203] CTA 2009, s 751(6), (7).
[204] CTA 2009, s 753(1).
[205] CTA 2009, s 753(3).
[206] CTA 2009, s 753(3).
[207] The sum capitalised for accounting purposes includes expenditure incurred on the acquisition of the asset, and also expenditure on improving or enhancing it: CTA 2009, s 727.

an intangible fixed asset either (a) by way of amortisation or (b) as a result of an impairment review then for corporation tax purposes a corresponding debit is brought into account.[208] Tax avoidance arrangements will prevent debits being brought into account for the purposes of writing down on an accounting basis, or the amount of such debits.[209]

As an alternative to writing down on an accounting basis a company can make an irrevocable election to write down the cost of an intangible fixed asset for tax purposes at a fixed rate (the election must be made within two years).[210] Where an election is made, a debit equal to either (a) 4% of the cost of the asset[211] or (b) if less, the balance of the tax written down value is made for tax purposes in each accounting period commencing with that in which the expenditure was incurred.[212] The purpose of the fixed rate relief is to provide a tax deduction for durable intangible assets.

7.9.6   Computer software

The Part 8 regime permits companies to use the relief available in connection with capital expenditure[213] on computer software under CAA 2001 (considered further in Chapter 10).[214] This is because tax relief may be available at a faster rate under the capital allowances code. To obtain the benefit of the CAA 2001 relief, a company must make an election within 2 years of the end of the accounting period in which the expenditure was incurred. Any receipts derived from realisation of the software that are not brought into account under the capital allowances rules will be recognised as taxable income under the intangible fixed asset regime.

7.9.7   Intangible fixed asset: disposals

As mentioned previously, any 'capital gain' arising from intangible fixed assets is taxed as income, provided that the asset is subject to the provisions of the regime (ie, that asset was created on or after 1 April 2002).[215] Where intangible fixed assets are realised together, there must be a just and reasonable apportionment of the consideration between the assets.[216] Broadly, the difference between the realisation proceeds of an intangible asset and its tax value are brought into account.[217] There is a

---

[208]   CTA 2009, s 729(1).
[209]   CTA 2009, s 864.
[210]   CTA 2009, s 730.
[211]   The tax cost is the amount capitalised for accounting purposes in respect of expenditure on the asset, unless any adjustment is required for tax purposes: CTA 2009, s 731.
[212]   CTA 2009, s 731.
[213]   See **7.8.4**.
[214]   CTA 2009, s 815.
[215]   CTA 2009, s 906.
[216]   CTA 2009, s 856(5).
[217]   CTA 2009, s 733.

realisation of an intangible fixed asset where, in accordance with UK GAAP, there is a transaction resulting in it ceasing to be recognised in the company's balance sheet, or in a reduction in the accounting value of the asset.[218]

The 'proceeds of realisation' are regarded as 'the amount recognised for accounting purposes as the proceeds of realisation, reduced by the amount so recognised as incidental costs of realisation'.[219] A part realisation is subject to rules which apportion the proportion of the tax written down value or else the cost of the asset to be set off.[220] Tax avoidance arrangements will be disregarded in determining whether a credit is to be brought into account in respect of a realisation, or the amount of such a credit.[221]

If any debits have been brought into account for tax purposes in respect of writing down on either an accounting basis or at a fixed rate, then realisation of a fixed intangible asset has the following results: (a) proceeds of realisation in excess of the tax written down value of an asset will be taxed as a credit (limited to the excess); (b) proceeds of realisation less than the tax written down value of an asset will be relieved as a debit (limited to the shortfall); and (c) if there are no proceeds of realisation a debit equal to the tax written down value of the asset will be brought into account.[222]

Where there is a realisation of a fixed intangible asset which has not been written down there are the following results:[223] (a) proceeds of realisation which exceed the cost of the asset[224] will be taxed as a credit (limited to the excess); (b) proceeds of realisation less than the cost of the asset will be relieved as a debit (limited to the shortfall); and (c) if there are no proceeds of realisation a debit equal to the cost of the asset will be brought into account.

Any proceeds of realisation derived from an intangible fixed asset not shown in a company's balance sheet will be taxed as a credit.[225] The type

United Kingdom
Taxation: General

---

[218] CTA 2009, s 734(1). *Reporting the Substance of Transactions* (FRS 5) states that an entire asset should cease to be recognised '[w]here a transaction involving a previously recognised asset transfers to others: (a) all significant rights or other access to benefits relating to that asset; and (b) all significant exposure to the risks inherent in those benefits ...' (para 22).

[219] CTA 2009, s 739(1). Although this amount is subject to any adjustment for tax purposes: CTA 2009, s 739(2).

[220] CTA 2009, s 737.

[221] CTA 2009, s 864(1).

[222] CTA 2009, s 735. The regime in Part 8, Chapter 4 defines how the tax written down value is calculated.

[223] CTA 2009, s 736.

[224] The cost of an asset is the cost recognised for tax purposes, which means the amount capitalised for accounting purposes in respect of expenditure on the asset, unless any adjustment is required for tax purposes: CTA 2009, s 736(5)–(7).

[225] CTA 2009, s 738.

of asset subject to this rule is one which has been wholly written off, or is an internally-generated asset which cannot be capitalised under FRS 10.

7.9.8 Assets excluded from relief

The following assets of relevance in the context of an internet business are excluded from the intangible fixed asset regime, except in relation to taxation of royalties[226] arising from them:master of a film or sound recording; and computer software treated as part of the costs of the related hardware.[227] Intangible assets held by a company that represent expenditure on R&D[228] are also broadly excluded from CTA 2009.[229] Where an asset is excluded from Part 8 of CTA 2009 the general provisions of the Corporation Tax Acts will apply as appropriate.[230]

7.9.9 Application of intangible fixed asset regime

As discussed previously, the all-income basis of taxation applies solely to intangible fixed assets that were acquired on or after 1 April 2002. All intangible assets held prior to this date by a corporation or which remain within the ownership of the same economic group of companies will fall outside of the regime, and will continue to be taxed in accordance with the pre-CTA 2009, Part 8 regime. Any royalties derived from intellectual property held prior to 1 April 2002, and which are received after that date, will be taxed and relieved in accordance with Part 8.

Under the general corporation tax code for pre-1 April 2002 intangibles there is no uniform tax code: for example, capital expenditure is only deductible if specifically authorised by CAA 2001. The basis on which receipts derived from, and capital expenditure incurred on intellectual property will be relieved for intellectual property held before 1 April 2002 will depend on the particular provisions of CTA 2009.

Where the all income regime under Part 8 of CTA 2009 applies it will generally take precedence over other tax legislation applicable to companies. For example, s 54 of CTA 2009, which prohibits the deduction of revenue expenditure not wholly and exclusively incurred for the purposes of a trade, will not apply. Instead the basis for charging to tax and allowing a deduction for intangible fixed assets is determined by Part 8. However, it is important to note that there are some circumstances

---

[226] For this purpose the term 'royalty' is defined as 'a royalty in respect of the enjoyment or exercise of rights that constitute an intangible fixed asset': CTA 2009, s 714.

[227] See CTA 2009, ss 902, 810(1), 811 (sound recordings) and 812 (master version of films where principal photography commenced before 1 January 2007 or the acquisition was before 1 October 2007), 813 (costs related to hardware).

[228] The definition of R&D in CTA 2010, s 1138 is adopted for the purposes of the CTA 2009, Part 8 regime.

[229] CTA 2009, s 814.

[230] CTA 2009, ss 802(2), 902.

in which other parts of the corporation tax legislation will apply in priority to this regime. In this regard, see generally s 1308 of CTA 2009, which applies if expenditure is brought into account in determining the value of an intangible asset, and allowed as a deduction in calculating profits where a company has incurred expenditure on R&D which is not of a capital nature and the company has brought the expenditure into account in determining the value of an intangible asset.[231] In these circumstances the company is not permitted to make a deduction in calculating its profits of any amount in respect of the writing down of so much of the value of the intangible asset as is attributable to the expenditure.[232]

7.9.10 Intellectual property outside the intangible fixed asset regime

The tax consequences of owning and exploiting intellectual property rights held prior to 1 April 2002 is outside the scope of this chapter. The tax position can be complicated as the prior regime did not apply in a uniform manner. Broadly, intellectual property held prior to the commencement of the CTA 2009, Part 8 regime will be subject to corporation tax on chargeable gains in respect of any disposal, provided that the asset was held on an investment basis. Such a chargeable gain is calculated by deducting from the disposal proceeds the expenditure incurred in acquiring the asset,[233] as increased by indexation.[234] The gain may be reduced by the carry forward of capital losses from previous accounting periods, or by the set off of losses in the current period.[235] This is in clear contrast to any proceeds from the disposal of an intangible fixed asset acquired on or after 1 April 2002, which will be taxed as income.. This means that it is not possible to use capital losses against receipts derived from the disposal of intangible fixed assets acquired on or after 1 April 2002.

7.10   TRADING LOSSES

7.10.1   Trade losses against total profits of current and preceding accounting period

A company is entitled to claim relief for a trading loss arising in an accounting period to be used as a deduction against its total profits (of any kind) of the same accounting period.[236] Further, the company is entitled to make a claim for the current year's trading loss to be offset

---

[231]   CTA 2009, s 1308(1), (4).
[232]   CTA 2009, s 1308(5).
[233]   TCGA 1992, s 38(1).
[234]   TCGA 1992, s 53(1).
[235]   TCGA 1992, s 2.
[236]   CTA 2010, s 37.

against profits of any kind arising in an immediately preceding accounting period.[237] This means that a trading loss can only be carried back a maximum of 12 months.[238] A claim for relief must be made within 2 years from the end of the accounting period in which the loss is incurred.[239] Relief is denied where the trade in which the loss arises is not carried out on a commercial basis, and with a view to the making of a profit in the trade or so as to afford a reasonable expectation of making such a profit.[240] The loss permitted to be used as a deduction for an accounting period is restricted to the amount of the loss that cannot be deducted for a subsequent accounting period.[241] If the company ceases to carry on its trade, then the terminal loss can be carried back over a period of 3 years.[242]

Example 7.8

Alpha Computer Component Manufacturers Ltd achieves profits of £60,000, £80,000 and £100,000 for the 2011/12, 2012/13 and 2013/14 tax years respectively. A trading loss of £180,000 is incurred in the 2014/15 tax year. The taxpayer may elect to offset the loss against profits of the earlier accounting period in the following way. For the purposes of this example it is assumed that the tax rate throughout these years is fixed at 25%.

	2011/12	2012/13	2013/14	2014/15
Taxable profits	£60,000	£80,000	£100,000	–
Tax payable	£15,000	£20,000	£25,000	
Trading loss	–	–	£100,000 (carried back)	£180,000 (carry back under CTA 2010, s 37)
Tax repayment	No	No	Yes	–

A trading loss is calculated in the same way as trading profits would be calculated.[243] No claim to relief can be made if during the loss-making period the company carried on the trade wholly outside the UK.[244] Where

---

[237] CTA 2010, s 37(3).
[238] CTA 2010, s 37(3).
[239] CTA 2010, s 37(7).
[240] CTA 2010, s 44.
[241] CTA 2010, s 37(4).
[242] CTA 2010, s 39.
[243] CTA 2010, s 35(3); CTA 2009, s 47.
[244] CTA 2010, s 37(5).

a claim to relief is made to carry back a loss against trading profits, it is necessary for the trade not to have been carried on wholly outside the UK.[245]

7.10.2   Transfer of losses against trading profits of later accounting periods

Once allowable expenditure is deducted from revenue receipts the resulting computation may establish a trading loss. A trading loss can be used to reduce the level of taxable profits in subsequent or earlier accounting periods of the company.[246] The company has the right to use trading losses in this way provided it continues to carry on a trade.[247] Where the loss is only partially absorbed by trading profits of a subsequent period, this is carried forward to trading profits arising in later accounting periods.[248] In this way, the trading loss is absorbed throughout subsequent accounting periods.

Example 7.9

E-commerce Ltd incurs a trading loss of £80,000 (2011/12) from the licensing of e-commerce payment technology. Trading profits in subsequent accounting periods are £25,000 (2012/13), £45,000 (2013/14), £250,000 (2014/15). The trading loss will be absorbed in the following way:

	2011/12	2012/13	2013/14	2014/15
Trading profits		£25,000	£45,000	£250,000
Trading loss	£80,000	£55,000 c/f	£10,000 c/f	–
Taxable profit	0	0	0	£240,000

A trading loss is determined by the same rules that apply to the computation of trading profits.[249] In certain circumstances where trading profits are insufficient to absorb the trading loss, it is possible to use the loss against income arising in respect of trade-related interest and dividends.[250]

---

[245] CTA 2010, s 37(6).
[246] CTA 2010, s 36.
[247] CTA 2010, s 45(4).
[248] CTA 2010, s 45(4).
[249] CTA 2010, s 35(3); CTA 2009, s 47.
[250] CTA 2010, s 46. For this purpose the provisions apply to interest or dividends from investments, and which would be brought into account as trading receipts in calculating the profits of the trade of the company but for the fact that they have been subjected to tax under other provisions of the Tax Acts: CTA 2010, s 46(3).

United Kingdom Taxation: General

7.11   CHARGEABLE GAINS

7.11.1   Introduction

A company is subject to corporation tax on any chargeable gains arising from the disposal of assets.[251] This tax charge is important for a company because it can potentially touch upon all assets used within the world of e-commerce and e-infrastructure activities. A chargeable gain is calculated using many of the principles that are applied for the purposes of computing an individual's liability to capital gains tax.[252] A chargeable gain is calculated by reference to the company's accounting period.[253]

A non-UK resident company is also subject to corporation tax on chargeable gains, where it carries on a trade through a permanent establishment within the UK.[254] The tax charge arises in respect of the disposal of assets which are situated in the UK and are used for the purposes of a trade.[255] The tax charge also applies to gains from the disposal of assets situated in the UK which are used or held for the purposes of a permanent establishment.[256] No tax can be imposed in respect of this charge unless the company is carrying on a trade through a permanent establishment in the UK.[257]

In the context of chargeable gains it is necessary to consider whether:

(1)   the company owns an asset;

(2)   the company makes a disposal of an asset;

(3)   the company is entitled to disposal proceeds; and

(4)   the company can deduct allowable costs.

These aspects are considered in the following parts of this section.

> *Example 7.10*
>
> E-commerce Ltd operates an internet site, established in 1995, whereby other companies purchase a presence on the internet site for the purposes of carrying on their own e-commerce activities. The site has built up considerable goodwill with the result that it is valued at £1 million. The company disposes of the site at market value. The transfer involves the

---

[251]   TCGA 1992, s 1(2).
[252]   TCGA 1992, s 8(3).
[253]   TCGA 1992, s 8(1).
[254]   CTA 2009, s 5(2), (3).
[255]   TCGA 1992, s 10B(1)(a).
[256]   TCGA 1992, s 10B(1)(b).
[257]   TCGA 1992, s 10B.

disposal of computer software, trade marks and goodwill. Circumstances such as these will trigger a tax corporation charge on the disposal of assets.[258]

7.11.2   Assets

An asset is broadly defined to include all forms of property,[259] and specifically any form of property created by the company disposing of it.[260] All tangible property used by IT or e-commerce businesses will therefore potentially be subject to corporation tax on chargeable gains.

Example 7.11

Intranet Ltd owns satellite receivers that are used to distribute telecommunications. Another company is interested in acquiring the receivers for a payment of £25 million. In this situation the transfer of the equipment is potentially a taxable disposal under TCGA 1992.

Intangible rights are also capable of being subject to corporation tax on chargeable gains unless they comprise intangible fixed assets, which are subject to CTA 2009 (see **7.9**).

7.11.3   Disposal

In simple terms, an asset is disposed of, where there is a conveyance of the asset, by sale or by operation of law. The time of a disposal is fixed at when the contract is entered into for the disposal and acquisition of the asset.[261] The fact that the asset is transferred at a different time from the period of entering into the contract is wholly irrelevant.[262] In addition, a disposal occurs where a capital sum[263] is derived from an asset.[264] In this situation, the time of disposal is the period when the capital sum is received.[265] TCGA 1992 makes particular reference to capital sums derived from the surrender of rights, or for refraining from exercising rights, and such sums received as consideration for the use or exploitation of assets.[266] A disposal is also deemed to occur where the asset is destroyed, irrespective of whether any capital sum is received by way of compensation for the destruction of the asset.[267] In the event that a

United Kingdom
Taxation: General

---

[258]   If the assets fall within Part 8 of CTA 2009 they will be subject to an all income basis of taxation: see **7.8**.

[259]   TCGA 1992, s 21(1).

[260]   TCGA 1992, s 21(1)(c).

[261]   TCGA 1992, s 28(1).

[262]   TCGA 1992, s 28(1).

[263]   A capital sum is defined as 'any money or money's worth which is not excluded from the consideration taken into account in the computation of the gain': TCGA 1992, s 22(3).

[264]   TCGA 1992, s 22.

[265]   TCGA 1992, s 22(2).

[266]   TCGA 1992, s 22(1)(c), (d).

[267]   TCGA 1992, s 24(1).

disposal is subject to a conditional contract, such as the exercise of an option, the time of the disposal is when the contract becomes unconditional.[268]

7.11.4   Disposal consideration

Normally, HMRC will not be able to interfere with the consideration agreed upon for the disposal of an asset. However, there are circumstances in which HMRC is entitled to substitute another amount as the disposal consideration. This occurs where an asset is acquired or disposed of otherwise than on an arm's length basis.[269] Where an asset is transferred between connected persons, there is an assumption that the disposal consideration will not be at arm's length.[270] Other detailed provisions may also apply for fixing the value of the disposal.[271]

7.11.5   Allowable deductions

In the computation of a chargeable gain a company is entitled is entitled to make a number of deductions. The permitted deductions are as follows:[272]

(1)   the amount given wholly and exclusively for the purposes of acquiring the asset;

(2)   the incidental costs of acquisition;

(3)   any amount incurred wholly and exclusively for the purposes of enhancing the value of the asset;

(4)   any expenditure wholly and exclusively incurred in establishing, preserving or defending title to the asset, or a right over the asset;

(5)   any incidental costs incurred in the disposal of the asset.[273]

A company is not permitted to make any deduction in respect of expenditure that has been deducted for the purposes of ascertaining the profits or gains or losses of a trade.[274]

---

[268]   TCGA 1992, s 28(2).
[269]   TCGA 1992, s 17(1).
[270]   TCGA 1992, s 18.
[271]   TCGA 1992, ss 18–20.
[272]   TCGA 1992, s 38(1).
[273]   For example, fees, commission or remuneration paid for professional services: TCGA 1992, s 38(2).
[274]   TCGA 1992, s 39.

Example 7.12

Alpha Electronic Merchandising Ltd (AEM) acquired computer software in 1991 for £50,000, which was used to carry on a trade across the internet supplying software in an electronic format. In 2010 AEM disposed of the computer software for £60,000, and the trademarks associated with the internet business for £100,000, and copyright in the software sold via the internet, for £200,000. The original cost of acquiring the copyright and trademarks by AEM amounted to £65,000.

	2010	
	£	£
Disposal consideration		360,000
Acquisition costs	(65,000) + (50,000)	
Chargeable gains		245,000

NB: This example does not take into account indexation; and strictly the gains would be calculated on an asset-by-asset basis.

7.11.6   Wasting assets

Where an asset is disposed of a chargeable gain may arise for the purposes of TCGA 1992. Where such an event occurs, a deduction must be made for the acquisition cost against the disposal proceeds to ascertain any chargeable gain.[275] However, the acquisition cost is restricted when an asset is regarded as a 'wasting asset'. Expenditure on wasting assets must be written off on a straight-line basis,[276] unless capital allowances were available for a trader.[277]

An asset will be regarded as a wasting asset where its 'predictable life [does] not exceed 50 years'.[278] No definition is given of 'predictable life' for the purpose of intangible assets. Plant and machinery is deemed to have a predictable life of less than 50 years.[279] In some cases the wasting asset provisions will not be relevant. For example, the typical duration of copyright is the author's life plus 70 years.[280]

United Kingdom
Taxation: General

---

[275] TCGA 1992, s 38(1)(a).
[276] TCGA 1992, s 46.
[277] TCGA 1992, s 47.
[278] TCGA 1992, s 44(1)(c).
[279] Where a licence is acquired in respect of computer software, the capital expenditure is deemed to be on plant (CAA 2001, s 71). As a result, under TCGA 1992 it is regarded as having a predictable life of less than 50 years. Such an item will always be regarded as a wasting asset to the extent it is within the capital gains code, and is not an intangible fixed asset (CTA 2009, s 906).
[280] See CDPA 1988.

7.11.7 Relief for gain arising on the disposal of business assets

A chargeable gain accruing on the disposal of business assets can be deferred by the acquisition of further business assets with the consideration arising on the disposal.[281] This is known as roll-over relief. Where a claim is made for this relief, it is deemed that the consideration received is adjusted so that neither a gain nor a loss arises to the company.[282] The relief also operates to reduce the value of the acquired asset by the excess of the amount accruing from the asset disposed of over the adjusted value (ie the otherwise chargeable gain is rolled into the new asset so that the value of the new asset is reduced by the amount of the chargeable gain, so that on any subsequent disposal of the asset the rolled-over gain will potentially be subject to tax). The operation of this relief does not affect the value of the consideration paid by the person acquiring the old asset, or the other party selling the new asset.[283] The relief is not available where the new assets are not acquired for the purposes of use in a trade.[284]

Roll-over relief only operates in respect of assets specified in TCGA 1992 (see **7.11.8**).[285] There is no requirement for the disposal consideration accruing from an asset to be invested in exactly the same type of asset. The only requirement is that the consideration is used to acquire an asset within the specified classes of business assets that qualify for roll-over relief.[286] The relief is excluded where the new asset is not acquired, or an unconditional contract is not entered into for the acquisition of the new asset, 12 months before the disposal of the old asset or within 3 years of the disposal of the old asset.[287] Where an unconditional contract is entered into the relief is given on a provisional basis.[288] Where the asset is not acquired under such a contract all necessary adjustments will be made.[289] There are provisions that deal with the appropriation of an asset to trading stock.[290]

7.11.8 Assets qualifying for roll-over relief

The assets in which disposal consideration must be reinvested to qualify for roll-over relief are as shown in Table 7.4.[291]

---

[281]   TCGA 1992, s 152.
[282]   TCGA 1992, s 152(1)(a).
[283]   TCGA 1992, s 152.
[284]   TCGA 1992, s 152(5).
[285]   TCGA 1992, s 152(1). For the procedure to claim relief, see TCGA 1992, s 153A.
[286]   These assets are listed at TCGA 1992, s 155.
[287]   TCGA 1992, s 152(3).
[288]   TCGA 1992, s 152(4).
[289]   TCGA 1992, s 152(4).
[290]   TCGA 1992, s 161.
[291]   TCGA 1992, s 155.

Table 7.4: Qualifying categories for roll-over relief

Class	Type of asset
Class 1	Head A Any building or part of a building occupied, or used only for the purpose of a trade. Head B Fixed plant or machinery not forming part of a building.
Class 2	Ships, aircraft and hovercraft.
Class 3	Satellites, space stations and spacecraft, launch vehicles.
Class 4 *	Goodwill.
Classes 5–8	Not relevant for e-commerce.

* NB: Class 4 does not apply for corporation tax purposes in respect of the acquisition of new assets that are chargeable intangible assets for the purposes of Part 8 of CTA 2009. A form of roll-over relief is available in respect of such assets under the intangible fixed asset regime.[292]

7.11.9 Other reliefs

TCGA 1992 provides a number of other reliefs from corporation tax on chargeable gains. The primary reliefs relate to intra-group transfers (s 171), schemes relating to reconstruction or amalgamation of a company's business (s 139) and mergers (s 181). Gifts of business assets by an individual qualify for relief (s 165), the effect of which is to hold over the gain. An examination of these reliefs is beyond the scope of this book.

---

[292] CTA 2009, Part 8, Chapter 7.

CHAPTER 8

OUTBOUND UK AND INTERNATIONAL E-COMMERCE: SCOPE OF CHARGE TO TAX

8.1 INTRODUCTION

Any person carrying on an internet business will need to organise its legal and commercial structure to minimise the level of taxation which will be incurred on its activities, including on cross-border activities. If the owners of a business wish it to expand, they must recognise that the rate of that expansion will depend upon their ability to maximise the amount of funds actually retained by the business from its profits, and accordingly it is desirable to eliminate unnecessary tax costs.

Many of the issues examined in Chapter 6 (Inbound UK E-Commerce) will be relevant to outbound UK internet business (ie the provision of goods and/or services to another country) since most double taxation agreements (DTAs) will have been influenced by the OECD Model Tax Convention. Chapter 6 examined the connecting factors that must exist before a company (whether incorporated in or outside the UK) is subject to UK corporation tax and income tax, and in this regard many countries will have similar rules (but they will not be identical: accordingly advice should always be taken from local tax advisers). Where a UK resident is taxed in another country the issue of how the non-UK taxation is relieved against that person's UK tax liability arises. Relief will typically be provided as a credit for the foreign taxes, but it is possible to elect for the profits of a non-UK permanent establishment to be exempt from UK tax so that it incurs solely the tax of the other country (see Chapter 6).

The role of DTAs is also examined in Chapter 6 since such agreements operate as a limitation on the UK's domestic tax charge (see **6.5–6.8**), and in this regard the UK's DTAs with other countries should operate to limit the domestic tax charge in those countries. Chapter 6 also considers the views of the OECD on the application of DTAs to e-commerce (see **6.9**) since many of the UK's DTAs mirror the fundamental principles reflected in the OECD Model Tax Convention. In this regard many countries will be influenced by the OECD Model.

8.2 RESIDENT AND NON-RESIDENT CORPORATIONS

The problem with the supply of goods and/or services on a cross-border basis is that there is often no single system for the taxation of business income and asset transfers between the country of residence and country of source (ie the country in which the economic activity is carried on). The exception to this is the EU, which operates a common system of VAT (see Part V) and a core set of principles in relation to the payment of dividends, interest and royalties between associated companies (see Chapter 6). The consequences of not having a single tax base are very often that the taxation of income and capital is dependent on the location of the holding company and subsidiaries; tax rates vary between countries leading to competition to attract business; and the allocation of taxing rights between countries is not consistent.

In developing a structure for a holding company and cross-border business operations it is necessary to take account of a number of tax-related objectives. In establishing a trading presence in another country it is often necessary to determine whether a company should be incorporated, or whether a branch or agency (ie a permanent establishment) should be set up in that country. Each of these choices is likely to result in the profits of the business in the other country being subject to local taxes. Where this is the case it will be necessary to consider the extent to which DTA will extinguish, reduce or otherwise provide relief for any element of double taxation between the home country and country of source in which the business is carried on (see **8.5** on the nature of DTAs).

If the decision is made to incorporate a company in another country it is necessary to consider issues such as the rate of taxation in that country, whether inbound/outbound dividends/royalties/interest are subject to withholding taxes, whether the country has an extensive DTA network, OECD-compliant transfer pricing rules, whether there are any capital/stamp duties on establishing or transfer of shareholdings and VAT issues. In developing a structure it is necessary to identify the tax objectives of the structuring operation. These objectives are typically to achieve profitable growth by minimisation of taxes on operating income or any capital arising on the disposal of an investment and to minimise taxes on profit, capital distributions and intra-group supplies.

Unless an internet business activity is within a specific charge to corporation tax or income, there is no right for the UK tax authorities to impose tax on the economic activity.[1] As discussed in Chapter 6, a company, irrespective of where it is incorporated, is subject to corporation tax if it is a resident of the UK. A company is a UK resident

---

[1] Tax can only be charged on a taxpayer if the charging statute clearly and unambiguously applies. Otherwise HMRC has no right to charge tax: see *Partington v Attorney-General* (1869) LR 4 100, at 122, HL.

if either (a) it is incorporated in the UK[2] or (b) it has its central management and control in the UK.[3] A UK resident company is subject to corporation tax on all of its profits (both income and chargeable gains) irrespective of where they arise. Where a non-resident company is not incorporated in the UK it is important to ensure that it is not centrally managed and controlled in the UK, otherwise its worldwide profits will be subject to corporation tax.

A non UK-resident company is subject to corporation tax if it carries on a trade through a permanent establishment in the UK.[4] The chargeable profits of a permanent establishment will comprise trading income, any non-trading income from property or rights used by or held by or for the permanent establishment (such as interest or income derived from patent rights) and capital gains arising from assets held for the purposes of the trade of the permanent establishment.[5]

The nature of the charge to tax on resident and non-resident companies is considered in further detail in Chapter 6.

8.3   UK TAXATION OF FOREIGN PROFITS

A UK resident company is subject to corporation tax on all of its profits (both income and chargeable gains) irrespective of where they arise (the basis on which profits are calculated is explored in Chapter 7).[6] Trading profits from a non-UK trade will be calculated on the same basis as a UK trade.[7] However, where appropriate, relief will typically be given for foreign taxes.[8] A non UK-resident company is subject to corporation tax if it carries on a trade through a permanent establishment in the UK.[9] It may also be subject to UK income tax if it is trading in the UK without having a permanent establishment (although this is usually covered by an applicable double tax treaty).The chargeable profits of a permanent establishment will comprise trading income, any non-trading income from property or rights used by or held by or for the permanent establishment (such as interest or income derived from patent rights) and capital gains arising from assets held for the purposes of the trade of the permanent establishment.[10]

United Kingdom
Taxation: General

---

[2]   CTA 2009, s 14(1). This is the case even if a different place of residence is given by a rule of law.

[3]   *De Beers Consolidated Mines Ltd v Howe* 5 TC 198 at 213; *Unit Construction Co Ltd v Bullock (Inspector of Taxes)* [1959] All ER 831; *American Thread Co v Joyce* 6 TC 163 at 165.

[4]   CTA 2009, s 5(2).

[5]   CTA 2009, s 19(2), (3).

[6]   CTA 2009, s 5(1).

[7]   CTA 2009, s 35.

[8]   Relief will be given in accordance with the provisions of the Taxation (International and Other Provisions) Act 2010 (TIOPA 2010).

[9]   CTA 2009, s 5(2).

[10]   CTA 2009, s 19(2), (3).

Where a UK company receives profits from a foreign permanent establishment it may opt to elect for exemption from corporation tax for those foreign profits.[11] If profits are exempt from corporation tax due to the election then any losses will be excluded to the extent that they arise from the foreign permanent establishment. Once made the election is irrevocable.[12] Specific rules govern the basis on which the profits of the foreign permanent establishment will be calculated (either in accordance with a DTA or by reference to the OECD Model Tax Convention (July 2010)).[13] It is not possible to make this election if the company is a small company with a permanent establishment that is not in what is called a full treaty territory.[14]

8.4   UNILATERAL RELIEF FOR FOREIGN TAX

Where income (such as royalties) is received under deduction of withholding taxes from the country of source and relief under a DTA is not available, it is possible for a UK company to claim credit for (ie the country in which the royalties arise) the withholding by way of unilateral relief. The rules give credit for tax incurred in a territory outside the UK in respect of income or gains arising in that territory.[15] Any tax paid under the law of another territory on income or gains accruing in that territory is allowed as a deduction against any UK income tax, capital gains tax or corporation tax in respect of that income or gain.[16]

This relief is effective where, for example, copyright is owned by a UK resident in a country with which the UK has no DTA. However, this relief does have restrictions in that it only applies to income arising or chargeable gains accruing in the foreign territory.[17] By way of concession HMRC permit unilateral relief to be claimed in other circumstances in respect of intellectual property.[18] The concession applies to copyright, patent rights, industrial designs, secret processes, formulae, trade marks or

---

[11]   CTA 2009, s 18A.
[12]   CTA 2009, s 18F.
[13]   CTA 2009, s 18A(4)–(6).
[14]   CTA 2009, s 18P. A full treaty territory is one with which the UK has entered into a DTA, and which includes a non-discrimination article that applies to permanent establishments in that territory: CTA 2009, s 18R.
[15]   TIOPA 2010, s 18.
[16]   TIOPA 2010, s 9.
[17]   TIOPA 2010, s 9.
[18]   Extra-Statutory Concession B8 (1994) *Double Taxation Relief: Income Consisting of Royalties and 'Know-How' Payments*. The concession provides as follows: 'Payments made by a person resident in an overseas country to a person carrying on a trade in the United Kingdom as consideration for the use of, or for the privilege of using, in the overseas country any copyright, patent, design, secret process or formula, trade-mark or other like property may in law be payments the source of which is in the United Kingdom, but are nevertheless treated for the purpose of credit (whether under double taxation agreements or by way of unilateral relief) as income arising outside the United Kingdom except to the extent that they represent consideration for services (other than merely incidental services) rendered in this country by the recipient to the payer.'

other similar property. A UK resident may licence intellectual property for use abroad; however, the source of the revenue or gains may in law be regarded as arising in the UK. If withholding tax is imposed upon the payments in the foreign territory, it is clear that the unilateral relief provision would not apply. HMRC by concession permits the relief to be claimed in the aforementioned circumstances despite the fact that the source of the payments is within the UK.

8.5 DOUBLE TAXATION AGREEMENTS

Many countries impose some form of tax on income or profits that are created by a non-resident in that country. In each case it will always be necessary for a non-resident to examine the precise circumstances in which a charge to tax will arise on business profits derived from a permanent establishment, or in respect of payments of royalties, interest and dividends. Where tax charges do arise in another country it should be possible to ensure that the tax is reduced or eliminated or that credit is available against home country taxes (ie, UK tax) by virtue of the terms of a DTA, provided such an agreement exists between the UK and that country. However, to qualify for the benefits of a DTA it is often necessary, among other things, to ensure that the UK taxpayer is the beneficial owner of the relevant income, otherwise the benefits of the DTA will usually be denied.

The UK has entered into over one hundred DTAs with other countries, the purpose of which is to eliminate or reduce double taxation that would otherwise arise in the country of source of business activities and the country of residence of a taxpayer. Many of the UK's DTAs are based on the OECD Model Tax Convention on Income and on Capital (the OECD Model Convention). In considering how tax will be applied to internet business activities carried on by a UK resident in another country, it is appropriate to refer to the principles of the Model Convention. Since the development of the OECD Model Convention, most of the UK's DTAs are based upon the concepts of the Model. In this regard, the OECD Commentary on the OECD Model Convention should also be referred to in applying the provisions of a DTA given the influence that the OECD Model Convention has had on the negotiation of tax treaties between countries.

8.5.1 Elimination of double taxation

Double taxation arises where two countries claim tax in respect of the same income, profits or capital gains. The nature of double taxation varies. It could arise where both countries tax the same person in respect of the same item of income, profit or gain (e g royalties taxed in the source country in which they arise and the country of residence of the recipient). There may also be economic double taxation which arises where both countries tax the same item of income, profit or gain, but in the hands of different recipients (e g tax paid by a company on profits in the country of its residence and tax imposed in another country on dividends distributed to shareholders who are residents of that other country). The function of any DTA is to eliminate double taxation that would otherwise arise under the taxation laws of different countries.

The scope of relief will depend upon the terms of the relevant DTA. The relief of double taxation under DTAs is usually achieved by employing different mechanisms which include: (1) exempting certain types of income from tax in one Contracting State such as the country of source (e g interest and royalties under Arts 11 and 12 of the OECD Model Convention); (2) reducing the rate of tax imposed by the Contracting State of source in which the income arises (e g by a reduction in the rate of withholding tax imposed on royalties: see Art 12 of the OECD Model Convention); (3) provision of credit relief by the Contracting State of residence of the recipient for the taxes incurred on income, profit or gains which are imposed by the source Contracting State (e g see Art 23A of the OECD Model Convention).

Alternatively, it is sometimes possible for a UK taxpayer to claim 'unilateral relief' which permits foreign tax chargeable on income or gains to be allowed as a credit against the UK income or corporation tax liability on the same income or gains.[19] The following paragraphs discuss the generic nature of certain articles which are usually to be found in DTAs, and which are likely to be relevant to an internet business. Many of the DTAs will be based on the OECD Model Convention. But it is important to examine in each case the extent of the relief available under a specific DTA.

8.5.2   Business profits

The OECD Model Convention provides that a company resident in one country (e g the UK) cannot be taxed on its business profits in another country unless it carries on business in that other country through a permanent establishment.[20] The business profits article will often restrict the provisions of domestic tax laws to the scope of activities that are attributable to the country of source (see Chapter 6 at **6.2** for the UK's domestic rules).

Where a company does carry on a business in another country through a permanent establishment, that enterprise may be taxed only on the profits attributable to the permanent establishment. Article 7 of the OECD Model Convention will determine the extent to which a Contracting State can tax the business profits derived from a permanent establishment under its domestic tax laws. Usually, the business profits article will

---

[19]   See **8.4**.
[20]   See OECD Model Convention (July 2010), Art 7(1).

require that the profits of the permanent establishment are to be calculated as if that establishment were a separate and independent enterprise engaged in the same or similar activities under the same or similar conditions, taking into account the functions performed, assets used and risks assumed by the enterprise through the permanent establishment and through other parts of the enterprise: see Chapter 6 at **6.10** for a review of the UK's approach to the allocation of profits.

8.5.3 Permanent establishment

The definition of permanent establishment is often of critical importance to many articles of a DTA (such as the business profit, interest and royalty articles). The business profits article (see above), will often provide that a resident of one country is not to be taxed in another country on business profits unless it carries on business in that other country through a permanent establishment. The concept is defined as meaning 'a fixed place of business through which the business of an enterprise is wholly or partly carried on'.[21] The term 'permanent establishment' in Art 5 of the OECD Model Convention is defined as including a 'place of management', 'branch', 'office' and 'factory'. The nature of the UK's domestic tax definition of permanent establishment is examined in Chapter 7.

The OECD Commentary on the concept of permanent establishment makes the following points on the definition of permanent establishment:[22]

- there must be a 'place of business', that is, a facility such as premises or, in certain instances, machinery or equipment;

- the place of business must be 'fixed', that is, it must be established at a distinct place with a certain degree of permanence; and

- the business of the enterprise must be carried on through the fixed place of business.

The business profits article will normally state that various activities within a country cannot constitute a permanent establishment, and as such imposes a fundamental limitation on the ability of a country to tax those activities. The activities that typically do not comprise a permanent establishment will include the following:[23]

(a) the use of facilities solely for the purpose of storage, display or delivery of goods or merchandise belonging to the enterprise;

---

[21] See OECD Model Convention (July 2010), Art 5(1).
[22] OECD Commentary on the OECD Model Convention (July 2010), para 2 on Art 5.
[23] See OECD Model Convention (July 2010), Art 5(4).

(b)   the maintenance of a stock of goods or merchandise belonging to the enterprise solely for the purpose of storage, display or delivery;

(c)   the maintenance of a stock of goods or merchandise belonging to the enterprise solely for the purpose of processing by another enterprise;

(d)   the maintenance of a fixed place of business solely for the purpose of purchasing goods or merchandise, or of collecting information, for the enterprise;

(e)   the maintenance of a fixed place of business solely for the purpose of carrying on, for the enterprise, any other activity of a preparatory or auxiliary character;

(f)   the maintenance of a fixed place of business solely for any combination of the activities mentioned in (a)–(e), provided that the overall activity of the fixed place of business resulting from this combination is of a preparatory or auxiliary character.

The permanent establishment article will also normally identify the circumstances in which an agent operating in another country will be a permanent establishment. An agent is usually only capable of being a permanent establishment if the agent is a 'dependent agent'. This is an agent who acts on behalf of a person and has and habitually exercises an authority to conclude contracts that are binding on the person.[24] An independent agent is often excluded from being a permanent establishment; and in this regard an independent agent can usually never constitute a permanent establishment provided that the agent is acting in the ordinary course of its business as an independent agent.[25]

8.5.4   Interest

The OECD Model Convention provides that interest beneficially owned by a resident of one country cannot be taxed, by the country in which the interest arises, at a rate in excess of 10% of the gross amount of the interest.[26] However, it is often the case that both countries will agree for interest to be paid on a gross basis to the resident of a Contracting State who is beneficially entitled to the interest (in other words, the rate of withholding is nil). There will also often be an exception that preserves source taxation in respect of interest attributable to a permanent establishment located in the country of source.

---

[24]   See OECD Model Convention (July 2010), Art 5(5).
[25]   See OECD Model Convention (July 2010), Art 5(6).
[26]   See OECD Model Convention (July 2010), Art 11(0).

8.5.5 Royalties

The royalties article of many DTAs in the UK network, based on the OECD Model Convention, will provide an exclusive right of taxation to the country of residence of the recipient of royalties (ie the country of source will have no right to impose withholding tax on the royalties). However, there will usually be an exception that preserves source taxation in respect of royalties attributable to a permanent establishment located in the country of source (such as the UK). The definition of royalties will typically include:[27] (i) copyright of literary, artistic, or scientific work (including cinematographic films), (ii) any patent, (iii) trade mark, (iv) design or model, plan, (v) secret formula or process and (vi) information concerning industrial, commercial or scientific experience. Additionally, some older treaties include, in the royalties definition, payments for the use of or right to use industrial, commercial or scientific equipment.

Typically, the benefits of a royalties article will be denied or restricted where there is a special relationship between the payer and the recipient of the royalties, and the amount of royalties paid between those persons exceeds for whatever reason the amount which would have been paid in an arm's length situation. In such circumstances, the excess of the royalties over an arm's length rate do not qualify for the benefits of the article but remain taxable under the domestic laws of the two countries.

8.5.6　Relief from double taxation

In addition to the rules restricting the country of source from taxing income and gains (eg on 'business profits', 'interest dividends' or 'royalties'), the provisions of a DTA if based on the OECD Model Convention will also provide that double taxation is relieved by the country of residence of the recipient of income, profits or gains allowing exemption from tax or credit for taxes paid in the country in respect of which such income, profits or gains arise.[28] The normal basis for relief in the UK is by permitting a credit to be allowed for any non-UK tax payable on profits, income or chargeable capital gains from sources within the other country against the UK tax computed by reference to the same profits, income or chargeable capital gains. The nature and scope of available relief will need to be considered according to the specific circumstances of each case.

United Kingdom
Taxation: General

---

[27]   See OECD Model Convention (July 2010), Art 12(2).
[28]   See OECD Model Convention (July 2010), Arts 23A and 23B.

8.6   OECD COMMENTARIES RELEVANT TO E-COMMERCE

8.6.1   General

Considerable weight should be attached to the Commentaries of the OECD where a DTA is based on its provisions. They are used as an aid by the UK courts, and the Commentaries have also influenced the practice of HMRC. The concept of permanent establishment will be of importance in determining the extent to which corporation tax or income tax can be imposed upon a non-resident engaged in internet business activities in the UK. The Commentaries make a number of important observations that can assist in determining the extent to which the internet business will be captured by UK tax.

The term 'permanent establishment' is identified by the key characteristic of a 'distinct situs' and a 'fixed place of business'. The Commentaries draw the following inferences from the definition of permanent establishment, which must be satisfied for it to exist:[29]

- the existence of a 'place of business', ie a facility such as premises or, in certain instances, machinery or equipment;

- this place of business must be 'fixed', ie it must be established as a distinct place with a certain degree of permanence; and

- the carrying on of the business of the enterprise through this fixed place of business.

This usually means that persons who, in one way or another, are dependent on the enterprise (personnel) conduct the business of the enterprise in the State in which the fixed place is situated.

It is worth pausing to highlight the inference drawn in the Commentaries that 'machinery or equipment' is capable of forming the subject matter of a place of business. This must, therefore, extend to computer hardware from which an internet business is operated by computer software. Where a DTA is in place, a permanent establishment is relevant to a charge to UK income/corporation tax because this must exist in addition to a trade being exercised in the UK. The following observations from the Commentaries are of relevance in determining the extent to which an internet business comes within the concept of permanent establishment:

---

[29]   See OECD Commentary on the OECD Model Convention (July 2010), Art 5. See para 2.

- the fact that an establishment fulfils a 'productive character' to a whole organisation, it does not necessarily follow that it is a permanent establishment to which profits can be attributed (Commentary to Art 5, para 3);

- 'place of business' includes any facilities or installations used for carrying on the business (Commentary to Art 5, para 4);

- a place of business can exist whether premises, facilities or installations are owned or rented by the enterprise concerned (Commentary to Art 5, para 4);

- a place of business may be situated in the business facilities of another enterprise (Commentary to Art 5, para 4);

- a place of business must be a fixed one (Commentary to Art 5, para 5);

- equipment constituting a place of business does not have to be fixed on the soil on which it stands (Commentary to Art 5, para 5);

- the place of business must have a degree of permanency (Commentary to Art 5, para 6);

- a permanent establishment does not exist where the place of business has a purely temporary nature (Commentary to Art 5, para 6);

- an enterprise must carry on a business activity through the place of business either wholly or partially (Commentary to Art 5, para 7);

- there can be an interruption to the operation of the business activity, but the activity must be carried out on a regular basis (Commentary to Art 5, para 7);

- a permanent establishment may exist if the business of an enterprise is carried on mainly through automatic equipment, and the activities of personnel of an enterprise are restricted to setting up, operating, controlling and maintaining such equipment (Commentary to Art 5, para 10);

- the Commentaries give as an example the illustration of gaming or vending machines which are set up by an enterprise in a Contracting State. A permanent establishment may exist if the enterprise which sets up the machines also operates and maintains the machines for its own account (Commentary to Art 5, para 10).

Against this background, it appears that the existence of a computer server in the UK, which operates an internet trade in every sense of the

United Kingdom
Taxation: General

word would be sufficient to allow the UK to tax a non-resident. However, this is not HMRC practice (see Chapter 6 at **6.4**).

8.6.2   Specific Commentary

The OECD Commentary on the OECD Model Convention contains specific provisions on e-commerce.[30] In summary the conclusions reached are that:[31]

- a website cannot in itself constitute a permanent establishment;

- website hosting arrangements will not typically result in a permanent establishment for the enterprise that carries on business through that website; and

- the functions performed by internet service providers (ISPs) will not typically constitute a dependent agent of another enterprise so as to constitute a permanent establishment of that enterprise.

However, it is interesting to note that Spain and Portugal consider that physical presence is not a requirement necessary for a permanent establishment to exist, and accordingly consider that in some circumstances an enterprise carrying on a business in a State through a website could be treated as having a permanent establishment.[32]

The OECD Commentary draws a distinction between the tangible instruments of e-commerce, namely a computer server (IT), and the intangible instruments, namely software and data which is used by, or stored on, the computer equipment. The main conclusions adopted by the OECD are as follows:[33]

- A website of an e-commerce business is a combination of software and electronic data stored on and operated by a server. A website cannot of itself constitute a 'place of business' because it does not

---

[30]   These are based on the views of the Committee of Fiscal Affairs of the OECD published in a paper on permanent establishments in the context of websites and computer equipment, 'Clarification on the application of the permanent establishment definition in e-commerce: changes to the commentary on the model tax convention on article 5' (22 December 2000). This clarification paper reflects the changes to the Commentary on the Model Convention which were adopted by the Committee on Fiscal Affairs on 22 December 2000.

[31]   'Clarification on the application of the permanent establishment definition in e-commerce: changes to the commentary on the model tax convention on article 5' (22 December 2000), para 6.

[32]   Ibid, para 6.

[33]   Ibid, para 5.

constitute any form of tangible property. This is because there is no 'facility such as premises or, in certain circumstances, machinery or equipment'.[34]

- A server may constitute a permanent establishment because it is a piece of tangible equipment which requires a physical location and may thus be fixed and constitute a 'fixed place of business' within Art 5(1) of the OECD Model Convention.[35]

- A distinction must be made between an enterprise operating a computer server (ie an ISP), which hosts the website of another enterprise, and using the website to carry on a trade. The mere operation of a website by an enterprise from a server owned by another enterprise (ie an ISP) located in a country cannot constitute a permanent establishment since the fees paid for these servers are typically based on the amount of disk space used to store software and data required by the website, and the contracts do not as a rule result in the server being at the disposal of the enterprise. In these circumstances the non-resident does not have a physical presence in a country since the website is not tangible.[36]

- If a non-resident carries on business through a website on a server that is at its own disposal (whether owned or leased) and operates the server on which the website is stored and used, then the place where the server is located could constitute a permanent establishment of the non-resident (subject to the other conditions of the permanent establishment article being met).[37]

- Computer equipment, such as a server, may only constitute a permanent establishment if it is fixed for the purposes of Art 5 of the OECD Model Convention. The Commentary emphasises that in order to constitute a fixed place of business, a server will need to be located at a certain place for a sufficient period of time so as to be fixed within the meaning of Art 5.1 of the Model Convention.[38]

- Automated equipment which does not require on-site human assistance for its operation can constitute a permanent establishment.[39]

- No permanent establishment can exist where the operations of the computer equipment are restricted to preparatory or auxiliary activities within Art 5(4) of the OECD Model Convention. In

United Kingdom Taxation: General

---

[34] See Commentary on Art 5, para 42.2.
[35] See Commentary on Art 5, para 42.2.
[36] See Commentary on Art 5, para 42.3.
[37] See Commentary on Art 5, para 42.3.
[38] See Commentary on Art 5, para 42.4.
[39] See Commentary on Art 5, para 42.6.

assessing whether this is the case it is necessary to identify the functions being performed by the equipment. Examples of activities which would generally be regarded as preparatory or auxiliary include:[40]

- providing a communication link between suppliers and customers;
- advertising of goods or services;
- relaying information through a mirror server for security and efficiency purposes;
- gathering market data for the enterprise;
- supplying information.

- The Commentary emphasises that where the functions performed through the computer equipment include activities that form in themselves an essential and significant part of the commercial activity of an enterprise as a whole, then assuming the equipment is a fixed place of business it would constitute a permanent establishment (since the activities would go beyond preparatory or auxiliary activities).[41]

- In assessing what qualifies as preparatory or auxiliary activities it is necessary to examine the nature of the activities performed at a location in light of the business carried on by the enterprise. Thus if the activities are preparatory or auxiliary to the business of selling products on the internet, for example, the location is used to operate a server that hosts a website that is used exclusively for advertising, displaying a catalogue of products or providing information to prospective customers, then the location will not constitute a permanent establishment. By contrast if the functions related to a sale are performed at that location, for example, the conclusion of the contract with the customer, processing of the payment and delivery of the products, are performed automatically via the equipment at that location then the activities will not be regarded as preparatory or auxiliary.[42]

- Generally, ISPs hosting a website for another enterprise will not be a deemed permanent establishment within Art 5(5) of the OECD Model Convention. This is because the ISPs will not constitute agents of the enterprises because the ISPs will not have authority to conclude contracts in the name of the enterprises that own the websites, and neither will the ISPs regularly conclude contracts on their behalf. ISPs even if acting as agent will generally be doing so as independent agents acting in the ordinary course of business and so will not constitute a permanent establishment. The independent

---

[40] See Commentary on Art 5, para 42.7.
[41] See Commentary on Art 5, para 42.8.
[42] See Commentary on Art 5, para 42.9.

nature of the ISPs is often evidenced by the fact that they host the websites of many different enterprises.[43]

- A website is not a 'person' within Art 3 (definitions) of the OECD Model Convention, and consequently Art 5(5) cannot apply to deem a permanent establishment to exist by reason of the website being an agent of the enterprise.[44]

The OECD Commentary provides clarity and certainty in the application of DTAs based on the OECD Model Convention. The enduring problem of e-commerce for national tax authorities is the transitory and intangible nature of it. The concept of permanent establishment is not capable of dealing with intangible instruments such as software and data used to carry on an e-commerce trade.[45]

8.7   ATTRIBUTION OF PROFITS TO A PERMANENT ESTABLISHMENT

8.7.1   OECD Model Convention and Commentary

The profits to be attributed to a permanent establishment of a non-resident company will generally be determined in accordance with the provisions of a DTA, in combination with domestic tax rules. The problem with profit attribution is that the permanent establishment is part of a far larger company, and it has no legal personality that is separate and distinct from the overall company of which it forms a part. The OECD Model Convention provides that the profits to be attributed to a permanent establishment are those which it might be expected to make if it were a separate and independent enterprise engaged in the same or similar activities under the same or similar conditions, taking into account the functions performed, assets used and risks assumed by the enterprise through the permanent establishment and through the other parts of the enterprise.[46] The Commentary to the Model Convention makes the point that this principle corresponds to the 'arm's length principle' applicable to Art 9 of the Model Convention in respect of transactions between associated enterprises.[47]

The OECD Commentary explains a two-step approach that should be taken for determining the profits of a permanent establishment, which is as follows:[48]

---

[43]   See Commentary on Art 5, para 42.10.
[44]   See Commentary on Art 5, para 42.10.
[45]   See generally 'Clarification on the Application of the Permanent Establishment Definition in E-commerce: Changes to the Commentary on the Model Tax Convention on Article 5' (22 December 2000).
[46]   See OECD Model Convention (July 2010), Art 6.2.
[47]   OECD Commentary (para 16) on Art 7(2) of the Model Convention.
[48]   OECD Commentary (paras 21–22) on Art 7(2) of the Model Convention.

'Under the first step, a functional and factual analysis is undertaken which will lead to:

- the attribution to the permanent establishment, as appropriate, of the rights and obligations arising out of transactions between the enterprise of which the permanent establishment is a part and separate enterprises;
- the identification of significant people functions relevant to the attribution of economic ownership of assets, and the attribution of economic ownership of assets to the permanent establishment;
- the identification of significant people functions relevant to the assumption of risks, and the attribution of risks to the permanent establishment;
- the identification of other functions of the permanent establishment;
- the recognition and determination of the nature of those dealings between the permanent establishment and other parts of the same enterprise that can appropriately be recognised ..., and
- the attribution of capital based on the assets and risks attributed to the permanent establishment.

Under the second step, any transactions with associated enterprises attributed to the permanent establishment are priced in accordance with the guidance of the OECD Transfer Pricing Guidelines and these Guidelines are applied by analogy to dealings between the permanent establishment and the other parts of the enterprise of which it is a part. The process involves the pricing on an arm's length basis of these recognised dealings through:

- the determination of comparability between the dealings and uncontrolled transactions, established by applying the Guidelines' comparability factors directly (characteristics of property or services, economic circumstances and business strategies) or by analogy (functional analysis, contractual terms) in light of the particular factual circumstances of the permanent establishment; and
- the application by analogy of one of the Guidelines' methods to arrive at an arm's length compensation for the dealings between the permanent establishment and the other parts of the enterprise, taking into account the functions performed by and the assets and risks attributed to the permanent establishment and the other parts of the enterprise.'

8.7.2 OECD Discussion Draft on Attribution of Profit to a Permanent Establishment Involved in Electronic Commerce Transactions

The OECD issued in February 2001 a discussion paper, 'Attribution of Profit to a Permanent Establishment Involved in Electronic Commerce Transactions'.[49] The scope of the paper is limited to a review of the application of Art 7 of the OECD Model Convention (as it existed prior to that adopted in July 2010) to a permanent establishment constituted as a computer server, carrying on retail e-commerce activities. The principal conclusions of the paper are that the amount of profit to be attributed to

---

[49] February 2001. Available at www.oecd.org (2011). This is reproduced at Appendix E.

a permanent establishment will be related to the nature of the functions that it performs.[50] Further, that in the context of a stand-alone computer server the functional and factual analysis is likely to show that the permanent establishment is performing only routine functions and is reliant on the other parts of the enterprise, ie the head office to provide the intangible assets necessary for it to perform its functions.[51] Against such a background the activities of the computer server would not warrant the attribution of a substantial share of the profits associated with the distribution activities of the enterprise conducted through the computer server.[52]

The OECD paper also argues that the absence of personnel is likely to mean that tasks performed by the computer server are likely to be conducted under a 'contract service provider' arrangement that would leave all substantial assets and risks with the head office and attribute to the permanent establishment the profits associated with the physical operation of the computer server.[53] The paper also discusses the possibility that the permanent establishment could be considered an 'independent service provider'. If this was the case, the conclusion would be similar, given the requirement for the permanent establishment to recognise in computing its profits the arm's length value of tangible and intangible property that it uses and that were contributed by the other parts of the enterprise, namely the head office.[54]

The discussion paper comments that in applying Art 7(2) of the OECD Model Convention (which is similar to the July 2010 version), in attributing profits it is necessary to adopt a two-stage approach (which is similar to that described above in the subsequent commentary on the July 2010 version of the OECD Model Convention). The discussion paper remains relevant in how to approach these issues relating to computer servers. As to the approach, first, it is necessary to carry out a functional and factual analysis to hypothesise the permanent establishment and the remainder of the enterprise as if they were associated enterprises, each undertaking functions, using assets and assuming risks. Secondly, it is necessary to analyse the OECD Transfer Pricing Guidelines relevant to applying the arm's length principle to the hypothesised enterprises so undertaking functions, using assets and assuming risks.[55] Accordingly, the approach advocated in attributing profits is to apply the approach adopted in the OECD Transfer Pricing Guidelines. The key approach in this context is the carrying out of a functional analysis to determine what activities are undertaken by the enterprise as a whole, and then determine which activities (including the extent) of the enterprise that are associated

United Kingdom
Taxation: General

---

[50] 'Attribution of profit to a permanent establishment involved in electronic commerce transactions' (February 2001), para 8.
[51] Ibid, para 8.
[52] Ibid, para 8.
[53] Ibid, para 8.
[54] Ibid, para 8.
[55] Ibid, para 27.

with the permanent establishment.[56] Part of the functional analysis includes indentifying the assets used and risks assumed by the permanent establishment. The reason for this is that the use of assets should be taken into account in rewarding the functions performed by the permanent establishment.[57] The next step is to attribute to the permanent establishment the risks which are inherent in, or created by, its functions and the risks which arise from its activities.[58]

Once the functional analysis is completed the OECD paper discusses how the permanent establishment should obtain an arm's length return for its functions, taking into account the assets used and risks assumed, in the same manner as would a comparable independent enterprise.[59] A comparison would then be made of the 'dealings' between the permanent establishment and the enterprise, with transactions between independent enterprises.[60]

The OECD discussion paper contains extensive analysis on the attribution of profits to a computer server. The primary findings of the paper are summarised as follows:

- If the permanent establishment comprises solely a computer server supporting a website through which commercial transactions are executed and digitised products are transmitted, then the bulk of the benefit to the permanent establishment is derived from the exploitation of hardware and software and marketing intangibles. In such circumstances it is likely that the arrangements between the head office and the permanent establishment can be characterised as either a 'contract service provider', or an 'independent service provider' arrangement. Under the former, economic ownership and risks associated with the property and marketing intangibles (such as brand name) will remain with the head office. Under the latter, the head office will have transferred a package of assets to the permanent establishment, and an arm's length charge for such a transfer would attribute the bulk of the profits directly associated with the assets to the head office.[61] In these circumstances the computer server is regarded as performing functions which only represent a small part of the functions necessary to act as a full function retail outlet. The amount of profit to be attributed to the permanent establishment is accordingly likely to be small.[62]

- Where personnel are present in support of the computer server for the purposes of ensuring continuous operation of a website and

---

[56] Ibid, para 28.
[57] Ibid, para 29.
[58] Ibid, para 30.
[59] Ibid, para 32.
[60] Ibid, para 33.
[61] Ibid, para 140.
[62] Ibid, para 140.

providing technical support to customers, the permanent establishment should be attributed with the profits associated with such service functions. The profits associated with the exploitation of hardware and software created by the enterprise and from marketing intangibles would continue to be substantially attributed to the head office.[63]

- If hardware and software is developed and constructed by personnel of the permanent establishment so that the permanent establishment is treated as the economic owner of the intangible property, then the profit directly associated with the commercial exploitation of such assets should be attributable to the permanent establishment. If software is developed partly by the head office, then an appropriate proportion of the profits derived from the commercial exploitation of such asset should be allocated between the head office and the permanent establishment. The proportion allocated to the permanent establishment should reflect the value of the contribution made by it.[64]

8.8 CHARACTERISATION OF PAYMENTS AND E-COMMERCE ACTIVITIES

8.8.1 Introduction

Payments for the use of intellectual property rights (such as copyright), which are made by a licensee to a non-resident owner/licensor are typically subject to withholding tax.[65] However, a DTA may operate either partially to reduce or to extinguish the amount of tax withheld. Article 12 of the OECD Model Convention applies to royalty payments, and where it applies royalties should only be taxed in the country of residence of the beneficial owner (see **8.5.5**).[66] Many DTAs tend to follow the approach of the OECD Model Convention. If the royalty article does not apply it is likely that the payments will be treated as business profits and subject to Art 7 of the OECD Model Convention which applies to such profits (see **8.5.3**).

Before considering whether a DTA will reduce the amount of source taxation on a payment, it is first necessary to identify whether tax should be withheld at all. In other words, does the payment represent payment for the use of intellectual property, specifically copyright, in the context of e-commerce activities?

---

[63] Ibid, para 140.

[64] Ibid, para 140.

[65] See Chapter 6 for the circumstances in which UK withholding tax is imposed on some types of intellectual property payments.

[66] See OECD Model Convention (July 2010), Art 12(1).

8.8.2 Computer software payments

The characterisation of payments for the use of computer software is considered in the Commentary to the OECD Model Convention.[67] In this regard, the OECD considers that the characterisation of payments for computer software depends upon the qualitative nature of the rights that the transferee obtains under the arrangements for its use and exploitation.[68] Payments made for the right to use computer software on computer hardware or copying a program onto a computer's random access memory (RAM) or making an archival copy are regarded as utilisation rights.[69] Payments associated with this type of use relate to transactions associated with commercial income under the business profits article of the OECD Model Convention (see **8.5.2**). In other words, there should be no issue of withholding tax arising due to the point that the transferee/user is grated a limited right, namely only the right to copy the software/program into the user's hardware. In addition the point is made that payment for a site or network licence (ie which solely enables the licensee to use the program on its network of computers) will in most cases be dealt with as business profits under Art 7 of the OECD Model Convention.[70]

The OECD report on *Tax Treaty Characterisation Issues Arising from E-Commerce*[71] draws the distinction between payments for the use of copyright (which are regarded as royalties) and other payments (which are regarded as business profits) in the following way:[72]

> '14. Since the definition of royalties applies to "payments for" any of the various items listed in that definition, the Group has concluded that, in any given transaction, the main question to be addressed is the identification of the consideration for the payment. Under the relevant legislation of some countries, transactions which permit the customer to electronically download computer programs or other digital content may give rise to use of copyright by the customer, e.g. because a right to make one or more copies of the digital content is granted under the contract. Where the essential consideration is for something other than the use of, or right to use, rights in the copyright (such as to acquire other types of contractual rights, data or services), and the use of copyright is limited to such rights as are required to enable downloading, storage and operation on the customer's computer, network or other storage, performance or display device, such use of copyright should be disregarded in the analysis of the character of the payment for treaty purposes. This would be the case, for instance, where a payment is made by a person for the downloading and the operation of a copy of a computer program. Whilst electronic downloading of the program

---

67 See Commentary on Art 12 of the OECD Model Convention, paras 12–17.
68 Ibid, at para 12.2.
69 Ibid, at para 14.
70 Ibid, at para 14.2.
71 1 February 2001, available at www.oecd.org (2011). The paper is reproduced at Appendix D.
72 At paras 14 and 15.

may or may not constitute the use of a copyright by the user (as opposed to by the provider) depending on the relevant copyright law and contractual arrangements, the essential consideration for the payment is not that possible use of a copyright.

15. In the case of transactions that permit the customer to electronically download digital products (such as software, images, sounds or text), the payment is made to acquire data transmitted in the form of a digital signal for the own use or enjoyment of the acquiror.[73] This constitutes the essential consideration for the payment. To the extent that the act of copying the digital signal onto the customer's hard disk or other non-temporary media (including transfers to other storage, performance or display devices) constitutes the use of a copyright by the customer under the relevant law and contractual arrangements, this is merely an incidental part of the process of capturing and storing the digital signal. This incidental part is not important for classification purposes because it does not correspond to the essential consideration for the payment (ie, to acquire data transmitted in the form of a digital signal), which is the determining factor for the purposes of the treaty definition of royalties.'

The OECD Commentary on Art 12 draws the distinction made in the report.[74] The Commentary makes the point that in characterising payments concerning digital products the main issue is the identification of that for which the payment is essentially made.[75] For instance, if the payment is for something other than the use of copyright (such as to acquire other types of contractual rights, data or services) and the use of the copyright is limited to such rights as necessary to permit downloading, storage and operation on a computer, network or other storage, performance or display device then the use of copyright should not affect the character of the payment as being commercial income.[76] The Commentary notes that transactions where the essential consideration for the payment is the granting of the right to use a copyright in a digital product that is electronically downloaded for that purpose will give rise to royalties.[77]

A royalty payment for the right to reproduce and distribute computer software is regarded as being subject to withholding tax, and will be within the provisions of Art 12 of the OECD Model Convention.[78] This is because the payment is made to acquire a right to use the program in a

---

[73] The same result would apply regardless of whether the payment was made as regards the downloading of one specific product or in the form of a subscription fee for the right to access a website where that digital product may be downloaded.

[74] See Commentary on Art 12 of the OECD Model Convention, at para 17.2.

[75] Ibid, at para 17.2.

[76] Ibid, at para 17.2.

[77] Ibid, at para 17.4.

[78] However, if the consideration is not made for the use of the copyright but instead reflects payment for the transfer of ownership in the copyright, then the provisions of Art 12 will not apply. Instead such payments will either represent commercial income within Art 7 or capital gains within Art 13 of the OECD Model Convention. See paras 15 and 16 of the OECD Commentary on Art 12. The Commentary emphasises

manner that without such a licence would constitute an infringement of the copyright.[79] The acquisition of standardised software via the internet involves the acquisition of a licence which is classified as a utilisation right. In this context, there is no obligation upon the UK consumer to withhold tax upon the payment to a non-resident seller. The OECD Commentary describes the royalty point in the following way:[80]

> '... transactions where the essential consideration for the payment is the granting of the right to use a copyright in a digital product that is electronically downloaded for that purpose will give rise to royalties. This would be the case, for example, of a book publisher who would pay to acquire the right to reproduce a copyrighted picture that it would electronically download for the purposes of including it on the cover of a book that it is producing. In this transaction, the essential consideration for the payment is the acquisition of rights to use the copyright in the digital product, ie, the right to reproduce and distribute the picture, and not merely for the acquisition of the digital content.'

The Commentary emphasises that the method of delivery of the computer software, whether by disc or modem connection, is irrelevant to the characterisation of the payment.[81] Where a payment represents a package price for both hardware and computer software the consideration should where necessary be broken down by reference to the contract or by means of a reasonable apportionment for the purposes of allocating a portion of the consideration to the hardware and software.[82]

8.8.3   E-commerce transactions

In February 2001 the Treaty Characterisation Technical Advisory Group (TAG) released a report, *Tax Treaty Characterisation Issues Arising from E-Commerce*.[83] The TAG was given the mandate to consider the characterisation of various types of e-commerce payments under a DTA for the purposes of recommending any necessary clarification to the Commentary on the OECD Model Tax Convention. Annex 2 of the report provides an analysis of the characterisation of various categories of e-commerce payment in the context of the OECD Model Convention. A summary of the analysis is provided in Table 8.1.

---

that a transaction which is an alienation of rights cannot be for the use of the rights, and that an alienation cannot be altered by the form of the consideration (see para 16 of the Commentary).

[79]   See Commentary on Art 12 of the OECD Model Convention, at para 13.1.
[80]   Ibid, at para 17.4.
[81]   Ibid, at para 14.1.
[82]   Ibid, at para 17.
[83]   1 February 2001, available at www.oecd.org (2011). The report is reproduced at Appendix D.

Table 8.1: Summary of the TAG characterisation of various categories of e-commerce payment in the context of the OECD Model Convention

	Category of e-commerce transaction[84]	Characterisation of payment	
		Payment constitutes business profits (within Art 7 OECD Model Convention)	Payment of royalties for use of copyright or similar rights (within Art 12 OECD Model Convention)
1	Electronic order processing of tangible products	✔	X
2	Electronic ordering and downloading of digital products	✔	X
3	Electronic ordering and downloading of digital products for purposes of commercial exploitation of copyright	X	✔
4	Updates and add-ons related to Category 1	✔	X
5	Updates and add-on related to Category 2	✔	X
6	Limited duration software and other digital information licenses	✔	X
7	Single-use software or other digital product	✔	X
8	Application hosting – separate license	✔	X
9	Application hosting – bundled contract	✔	X
10	Application service provider	✔	X
11	Application service provider license fees	✔	X
12	Website hosting	✔	X

United Kingdom Taxation: General

---

[84] For a description of the nature of the category see *Tax Treaty Characterisation Issues Arising From E-Commerce*, Annex 2.

	Category of e-commerce transaction[84]	Characterisation of payment	
13	Software maintenance	✔[85]	X
14	Data warehousing	✔	X
15	Customer support over a computer network	✔	X
16	Data retrieval	✔	X
17	Delivery of exclusive or other high-value data	✔	X
18	Advertising	✔	X
19	Electronic access to professional advice (eg consultancy)	✔[86]	X
20	Technical information	X	✔[87]
21	Information delivery	✔	X
22	Access to an interactive website	✔	X
23	Online shopping portals	✔	X
24	Online auctions	✔	X
25	Sales referral programs	✔	X
26	Content acquisition transactions: payment for the right to display copyright protected material	X	✔
27	Content acquisition transactions: payment for creation of new content, and buyer becomes owner of the copyright	✔	X
28	Streamed (real time) web based broadcasting	✔	X
29	Carriage fees (eg payment to a website operator for content to be displayed on the website)	✔	X

---

[85] Part of the payment may represent technical fees.
[86] The payment may represent technical fees depending on the definition of technical fees used in a double taxation agreement.
[87] A payment for the supply of know-how.

	Category of e-commerce transaction[84]	Characterisation of payment	
30	Subscription to a website allowing the downloading of digital products	✔	X

8.8.4 Know-how and services

A further characterisation issue relates to the distinction between the provision of know-how and services. Article 12 of the OECD Model Convention applies to royalty payments, and the term 'royalties' is defined to include payments 'for information concerning industrial, commercial or scientific experience'.[88] Payments for the provision of services will be subject to the provisions of Art 7 (business profits) of the OECD Model Convention. The Commentary distinguishes between know-how and services in the following way. Contracts for the supply of know-how are concerned with information which is undivulged technical information that is necessary for the industrial reproduction of a product or process which is derived from experience, and that already exists; or concerns the supply of such information after its development or creation and includes specific provisions concerning the confidentiality of that information.[89] By contrast, contracts for the provision of services involve the supplier undertaking to perform services which may require the use, by that supplier, of special knowledge, skill or expertise (but not the transfer of such knowledge, skill or expertise to the other party).[90] The Commentary gives the following example in the context of e-commerce of what would be regarded as a payment for the provision of services:[91]

> '... payments for advice provided electronically, for electronic communications with technicians or for accessing, through computer networks, a trouble-shooting database such as a database that provides users of software with non-confidential information in response to frequently asked questions or common problems that arise frequently.'

Further, the Commentary makes the point that, in a contract for the provision of information by a supplier concerning computer programming, the payment will only be considered to be made in consideration for the provision of such information so as to constitute know-how where it is made to acquire information constituting ideas and principles underlying

---

[88]   Art 12(2). Most DTAs contain a royalty article, which allocates taxing rights to contracting states. Sometimes under such an agreement the country of source of a royalty payment will be permitted to tax a percentage of the payment. However, many DTAs permit royalty payments to be paid gross provided that the recipient is the beneficial owner. If the right in respect of which a royalty is paid is connected with a permanent establishment the royalty article is generally disapplied in favour of the business profits article (see Art 7 of the OECD Model Convention).

[89]   See Commentary on Art 12 of the OECD Model Convention, at para 11.3.

[90]   Ibid, at para 11.3.

[91]   Ibid, at para 11.4.

the program, such as logic, algorithms or programming languages or techniques, subject to the customer not disclosing such information without the authorisation of the supplier, and that information being subject to any available trade secret protection.[92]

---

[92]   Ibid, at para 11.5.

CHAPTER 9

TRANSFER PRICING

9.1 INTRODUCTION

9.1.1 The impact of e-commerce on functional profile

Transfer pricing is a significant business concern for multinational groups, with a plethora of legislative developments in recent years designed to limit the ability of multinational groups to engage in aggressive tax arbitrage planning. The basic rule is that taxable profits in a particular jurisdiction will be determined by the economic significance of functions performed, risks managed and assets employed in that jurisdiction to generate profits. The ability to shift functions, risks and assets is proportional to the arbitrage benefits that could be obtained and e-commerce is a forum in which that ability is heightened, given the following characteristics that will impact the functional profile of a business across the supply chain:

- increased visibility of information;

- reduced barriers to entry impacting competition;

- impact on the traditional longevity of supply chain relationships;

- increased speed of decision making;

- increased connectivity with customers and suppliers; and

- increased uncertainty.

Note that a business adopting e-commerce across the supply chain will not necessarily trigger transfer pricing issues unless the functional profile of the business is impacted across borders (whilst UK transfer pricing legislation applies to UK transactions for large companies,[1] the tax impact of domestic transactions is neutral in the majority of cases).

---

[1] See **9.3.4** for further details.

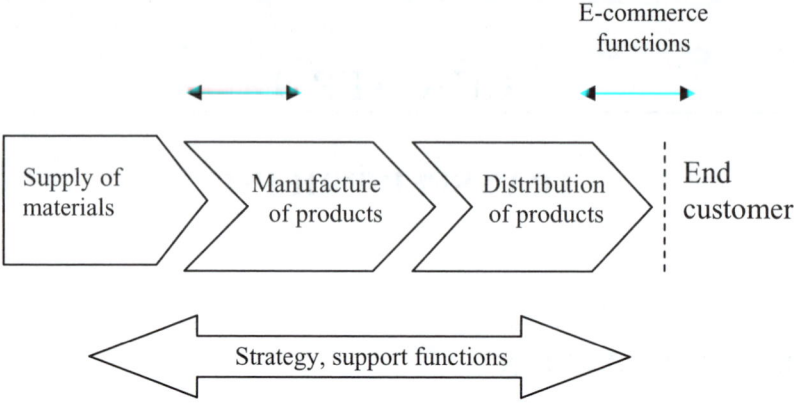

Figure 9.1: Basic supply chain for a retail business

9.1.2   Example of tax arbitrage through intra-group planning

Mechanisms for facilitating e-commerce across the supply chain, such as telecom networks, internet access points, routers, computer software, domain names etc, can be structured between associated companies in a multinational group. This structuring can lead to tax arbitrage through the transfer pricing allocation of profits from a high tax country to a low tax country by imposing an above market price on the supply of goods and/or services by a company in a low tax jurisdiction to an associated party in a high tax jurisdiction. The net effect of such a policy would, assuming the application of tax to 'profits', be a reduction in taxable profits in the high tax country due to the expense of the above market rate supply (and of course a corresponding increase of profits in the low tax country).

This is because, generally, to calculate profits of a trade a taxpayer is allowed to offset expenditure incurred in carrying on the trade, for example, expenditure relating to goods or services, against receipts derived from the trade (see Chapter 7 for how trading profits are calculated).

Example 9.1

Cayman Island Trading Ltd is the parent company of a UK subsidiary. Cayman Island Trading Ltd provides an internet service to its UK subsidiary, which carries on a trade. The price of the service provided to the UK subsidiary is fixed at £150,000 per year. The true market cost of the service if provided between independent parties dealing on an arm's length basis would only be £50,000. The UK subsidiary makes a trading profit of £300,000 in 2011/12. Assuming no other adjustments, the UK subsidiary seeks to deduct the expense of £150,000 paid to its parent company. If such a deduction were permitted, taxable profits would be £150,000. If the deduction is restricted to the market cost of the service, taxable profits would be increased to £250,000 (tax impact of £26,000 at 2011/2012 corporation tax rates in the UK of 26%* (£250,000–£150,000)). The UK and many other countries[2] operate transfer pricing rules, which means that it is necessary to ensure that goods and/or services are provided on an arm's length basis between associated parties. Note that the company could decide to move functions, assets and risks in relation to the trade from the UK to Cayman and this would increase arbitrage opportunities. One example would be to hold an electronic list of customers (a valuable trade secret) in Cayman with customer relationships managed by the Cayman entity. It is important to recognise that there may be commercial benefits from centralising functions in a particular entity such as scale leverage and improved strategic management.

* Reducing to 25% for 2012/13.

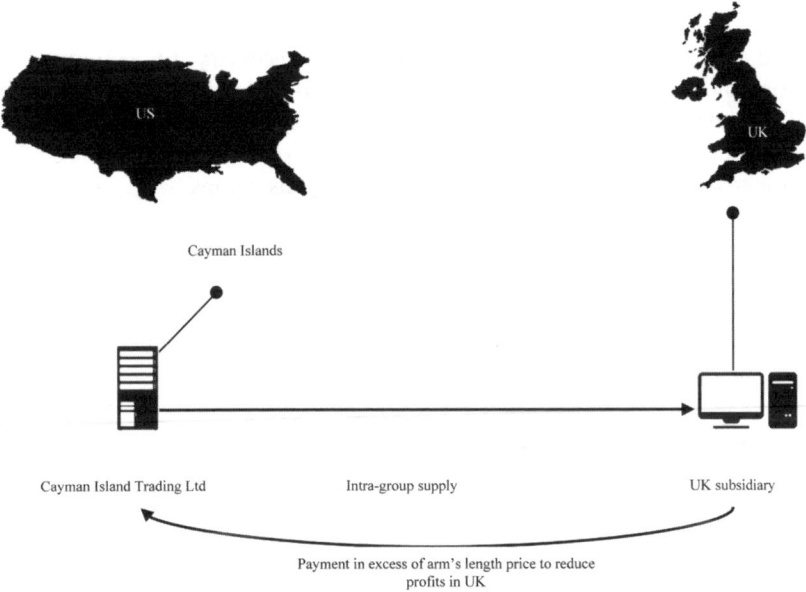

US

UK

Cayman Islands

Cayman Island Trading Ltd   Intra-group supply   UK subsidiary

Payment in excess of arm's length price to reduce
profits in UK

9.1.3 The approach of tax administrations to transfer pricing and e-commerce

Transactions between associated parties structured to take advantage of different tax regimes are the subject of ever increasing scrutiny by tax authorities throughout the world. The UK government's report *Electronic Commerce: The UK's Taxation Agenda* (26 November 1999) describes the concept of transfer pricing and its application to the e-commerce world in the following terms:[3]

'Transfer pricing is the term used to describe the process whereby prices are set by enterprises which are related to or "associated with" each other, in

---

[2]   About forty jurisdictions now impose transfer pricing regulations.
[3]   Chapter 8, at paras 8.6 and 8.7.

respect of dealings between them. Such dealings may include sales or transfers of goods or assets, both tangible and intangible, and the provision of services, including finance.

It is important to both taxpayers and tax administrations as it can have a considerable effect on the taxable profits of such associated enterprises. Where the transactions in question are between associated enterprises which are resident in different countries, the transfer prices affect more than one tax jurisdiction. If both jurisdictions do not agree on the appropriate transfer prices and thus the sharing of taxing rights, there is a risk of double taxation or of less than single taxation. These considerations apply to transactions conducted electronically as they do to transactions conducted by more conventional means.'

It is particularly important to ensure that all transactions between associated parties are made on an arm's length basis. As discussed above, to determine an arm's length price, it is necessary to examine the economic functions carried on, assets deployed and risks assumed by each of the related parties in building a functional profile of the business. This must be done because these factors, among other things, are used by unrelated parties to determine the price for transactions.

In practical experience, the following are particular areas of concern for tax administrations:

- the ability to trace transactions – it is difficult to audit what cannot be identified;

- integration/consolidation of supply chain functions rendering traditional comparisons invalid;

- e-commerce is an area in which tax administrations do not have significant experience (although this experience is improving over time); and

- lack of clear guidance on the subject from international bodies such as the OECD – perceived wisdom is that the current Transfer Pricing Guidelines are sufficient to address e-commerce transactions.

9.2 OECD GUIDELINES

Many tax authorities have implemented legislation requiring taxable profits from transactions between associated parties to be calculated on the basis of arm's length prices. The theory and practice of transfer pricing is contained in a looseleaf work published by the OECD called *Transfer Pricing Guidelines for Multinational Enterprises and Tax Administrations* (2010). The source of authority to alter the pricing structure between associated parties for UK purposes is contained in the

Taxation (International and Other Provisions) Act 2010 (TIOPA 2010) and relevant double taxation agreements (DTAs): these aspects are discussed in this chapter.

9.3 UK TRANSFER PRICING LEGISLATION

9.3.1 Double taxation agreements

A DTA is the result of bilateral negotiations between two countries. The purpose of a DTA is to reduce or extinguish the double taxation of profits, income or capital, which is derived from a country by a non-resident who is taxable in respect of that amount in its own country. A DTA has force of law within the UK.[4] Many DTAs are based upon the OECD Model Tax Convention on Income and Capital (the OECD Model Convention),[5] which provides under Art 9 a right to adjust the profits of a party and to apply tax to the altered amount. The adjustment permitted is that which provides an arm's length value for a transaction between associated parties. The wide ambit of Art 9(1) is shown below:

> 'Where ... conditions are made or imposed between ... two enterprises in their commercial or financial relations which differ from those which would be made between independent enterprises, then any profits which would, but for those conditions, have accrued to one of the enterprises, but, by reason of those conditions, have not so accrued, may be included in the profits of that enterprise and taxed accordingly.'

Provisions will also usually apply in a DTA for an adjustment to be made by a contracting State for profits that should be taxed in the other contracting State in consequence of an adjustment to an arm's length pricing of a transaction.[6]

Example 9.2

> UK Ltd enters into an agreement to obtain loan finance from Netherlands BV, which holds the majority of shares in UK Ltd. The interest payments agreed by UK Ltd are higher than would have been agreed between independent parties. In other words, but for the relationship, interest payments would have been lower. In consequent it follows that the taxable profits of UK Ltd would have been higher, due to lower interest payment deductions. In circumstances such as these the profits of the UK company could be increased by HMRC because of the non-arm's length interest payments.

United Kingdom
Taxation: General

---

[4] TIOPA 2010, s 2.
[5] See www.oecd.org.
[6] OECD Model Convention, Art 9(2).

9.3.2 UK rules

The UK's rules on transfer pricing apply to both UK and cross-border transactions between connected parties. The rules can potentially apply to a broad range of situations, including transactions entered into in the context of e-commerce and e-infrastructure business activities.

The rules are focussed on 'provisions' made or imposed otherwise than on arm's length basis between related parties.[7] In summary, the transfer pricing rules apply where:[8]

(1)   provision (the 'actual provision') has been made or imposed as between any two persons (the 'affected persons') by means of a transaction (or series of transactions);

(2)   the participation condition is met; and

(3)   the actual provision differs from the provision ('arm's length provision') that would have been made as between independent enterprises.

Where these rules apply, the profits and losses of a potentially advantaged person must be calculated for tax purposes as if the arm's length provision had been made or imposed instead of the actual provision.[9] This requirement is imposed where a basic precondition is met and the actual provision confers a potential advantage in relation to UK tax on one of the affected persons.[10] There are certain exemptions from the rules for dormant companies, and small and medium-sized enterprises (SMEs) (see **9.3.4**).[11]

'Provision' is not defined, but it appears to be intended to be a reference to the terms of, and effects brought about by, the transaction.[12] It probably corresponds to the term 'conditions' in Art 9 of the OECD Model Convention. It should be noted that a 'provision' can arise from a series of transactions, which need not all involve the parties that have made the provision.

Transaction

The concept of 'transaction' is defined as including 'arrangements, understandings and mutual practices (whether or not they are, or are

---

[7]   TIOPA 2010, s 147.
[8]   See generally TIOPA 2010, Part 4.
[9]   TIOPA 2010, s 147(3).
[10]   TIOPA 2010, s 147(2).
[11]   TIOPA 2010, s 147(6).
[12]   TIOPA 2010, s 147.

intended to be, legally enforceable)'.[13] The term 'arrangement' is given a broad meaning of 'any scheme or arrangement of any kind (whether or not it is, or is intended to be, legally enforceable)'.[14]

Example 9.3

> UK Internet Trading Ltd has an associated company located in the US, called US internet Trading Inc. Various formal written agreements exist between the two parties, which include (1) a finance agreement and (2) a distribution agreement relating to orders placed by UK consumers via the US internet site and US consumers via the UK internet trading site. Various informal unwritten arrangements exist whereby when UK site access is heavy consumers are diverted to a mirror site operated by the US company in Canada. This site processes the diverted orders, issues acceptance notices and accepts payment for orders on behalf of the UK company. Formal and informal arrangements of this type are all potentially subject to UK transfer pricing legislation.

The rules also apply to a series of transactions which include references to a number of transactions each entered into in pursuance of, or in relation to, the same arrangement.[15] The concept of series of transactions is particularly wide since the following matters do not prevent there being a series of transactions: (a) there is no transaction in the series to which both the persons are parties; (b) that the parties to any arrangement in pursuance of which the transactions in the series are entered into do not include one or both of those persons; and (c) and there is one or more transactions in the series to which neither of those persons is a party.[16]

Participation

The participation condition refers to a requirement that at the time of the making or imposition of the actual provision:[17]

(a)   one of the affected persons was directly or indirectly participating in the management, control or capital of the other party; or

(b)   the same person (ie a third party) or persons was or were directly or indirectly participating in the management, control or capital of each of the affected persons.

There is another condition for participation which relates to 'financing arrangements',[18] and this is met in relation to the actual provision if at the

---

[13]   TIOPA 2010, s 150(1).
[14]   TIOPA 2010, s 150(5).
[15]   TIOPA 2010, s 150(3).
[16]   TIOPA 2010, s 150(4).
[17]   TIOPA 2010, s 148(3).
[18]   This refers to arrangements made for providing or guaranteeing, or otherwise in connection with, any debt, capital or other form of finance.

time of the making or imposition of the actual provision or within the period of 6 months beginning with the day on which the actual provision was made or imposed either of (a) or (b) above are met.[19]

In relation to the concept of participation a person participates directly in the management, control or capital of another person where:[20]

- the other person is a corporation or a partnership; and

- is controlled by the first person

> *Example 9.4*
>
> Internet Access (Corporate Intranet) Ltd is a wholly owned subsidiary of Internet Access (World Wide) BV. In circumstances such as these the Netherlands parent directly participates in the capital of the UK company. Any transaction between them would be subject to the UK transfer pricing rules.

These are further tests relating to what is called 'indirect participation' to prevent potential loopholes.[21] Broadly, a person indirectly participates in the management, control or capital of another person where:[22]

(1)   That person (P) would be taken to be directly participating in the management, control or capital of another person (A) if the rights and powers attributed to P included all of the rights and powers that:

   (a)   P is entitled to acquire at a future date or which P will be entitled to acquire at a future date;[23]
   (b)   are rights and powers of third parties, that P can have or could have exercised on P's behalf, under the direction of P, or for the benefit of P;[24]
   (c)   any person has with whom P is connected.

(2)   That person (P) is one of a number of major participants in that other person's (A) enterprise.[25] P is a major participant A if that other person is a body corporate or partnership and the so-called '40% test' is met.[26] The 40% test is satisfied if in the case of *each* of the two persons who, taken together, control the subordinate (A),

---

[19]   TIOPA 2010, s 148(2).
[20]   TIOPA 2010, s 157.
[21]   TIOPA 2010, ss 158–163.
[22]   TIOPA 2010, s 158.
[23]   TIOPA 2010, s 159.
[24]   TIOPA 2010, s 159.
[25]   TIOPA 2010, s 160.
[26]   TIOPA 2010, s 160(3).

and of whom one is the major participant (P).[27] For the purposes of determining the 40% test, each person must have attributed to them all the rights and powers that are attributed to a potential participant.[28]

An in-depth examination of these rules is beyond the scope of this chapter.

9.3.3 Adjustment to arm's length price

If a 'provision' exists which differs from that which would have been made between independent parties and which confers a potential advantage in respect of UK tax on one or both parties, the profits or losses of the potentially advantaged party are altered for tax purposes as if the arm's length provision has been made.[29] A potential advantage is conferred by the actual provision where the effect of making or imposing the actual provision, instead of the arm's length provision, would be one or both of the following:[30]

- that a smaller amount (which may be nil) would be taken for UK tax purposes to be the amount of that person's profits (eg by payment of an excessive expense); or

- that a larger amount (or if there would not otherwise have been losses, any amount of more than nil) would be taken for UK tax purposes to be the amount of that person's losses.

Example 9.5

US Satellite Support Services Inc supplies data carrier services to a related party (ie one which is indirectly participating in the other), called Internet Access Ltd. The price paid for the supply of the carrier services is £700,000 per year. The UK company receives trading receipts of £2.7 million in 2012/13. Assuming no other deductions, the profit would be £2 million. The price paid for the carrier service is in excess of an arm's length price by £200,000. This excessive pricing thus confers an advantage in respect of UK tax by decreasing the taxable profits of Internet Access Ltd. UK transfer pricing legislation will operate to adjust the deductible expense from £700,000 to £500,000, which represents the true arm's length price for the carrier service.

9.3.4 Exclusions, advance pricing agreements and adjustments

There are various exclusions contained in the legislation that prevent the transfer pricing rules from applying, and these are summarised below.

---

27 TIOPA 2010, s 160(3).
28 TIOPA 2010, s 160(5).
29 TIOPA 2010, s 147(3).
30 TIOPA 2010, s 155(2).

Dormant companies

The rules do not apply where the potentially advantaged person is a dormant company.[31] A company is 'dormant' during any period in which it has no significant accounting transaction.[32]

Small and medium-sized enterprises

The rules do not apply where the potentially advantaged person is an SME.[33] Whether a company is an SME is determined by reference to Commission Recommendation 2003/361/EC (6 May 2003).[34] The definition is reproduced at Appendix G, but is applied with certain modifications.

Recommendation 2003/361/EC defines enterprises as micro, small or medium by reference to ceilings relating to staff headcount, annual turnover and balance sheet totals.

A medium-sized enterprise is one that falls with the category of micro, small and medium-sized enterprises, but which is not a small enterprise as defined in the Annex to the Recommendation (this is an adjustment imposed by tax law[35]).[36]

To come within a particular category an enterprise must meet the 'staff headcount' test and at least one of the 'turnover' or 'balance sheet total' tests shown in Table 9.1.

Table 9.1: SMEs: categorisation of enterprises

Enterprise category	Staff headcount	Turnover	Balance sheet total
Medium sized	< 250	not exceeding €50m	not exceeding €43m
Small	< 50	not exceeding €10m	not exceeding €10m

---

[31] TIOPA 2010, s 165.

[32] CA 2006, s 1169.

[33] TIOPA 2010, s 167.

[34] TIOPA 2010, s 172.

[35] Where any enterprise is in liquidation or administration the rights of the liquidator or administrator are left out of account for certain purposes when deciding whether that enterprise or another is an SME: TIOPA 2010, s 172(4). Additionally, Art 3, para 5 is omitted; and the first sentence of Art 4(1) has effect as if the data to apply to the headcount of staff and financial amounts were the data relating to the chargeable period referred to in TIOPA 2010, s 166 (and calculated on an annual basis). Art 4 also has effect with the omission of (a) the second sentence of para 1 (data to be taken into account from date of closure of accounts); (b) para 3 (no change of status unless ceilings exceeded for two consecutive periods); and (c) para 3 (genuine estimate in case of newly established enterprise): see TIOPA 2010, s 172.

[36] TIOPA 2010, s 172(1).

| Micro | < 10 | not exceeding €2m | not exceeding €2m |

The SME exemption is not available if the taxpayer makes an election to fall outside its scope, but the effect of this irrevocable.[37] Additionally, the exemption does not apply where an SME enters into a transaction with a person in a country that does not have a DTA with the UK that contains an appropriate non-discrimination article.[38] An appropriate non-discrimination article is one that ensures the nationals of a contracting state may not be less favourably treated in the other contracting state than nationals of that latter state in the same circumstances.[39]

Advance pricing agreement

It is possible to enter into an advance pricing agreement (APA) with HMRC for the purposes of resolving complex transfer pricing and attribution of income issues on a prospective basis.[40] An APA is a bilateral agreement with HMRC, which is binding on the parties.[41] An APA may be requested by any person (A) with HMRC for the purposes of clarification by agreement of the effect in A's case of provisions by reference to which questions relating to any one or more of the following matters are to be determined:[42]

(1) the attribution of income to a branch or agency through which A has been carrying on a trade in the UK or is proposing to carry on a trade in the UK;

(2) if A is a company, the attribution of income to a permanent establishment through which A has been carrying on a trade in the UK or is proposing to carry on a trade in the UK;

(3) the attribution of income to any permanent establishment of A's, wherever situated, through which A has been carrying on, or is proposing to carry on, any business;

(4) the extent to which income has arisen or may arise to A is to be taken for any purpose to be income arising in a country or territory outside the UK; and

---

[37] TIOPA 2010, s 167(2).
[38] TIOPA 2010, s 167(3).
[39] See TIOPA 2010, ss 167(3) and 173. A list of countries that meet this condition is provided in HMRC's *International Manual* at 432112.
[40] TIOPA 2010, ss 218–230. Guidance on the application of the legislation by HMRC is contained in SP 3/99, *Advance Pricing Agreements* (31 August 1999). This SP is due to be updated: see www.hmrc.gov.uk/cap/index.htm (2011).
[41] TIOPA 2010, s 220. The APA can be revoked in specific circumstances, such as failure on the part of the taxpayer to comply with the provisions of the APA: see TIOPA 2010, s 221.
[42] TIOPA 2010, s 223.

(5)   the treatment for tax purposes of any provision made or imposed, whether before or after the date of the agreement, as between A and any associate of A's.[43]

As can be seen from the foregoing, the advantages of an APA are material in the context of ensuring no significant issues arise in connection with the application of transfer pricing rules and the attribution of income to a permanent establishment. The foremost advantage is the relative certainty and likely absence of costly investigations and negotiations with tax authorities in respect of pricing arrangements.

It is important to emphasise that an APA will confirm a taxpayer's tax treatment only within the UK. It will not determine the tax treatment within another jurisdiction. To determine the cross-border issues comprehensively, HMRC would need to reach an agreement with the related parties' tax authority. Where a DTA is in existence, this is achieved through the mutual agreement procedure (MAP) article.[44] The MAP article is concerned with the interpretation and handling of problems arising from the application of a DTA. This provides HMRC with authority for entering into negotiations with another DTA partner. Where conditions for the use of the MAP article are in existence, HMRC can participate in another treaty partner's APA process. This enables HMRC to agree with a treaty partner how the terms of the treaty, particularly the concept of arm's length transactions, are to apply in a particular case. In this context, APA participation is limited by the MAP article.

Adjustments

It is possible to make an adjustment under the transfer pricing rules so that a person is treated as though a transaction had occurred on an arm's length basis. Where one of the affected persons (A) has a potential advantage in relation to UK taxation which is conferred by the actual provision and the other affected person (B) is within the charge to income tax or corporation tax in respect of profits arising from 'relevant activities', then it is possible for the disadvantaged person to make a claim for its profits and losses to be calculated for tax purposes as if the arm's length provision had been made.[45] However, a claim may not be made by the disadvantaged person unless a calculation (filed by way of a return to HMRC) has been made in the case of the advantaged person on the basis that the arm's length provision was made instead of the actual provision.[46] It is also possible for the parties to make balancing payments

---

[43]   TIOPA 2010, s 218(2).
[44]   See Art 25 of the OECD Model Convention.
[45]   TIOPA 2010, s 174(2). There are certain restrictions which apply where the claim relates to a guarantee in relation to a security: TIOPA 2010, s 175.
[46]   TIOPA 2010, s 176.

in order to correct the cash flow positions which have arisen in consequence of adverse transfer pricing arrangements.[47]

9.4 OECD TRANSFER PRICING GUIDELINES

The transfer pricing rules are required to be constructed in such a manner as 'best secures consistency' between UK law, which requires an arm's length provision between related parties, and 'the effect which, in accordance with the transfer pricing guidelines is to be given, in cases where double taxation agreements incorporate the whole or any part of the OECD Model, to so much of the arrangements as does so'.[48] The term 'transfer pricing guidelines' are defined as all documents approved by the OECD on 22 July 2010 as part of their *Transfer Pricing Guidelines for Multinational Enterprises and Tax Administrations*.[49]

The UK's domestic transfer pricing rules and the articles in DTAs are comparable to Art 9 of the OECD Model Convention, which requires the profits for transactions between associated parties to be on an arm's length basis otherwise an adjustment will be made to achieve this objective. The OECD *Transfer Pricing Guidelines* provide analysis of the ways in which the arm's length price for transactions is to be ascertained. The appropriate method to adopt in determining an accurate arm's length price will depend heavily upon obtaining professional advice from transfer pricing specialists who can draw on the skills of economists and tax advisers and corporate finance expertise. The main methods are summarised below.

9.4.1 Comparable uncontrolled price

Under comparable uncontrolled price (CUP), the parties identify what would have been charged between independent parties in respect of the transaction for goods or services that have been entered into between the associated parties. The main requirement is that only comparable transactions between unrelated entities are used as benchmarks.[50] In other words, all the essential indicia of the supply are ascertained, and then relevant comparable transactions are identified.

9.4.2 Resale price method

This method is used where products are transferred between associated parties and then resold to an independent person. Under this method, the

United Kingdom Taxation: General

---

[47]   See generally TIOPA 2010, Part 4, Chapter 6.

[48]   TIOPA 2010, s 164(1).

[49]   TIOPA 2010, s 164, as amended by FA 2011, s 58. It also includes any document approved by the OECD, which is designated by order made by the Treasury.

[50]   See OECD *Transfer Pricing Guidelines for Multinational Enterprises and Tax Administrations*, Part II, B1, which explores the issues relating to the application of CUP in determining arm's length price.

parties approach the arm's length issue from the starting point of the price paid for products by an independent person at the end of the supply process. This price represents the resale price. The method requires the resale price to be reduced by an arm's length 'resale margin', which represents the costs and profits the reseller would seek to recover. Once the margin is deducted, what is left is the arm's length price for the original transfer of the product between associated parties.[51] Again, the benchmark transactions must be comparable and involve unrelated parties.

Example 9.6

Alpha Computer Services Inc, a US company, makes a supply of computer software to Beta Software Ltd (UK) for £20,000. The UK company then makes an onward supply of the software to a business consumer for £37,000. Transactions of this nature are typical for the UK company. HMRC challenge the expenditure by saying that a true arm's length price is £15,000 for the supply from the US. In applying the resale price method to determine the arm's length price, the parties would need to deduct a 'resale margin' from the resale price of £37,000. Once the reseal margin, representing costs and a mark-up for profit, are deducted this should leave the arm's length price.

9.4.3   Cost plus method

By this approach the arm's length price is ascertained by determining the amount of the costs incurred by the supplier of products or services in their provision to an associated person. A mark-up is then added to the costs to reflect an appropriate profit to the supplier against the background of the functions performed, risks assumed by the supplier and market conditions.[52] This method is approached by determining the costs plus mark-up which would be applied in a comparable uncontrolled transaction for the supply of relevant products and services.

Example 9.7

UK Intranet Ltd uses the telecom carrier services of a related party, called USA Access Inc. HMRC challenges the payments for the carrier services on the basis that they are in excess of an arm's length price. One method of defending the claim is for the UK company to compute an arm's length price for the same type of service. Assume the cost-plus approach is the appropriate approach in this case. In other words, we must ask what would be the costs of providing a telecom carrier service, and what would be the profit or mark-up for a comparable supplier in an uncontrolled transaction. The figure reached at the end of this process is an arm's length price.

---

[51] *Transfer Pricing Guidelines*, Part II, C1.
[52] *Transfer Pricing Guidelines*, Part II, D1.

9.4.4 Other methods

Where difficulties are experienced in applying the above methods, perhaps because of inability to obtain details of comparable transactions, the OECD guidelines identify two further methods. These are the 'profit split' and 'transactional net margin' methods.[53] The profit split method[54] is useful where two associated entities enter into a collaborative venture and split the profits between themselves. The purpose of this method is to determine the appropriate profit split by reference to economic analysis of the transaction and the function performed by each of the associated parties. Broadly, the party which contributes the most resources and incurs more risk in the collaboration is entitled to a higher percentage of the profit split. Under the net margin method[55] the arm's length price is determined by reference to the net margin, ie the margin the party would earn on a comparable uncontrolled transaction by reference to a certain factor, such as its cost base or its capital employed.

9.4.5 Documentation

Chapter V of the OECD *Transfer Pricing Guidelines for Multinational Enterprises and Tax Administrations* gives guidance on the type of documentation that a taxpayer should seek to compile for the purposes of handling transfer pricing investigations. As the guidelines rightly observe, the individual circumstances of each case vary and it is impossible to give guidance for every single scenario. However, on a general level the compilation and retention of documentation should be a matter of common sense.

In order to evaluate whether a transaction is at an arm's length price, it is necessary for both the tax administration and the taxpayer to possess full information about the particular circumstances of the associated parties and the transaction. Documentation relating to a business activity should inform the tax administration about the following matters, although this is not an exhaustive list:

- the associated parties to the transaction;

- the economic functions of each of the associated parties to the transaction, such as manufacturing, marketing, carriage and warehousing activities, training of personnel, finance provision etc;

- the risks and obligations assumed by each of the parties to the transaction;

United Kingdom
Taxation: General

---

[53] *Transfer Pricing Guidelines*, Part II, D1.
[54] *Transfer Pricing Guidelines*, Part III, C1.
[55] *Transfer Pricing Guidelines*, Part III, B1.

- information concerning comparable uncontrolled transaction with independent third parties (or the lack thereof);

- market conditions within which the controlled transactions are implemented;

- nature and terms of individual transactions between associated parties, including precise identification of products and/or services supplied;

- how the transactions operate between associated parties;

- documentation of location of ownership rights in intangible assets exploited between associated parties;

- full legal documentation should ideally be maintained which records accurately the economic transactions between associate parties;

- full legal documentation of arrangements with related and unrelated commercial intermediaries which reflects the allocation of risks between the parties, for example, responsibility for damage to products, liability for defective products etc;

- the pricing strategy, including reasons for various margins allowed under arrangements;

- sales information, such as of products, services rendered, lease of property;

- research and development ('R&D') documentation that reflects ownership of rights in R&D, as well as the finance, risks assumed, assets contributed under the R&D venture; and

- market conditions such as scope of competition.

9.4.6   Intra-group services

IT is of particular use in the provision of effective channels of communication between associated parties. The parties are likely to have their own information superhighway in the form of an intranet. The parties could use their intranet as a means of providing technical data between a parent and subsidiary, provision of IT services (such as computer advice), financial advice, legal advice etc. In fact, it is entirely possible for a headquarters company to provide extensive management services to its subsidiaries and other associated parties by use of IT.

Chapter 7 of the OECD *Transfer Pricing Guidelines for Multinational Enterprises and Tax Administrations* gives guidance on the issues relating to applying an arm's length standard to intra-group service provision. Generally it is desirable to identify as specifically as possible what services are provided on an intra-group basis, and the extent to which these services are charged for between the parties. The method of charge for the intra-group services should also ideally be reflected. In setting the price for intra-group services the parties should have regard to the transfer pricing methods detailed in the guidelines.

9.4.7   Impact of e-commerce and transfer pricing

As discussed at the outset of this chapter, e-commerce is a relatively new method of doing business and presents tax administrations with areas of uncertainty and subjective treatment. However, the transaction differences have not (as of yet) led to specific OECD Guidance in this area (as there are for financial services and insurance by way of example).

It is true that supply chain considerations are quite distinct; e-commerce offers entrepreneurs, developers, manufacturers and other suppliers the opportunity of eliminating the need for commercial intermediaries and supplying direct to the consumer. Cost savings and profit enhancements from this will usually be replaced with other costs associated with e-commerce, such as investment in technology and management of intellectual property. The refocusing of expenditure away from a physical asset base makes transactions difficult to accurately identify, trace and price.

In ascertaining the correct arm's length price for e-commerce, both the taxpayer and the tax authority must determine the functional profile of the business. The allocation of cost to specific areas will vary according to the nature of the business. The significant cost for an e-commerce seller is likely to be advertising, for example, via internet search engine sites. Each e-commerce seller is competing with all the other millions of sellers for space on the individual consumer's desktop computer monitor. By contrast the costs of a developer of IT would be very different.

Functional analysis to determine the correct arm's length price is a complex operation. A number of factors must be considered in establishing and defending a price which is claimed to represent an arm's length price. These include the following:

- Determination of research and development costs.

- The legal nature of the delivery process. For example, does the transfer of electronic material represent payment by the customer for the use of copyright? The answer will be yes where the transfer is made under a licence for the reproduction and exploitation of the material.

- The method and number of intermediaries used in the delivery process. If fewer intermediaries are used to deliver electronic products, the costs which would have existed in respect of physical media may still be incurred in other ways because of the e-commerce delivery process. For example, the e-commerce seller may incur new costs such as payments for maintaining a dedicated delivery computer server with associated permanent internet connections. The new costs must be identified because these will be relevant to determining an arm's length price.

- In determining the value to be allocated to a particular service it will be necessary to take into account the benefits conferred by the related party. For example, the existence of a computer server with a fast and permanent telecommunication delivery between a supplier and other parties facilitating the supplier's e-commerce business must be taken into account in ascertaining an arm's length price. In designing a transfer pricing strategy for e-commerce it is necessary to ascertain precisely where value is added by a supply. Those businesses which assist in the provision of e-commerce will need to identify precisely the nature of the value which they are providing. For instance, the value of these support services will be determined by durability, effectiveness, speed, employment of new technologies, security etc.

- The value of providing access to an infrastructure for e-commerce will turn upon the cost of plant and machinery, such as satellite earth stations, fibre optic cables etc. It will be necessary to determine the extent to which there is any cost attributable to use of intellectual property by recipients.

- The cost of manufacturing products for electronic distribution may be minimal. However, businesses will probably find that costs will be attributed to other elements, such as R&D, advertising and intellectual property.

Whist e-commerce may not create unique problems in the application of transfer pricing law, it will be necessary to identify where costs are being incurred and where value is added across the supply chain.

CHAPTER 10

COMPUTER SOFTWARE

10.1 SOFTWARE: WHAT IS IT?

Software (otherwise known as a program) represents the instructions which cause IT hardware to operate in a particular way, such as displaying and moving images for a game on a television or computer screen in response to motion sensors in a hand-held device. The European Commission has defined the concept of 'computer program' as including the following:[1]

> '... the term "computer program" shall include programs in any form, including those which are incorporated into hardware. This term also includes preparatory design work leading to the development of a computer program provided that the nature of the preparatory work is such that a computer program can result from it at a later stage.'

Computer software can contains thousands, sometimes millions, of separate instructions. The instruction is given in the form of a binary notation, which uses two digits (0 and 1). A computer is able to process the binary notation and comply with the instructions for operating the IT (the nature of IT and how computers operate is explored in Chapter 1).

Computer software and data (information used for processing by the software) is stored on a physical piece of IT. For example, information/data may be stored on a CD or DVD as a series of 'etches' created by a laser. Where these physical carriers are produced on a mass-market basis, the plastic carrier will have been stamped by a metal master disc, which creates the necessary mould on the disc (which is then coated with protective layers). The disc may be capable of only being read by a device, or it may be possible for data on the disc to be recorded and then altered. The physical carrier usually costs very little to manufacture. Software may be stored on a variety of physical carriers such as computer hard drives, external hard drives, memory sticks etc.

The value of the software resides in the information/instructions and the intellectual property rights which protect the owner from unlawful

---

[1]   Directive 2009/24/EC on the legal protection of computer programs, OJ L111/16.

copying. The type of intellectual property rights that exist in software is varied (this aspect is considered at **10.1.1**).

The purpose of this chapter is to provide an overview of the tax aspects relating to the exploitation of computer software. In dealing with the taxation of software it is necessary to identify the constituent elements of the software and how it is classified for the purposes of taxation. For example, if software is classified as goods it will be subject to VAT as a supply of goods, whilst software classified as services will be subject to VAT as a supply of services. The difference is sometimes of critical importance because the application of VAT can differ materially for goods and services. The VAT aspects of computer software are explored in Chapter 21.

10.1.1   Intellectual property

The value of software from a development and manufacturing perspective lies in the proprietary rights, which can be used to prohibit the reproduction of the software by competitors. Computer software is essentially pure information/instructions recorded on a physical device as a series of 0s and 1s (ie as a binary code). In itself, this information is subject to no proprietary right.[2]

Computer software is protected by copyright to the extent that it is a literary work.[3] This is the primary form of intellectual property right by which computer software is exploited. Copyright will also exist in a computer database.[4] Payment for use of software or a database involves the grant of a licence to the end-user, although a licence will also be granted where use of a computer program is made available without consideration.

Depending on the circumstances, a licence can be granted on either express or implied terms. However, the norm will be for commercially exploited computer software to be on the basis of express terms incorporated as part of the package, where it is sold on a retail basis, or, where software is developed on a bespoke basis, through express terms incorporated in a written agreement between the licensor and licensee. Typically a licence granted for use of retail software will state that the end-user is entitled to install one copy of the software on one computer (or at least on a limited number of computers), that the content (such as icons, sounds and media) are for non-commercial use only and that the

---

[2]   *Boardman v Phipps* [1967] 2 AC 46, at 128, HL; *Oxford v Moss* (1978) 68 Cr App R 193.

[3]   CDPA 1988, s 3(1)(b).

[4]   CDPA, s 3(1)(d). CDPA 1988, s 3A defines a 'database' as: '(1) … a collection of independent works, data or other materials which – (a) are arranged in a systematic or methodical way, and (b) are individually accessible by electronic or other means. (2) For the purposes of this Part a literary work consisting of a database is original if, and only if, by reason of the selection or arrangement of the contents of the database the database constitutes the author's own intellectual creation.'

software cannot be licensed, sold, rented or leased. Where the software is purchased and digitally downloaded online, the end-user will typically be granted a right to make one copy of the software on a disc for the purposes of using it as a backup copy.

UK Patent rights cannot be granted in respect of computer programs to the extent the application relates a program for a computer 'as such'.[5] It has proved difficult for inventions with a computer program to qualify for patent right protection.[6]

10.1.2 Multimedia products

Multimedia products include computer software, which produces multiple types of media, such as text, images and sound on a computer, television or mobile device. The intellectual property rights that exist in this type of media are potentially very wide. Copyright is capable of existing in computer software as a literary work. It should also be possible for multimedia products to be protected as a film. The Copyright, Designs and Patents Act 1988 (CDPA 1988) defines a film as 'a recording on any medium from which a moving image may by any means be produced'.[7] There will also be other aspects of copyright protection under CDPA 1988 in multimedia products, such as the instruction book (literary work), graphic images (artistic work) and sounds produced by the computer program (sound recording). Payment for use of multimedia software will involves the grant of a licence to the end-user, although a licence will also be granted where use of a computer program is made available without consideration.

10.1.3 Off-the-shelf software/standardised software

Many forms of software can be acquired by customers directly through retail outlets, e-commerce or direct digital download over the internet. This off-the-shelf/standardised software is characterised by the fact that it is mass-produced and readily available to the general public – for example, Microsoft or Apple products. If the physical product is examined, a sticker is usually to be found stating that the opening of the package is deemed to be acceptance of the manufacturer's licence of the computer software. Upon the installation of software directly onto a computer, the user is typically asked to input an activation code and/or to accept the terms of a licence of the software by 'ticking' a box and then clicking OK.

For tax purposes it is important to identify the nature of what has been supplied. Where software is downloaded directly over the internet the end-user has paid consideration for a licence to use the software; and

United Kingdom Taxation: General

---

[5] Patents Act 1977, s 1(2).
[6] See *Merril Lynch's Application* [1989] RPC 561; *Gale's Application* [1991] RPC 305; *Fujitsu's Application* [1991] RPC 305.
[7] CDPA 1988, s 5B(1).

where acquired off-the-shelf software the supply could be categorised as two things, namely payment for the device upon which the software is stored and for the licence to use the computer software.

The fact that payment can be categorised in this way raises the question of how the purchase of this type of software is to be classified. As discussed in Chapter 21, for VAT purposes software digitally downloaded directly onto a computer is a supply of services, whilst the purchase of a device storing the software (such as a DVD) is often a supply of goods.

10.1.4   Specific software

Specific software is computer software that is custom-made by a computer developer for a specific client. It is characterised by the fact that it is not mass-produced and is not readily available to the general public. Procuring the services of a person to develop software raises the issue of whether the contract is one for the supply of goods or for the supply of services. This classification is important for tax purposes, and is discussed below.

10.1.5   Internet downloaded software

Software downloaded over the internet (eg from a retailer's website) is computer software which a consumer obtains by an electronic download via the telecommunication network. Software available for download can be acquired either from retailers for payment of a fee, or sometimes free of charge from software developers. The characterisation of this type of software is that its acquisition lacks any type of physical existence. The consumer acquires software that is transferred as a binary code from the retailer's computer network and installed directly onto the recipient's hard disk in their computer. This type of supply is of services.

10.1.6   Software incorporated on hardware

Hardware such as a microprocessor, graphics card or a hard drive in a computer are supplied with pre-encoded software. When the hardware is purchased the consumer acquires not only the device, but also a licence for use of the software encoded on the device. These classifications have different tax consequences.

10.2   TAX POINTS AND RELIEFS

The tax legislation of the UK can apply in a number of different situations to transactions in respect of computer software. The principal corporation tax issues arising on the setting up and operation of an internet business are considered in Chapter 7. The nature of the corporation tax charges that arise on the exploitation of intellectual property rights (including copyright in computer software) are also examined in Chapter 7. The purpose of this chapter is to explain areas of the corporation tax regime which apply specifically to computer software.

10.2.1 Expenditure on computer software

The key tax consequences relating to the development and exploitation of computer software are provided in this chapter.

In summary, the tax consequences are as follows:

- Expenditure on an intangible fixed asset (represented by copyright in, or a licence of, computer software) is relieved in accordance with the accounting treatment of the expenditure (irrespective of whether the expenditure is revenue or capital in nature): see **10.2.2**; an election can be made so that capital expenditure on computer software qualifies for capital allowances (see **10.2.3**).

- Expenditure on computer software (eg where it is integral to hardware) that does not fall to be treated as being on an intangible fixed asset is relieved in accordance with the rules relating to whether it is revenue or capital expenditure: see **10.2.3**.

- Computer software that has been created on a bespoke basis is considered at **10.2.4**.

10.2.2 Intangible fixed assets

Expenditure on computer software may either be classified as being solely on the purchase of copyright in, or a licence to use, the software, or on the IT hardware which holds the software. If the expenditure is on the former it will be relieved as expenditure on intangible fixed assets, which is based on the accounting treatment of such assets, as adjusted by any rules provided in Part 8 of CTA 2009: this regime is considered in detail in Chapter 7.

The concept of an 'intangible fixed asset' owned by a company is defined as meaning 'an intangible asset acquired or created by the company for use on a continuing basis in the course of the company's activities'.[8] An 'intangible asset' is given the same meaning as it has for UK accounting purposes.[9] Financial Reporting Standard 10 (FRS 10) defines intangible

United Kingdom Taxation: General

---

[8] CTA 2009, s 713(1). Intangible assets which are held as trading stock are outside this definition.

[9] CTA 2009, s 712(1). The intention is to bring within the regime assets that are within the scope of the Accounting Standards Board's Financial Reporting Standard 10, *Goodwill and Intangible Assets* (December 1997, as amended) (FRS 10), available at www.frc.org.uk. Since the regime was introduced International Accounting Standards have become applicable to many UK companies and are acceptable for the Intangible

assets as 'non-financial assets that do not have physical substance but are identifiable and are controlled by the entity through custody or legal rights'.[10] It is not necessary for an intangible asset to be included on the company's balance sheet for it to be regarded as a fixed asset.[11] The rules provide that the definition of an 'intangible asset' shall include any 'intellectual property', which is defined as including copyright, any right under the law of a country or territory outside the UK corresponding to, or similar to copyright, and any licence of such rights.[12]

Intangible fixed assets: credits and debits

The tax treatment of credits (ie receipts) and debits (ie expenditure) in respect of intangible fixed assets is determined by reference to the purpose for which such assets are held by the company.[13] The tax treatment of credits and debits brought into account under the corporate tax regime in respect of intangible fixed assets is determined by reference to the purpose for which such assets are held by the corporate recipient.[14] In the case of a trade the deductible debits and taxable credits which are brought into account under the regime are regarded as receipts and expenses of the company's trade.[15] This means that the usual corporation tax rules will then apply to the amounts that are brought into account as part of the taxpayer's trading activities. This regime is considered in Chapter 7.

10.2.3   Revenue expenditure

A person will normally be is entitled to deduct revenue expenditure incurred in earning the revenue receipts derived from a trade.[16] If expenditure on software does not come within the intangible fixed asset regime (other than by way of an election to fall within the capital allowance regime), then the expenditure should be relieved as revenue expenditure if it does not have an enduring benefit for the purposes of the person's trade. However, it would typically be the case that if intangible fixed assets are not capitalised then the costs will immediately be taken to the profit and loss account, and then relieved in accordance with the intangible fixed asset regime (see **10.2.2**).

Fixed Assets regime. For simplicity we refer simply to the old UK GAAP regime. In any event, certain assets are specifically excluded from the definition of intangible assets such as oil licences, financial assets, and rights in companies or trusts. See generally CTA 2009, Part 8, Chapter 10.

[10]   FRS 10, para 2.
[11]   CTA 2009, s 713(3).
[12]   CTA 2009, s 712(3). However, the definition is subject to the list of excluded assets: see Part 8, Chapter 10.
[13]   CTA 2009, s 745.
[14]   CTA 2009, s 745(1).
[15]   CTA 2009, s 747.
[16]   See Chapter 7.

Pre-trade expenditure

The tax legislation allows revenue expenditure incurred prior to a trade to be deducted from revenue receipts derived from that trade once it has commenced.[17] This relief is available where expenditure is incurred no more than 7 years before the trade is started.[18] However, a deduction is permitted only if it would be allowed for the purposes of computing profits from a trade.[19]

Trade-related expenditure

Revenue expenditure that is brought into account on the basis of generally accepted accountancy practice must be adjusted for any prohibited expenditure contained in the tax legislation. Of principal importance is the rule that no deduction can be made under general principles unless the expenditure is incurred wholly and exclusively for the purposes of a trade, or losses not connected with or arising out of the trade.[20] Expenditure would not, for example, be capable of deduction where a company carrying on a trade solely of manufacturing computers pays rent for separate office space that is occupied by its distribution and marketing companies (who are carrying on separate trades). See generally Chapter 7.

Capital expenditure

Capital allowances in respect of plant or machinery expressly extends to capital expenditure incurred by a trader on the right to use or otherwise deal with computer software.[21] This form of relief is available where an election is made to exclude capital expenditure on software from the intangible fixed asset regime (see **10.2.2**).[22] A company is entitled to claim capital allowances at the rate of 20% (2011/12; reducing to 18% from April 2012) per annum on a reducing balance basis in connection with capital expenditure incurred on plant and machinery.[23] See generally Chapter 7.

The term 'computer software' is not defined in the capital allowances legislation. Computer software and the right to use it is treated as plant (whether or not it would constitute plant), where a trader incurs capital expenditure, for the purposes of a trade, on the acquisition of a right to

United Kingdom Taxation: General

---

[17] CTA 2009, s 61.
[18] CTA 2009, s 61(1).
[19] CTA 2009, s 61(2).
[20] CTA 2009, s 54(1). See also *Mallalieu v Drummond* [1983] STC 665. If an expense is incurred for more than one purpose the expense is not prohibited if any identifiable part or identifiable proportion of the expense is incurred wholly and exclusively for the purposes of the company's trade: CTA 2009, s 54(2).
[21] CAA 2001, s 71.
[22] CTA 2009, s 815.
[23] CAA 2001, s 56.

use or otherwise deal with computer software.[24] The taxpayer must be entitled to the right to use the software otherwise the taxpayer will not be treated as owning the plant (ie the software).[25]

Some guidance on the application of the plant allowance is contained in HMRC's guidance manuals. The *Capital Allowances Manual* states that all computer programs and data of any type should be treated as computer software.[26] The manual also states that where software is transferred by 'electronic means' (eg by download over the internet) in circumstances where there is no physical asset, the legislation will nonetheless apply.[27]

HMRC's *Business Income Manual* provides guidance on how expenditure should be classified in the context of the revenue and capital divide (the text is reproduced in Appendix F).[28] In the context of software acquired under a licence, regular payments akin to a rental are treated as revenue expenditure (which if incurred by a corporate would be subject to the intangible fixed asset regime). The deduction of such payments is governed by accounting practice. In respect of a lump sum payment the first issue in determining tax treatment is to identify whether the licence is a capital asset. In general terms a licence is a capital asset if it has a 'sufficiently enduring nature'. Where the software has a useful economic life of less than 2 years then HMRC will accept that the expenditure is revenue.

The manual also deals with equipment acquired as a package and software owned outright. In this regard, where IT hardware and the licence to use software are purchased as a package for a single payment the expenditure has to be apportioned between the IT hardware and the software.[29] Capital allowances under the general plant and machinery rules will be applied to the IT hardware expenditure,[30] and how the balance of the expenditure attributable to the software licence is treated will depend on whether it is classified as revenue or capital. However, HMRC acknowledges that where the hardware and software are acquired on capital account, and the expenditure is all within the general machinery and plant 'pool', then no apportionment will be necessary in practice.[31]

In various prescribed circumstances a taxpayer is required to deduct disposal value of an asset from qualifying expenditure incurred in

---

[24]   CAA 2001, s 71(2).
[25]   CAA 2001, s 71(2).
[26]   HMRC Guidance Manual CA23410 – *PMA: Computer Software*: www.hmrc.gov.uk/ manuals/camanual/CA23410.htm.
[27]   HMRC Guidance Manual CA23410 – *PMA: Computer Software*.
[28]   HMRC's *Business Income Manual*, at para 35810.
[29]   HMRC's *Business Income Manual*, at para 35810.
[30]   See **7.8.4** for details relating to the general plant and machinery allowance.
[31]   HMRC's *Business Income Manual*, at para 35810.

acquiring that asset. The disposal value that must be brought into account for computer software is summarised in Table 10.1.

Disposal value must be brought into account when one of the following events shown in Table 10.1 occur.[32] The amount of the disposal value that must be brought into account is also shown.

Table 10.1: Amount of disposal value on a disposal event

	Computer software	
	Prescribed event	*Disposal value*
(a)	Grant of software right for a consideration not consisting entirely of money.	Market value of the right granted at the time of the grant.
(b)	Sale at a price below the market value, there is no charge to tax under ITEPA 2003 (employment income), and either the grantee is not entitled to relief under Part 2 (plant) or Part 6 (R&D) of CAA 2001 or the grantee is a dual resident investing company which is connected with the grantor.	Market value of the right granted at the time of the grant.
(c)	Grant is made in circumstances other than those given in (a) and (b) above.	The net consideration in money received for the grant, together with (i) any insurance money received in respect of the software as a result of an event affecting the consideration obtainable on the grant and (ii) any other compensation of any description so received, so far as it consists of a capital sum.

The disposal value brought into account is not permitted to exceed the capital expenditure incurred by the taxpayer.[33] Thus, if a computer software company incurred capital expenditure of £50,000 in the acquisition of a computer server, which is subsequently destroyed in a fire, and receives insurance money of £60,000 to buy a replacement, the taxpayer is not required to bring into account disposal value in excess of £50,000 (albeit that the excess may constitute a capital gain subject to corporation tax on chargeable gains).

United Kingdom
Taxation: General

---

[32] In CAA 2001, s 72 (software).
[33] CAA 2001, s 73. Connected party transactions are subject to special rules governing the amount of the limit on disposal value: CAA 2001, s 62.

Short-life assets

The plant and machinery allowance of 20% (2011/12; reducing to 18% from April 2012), on a reducing balance basis, can cause problems where the economic life of the plant or machinery is less than the time it takes for the value to be written-off for tax purposes. In order to ameliorate this problem, relief is available which accelerates the rate of depreciation on what are known as 'short-life' assets (namely, assets with a life of less than 8 years).[34] To qualify for relief, an election must be made to HMRC.[35] The election must be within 2 years from the end of the relevant chargeable period (meaning the chargeable period in which the expenditure is incurred).[36] This is considered further in Chapter 7.

Long-life assets

Where capital expenditure is incurred for the purposes of a trade or other qualifying activity, and it is expenditure on plant or machinery with a useful economic life of 25 years or more, then it will be treated as a long-life asset.[37] The effect of this scheme is to limit the rate of depreciation to 10% rather than 20% (2011/12; reducing to 8% from April 2012).[38] The long-life asset provisions do not apply unless the expenditure incurred within a chargeable period is in excess of £100,000.[39] This is considered further in Chapter 7.

A similar 10% rate (reducing to 8% from April 2012) applies to certain 'integral fixtures' in buildings.

Alternative investment allowance

An alternative investment allowance (AIA) of £25,000 (from April 2012) per annum is available to all businesses in respect of qualifying expenditure.[40] It is necessary that the person owns the plant and machinery at some time during the chargeable period to qualify for the relief.[41] The expenditure covered by the £25,000 qualifies for full tax relief. This is considered further in Chapter 7.

---

[34]　CAA 2001, s 86.
[35]　CAA 2001, s 85.
[36]　CAA 2001, s 85(3).
[37]　CAA 2001, s 91.
[38]　CAA 2001, s 104D.
[39]　CAA 2001, s 99.
[40]　CAA 2001, ss 38A, 51A–51N. The AIA is made only in the chargeable period in which the qualifying expenditure is incurred with the consequence that it cannot be deferred to a later period.
[41]　CAA 2001, s 51A(1).

10.2.4 Software owned outright: 'bespoke software'

For accounting purpose, the costs of developing software on a bespoke basis that are directly attributable to bringing a computer system or other computer-operated machinery into working condition for its intended use within a business are treated as part of the cost of the related hardware rather than as a separate intangible asset for accounting purposes.[42] Where expenditure is treated as being on an intangible asset for accounting purposes under FRS 10 then corporation tax relief should be given in accordance with the intangible fixed asset regime (see **10.2.2**).[43]

10.3 DEDUCTION OF TAX AT SOURCE ON LICENCE PAYMENTS

The payment of royalties or licence fees for the use of intellectual property (including copyright in computer software) by a licensee to a licensor may be subject to deduction of tax at source, with the obligation on the licensee to make the deduction. Certain payments to a non-resident licensor are also subject to deduction of tax at source. Chapter 6 examines the nature of the withholding tax obligations, and the following is a summary of the position where there are specific withholding tax obligations in relation to computer software. Chapter 8 examines the characterisation of payments made on a cross-border basis, and the circumstances in which they will be treated as being made in respect of copyright.

In summary, the nature of the withholding obligations (for details see Chapter 6 at **6.11**) are:

(1) an individual licensee who pays certain annual payments which are made for genuine commercial reasons in connection with the individual's trade, profession or vocation is required to deduct tax at source at the basic rate of income tax from such payments (see ITA 2007, s 900);

(2) any corporate licensee who pays certain annual payments must deduct tax at source from such payments, at the basic rate of income tax (see ITA 2007, s 901);

(3) any licensee (whether an individual or corporation) who pays royalties for the use of patent rights must deduct tax at source at the basic rate of income tax from such payments (see ITA 2007, s 903);

United Kingdom
Taxation: General

---

[42] FRS 10, para 2 (intangible assets).
[43] CTA 2009, s 712.

(4)   any payment of royalties/periodic sums in respect of copyright or right in a design to an owner whose usual place of abode is outside the UK must be made under deduction of income tax at the basic rate (see ITA 2007, s 906);

(5)   inter-company royalty payments can be made on a gross basis subject to certain qualifying conditions (see Chapter 6 at **6.11.5**);

(6)   payments may be made on a gross basis with the benefit of a double taxation agreement (see Chapter 6 at **6.11.6**); and

(7)   payments may be made on a gross basis between member of an EU corporate group (see Chapter 6 at **6.11.8**).

Any payment of royalties and/or periodic sums in respect of copyright[44] (referred to in the tax legislation as the 'relevant intellectual property right') to an owner whose usual place of abode is outside the UK must be made under deduction of tax at the basic rate of income tax,[45] except where that licensor has the benefit of a double taxation agreement between the country of its residence and the UK, whereby the rate of such withholding tax is reduced, or the obligation to deduct is removed altogether.

The obligation to withhold will only arise in connection with a payment where:[46]

(1)   it is a payment of any royalties, or sums payable periodically, in respect of a relevant intellectual property right;

(2)   that payment is one that is charged to income tax or corporation tax; and either:

   (a)   the usual place of abode of the owner of the right is outside the UK; or
   (b)   a person ('the seller') has assigned the intellectual property right to another person, the usual place of abode of the seller is outside the UK, the seller is entitled to periodical payments in respect of the right, and the payments are in respect of that entitlement.

No withholding obligation is imposed where the payment is made in respect of copies of works or articles that have been exported from the

---

[44]   For this purpose the term 'copyright' is defined as excluding any copyright in (a) a cinematographic film or video recording or (b) the sound-track of a cinematographic film or video recording, except so far as it is separately exploited: ITA 2007 s 907(2).
[45]   ITA 2007, s 906(5).
[46]   ITA 2007, s 906(1)–(3).

UK for distribution outside the UK.[47] It should also be noted in connection with payments of royalties of relevant intellectual property (within the meaning given by ITA 2007) to a non-UK resident owner that are made through an agent resident in the UK with regard to which the agent is entitled as against the owner of the right to deduct any sum by way of commission in respect of services rendered, the amount of the payment from which the tax must be deducted is that payment less the commission.[48] However, if the person by or through whom the payment is made does not know the commission is payable, or does not know its amount, the sum representing income tax required to be deducted must be calculated on the total amount of the payment.[49] Any agreement to make the payment for the relevant intellectual property without deduction for income tax is void.[50]

---

[47] ITA 2007, s 906(4).
[48] ITA 2007, s 908(1).
[49] ITA 2007, s 908(2).
[50] ITA 2007, s 909(2).

PART IV

SHARE-BASED EMPLOYEE INCENTIVES

CHAPTER 11

SHARE-BASED EMPLOYEE INCENTIVES FOR PRIVATE TECHNOLOGY COMPANIES

11.1   INTRODUCTION

Part IV deals with shares and options to acquire shares held by directors and employees in private technology and e-commerce companies (referred to as 'technology companies'). Different considerations apply to public companies, listed companies and carried interests in partnerships and these are not discussed here.

Equity is critical to technology companies as it enables incentives to be provided to employees, often at little or no cash cost to the business. Arrangements of this sort usually work best where an exit is likely to be achieved in the short to medium term. The objective is typically to structure these arrangements so as to allow gains made by employees to be taxed as capital whilst at the same time avoiding (or minimising) any cash costs until they are in a position to raise cash through share sales. In group situations, the shares will typically be in shares in the parent or otherwise in the company within the group most likely to exit. Reference to 'exit' is to a sale of the entire issued share capital of the company to a third party purchaser or an initial public offering (IPO) (although the latter is less common).

The main income tax legislation is contained in the Income Tax (Earnings and Pensions) Act 2003 (ITEPA 2003). Section 62 of ITEPA 2003 imposes income tax on 'general earnings' (which includes shares acquired by reason of employment), Part 7 of ITEPA 2003 imposes income tax charges on employment-related securities and employment-related securities options and Part 7A of ITEPA 2003 contains anti-avoidance rules designed to impose income tax charges on so-called 'disguised remuneration' provided by third parties. The main social security legislation is contained in the Social Security Contributions and Benefits Act 1992 (SSCBA 1992). The main capital gains tax legislation is contained in the Taxation of Chargeable Gains Act 1992 (TCGA 1992). For UK incorporated companies, the main company law legislation is contained in the Companies Act 2006 (CA 2006).

It is essential to ensure, so far as possible, that gains are taxed as capital rather than income as the differential is stark. The highest effective rate on gains taxed as income is 58.9% for 2011/12 (including employees' and employers' National Insurance contributions (NIC) where the employers' NIC cost is passed on to employees), whereas the lowest rate on gains taxed as capital is 10% (for office-holders and employees who qualify for entrepreneurs' relief),[1] a differential of 48.9%.

Technology companies are typically wholly owned by 'founder directors' in the early stages, and in the later stages (after a funding round or two) by a mixture of founder directors and investors. Occasionally companies may be owned wholly by investors (eg after a rescue funding round), but management are likely to receive fresh equity in these circumstances to protect the interests of investors. At any stage from start up to exit it may be necessary to recruit or retain employees using share-based incentives.

The thrust of Part IV is to examine the share-based incentive arrangements which technology companies put in place in practice. Part 7 of ITEPA 2003 was introduced in 2003 to subject artificial gains to income tax and Part 7A was introduced on 10 December 2010 to subject so-called 'disguised remuneration' provided through third parties to income tax. In the author's experience, the vast majority of technology companies are interested in rewarding employees only for genuine commercial growth, so most of the anti-avoidance rules are irrelevant. There are, however, some cases where commercial growth can be taxed as income, so arrangements have to be structured carefully to avoid unwelcome tax results.

11.1.1   Options

Traditionally the most common incentive arrangements operated by technology companies have involved granting options to employees to subscribe for shares. These options are usually structured so as to become exercisable only on an exit to avoid the need to purchase shares pre-exit.

It is essential to ensure options qualify for tax relief using one of the two discretionary tax advantaged share options plans, namely the enterprise management incentive plan (EMI) or the company share option plan (CSOP). EMI is the more generous of the two, so should be the first port of call.

Options have a number of advantages over shares, the main ones being cash flow and simplicity. Employees do not need to pay anything for the grant of an option – if the option is only capable of exercise on exit it is possible to fund the exercise price out of the proceeds realised from the sale of option shares. Exit only options can be structured so as to lapse on cessation of employment thereby freeing up share capital to provide

---

[1]   TCGA 1992, s 169N.

future incentives. Alternatively, exit only options can be structured so as to continue after cessation of employment but to become exercisable only on an exit being achieved.

Option-holders can be required to enter into a power of attorney authorising a director to exercise options on an exit and to sell the option shares to a purchaser by entering into the sale and purchase agreement on their behalf. Options structured in this way are straightforward to operate as it is possible to deliver 100% control to a purchaser. The option shares are never owned by the option-holder (other than for a short period prior to completion) so there is no need to put in place arrangements to acquire forfeited shares from participants.

EMI options can be structured to qualify for tax relief on grant and exercise, allowing gains to be taxed as capital on the sale of the option shares. In addition, the employing company will usually qualify for a corporation tax deduction for the accounting period of exercise equal to the spread (ie the difference between the market value of the option shares on the date of exercise and the exercise price). The deduction is often treated as a 'deferred tax asset' in completion statements, increasing the value of the company to the purchaser (see Chapter 13 at **13.3**, Corporation Tax Relief).

Options that are structured to allow exercise pre-exit can be more complicated to operate than exit only options if it is also intended to purchase the shares pre-exit (eg from leavers on cessation of employment). Many of the comments below concerning shares apply equally to option shares acquired pursuant to the exercise of options pre-exit.

11.1.2   Shares

There has been a shift from providing incentives in the form of options to shares in recent years, for several reasons.

It is necessary for individuals to hold shares (as opposed to options) to qualify for entrepreneurs' relief (ER). Individuals who qualify for ER are taxed at a rate of 10% on the first £10 million of lifetime chargeable gains[2] whereas the top rate of CGT is 28%[3] (a maximum saving of £1.8 million). An individual qualifies for ER on gains made on the sale of shares in his 'personal company'.[4] To qualify, the shares must be in a trading company (or the holding company of a trading group) for the 12 months prior to disposal, the shares must be held by an office-holder or employee, they must represent at least 5% of the ordinary share capital (when tested by nominal value) and the holder must be entitled to at least 5% of the

---

[2]   TCGA 1992, s 169N.
[3]   TCGA 1992, s 4(3).
[4]   TCGA 1992, s 169S(3).

voting rights.[5] When ER first came into effect on 5 April 2008 it was not particularly valuable due to the lifetime limit of £1 million. A succession of increases in the limit (the last being from £5 million to £10 million for disposals after 5 April 2011[6]) and the introduction of a top rate of capital gains tax (CGT) of 28%[7] have made ER progressively more valuable. Consequently, many technology companies that qualify for EMI have recently started offering shares to (usually more senior) employees to allow them to benefit from ER.

Venture owned (as opposed to venture backed) technology companies often do not satisfy the EMI conditions (as they are not 'independent' for the purposes of the EMI legislation).[8] Many of these companies award shares (as opposed to options) to allow gains made by all employees to be taxed as capital.

Many technology companies operate internationally. EMI and CSOP options only afford relief from UK income tax and NIC so it is often more tax efficient to award shares (as opposed to options) to non-UK resident employees to allow gains to be taxed as capital. The same applies to awards made to UK resident individuals who do not qualify for EMI (such as non-executive directors who do not meet the EMI 'full-time working' requirement).

Equity is often the only significant benefit that technology companies are able to offer to employees. In recent years there has been a trend towards prospective employees taking advice in relation to the equity component of their proposed package. Advisers often request arrangements involving shares if these are more tax efficient. Advisers also favour shares as shareholders benefit from minority shareholder rights, which are not available to option-holders.[9]

There are a number of additional issues which need to be considered if arrangements involve shares, the main ones being cash flow and the mechanics of how to impose vesting and forfeiture conditions.

11.1.3   Cash flow issues

If employees are awarded shares, as opposed to options, they will need to find some funds on acquisition to pay the subscription or purchase monies. In addition, if the shares are acquired at an under-value there may be a charge to income tax, which also has to be funded.

---

[5]   TCGA 1992, s 169S.
[6]   Finance Act 2011, s 9.
[7]   Finance (No 2) Act 2010, s 2, with effect for gains accruing on or after 23 June 2010.
[8]   ITEPA 2003, Sch 5, para 9.
[9]   CA 2009, Part 30.

It is preferable to ensure shares awarded to directors and employees have a market value of no more than a nominal amount at the time the award is made to avoid or minimise the amount the employee has to pay for the shares and to avoid or minimise any income tax exposure. It is not possible to agree the value of shares with HMRC in advance of acquisition. Any income tax is payable through self-assessment unless the shares are readily convertible assets (RCAs), in which case the employer is required to operate PAYE and NIC on a 'reasonable estimate' of the market value.[10]

If the market value of shares is substantial (and therefore likely to trigger unacceptable income tax charges on acquisition) there are, broadly, three solutions outlined below. There are some commercial differences between them which are best illustrated using an example.

Example 11.1: Solutions to cash flow issue

Suppose Company A is worth £10 million (arrived at by applying a multiple of 1 to turnover) and has 95,000 ordinary shares of 1p each in issue held by two founder directors. It is intended to award an interest in 5% of the fully diluted share capital to a new CEO to reward him for increases in the value of the shares to exit. The value would be in the region of £100 per share calculated on a pro rata basis (£10 million/100,000) or £40 per share after applying a discount of 60% for minority holdings.[11]

(1) Growth shares

The articles of association of the company could be amended to create a new class of growth shares with a nominal value of 1p each, which have no rights other than to participate in exit consideration achieved in excess of £10 million. The ordinary shares would be entitled to all exit consideration up to £10 million and the ordinary shares and growth shares would rank pro rata to holdings as if they constituted one class for exit consideration achieved above £10 million. The CEO could be permitted to subscribe at par for 5,000 growth shares representing 5% of the fully diluted share capital.[12] If the company were to go into liquidation, the CEO would have no liability as the growth shares would have been issued fully paid. The rights attaching to the growth shares need to be set out in the articles (so it is clear the rights are not personal to the holder) for reasons explained in Chapter 12 at **12.2**.

(2) Joint share ownership plans (JSOPs)

---

[10] ITEPA 2003, s 696.
[11] All examples in Part IV assume that where is it appropriate to apply a minority discount, it is 60% as that is the top end of the range HMRC usually allows for technology companies. It may be possible to justify a higher discount based on valuation case-law but HMRC tends to resist higher discounts – it assumes that if a company establishes share-based incentive arrangements it is an indication that the company intends to exit in the short to medium term. A discount of 60% takes into account the prospect of an exit.
[12] (95,000/95 x 5).

The company could establish an employee share ownership plan (ESOP) trust. The CEO and trustee of the ESOP would then subscribe jointly for 5,000 ordinary shares at a subscription price of £40 per share with the CEO paying a nominal amount and the balance of the subscription monies being paid by the trustee. The ownership terms would be set out in a JSOP agreement between the CEO, the trustee and the company. The JSOP agreement would entitle the CEO to the sale consideration achieved in excess of £40 per share. If the company were to go into liquidation, neither the CEO nor the ESOP trustee would have any further liability as the shares would have been issued fully paid.

(3) Nil paid shares

The CEO could subscribe for 5,000 ordinary shares at a subscription price of £40 per share (ie subscription monies of £40 x 5,000 = £200,000), but with the subscription monies left outstanding until called. In practice the company would only call the shares when they are sold, at which point the CEO would have the funds with which to pay the call (assuming the shares are sold for more than £200,000). If the company goes into liquidation, the liquidator would be obliged to call the shares, leaving the CEO with a liability of £200,000 and no funds with which to pay the call. It is not possible to override the obligation of the liquidator to call the shares in the articles of association (or subscription agreement).[13] It is possible to circumvent the obligation of the liquidator to call the shares by arranging for the shares to be issued fully paid to a third party such as an ESOP trust which then sells the shares to the CEO on deferred payment terms. This approach should generally be avoided as it risks a punitive PAYE and NIC charge arising under the disguised remuneration rules in ITEPA 2003, Part 7A.[14] The disguised remuneration rules are discussed in Chapter 15.[15]

The key commercial difference between the three suggested routes in this example is that the CEO is required to take a real commercial risk using nil paid shares whereas his liability is nominal and paid up front using growth shares and JSOPs.

---

[13] *Re Cordova Gold Co* [1891] 2 Ch 580.

[14] ITEPA 2003, s 695A.

[15] The disguised remuneration rules impose PAYE and NIC charges when a 'relevant third party' such as an ESOP takes a 'relevant step' which includes the transfer of an asset (such as the shares) and the earlier 'earmarking' of the shares (unless the earmarking occurs at the same time as the transfer). If the disguised remuneration rules apply: they operate by imposing a PAYE and NIC charge on the full value of the shares earmarked or transferred (none of the reductions would apply here as nothing is assessed to income tax when the steps occur and the CEO pays nothing for the shares at the time the shares are transferred). There is an exemption from the transfer charge if the shares are subject to short-term risk of forfeiture but no exemption applies to an earlier earmarking of the shares by the trustee. Therefore, if an ESOP is to be used as suggested it is essential for the growth shares sold to the CEO on deferred payment terms to be subject to short-term risk of forfeiture and to ensure the trustee is not informed of the identity of the CEO until the shares are transferred so as to avoid an earlier earmarking of the shares.

The JSOP and nil paid share routes reward increases in value above £40 per share (because it is possible to discount the value of the ordinary shares by 60% to the pro rata price), whereas the growth share route, in effect, rewards increases in value above £100 per share (£10 million/100,000 = £100). If the growth shares were structured so the threshold above which the growth shares participate is reduced by 60% to £4 million, the intrinsic value of the shares would be £60 per share (£10 million – £4 million/100,000), calculated on a pro rata basis or £24 per share (£60 x 40%) calculated after applying a 60% discount for minority holdings. Accordingly it would not be possible to argue the up front value of the growth shares is nominal. Growth shares tend to be structured so the threshold is at least equal (if not at a premium) to the value of the company as a whole at the time the awards are made so it is possible to argue the value of the growth shares is nominal on acquisition.

There is no need to establish an ESOP using growth shares or nil paid shares (at least, not when the awards are made); both of these routes potentially allow the CEO to qualify for ER whereas the JSOP route generally does not (see Chapter 13 at **13.4.1**).

When one works through the pros and cons, the optimum route is usually to create a new class of growth shares as it involves no commercial risk for the employee, it allows him to qualify for ER and does not require (at least initially) the company to establish an ESOP. There may be some risk of an up front tax charge but this should be minimal if the threshold is set correctly.

11.2 SHARES – VESTING AND FORFEITURE CONDITIONS

Arrangements involving shares need to be structured carefully in order to provide an effective incentive. Vesting and forfeiture conditions will usually be required, although there may be exceptions where these are inappropriate (such as shares awarded in recognition of past service or shares held by founder directors).

Vesting is not a defined term, its meaning depends on what the relevant documentation provides. Vesting can govern the extent to which shares can be sold at a gain on an exit, the extent to which shares can be retained following cessation of employment, the extent to which shares are required to be offered for sale (usually at fair value) on cessation of employment or the extent to which any performance conditions are met. Shares which fail to vest often have to be forfeited either for no payment or for a payment equal to the lower of cost and fair value. Once vested, shares may be required to be forfeited in certain 'bad leaver' situations (such as gross misconduct or breach of non-compete clauses) or leavers may be required to offer shares for sale on ceasing employment at 'fair value'. The subject that requires careful consideration (particularly for technology companies with no distributable reserves) is the mechanics of vesting and forfeiture.

Private companies that are UK incorporated are not permitted to hold shares in treasury[16] so the choices are usually to use an ESOP (or arrange for a friendly shareholder) to 'warehouse' the shares pending redistribution, arrange for the company to purchase and cancel the shares or convert the shares to deferred shares.

11.2.1   Conversion to deferred shares

The articles of association of the company could allow the board to convert shares held by employees to deferred shares in specified circumstances. The deferred shares would typically have no rights other than to the return of the original subscription price on an exit being achieved. This is by far the simplest solution but it does not allow participants to receive any cash until an exit is achieved. Note: it is not possible under UK company law to redesignate irredeemable shares as redeemable shares (with a view to redeeming them shortly thereafter) as redeemable shares have to be issued as such.[17]

11.2.2   Purchase of own shares

Private companies are permitted to purchase and cancel their own shares, but the rules can be difficult to comply with. The purchase must be funded out of distributable reserves or the proceeds of a fresh issue of shares.[18] This requirement is impossible for many technology companies to satisfy as often they have no distributable reserves. The purchase contract must be approved in advance of the purchase by a special resolution of shareholders and that process requires the contract (or a memorandum of its terms) to be circulated to all shareholders.[19] It is possible, however, for the company and prospective seller to enter into a contingent purchase contract (CPC) and for the CPC to be approved only when the company wishes to purchase the shares.[20]

Private companies are permitted to fund the purchase of own shares out of capital but the procedural requirements can be onerous.[21] The directors are required to prepare a statement of solvency backed by an auditors'

---

[16]   CA 2009, s 724.
[17]   CA 2006, s 684(1).
[18]   CA 2006, s 692.
[19]   CA 2006, s 696(2).
[20]   CA 2006, s 694(2)(b).
[21]   CA 2006, s 713.

report.[22] Following a purchase out of capital, the company is required to issue a notice in the *Gazette* and either to notify creditors directly or via a national newspaper.[23]

The price paid by a company when it purchases its own shares is taxed as a distribution to the extent it exceeds the original subscription price paid for the shares.[24] The amount of the distribution is added to the individual's taxable income and charged at an effective tax rate of 25% for income between the higher and additional rate income tax thresholds and at an effective rate of 36.1% for income above the additional rate tax threshold. If certain conditions are met, however, capital treatment applies. The capital treatment conditions are stringent, the main ones being the shares being purchased must have been held by the shareholder for at least 5 years, the purpose of the purchase must be wholly or mainly to benefit the company's trade and the shareholder's interest in the company must be substantially reduced as a result of the purchase.[25] If the conditions are met, capital treatment applies automatically. It is possible to apply for clearance from HMRC in advance as to whether the capital conditions are met.[26]

11.2.3 Friendly shareholder

If the shares are required to be offered for sale at fair value it may be possible to find a purchaser (eg the shares could be sold to a new recruit or to an investor as a condition of a fundraising). If the shares are required to be offered for sale at an under-value, however, it is best to avoid sales to a 'friendly' shareholder with the intention of warehousing the shares pending redistribution. If the purchaser is a director or employee, the acquisition will give rise to a tax charge on the amount of the under-value (see Chapter 12 at **12.1.1**). Any shareholder warehousing the shares (whether or not an employee) will be treated as a third party for the purposes of the disguised remuneration rules in ITEPA 2003, Part 7A, causing a further layer of complexity and risking inadvertent PAYE and NIC charges depending on how the shares are distributed (see Chapter 15).

11.2.4 ESOPs

The company could establish a discretionary trust for the benefit of employees and former employees (referred to as an ESOP). The ESOP could purchase the shares as and when requested to do so by the company funded (usually) by an interest free loan from the company. The shares could be held in an ESOP pending redistribution to employees. There is

---

[22]   CA 2006, s 714.
[23]   CA 2006, s 719.
[24]   CTA 2010, s 1000(1).
[25]   CTA 2010, ss 1033–1045.
[26]   CTA 2010, s 1044.

IV **Share-based Employee Incentives**

usually no need to establish the ESOP until shares are first required to be purchased, thereby deferring set-up fees.

ESOPs have several advantages over own share purchases and tend to be the preferred solution. ESOP trustees can purchase shares by private agreement or through pre-emption with no need for the contract to be approved by shareholders; capital treatment applies on the sale of shares to an ESOP; and there is no requirement for ESOPs to be funded out of distributable reserves. There are, however, a number of significant tax and other issues which need to be considered.

If the trustee of the ESOP is UK resident, the trustee will be subject to CGT.[27] Consequently most ESOPs are run by professional trustees resident in a low tax jurisdiction such as Jersey or Guernsey to avoid gains made by the ESOP from being subject to CGT. It is necessary to demonstrate that the ESOP is managed and controlled outside the UK to obtain the desired CGT treatment,[28] so careful communication is required between the establishing company and the trustee. Trust law requires the trustee to act in the best interests of its beneficiaries and prevents the trustee acting in a manner which fetters its discretion, so the trustee is not always in a position to act as the establishing company may request.

ESOPs have to be drafted such that the beneficiaries are confined to employees, former employees and their dependents (to ensure that they meet the definition of 'employees share scheme'[29] and to ensure they qualify as 'section 86 trusts' for inheritance tax (IHT) purposes[30]). If the trust deed is so drafted, the trustee will be unable to provide benefits to the establishing company or any company within the same group. Consequently funds should usually be provided in the form of loans (as opposed to contributions) to enable any surplus cash to be extracted from the ESOP in the form of loan repayments.

If a close company makes a loan to an ESOP, it is required to pay a deposit to HMRC equal to 25% of the loan if the loan is still outstanding 9 months after the end of the accounting period in which it is made.[31] The deposit can only be reclaimed as and when the loan is repaid.[32] Most private technology companies fall within the definition of a close company which is, broadly, a company controlled by five or fewer shareholders or its directors, however many.[33] The deposit requirement can be particularly harsh for companies that are short of cash (as is the case with many technology companies).

---

[27]   TCGA 1992, s 2.
[28]   *De Beers Consolidated Mines Ltd v Howe (Inspector of Taxes)* [1906] AC 455.
[29]   CA 2006, s 1166.
[30]   Inheritance Tax Act 1984 (IHTA 1984), s 86.
[31]   CTA 2010, s 455(3).
[32]   CTA 2010, s 458.
[33]   CTA 2010, s 439.

Contributions to ESOPs by close companies can trigger IHT charges in the hands of the company.[34] These can be avoided by excluding 5% plus participators from benefiting from the trust.[35] The so-called 'section 13 exclusion' still permits 5% plus participators to receive benefits if these are provided in a form which is subject to income tax.[36] It is advisable to incorporate the s 13 exclusion (even though it makes the operation of the ESOP restrictive) as there are occasions when it is necessary for close companies to make contributions to an ESOP. If an ESOP is closed following an exit, for example, it may be necessary to 'write off' outstanding loans from the establishing company to the ESOP. Unfortunately, if the loans were to be written off it would trigger an income tax charge in the hands of the trustee.[37] The income tax charge can be avoided if the trustee is put in funds by way of a contribution which it then uses to repay the loan.

The introduction of the disguised remuneration rules in ITEPA 2003, Part 7A has added a further complication in that inadvertent PAYE and NIC charges can now arise when shares are provided to employees or 'earmarked' by 'third parties'. The trustee of an ESOP will be a third party for these purposes, so advice is required whenever the trustee acts in order to avoid inadvertent tax charges arising under the rules.

The tax and other complications associated with running ESOPs mean it is usually preferable for technology companies to avoid establishing them unless absolutely necessary. The Office of Tax Simplification will be considering unapproved share plan arrangements following the enactment of the Finance Act in 2012.[38] The author suggests what is necessary is a qualifying ESOP or 'QuESOP', which would be exempt from the above tax charges to allow private companies to provide incentives using shares without incurring the current exposure, expense and difficulty associated with operating ESOPs (see Chapter 16 at **16.2.3**, Suggested Reforms).

11.2.5   Meaning of fair value

It is common for articles of association to require 'good leavers' to offer their shares for sale at 'fair value', being the price agreed between the leaver and the directors or the fair value determined by an independent valuation expert if agreement cannot be reached.

Often articles prescribe how fair value is to be determined in these circumstances and state that the size of holding is to be ignored in arriving at the value. It is often possible to apply a discount of between

---

[34]   IHTA 1984, s 94.
[35]   IHTA 1984, s 13.
[36]   IHTA 1984, s 13(4)(a).
[37]   ITTOIA 2005, s 420.
[38]   HM Treasury press release, 'Tax Simplification team to review pensioner taxation and share schemes', 11 July 2011.

40% and 60% for minority holdings, whereas these provisions may allow a leaver to insist on his shares being offered for sale at an undiscounted price. If shares are sold at an undiscounted price, HMRC may take the view the shares were sold at an over-value, triggering PAYE and NIC charges on the amount of the over-value under ITEPA 2003, Part 7, Chapter 3D.[39] Alternatively, HMRC may take the view the sale was at an arm's length price thereby making it impossible to agree a discounted valuation should the company wish to make further awards using the same class of shares in the future. More likely, no purchaser will be found for the shares, allowing the shareholder to retain the shares to exit (when the commercial intention may have been only to allow the leaver to benefit from gains made to cessation of employment).

Leaver provisions of this sort are much better drafted by providing that fair value is the price agreed between the seller and the directors or the fair value determined by an independent valuation expert without specifying what factors the expert is required to take into account or ignore. The meaning of 'fair value' allows the valuer to take all factors into account, including the size of holding. It is more likely the fair value determined on that basis will equate to market value for tax purposes thereby minimising the risk of PAYE and NIC charges arising on the sale of the shares.

Example 11.2: Vesting and forfeiture conditions

In our example suppose Company A decides to make an award to its new CEO by creating a new class of growth shares that participate in exit consideration above £10 million. The company is attracted to this proposal as it allows the CEO to qualify for ER, it does not involve him taking any commercial risk and it avoids the need to establish an ESOP (at least initially).

The terms of the award are the CEO's shares vest 25% on the first anniversary of the vesting commencement date (being his start date) and thereafter 6.25% quarterly until fully vested on the fourth anniversary of the vesting commencement date. If he leaves, his unvested shares are required to be forfeited for no payment and his vested shares are required to be offered for sale at fair value (being the price agreed between him and the board or, failing that, fair value determined by an independent valuation expert taking all relevant factors into account, including the size of holding). The company has no ESOP and has no intention of establishing one due to the complexity and cost, unless it is necessary later. The arrangements could be structured as follows.

The articles of Company A are amended to create the new class of growth shares and (if necessary) a new class of deferred shares. The nominal value of the growth shares and ordinary shares is 1p per share and both classes are entitled to one vote per share. By structuring this way it is hoped the CEO

---

[39]   ITEPA 2003, ss 446Y and 698.

will meet the relevant ER conditions by satisfying the 5% tests.[40] Shortly after the shareholder resolutions are passed, the CEO enters into a subscription agreement and a related contingent purchase contract (CPC). The CPC contains a vesting schedule and which gives the company the right to buy shares (or to designate another person to do so) if the CEO leaves for any reason. Vested shares can be bought at fair value and unvested shares at the lower of cost and fair value. The amended articles allow the board to redesignate growth shares as deferred shares in circumstances where it has been determined that they cannot vest. The CPC includes powers of attorney to force the completion of share sales should the CEO prove unco-operative.

If the CEO were to leave, the company could redesignate all unvested shares as deferred shares. It may be the company is able to find a purchaser who is willing to buy the vested shares at fair value (e g an investor may be prepared to buy the shares as a condition of a fundraising or they could be sold to a replacement CEO). In the absence of a purchaser, the company could establish an ESOP and put it in funds to purchase the shares or it could purchase and cancel the shares. If the own share purchase route is used, the company would need sufficient distributable reserves (or be prepared to fund the purchase out of capital using the more complex procedure) and the CPC would need to be approved by a special resolution of shareholders prior to the purchase (there is no need to seek shareholder approval for the CPC when it is entered into).[41]

In the past it was common for vesting schedules and good/bad leaver provisions to be set out in the articles of association. The author considers the arrangement suggested above (in which the vesting schedule is contained in the CPC) is a better approach. The CPC is more flexible, allowing different vesting schedules and performance conditions for each participant. The CPC is a private agreement (unless and until it needs to be circulated to shareholders and that is only necessary if the company purchases the shares). The legal title to shares can be put in the name of a nominee to prevent the number of shares held by an employee from becoming public knowledge. In addition, the redesignation facility allows unvested shares to be converted to deferred shares requiring a purchaser to be found only for the vested shares.

---

[40]   TCGA 1992, s 169S(3).
[41]   CA 2006, s 694(2)(b).

CHAPTER 12

CHARGING PROVISIONS UNDER ITEPA 2003, PART 7

12.1 OVERVIEW OF RELEVANT TAX CHARGING PROVISIONS AND RELIEFS

Shares acquired at an under-value by reason of employment are taxed as general earnings under the Income Tax (Earnings and Pensions) Act 2003 (ITEPA 2003), s 62. Part 7 of ITEPA 2003 was introduced on 16 April 2003 and supplements the basic general earnings charge under s 62. The main chapters are as follows:

- Chapter 1: Introduction;

- Chapter 2: Restricted securities;

- Chapter 3: Convertible securities;

- Chapter 3A: Securities with artificially depressed market value;

- Chapter 3B: Securities with artificially enhanced market value;

- Chapter 3C: Securities acquired for less than market value;

- Chapter 3D: Securities disposed of for more than market value;

- Chapter 4: Special benefits from securities;

- Chapter 4A: Shares in research institution spin-out companies; and

- Chapter 5: Securities options.

The most important charging provisions in practice are the general earnings charge under s 62 as supplemented by charges arising in relation to restricted securities imposed pursuant to Chapter 2 of ITEPA 2003, Part 7. Chapter 3C (securities acquired for less than market value) is largely only relevant where shares are acquired nil paid or partly paid (it imposes charges on the amount left unpaid by treating it as a 'notional loan'). Chapter 3D (securities disposed of for more than market value) is relevant as it can give rise to valuation issues on share sales. Chapter 5 (securities options) is relevant to explain why options should be structured so as to qualify for EMI where possible, it also impacts on the structure of earn-outs capable of settlement only in securities.

Chapter 3 of ITEPA 2003, Part 7 deals with convertible shares and is relevant only to explain why arrangements should be structured so shares are not convertible. Chapters 3A and 3B of ITEPA 2003, Part 7 are designed to prevent artificial manipulation of share values. Chapter 4 of ITEPA 2003, Part 7 (special benefits from securities) allows HMRC to impose income tax charges in cases of avoidance not covered elsewhere. This chapter does not deal with Chapters 3, 3A, 3B or 4 in any detail and does not cover the special reliefs for shares in research institution spin-out companies in Chapter 4A. All the Chapters in Part 7 contain anti-avoidance provisions, which are not dealt with in any detail.

Part 7A of ITEPA 2003 was introduced on 10 December 2010 to combat so-called 'disguised remuneration' provided using employee benefit trusts. The rules are only relevant where 'third parties' (typically ESOPs and individual shareholders) warehouse shares pending distribution to employees. Careful structuring is required to avoid these charges. The disguised remuneration rules are dealt with in Chapter 15.

The most useful reliefs are contained in:

- ITEPA 2003, Part 7, Chapter 9 (EMI (enterprise management incentive plan) tax reliefs as supplemented by the EMI conditions in ITEPA 2003, Sch 5);

- Corporation Tax Act 2009 (CTA 2009), Part 12 (Corporation tax deduction for employee share acquisitions);

- Taxation of Chargeable Gains Act 1992 (TCGA 1992), Part 5, Chapter 3: Entrepreneurs' relief;

- Income Tax Act 2007 (ITA 2007), Part 8, Chapter 1 (Tax relief for interest on borrowings to buy shares); and

- ITA 2007, Part 4, Chapter 6 (Loss relief against income on disposal of shares).

The first three of these reliefs are dealt with in Chapter 13. In most cases where income tax charges arise, the base cost of the shares is uplifted for capital gains tax (CGT) purposes by the amount assessed to income tax to avoid a double charge to tax.[1] Many of the charging provisions and reliefs deserve chapters in their own right, so what follows necessarily focuses on

---

[1]   TCGA 1992, s 119A.

the key issues that arise for technology companies in practice. It is assumed employees are resident, ordinarily resident and domiciled in the UK for the purposes of Part IV.

12.1.1   Acquisition of shares: the general earnings charge under ITEPA 2003, s 62

The case of *Weight v Salmon*[2] establishes that shares acquired by reason of employment are subject to income tax on the amount of any under-value; it is an emolument which is a category of general earnings brought into charge by ITEPA 2003, s 62.

The charge applies to any shares acquired by reason of employment not just shares in the employer or a company in the same group as the employer. ITEPA 2003, s 5 treats all office-holders as if they were employees for the purposes of the Act so the charge applies, for example, to directors who are not employees (such as non-executive directors).

The 'money's worth' basis of valuation applies to emoluments so applies to charges under s 62. The basis of valuation is a subjective one in that it takes into account the value of the benefit to the employee in question. Consequently the value of the shares will be depressed by all restrictions (and enhanced by all entitlements) whether these are contained in the articles or elsewhere and whether these are intrinsic to the shares or personal to the holder. The seller of the shares for the purposes of the money's worth valuation is the actual employee, so any information known to him is taken into account. There is a long line of case-law establishing the money's worth basis of valuation.[3] The money's worth charge itself has been replaced by the benefit in kind rules for employees earning over £8,500 per year, but still applies to emoluments.

12.1.2   Capital gains tax basis of valuation

The money's worth basis of valuation applicable for the purposes of the general earnings charge under ITEPA 2003, s 62 contrasts to the CGT basis of valuation that applies to charges arising under ITEPA 2003, Part 7. The CGT definition of market value in the context of unquoted shares is the price which the shares 'might reasonably be expected to fetch on a sale in the open market'.[4] The legislation stipulates that:[5]

> '... it shall be assumed that, in the open market which is postulated for the purposes of that determination [of market value], there is available to any prospective purchaser of the asset in question all the information which a

---

[2]   (1935) 19 TC 174.
[3]   HMRC *Employment Related Securities Manual* ERSM220030 (Valuation Issues).
[4]   TCGA 1992, s 273(1).
[5]   TCGA 1992, s 273(3).

IV Share-based Employee Incentives

prudent prospective purchaser of the asset might reasonably require if he were proposing to purchase if from a willing vendor by private treaty and at arm's length.'

The CGT definition assumes a hypothetical sale of the shares in the open market negotiated freely at arm's length between hypothetical parties for the best price reasonably obtainable. It is irrelevant if the shares are in fact unmarketable or subject to transfer restrictions. Any such restrictions are not binding upon the hypothetical purchaser, who must be assumed to be entitled to acquire and to hold the shares subject to the company's articles (though the existence of transfer and other restrictions may affect the price which the hypothetical purchaser would be prepared to pay).

HMRC states that in most cases there will be no difference between the money's worth and CGT basis of valuation.[6] There is, however, one instance where there can be a substantial difference. If a director acquires shares whilst in possession of confidential information (eg because he has been negotiating a sale or funding round) the money's worth basis of valuation takes his knowledge into account. It is common (for the reasons explained at **12.2.8**) for employees and employers to make a joint election pursuant to ITEPA 2003, s 431(1) to pay income tax on the unrestricted market value (UMV) of shares within 14 days of acquisition. If such an election is made, the CGT basis of valuation applies for the purposes of determining the UMV.[7] It may be beneficial for the director to make such an election in these circumstances as it is then possible to argue, under the information standard applicable to the CGT basis of valuation, that it would be unreasonable for a hypothetical purchaser of a small minority holding to be made aware of confidential information. HMRC confirms that where a director acquires shares whilst in possession of confidential information, it may add substantially to the taxable value of the shares for the purposes of the money's worth charge compared with the CGT basis of valuation.[8]

12.1.3   Scope of ITEPA 2003, Part 7

Before the introduction of ITEPA 2003, Part 7 it was common to argue that shares were not acquired by reason of employment for the purposes of the tax charge on acquisition pursuant to s 62 but for some other reason such as 'qua founder'. The scope of Part 7 is drafted widely and is designed to put an end to this type of argument.

---

[6]   HMRC *Employment Related Securities Manual* ERSM20400 (Employment Related Securities and Options: meaning of 'market value').

[7]   ITEPA 2003, s 431(1) provides that if an election is made and the shares are subject to restrictions, for 'relevant tax purposes' their 'market value' is to be calculated as if they were not. The CGT market value (rather than the money's worth value) ignoring restrictions determines the amount brought into charge by s 62.

[8]   HMRC *Shares and Assets Valuation Manual* SVM109030 (Normal Rules Charge: ITEPA 2003, s 62).

ITEPA 2003, Part 7, Chapters 2–4A apply to 'securities' and 'interests in securities' acquired by a person where the right or opportunity is made available by virtue of the employment of that or any other person.[9] Securities are widely defined to include shares and interests in shares but not options (which are dealt with separately in Chapter 11).[10] 'Employment' includes former and prospective employment and office-holders are treated as employees for these purposes.[11] Securities made available by an employer (or person connected to an employer) are deemed to have been made available by reason of employment unless in the 'normal course of domestic, family or personal relationships'.[12] Consequently, whilst there may be very limited circumstances in which Chapters 2–4A do not apply, the working assumption should be that they do.

The acquisition occurs upon receipt of beneficial entitlement to the security or interest in the security.[13] Chapter 2 applies to securities acquired on or after 16 April 2003 and Chapters 3 and 4 apply whenever the shares were acquired. Where shares are acquired by an 'associated person' of the employee,[14] charges apply to the employee. Transfers of shares to or between associated persons are ignored, with the effect that charges on disposals only occur when the securities are disposed of to a person who is not associated.[15] The rules cease to apply on disposal of the securities or interest in securities to a person who is not associated (or to securities or interests in securities held 7 years after cessation of employment[16] or immediately prior to death[17]).

Before the introduction of ITEPA 2003, Part 7 it was also common in start-up situations to arrange for a swamping bonus issue shortly after the issue of shares to an employee and to argue the bonus issue shares were acquired 'qua shareholder'. Part 7 counteracts this by deeming replacement or additional shares to have been received at the same time and by virtue of the same employment opportunity as the original shares.[18] Where the market value of the original shares is reduced by the issue of replacement or additional securities, the reduction in value is treated as consideration for the new shares.[19] Consequently, the issue of shares pursuant to a proportionate share issue does not give rise to tax

---

[9] ITEPA 2003, s 421B(1).
[10] ITEPA 2003, s 420.
[11] ITEPA 2003, s 5.
[12] ITEPA 2003, s 421B(3).
[13] ITEPA 2003, s 421B(2)(a).
[14] ITEPA 2003, s 421C.
[15] ITEPA 2003, s 427(3)(c).
[16] ITEPA 2003, s 421B(7).
[17] ITEPA 2003, s 421B(6).
[18] ITEPA 2003, s 421.
[19] ITEPA 2003, s 421D(3).

IV Share-based Employee Incentives

charges on acquisition under Part 7 but the shares may nonetheless be subject to subsequent charges under Part 7 in the same way as the original shares.

The deeming provisions do not apply to the general earnings charge arising under ITEPA 2003, s 62, so it is possible to argue that shares were not acquired by reason of employment for the purposes of s 62 whilst accepting they were deemed to have been acquired by reason of employment for the purposes of ITEPA 2003, Part 7, Chapters 2–4A. There is generally no advantage in advancing this argument, however, as Chapter 3C applies to the acquisition of shares at an under-value.[20] Chapter 3C treats the amount of the under-value as a 'notional loan' whilst outstanding[21] and operates to bring the full amount into charge when the shares are disposed of to a person who is not associated.[22] This treatment does not apply if the undervalue is brought into charge under s 62 on acquisition as the amount assessed to income tax is deducted in assessing the value of the notional loan, resulting in a nil charge.[23] Consequently, most practitioners now accept that s 62 applies in the same circumstances as Part 7 of ITEPA 2003.

The CGT definition of market value in TCGA 1992, Part 8 applies for the purposes of Chapters 2–5 of ITEPA 2003, Part 7.[24] Consideration given for an asset cannot be counted twice and does not include the performance of any duties of employment or in connection with employment.[25]

12.2   CHAPTER 2: RESTRICTED SECURITIES AND RESTRICTED INTERESTS IN SECURITIES

The mischief with which ITEPA 2003, Part 7, Chapter 2 is designed to deal is where an employee acquires shares subject to restrictions that later lift. It would be relatively straightforward, for example, to impose personal restrictions by private agreement which later lift, allowing the employee to pay income tax only on the depressed value of the shares.

Chapter 2 applies to securities or interests in securities if these are subject to restrictions and the market value is less than it would be but for the restrictions.[26] Chapter 2 creates the concept of UMV and actual market value (AMV). UMV is the CGT market value ignoring restrictions[27] and

---

[20]   ITEPA 2003, s 446Q.
[21]   ITEPA 2003, s 446S.
[22]   ITEPA 2003, s 446U(1).
[23]   ITEPA 2003, s 446T(3)(b).
[24]   ITEPA 2003, s 421.
[25]   ITEPA 2003, s 421A.
[26]   ITEPA 2003, s 423(1).
[27]   ITEPA 2003, s 428(2).

AMV is undefined,[28] but is implicitly the CGT market value taking account of restrictions. If Chapter 2 applies, it does not generally displace the general earnings charge on acquisition under ITEPA 2003, s 62 but imposes additional income tax charges on the occurrence of later 'chargeable events' (being the lifting or variation of restrictions or the disposal of the shares).[29] Charges under Chapter 2 are imposed on a proportion of the UMV of the shares at the time of the chargeable event calculated using a formula in ITEPA 2003, s 428. If the shares are subject to short-term risk of forfeiture (ie forfeiture conditions which lift within 5 years of acquisition), there is no charge under s 62 on the acquisition of the shares,[30] but charges apply instead when the forfeiture conditions (or any other restrictions) lift on a proportion of the UMV at the time of the relevant event.[31]

Restrictions can be contained in any 'contract, agreement, arrangement or condition' and may relate to forfeiture, the freedom to dispose of the shares or to retain the sale proceeds or to any other disadvantage.[32] There is an important distinction between restrictions that are personal to the holder and rights which are intrinsic to the shares. If an employee is awarded a new class of growth shares (eg) in which the articles specify the growth shares as a class have no voting rights, no dividend rights and only a right to participate in winding-up or exit consideration achieved above a threshold, HMRC accepts that these are not 'restrictions' but intrinsic rights attaching to a separate class of shares.[33] It is essential for these rights to be set out in the articles of association so they bind any purchaser (otherwise they would be personal restrictions for the purposes of Chapter 2).

If the shares are also subject to vesting/forfeiture conditions (whether contained in the articles or elsewhere), by contrast, these are personal to the holder and hence restrictions for the purpose of Chapter 2.[34] There is no tax reason to include personal restrictions in the articles of association and it is usually preferable not to, as it makes the arrangements more flexible.

Chapter 2 only applies if the market value of the employment-related securities is less than it would be but for the restrictions.[35] The working assumption is that Chapter 2 does apply if the shares are subject to restrictions, as they must reduce the market value of the shares (even if only by a fractional amount). Chapter 2 is drafted defectively, however, as it asks whether the CGT market value is less than it would be but for the

---

[28] AMV is referred to without definition at ITEPA 2003, s 428(5).
[29] ITEPA 2003, s 427.
[30] ITEPA 2003, s 425.
[31] ITEPA 2003, s 426.
[32] ITEPA 2003, s 423.
[33] HMRC *Employment Related Securities Manual* ERSM30310 (Restricted Securities).
[34] ITEPA 2003, s 423.
[35] ITEPA 2003, s 423(1)(b).

restrictions. The seller and purchaser are hypothetical for the purposes of the CGT definition so it cannot be assumed any restrictions which are personal to the actual seller will apply to the hypothetical purchaser. Consequently, the CGT market value cannot be reduced by personal restrictions as they are ignored anyway. What the legislation should compare is the CGT market value (ie the value ignoring personal restrictions) with the CGT market value calculated as if the hypothetical purchaser were subject to the same restrictions as apply to the seller. Unfortunately it is necessary to suspend disbelief by pretending the legislation says this in order to make any sense of it!

There is an awkward category of restrictions that can be contained in the articles and framed so as to be intrinsic to the shares by applying to all shareholders (such as a directors' discretion to refuse to register share transfers or general pre-emption rights which require all shares to change hands on the same basis regardless of the identity of the seller). The definition of restrictions is wide enough to include all restrictions whether personal or intrinsic.[36] The CGT definition of market value ignores personal restrictions but it takes into account intrinsic restrictions, whereas the UMV requires all restrictions to be ignored. Consequently, when determining the UMV of shares that are subject to intrinsic restrictions, one is in effect required to value a separate class of shares which do not exit.

12.2.1   ITEPA 2003, s 431(1) elections

The charges under ITEPA 2003, Part 7, Chapter 2 can be avoided if the employee and employer make a joint election pursuant to s 431(1) of ITEPA 2003 for the employee to pay income tax on the UMV of the securities or interest in securities. The election must be made within 14 days of acquisition.[37] The election ensures all gains thereafter are taxed as capital absent the application of Chapters 3–4. It is common practice to make elections pursuant to s 431(1) to avoid income tax charges arising under Chapter 2. Consequently, the most common valuation issue which arises in practice is whether the employee paid UMV for the securities. The UMV for these purposes is the CGT definition of market value calculated ignoring all restrictions.[38]

Section 431 elections must be made jointly by the employee and employer within 14 days of acquisition, there is no need to file the election with HMRC.[39]

---

[36]   ITEPA 2003, s 423(2)–(4).
[37]   ITEPA 2003, s 431(5).
[38]   ITEPA 2003, s 431(1).
[39]   ITEPA 2003, s 431(5).

12.2.2   Employee pays UMV or more

If the employee acquires securities without making an ITEPA 2003, s 431(1) election but pays UMV or more for the securities, no charges can arise under Chapter 2 due to the way the formula in ITEPA 2003, s 428 works to calculate the chargeable amount.[40]

12.2.3   Shares not subject to short-term risk of forfeiture

If an employee acquires securities without making a s 431(1) election and the shares are not subject to short-term risk of forfeiture (ie forfeiture conditions which lift within 5 years of acquisition), he will be subject to income tax on any under-value under the general earnings charge in ITEPA 2003, s 62.[41]

If the amount paid for the shares on acquisition plus the amount assessed to income tax under s 62 is equal to or exceeds the UMV at the time of acquisition, no charges can arise under Chapter 2 due to the way the formula in ITEPA 2003, s 248 works. It is possible for the money's worth value to exceed UMV, for example, if the shares were acquired by a director whilst in possession of confidential information due to the different information standards applicable to the money's worth and CGT basis of valuation.

If the amount paid for the shares plus the amount assessed to income tax on acquisition under s 62 is less than the UMV on acquisition, no tax charges arise under Chapter 2 provided no restrictions are lifted or varied and the shares are sold subject to the same restrictions as applied on acquisition. If any of these events occur, however, they will be 'chargeable events' for the purposes of Chapter 2.[42]

It is common for shares acquired by founder directors to be acquired without making a s 431(1) election and for the shares not to be subject to vesting and forfeiture conditions. No charges will arise under Chapter 2 on disposal if these shares are sold subject to the same restrictions as applied on acquisition (and that is usually the case on an exit by way of a sale). If the shares were acquired at an under-value, any charge relates to the tax year of acquisition not the tax year of disposal. If the shares were not readily convertible assets[43] (RCAs) at the time of acquisition, any tax should have been paid by the director through self-assessment.

---

[40]   ITEPA 2003, s 428.
[41]   *Weight v Salmon* (1935) 19 TC 174.
[42]   ITEPA 2003, s 427.
[43]   ITEPA 2003, s 702.

IV Share-based Employee Incentives

12.2.4   Shares subject to short-term risk of forfeiture

If the employee acquires securities without making a s 431(1) election and the securities are subject to short term risk of forfeiture (ie forfeiture conditions that lift within 5 years of acquisition), no charge will arise on acquisition as the charge under s 62 is exempt.[44] Charges arise instead when forfeiture conditions (or other restrictions) are lifted or varied or when the shares are disposed of.[45] The charge is based on a proportion of the UMV of the shares immediately after the event.[46]

12.2.5   The formula in ITEPA 2003, s 428

The amount on which income tax is charged upon the occurrence of a chargeable event is determined by the following formula:

$$(UMV \times (IUP - PCP - OP)) - CE$$

where:

- UMV is what would be the CGT market value of the securities immediately after the chargeable event but for any restrictions.

- IUP is the initial uncharged portion, being IUMV – DA / IUMV where:

- IUMV is the initial UMV of the securities at the time of acquisition.

- DA is the sum of the following deductable amounts:

  – any amount paid for the shares;
  – any amount charged to income tax as general earnings;
  – any amount charged to income tax upon the exercise of an option;
  – any amount relieved from income tax upon the exercise of an EMI option;
  – certain amounts subject to income tax under rules applicable before the introduction of ITEPA 2003, Part 7, which are no longer likely to be relevant.

- PCP is the previously charged portion being the aggregate of the result of applying the formula:

  – IUP – PCP – OP on each previous chargeable event (PCP is nil if there has not been an earlier chargeable event)

---

44   ITEPA 2003, s 425(2).
45   ITEPA 2003, s 426.
46   ITEPA 2003, s 428.

- OP is the outstanding portion, calculated as UMV – AMV / AMV where:

- AMV is the actual market value of the shares immediately after the chargeable event (AMV is not defined but is taken to be the CGT market value taking into account all restrictions whether personal or intrinsic).

- CE is any consideration given and expenses incurred by the holder in connection with the chargeable event itself plus, if the event is the lifting or variation of a restriction, any consideration given for that.

Example 12.1 (see **12.2.7**) illustrates how the formula works when shares are acquired subject to short-term risk of forfeiture. Some further examples are given in HMRC's *Employment Related Securities Manual* ERSM30420 and ERSM30430.

12.2.6   Other elections

An election can be made pursuant to ITEPA 2003, s 431(2) within 14 days of acquisition to pay income tax on the CGT market value of the securities or interest in securities calculated ignoring only specified restrictions[47] (whereas the more common s 431(1) election requires all restrictions to be ignored[48]). This more targeted election makes it possible, for example, to distinguish between intrinsic restrictions (which are likely to remain) and personal restrictions (which are likely to fall away) and to elect to pay income tax ignoring only those restrictions which are likely to fall away. These elections are less common as employers usually prefer to remove any risk of tax charges arising under ITEPA 2003, Chapter 2 and that is only possible by making a 431(1) election to ignore all restrictions.

The charge on the acquisition of shares under ITEPA 2003, s 62 does not apply where the securities or interest in securities are subject to short-term risk of forfeiture.[49] The employee can elect to pay income tax on acquisition under s 62 in these circumstances.[50] The election must be made within 14 days of acquisition.[51] The advantage of making the election is to reduce the amount brought into charge later when restrictions are lifted or varied or when the securities are disposed of (the initial untaxed portion is reduced by the amount assessed to income tax under s 62 so reducing the proportion brought into charge on later chargeable events).[52]

---

[47]   ITEPA 2003, s 431(2).
[48]   ITEPA 2003, s 431(1).
[49]   ITEPA 2003, s 425(2).
[50]   ITEPA 2003, s 425(3).
[51]   ITEPA 2003, s 425(5).
[52]   ITEPA 2003, s 428.

IV Share-based Employee Incentives

An election can be made within 14 days of a chargeable event to pay tax on the remaining untaxed portion of the UMV at the time of the event.[53] This form of election can be useful, for example, where a s 431(1) election was not made when the shares were acquired originally

12.2.7 Exemption for lifting of restrictions applicable to whole share class

Where restrictions are lifted or varied or the shares are sold pursuant to an event which affects the whole share class, no charge arises under ITEPA 2003, Chapter 2 if the majority of the shares of the class are not employment-related securities or the company is 'employee-controlled' by virtue of the share class concerned.[54] The exemption may be of assistance, for example, if restrictions are removed immediately prior to an IPO.

Example 12.1: Charges arising under ITEPA 2003, Chapter 2

In our example the CEO of Company A subscribed for 5,000 growth shares paying nominal value of 1p per share.

(1) Section 431(1) election – no tax to pay

Suppose the CEO and Company A made a joint election pursuant to ITEPA 2003, s 431(1) to pay income tax on the UMV of the growth shares within 14 days of acquisition. The shares are not RCAs or deemed to be RCAs as Company A is independent and there are no arrangements in place to create a market in the shares.[55] Advisers acting for the company apply to HMRC for a post-transaction valuation check to agree the UMV of the shares on the CEO's behalf.

The valuation application suggests Company A can be valued at no more than £10 million as a whole by applying a multiple of 1 to turnover as stated in the most recent accounts. The growth shares have no rights other than to voting rights and rights to participate in exit consideration achieved above £10 million, so have an intrinsic value of no more than par. The valuation is arrived at without regard to personal or intrinsic restrictions applicable to the growth shares, so it is submitted the shares have a UMV of 1p per share. If HMRC agrees UMV of 1p per share the CEO has no income tax to pay as a result of making the election and all gains thereafter will be taxed as capital (absent the application of Chapters 3 and 4, but there is no reason to suppose these will apply).

(2) Section 431(1) election – acquisition at an under-value

Suppose HMRC disagrees with the valuation put forward and suggests instead that Company A should be valued using a multiple of 1.2 times historic turnover. The intrinsic value of the growth shares would then be £12

---

[53] ITEPA 2003, s 430.
[54] ITEPA 2003, s 429.
[55] ITEPA 2003, s 702.

million – £10 million x 5% = £100,000, calculated using an undiscounted basis or £40,000 after applying a discount of 60% to reflect the fact the growth shares represent a minority holding. The valuation was arrived at without any regard to personal or intrinsic restrictions applicable to the growth shares so constitutes the UMV of the shares. If £40,000 is agreed to be the UMV of the growth shares on acquisition, the CEO would have income tax to pay on a benefit of £39,950 (being the UMV of £8 per share (£40,000/5,000) less the subscription price of £50). The tax would be payable through self-assessment for the tax year of acquisition.

(3) No s 431(1) election

Suppose the CEO made no s 431(1) election when he acquired the growth shares. It is first necessary to establish whether the shares were subject to short-term risk of forfeiture (ie are capable of forfeiture within 5 years of acquisition) to determine whether the charge on acquisition under ITEPA 2003, s 62 is exempt. In this case the shares vest as to 25% on the first anniversary of his joining date and quarterly thereafter in equal tranches until fully vested on the fourth anniversary of his joining date. Unvested shares are forfeited on cessation of employment for any reason and can either be redesignated as worthless deferred shares or bought back by the company or anyone designated by the company at the lower of cost and fair value. Consequently, all the shares are subject to short-term risk of forfeiture.[56] The CEO is therefore exempt from income tax charge on acquisition under s 62.[57]

No tax charges will arise on any later chargeable event if the 1p subscription price paid was equal to or more than UMV at the time of acquisition. All charges arising under the formula in ITEPA 2003, s 428 require there to be an initial uncharged portion of less than one and that is only possible were the deductable amounts are less than the initial UMV. Deductable amounts include the amount paid for the shares (ie 1p per share in this case) and the amount assessed to income tax on acquisition under s 62 (ie nil in this case).

Advisers acting for Company A apply for a post-transaction valuation check, suggesting the UMV was no more than par. Suppose HMRC rejects the application and suggests instead UMV of £8 per share (calculated as in (2) using a multiple of 1.2 times historic turnover). The initial uncharged portion would then be £8 – £7.99/£8 or 0.00125.

The first chargeable event occurs when 25% of the shares (ie 1,250 shares) vest on the first anniversary of the CEO joining. The vesting and forfeiture conditions are personal restrictions which cease to apply on vesting. In addition, suppose all growth shares as a class are subject to a directors' discretion to refuse to register transfers that is contained in the articles. This is an intrinsic restriction which continues to apply to the vested shares after the chargeable event. HMRC agrees the UMV of the growth shares

---

[56]   ITEPA 2003, s 425(1)(b).
[57]   ITEPA 2003, s 425(2).

IV   **Share-based Employee Incentives**

immediately after the event is £10 per share and the AMV is £9, representing a discount of 10% to reflect the intrinsic restriction still applicable to the vested shares.

The amount assessed to income tax for the tax year in which 25% vesting occurs would be £8.9875 per share or £11,234.375 in total (1,250 x £8.9875). The amount per share is calculated using the formula in s 428 being:

$$(UMV \times (IUP - PCP \leq OP)) - CE$$

Whiic.

- UMV (the unrestricted market value of the shares immediately after the event) = £10.

- IUP (the initial uncharged portion being UMV on acquisition less the deductable amount, which includes the subscription price paid for the shares of 1p and any amount assessed to income tax on acquisition pursuant to s 62 of nil) = £8 – (£0.01 + nil) / £8.

- PCP (the previously charged portion) = nil.

- OP (the outstanding proportion being UMV – AMV / UMV immediately after the event) = £10 – £9 / £10.

- CE (the consideration given and expenses incurred by the holder in relation to the chargeable event) = nil.

    $$(£10 \times (0.99875 - 0 - 0.1)) - 0 = £8.9875$$

(4) Section 430 election

The shares vest quarterly after the first anniversary of the CEO's start date and similar charges arise on each quarter thereafter over the following 3 years as the remaining 75% of the growth shares vest. It is possible to prevent further income tax charges arising, however, by making an election within 14 days of a chargeable event to pay tax on a proportion of the UMV immediately after the event.[58] The election uses the formula in s 428, but ignores 'OP' so the amount assessed to income tax as a result of making the election would be £9.9875 per share (£10 x 0.99875) or £49,937.5 in total (assuming the election is made in respect of all 5,000 growth shares).

12.2.8   Advantages of s 431(1) elections

It is essential to require employees to elect to pay income tax on the acquisition of securities pursuant to ITEPA 2003, s 431(1) where the shares are subject to vesting and forfeiture conditions. The election removes the possibility of further income tax charges arising under ITEPA 2003, Chapter 2. These charges can be complicated to calculate

---

[58]   ITEPA 2003, s 430.

and can subject employees to income tax on a proportion of commercial growth. Worse still, the charges trigger reporting requirements for the employer[59] and can also trigger PAYE and NIC obligations if the underlying shares are RCAs at the time of the relevant event (or on disposal even if the shares are not RCAs at the time unless the consideration is in the form of securities which are not RCAs).[60]

The employee takes a risk by making a s 431(1) election in that he may pay income tax on a benefit he may never receive (e g because the shares later become worthless or are required to be forfeited). It is not generally possible to recover the tax in these circumstances, but it may be possible to recover tax indirectly under ITA 2007, Part 4, Chapter 6 (which allows capital losses to be set off against income if the relevant conditions are met).

12.3 CHAPTERS 3–3B: CONVERTIBLE SHARES AND OTHER ANTI-AVOIDANCE RULES

The mischief with which Chapter 3 of ITEPA 2003, Part 7 is designed to deal is where an employee acquires worthless deferred shares that later convert to a class of more valuable shares, with the objective of paying income tax only on the value of the deferred shares. The legislation is effective in blocking this device and means convertible shares should be avoided.

The legislation modifies the tax charge on acquisition under ITEPA 2003, s 62 so it applies to the value of the shares ignoring the right to convert.[61] Income tax applies to chargeable events, which include conversion, release, disposal and receipt of any benefit in connection with the securities.[62] The amount brought into charge is determined by a formula.[63] In the case of conversion the charge is based on the difference in value between the new securities and the old securities, ignoring the right to convert.[64] There is no charge under the formula where valuable shares convert to a less valuable class, so it is acceptable, for example, for growth shares to convert to deferred shares as illustrated in Example 11.2 (see Chapter 11 at **11.2.5**).

The definition of convertible securities is wide as it includes any contract, arrangement, agreement or condition.[65] The convertible share legislation only applies, however, if securities are convertible to another class in

---

[59] ITEPA 2003, s 421K(3)(b).
[60] ITEPA 2003, s 698.
[61] ITEPA 2003, s 437(1).
[62] ITEPA 2003, s 439.
[63] ITEPA 2003, s 440.
[64] ITEPA 2003, s 441.
[65] ITEPA 2003, s 436.

accordance with their terms.[66] If the securities are simply exchanged for securities of a more valuable class, ITEPA 2003, Part 7, Chapter 3D (sale of securities at an over-value) would apply instead.

Chapters 3A and 3B of ITEPA 2003, Part 7 counter artificial arrangements designed to avoid tax by reducing the value of shares prior to acquisition and/or enhancing the value of shares post-acquisition. These provisions are not covered in Part IV.

12.4   CHAPTER 3C. ACQUISITION OF SHARES AT AN UNDERVALUE (NIL PAID SHARES)

The mischief with which ITEPA 2003, Part 7, Chapter 3C is designed to deal is where an employee acquires shares on deferred payment terms. Chapter 3C treats the consideration outstanding as a notional loan, which is taxed in a similar way to a real interest free loan.[67] It also taxes the amount of the deferred consideration if it is written off (or if the shares are sold with the obligation to pay outstanding).[68]

The disguised remuneration rules in ITEPA 2003, Part 7A have effectively blocked arrangements involving the sale of fully paid shares by a 'third party' (such as an ESOP or shareholder) to an employee on deferred payment terms by imposing a PAYE and NIC charge on the full value of the shares on acquisition.[69] Chapter 3C is still relevant, however, where shares are issued nil paid (or partly paid) by a company to employees or directors within the same group as these arrangements are exempt from the disguised remuneration rules.

If an employee acquires shares for £1 with the amount payable left outstanding until called by the company, he will have no income tax to pay on acquisition under ITEPA 2003, s 62 or s 431(1) if HMRC agrees the relevant value is no more than £1. In determining whether the shares were acquired at an under-value, it is the amount which the employee agreed to pay that is relevant, whether or not it is actually paid.

Chapter 3C applies where no payment is made for the shares on acquisition (or any payment is less than market value)[70] and the under-value is not otherwise subject to tax.[71] For these purposes, market value is the CGT market value determined ignoring the obligation to pay the call.[72]

---

[66]   ITEPA 2003, s 435.
[67]   ITEPA 2003, s 446S.
[68]   ITEPA 2003, s 446U.
[69]   ITEPA 2003, s 695A. Note: The charge is exempt if the shares are subject to short-term risk of forfeiture. This is dealt with in more detail in Chapter 15.
[70]   ITEPA 2003, s 446Q(1).
[71]   ITEPA 2003, s 446T(3)(b).
[72]   ITEPA 2003, s 446Q(3).

12.4.1   Notional loan charge

Where ITEPA 2003, Part 7, Chapter 3C applies, an interest free loan (or 'notional loan') is treated as having been made when the shares were acquired.[73] The employee is taxed as if he had received a real interest free employer-related loan.[74] The taxable benefit is the interest he would have paid on a real loan at the official rate of interest[75] (which is 4% for 2011/12).

The amount of the notional loan initially outstanding is MV – DA where:

- MV is the CGT market value of fully paid up shares of the same class at the time of acquisition; and

- DA is total deductible amounts (which include the amount (if any) paid for the shares and the amount assessed to income tax on acquisition).[76]

If the shares are subject to short-term risk of forfeiture, (ie forfeiture conditions which lift within 5 years of acquisition) the notional loan charge is delayed until the first risk of forfeiture lifts and the amount of the notional loan is calculated by reference to the CGT market value of the shares at the time.[77] If the market value of the shares has increased (as hoped) when the risk of forfeiture lifts, this not only increases the amount of the notional loan brought into charge but can also create an exit charge to income tax (as the notional loan will exceed the amount payable when the shares are called, leaving an outstanding notional loan equal to the difference, which is treated as being written off when the shares are sold).[78] It is possible to avoid this outcome by making a s 431(1) election within 14 days of acquisition, with the effect that the notional loan is calculated by reference to the CGT market value when the shares were acquired. It is advisable to make such an election anyway if shares are subject to short-term risk of forfeiture to avoid tax charges arising under ITEPA 2003, Part 7, Chapter 2 for reasons explained at **12.2.8**.

The notional loan charge does not apply if the employee's total actual and notional loans do not exceed £5,000.[79]

The notional loan charge does not apply where the employee would have obtained tax relief on interest payments had he borrowed money to buy the shares.[80] The main type of interest relief available is on borrowings to

---

[73]   ITEPA 2003, s 446S.
[74]   ITEPA 2003, s 446S(2).
[75]   ITEPA 2003, s 175.
[76]   ITEPA 2003, s 446T.
[77]   ITEPA 2003, s 446Q(4).
[78]   ITEPA 2003, s 446U.
[79]   ITEPA 2003, ss 446S(2) and 180(1).
[80]   ITEPA 2003, ss 446S(2) and 178.

IV   Share-based Employee Incentives

buy shares in close companies.[81] The shares must be ordinary shares in a close company (which is not a close investment-holding company).[82] The individual must own at least 5% of the ordinary share capital[83] or spend the greater part of his time in the 'actual management or conduct of the company' or any associated company.[84] HMRC interprets the actual management or conduct test quite narrowly so as to confine it (in effect) to executive directors of the main board. HMRC also says that the 'greater part of the time' requirement should normally be interpreted as more than half of the normal working day, an interpretation which excludes non-executive directors.[85]

The notional loan charge ceases to apply on death or on the seventh anniversary of the employee ceasing to be in relevant employment.[86]

12.4.2 Income tax on disposal or write-off

The amount of the notional loan is brought into charge if the amount payable is written off or if the shares are sold subject to the obligation to pay the call.[87] There is no charge if the shares are paid up prior to disposal.[88] The notional loan is treated as paid up tax free if the employee dies.[89]

The legislation creates a trap if the shares are sold subject to the obligation to pay the call as the notional loan is brought into charge even if the price paid reflected the obligation. HMRC accepts, however, that if the shares were paid up out of the sale proceeds as part of one transaction, the repayment will be treated as having occurred first, thereby avoiding the charge.[90] HMRC proposed an amendment to the legislation in the 2009 Budget to remove this trap but the amendments were dropped due to lack of space.

12.4.3 PAYE and NIC

PAYE does not apply to the annual notional loan charge which is reported as a benefit in kind on Form P11D. PAYE arises on acquisition of the nil paid shares, however, as they do not meet the conditions for

---

81 ITA 2007, ss 392–395.
82 ITA 2007, s 392(2)(a).
83 ITA 2007, s 394.
84 ITA 2007, s 393(3).
85 HMRC *Savings and Investment Manual* SAIM10230 (Relief for Interest Paid: interest in a close company the 'full time working conditions').
86 ITEPA 2003, s 421B(6) and (7).
87 ITEPA 2003, s 446U(2).
88 ITEPA 2003, s 446U(4)(a).
89 ITEPA 2003, s 446U(4)(1).
90 HMRC *Employment Related Securities Manual* ERSM70120 (Securities Assigned for less than market value, Example 3).

corporation tax relief in CTA 2009, Part 12 so are deemed to be RCAs.[91] PAYE also arises on the discharge of the notional loan whether by way of write-off or on sale.[92]

The annual notional loan charge is subject to Class 1A NICs (ie the employer-only NIC charge on benefits in kind)[93] and the income tax charge on write off or disposal is subject to Class 1 NICs (ie employer and employees NICs).[94] The employer's NIC liability cannot be passed on to employees.[95]

12.4.4 Anti-avoidance

If the main purpose or one of the main purposes in entering into the nil paid share arrangements is to avoid income tax or NIC, PAYE and NIC apply to the value of the notional loan on acquisition.[96] It is suggested that tax effective planning of the sort illustrated in Example 12.2 is not subject to the anti-avoidance rule, otherwise ITEPA 2003, Part 7, Chapter 3C would be otiose other than the anti-avoidance rule itself.

Example 12.2: NED acquiring nil paid shares

Suppose Company A recruits a non-executive director shortly after the CEO acquired his growth shares. The terms are the NED will be permitted to subscribe for 1,000 growth shares of the same class as the CEO. Following the subscription the issued share capital of Company A will be held as follows:

- 95,000 ordinary shares of 1p each held by the two founder directors;

- 5,000 growth shares of 1p each held by the CEO; and

- 1,000 growth shares of 1p each held by the NED.

Suppose HMRC agreed the UMV of the growth shares was £8 each (based on a multiple of 1.2 times turnover per the last accounts) for the purposes of the CEO's tax return. Company A anticipates the growth shares are still worth £8 each when the NED subscribes for them. The NED subscribes for 1,000 growth shares at a subscription price of £8 per share.

The shares are acquired nil paid with the company only entitled to call the shares immediately prior to sale. The shares are intended to vest in full on the first anniversary of the NED's joining date. If the NED ceases to be a director for any reason, vested shares are required to be offered for sale at fair value and unvested shares at the lower of cost and fair value. The NED

---

[91] ITEPA 2003, s 702(5A) and CTA 2009, s 1008(1).
[92] CTA 2009, s 698.
[93] Social Security Contributions and Benefits Act 1992 (SSCBA 1992), s 10.
[94] Social Security (Contributions) Regulations 2001 (SCCR 2001), SI 2001/1004, reg 22(7).
[95] SSCBA 1992, Sch 1, para 3A.
[96] ITEPA 2003, s 446UA.

IV Share-based Employee Incentives

is required to enter into a contingent purchase contract that includes the vesting terms and entitles Company A to purchase the shares or to direct any other person to do so if the NED ceases to be a director. Fair value for these purposes is determined on the same basis as for the CEO (ie the fair value agreed between the board and the NED or, if agreement cannot be reached, the fair value determined by an independent valuation expert taking everything into account including the size of holding).

The unpaid subscription monies are not a loan, nor are they a debt until the call is made and left unpaid.[97] Consequently, there is no need to obtain shareholder approval under the Companies Act 2006 (CA 2006) s 197 (loans to directors) and there is no need for Company A to pay a deposit to HMRC pursuant to the Corporation Tax Act 2010 (CTA 2010), s 455 (charge on loans to participators by close companies).

The shares are deemed to be RCAs as nil paid shares do not qualify for corporation tax relief.[98] Company A is the employer for these purposes and is required to operate PAYE and NIC on a reasonable estimate of the liability.[99] Company A takes professional advice to the effect that a reasonable estimate of the PAYE exposure is nil as £8 was recently agreed as the UMV of the shares for the CEO and nothing material has happened since to affect the value. Company A does not operate PAYE or NIC and does not apply to HMRC for a PAYE valuation health-check.

(1) UMV equal to unpaid amount with s 431(1) election

Suppose the NED and Company A make a joint election pursuant to ITEPA 2003, s 431(1) to pay income tax on the UMV of the growth shares within 14 days of acquisition. Advisers acting for Company A apply to HMRC for a post-transaction valuation check for the purposes of the NED's tax return. Suppose HMRC agrees the UMV on acquisition is £8 per share so the NED has no income tax to pay as a result of making the s 431(1) election.

No account is taken of the fact the shares are issued nil paid in assessing UMV for these purposes so ITEPA 2003, Chapter 3C applies as the benefit is not otherwise subject to income tax.[100] The amount of the notional loan is the CGT market value less deductible amounts.[101] The CGT market value ignores personal restrictions but takes account of intrinsic restrictions. The growth shares are subject to a directors' discretion to refuse to register share transfers, which is an intrinsic restriction. HMRC agrees that the CGT market value is £7.20 per share, being 10% less than UMV of £8. There are no deductible amounts in this case as the NED has not paid anything for the shares on acquisition and he was not subject to income tax on any undervalue on acquisition. The notional loan outstanding would be £7.20 x 1,000 = £7,200.

---

[97]   *Whittaker v Kershaw* [1890] 34 ChD 320.
[98]   CTA 2009, Part 12.
[99]   ITEPA 2003, s 696(2).
[100] ITEPA 2003, s 446T(3)(b).
[101] ITEPA 2003, s 446T.

The annual notional loan charge would be 4% x £7,200 = £288, assuming an official rate of interest of 4%. The NED is not exempt from the annual notional loan charge as he would not qualify for interest relief on borrowing to buy shares in Company A.[102] The holding represents less than 5% of the ordinary share capital and he does not spend the 'greater part' of his time in the actual management or conduct of the company. The notional loan charge is reported on the NED's Form P11D as a benefit in kind and is subject to Class 1A employers' NIC.[103]

Suppose the NED resigns after one year when his shares have vested and the fair value of the shares is agreed to be £10 per share. The NED is required to sell 1,000 vested shares for £10 each. Company A does not have any distributable reserves so establishes an ESOP to buy the shares. It lends the ESOP £10,000 to fund the purchase.

Company A must ensure the shares are called immediately prior to sale. If the shares were to be sold to the ESOP with the call outstanding, the NED would be subject to an income tax charge on the full value of the notional loan outstanding of £7,200.[104] HMRC accepts that the call can be funded out of the sale proceeds, however, providing it is part of one transaction.[105] Consequently, the paperwork needs to make it clear that the company called the shares and the NED authorised the ESOP trustee to apply £8,000 of the £10,000 sale proceeds in satisfaction of the call. The shares will then be treated as having been sold fully paid and the £2,000 gain on the sale of the vested shares is taxed as capital.

(2) UMV exceeds unpaid amount with s 431(1) election

If HMRC had agreed the UMV of the shares on acquisition was (say) £9 per share (instead of £8 per share in example (1)), income tax will be payable on the under-value of 1,000 x (£9 – £8) = £1,000. PAYE and NIC are required to be operated on a reasonable estimate of the value of the shares.[106] If £8 was a reasonable estimate, no PAYE and NIC need to be operated, the tax is payable by the NED through self-assessment.

If HMRC agrees that the CGT market value is 10% less than UMV (to reflect the directors' discretion to refuse to register share transfers being an intrinsic restriction taken into account for the purposes of the CGT market value), the CGT market value would be £8.10 per share. The amount of the notional loan is the CGT market value less deductable amounts, which includes the £1,000 subject to income tax on acquisition so the notional loan would be 1,000 x (£8.10 – £1) = £7,100.

---

[102] ITA 2007, ss 392–395.
[103] SSCBA 1992, s 10 applies Class 1A NICs to general earnings not subject to Class 1 NICs. SSCR 2001, reg 40(2) excludes benefits listed in Sch 3, Part IX from being brought into the charge to Class 1A NICs. The notional loan charge in ITEPA 2003, Part 7, Chapter 3 is not listed in Sch 3, Part IX and is therefore brought within the charge to Class 1A NICs.
[104] ITEPA 2003, ss 446U(1)(b) and 446U(2).
[105] HMRC *Employment Related Securities Manual* ERSM70120 (Securities Acquired for less than market value, Example 3).
[106] ITEPA 2003, s 696(2).

(3) No s 431(1) election

If the NED did not make a s 431(1) election, there would be no annual notional loan charge until the risk of forfeiture lifts when the charge vest.[107] The notional loan charge is calculated by reference to the CGT market value at the time the risk of forfeiture lifts.[108]

If the CGT market value is £10 when the shares vest, the notional loan would be 1,000 x £10 = £10,000, resulting in an annual notional loan charge of £400 (£10,000 x 4%), assuming an official rate of interest is 4%. The charge runs from the vesting date rather than to the date of acquisition.[109]

Company A would call the shares immediately before purchase by the ESOP. The amount payable is £8 per share, leaving an outstanding notional loan of £10,000 – £8,000 = £2,000. The shares are disposed of subject to an outstanding notional loan of £2,000, which is brought into the charge to income tax.[110] This charge is subject to PAYE and NIC irrespective of whether the shares are RCAs at the time.[111]

Additional income tax charges may arise under ITEPA 2003, Part 7, Chapter 2 in relation to the lifting of the forfeiture conditions. These were illustrated in Example 12.1 (see **12.2.7**) in relation to the CEO so are not repeated here. The purpose of this example is to illustrate only the notional loan charges arising under Chapter 3C. It should be clear from this example that it is necessary to make a s 431(1) election on the acquisition of nil paid shares to avoid income tax charges arising on disposal.

12.5   CHAPTER 3D: SALES OF SHARES AT AN OVERVALUE

The mischief with which ITEPA 2003, Part 7, Chapter 3D is designed to deal is where an employee sells shares at an over-value. The amount of the over-value is brought into charge to income tax with no credit for any amount assessed to income tax earlier.[112] Charges arising under Chapter 3D are subject to PAYE and NIC even if the underlying shares are not RCAs (unless the sale consideration consists of assets which are not RCAs).[113] The CGT definition of market value applies as with other charges arising under Part 7.[114]

---

[107]   ITEPA 2003, s 446Q(4).
[108]   ITEPA 2003, s 446T(3)(c).
[109]   ITEPA 2003, s 446Q(4).
[110]   ITEPA 2003, s 446U(1)(b) and (2).
[111]   ITEPA 2003, s 698(1)(e).
[112]   ITEPA 2003, s 446Y.
[113]   ITEPA 2003, s 698.
[114]   ITEPA 2003, s 421.

12.5.1 The *Gray's Timber* case

The Supreme Court case of *Gray's Timber Products Ltd v Revenue and Customs Commissioners*[115] illustrates one of the circumstances in which ITEPA 2003, Part 7, Chapter 3D applies. The case involved the sale of ordinary shares by a director (Mr G) for disproportionate sale consideration. Mr G subscribed for ordinary shares in the company for a total subscription price of £50,000 and shortly thereafter entered into a subscription agreement with three major shareholders together holding 84% of the issued share capital. They agreed to procure that he would be paid one-third of the increase in value of the company from the date of subscription if an exit occurred 2 years or more after he acquired the shares. On exit Mr G was duly paid £1.45 million, being nearly four times what his pro rata entitlement would have been had all ordinary shares been sold at the same price. HMRC assessed the over-value to PAYE and NIC pursuant to Chapter 3D. The case was brought by Gray's Timber as it was required to pay employers' NIC on the over-value. The Supreme Court (and every lower court prior to it) held for HMRC on the basis the subscription agreement was a private agreement which ceased to exist on exit. The rights were personal to Mr G and of no value to the purchaser, so were required to be ignored for the purposes of the CGT market value.

Mr G acquired his shares in November 1999 before ITEPA 2003, Part 7 was introduced. It is not stated what (if any) income tax Mr G paid in relation to the acquisition of his shares. but he would have been subject to income tax on the amount of any undervalue.[116] His shares would have been valued using the money's worth basis of valuation, which takes into account all entitlements whether personal or intrinsic, so it is possible that Mr G paid income tax on any undervalue calculated so as to take into account personal entitlements in the subscription agreement. Any income tax paid by Mr G on acquisition cannot be claimed as a credit against the income tax charge arising on sale. There are two ways in which this double charge to income tax could be avoided if a similar arrangement were to be implemented now.

(1) If Mr G had acquired his shares after 16 April 2003 when Chapter 2 came into force, he could have made a s 431(1) election to pay income tax on the UMV of the ordinary shares within 14 days of acquisition. The CGT value would then have applied[117] and would have ignored the personal rights specified in the subscription agreement, causing him to pay income tax only on the value of the ordinary shares ignoring the additional rights. The same over-value charge would have applied on disposal, but the election would at

---

[115] [2010] UK SC4.

[116] ITEPA 2003, s 62.

[117] ITEPA 2003, s 431(1) provides that if an election is made the 'amount' which is brought into charge by ITEPA 2003, Part 7, s 62 is determined by reference to the CGT definition of market value ignoring restrictions.

IV Share-based Employee Incentives

least have prevented any income tax charge arising on acquisition relating to the value of the additional rights.

(2)   The arrangements could have been structured by creating a new class of preference shares with the enhanced rights specified in the articles and framed so as to be applicable to any purchaser of the preference shares. Mr G would have paid income tax on the same benefit on acquisition, but the over-value charge on disposal would have been avoided as the consideration would have reflected the intrinsic rights attaching to the shares.

12.5.2   Fair value transfer provisions

It is common for articles of association to require 'good leavers' to offer their shares for sale at 'fair value', being the price agreed between the leaver and the directors or the fair value determined by an independent valuation expert if agreement cannot be reached. Often articles prescribe how fair value is to be determined in these circumstances and state that the size of holding is to be ignored in arriving at the value. It is often possible to apply a discount of anything from 40% to 60% for minority holdings, so these provisions may allow a leaver to insist on his shares being offered for sale at an undiscounted price. If the shares are sold at an over-value, ITEPA 2003, Part 7, Chapter 3D imposes PAYE and NIC charges on the amount of the over-value even if the shares are not RCAs.[118]

If the parties agreed to sell at a discounted price regardless of what the articles say, HMRC may accept that this is what happened, in which case no charges will arise under Chapter 3D. If the parties agreed to trade the shares at the pro rata price in accordance with the articles and HMRC accepts that this was an arm's length price, there would be no charge arising under Chapter 3D but HMRC would almost certainly seek to apply the same basis of valuation consistently, making it impossible to agree a discounted valuation should the company wish to make further awards using the same class of shares in the future.

Leaver provisions of this sort are much better drafted by providing that fair value is the price agreed between the seller and the directors or the fair value determined by an independent valuation expert without specifying what factors the expert is required to take into account or ignore. The meaning of 'fair value' allows the valuer to take all factors into account, including the size of holding. It is more likely the fair value determined on that basis will equate to the CGT market value (although the two may not be exactly the same[119]).

---

[118]   ITEPA 2003, s 698(1)(f).
[119]   HMRC *Employment Related Securities Manual* ERSM80110 (Disposals for more than Market Value).

12.5.3 Earn-outs

It is common for shares held by management to be subject to an earn-out on an exit structured as a sale. It is also common for the earn-out to be disproportionate to shareholdings by applying only to shares held by members of the management team who intend to stay after the change of control. The question arises as to whether staying management are selling their shares at an over-value equal to the net present value of the earn-out for the purposes of Chapter 3D. This question is considered further at **14.4.2**.

12.6 CHAPTER 4: SPECIAL BENEFITS FROM SECURITIES

ITEPA 2003, Part 7, Chapter 4 applies if an associated person receives a benefit 'in connection with' employment-related securities which is not otherwise subject to income tax.[120] This is a catch-all provision designed to give HMRC the ability to tax arrangements not otherwise brought into the charge to income tax. Dividends are already subject to income tax and HMRC can in any case recategorise dividends as earnings taxed under ITEPA 2003, s 62 without invoking Chapter 4.

In 2004 HMRC changed its FAQs so as to subject the operation of ratchets to income tax. It used Chapter 4 as the statutory basis for this change of stance. This move was controversial as HMRC stated that the charge would apply to ratchets built into the shares on acquisition which operated in accordance with their terms. Two challenges to HMRC's view were due to be heard by the Special Commissioners, so HMRC took advice on the applicability of Chapter 4 in advance of the hearings. The advice was that it was 'unsustainable' to apply a Chapter 4 charge where the ratchets were imbedded in the shares on acquisition. In August 2006, HMRC withdrew its guidance (in what was then FAQ4(a) and FAQ4(c)). Consequently, it is difficult to see how Chapter 4 could apply where share rights are intrinsic to the share class and operate in accordance with their terms.

12.7 CHAPTER 5: SECURITIES OPTIONS

Options granted to an employee by reason of employment are taxed under ITEPA 2003, Part 7, Chapter 5. No tax arises on grant but the full spread is subject to income tax on exercise.[121] It is highly likely that options will be exercised immediately before an exit (if the exit is a sale). The exit will usually mean the option shares are RCAs at the time of

---

[120] ITEPA 2003, s 447(4).
[121] ITEPA 2003, ss 475 and 476.

exercise so PAYE and NIC will apply.[122] The employer's NIC is a cost of the employing company but can be passed on to the option-holder by agreement or election.[123] If the employee bears the employer's NIC cost it is deducted from the amount assessed to income tax (but not from the amount subject to employee's NIC).[124]

The effective tax rate depends on whether the option-holder bears the employer's NIC cost. For 2012/13 the effective tax rate for an additional rate taxpayer is 58.9% if he pays the employer's NIC. On £100 of option gains, tax and NIC would be calculated as follows:

$$((£100 - £13.8) \times 50\%) + (£100 \times 2\%) = £58.9.$$

If options are exercised immediately before an exit, the exercise price and any PAYE and NIC can be funded out of the sale proceeds providing authority is in place to allow the employer to sell sufficient shares to meet these liabilities. Options will usually be granted subject to plan rules that include suitable authority. It is also standard practice to require option-holders to execute a power of attorney as a condition of grant authorising the option to be exercised immediately prior to exit and authorising the option shares to be sold to the purchaser pursuant to the sale and purchase agreement. The power of attorney will also give the attorney authority to direct the sale proceeds to be applied in satisfaction of the option exercise price, PAYE and NIC liabilities and deal costs and to pay the option-holder the net sale proceeds. If the employer pays the employers' NIC, the cost will generally be factored into the statement of assets and liabilities as at completion and will be reflected in the purchase price.

Options are usually granted for no consideration by deed or agreement, and if exercised in a cashless manner on exit there need be no cash flow issue for the option holder at any stage. The difficulty with unapproved or non-qualifying options is the amount of tax payable as the full commercial gain is subject to income tax. Consequently, options should be avoided unless they qualify as EMI options (see Enterprise management incentive plans at **13.1**) or possibly as CSOPs (see Company share option plans at **13.2**). If the company cannot qualify for EMI or the individual does not meet the relevant EMI conditions, one of the arrangements outlined in Example 11.1 at **11.1.3** should generally be considered instead.

ITEPA 2003, Part 7, Chapter 5 contains similar deeming provisions for securities options as those that apply to securities acquired by reason of employment in ITEPA 2003, Part 7, Chapter 1.[125] Chapter 5 applies to

---

[122] ITEPA 2003, s 700.
[123] SSCBA 1992, Sch 1, paras 3A and 3B.
[124] ITEPA 2003, s 481.
[125] ITEPA 2003, s 471.

any right to acquire securities so includes rights to acquire shares where no exercise is required (eg 'restricted stock units' structured as a contractual right to receive shares for no payment at the end of a performance period). Chapter 5 also applies to earn-outs that are capable of settlement only in securities (such as loan notes or shares) issued by the purchaser as the earn-out is a right to acquire securities and is deemed to have been acquired by reason of employment (see Earn-outs at **14.4**).

The charge on the exercise of an option is calculated by reference to the CGT market value of the option shares on the date beneficial ownership is acquired less certain deductable amounts, which include the exercise price and any amount paid for the grant of the option.[126] Chapter 5 also imposes income tax charges on the assignment or release of an option (on the consideration received) and on the receipt of any compensation or benefit in connection with the option (on the amount received or the market value of the benefit).[127]

Employers can claim a corporation tax deduction equal to the spread for the accounting period in which options are exercised if the relevant conditions are satisfied[128] (see Chapter 13 at **13.3**).

Options can be exchanged for options to acquire different securities without triggering tax charges until exercise of the new option.[129] This contrasts to the employment-related securities rules in Chapters 2–4 of Part 7, which treat share exchanges as disposals giving rise to a chargeable event.

Once the option-holder has exercised the option, Chapters 2–4 will generally apply to the option shares. If the option shares are restricted securities, the option-holder and employer should consider making a s 431(1) election within 14 days of acquisition.

12.8 ACCOUNTING FOR INCOME TAX UNDER PAYE

If any income tax charges arise it is necessary to determine whether the tax should be accounted for through PAYE or self-assessment.

PAYE is required to be operated where the securities acquired are 'readily convertible assets' (RCAs).[130] Charges arising under ITEPA 2003, Part 7 are subject to PAYE if the underlying shares are RCAs. PAYE is also required to be operated on certain charges arising under Part 7 even if the shares are not RCAs (the charges include the disposal of restricted securities brought into charge by Chapter 2 and the disposal of

---

[126] ITEPA 2003, s 478.
[127] ITEPA 2003, s 477(3).
[128] Chapter 3 CTA 2009, Part 12.
[129] ITEPA 2003, s 483.
[130] ITEPA 2003, s 696.

employment-related securities at an over-value brought into charge by Chapter 3D) unless the consideration for the disposal is provided in the form of assets which are not themselves RCAs.[131]

The definition of RCAs includes assets for which 'trading arrangements' exist or 'are likely to come into existence' in accordance with arrangements existing when the asset is provided or in accordance with an understanding existing at the time.[132] As a rough guide it is not enough that the company intends to achieve an exit in the future or that it has established an ESOP. If the company has an ESOP, trading arrangements may exist if employees are made aware that the ESOP trustee is willing and able to purchase shares. Trading arrangements may exist if the company has taken concrete steps to exit (such as instructing brokers in relation to an IPO or entering into negotiations to sell the company), although it is unclear from HMRC guidance whether this information needs to be communicated to employees.[133]

Shares are deemed to be RCAs if the employing company does not qualify for a corporation tax deduction in relation to the shares.[134] The conditions for shares to be 'corporation tax deductible' are explained in Chapter 13 at **13.3**). The deeming provision expands the scope of RCAs to include subsidiaries where the parent is not listed on a recognised stock exchange and shares that are not issued fully paid.[135] Many venture-backed technology companies are controlled by venture capital companies (VCs) that are not listed on recognised stock exchanges. Shares acquired by employees in such companies can give rise to a 'dry' PAYE charge.

The employer is usually required to operate PAYE. Where shares are provided by a third party such as an ESOP, the employer is treated as the payer and therefore required to operate PAYE unless the actual payer does so.[136]

Where an employee is provided with income in the form of RCAs, the employer is treated as making a payment of income for PAYE purposes and is required to operate PAYE on the 'best estimate' that can 'reasonably be made' of the taxable earnings arising in connection with the provision of the asset.[137] The employer can request a PAYE health check from HMRC in advance of the date on which PAYE is required to be operated for the PAYE month concerned, but the health check is purely to confirm a reasonable estimate of the amount due. If the considered

---

[131] ITEPA 2003, s 698.

[132] ITEPA 2003, s 702(1).

[133] HMRC *Employment Income Manual* 11910 (PAYE: meaning of readily convertible assets: trading arrangements: definition).

[134] ITEPA 2003, s 702(5A).

[135] CTA 2009, s 1008(1).

[136] ITEPA 2003, s 687.

[137] ITEPA 2003, s 696.

value later agreed with HMRC for the purposes of the employee's tax returns is more than the reasonable estimate on which PAYE was operated, the balance of tax due is payable by the employee through self-assessment. It is generally sufficient for an employer to discharge its obligation to operate PAYE on a reasonable estimate by taking professional advice without seeking a PAYE health check.

It is advisable to ensure that the employer is able to recover funds from the employee to meet the costs of operating PAYE. This is straightforward to achieve where PAYE arises on a disposal of shares for cash (e g on an exit) – all that is required is authorisation from the employee for the employer to deduct sufficient funds from the sale proceeds. The authorisation can be built into the award documentation. Where a so-called 'dry' PAYE charge arises, however, the operation of PAYE can be problematic if there is no market for the shares.

Where shares are provided in the form of RCAs or in other circumstances where PAYE applies, the employer is treated as making a 'notional payment'.[138] If the employer is not 'made good' by the employee within 90 days, the amount of the tax is treated as an emolument in the hands of the employee.[139] There is no off-set if the employee makes good the employer after the 90-day period. Tax on the emolument is payable through self-assessment (as there is neither a payment nor a notional payment) but the emolument is subject to Class 1 NICs.[140] There is an argument that if the employer is authorised to sell sufficient shares to enable the employer to recover the amount due, the employee has made good that amount even if the employer did not in fact exercise its right to sell any shares.

The better solution by far is to structure arrangements involving share awards so any income tax arises only on acquisition of the securities and so the value of the interest at that point is nominal. It should then be possible to take the view a 'reasonable estimate' of the amount due is nil so PAYE need not be operated.[141] Options should usually be structured as EMI or CSOP options or the alternatives illustrated in Example 11.1 at **11.1.3** should be considered instead.

12.9 ACCOUNTING FOR INCOME TAX UNDER SELF-ASSESSMENT

Individuals are required to report income and gains not taxed in full under PAYE or through deduction at source through self-assessment by 5 October following the tax year of assessment. If the income or gains arise from options or shares and the tax is less than £2,000, the taxpayer

---

[138] ITEPA 2003, s 222(1)(a).
[139] ITEPA 2003, s 222(2).
[140] SSCR 2001, reg 22(4).
[141] ITEPA 2003, s 696(2).

can contact HMRC and arrange for the tax to be collected through PAYE without completing a self-assessment tax return. Otherwise a self-assessment tax return will generally be required. Any income tax is payable by 31 January following the tax year in which the income arose.

An employee is required to report capital gains arising on share sales if total gains from all disposals exceed the annual exempt amount for the tax year concerned and/or the sale proceeds exceed four times the annual exempt amount for that tax year.

12.10   NATIONAL INSURANCE CONTRIBUTIONS

The main NIC legislation is the Social Security Contributions and Benefits Act 1992 (SSCBA 1992), ss 4–10 and Sch 1, as supplemented by the Social Security (Contributions) Regulations 2001[142] (SSCR 2001), para 22 and Schs 2–5.

The legislation generally applies Class 1 NICs to employment-related securities in the same circumstances and on the same amount as PAYE.[143]

There are some exceptions where PAYE and NIC are not aligned. The Class 1A NICs (the employers-only charge) applies to general earnings not subject to Class 1 NICs and includes the annual notional loan charge arising under ITEPA 2003, Part 7, Chapter 3C. This is a benefit in kind subject to Class 1A employers' NIC but is not subject to PAYE.[144] The tax on tax charge arising on notional payments not made good within 90 days is an emolument subject to Class 1 NICs but is not subject to PAYE.[145] In cross-border situations NIC is governed by international agreements (or regulations in the case of EU Member States) and the provisions differ from double tax treaties applicable to income tax.

---

[142]   SI 2001/1004.

[143]   SSCBA 1992, s 3(1) imposes Class 1 NIC on 'earnings', which includes remuneration or profit derived from employment. SSCBA 1992, s 4(4) treats as remuneration any gain charged to income tax under ITEPA 2003, s 479 (exercise, release, assignment or receipt of a benefit in connection with a securities option). SSCBA 1992, s 4(6) allows regulations to be made to treat other amounts chargeable to income tax under ITEPA 2003 as remuneration. SSCR 2001, reg 22(7) provides that 'earnings' are taken to include any amount which counts as employment income in relation to employment-related securities and to which PAYE applies. SSCR 2001, Sch 3, Part IX then disregards certain payments by way of securities, restricted securities and restricted interests in securities, including where what is acquired is not an RCA (whether acquired upon the exercise of an option or otherwise). SSCBA 1992, Sch 2(5) provides in the case of RCAs, NIC is levied on the best estimate that can reasonably be made in line with the PAYE obligation.

[144]   SSCBA 1992, s 10 applies Class 1A NICs to general earnings not subject to Class 1 NICs. SSCR 2001, reg 40(2) excludes benefits listed in Sch 3, Part IX from being brought into the charge to Class 1A NICs. The notional loan charge in ITEPA 2003, Part 7, Chapter 3C is not listed in Sch 3, Part IX and is brought within the charge to Class 1A NICs.

[145]   SSCR 2001, reg 22(4).

If a third party such as an ESOP provides benefits in the form of RCAs it will trigger a Class 1 NIC charge in the hands of the employer. This is a trap as the employer has no right of recovery against the third party (indeed the employer may be unaware that such a benefit is even being provided).

It is generally illegal to recover employers' Class 1, 1A or 1B NICs from employees.[146] In the dotcom boom many listed technology companies were faced with the problem of having to provide for anticipated employers' NIC liabilities arising in connection with share options by 'marking to market', as required by UITF Abstract 25. The combination of soaring share prices and the accounting charge could have led to technical insolvency. The government agreed to allow employers' NIC arising in connection with options to be transferred to employees in order to solve the problem. This is an unusual provision compared with other jurisdictions, which do not normally allow employers' social security liabilities to be transferred in any circumstances (despite having the same problem often compounded by higher employers' social security rates).

Secondary NIC liabilities arising in connection with 'relevant employment income' can be recovered from employees by agreement or can be transferred to employees by joint election.[147] Relevant employment income includes NIC arising in connection with the exercise, assignment or release of rights to acquire securities including options, NIC charges arising in respect of post-acquisition chargeable events and convertible securities. The form of any joint election needs to be agreed with HMRC even if the pro forma election on HMRC's website (see ERSM 170750) is used.[148] The definition of 'agreement' is very wide and includes any arrangement or understanding, whether legally enforceable or not.[149] Consequently, it is more straightforward to require reimbursement by agreement by including the necessary wording in the relevant documentation that the employee is required to sign. The ability to pass on secondary Class 1 NIC does not apply to the acquisition of shares (other than pursuant to the exercise of a securities option), so does not apply, for example, to NIC arising on the acquisition of shares at an undervalue taxable pursuant to ITEPA 2003, s 62.

Most plan documentation includes contractual authority for the employer to sell sufficient shares to cover PAYE and NIC liabilities and to recover employers' Class 1 NICs from the employee where permitted. There may be instances, however, where it is not possible to sell shares to cover the liability (such as where dry PAYE and NIC charges arise). SSCR 2001 was amended by the National Insurance Contributions Act 2004 to allow employers to recover NIC from salary paid after the month of the

---

[146] SSCBA 1992, Sch 1, para 3A(1)(a)–(c).
[147] SSCBA 1992, Sch 1, paras 3A and 3B.
[148] SSCBA 1992, Sch 1, para 3A(1)(b).
[149] SSCBA 1992, Sch 1, para 3A(4).

relevant chargeable event. The amendment allows the employer to deduct Class 1 NIC from salary from the same or following tax year.[150] The employer is also allowed to retain or sell sufficient securities to meet any primary Class 1 NIC liability with the prior written consent of the employee.[151] The trustee of an ESOP can also sell or retain shares in this way, but it must do so as agent for the employer.

12.11   REPORTING

ITEPA 2003, Part 7, Chapter 1 contains extensive reporting requirements.[152] They require companies to report the grant and exercise of both HMRC-approved and unapproved options on an annual basis. The legislation also requires the report of the acquisition, disposal and other chargeable events relating to employment-related securities such as restricted securities.

Forms are available for each of the HMRC tax advantaged plans and Form 42 is used to report reportable events relating to unapproved share arrangements. All the forms can be found on HMRC's website[153] and can be filed electronically.

The relevant form(s) must be filed with HMRC by 6 July following the end of the tax year in which the reportable events take place. Significant penalties can apply if the returns are not filed with HMRC in time and so it is important for companies to have appropriate procedures in place to ensure that their annual employee share plans are completed and filed in a timely and accurate way.

---

[150] SSCR 2001, Sch 4, para 7.
[151] SSCR 2001, Sch 4, para 12.
[152] ITEPA 2003, ss 421J–421L.
[153] www.hmrc.gov.uk/sharschemes/ann_app_schemes.htm.

CHAPTER 13

RELIEFS

13.1 ENTERPRISE MANAGEMENT INCENTIVE PLANS (EMI)

The purpose of EMI is to help small, higher-risk companies to recruit and retain skilled employees by offering them tax advantaged share options. The EMI tax reliefs are set out in the Income Tax (Earnings and Pensions) Act 2003 (ITEPA 2003), Part 7, Chapter 9 and the conditions are set out in ITEPA 2003, Sch 5.

13.1.1 Tax advantages

The tax treatment of EMI options is very generous. If the relevant conditions are met, no income tax arises on exercise if the exercise occurs within 10 years of grant and the option was not granted at a discount.[1] If the option was granted at a discount, only the amount of the discount on grant is subject to income tax on exercise.[2] If the option was granted at a discount and the market value of the option shares is lower on exercise than on grant, the amount assessable to income tax is restricted to the difference between the market value on exercise and the exercise price.[3]

PAYE and NIC apply to any amount assessed to income tax if the option shares are readily convertible assets (RCAs) at the time. In the normal course of events, options granted at market value can be exercised income tax and NIC free on an exit.

There is no minimum holding period for the option before it can be exercised and there is no minimum holding period for the option shares once acquired. Accordingly it is possible to exercise an EMI option immediately before an exit and to sell the option shares to the purchaser (even if the options are granted only shortly prior to heads of terms being signed).

---

[1]   ITEPA 2003, s 530.
[2]   ITEPA 2003, s 531.
[3]   ITEPA 2003, s 531(3)(b).

The employer can claim a corporation tax deduction equal to the spread if the relevant conditions are met (in the same way as for non-qualifying options) even where the exercise is fully tax relieved.[4]

HMRC allows valuations to be agreed in advance of the grant of EMI options so it is possible to set the exercise price at not less than market value to avoid granting options at a discount. EMI options are subject to an individual limit of £120,000 on the value of shares which may be subject to subsisting options,[5] but it is possible to grant EMI options over a corporate class of growth shares (gg) to allow the limit to go further (see Example 13.1 at **13.1.5**).

EMI option holders are deemed to make an ITEPA 2003, s 431(1) election on the date of exercise if the option was not granted at a discount.[6] The election does not trigger any tax liability and results in the option shares being exempt from charges under ITEPA 2003, Part 7, Chapter 2 on the occurance of later chargeable events.[7] The election is voluntary in the case of EMI options granted at a discount, but there is no downside in making such an election if the market value has increased since grant as the amount brought into charge is still the amount of the discount on grant.[8]

Gains on the sale of EMI option shares will not normally qualify for entrepreneurs' relief (ER). An individual must own 5% or more of the ordinary share capital and exercise at least 5% of the voting rights for at least one year prior to disposal to qualify for ER[9] (see Entrepreneurs' relief at **13.4**). If an individual exercises an EMI option immediately prior to an exit and sells the option shares to the purchaser, he will not qualify for ER if he has no other holdings of securities in the company. If he meets the 5% ER tests by virtue of other holdings of securities, however, he will be able to claim ER on the disposal of option shares as ER is available for any disposals of securities or interests in securities in the same company if an individual qualifies.[10]

Tax relief is lost for increases in value after any 'disqualifying event', but gains to the point of the event still qualify for relief.[11] Shareholders will usually be required to warrant no PAYE and NIC liabilities arise in relation to EMI options on an exit by way of a sale. The possibility of an historic disqualifying event having arisen prior to sale represents a potential risk for sellers.

---

[4]   Corporation Tax Act 2009 (CTA 2009), Part 12, Chapter 3.
[5]   ITEPA 2003, Sch 5, para 5.
[6]   ITEPA 2003, s 431A(2)(d).
[7]   ITEPA 2003, s 431(1)(b).
[8]   ITEPA 2003, s 531(3).
[9]   Taxation of Chargeable Gains Act 1992 (TCGA 1992), s 169S(3).
[10]   TCGA 1992, s 169I(6).
[11]   ITEPA 2003, s 532.

13.1.2 Flexibility

There are very few prescriptive requirements in the EMI legislation relating to the option terms. The main ones are that options cannot be transferred,[12] they must lapse within 12 months of death[13] and it must be clear that the option is a right to acquire shares (so cannot contain excessive discretion).[14] Tax relief is secured using a self-certifying procedure by filing Form EMI 1 with the Small Companies Enterprise Centre within 92 days of grant.[15] There is no need to obtain prior HMRC approval for an EMI plan, unlike company share option plans (CSOPs) and other approved plans (indeed the only clearance permitted is from the Small Companies Enterprise Centre, which will only confirm if the relevant corporate conditions are satisfied). There is no requirement for options to be granted pursuant to a set of plan rules so the conditions can, for example, be contained in an option agreement which modifies the terms of an existing plan. Consequently, it is possible to tailor EMI to fit most commercial requirements and to put these plans in place quickly and easily.

13.1.3 Conditions

Options must satisfy certain conditions relating to the purpose of the option grant, limits, the eligibility of an employee, the company, the option terms and the type of shares. The Small Companies Enterprise Centre has 12 months from the date the Form EMI 1 is filed to challenge the qualifying status of EMI options, and thereafter EMI options will be taken to meet the conditions.[16] This section **13.1.3** deals with the conditions, with a focus on the more problematic areas that apply to technology companies.

The purpose test

Options must be granted for commercial reasons in order to recruit or retain an employee and not as part of a scheme or arrangement the main purpose (or one of the main purposes) of which is to avoid tax.[17] If this provision were interpreted strictly, no EMI option would qualify for tax relief. Fortunately HMRC is unlikely to invoke the provision other than in aggressive tax avoidance cases.

---

[12] ITEPA 2003, Sch 5, para 38 prohibits the option from being transferred other than to personal representatives on death.
[13] ITEPA 2003, Sch 5, para 38(2).
[14] ITEPA 2003, Sch 5, para 35.
[15] ITEPA 2003, Sch 5, para 44.
[16] ITEPA 2003, Sch 5, para 6.
[17] ITEPA 2003, Sch 5, para 4.

IV Share-based Employee Incentives

Limits

An individual may not hold unexercised qualifying options that are in respect of shares worth more than £120,000[18] (the limit was £100,000 for options granted before 5 April 2008). There is also a limit of £3 million on the total value of unexercised qualifying options.[19] Market value for the purposes of these two limits is the unrestricted market value (UMV) of the option shares at the time of grant.[20]

Options granted over the limit are treated as non-qualifying options Options cease to count towards the limit upon exercise, lapse or surrender. If an individual is granted options over exactly the maximum £120,000-worth of shares, further qualifying options cannot be granted to him for another 3 years.[21] The 3-year rule can be avoided by stating a limit of £119,999 in the plan rules so as to prevent the maximum from being granted. If an individual already holds subsisting CSOP options, these are treated as if they are qualifying EMI options for the purposes of calculating the limit.[22]

Option shares

Option shares must be fully paid up, non-redeemable shares that form part of the ordinary share capital as defined in the Income Tax Act 2007 (ITA 2007), s 989 (ie any shares other than shares with a right to a dividend at a fixed rate but with no other right to share in the company's profits).[23]

It is possible to create a separate class of shares (such as growth shares in Example 13.1 at **13.1.5**) to allow the £120,000 limit to go further. It is also possible to impose restrictions on option shares. Option-holders can, for example, be required to enter into a power of attorney as a condition of grant or exercise authorising the attorney to sell the option shares to a purchaser on an exit.

Exercise price

Options can be granted at any exercise price or for a nil exercise price. Options are usually granted at a price equal to market value at the time of grant in order to prevent any income tax arising on the amount of the discount on grant when the option is exercised.[24] Market value for these

---

[18] ITEPA 2003, Sch 5, para 5.
[19] ITEPA 2003, Sch 5, para 7.
[20] ITEPA 2003, Sch 5, paras 5(7) and 7(6).
[21] ITEPA 2003, Sch 5, para 46.
[22] ITEPA 2003, Sch 5, para 5(4).
[23] ITEPA 2003, Sch 5, para 35.
[24] ITEPA 2003, s 530.

purposes is the capital gains tax (CGT) market value (ie it ignores personal restrictions but takes into account intrinsic restrictions).[25]

Option terms

Options must be granted by way of an agreement that contains prescribed information such as the grantor, the grant date, the maximum number of shares that may be required (or a formula that may be used to calculate this), the exercise price (if any) or how it will be determined, when and how the option may be exercised, any performance conditions and any restrictions applicable to the option shares.[26] HMRC allows documents containing restrictions (such as the articles of association) to be annexed to the agreement instead of the restrictions being specified in the agreement.

It is unusual for option plans to incorporate performance targets but the most common target (if one is used) relates to the value achieved on an exit.

Options cannot be assigned (other than to personal representatives following death)[27] and must be capable of exercise within 10 years of grant.[28] Options which become exercisable only on an exit satisfy this requirement as an exit could occur at any time, making the option capable of exercise within 10 years of grant.

Option terms can be altered but there are two traps to be wary of. The alteration may be a disqualifying event if it increases the value of the option shares or results in any of the requirements of Sch 5 ceasing to be met (see Disqualifying events at **13.1.4**). If the alteration is to a fundamental term (such as the number of shares subject to option, the exercise price or the timing of exercise), it would amount to the grant of a new option, requiring a new Form EMI 1 to be filed within 92 days of grant.[29] If the market value of option shares has increased since the grant of the first option, the new option may be granted at a discount, causing income tax charges to arise on exercise.[30]

HMRC allows options to be granted by block deed of grant.[31] If this procedure is used the option grant will usually be confirmed by a certificate and participants will be required to sign a form of acceptance

---

[25] ITEPA 2003, s 421.
[26] ITEPA 2003, Sch 5, para 37.
[27] ITEPA 2003, Sch 5, para 38(2).
[28] ITEPA 2003, Sch 5, para 36.
[29] HMRC *Employee Share Schemes Unit Manual* 54600 (Requirements relating to options: Grant of option by deed).
[30] ITEPA 2003, s 531.
[31] HMRC *Employee Share Schemes Unit Manual* 54600 (Requirements relating to options: Grant of option by deed).

IV Share-based Employee Incentives

shortly after the legal grant in which they agree to be bound by the terms of the plan and to pay any employers' NIC.

Eligible employees

An individual is eligible if he is an employee of the company or one of its qualifying subsidiaries at the time of grant, he satisfies the commitment of working time requirement and he does not have a material interest.[32]

The commitment of working time requirement is the employee must work at least 25 hours per week on average for the company (or its 51% subsidiaries) or 75% of his 'working time' if less.[33] Periods of absence are ignored for specified reasons such as reasonable holiday, garden leave, ill health, pregnancy, childbirth, maternity and paternity leave and parental leave.[34]

The material interest test is (broadly) that an employee cannot be granted an EMI option if he (and associates) beneficially owns or has the ability to control more than 30% of the ordinary share capital of the company (or more than 30% of assets on a winding-up in the case of a close company).[35] The EMI option itself does not count towards the limit, so if an individual (with associates) beneficially owns 20% of the ordinary share capital it would be possible to grant him an EMI option to acquire a further 20% without breaching the limit. The rules that attribute certain holdings of associates to the individual for the purposes of the test are complex and not dealt with here.

Qualifying companies test

At the time of grant the company must meet tests relating to independence, gross assets, number of employees, status of subsidiaries and trading actives.[36] The rules were relaxed for option grants after 16 December 2010 so at least one group company must have a permanent establishment in the UK (whereas previously at least one group company had to trade mainly in the UK).[37] There is no requirement for the company to be UK incorporated so it is possible, for example, for US-incorporated technology companies to grant EMI options to their UK employees.

---

[32] ITEPA 2003, Sch 5, para 24.
[33] ITEPA 2003, Sch 5, paras 26 and 27.
[34] ITEPA 2003, Sch 5, para 26(3).
[35] ITEPA 2003, Sch 5, paras 28–33.
[36] ITEPA 2003, Sch 5, para 8.
[37] ITEPA 2003, Sch 5, para 14A.

Independence test

The company cannot:

(1)   be a 51% subsidiary of another company; or

(2)   be under the control of another company (or of another company and persons connected with the other company) without being a 51% subsidiary of that other company,

and there cannot be arrangements in place by virtue of which the company could become such a subsidiary or fall under such control.[38]

The independence test precludes venture owned companies from qualifying for EMI and needs to be considered carefully in borderline cases as it can even exclude venture backed companies if the investors are connected to each other.

A company is a 51% subsidiary[39] if more than 50% of its 'ordinary share capital'[40] is owned directly or indirectly by another company.[41] The test is applied by reference to the relative nominal value of the ordinary share capital in issue.[42] Ordinary share capital for these purposes is as defined in ITA 2007, s 989 (ie all the issued share capital of the company by whatever name called other than capital the holders of which have a right to a dividend at a fixed rate but have no other right to share in the profits of the company).[43]

A company is under the control of another company if (broadly) that company is able to secure that the affairs of the company are conducted in accordance with its wishes by means of the holding of shares, possession of voting power or by virtue of powers conferred in the articles or in some other document.[44] The rule that one has to include persons connected with a company to determine whether it has control can cause difficulties.[45] Venture backed companies will not qualify if the majority of the share capital is held by funds that are connected to each other. Read strictly, if an individual controls the company by holding a majority of the shares in his own name and some shares via his personal company, the personal company will be treated as having control (as he is connected to it). It is understood that HMRC will treat the independence test as

---

[38]   ITEPA 2003, Sch 5, para 9.
[39]   Schedule 5, para 59 applies the definition in ITA 2007, s 989 which in turn applies definition of '51% subsidiary' in CTA 2010, s 1154.
[40]   As defined in ITA 2007, s 989.
[41]   The direct and indirect ownership tests are set out in CTA 2010, ss 1155–1156.
[42]   *Canada Safeway Limited v IRC* [1973] Ch 374 and *South Shore Mutual Insurance Co Ltd v Blair* [1999] STC 296.
[43]   Sch 5, para 59 applies this definition in ITA 2007, s 989.
[44]   ITA 2007, s 995.
[45]   The definition of connected is as ITA 2007, s 993.

IV Share-based Employee Incentives

satisfied in these circumstances if the individual owns sufficient shares in his own name to control the company.

A company will fail the independence test if 'arrangements' are in place by which the company could become a 51% subsidiary or fall under the control of another company.[46] 'Arrangements' are widely defined.[47] It is understood that the Small Companies Enterprise Centre considers signed heads of terms for the sale of the company to be an arrangement for these purposes.

Gross assets test

The value of the company's gross assets cannot exceed £30 million at the time of grant.[48] In group situations the assets of all 51% subsidiaries are included. The value can normally be taken from the most recent balance sheet.[49] In group situations it is normally possible to use the consolidated balance sheet. Intra-group debt and shares held by group companies in each other are excluded (but these items will usually be excluded from the consolidated balance sheet anyway). It is necessary to include amounts payable on nil paid or partly paid shares. The HMRC Statement of Practice SP2/06 outlines how the value of assets is calculated for the purposes of venture capital trusts and the Enterprise Investment Scheme. If the company exceeds the gross assets test, this is not a disqualifying event (as that would penalise success) – it merely means options cannot be granted whilst the limit is exceeded.

Number of employees

Since 21 July 2008 a company must have less than 250 full-time equivalent employees at the time of grant.[50] For these purposes an employee includes a director but excludes an employee on maternity or paternity leave or students on vocational training. In group situations employees of all qualifying subsidiaries are included even if these are outside the UK. The test is a snap shot not an average, so borderline companies with seasonal employees may qualify by careful timing of option grants.

A full-time employee is not defined in the legislation but is taken by HMRC to mean at least 35 hours per week excluding lunch breaks and overtime.[51] An employee who works more than 35 hours is taken to be one full-time employee. It is necessary to add to the number of full-time

---

[46]   ITEPA 2003, Sch 5, para 9(4).
[47]   ITEPA 2003, Sch 5, para 58.
[48]   TEPA 2003, Sch 5, para 12.
[49]   HMRC *Employee Share Schemes Unit Manual* 52200 (Qualifying Companies: Gross Assets Requirements).
[50]   ITEPA 2003, Sch 5, para 12A.
[51]   HMRC *Employee Share Schemes Unit Manual* 52300 (Qualifying Employees: Number of Employees Requirement).

employees a 'just and reasonable' fraction for each employee who is not a full-time worker. If a company exceeds the limit it is not a disqualifying event (as that would penalise success) – it merely means options cannot be granted whilst the limit is exceeded.

Qualifying subsidiaries

A company is not a qualifying company unless all its subsidiaries are qualifying subsidiaries at the time of grant.[52] A subsidiary for these purposes is any company that the company controls either on its own or together with any person connected with it.[53]

A company is a qualifying subsidiary if it is a 51% subsidiary of the holding company, no other person (other than the holding company or another of its subsidiaries) has control of the subsidiary and there are no arrangements in existence by virtue of which these conditions would cease to be met.[54]

This test frequently causes difficulties in 50:50 joint venture (JV) situations where the company will be treated as acting together with the JV partner to control the JV. The Small Companies Enterprise Centre takes the view that in 50:50 deadlock situations the JV partners must be acting together to secure control for the purposes of the test. In these circumstances it is often necessary to alter the share capital held by the company in the JV so that it holds more than 50% by nominal value (whilst retaining only 50% economic rights) in order to ensure the JV is a 51% subsidiary. If the JV vehicle is not incorporated in the UK it may not have 'ordinary share capital', so it is then necessary to examine HMRC practice in relation to the share capital of the jurisdiction in which the JV is incorporated to ascertain whether HMRC is prepared to recognise it as ordinary share capital for the purposes of the test. If a company ceases to meet the qualifying subsidiary test it is not a disqualifying event; it merely means that further EMI options cannot be granted whilst the test is failed.

The qualifying subsidiary and independence tests are the two most problematic areas of the EMI legislation and it is frequently necessary to obtain clearance from the Small Companies Enterprise Centre in borderline cases.

Trading activities

A single company must exist wholly for the purpose of carrying out a qualifying trade or be preparing to do so.[55] A parent company must have at least one group company that exists wholly for the purpose of carrying

---

[52] ITEPA 2003, Sch 5, para 10(1).
[53] ITEPA 2003, Sch 5, para 10(2).
[54] ITEPA 2003, Sch 5, para 11.
[55] ITEPA 2003, Sch 5, para 13.

out a qualifying trade, or be preparing to do so, and the business of the group as a whole must not consist (wholly or as to a substantial part) in carrying out a non-qualifying trading activity.[56] Certain activities are disregarded for these purposes including research and development and holding property.[57]

For options granted on or after 16 December 2010 a single company must have a permanent establishment in the UK and a parent company must have at least one group company with a permanent establishment in the UK.[58] The test was more difficult to satisfy before 16 December 2010 when a single company had to carry out a qualifying trade wholly or mainly in the UK and a parent company had to have at least one group company that carried out a qualifying trade wholly or mainly in the UK. The relaxation now means, for example, US technology companies need only have one group company with a permanent establishment in the UK to satisfy the test.[59] Before this date it was often necessary to establish a service company in the UK which charged a mark up to satisfy the test.

A trade is a qualifying trade if it is conducted on a commercial basis with the view to realising profit and it does not consist (either wholly or as to a substantial part) in the carrying on of excluded activities.[60] 'Substantial' is not defined in the legislation but is taken by HMRC to mean not more than 20% of turnover, assets, expenses and staff time using the same tests as HMRC applies to determine whether a company is a trading company for ER purposes.[61] The excluded activities are listed in ITEPA 2003, Sch 5, para 16 and consist of:

- dealing in land, commodities, futures, shares, securities and other financial instruments;

- dealing in goods other than other than as part of a trade of retail or wholesale distribution;

- banking, insurance, money-lending and other financial trades;

- leasing;

- receiving royalties or licence fees;

- legal or accountancy services;

- property development;

---

[56] ITEPA 2003, Sch 5, para 14.
[57] ITEPA 2003, Sch 5, para 14(3).
[58] ITEPA 2003, Sch 5, para 14A.
[59] See HMRC guidance at ESSUM 52400 relating to permanent establishments.
[60] ITEPA 2003, Sch 5, para 15.
[61] HMRC *Capital Gains Manual* CG64090 (Entrepreneurs' Relief: trading company and holding company of holding group: The meaning of 'substantial').

- farming or market gardening;

- activities connected with woodlands;

- shipbuilding;

- coal production;

- steel production;

- operating or managing hotels and similar businesses;

- operating nursing, care or residential homes; and

- provision of services or facilities to businesses carrying on excluded activities.

The activities listed above are further defined in ITEPA 2003, Sch 5, para ss 17–23 and explained further in HMRC's *Employee Share Scheme Unit Manual* ERSM52600–52680.

'Leasing' includes the receipt of royalties and licence fees, so potentially applies to many technology companies that develop and licence software and other products. There is an exclusion if the royalty or licence fees relate to 'relevant intangible assets', being assets where the whole or greater part of the value was created by the company or one of its qualifying subsidiaries.[62] The exclusion means that it is necessary for group companies to have developed the greater part of the value. In group reorganisations where a new company is put on top of an existing company, the new company stands in the shoes of the old company for the purpose of the exclusion.[63]

13.1.4 Disqualifying events

The legislation prescribes certain 'disqualifying events'. If one occurs it has no effect if the option is exercised within 40 days of the event. If an option is exercised more than 40 days after a disqualifying event, however, gains in excess of market value at the time of the event are subject to income tax (and PAYE and NIC if the options are exercised when the option shares are RCAs).[64] The disqualifying events are as follows:

(1) Loss of independence occurring when a company becomes a 51% subsidiary of another or comes under the control of another company or persons connected with the other company.[65] It is not a

---

[62] ITEPA 2003, Sch 5, para 19.
[63] ITEPA 2003, Sch 5, para 19(8).
[64] ITEPA 2003, s 532.
[65] ITEPA 2003, s 534(1)(a) and (b).

disqualifying event, however, when arrangements exist whereby independence could be lost. If heads of terms are signed for the sale of a company, for example, it is not a disqualifying event until the actual change of control occurs. It is also possible to grant qualifying replacement options in certain change of control situations without triggering a disqualifying event (see **13.1.5**, Company reorganisations).

(2)   Ceasing to meet the trading activities requirement.[66]

(3)   Ceasing to be an eligible employee, which occurs if an option-holder leaves or ceases to meet the commitment of working time requirement.[67] EMI plan rules often allow exercise of vested options within 40 days of cessation to give a leaver the opportunity to exercise his options tax free. The option shares can then be retained to exit, allowing all gains to be taxed as capital. If the option-holder is permitted to retain the option to exit without exercising it until then, by contrast, gains from the date of the disqualifying event will be subject to income tax on exercise.[68]

(4)   Varying the terms of an option either so as to increase the market value of the shares subject to option or so as to cause the requirements of Sch 5 to cease to be satisfied.[69]

(5)   An alteration to the share capital of the company which (a) affects (or would but for some other event affect) the value of shares under option and causes the requirements of Sch 5 to cease to be satisfied[70] or (b) increases the market value of shares subject to option and is either done for non-commercial reasons or the main purpose (or one of the main purposes) is to increase the market value of the shares subject to option.[71] 'Alterations' for these purposes include the creation, variation or removal of rights relating to any shares in the company, the imposition of restrictions on any shares and the variation or removal of restrictions applicable to the shares subject to option.[72]

(6)   Conversion of any of the option shares into shares of a different class.[73] The conversion is not a disqualifying event, however, if the conversion of shares is of one class only into shares of one other class only, all the shares of the original class are converted and immediately before the conversion either (a) the majority of the

---

[66]   ITEPA 2003, s 534(1)(c).
[67]   ITEPA 2003, s 535.
[68]   ITEPA 2003, s 532.
[69]   ITEPA 2003, s 536(1)(a).
[70]   ITEPA 2003, s 536(1)(b).
[71]   ITEPA 2003, s 536(1)(c).
[72]   ITEPA 2003, s 537(2).
[73]   ITEPA 2003, s 536(1)(d).

shares of the original class were held otherwise than by or for the benefit of directors or employees or (b) the company was employee-controlled by virtue of holdings of shares of the original class.[74] This can be a trap where an exit is by way of an IPO effected by way of a conversion of different classes into one new class of shares. More typically, however, the IPO will be affected by putting a new holding company on top in which case the existing EMI options would be exchanged for replacement options of equivalent value over shares in the new holding company, the exchange would not be a conversion for these purposes.

(7) Grant of a CSOP option causing the £120,000 limit to be exceeded.[75] CSOP options count towards the EMI limit[76] but the effect depends on the order in which options are granted. If an EMI option is granted after a CSOP option, causing the limit to be exceeded it is not a disqualifying event – the excess is merely treated as a non-qualifying option.[77] If the grant of a CSOP option causes the limit to be exceeded, by contrast, it is a disqualifying event.[78]

13.1.5 Company reorganisations

On a company reorganisation, option holders can be granted replacement options over shares in the new holding company, which continue to qualify for tax relief if certain conditions are met.[79] The 'normal' EMI conditions must be met save that the new holding company need not satisfy the £30 million gross assets or 250 employee tests.[80] The limits applicable to the replacement options are modified so as to be calculated by reference to the UMV and actual market value (AMV) on the grant of the original option not the replacement option.[81] The 10-year period during which options can be exercised in a manner which qualifies for tax relief runs from the grant of the original option.[82] The total exercise price and market values of the original and replacement options must be the same, so it is normally necessary to agree the exchange ratio with HMRC.[83] There is no need, however, for the other terms of the replacement options to be identical. The replacement options can only be granted by agreement and Form EMI 1 must be filed within 92 days of the grant of the replacement option.[84]

---

[74] ITEPA 2003, s 538.
[75] ITEPA 2003, s 536(1)(e).
[76] ITEPA 2003, Sch 5, para 5(4).
[77] ITEPA 2003, Sch 5, para 5(3).
[78] ITEPA 2003, s 536(1)(e).
[79] ITEPA 2003, Sch 5, paras 39–43.
[80] ITEPA 2003, Sch 5, para 43.
[81] ITEPA 2003, Sch 5, para 43(4).
[82] ITEPA 2003, Sch 5, para 41(5), (6).
[83] ITEPA 2003, Sch 5, para 43(6) and (7).
[84] HMRC *Employee Share Schemes Unit Manual* 55300 (Company reorganisations: Grant of replacement options).

The replacement option provisions are most useful in reorganisations where a new holding company is placed on top of the existing EMI company. It is necessary to put proposals to option-holders to obtain their agreement to the grant of the replacement options and to obtain signatures to the Form EMI 1s. EMI plan rules should be drafted so option exercise is not triggered by a reorganisation of this sort and so that options cease to be exercisable and lapse after a short period if qualifying replacement options are offered.

Example 13.1: EMI option grant following funding round

Company A has a series A funding round in which a VC investor subscribes £10 million in exchange for the issue of a new class of preference shares of 1p each equating to 30% of the fully diluted share capital. The investor agrees that two EMI options will be granted to two new directors over a total of 5% of the fully diluted share capital post funding round. Each director will receive 2.5% so would not qualify for ER were they to be issued with shares. The preference shares issued to the investor have a 1x liquidation and exit preference, anti-dilution protection and benefit from investor consents.

After the funding round and option grants the issued and issuable share capital will be held as follows:

Number	Class	Percentage by nominal value	Shareholder
46,154	Prefs	30%	Venture capital investor
95,000	Ords	61.75%	Founder directors
5,000	Growth	3.25%	CEO
7,692	Growth	5%	Two option-holders
Total: 153,846			

The 1,000 growth shares held by the employee share ownership plan (ESOP) are ignored for these purposes as they will be used to satisfy EMI options. The order of priority on a liquidation or exit is as follows:

- £10 million to the preference shares;

- £10 million to the ordinary and preference shares pro rata to holdings as if they constituted one class.

- The balance of the consideration to the holders of preference, ordinary and growth shares pro rata to holdings as if they constituted one class.

The existing growth shares would be valued as follows:

- Value of company A as a whole: £10 million / 30 x 100 = £33.333333 million.

- Less liquidation and exit preference: (£10 million).

- Value implied by the investment: £23.333333 million.

- Less exit consideration payable to preference and ordinary shares below the threshold: (£10 million).[85]

- Total available for distribution above the threshold: £13.333333 million.

- Intrinsic value of growth shares as a class: 8.25% x £13,333,333 = £1,100,000.

- Undiscounted value per share: £1,100,000/12,692 = £86.67.

- Discounted value: 40% x £143 = £34.67.

The discounted value of £34.67 per share was arrived at without taking account of any restrictions applicable to the growth shares so represents the UMV. The growth shares are subject to a directors' discretion to refuse to register share transfers so the AMV of the growth shares is likely to be £31.2 per share (representing a discount of 10%) to reflect these restrictions.

The UMV determines whether the EMI option was granted within the £120,000 limit. If each director were to be granted an option to acquire 3,846 growth shares and HMRC were to agree UMV of £34.67 per share, the UMV of each tranche of options would be £133,341 (ie in excess of the £120,000 limit).

Consequently, it is decided to create a new class of growth shares (series 2 growth shares), which have identical rights to the existing growth shares save that they participate in exit consideration achieved in excess of £23.3 million. The UMV and AMV of the series 2 growth shares can then be argued to be equal to the par value of 1p per share, allowing options to be granted within the £120,000 limit.

The trustee of the ESOP is asked to sign an operating agreement in which it agrees to satisfy options granted by Company A to acquire growth shares if requested to do so by the company to the extent it has sufficient growth shares available in the trust. The operating agreement does not mention the names of the proposed option holders so as to prevent earmarking

---

[85] The growth shares in issue have a threshold of £10 million. The articles would usually allow the threshold to be adjusted for fund raisings but no adjustment will be made here as the liquidation preference attaching to the preference shares is paid in full in priority to any distributions to other shareholders. It would be necessary to adjust the threshold to £20 million if the first £10 million of exit consideration were to count towards the threshold. The adjustment would be required so as to avoid rewarding the CEO for increases in value not attributable to commercial growth.

IV Share-based Employee Incentives

occurring for the purposes of the disguised remuneration rules (see Chapter 15). The trustee is asked to sign the operating agreement prior to the option grants so the trustee can be comfortable it is not benefiting Company A by relieving it of an obligation to satisfy options it has already granted. The trustee holds series 1 growth shares whereas the options are granted over series 2 growth shares, so it will be necessary to redesignate the shares held by the ESOP. Company A could make a contribution to the ESOP in exchange for the trustee waiving any claims in relation to the redesignation. The cash could be extracted by Company A demanding repayment of part of the outstanding loan to the ESOP equal to the amount of the contribution.

The nominal value of the preference shares was set at 1p to ensure Company A is not a 51% subsidiary of the investor for the purposes of the EMI independence test.[86] The preference shares are ordinary share capital for these purposes so it is necessary to ensure no company owns more than 50% of the ordinary share capital when tested by nominal value.

13.2 COMPANY SHARE OPTION PLANS (CSOP)

A CSOP is the other type of discretionary tax advantaged share option plan. The CSOP tax reliefs are set out in ITEPA 2003, Part 7, Chapter 8 and the conditions are in Sch 4. The tax relief is less generous than EMI as the limit is only £30,000[87] and participants qualify for tax relief only if the option is exercised more than 3 years after grant (or before then in certain 'good leaver' situations).[88] Options can be exercised at any time after 3 years in a manner that qualifies for tax relief until the tenth anniversary of grant.[89] Former employees qualify for tax relief if this option is exercised more than 3 years after grant irrespective of the reason for leaving.

The company must not be under the control of another company (unless it is a company listed on a recognised stock exchange)[90] but, in contrast to EMI, there is no trading activities requirement, no gross asset test and no 250-employee limit. Consequently, the main use of CSOPs is for larger, independent technology companies that do not meet the EMI conditions.

It is not generally possible to create a separate class of shares for CSOPs due to the requirement that the majority of shares of the class used for the plan must either give employees control of the company or be so-called 'open market' shares (ie held by persons who acquired their shares otherwise than by reason of employment).[91] The CSOP plan rules and

---

[86] ITEPA 2003, Sch 4, para 9.
[87] ITEPA 2003, Sch 4, para 6.
[88] ITEPA 2003, s 524.
[89] ITEPA 2003, s 524(2).
[90] ITEPA 2003, Sch 4, para 17.
[91] TEPA 2003, Sch 4, para 20.

grant documentation must be approved by HMRC in advance of grant.[92] Options cannot be granted at an exercise price which is 'manifestly less' than the market value at the time of grant.[93] HMRC suggests the market value of shares is agreed in advance of grant[94] although it is not strictly a requirement of the legislation.

Plan shares cannot be subject to restrictions unless they apply to all shares of the same class.[95] There is a narrow exception that allows leavers to be required to offer shares for sale on cessation of employment (or upon acquiring shares after cessation of employment), but the requirement cannot apply to their transferees.[96] CSOP options should generally be structured as 'exit only' options as it is then possible to amend the articles so no restrictions (with the exception of drag and tags) apply to plan shares. Provisions of this sort allow the shares to meet the CSOP conditions without disturbing commercial restrictions applicable to other shares of the same class. It is acceptable for drag and tag provisions to apply to plan shares if they apply equally to all shares of the same class. The rules on restrictions mean that it is not possible to require option-holders to sign powers of attorney in which they authorise exercise and sale on an exit.

CSOPs tend to work best for broad-based awards to employees to acquire ordinary shares where the EMI conditions cannot be satisfied. If an exit by way of sale is achieved within 3 years of grant, option-holders will not qualify for tax relief (although it is possible to offer replacement options which enable them to qualify).[97] If the likely exit is an IPO, the 3-year period before participants qualify for tax relief can continue to run post IPO so need not be the disadvantage it at first appears.

13.3 CORPORATION TAX RELIEF

The Finance Act 2003 introduced corporation tax relief in respect of employment-related securities. The provisions are now contained in CTA 2009, Part 12. The rules allow an employing company to obtain a corporation tax deduction equal to the spread on the exercise of options for the accounting period in which options are exercised by its employees.[98] The relief applies irrespective of whether the option-holder was subject to income tax, or the cost of providing the shares or how the shares are sourced. Relief is also available upon the receipt of securities

---

[92] ITEPA 2003, Sch 4, para 28.
[93] ITEPA 2003, Sch 4, para 22.
[94] HMRC *Employee Share Schemes Unit Manual* 44135 (Requirements Relating to Options: MV to be agreed in advance of grant).
[95] ITEPA 2003, Sch 4, para 19(1).
[96] ITEPA 2003, Sch 4, para 19(2).
[97] ITEPA 2003, Sch 4, paras 26–27.
[98] CTA 2009, Part 12, Chapter 3.

acquired by reason of employment or upon later chargeable events and in those cases the amount of the relief broadly mirrors the amount assessed to income tax.[99]

Consequently, relief is available for the full spread on the exercise of EMI and CSOP options even though participants may also be relieved from income tax. This gives EMI options (and CSOPs) a significant tax advantage compared with awards of shares (where the only deduction is likely to be on the amount (if any) assessed to income tax on acquisition).

The conditions relating to shares have a further significance as shares that are not 'corporation tax deductible' are deemed to be RCAs for PAYE purposes.[100] Shares must be ordinary shares that are fully paid up and non-redeemable. Shares must be in a company which is not controlled by another company (or in a company listed on a recognised stock exchange or in a company controlled by a listed company). Shares must be in the employing company or a parent of the employing company or a member of a consortium which owns either the employing company or its parent.[101] The employer must be within the charge to corporation tax and the options must be granted by reason of the business the employer undertakes.[102] The relief applies to option exercises by leavers, replacement options and options exercised by personal representatives following death.[103] The 'spread' for these purposes is the CGT market value of the shares on the date of exercise less the exercise price and is not reduced by any employers NIC passed on to the employee.[104]

In exit situations it is usually necessary to ensure options are exercised immediately before completion when the company is still independent (to ensure the employer qualifies for a corporation tax deduction).[105] HMRC accepts that EMI option plans can be amended to allow exercise immediately prior to a change of control without the amendment being treated as an alteration to a fundamental term causing a new option to be granted.[106] The deduction must be claimed by the employing company for the accounting period in which options are exercised.[107] If the employing company does not pay corporation tax, the claim may generate a loss, which can be group relieved. In exit situations, the loss can be recognised as a deferred tax asset in the completion statements and it is then a matter of negotiation as to whether sellers are given credit for it in the sale price.

---

[99]   CTA 2009, Part 12, Chapter 2.
[100] ITEPA 2003, s 702(5A)–(5D).
[101] CTA 2009, s 1016.
[102] CTA 2009, s 1015.
[103] CTA 2009, ss 1002(2), 1022 and 1017(5).
[104] CTA 2009, ss 1018 and 1019.
[105] CTA 2009, s 1016(1).
[106] Note of Technical Meeting between Share Plan Lawyers Group and HMRC on 7 December 2005 at A2(iii).
[107] CTA 2009, s 1021.

13.4 ENTREPRENEURS' RELIEF

Individuals who qualify for ER are taxed at the rate of 10% on capital gains up to a lifetime limit of £10 million.[108] The relief must be claimed on or before the first anniversary of 31 January following the tax year of disposal (ie by 31 January 2015 if the disposal occurs in 2012/13).[109] The relief is available for disposals of securities (or interests in securities) if conditions A or B are satisfied.[110]

Condition A is that throughout one year prior to the disposal:

(a) the company is the individual's 'personal company' and is either a trading company or the holding company of a trading group; and

(b) the individual is an officer or employee of the company or one or more companies in the same group.[111]

A personal company in relation to an individual means a company:

(a) at least 5% of the ordinary share capital of which is held by the individual; and

(b) at least 5% of the voting rights in which are exercisable by the individual by virtue of that holding.[112]

Condition B allows the relief to be claimed for disposals that occur within 3 years of the company ceasing to be a trading company if the conditions in A were met for the one-year period prior to cessation.[113]

The relief can be claimed on any disposal of securities or interest in securities in the same company if an individual qualifies.[114] It would be possible, for example, for an employee who qualifies for ER (because he held sufficient shares for more than one year to meet the 5% and other tests) to exercise an EMI option immediately prior to an exit, sell the option shares and qualify for ER on the disposal of the option shares.

13.4.1 5% tests

The 5% tests can be complicated where there is more than one class of share in issue.

---

[108] TCGA 1992, s 169N.
[109] TCGA 1992, s 169M.
[110] TCGA 1992, ss 169H(2) and 169I(2)(c).
[111] TCGA 1992, s 169I(6).
[112] TCGA 1992, s 169S(3).
[113] TCGA 1992, s 169I(7).
[114] TCGA 1992, s 169I(5).

The 5% of ordinary share capital test is calculated by reference to the nominal value of the ordinary shares in issue.[115] For these purposes, ordinary share capital is as defined in ITA 2007, s 989 (ie any shares by whatever name called other than shares which give the holder a right to participate in a fixed dividend at a fixed rate but which have no other right to share in the company's profits).[116]

The 5% test does not relate to the economic rights attaching to the shares so it is possible, for example, to create a special class of shares (such as growth shares in Example 11.2 at **11.2.5**) with economic rights of less than 5% which nonetheless satisfy the test.

There is no requirement in the legislation for the shares to be paid up so it seems to be possible for nil paid shares to satisfy the 5% by nominal value test.

The relief applies to shares and 'interests in shares',[117] so jointly owned shares can qualify. The legislation requires an apportionment, however, for the purposes of the 5% test where the shares are held jointly so as to treat the holder as the beneficial owner of only so many shares as is 'proportionate to the value of the individuals share'.[118]

Options are usually exercised immediately before an exit by way of a sale. The issue of additional shares may cause other holdings to be reduced to below 5% momentarily prior to disposal. The legislation requires the 5% tests to have been met 'throughout the the period of one year ending with the date of disposal'.[119] HMRC have confirmed they will not regard the 5% tests as failed in these circumstances.[120]

It is understood the Office of Tax Simplification is in favour of removing the 5% threshold. It is an anomalous test as ER is available for other asset classes (such as business assets and partnership interests) with no equivalent threshold.

13.4.2 Trading company test

The company must be a trading company or the holding company of a trading group throughout the period of one year prior to the disposal.[121]

---

[115] *Canada Safeway Limited v IRC* [1973] Ch 374 *and HMRC Commissioners v 1) Taylor and 2) Hainendorf* [2010] 417 (TCC) at paras 14–18. See also ICAEW Tax Facility Guidance note of 25 January 2012, Example B1.

[116] TCGA 1992, s 169S(5) imports the definition of ordinary share capital in ITA 2007, s 989.

[117] TCGA 1992, s 169I(2)(c).

[118] TCGA 1992, s 169S(4).

[119] TCGA 1992, s 169I(6).

[120] ICAEW Tax Faculty Guidance Note, 25 January 2012, Example A7.

[121] TCGA 1992, s 169I.

A trading company has the same meaning as in TCGA 1992, s 165.[122] HMRC guidance suggests a company is broadly a trading company if no more than 20% of turnover is from investments, no more than 20% of assets on the balance sheet are non-trading assets and no more than 20% of management time is spent on non-trading activities.[123]

The biggest problem in practice is too much cash on the balance sheet. Whilst many technology companies are short of cash they tend not to have much in the way of other assets either, causing the 20% test to be breached. It is possible to add goodwill and intangible assets not shown the in balance sheet to expend the denominator for these purposes and HMRC will in any case accept the test is met where the cash represents necessary working capital. It is possible to apply to the HMRC Clearances Team to request confirmation that a company is a trading company under the non-statutory business clearance procedure.

13.4.3   Office or employment

The definition of an officer has the same as in ITEPA 2003, s 5A(3) being 'any position which has an existence independent of the person who holds it and may be filled by successive holders'.[124] HMRC's *Employment Status Manual* ESM2502 (Offices: definition) extends this to include a 'permanent, substantive position', its interpretation is based on case-law, in particular on dicta by Rowlatt J in *Great Western Railway Company v Bater*.[125]

There is no minimum number of hours per week that an employee must work in order to meet the employment requirement.

---

[122]   TCGA 1992, s 169S(5).
[123]   HMRC *Capital Gains Manual* CG64090 (Entrepreneurs' Relief: Trading Company and Holding Company of a Trading Group: meaning of 'substantial').
[124]   TCGA 1992, s 169S(5) imports the definition of officer from ITEPA 2003, s 5(3).
[125]   [1920] 3 KB 266. Useful guidance on this point can be found at HMRC *Capital Gains Manual* CG64110 (Entrepreneurs' Relief: Officers and Employees).

IV   Share-based Employee Incentives

CHAPTER 14

EXITS BY WAY OF A SALE

Exits by way of a sale of the entire issued share capital of a target company to a third party purchaser usually consist of initial consideration (some of which may be deferred) and an earn-out. Sellers will be concerned to minimise capital gains tax (CGT) and to avoid any income tax/NIC charges. This chapter examines the tax issues involved in structuring sales tax efficiently for sellers who are also employees of the target.

14.1 INITIAL CONSIDERATION

If the initial consideration is settled in cash, it will trigger a disposal for CGT purposes on which the seller may claim entrepreneurs' relief (ER) if he qualifies, allowing him to pay tax at the rate of 10% on the first £10 million of lifetime gains.[1]

If the initial consideration is settled in shares in the purchaser, reorganisation treatment will apply automatically if the relevant conditions are met, with the result that the new shares are treated as having been acquired when the old shares were acquired for the same base cost.[2] The ER rules allow sellers to elect to disapply reorganisation treatment so triggering a disposal on the exchange of old shares for new ones.[3] It may be beneficial to make such an election, for example, if the seller qualifies for ER on shares held in the target but will cease to qualify for ER post completion. The election must be made by the first anniversary of 31 January following the tax year of disposal (ie within the same time-limit for claiming ER).[4]

If the initial consideration is to be settled in cash, the purchaser may be prepared to offer a loan note alternative. If the loan notes are structured as non-qualifying corporate bonds (non-QCBs), the tax treatment is the same as for shares in the purchaser causing the tax point to be deferred until sale or redemption of the loan note. A seller who meets the ER conditions on completion but who ceases to satisfy these conditions post completion will usually be unable to claim ER on the sale or redemption

---

[1]   TCGA 1992, s 169N.
[2]   TCGA 1992, ss 127 and 135.
[3]   TCGA 1992, s 169Q.
[4]   TCGA 1992, s 169Q(4).

of the loan notes. Sellers in this position typically face a choice between paying CGT at the 10% rate for the tax year of completion or CGT at the top rate of 28% on the later sale or redemption of the loan notes. Given that choice it will usually be advantageous to opt for cash (or take the loan notes and elect to treat the exchange as a disposal) so as to be able to claim ER.[5]

There are some instances, however, where it may be beneficial to take loan notes. Sellers who do not qualify for ER on completion (eg because they have exhausted the limit or do not meet the 5% tests) may wish to take loan notes so as to defer tax until sale or redemption of the loan note and/or take advantage of annual exemptions/lower CGT rates/transfers to registered partners, etc. In the High Court case of *Snell v HMRC*,[6] Mr Snell hoped to avoid CGT completely by taking loan notes with the intention of redeeming them after shedding his UK residence. The High Court held that reorganisation treatment did not apply to the loan notes issued in consideration for shares in the target causing the tax point to arise on completion (when Mr Snell was still UK resident). The Taxation of Chargeable Gains Act 1992 (TCGA 1992), s 137 disapplies reorganisation treatment for 5% plus shareholders if the transaction is not for bona fide commercial reasons or the main purpose (or one of the main purposes) is the avoidance of CGT or corporation tax.[7] The court found one of the main purposes was to avoid CGT as Mr Snell took the loan notes intending to redeem them after shedding his UK residence (it is unclear from the case what the position would have been if the intention to avoid CGT was formed after taking the loan notes). Section 137 does not apply if the intention is to defer (as opposed to avoid) CGT.[8] It is advisable to obtain clearance from HMRC that reorganisation treatment applies. The application can be made in advance of completion on behalf of 5% plus shareholders.[9] Mr Snell did not obtain clearance.

It is possible (although unlikely) that the seller will qualify for ER on the sale or redemption of loan notes issued by the purchaser by virtue of holding sufficient shares in the purchaser to meet the 5% and other ER tests. ER applies to securities[10] and loan notes issued by the purchaser in exchange for shares in the target are deemed to be securities[11] for these purposes. The loan notes will not themselves entitle the seller to qualify for ER (as they are not ordinary share capital and will not carry voting rights), but if the seller owns sufficient ordinary shares in the purchaser to meet the ER tests he will qualify for ER on the sale or redemption of the loan notes.

---

[5]   TCGA 1992, s 169Q(4).
[6]   [2006] EWCH 3350 (Ch).
[7]   TCGA 1992, s 137(1).
[8]   TCGA 1992, s 137(1).
[9]   TCGA 1992, s 138.
[10] TCGA 1992, s 169(5).
[11] TCGA 1992, s 251(6).

If it is intended to take loan notes they need to be structured carefully so as to ensure reorganisation treatment applies. The loan notes must be issued by the purchasing vehicle (as opposed to any other company in the purchasing group)[12] and should not be capable of redemption within 6 months of issue so that HMRC is satisfied they are not a mere proxy for cash.[13] Loan notes issued by the purchaser in exchange for shares in the target will be deemed to be securities by virtue of TCGA 1992, s 251(6) so it is not strictly necessary to ensure they are securities as defined by case-law, ie they need not be capable of being held as an investment, realised at a profit or freely transferable (although they often are drafted to meet these conditions too).

It is advisable to structure the loan notes so as not to be QCBs. QCBs operate by freezing the gain on completion and bringing it into charge on sale or redemption of the QCB.[14] If the purchaser defaults on the QCB, the frozen gain will be brought into charge,[15] whereas no gain arises if the purchaser defaults on a non-QCB (indeed it is possible to claim a loss equal to the base cost of the non-QCB in these circumstances). It is straightforward to structure loan notes as non-QCBs by causing one of the QCB conditions to be failed (eg by making the loan note capable of redemption in a currency other than sterling with a tight collar and cap to avoid it being a deep discounted security).[16] Before 23 June 2010 ER operated by reducing the gain brought into charge, this gave QCBs an advantage as it was possible to claim ER so as to reduce the frozen gain held-over into the QCB with the result that tax on the lower gain to be deferred until sale or redemption of the QCB. This advantage ceased to apply on 23 June 2010 when ER was altered so as to operate by applying a 10% rate rather than as a reduction in the gain. At the same time QCBs were put on a supposedly level footing with non-QCBs by permitting QCB holders to elect to treat the exchange into QCBs as a disposal for ER purposes in the same way as for shares and non-QCBs issued by the purchaser.[17] The unfavourable position on default by the purchaser, however, remains unaltered and now means that QCBs should be avoided.

14.2   DEFERRED CONSIDERATION

It is common for some initial consideration to be held back and paid net of warranty and indemnity claims. The full value of any deferred consideration of this sort is brought into charge for the tax year of completion.

---

[12]   TCGA 1992, s 135(1).
[13]   ICAEW Technical Release 657.
[14]   TCGA 1992, s 116(10).
[15]   TCGA 1992, s 24 deems a disposal to occur where assets become of negligible value.
[16]   TCGA 1992, s 117(1).
[17]   TCGA 1992, s 169R.

TCGA 1992, s 48 applies to deferred consideration the amount of which is known at the time of disposal or to consideration which is capable of being ascertained by reference to events which occurred prior to disposal or to consideration which is ascertainable but contingent on events which occur after disposal.[18] The full amount of the consideration is brought into charge for the tax year of disposal with no reduction for time use of money, risk of recoverability or contingencies. If any of the consideration subsequently proves irrecoverable, it is possible to adjust the amount brought into charge by making a claim.[19] Sellers are permitted to request payment of tax by instalments where the consideration is payable in instalments over a period exceeding 18 months.[20]

There is no provision for adjustment of ER claims in the ER legislation but HMRC has confirmed[21] that it is possible to make such adjustments within the time-limit for claiming ER. Sellers may want to adjust ER claims in circumstances where they claimed ER on the maximum amount of any deferred consideration and some of it subsequently proves to be irrecoverable.

14.3   CONTINGENT LIABILITIES

It is common for sellers to be required to make post-completion payments to the purchaser if certain contingencies arise (such as indemnity payments and claims for breach of warranties). The case of *Randall v Plumb*[22] establishes that the value of the consideration brought into charge on completion is discounted to take contingent liabilities into account. It is not possible to adjust the computation (either way) if the valuation of the contingency proves to be wrong.[23]

TCGA 1992, s 49 reverses *Randall v Plumb* for certain contingent liabilities, including those relating to warranties and representations, with the effect that the amount brought into charge on completion cannot be reduced for these contingencies.[24] If sellers are required to make such payments, they are permitted to adjust the CGT computation.[25] Section 49 does not apply to indemnity claims so the value of the initial consideration on completion should, strictly, be reduced for the risk of having to pay indemnities. Paragraph 13 of ESC D33 confirms it is

---

[18]   HMRC *Capital Gains Manual* CG14875–14890 contains some examples of consideration to which TCGA 1992, s 48 applies.
[19]   TCGA 1992, s 48(1).
[20]   TCGA 1992, s 280 and CG14910–CG14911.
[21]   HMRC *Capital Gains Manual* CG63970.
[22]   50 TC 392.
[23]   HMRC *Capital Gains Manual* CG14800–14802.
[24]   TCGA 1992, s 49(1).
[25]   TCGA 1992, s 49(2).

possible to adjust CGT computations should sellers be required to make indemnity payments in the same way as adjustments are permitted for warranty payments.[26]

14.4 EARN-OUTS

For tax purposes earn-outs can be structured in one of three ways:

- ascertainable but contingent;

- unascertainable and capable of settlement in cash; or

- unascertainable and capable of settlement only in securities issued by the purchaser.

If the earn-out is structured so as to be ascertainable but contingent, the maximum amount payable is brought into charge on completion, so allowing ER to be claimed on the maximum value of the earn-out. No further disposals occur as and when the earn-out payments are made.[27]

If the earn-out is structured so as to be unascertainable on completion and capable of settlement in cash, '*Marren v Ingles*'[28] treatment applies. The net present value (NPV) of the earn-out is brought into charge for the tax year of completion allowing the seller to claim ER only on the NPV of the earn-out. If the earn-out pays out more than its NPV on completion, the payment will be a part disposal of the earn-out right triggering further CGT charges on which ER cannot be claimed (as the earn-out right is a chose in action and not a security for ER purposes). If the earn-out pays out less than its NPV on completion, the disposal will trigger a loss which (amongst other things) can be carried back and used to reclaim excess CGT paid for the tax year of completion.[29]

If the earn-out is structured so it is capable of settlement only in shares or loan notes issued by the purchaser, reorganisation treatment will usually apply so deferring any disposal until the sale or redemption of the loan notes issued in settlement of the earn-out. The seller will not usually qualify for any ER on these disposals as he is unlikely to hold sufficient (or indeed any) ordinary share capital in the purchaser to meet the ER conditions.

---

[26] HMRC *Capital Gains Manual* CG14825.
[27] TCGA 1992, s 48(1).
[28] [1980] STC 500.
[29] TCGA 1992, s 280 and CG14910.

IV Share-based Employee Incentives

14.4.1   Methods of structuring earn-outs

Suppose heads of terms for the sale of Company B provide for initial consideration of £2 million and an earn-out of up to a further £3 million based on a price:earnings (PE) ratio applied to profits for the 3 financial years (FYs) following completion, capped at £1 million per year.

(1) Ascertainable but contingent earn-outs

The earn-out could be structured so as to be ascertainable and contingent by providing in the sale and purchase agreement (SPA) that a payment of £3 million will be made in three instalments of £1 million each after finalising the accounts for the three FYs following completion. Sellers are required to warrant Company B will achieve specified profits for FYs 1 to 3 and will be required to pay damages (capped at £1 million for each FY) to the extent profits fall short of the warranted amounts. Damages for breach of warranty will be off-set from the amounts payable pursuant to the earn-out assuming the earn-out would be settled in cash).

The consideration is ascertainable on completion (£3 million) so falls to be taxed in full under TCGA 1992, s 48 for the tax year of completion. TCGA 1992, s 49(1) prevents any reduction in the amount brought into charge for the possibility of damages payments for breach of warranty. No disposal occurs when the earn-out payments are made. The advantage of this method is that it allows sellers to claim ER on the maximum £3 million earn-out (assuming they qualify for ER on completion). If the profits targets are not met, TCGA 1992, s 49(2) allows the consideration in the CGT computation for the tax year of completion to be adjusted for the amount of damages paid for failure to meet the profits targets.

CGT is payable by 31 January of the tax year following the tax year of completion on the maximum value of the earn-out (but sellers would normally claim ER by that date so tax need only be paid at the 10% rate). In addition, it is possible to apply to HMRC for the tax to be paid in instalments where the consideration is payable in instalments over more than 18 months.[30]

ER may be wasted to the extent the earn-out pays out below the maximum. HMRC has confirmed it is possible to make a claim to adjust the amount of ER if the adjustment claim is made within the time-limit for making the ER claim itself (ie by the first anniversary of 31 January following the tax year of disposal).[31] Example 14.1 (see **14.4.2**) illustrates the timing issues with making ER claims and subsequent adjustments.

---

[30]   TCGA 1992, s 280 and HMRC *Capital Gains Manual* CG53970 (Deferred consideration: ascertainable: payment by instalments: conditions).
[31]   TCGA 1992, s 169M.

Care needs to be taken in structuring these arrangements to ensure the consideration is ascertainable at completion. The case on the border between ascertainable and unascertainable consideration is *Marson (Inspector of Taxes) v Marriage*,[32] in which the taxpayer sold land to a developer shortly before the introduction of CGT in 1965 for £1,000 per acre plus a further £7,500 per acre (subject to a formula which adjusted the price depending on density of housing) if planning permission was achieved. The developer obtained outline planning permission in 1975 and made a further payment in settlement of its obligations. The taxpayer argued the consideration was ascertainable on completion but contigent and so taxable under what is now TCGA 1992, s 48; the sale occurred before the introduction of CGT so no tax arose on completion or upon receipt of the subsequent payment. The contract contained a third possibility, however, as it required the purchaser to pay half of any compensation should the land be compulsorily purchased. The compulsory purchase possibility meant the consideration was unascertainable so the additional payments were taxed under *Marren v Ingles* for the tax year of receipt.

In the author's view it preferable to structure the earn-out as a fixed amount which is, in effect, adjusted through warranties and damages so it is clear the amount of the earn-out is ascertainable at completion. If the earn-out is structured instead as a series of specified amounts subject to various contingencies it may be open to challenge as being unascertainable. The example which HMRC give of ascertainable consideration which is contingent on achieving post-completion profits at CG14885 involves only two possible outcomes, namely £250,000 or zero and HMRC states at CG14887: 'The consideration will be unascertainable if events which establish the AMOUNT do not occur until after the date of the disposal.'

It is common for earn-outs payable to sellers who are to remain as employees of the target post completion to be forfeitable due to cessation of employment. The preferable way to structure forfeiture provisions is to require employees to warrant they will remain in employment and to require them to pay damages for breach of warranty to avoid any possible argument the forfeiture provisions cause the amount of consideration on completion to be unascertainable.

If the earn-out were to be settled in shares or loan notes issued by the purchaser, the tax treatment would be the same as for ascertainable earn-outs settled in cash, but it would cause some cash flow issues as the sellers would have to fund damages claims from their own resources. This method works better if the earn-out consideration is settled in cash so the damages can be netted off against the cash.

---

[32] [1980] STC 177.

(2) Unascertainable earn-out capable of settlement in cash

The earn-out could be structured so as to be unascertainable on completion based on a PE of profits for FYs 1 to 3 capped at £1 million per FY. It is assumed the earn-out would be capable of settlement only in cash (but the tax position is the same if the earn-out is also capable of settlement in some other way, such as the issue of securities in the purchaser).

If the earn-out is structured in this way, the House of Lords case of *Marren v Ingles* applies and brings the NPV of the earn-out into charge for the tax year of completion. The earn-out is a separate asset,[33] the base cost of which is the NPV on completion. Any earn-out payments represent a capital sum derived from an asset which gives rise to further disposals for CGT purposes.[34] If there is more than one earn-out payment, each payment bar the last represents a part disposal of the asset, requiring the base cost to be apportioned by reference to the value of the asset at the time using the part disposal rules.[35] If the amount paid exceeds the apportioned base cost, further chargeable gains arise for the tax year in which the part disposal occurs. If the amount paid is less than the apportioned base cost, the disposal will trigger a loss which (amongst other things) can be carried back and used to reclaim surplus tax paid for the tax year of completion.[36]

ER can be claimed only on gains calculated by reference to the NPV of the earn-out on completion. It is not possible to claim ER on subsequent gains in excess of the NPV when the earn-out is paid as the earn-out is a chose in action which is not a security for ER purposes.[37] Consequently, sellers who qualify for ER will typically pay CGT at 10% on gains calculated by reference to the NPV of the earn-out on completion and at the top rate of 28% on earn-out payments in excess of the NPV on completion. It is not possible to apply to pay tax in instalments (in contrast to the ascertainable but contingent route) as the earn-out is unascertainable so cannot be paid in fixed instalments.[38]

The NPV of the earn-out would normally be agreed with HMRC before the tax is due on 31 January of the tax year following that of completion. Sellers will usually claim ER by that date to minimise the tax payable. If this route is taken it makes sense for sellers to agree with HMRC a value for the earn-out that is as accurate as possible so as to avoid paying CGT at top rates on earn-out payments in excess of NPV on completion. The valuation is as at completion and normal valuation principles suggest the

---

[33]   The earn-out is incorporeal property for the purposes of TCGA 1992, s 21(1)(a).
[34]   TCGA 1992, s 22(1).
[35]   TCGA 1992, s 42.
[36]   TCGA 1992, ss 279A–279D.
[37]   TCGA 1992, s 169S(5).
[38]   TCGA 1992, s 280.

NPV should be heavily discounted at that point for time use of money and for the possibility the earn-out conditions will not be met. If the earn-out is going better than expected by the time the valuation is requested, HMRC cannot necessarily be relied upon to agree a high up-front value. If the earn-out pays out less than the NPV on completion, some ER may be wasted. It is possible to apply to adjust the ER claim, but only within the time-limit for claiming ER itself (ie by the 31 January after 31 January following the tax year of completion).[39]

It is possible to structure any forfeiture conditions on cessation of employment by providing that future earn-out is forfeited (there is no need to structure using warranties and damages payments as suggested for ascertainable but contingent earn-outs).

(3) Unascertainable and capable of settlement only in securities issued by the purchaser

The earn-out could be structured so as to be unascertainable on completion based on a PE of profits for FYs 1 to 3 capped at £1 million per FY and capable of settlement only in shares or loan notes issued by the purchaser.

If the earn-out is structured in this way, reorganisation treatment will usually apply, so deferring any CGT charges until the sale of shares issued in settlement of the earn-out (or sale/redemption of the loan notes).[40] The seller will not usually qualify for ER on these disposals as he is unlikely to meet the ER conditions at the time of sale or redemption. The advantage of this route is it defers the tax point until receipt of the cash and allows sellers to take advantage of planning techniques (other than ER) in future tax years, such as utilisation of annual exemptions/transfers to registered partners, etc.

TCGA 1992, s 127 applies reorganisation treatment to conventional reorganisations, TCGA 1992, s 135 extends this to acquisitions involving the issue of securities in the purchaser and TCGA 1992, s 138A extends s 135 to unascertainable consideration. The conditions in s 138A require the earn-out to be unascertainable, capable of settlement only in securities issued by the purchaser and that s 135 is not disapplied by the anti-avoidance rule applicable to 5% plus shareholders in TCGA 1992, s 137.[41] If the conditions are met, reorganisation treatment applies automatically unless the seller elects for it to be disapplied (in which case *Marren v Ingles* treatment applies instead).[42]

---

[39] HMRC *Capital Gains Manual* CG63970 (Entrepreneurs' Relief: claims to relief).
[40] TCGA 1992, ss 127, 135 and 138A.
[41] TCGA 1992, s 138A(1) and (2).
[42] TCGA 1992, s 138A(2A).

If reorganisation treatment applies, the earn-out is deemed to be a security which is a non-QCB (even if the earn-out is settled in QCBs).[43] If the earn-out is settled in shares or non-QCBs issued by the purchaser, a further reorganisation applies at that point thereby deferring the tax point until sale of the shares (or sale/redemption of the non-QCB).[44] If the earn-out is settled in QCBs, the gain is calculated at that point but held over until sale or redemption of the QCB.[45] QCBs should generally be avoided due to the position on default by the purchaser (see **14.1**).

Sellers will not qualify for ER on sale or redemption of loan notes issued in settlement of an earn-out unless they hold sufficient shares in the purchaser to meet the 5% test and other ER conditions. Sellers who qualify for ER on completion could elect to disapply reorganisation treatment, causing *Marren v Ingles* treatment to apply.[46] ER can then be claimed on the gain arising for the tax year of completion which is calculated by reference to the NPV of the earn-out at that point. The time-limit for the election to disapply reorganisation treatment is the same as the deadline for claiming ER (ie on or before the first anniversary of 31 January following the tax year of completion).[47]

If the earn-out is capable of settlement only in shares or loan notes issued by the purchaser there is a risk that some or all of the earn-out will be subject to income tax. If the securities issued in settlement of the earn-out are RCAs (or deemed to be RCAs), PAYE and NIC will apply.[48] The risk arises because the earn-out is a right to acquire securities which is deemed to have been received by reason of employment in the case of shareholders in the target who are also employees or directors.[49] HMRC does not impose this tax treatment, however, if it is satisfied the earn-out is further consideration for the sale of shares in the target and not remuneration. HMRC has published guidance at ERSM110940 outlining the key indicators it applies in these circumstances, which are as follows:

> 'Key indicators in determining whether an earn-out is further sale consideration rather than remuneration are:
> a. The sale agreement demonstrates that the earn-out is part of the valuable consideration given for the securities in the old company.
> b. The value received from the earn-out reflects the value of the securities given up.
> c. Where the vendor continues to be employed in the business, the earn-out is not compensation for the vendor not being fully remunerated for continuing employment with the company.

---

[43] TCGA 1992, s 138A(3).
[44] TCGA 1992, s 138A(3).
[45] TCGA 1992, ss 138A(3) and 116(10).
[46] TCGA 1992, s 138A(2A).
[47] TCGA 1992, s 138A(5) and (6).
[48] ITEPA 2003, s 700.
[49] ITEPA 2003, s 471(3).

d. Where the vendor continues to be employed, the earn-out is not conditional on future employment, beyond a reasonable requirement to stay to protect the value of the business being sold.

e. Where the vendor continues to be employed, there are no personal performance targets incorporated in the earn-out.

f. Non-employees or former employees receive the earn-out on the same terms as employees remaining.

The following factors may also be relevant:

g. Negotiations between the seller and buyer as to the level of the earn out in relation to the value of the consideration given for securities in the old company.

h. Any clearance that might have been obtained under Section 138 and Section 707 demonstrating the bona fide nature of the transactions, and the level of the earn-out linked to profitability or other key performance indicators of the business.

i. Evidence that future bonuses were reclassified or commuted into purchase consideration would indicate that the earn-out was, at least partly, remuneration rather than consideration for the disposal of securities.

Where the earn-out is partly deferred consideration for the old securities and partly a reward for services or inducement to continue working for the business, then an apportionment of the value will need to be undertaken on a just and reasonable basis.'

These are indicators not conditions so it is possible to pass the test without the earn-out satisfying all the indicators. It is a common misconception that the indicators prevent earn-outs from being conditional upon continued employment. Indicator (d) makes it clear that it is permissible for an earn-out to be subject to forfeiture for cessation of employment provided the forfeiture condition is not capable of applying beyond a 'reasonable period'. It is understood HMRC takes this to be up to 3 years. Assuming employees continue to be fully remunerated post completion the biggest problem in practice is disproportionate earn-outs, considered at **14.4.2**.

It is possible to obtain clearance from the HMRC Employees Share Scheme Unit as to whether an earn-out will be treated as further sale consideration. If clearance is refused or if there is insufficient time to obtain clearance and it is considered there is a risk the earn-out will be taxed as remuneration, it may be advantageous to structure the earn-out so it is capable of settlement in cash. The earn-out will not then be a securities option and *Marren v Ingles* treatment will apply.

14.4.2 Disproportionate earn-outs

It is common (for understandable commercial reasons) for earn-outs to be restricted so as to apply only to shareholders who are employees of the

target and intend to remain so following completion. This can result in earn-outs being disproportionate to shareholdings.

For disproportionate earn-outs capable of settlement in cash, the question arises as to whether participants in the earn-out are selling their shares in the target at an over-value equal to the NPV of the earn-out. Sales of securities at an over-value are subject to income tax under the Income Tax (Earnings and Pensions) Act 2003 (ITEPA 2003), Part 7, Chapter 3D on the consideration given for the shares less the market value of the shares in the target after expenses.[50] Over-value charges are always subject to PAYE and NIC (unless the consideration is in the form of securities that are not themselves RCAs or deemed to be RCAs).[51] The CGT basis of valuation applies to determine the market value of the shares in the target for these purposes.[52]

Disproportionate earn-outs that are capable of settlement only in securities issued by the purchaser are subject to income tax as employment-related securities options. HMRC does not apply this treatment if it considers the earn-out to be further consideration for the sale of the shares and not remuneration. Disproportionate earn-outs do not satisfy indicator (f) in ERSM110940 so potentially cause HMRC to apply remuneration treatment. If the earn-out is treated as remuneration, PAYE and NIC will apply if the securities issued in settlement of the earn-out are RCAs or are deemed to be RCAs at the time.[53] These charges can be avoided by structuring the earn-out so it is capable of settlement in cash (so *Marren v Ingles* treatment applies), but if so structured it is necessary to consider whether shares in the target are being sold at an over-value equal to the NPV of the earn-out.

The author considers it would be very difficult for HMRC to justify an over-value charge if employees participating in the earn-out continue to be paid a commercial salary and benefits following completion. Earn-outs represent a price arrived at in the open market by the parties in arm's length negotiations. If an over-value charge were to apply it would involve substituting the real price with a hypothetical one arrived at by postulating a hypothetical purchaser who (in contrast to the real one) has no interest in protecting their investment by offering an earn-out to key employee shareholders.

> *Example 14.1: Sale of issued share capital of company a to a third party purchaser*
>
> The management of Company A enter into negotiations to sell the entire issued share capital to a purchaser for cash consideration of £25 million and

---

[50]   ITEPA 2003, s 446Y.
[51]   ITEPA 2003, s 698.
[52]   ITEPA 2003, s 421.
[53]   ITEPA 2003, ss 696 and 700.

an earn-out based on turnover for the 3 FYs following completion of up to a further £10 million payable only to employees and capped at a third of that for each FY. Earn-out payments are forfeited on cessation of employment within FYs 1 to 3 but payments made prior to cessation can be retained. Prior to signing heads of terms Company A grants further EMI options to acquire series 2 B ordinary shares at a strike price equal to the par value of 1p per share to five employees over an additional 2,000 shares in satisfaction of past commitments. Deal costs are ignored for these purposes. Completion occurs on 1 May 2012, FYs run to 29 April and the earn-out is required to be calculated and paid on 1 July following the end of each FY.

The exit consideration is distributed in accordance with the articles as follows:

- £10 million to the preference shares;

- £10 million to the preference and ordinary shareholders pro rata to holdings;

- between £20 million and £23.33333 million to preference shareholders, ordinary shareholders and Growth 1 shareholders pro rata to holdings; and

- above £23.333333 to preference, ordinary and growth 1 and 2 shareholders pro rata to shareholdings.

The earn-out is treated as the top slice of consideration for these purposes so is payable to all employee shareholders pro rata to holdings.

The fully diluted share capital table and distribution of the consideration is as follows:

Number	Class	Percentage (by nominal value)	Shareholder	Initial consideration £	Maximum earn-out £
46,154	Prefs	29.62%	Venture capital investor	14,815,982	–
95,000	Ords	60.96%	2 founder directors	9,912,862	8,660,613
5,000	Growth 1	3.21%	CEO	167,507	455,822
3,846	Growth 2	2.47%	Option-holder 1	41,130	350,618
3,846	Growth 2	2.47%	Option-holder 2	41,130	350,618
2,000	Growth 2	1.28%	5 new option-holders (400 shares each)	21,359	182,329
TOTAL 155,846				25,000,000	10,000,000

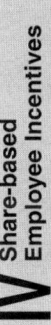

Founder directors

Each of the founder directors qualifies for ER. Each will receive initial consideration of £1,966,131 and an earn out of up to an additional £4,330,301 capped at £1,443,436 for each of the three FYs following completion. It is assumed the base cost of their shares is nominal and the £10 million ER lifetime limit is available to both directors in full.

If the initial consideration is paid in cash it would trigger a disposal in 2012/13 giving rise to a gain of £4.956 million. If the directors claim ER on the gain the tax bill for would be £495,641 and would be payable by 31 January 2014. The directors do not intend to move abroad in order to shed their UK residence and are content to pay tax at a rate of 10% so opt to take the initial consideration in cash.

The earn-out could be structured in one the three ways explained above.

Route 1: Ascertainable but contingent

If the earn-out is structured as ascertainable and contingent the directors would each be subject to CGT for the tax year of completion on the maximum value of the earn-out causing them to make additional gains for 2012/13 of £4,330,301. If ER is claimed on the gains the amount of tax due would be £433,030 and is payable by 31 January 2014. There would be no further tax to pay as and when the earn-out is settled. If the earn-out for FY 1 is determined to have failed on 1 July 2013, the directors would be required to pay damages of £1,443,436, which would be netted off against the first instalment of the earn-out of the same amount. Assuming the CGT computations for 2012/13 have not been agreed by 1 July 2013 they could adjust their draft computations relating to FY 1 to nil and not claim ER in respect of FY 1. If the earn-out for FY 2 is determined to have failed on 1 July 2014, they could apply to adjust the CGT computations for 2012/13 relating to FY 2 to nil and reclaim the CGT paid on 31 January 2014 relating to FY 2. They could also apply to adjust the ER claimed in relation to FY 2 as the time-limit for ER claims and adjustments is 31 January 2015. If the earn-out for FY 3 is determined to have failed on 1 July 2015, they could reclaim tax paid in relation to FY 3 but they would be out of time to adjust the ER claimed in relation to FY 3 so ER of £1,443,436 would be wasted. It is of no assistance to apply for tax relating to the earn-out to be paid in instalments. There is no relief for FY 1 as the earn-out is payable before the tax due date on 31 January 2014. The tax due in relation to FYs 2 and 3 is less than 50% of each instalment so the founder directors would not qualify for relief.[54] In summary, this route allows ER to be utilised against the full value of the earn-out but causes the directors to pay £433,030 of tax early on 31 January 2014. They can reclaim the tax to the extent the earn-out is failed but risk wasting £1,443,436 of ER.

Route 2: Unascertainable and settled in cash

---

[54] HMRC *Capital Gains Manual* CG14912–14913.

If the earn-out is unascertainable and settled in cash, the directors would each be subject to CGT for 2012/13 on the NPV of the earn-out. The directors have until 31 January 2014 to agree the NPV and pay the tax. If HMRC agrees the NPV of the earn-out is (say) 40% of the maximum, the NPV would be £1,732,204 (or £577,373 for each FY assuming it is fair to apportion the earn-out equally between FYs). ER can be claimed on the NPV of the earn-out for 2012/13 causing each director to pay additional tax of £173,220 by 31 January 2014.

If the earn-out for FY 1 were to pay out in full the directors would receive additional cash of £1,443,436 on 1 July 2013 and a gain of £866,062 would arise for 2013/14, the tax on which would be payable by 31 January 2015. ER would not be available for this gain so additional tax of £242,497 would be due on that date (assuming the directors pay CGT at the top rate of 28%). It the earn-out were to pay out in full for FYs 2 and 3 the same amounts of tax would be payable on 31 January 2016 and 2017. This route causes the directors to pay £900,657 of tax on the earn-out (an increase of £467,627 in comparison with route 1).[55] The difference arises because it is only possible to claim ER on the NPV of the earn-out rather than the full amount.

If the earn-out for FY 1 is failed, it would trigger a loss for CGT purposes of £577,373 in 2013/14. Assuming CGT computations for 2012/13 have not been agreed by 1 July 2013, it may be possible to establish and claim the loss against the gains arising in 2012/13 so tax need only be paid on 31 January 2014 on the net gain. ER need not be claimed in relation to the gain attributable to FY 1, which is eliminated by a loss of the same amount. If the earn-out for FY 2 is determined to have failed on 1 July 2014 it would trigger a loss of £577,373 for 2014/15, which could be carried back and set off against gains in 2012/13. The directors would be in time to adjust the ER claimed in relation to gains attributable to FY 2. If the earn-out for FY 3 is determined to have failed on 1 July 2015 it would trigger a loss for 2015/16, which could be carried back to allow tax relating to FY 3 to be reclaimed but the directors would be out of time to reclaim ER so ER of £577,373 would be wasted. There is no option to pay tax by instalments as the earn-out is unascertainable. In summary, this route causes the directors to pay £173,220 of tax early on 31 January 2014. They can reclaim tax through loss relief to the extent the earn-out is failed but they risk wasting ER of an estimated amount of £577,373 (the actual amount depends on what HMRC agree to be the NPV of the earn-out).

Route 3: Unascertainable and settled in loan notes

If the earn-out is unascertainable and capable of settlement only in loan notes issued by the purchaser, no tax would be payable in 2012/13 and no tax would be payable if the earn-out is failed. If the earn-out is successful tax would only arise when loan notes issued in settlement of the earn-out are sold or redeemed. If the founders pay CGT at the top rate of 28%, the

---

[55]   Note: strictly, the base cost of the earn-out should be apportioned using the formula A/A+B in TCGA 1992, s 42 when each part disposal of the earn-out right occurs on 1 July 2013 and 1 July 2014. The apportionment requires the earn-out to be revalued on each occasion. It has been assumed the value of the earn-out remains constant for the purposes of this example.

redemption of the loan notes would trigger a maximum tax liability of 28% x £4,330,301 = £1,212,484. The directors have a 'wait and see' option in that they could elect to disapply reorganisation treatment by 31 January 2015.[56] The election would trigger a tax charge on the NPV of the earn-out allowing them to claim ER on the same basis as in route 2.

The directors do not intend to move abroad to shed their UK residence so opt for route 1 in order to ensure they pay tax at 10% on the full value of the earn-out.

CDO

Unfortunately the CEO does not qualify for ER as his series 1 growth shares represent less than 5% of the issued ordinary share capital when tested by nominal value. The CEO will receive initial consideration of £167,507 and an earn-out of up to £455,822. It would make sense for his earn-out to be settled in loan notes so tax on the earn-out is deferred until sale or redemption of the loan notes and he may also prefer some of his initial consideration to be settled in loan notes. This would enable him to defer the bulk of the tax and to reduce the effective rate by utilising annual exemptions, etc.

The series 1 growth shares could have been structured so as to allow the CEO to benefit from ER by providing that series 1 growth shares are entitled to 5% voting rights as a class and by ensuring they represent at least 5% of the ordinary share capital when tested by nominal value. The nominal value test could be satisfied by specifying a higher nominal value for the series 1 growth shares than for other classes of ordinary shares or it could be done in a more targeted way by including anti-dilution protection, allowing him to subscribe for additional series 1 growth shares at par whenever additional ordinary shares are issued. The additional shares would not entitle him to further economic rights, the only purpose being to enable him to continue to meet the 5% by nominal value test. The economic rights attaching to the series 1 growth shares would be determined by reference to a formula in the articles (as opposed to the number of shares) in these circumstances.

Option-holders

All option-holders should be required to sign powers of attorney as a condition of the grant of options, authorising one of the directors to exercise their options and sell the option shares to the purchaser by entering into the SPA on their behalf. The power of attorney authorises the exercise price, any PAYE or NIC and deal costs arising in connection with the exercise of options to be deducted from the sale proceeds.

The new options were granted prior to heads of terms being signed. One of the EMI qualifying conditions is that company is independent when the options are granted, the test is failed if there are arrangements in place whereby independence could be lost.[57] The Small Companies Enterprise

---

[56]   TCGA 1992, s 138A(2A).
[57]   ITEPA 2003, Sch 5, para 9(3).

Centre takes the view that heads of terms constitute such arrangements. The new options were granted with a strike price of par. It should be possible to agree that is still the market value of the shares for EMI purposes as the CGT basis of valuation applies to determine the AMV and UMV of the shares.[58] The negotiations to sell Company A were not in the public domain at the time the options were granted so it can be argued these are not relevant (as the purchaser of a small minority holding of series 2 growth shares would not be made aware of confidential negotiations).

Options should be exercised immediately before completion (when the company is independent) to ensure that Company A qualifies for a corporation tax deduction equal to the spread. The purchaser is not listed on a recognised stock exchange (or controlled by a company that is) so Company A must be independent when the options are exercised to meet the tests in the Corporation Tax Act 2009 (CTA 2009), Part 12.[59]

The issue of additional shares may cause existing shareholdings to be reduced to below 5% momentarily prior to disposal. The legislation requires the 5% tests to have been met 'throughout the period of one year ending with the date of disposal'.[60] HMRC have confirmed they will not regard the 5% tests as failed in these circumstances.[61]

No option-holders will qualify for ER as they will have been shareholders for only a brief period prior to disposal. Option-holders 1 and 2 will be in a similar position to the CEO so are likely to want the earn-out to be settled in loan notes for the same reason. The five new option-holders will receive initial consideration of £4,278 and an earn-out of up to £36,466 (so they are likely to want all the initial consideration to be paid in cash and the earn-out to be settled in loan notes).

There is no need to obtain clearance pursuant to TCGA 1992, s 138 that reorganisation treatment applies as the only sellers it applies to have holdings of less than 5%. It is considered unnecessary to obtain clearance from the Employees Share Scheme Unit that the earn-out represents sale consideration as the indicators in ERSM110940 are met.

---

[58] ITEPA 2003, s 421.
[59] CTA 2009, s 1016(1).
[60] TCGA 1992, s 169I(6).
[61] ICAEW Tax Faculty Guidance Note, 25 January 2012, Example A7.

IV Share-based Employee Incentives

CHAPTER 15

DISGUISED REMUNERATION

15.1 INTRODUCTION

Part 7A of the Income Tax (Earnings and Pensions) Act 2003 (ITEPA 2003) is designed to prevent so-called disguised remuneration provided through third parties. The legislation took effect from 6 April 2011, with transitional provisions for certain steps taken between 10 December 2010 and 5 April 2011. The legislation imposes PAYE[1] charges on employees and steps taken after 5 December 2011 are also subject to NIC.[2] The legislation is referred to below as the 'DR rules'.

One of the abuses which the DR rules are designed to block is the use of employee benefit trusts (EBTs) to pay bonuses tax free. The typical structure involved an employer paying an amount equal to the intended bonus to an EBT, which the trustee then allocated to a revocable sub-trust for the benefit of the employee. No income tax arose at that point as the employee was not entitled to the money. The fund was then either lent to the employee (and the loan written off tax free on death) or invested (with the benefit of gross roll-up). The DR rules are effective in blocking this and other arrangements (which related to pensions) but have been drafted very widely so as to apply to legitimate share-based incentive arrangements operated by third parties, including employee share ownership plans (ESOPs).

Broadly, the DR rules apply where a 'third' person takes a 'relevant step' and it is 'reasonable to suppose' it is a means of providing rewards, recognition or loans in connection with a person's employment (or former or prospective employment). The relevant steps are the earmarking of money or assets, the payment of a sum or transfer of an asset and making an asset available. Where the legislation applies, the employee is subject to an immediate PAYE and Class 1 NIC charge with relief from later tax charges to avoid double tax.

---

[1] ITEPA 2003, ss 687A and 695A.
[2] Social Security (Contributions) Regulations 2001, SI 2001/1004, reg 22B and Sch 3, Part X, para 2A.

ITEPA 2003, Part 7A should be read in conjunction with the detailed HMRC guidance at EIM45000+.

15.2   THE GATEWAY

For the DR rules to apply an arrangement must pass what HMRC refers to in its guidance as the 'section 554A gateway'.[3] The gateway will be passed if:

* there is an *arrangement* that is wholly or partly a means of providing rewards, recognition or loans in connection with a person's employment;

* a *relevant step* has been taken; and

* the relevant step has been taken by a *relevant third person.*

The arrangement must be partly or wholly a means of providing, or partially or wholly concerned with the provision of, rewards, recognition or loans in connection with a person's employment (or former or prospective employment).[4] 'Arrangement' includes any agreement, scheme, settlement, transaction, trust or understanding (whether or not it is legally enforceable).[5] It also does not matter if the relevant arrangement does not include details of the steps that will or may be taken in connection with providing rewards, recognition or loans, so, for example, details of any sums or assets that will be involved or how or when or by whom or in whose favour any step will or may be taken need not be known.[6] It must be reasonable to suppose that, in essence, the relevant step is taken (wholly or partly) in pursuance of the relevant arrangement, or there is some other connection (direct or indirect) between the relevant step and the relevant arrangement.[7]

A relevant third person excludes the employer and the employee unless they are acting as trustees but includes any other third person such as an ESOP.[8] There is an exception for companies in the same group as the employer[9] provided there is no connection between the relevant step and a tax avoidance arrangement.

---

[3]   EIM45025 (Employment income provided through third parties: the Section 554A gateway).

[4]   ITEPA 2003, s 554A(1)(b) and (c)(i).

[5]   ITEPA 2003, s 554Z(3) and EIM45855 (Employment income provided through third parties: meaning of 'arrangement' and 'tax avoidance arrangement').

[6]   ITEPA 2003, s 554 A(6).

[7]   ITEPA 2003, s 554A(1)(e).

[8]   ITEPA 2003, s 554A(7).

[9]   ITEPA 2003, s 554A(8), which treats a group company in the same way as an employer. ITEPA 2003, s 554Z(5) defines group company by reference to the CGT definition in TCGA 1992, s 170(2)–(11), substituting 75% with 51%.

There are three types of 'relevant step', as follows.

15.2.1 Relevant step: earmarking of money or assets

It is a relevant step where a third party earmarks cash or assets for the benefit of an employee, with a view to a later relevant step being taken either by the third party or any other person in relation to the cash or asset.[10] Earmarking also occurs where cash or an asset starts being held by a person specifically with a view, so far as that person is concerned, to a later relevant step being taken in relation to the cash or asset[11] (often referred to as 'quasi-earmarking').

The terms of the later step need not be determined at the time the asset or money is earmarked. It can be unclear what the sum of money or what the asset will be, by whom or in whose favour the later step will be taken or how/when it will be taken.[12] It also does not matter that the later step is conditional such that the employee may never receive the money or assets,[13] nor that the employee (or any connected person) has no legal right to insist upon a relevant step being taken in the future.[14] It is therefore not possible to argue that the discretionary nature of arrangements prevents a charge arising.

15.2.2 Relevant step: payment of sum, transfer of asset etc

It is a relevant step if a third party pays a sum of money[15] or transfers an asset[16] to a 'relevant person', being the employee, a person chosen by the employee or within a class of people chosen by the employee.[17] A relevant step also includes a step taken by virtue of which a relevant person acquires securities, securities options or an interest in securities,[18] a step making available a sum of money or asset as security for a loan made or to be made to a relevant person,[19] or the grant of a lease to a relevant person for a term likely to exceed 21 years.[20] The grant of an option to an employee by an ESOP or another third party would therefore be a relevant step.

---

[10] ITEPA 2003, s 554B(1)(a).
[11] ITEPA 2003, s 554B(1)(b).
[12] ITEPA 2003, s 554B(2)(a).
[13] ITEPA 2003, s 554B(2)(b).
[14] ITEPA 2003, s 554B(2)(c).
[15] ITEPA 2003, s 554C(1)(a).
[16] ITEPA 2003, s 554C(1)(b).
[17] ITEPA 2003, s 554C(2).
[18] ITEPA 2003, s 554C(1)(c).
[19] ITEPA 2003, s 554C(1)(d).
[20] ITEPA 2003, s 554C(1)(e).

15.2.3   Relevant step: making asset available

A relevant step occurs if, without transferring the property in an asset to an employee or relevant person, a third party makes the assets available so that the employee or relevant person benefits as if the property had been transferred outright.[21] There is also a relevant step where an asset is made available for the employee or relevant person after cessation of employment. If the asset is made available within 2 years of cessation, the relevant step is deemed to have occurred 2 years following cessation of the employee's employment.[22]

15.2.4   Comment

It is preferable to avoid the DR rules by structuring arrangements so they do not involve a 'relevant third person' by involving only the employer or a company within the same group as the employer.

15.3   EXCLUSIONS AND RELIEFS

If the gateway is passed the next step is to determine whether any exclusions[23] or reliefs[24] apply.

There are two types of exclusions: full exclusions[25] and exclusions which relate only to earmarking.[26] A full exclusion applies to securities acquired subject to short-term risk of forfeiture,[27] the grant of employment-related securities options,[28] post-acquisition chargeable events relating to restricted securities (lifting or variation of restrictions or disposal of shares),[29] events that would be chargeable events but for making a s 431(1) election,[30] post-acquisition chargeable events relating to convertible securities, chargeable events relating to employment related securities options (exercise, assignment or release)[31] and disposal of employment-related securities at an over-value.[32] A full exclusion applies to later relevant steps taken after assets have been acquired by an employee (etc) providing he paid consideration of market value or more or the employee was charged to income tax on the undervalue pursuant to ITEPA 2003, s 62.[33] The exemption applies also to relevant steps taken after the

---

[21]   ITEPA 2003, s 554D(1).
[22]   ITEPA 2003, s 554D(1)(b) and (2).
[23]   ITEPA 2003, ss 554E–554X.
[24]   ITEPA 2003, s 554Z4–554Z15.
[25]   ITEPA 2003, ss 554E and 554N.
[26]   ITEPA 2003, ss 554H, 554J, 554K, 554L and 554M.
[27]   ITEPA 2003, s 554N(1).
[28]   ITEPA 2003, s 554N(2).
[29]   ITEPA 2003, s 554N(4) and (5)(a).
[30]   ITEPA 2003, s 554N(6).
[31]   ITEPA 2003, s 554N(5).
[32]   ITEPA 2003, s 554N(4) and (5)(c).
[33]   ITEPA 2003, s 554N(7) and (11).

acquisition of securities pursuant to the exercise of an employment related securities option.[34] A full exclusion is also available for tax advantaged plans such as enterprise management incentive (EMI) and CSOPs.[35]

If none of the exclusions apply, a PAYE and Class 1 NIC charge arises at the time the relevant step is taken (or, if later, the date on which the employee starts employment)[36] on the value of the relevant step. The value of a relevant step is, if the relevant step involves a sum of money, the sum of money,[37] or, in any other case, the market value of the asset which is the subject of the step.[38] The tax is payable via PAYE even where the asset is not cash or a readily convertible asset (RCA)[39] and a Class 1 NIC charge is also due in relation to relevant steps made on or after 6 December 2011. The amount of taxable employment income is based on the 'best estimate' of value.[40]

The amount brought into charge can be reduced by the consideration given by an employee for the transfer of the asset,[41] the amount assessed to income tax as general earnings under ITEPA 2003, s 62,[42] the value of a previous relevant step relating to the same asset,[43] for certain residence issues[44] and by the exercise price of an option (in the case of an earmarking charge relating to options).[45] If the amount is reduced to nil, no DR charge will apply. Where later events give rise to an income tax liability and it is just and reasonable to avoid a double tax charge, the later income tax liability will be relieved.[46] Relief can be claimed for an earmarking charge which is followed by an event which is not a relevant step and means the cash or assets will not be subject to a further relevant step.[47]

It is irrelevant whether the employer or the employee is aware that a relevant third person has taken a relevant step that has given rise to a DR charge, the PAYE liability will still arise. Any DR charge is also subject to ITEPA 2003, s 222 so that if an employee does not 'make good' the PAYE liability within 90 days from the date that the liability arises, that amount

---

[34] ITEPA 2003, s 554N(10) and (11).
[35] ITEPA 2003, s 554E.
[36] ITEPA 2003, ss 687A(3) and 695A(3).
[37] ITEPA 2003, s 554Z3(1).
[38] ITEPA 2003, s 554Z3(2) and (4). Note: the value of the relevant step is the higher of the market value of an asset and its cost but this does not apply where the asset is a security, an interest in a security or a securities option.
[39] ITEPA 2003, ss 687A(1) and 695A(1).
[40] ITEPA 2003, s 687A(2) and 695A(2).
[41] ITEPA 2003, s 554Z8.
[42] ITEPA 2003, s 554Z6.
[43] ITEPA 2003, s 554Z5.
[44] ITEPA 2003, s 554Z4.
[45] ITEPA 2003, s 554Z7.
[46] ITEPA 2003, s 554Z13.
[47] ITEPA 2003, s 554Z14.

IV Share-based Employee Incentives

will itself be treated as a taxable benefit.[48] It does not matter whether the employer actually accounted for the PAYE or whether the employee makes good the tax after the 90 days, the s 222 charge will still apply. Oddly, there are no reporting requirements under the DR rules.

15.3.1   Comment

The scope and complexity of the exclusions and reliefs is too great to cover in detail here. The examples examine the application of the DR rules to some common scenarios which apply to technology companies.

15.4   EXAMPLES RELATING TO TRANSFER OF ASSETS

The examples given at **15.4.1** to **15.4 5** relate to the application of the DR rules to typical situations involving the transfer of assets by an ESOP to employees. Some of these steps may also involve earmarking and these are considered separately (as this is a separate step under the DR rules). The step of making assets available for use is not considered as it rarely occurs in the context of share-based awards.

If an ESOP buys shares from an employee at market value or less (or sells shares to an employee at market value or more) it is arguable whether the gateway is passed as no quantifiable benefit is provided, it is assumed the test is passed for these purposes.

15.4.1   Purchase of shares by ESOP from employee

If the ESOP buys shares from an employee at market value or less, a relevant step occurs as the trustee pays a sum of money to a relevant person.[49] The DR charge will be reduced to nil as the employee gives full consideration (namely the shares).[50] It makes no difference if the trustee pays the consideration on deferred terms[51] but the employee must transfer the shares to the trustee 'before, or at or about' the same time as the payment (or first payment if there are several) for the reduction to apply.[52]

If the ESOP buys shares from an employee at an over-value, the amount of the over-value is exempt from the DR rules[53] (it is brought into charge instead by ITEPA 2003, Part 7, Chapter 3D and is subject to PAYE and NIC).

---

[48]   ITEPA 2003, s 222.
[49]   ITEPA 2003, s 554C(1)(a).
[50]   ITEPA 2003, s 554Z8.
[51]   There may, however, be an earmarking issue if funds are held back by the trustee for later payment.
[52]   ITEPA 2003, s 554Z8(1)(c).
[53]   ITEPA 2003, s 554N(4) and (5)(c).

15.4.2 Gift or sale of shares by ESOP to employee

If an ESOP gifts shares to an employee or sells them to an employee at market value or less, a relevant step occurs as the trustee transfers an asset (the shares) to a relevant person.[54] The position depends on whether the shares are subject to short-term risk of forfeiture (ie capable of being forfeited within 5 years of acquisition).[55]

If the shares are subject to short-term risk of forfeiture, the transfer is exempt from the DR rules.[56] No charge to income tax arises on acquisition unless the employee makes an election (eg, pursuant to ITEPA 2003, s 431(1) to pay income tax on the UMV of the shares).

If the shares are not subject to short-term risk of forfeiture, the DR charge is reduced by the consideration given by the employee for the shares[57] and the amount of any undervalue which is subject to tax as general earnings pursuant to ITEPA 2003, s 62.[58] It is essential for the employee to pay any consideration for the shares 'before, or at or about' the time of the transfer (otherwise the reduction for the consideration will not apply).[59]

Any subsequent chargeable events (or events which would have been chargeable but for making a s 431(1) election) are also exempt from the DR rules.[60]

15.4.3 Sale of shares by ESOP to employee on deferred payment terms

If an employee purchases shares from an ESOP on deferred payment terms, the arrangement will usually be structured so the amount payable is equal to the UMV of the shares on acquisition. The arrangement will be structured this way to prevent any income tax charge arising on acquisition (see **12.4**, ITEPA 2003, Part 7, Chapter 3C: acquisition of shares at an undervalue). The employee will usually make a s 431(1) election for the reasons explained at **12.4**.

If the shares are subject to short-term risk of forfeiture, the transfer of shares to the employee will be exempt from the DR rules,[61] as will later chargeable events.[62] The tax position will be the same as for the subscription of shares nil paid outlined at **12.4**.

---

54   ITEPA 2003, s 554C(1)(b).
55   ITEPA 2003, s 425(1).
56   ITEPA 2003, s 554N(1).
57   ITEPA 2003, s 554Z(8).
58   ITEPA 2003, s 554Z(6).
59   ITEPA 2003, s 554Z8(1)(c).
60   ITEPA 2003, s 554N(5) and (6).
61   ITEPA 2003, s 554N(1).
62   ITEPA 2003, s 554N(4) and (5)(a).

If the shares are not subject to short-term risk of forfeiture, there will be no reduction for the consideration ultimately payable as the employee is not required to pay for the shares 'before, or at or about' the time of the transfer.[63] The transfer will therefore result in a DR charge when the step is taken with no exemption or relief. The amount brought into charge under the DR rules reduces the amount of the notional loan brought into charge under ITEPA 2003, Part 7, Chapter 3C.[64] There is no provision for obtaining repayment of the DR charge, however, when the employee later pays the outstanding consideration to the trustee.

It is common for shares purchased on deferred payment terms as part of an incentive arrangement to be subject to vesting and forfeiture conditions so arrangements of this sort would not normally be subject to the DR rules. There is, however, a danger of an earmarking charge arising (see **15.5.3**), which means it is preferable to avoid the DR rules by structuring so the company issues shares nil paid.

15.4.4   Grant and exercise of options

The grant of any option by a trustee of an ESOP to an employee is a relevant step[65] that is exempt.[66] The exercise of such an option results in a relevant step, namely the transfer of an asset (the option shares),[67] which is also exempt.[68] The exemptions apply to all options including EMI and CSOP.

15.4.5   Loans by ESOP to employee

A loan by an ESOP to an employee will give rise to a DR charge on the full amount of the loan (as it involves the payment of a sum of money)[69] with no relief for later repayment of the loan. There is no relief for tax arising in relation to taxable cheap loans under ITEPA 2003, ss 173–191 and no £5,000 threshold. There are exceptions for commercial loan transactions[70] and all-employee benefit packages,[71] but these are unlikely to apply. Consequently, if it is intended to lend money to an employee the loan should be made by his employer or another company in the same group.

---

[63]   ITEPA 2003, s 554Z8(1)(c).
[64]   ITEPA 2003, s 446T(3)(f).
[65]   ITEPA 2003, s 554C(1)(c).
[66]   ITEPA 2003, s 554N(2).
[67]   ITEPA 2003, s 554C(1)(b).
[68]   ITEPA 2003, s 554N(5).
[69]   ITEPA 2003, s 554C(1)(a).
[70]   ITEPA 2003, s 554F.
[71]   ITEPA 2003, s 554G.

Loans by third parties to fund option exercises are exempt but certain conditions apply, in particular, the loan must be repaid within 40 days.[72]

15.5 EXAMPLES RELATING TO EARMARKING

All the steps mentioned above in relation to asset transfers potentially involve the trustee earmarking assets prior to the transfer. Separate charges arise under the DR rules when earmarking occurs (even if the later relevant step is itself exempt) so it is necessary to examine the same examples to analyse the exemptions and reliefs as they apply to earmarking.

15.5.1 Purchase of shares by ESOP from employee

An earmarking potentially occurs in relation to the cash the trustee sets aside to fund the purchase of shares from an employee[73] with no applicable exemption or reduction.

HMRC has confirmed at EIM54110 that no separate earmarking occurs where there is a simultaneous earmarking and transfer of cash or assets (as there is no 'later' relevant step). Care is therefore required not to reveal the identity of the employee to the trustee until the money is due to be transferred.

If an earmarking occurs in relation to the cash set aside by the ESOP, a DR charge would arise at that point on the amount of the cash set aside for the PAYE month in which the earmarking occurs.[74] When the ESOP pays the cash to the employee there will be a subsequent relevant step, the value of which is reduced using overlap relief by the value of the earlier relevant step.[75] The overlap relief is usually of no use as the value of the later step would have been reduced to nil anyway by the consideration given by the employee (see the example at **15.4.1**). Overlap relief operates by reducing the value of a subsequent relevant step by the value of the first. There is no reduction in the value of the first relevant step with the harsh result that the full amount of the cash set aside to purchase the shares is subject to a DR charge without relief.

If the trustee pays consideration on deferred payment terms, it may be difficult to avoid an earmarking in relation to any cash in this trust held back to fund deferred payments. One solution may be to ensure the trustee is only put in funds when required to make the deferred payments.

---

[72]   ITEPA 2003, s 554N(13)–(16).
[73]   ITEPA 2003, s 554B(1)(a).
[74]   ITEPA 2003, s 554Z3(1).
[75]   ITEPA 2003, s 554Z5.

15.5.2   Gift or sale of shares by ESOP to employee

An earmarking potentially occurs in relation to an asset (namely the shares) which the trustee sets aside to gift or sell to the employee.[76]

HMRC has confirmed at EIM54110 that no separate earmarking occurs where there is a simultaneous earmarking of the asset and transfer (as there is no later relevant step). Care is therefore required not to reveal the identity of the employee to the trustee until the shares are due to be transferred

If an earmarking occurs in relation to the shares set aside by the ESOP, a DR charge would arise on the value of the shares set aside[77] on the day the earmarking occurs.[78] When the shares are later transferred to the employee there will be a subsequent step, the value of which is reduced by the value of the earlier step.[79] The reduction in the value of the later step is usually of no use as the second step would either have been exempt or reduced to nil anyway (see the example at **15.4.2**). There is no relief for the value of the first step.[80]

Double tax relief is available for any subsequent income tax charges on a just and reasonable basis.[81] Consequently the amount of tax arising under ITEPA 2003, s 62 on the acquisition of the shares (or any tax arising under ITEPA 2003, Part 7 when later chargeable events occur) is reduced by the amount of the DR charge.[82] If the value of the shares is lower on the date of gift or sale than when the earmarking occurred, the employee would pay a DR charge on the higher value and obtain relief for tax paid only on the lower value.

There is no reduction for the consideration given by the employee for the shares (as the consideration is not given for the earmarking).[83] Consequently, if shares are earmarked and later sold to the employee at market value, a DR charge will apply to the full value of the shares when the earmarking occurs with no relief for the consideration given by the employee when the shares are later transferred.

There are two earmarking only exemptions for plans involving awards of shares – ITPEA 2003, s 554J (Deferred Share Awards) and s 554K (Exit Only Share Awards) and an exception involving cash and assets

---

[76]   ITEPA 2003, s 554B(1)(a).
[77]   ITEPA 2003, ss 554Z3(2) and 554Z(4). Note: the requirement that the value is determined by reference to the higher of the market value and cost does not apply to securities, interests in securities and securities options by virtue of s 554Z3(4).
[78]   ITEPA 2003, s 695A(3).
[79]   ITEPA 2003, s 554Z5.
[80]   ITEPA 2003, s 554Z5.
[81]   ITEPA 2003, s 554Z13.
[82]   ITEPA 2003, s 554Z13.
[83]   ITEPA 2003, s 554Z8.

earmarked pursuant to deferred remuneration plans.[84] The exemptions do not apply to the straight gift or sale of shares; they are designed to apply to deferred share award plans. It is unusual for private companies to operate plans of this sort but the conditions are summarised below.

An earmarking made pursuant to a pre-exit deferred share plan is exempt if the award allows the employee (etc) to receive shares in the future. The main purpose must be to defer receipt of the shares until a later specified fixed date that is within 10 years of the award date. The award must be subject to specified conditions which cause the award to lapse if failed. Shares must be transferred by the specified date but may vest and be transferred earlier. There must be a reasonable chance the conditions will not be met. A transfer prior to the specified date is permitted for good leavers and on a change of control provided that is not the main purpose of the award. Shares can be transferred to bad leavers before the specified date at the discretion of the board or remuneration committee. Awards may be cash settled.[85]

A separate earmarking only exemption applies to the earmarking of cash or assets pursuant to a deferred remuneration plan.[86] It applies to cash or assets earmarked pursuant to awards subject to a specified vesting date which is 5 years or less after the award date. The award must be subject to forfeiture and there must be a reasonable chance the conditions will not be met. Fallback charges apply if the shares cease to be required to satisfy the award but remain earmarked. The exemption is more flexible than the exemption for pre-exit deferred share awards as it is applies to any cash or assets and it is not prescriptive as to leaver provisions. The maximum 5 year vesting date, however, means the exemption is only suitable for deferred bonus awards as opposed to long term incentive awards.

An earmarking made pursuant to an exit only deferred share plan is exempt if the transfer of shares is subject to an exit being achieved. The main purpose of the award must be that shares are only transferred on an exit event and there must be a reasonable chance the exit event will occur. The award must be over shares in a trading company (or holding company of a trading group). The transfer of shares may be subject to additional conditions in addition to achieving an exit. Leavers may retain the award to exit but shares cannot be transferred pre-exit. Shares should be transferred within 6 months of an exit (to avoid fallback charges) and awards may be cash settled.[87]

---

[84] ITPEA 2003, s 554H.
[85] ITEPA 2003, s 554J.
[86] ITEPA 2003, s 554H.
[87] ITEPA 2003, s 554K.

IV Share-based Employee Incentives

15.5.3   Sale of shares by ESOP to employee on deferred payment terms

An earmarking potentially occurs in relation to an asset (namely the shares) which the trustee sets aside to sell to the employee.[88] The earmarking can be avoided by ensuring it occurs simultaneously, as confirmed by HMRC at EIM54110.

If an earmarking charge arises because the ESOP sets aside the shares prior to the transfer, a DR charge arises on the full value of the shares at the time.[89] The further relevant step occurs when the shares are transferred and is reduced by the value of the first step.[90]

If the shares are subject to short-term risk of forfeiture, the reduction is usually of no assistance as the later step would be exempt from the DR charge anyway (see the example at **15.4.3**). There is no credit for the consideration ultimately payable for the shares against the earmarking charge (as the consideration is not given for the earmarking).[91] It is possible to reduce any later income tax charges by the amount of the DR charge if that is just and reasonable,[92] but deferred shares would normally be structured so no later income tax charges arise (other than on the benefit of the notional loan).

If the shares are not subject to short-term risk of forfeiture, the value of the second step will be reduced by the value of the first, avoiding a double charge to tax under the DR rules.[93]

15.5.4   Grant and exercise of options

HMRC considers the grant of an option by a trustee gives rise to two steps, the grant itself (which is exempt)[94] and a separate earmarking by the trustee (the later relevant step being the transfer of shares to satisfy the option).[95] Options should be granted by the employing company (or a company within the same group as the employer) to avoid earmarking occurring on grant.

If one of the ways in which the option could be satisfied is by the transfer of shares held in the ESOP, it will be necessary to seek the agreement of the trustee (usually in advance of the grant). Consequently, there will

---

[88]   ITEPA 2003, s 554B(1)(a).
[89]   ITEPA 2003, s 554Z 3(2) and s 555Z 3(4).
[90]   ITEPA 2003, s 554Z5.
[91]   ITEPA 2003, s 554Z8.
[92]   ITEPA 2003, s 554Z13.
[93]   ITEPA 2003, s 554Z5.
[94]   ITEPA 2003, s 554 N(2).
[95]   HMRC Employment Income Manual 45325. Employment income provided through third parties excluding priority of Part 7, ITEPA 2003 over Part 7A Rules.

often be a linking agreement between the company that established the ESOP and the trustee, in which the trustee agrees to satisfy options if requested to do so by the company.

HMRC has confirmed that no earmarking will arise if the trustee knows that a specified number of shares have been granted to named employees without knowing the numbers attributable to each or that a specified number of shares have been awarded to a specified number or employees without knowing the names of the employees.[96] Consequently, it may be necessary to draft the linking agreement (or amend the terms of an existing linking agreement) to prevent earmarking occurring when the trustee is requested to agree to satisfy options.

If an earmarking charge arises, the amount of the charge is reduced by the exercise price.[97] If the earmarking occurs when the option is 'in the money', the earmarking charge may not be reduced to nil, so it is necessary to consider whether an exemption applies.

EMI and CSOPs benefit from a full exemption from all DR charges (including earmarking) if certain conditions are met.[98] Unapproved options benefit from one of two earmarking only exemptions depending on whether options are exercisable before an exit[99] or only on an exit being achieved.[100]

These exemptions[101] are qualified as they require only a 'reasonable number' of shares to be earmarked. HMRC guidance confirms that the 'maximum number which one might reasonably expect will depend on the facts of the case but, apart from exceptional cases, up to 100% is likely to be reasonable'.[102] The exclusions only apply if there is no connection to a tax avoidance arrangement.[103]

The exemption relating to CSOP and EMI imposes 'fallback' charges if the shares are no longer required to satisfy options but continue to be earmarked.[104] It is unclear whether a fallback charge arises if EMI options lose their qualifying status. The unapproved option exemptions impose conditions relating to the option terms and default charges if

---

[96] HMRC *Employment Income Manual* EIM45110 (Employment income provide through third parties: relevant steps: Section 554B: meaning of 'earmarked' in Section 554B(1)(a)).

[97] ITEPA 2003, s 554Z7.

[98] ITEPA 2003, s 554E.

[99] ITEPA 2003, s 554L.

[100] ITEPA 2003, ss 554M.

[101] ITEPA 2003, ss 554Z(7), 554E, 554L and 554M.

[102] HMRC *Employment Income Manual* 45470 (Employment income provided through third parties: exclusions: earmarking for employee share and share option schemes: meaning of 'maximum reasonably expected').

[103] ITEPA 2003, ss 554L(3)(c) and 554M(2)(c).

[104] ITEPA 2003, s 554E(10)–(11).

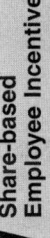

IV Share-based Employee Incentives

options are not granted within 3 months of an earmarking. Consequently, it is preferable to avoid earmarking occurring rather than to rely on the exemptions.

If an earmarking charge arises in connection with an unapproved option there is, in effect, a delayed relief as the amount assessed to income tax on the spread is reduced by the amount brought into charge under the DR rules.[105]

Unapproved options should preferably be structured so as to comply with the earmarking exemptions, so the conditions are summarised below.

An earmarking made pursuant to an exit only option plan is exempt if the plan allows exercise only on an exit being achieved and there is a reasonable chance an exit will be achieved. The options must be granted over shares in a trading company (or a holding company of a trading group). Options must be exercisable only upon an exit being achieved (although additional performance conditions are permitted). Leavers can retain options but options cannot be exercised until exit. Shares must be transferred within 6 months of exit (or, if earlier, by the latest date provided for in the plan) and may be cash settled.[106]

An earmarking made pursuant to a pre-exit option plan is exempt if the plan allows options to be exercised on or before a specified vesting date that is within 10 years of grant. For these purposes 'vesting' means the date the option becomes exercisable, and it need not be a specified date so could, for example, be the date on which a performance condition is determined to have been met causing the option to become exercisable. Options should lapse on or before the tenth anniversary of grant to avoid fallback charges. The option must include conditions which, if not met, will cause the option to cease to be exercisable on or before the vesting date. Options may be exercised prior to the vesting date (eg on an exit or by good leavers) providing it is not the main purpose of the option. Bad leavers can be permitted to exercise the option at the discretion of the board or remuneration committee. Options may be cash settled.[107]

15.5.5   Loan by ESOP to employee

An earmarking potentially occurs in relation to the cash the trustee sets aside to lend to the employee.[108] The earmarking can be avoided by ensuring the identity of the employee is not known to the trustee until the loan is advanced, as confirmed by HMRC at EIM54110.

---

[105] ITEPA 2003, s 480(5)(d).
[106] ITEPA 2003, s 554M.
[107] ITEPA 2003, s 554L.
[108] ITEPA 2003, s 554B(1)(a).

If an earmarking occurs in advance of the payment to the employee, a DR charge arises on the full amount of the cash set aside[109] with no exemption or relief.

When the loan is advanced to the employee the value of the relevant step is reduced by the value of the earlier step[110] thereby avoiding a double charge under the DR rules.

[109] ITEPA 2003, s 554Z3(1).
[110] ITEPA 2003, s 554Z5.

IV Share-based Employee Incentives

CHAPTER 16

REFORMS

16.1 GOVERNMENT REVIEW OF GEARED GROWTH ARRANGEMENTS

Part IV would be incomplete without mentioning two recent developments in relation to geared growth arrangements. In the first Budget of 2010 the then Labour Government announced 'there will be a review and consultation, during 2010, on taxation of geared growth arrangements used in connection with employment related securities, to ensure employment income is subject to correct tax and National Insurance contributions'.[1] No proposals have been announced in connection with this review.

On 22 June 2011, HMRC issued a consultation paper on whether to treat geared growth arrangements as discloseable for the purposes of the Disclosure of Tax Avoidance Scheme rules. The reason for the interest is so that HMRC can monitor whether geared growth arrangements are being used as a substitute form of bonus planning following the introduction of the disguised remuneration rules. The definition of growth shares that HMRC uses in the paper, however, extends to growth shares used by technology companies to reward commercial growth.[2]

As should be apparent from Chapters 11 and 12, tax-efficient planning for technology companies often hinges on being able to create geared interests with a low up-front value to avoid cash flow issues and to allow future gains to be taxed as capital. The arrangements are unnecessary when there is already a class of ordinary shares available with a low up-front value (ordinary shares of this sort are likely to be highly geared in these circumstances). Whichever class of shares is used, it should also be apparent that these arrangements are not used by technology companies as a form of bonus planning but as a method of isolating and

---

[1]   Budget 2010 'Enforcement and Compliance'.

[2]   In para 4.8 HMRC says: 'By "growth" share scheme HMRC is referring to schemes of various descriptions, the common feature of which is that they involve a class of shares, not available to ordinary investors, whose rights are such that they have low value at issue, or acquisition, but the potential for significant appreciation if the company grows in value. In tax terms they usually involve a relatively low up-front income tax charge to the employee, with capital gains tax treatment on disposal of the shares.'

rewarding employees for genuine commercial growth. If these arrangements were to be blocked, it would be highly damaging for many technology companies that rely on equity to attract talented employees.

The definition of 'growth shares' in the consultation paper excludes ordinary shares held by both management and investors, yet ordinary shares of this sort can be highly geared too. There are some examples of arrangements involving ordinary shares in the two memoranda agreed between HMRC and the British Venture Capital Association on 23 July 2003. The memoranda relate to the application of the Income Tax (Earnings and Pensions) Act 2003 (ITEPA 2003), Part 7 to the tax treatment of managers' equity investments in venture capital and private equity-backed companies and to carried interests in venture capital and private equity limited partnerships. The memorandum creates safe harbour treatment if the conditions are met by treating management as having paid unrestricted market value (UMV) for their shares or carried interests. The example in the memorandum relating to shares assumes Newco is established with £50 million of funding, of which £300,000 is provided by management in exchange for 15% of the ordinary share capital. The ordinary shares rank last in order of priority behind various classes of debt and preference shares. The example in memorandum relating to carried interests assumes management pay £2,500 for a 20% carried interest in a £100 million fund.

The memoranda do not deal with the situation where a new recruit is awarded equity some time after the original arrangements have been established, when the value of the ordinary shares (or carried interest) may have increased substantially. Nor do the memoranda deal with the situation where an outside investor does not acquire shares of the same class (or the same carried interests) as management. It is frequently necessary for investors to own a separate class of shares to management for commercial reasons.

In the author's view the abuse is not creating (or using) a class of geared shares owned only by employees but creating (or using) any shares in a way which is designed to deliver a bonus. Any abuse is better dealt with using an anti-avoidance rule.

16.2 SUGGESTED REFORMS

The author would like to suggest three reforms that could greatly assist technology companies.

16.2.1 Entrepreneurs' relief

The 5% threshold for ER should be removed and the one-year holding period should run from the grant of enterprise management incentive

(EMI) options (as it did previously for business asset taper relief). The 5% threshold encourages companies to offer shares to senior employees to allow them to qualify for ER, but shares are more complicated than options due to the mechanisms that need to be put in place to acquire forfeited shares prior to exit. This proposal would allow technology companies to deliver more incentives using EMI options which are much simpler to operate.

16.2.2   Valuations

HMRC should agree valuations in advance for s 431 elections in the same way as it currently allows for EMI options. This would remove uncertainty for employees acquiring shares.

16.2.3   Qualifying employee share ownership plans (QuESOPs)

There should be tax relief for trusts that satisfy the following conditions (referred to as 'QuESOPs').

The trust should be a discretionary trust with the class of beneficiaries confined to employees, former employees and their dependents. The purpose of trust should be for it to be an employees' share scheme as defined in the Companies Act 2006, s 1166 (ie to encourage or facilitate the holding of shares in the establishing company or any company in the same group). The trust deed should require the trust to be operated so the only assets it holds are:

- 'qualifying shares' (being shares in the settlor company or company within the settlor group);

- the proceeds of sale from qualifying shares;

- cash contributed or loaned by the settlor to the QuESOP for the purpose of acquiring qualifying shares.

Any cash could only be applied to repay loans/pay trust expenses or acquire shares within 2 years of receipt. Any shares could only be applied for the benefit of beneficiaries if the event is subject to income tax under ITEPA 2003, s 62 or Part 7. Shares could also be transferred to satisfy EMI and other tax-advantaged options and assets held in a QuESOP could be transferred to another QuESOP.

Breach of the above would be a disqualifying event resulting in loss of tax protection. A Form 'QuESOP 1' would be required to be submitted to the Small Companies Enterprise Centre by the settlor within 92 days of establishing the trust for it to qualify, with a transitional period of one year during which settlors may apply to register existing ESOPs as

IV   Share-based Employee Incentives

QuESOPs. The Small Companies Enterprise Centre would have a year from filing to challenge status otherwise the trust would qualify.

The tax advantages would be as follows:

- the QuESOP trustee would be exempt from all income tax, all CGT and all IHT;

- the disguised remuneration rules would be inapplicable;

- the loans to participators rules for close companies would be inapplicable; and

- the settlor and participators would be exempt from related close company IHT charges.

The tax charges listed above are seldom incurred in practice because technology companies usually take advice and structure so as to avoid the charges. A QuESOP would allow technology companies to operate share incentives flexibly without the cost of the advice at very little cost to the Exchequer.

PART V

VALUE ADDED TAX: EUROPEAN UNION TRADE

CHAPTER 17

VALUE ADDED TAX

17.1 INTRODUCTION

Value added tax (VAT) is a tax charge on the consumption of supplies of goods or services for a price (otherwise known as 'consideration'). VAT is a common tax imposed in the territory of the EU.[1] If goods are supplied from outside the EU to a Member State of the EU then import VAT may be payable (see Chapter 19), and certain services supplied from outside the EU to the EU may be subject to VAT (see Chapter 22). The export of goods from a Member State of the EU to outside the EU is not generally subject to VAT (see Chapter 20).

The scope of the charge to VAT is wide, and includes numerous forms of consumption by a consumer that are supplied for consideration. The principle of VAT in the EU is stated in Art 1 of the EU's 'VAT Directive',[2] in the following terms:

> 'The principle of the common system of VAT entails the application to goods and services of a general tax on consumption exactly proportional to the price of the goods and services, however many transactions take place in the production and distribution process before the stage at which tax is charged.

---

[1] The countries which comprise the VAT territory of the EU are: Austria, Belgium, Bulgaria, Cyprus, Czech Republic, Denmark (excluding Busingen and the Isle of Heligoland), Greece, Hungary, the Republic of Ireland, Italy (except the communes of Livigno and Camione d'Italia and the Italian waters of Lake Lugano), Latvia, Lithuania, Luxembourg, Malta, The Netherlands, Poland, Portugal (including the Azores and Madeira), Romania, Slovakia, Slovenia, Spain (including the Balearic Islands but excluding Ceuta and Melilla), Sweden and the United Kingdom (including the Isle of Man). Territories of some of the foregoing are not within the VAT territory of the EU, and accordingly supplies of goods from these territories will be treated as imports. The territories are: Andorra, the Åland Islands (Finland), the Channel Islands (Jersey, Guernsey, Sark), the Canary Islands (Spain), the overseas departments of France (Guadeloupe, Martinique, Reunion and French Guiana) and Mount Athos (Greece). To check on any alterations in the extent of the VAT territory see www.hmrc.gov.uk, and Value Added Tax Regulations 1995, SI 1995/2518, regs 136–139. Gibraltar is not part of the EU.

[2] Council Directive 2006/112/EC on the common system of value added tax, OJ L 347, 28/11/2006 p 1.

> On each transaction, VAT, calculated on the price of the goods or services at the rate applicable to such goods or services, shall be chargeable after deduction of the amount of VAT borne directly by the various cost components.
>
> The common system of VAT shall be applied up to and including the retail trade stage.'

The effect of Art 1 is to emphasise that VAT is a tax applied to the price of goods and services supplied to the end consumer, but only after deduction of the amount of VAT which has been incurred directly in connection with the cost components of the goods and services supplied to such consumer. Accordingly, the main principle of VAT is that it will be borne by the final consumer. This is the reason why a supplier who incurs VAT on components used for the purposes of making a supply is generally entitled to deduct 'input tax' from the VAT charged on supplies made by it, known as 'output tax'.

As a consumption tax, VAT is capable of being applied in many areas of e-commerce and e-infrastructure activities. Consider the following forms of supply:

(1) communication services, whether satellite or earth-based, to an internet access provider;

(2) grant of a copyright licence permitting the use of a search engine database by the provider of a mirror-site in another country;

(3) sale of computer software 'off-the-shelf';

(4) sale of computer software devised specifically for a business ('bespoke software');

(5) sale of micro-processors and other forms of IT equipment;

(6) sale of computer software via an internet transaction;

(7) sale of digital content via internet, phone or pay TV transactions, such as ebooks, films, games;

(8) sale of physical goods via the internet or phone transactions with delivery via a courier;

(9) financial or insurance services accessed by subscribers via the internet;

(10) purchase of computer hardware, with pre-installed computer software, licensed for use by the end user.

Each of the situations noted above has the potential to come within the scope of VAT, with a consequence for the supplier and/or consumer.

The application of VAT law in the area of e-commerce and e-infrastructure activities mainly falls to be determined by the general framework for VAT legislation created under EU laws and as implemented by national laws (see **17.2**) such as the UK's Value Added Tax Act 1994 (VATA 1994). To understand how VAT is applied in this area, it is first necessary to understand the general ingredients of the VAT charge and how it is applied. These aspects are considered in this chapter (for an overview see **17.3**), primarily from a UK VAT perspective.

Essentially, e-commerce transactions comprise two distinct categories for VAT purposes, namely (a) the supply of physical 'goods' ordered via e-commerce that are delivered to either businesses or private consumers and (b) the supply of services through e-commerce, such as downloads of digital content. Supplies of physical goods ordered and sold using the internet (ie e-commerce) should not of itself create any unusual issues, since the physical goods sold must still be delivered by conventional methods. Accordingly, the tax authorities would continue to be able to collect VAT, for example, on goods imported from outside the EU at the time of importation and via 'distance selling' arrangements affecting the VAT treatment of, for example, mail order sales within the EU.[3] In contrast, the supply of 'services' relating to e-commerce raises interesting VAT issues. One of the principal issues relating to the application of VAT to e-commerce activities is the place of supply rules, which seek to determine where VAT must be accounted for in relation to the services supplied.[4]

17.2 EUROPEAN LAW

As noted above, VAT in the EU is implemented by a series of EU laws and national implementing laws; for example, at the UK national level by VATA 1994. This will be the position for each Member State (ie any country or territory in the VAT territory of the EU).

By way of further background, the Treaty establishing the European Economic Community (EEC) (signed in March 1957 and known as the Treaty of Rome or the EEC Treaty) established the common European market and the institutions that implement the objectives of the EU. The Treaty of Maastricht[5] (known as the Treaty on European Union or 'TEU') established the 'European Union' (introducing new areas and forms of co-operation between Member States), and reclassified the EEC as simply the 'European Community' (so the EEC Treaty became known

---

[3]   See Chapter 18.
[4]   See particularly Chapter 22.
[5]   This treaty came into force on 1 November 1993.

as the EC Treaty). The TEU and the EC Treaty have both recently been amended, consolidated and renumbered following the Treaty of Lisbon to modernise the EU, which came into force on 1 December 2009, and the EC Treaty has been renamed the 'Treaty on the Functioning of the European Union' (TFEU). The TEU and TFEU (together, the 'Treaties') on which the EU is presently founded have the same legal value.

Under the EC Treaty (now repackaged as the 'TFEU'), each Member State surrendered part of its sovereignty to the institutions of the EU.[6] The principal institutions are the Commission,[7] the Parliament,[8] the Council[9] and the Court of Justice of the European Union (ECJ)[10] (collectively, 'the Institutions'). On issues concerning the interpretation and application of EU law, the ECJ is the final forum for deciding the point in issue. The ECJ is assisted by an Advocate General, whose role is to issue an impartial Opinion to assist the court in its decision-making, although such Opinion does not bind the ECJ. A national court may refer a matter concerning the interpretation and application of EU law to the ECJ for its decision on such interpretation and application (called a 'preliminary ruling').[11] The ECJ's decision would then be applied by the

---

[6]   *Costa v ENEL* [1964] ECR 585, at 593–594. See also *Factortame* (C-213/89) [1990] 1 ECR 2433.

[7]   The Commission initiates legislation, and is responsible for drafting proposals that are placed before the Parliament and the Council (see Art 17, para 1 TEU (formerly Art 211 EC Treaty)).

[8]   The Parliament has powers relating to implementing legislation and supervising the Commission.

[9]   The Council of the EU comprises representatives appointed by each Member State, and its responsibilities include legislating with the Parliament on proposals put forward by the Commission and entering into international agreements between the EU and international organisations. The decisions of the Council are reached on the basis of qualified majority voting as a general rule (Art 16, paras 3, 4 and 5 TEU and Art 238 TFEU) (broadly, each Member State has a specified number of votes based upon the size of its population) unless a decision must be unanimous, e g on sensitive topics such as taxation. The Council's qualified majority voting system will be subject to certain changes in the future, such as the introduction of the 'double majority voting' system in November 2014. See further Art 16 TEU and Art 238 TFEU. The Council of the EU is not to be confused with the Council of Europe, which is not an EU body, nor with the European Council – another institution, where EU leaders meet around four times a year, convened by its President who is elected for a once-renewable term of office of 2.5 years, to discuss the EU's broad political priorities and major initiatives but which does not have the power to pass laws – see Art 15 TEU.

[10]   The ECJ is responsible for ensuring that the Treaties and laws implemented in accordance with the Treaties are properly interpreted and applied in the same way within the EU (Art 19 TEU (formerly Art 220 EC Treaty)). A decision of the ECJ on a question of interpretation is final and binding upon the national courts of each Member State. As noted above, the ECJ is assisted by Advocates General, who are required to make reasoned submissions on cases which are to be decided by the ECJ (Art 252 TFEU (formerly Art 222 EC Treaty)).

[11]   A reference to the ECJ is made under Art 267 TFEU (formerly Art 234 EC Treaty). For the principles relating to making a reference to the ECJ see the judgment of Chadwick LJ in *Trinity Mirror plc (formerly Mirror Group Newspapers Ltd) v Customs and Excise Comrs* [2001] EWCA Civ 65, at [48]–[57], [2001] STC 192, at [48]–[51].

national court to the facts of the case as it is the national court that remains exclusively entitled to assess and rule specifically on the facts of a dispute.[12]

In accordance with the TEU, the EU only has competence to act and legislate on matters conferred directly by the Treaties.[13] Competences not conferred upon the EU in the Treaties remain with the Member States, for example, national security. Nonetheless, even if the EU does not have exclusive competence in a particular area, it is entitled to take action in accordance with the principle of 'subsidiarity'. Under that principle, the EU shall act only if, and so far as the objectives of the proposed action 'cannot be sufficiently achieved by the Member States ... but can rather, by reason of the scale or effects of the proposed action, be better achieved at Union level'.[14] Any such action by the EU should not, however, go beyond what is necessary to achieve the objectives of the Treaties (under the principle of 'proportionality').

The ECJ established the principle that EU law provisions have supremacy[15] over the national law of Member States (including the UK) in the event of conflict, and certain of the Institutions established under the Treaties have the power to adopt rules, which can be 'directly applicable' in Member States, meaning that those rules automatically form part of national law without further enactment by government and cannot be overridden by conflicting national law. Other EU rules (including certain of the Articles of the Treaties themselves) only have effect at a national level when brought into force by domestic laws. The rules that can have 'direct application' in each Member State are those applied by:

(1) a 'regulation',[16] which is of general application so has an immediate and binding effect in each Member State (eg the Council Regulation laying down implementing measures for the VAT Directive,[17] hereinafter the EU Implementing Regulation – see below); and

---

12 See *CLT-UFA SA v Finanzamt Koln-West* (Case C-253/03) [2006] ECR I-1831, paras 35–36; *Denkavit Futtermittel* (Case 36/79) [1979] ECR 3439, para 12. See also Art 267 TFEU as above – the functions of the ECJ and those of the referring national court are clearly separate, and it falls exclusively to the latter to interpret national legislation.

13 Art 5 TEU.

14 Art 5 TEU.

15 The principle of supremacy of EU law was considered and introduced by the ECJ in the *Costa v ENEL* case (Case 6/64). See note 6 above.

16 See Art 288 TFEU (formerly Art 249 EC Treaty) and note 20.

17 Council Implementing Regulation 282/2011/EU, laying down implementing measures for Directive 2006/112/EC on the common system of value added tax (recast), OJ L77/1, 15/03/2011, pp 1–22.

(2)   a 'decision',[18] which is a ruling that is binding and therefore directly
      applicable on a particular matter but only to whom it is specifically
      addressed.

A 'directive'[19] is in effect instructions addressed to each Member State to
implement a specific objective into domestic law. These are binding as to
the result to be achieved upon each such Member State, but they leave the
form and method of achieving the desired result to the discretion of
individual Member States (eg the VAT Directive), so to that extent they
are not 'directly applicable', as they must be implemented into national
law. It is also the case that even if an EU law provision is not 'directly
applicable', it may still have 'direct effect' (a concept developed by the
ECJ) at a national level, so that it gives rise to rights or obligations that
may be directly enforced in actions brought before a national court in a
Member State against either (or both) such State and/or other individuals
or businesses. EU law is generally capable of 'direct effect' if the provision
is clear, precise and unconditional and its operation does not call for
additional measures being taken at EU or national level or leave any
discretion for implementation of the provision in question. Therefore,
regulations[20] and decisions can be both 'directly applicable' and capable
of having 'direct effect'. There are also some examples of specific Treaty
Articles that have 'direct effect', and which can accordingly be relied upon
and enforced directly within a Member State, such as the right to freedom
of establishment (Art 49 TFEU), and the right to free movement of
capital and payments (Art 63 TFEU).[21]

As regards directives, the ECJ has held that where a Member State has
failed to implement a directive into national law by the relevant
implementation date, or where the national law has not been implemented
correctly or its application is inconsistent with a directive, then such
directive can be capable of having 'direct effect' in the UK or any other
Member State contrary to any domestic legislation, provided that its
provisions are 'unconditional and sufficiently precise', and the directive
'define[s] rights which individuals are able to assert against the State'.[22]

---

[18]   Art 288 TFEU (formerly EC Treaty, Art 249).
[19]   Art 288 TFEU (formerly EC Treaty, Art 249).
[20]   Under Art 288 TFEU regulations are expressly stated to be 'directly applicable', and the
       ECJ clarified in the *Politi* judgment of 14 December 1971 (Case 43/71 [1971] ECR 1039)
       that regulations are also capable of full 'direct effect', ie its provisions can be invoked
       against a Member State as well as against private individuals and other businesses.
       Decisions are only capable of direct effect in actions against a Member State who is the
       addressee of such decision.
[21]   See *Metallgesellschaft Ltd and others v IRC* (Case C-397/98) ECR I-1727; *Hoechst AG v
       IRC* (Case C-410/98) [2001] ECR I-1727, [2001] STC 452, [2001] 1 All ER (EC) 496; and
       Test Claimants in the FII Group Litigation v IRC (No 1) (Case C-446/04) [2007] STC
       326, 9 ITLR 426.
[22]   See *Becker v Finanzamt Munster-Innenstadt* [1982] ECR 53, paras 17–25. In *Marks &
       Spencer plc v Commissioners of Customs & Excise* (Case C-62/00) [2002] STC 1036, the
       ECJ summarised the position as follows (at para 25): 'whenever the provisions of a
       directive appear, so far as their subject-matter is concerned, to be unconditional and

Directives are only capable of partial 'direct effect' in a national court, ie their provisions can only be invoked in an action against the State and not against another private individual or business.

The concepts of supremacy of EU law, 'direct applicability' and 'direct effect' are given statutory effect in the UK as a result of the European Communities Act 1972, which provides that legal effect must be given to EU law in the UK. Section 2(1) of the Act states:

> 'All such rights, powers, liabilities, obligations and restrictions from time to time created or arising by or under the Treaties, and all such remedies and procedures from time to time provided for by or under the Treaties, as in accordance with the Treaties are without further enactment to be given legal effect or used in the United Kingdom shall be recognised and available in law, and be enforced, allowed and followed accordingly ...'

Section 2(4) of the Act provides that 'any enactment passed or to be passed, other than one contained in this Part of this Act, shall be construed and have effect subject to the foregoing provisions of this section'.

Accordingly, the UK courts must give legal effect to the Treaties and all provisions created or arising by or under the Treaties. In the event of any incompatibility between domestic law and the Treaties, a UK court will seek to give effect to the UK's treaty obligations.[23]

In the event of any inconsistency between domestic law and any directive, a UK court will give effect to the directive (provided it has direct effect) in any dispute between a UK taxpayer and the UK tax authorities.[24] As discussed above, a directive is only of direct effect if in connection with its subject-matter the terms of the directive are unconditional and sufficiently precise.[25] However, there is also an additional concept of 'indirect effect', which requires a court to interpret national law as far as possible to be consistent with EU law if it lacks direct effect, such that, through judicial interpretation, the provisions of a directive may be given effect 'indirectly' in a dispute between UK taxpayers.[26] In this respect, the ECJ has held that a national court is obliged, to the extent possible, to interpret domestic legislation in the context of the wording and the purpose of an applicable directive in order to secure the result sought to be achieved by the directive.[27] In addition, where a treaty Article has

---

sufficiently precise, they may be relied upon before the national courts by individuals against the State where the latter has failed to implement the directive in domestic law by the end of the period prescribed or where it has failed to implement the directive correctly ...'. See also *Francovich v Italian State* [1991] ECR I-5357.

[23] See *Litster v Forth Dry Dock and Engineering Co Ltd* [1990] 1 AC 546, HL.

[24] See *Robert Gordon's College v Customs and Excise Comrs* [1995] STC 1093, HL.

[25] See *Becker v Finanzamt Munster-Innenstadt* [1982] ECR 53, at paras 17–25.

[26] See *Von Colson and Kamann v Land Nordrhein-Westfalen* (Case 14/83) [1984] ECR 1891.

[27] See *Marleasing SA v La Comercial Internacional de Alimentacion SA* (Case C-106/89)

direct effect, a UK court must seek to interpret any domestic legislation as if its provisions were without prejudice to the directly enforceable rights conferred by the treaty Article.[28]

The approach of a UK court in construing domestic legislation in conformity with a directive concerning VAT was considered in *The Commissioners for Her Majesty's Revenue and Customs v IDT Card Services Ireland Ltd*,[29] in which the Court of Appeal made the following comments in relation to VATA 1994 and the Sixth Council Directive 77/388/EEC (now replaced by the VAT Directive – see below):[30]

> 'There are two different levels at which the court undertakes the task of interpretation in this case. The first level is that of the Sixth Directive, because, although that has no legal force as such in the United Kingdom, it is now well-established that the court must interpret domestic legislation in accordance with any applicable European directive. So the Court has to satisfy itself as to the meaning of that underlying legislation. The second level at which the court must undertake the task of interpretation is at the level of the VATA 1994. This of course is domestic law. The former task must be carried out in accordance with the principles laid down by the Court of Justice, which is the final arbiter on what Community legislation means. The latter task, however, is conducted under the principles of domestic law but for the purpose not of interpreting the statute in the ordinary way but of fulfilling the requirement of European Union law that a national court should interpret a statute which implements a directive, so far as possible, in the light of the wording and purpose of that directive.'

Against the above background, for VAT purposes, Art 113 TFEU (formerly Art 93 EC Treaty) imposes an obligation on the Council to adopt provisions for the harmonisation of turnover taxes (such as VAT) to ensure the establishment and the functioning of the single market within the EU. In particular, the Council is authorised, acting unanimously and after consulting with the Parliament, to issue directives for the approximation of laws on turnover taxes.[31] Generally therefore, EU laws on VAT take the form of directives.

Specifically, VAT was originally adopted in the EU by the First and Second Council Directives (67/227/EEC and 67/228/EEC) of 11 April 1967.[32] A framework for the rules, uniform basis of assessment and principles on the application of VAT in each Member State was then more

---

[1990] ECR 1-4135, at para 8. The obligation to interpret domestic law in conformity with EU law may also arise in circumstances where the domestic law was enacted before the EU law: see *Webb v EMO Air Cargo (UK) Ltd* [1994] QB 718.

[28] See *Imperial Chemical Industries plc v Colmer (Inspector of Taxes)* [1999] 1 WLR 2035, at 2041, HL; *Foulser and Foulser v David MacDougall (HM Inspector of Taxes)* [2005] EWHC 2958, at [61].

[29] [2006] EWCA Civ 29.

[30] See at [68] of the judgment of the Court of Appeal.

[31] Art 115 TFEU (formerly EC Treaty, Art 94).

[32] OJ L 71, 14/4/1967, pp 1301 and 1303.

substantially laid down in the Sixth Council Directive 77/388/EEC of 17 May 1977, providing for a common system of VAT.[33] Subsequently, for reasons of clarity and rationalisation, the VAT Directive was adopted as a recast of the Sixth Council Directive, which had been amended over the years, and consolidates various earlier EU VAT provisions. Hence the VAT Directive is now the essential piece of legislation from the EU on VAT. In addition, although, as noted above, directives are not generally 'directly applicable', Art 397 of the VAT Directive allows the Council to adopt measures necessary to implement the VAT Directive. Such measures include the EU Implementing Regulation, as mentioned earlier in this section, which has been adopted to provide binding rules on the application of certain provisions of the VAT Directive and to give legal certainty to a number of non-binding guidelines previously agreed by the EU concerning VAT.

The VAT rates vary throughout the Member States, but a summary of the standard VAT rates (1 January 2012) and, by way of example, the local rate of VAT imposed on supplies of physical books is given in Table 17.1.[34]

Table 17.1: VAT imposed on suppliers of physical books

Member State	Standard rate of VAT (%)	Rate of VAT on books (%)
Austria	20	10
Belgium	21	6
Bulgaria	20	20
Cyprus	15	5
Czech Republic	20	14
Denmark	25	25
Estonia	20	9
Finland	23	9
France	19.6	7
Germany	19	9
Greece	23	6.5
Hungary	27	5

[33] OJ L 145, 13/6/1977, p 1.
[34] For up-to-date details, refer to the website of each tax authority of the appropriate Member State. A summary of VAT rates can be found at http://ec.europa.eu/taxation_customs/taxation/vat/how_vat_works/rates/index_en.htm (2012).

Member State	Standard rate of VAT (%)	Rate of VAT on books (%)
Republic of Ireland	23	0
Italy	21	4
Latvia	22	12
Lithuania	21	9
Luxembourg	15	3
Malta	18	5
The Netherlands	19	6
Poland	23	5
Portugal	23	6
Romania	24	9
Slovak Republic	20	10
Slovenia	20	8.5
Spain	18	4
Sweden	25	6
United Kingdom	20	0

17.3   INGREDIENTS OF THE UK VAT CHARGE

A UK VAT charge will arise where there is:[35]

- a supply of goods or services;

- the place of supply of which is in the UK;

- the supply is a taxable supply;

- made by a taxable person;

- in the course or furtherance of business[36] carried on by the supplier; and

---

[35]   VATA 1994, s 4.

[36]   A business is defined in VATA 1994 as including any 'trade, profession or vocation' (s 94(1)). The comments made in relation to a trade in the context of corporation tax are equally valid in determining whether a trade is carried on for the purposes of VAT.

- the supply is not an otherwise 'exempt supply'.

Where UK VAT applies to a supply there are, for the purposes of e-commerce and e-infrastructure businesses, two main types of VAT rate. A VAT charge of 20% (2011) applies on standard-rated supplies,[37] while the charge is nil for zero-rated supplies (see further at **17.16**).[38] Certain supplies are subject to a reduced rate of tax of 5% (2011); this relates to a limited class of goods and services none of which are likely to be very relevant to e-commerce.[39] Where VAT applies to a supply it will normally be payable on top of the advertised purchase price (because the VAT is normally specified as being in addition to the purchase price, ie 'VAT exclusive', and this should be specified – if the contract is silent, VAT is treated as included in the purchase price).[40]

A taxable person who charges VAT on supplies made by him to a consumer is required to account for that VAT amount to HMRC.[41] In accounting for VAT to HMRC the taxable person is entitled to subtract the amount of VAT incurred by him in making those supplies, known as 'input tax', against the VAT that has been charged to the consumer (known as 'output tax').[42] The right of set-off only exists where a person makes taxable (ie standard-rated or zero-rated) supplies. Where a person makes wholly exempt supplies there is no right of set-off (see **17.17**).[43]

17.4   WHAT IS A SUPPLY, AND IS IT A SINGLE OR MULTIPLE SUPPLY?

17.4.1   Is there a supply?

A supply is defined as including 'all forms of supply, but not anything done otherwise than for consideration'.[44] The meaning of supply has been considered in a number of contexts outside the VAT legislation. It has been described as meaning in its ordinary sense, 'to furnish or to serve'.[45] Moreover, the breadth of the word has been emphasised on a number of

---

[37] VATA 1994, s 2(1).

[38] VATA 1994, s 30, Sch 8.

[39] VATA 1994, s 29A, Sch 7A (such as contraceptive products, women's sanitary products, domestic fuel, installation of energy-saving materials).

[40] VATA 1994, s 19(2).

[41] VATA 1994, s 25(1).

[42] VATA 1994, s 25(2). In order to have a right to deduct input tax the goods or services purchased must have a direct and immediate link with a taxable transaction: *BLP Group Plc v Customs and Excise Commissioners* (Case C-4/94) [1995] STC 424, [1996] 1 WLR 174, ECJ.

[43] VATA 1994, s 4(2).

[44] VATA 1994, s 5(2)(a).

[45] See *Williams v Pearce* (1916) 114 LT 898, at 901, per Lord Reading CJ (in a Licensing Act case), adopted in *Carlton Lodge Club v Customs and Excise Commissioners* [1974] STC 507.

occasions.[46] This is also inherent in the words of the legislation, which refers to 'anything ... done for consideration'.[47]

Example 17.1

Hardware Technologies Ltd, a UK supplier, sells 1,000 computers to a UK retailer for a lump sum of £1 million, plus VAT. It will charge VAT on the supply at the standard rate (ie £200,000 of VAT is paid by the retailer to Hardware Technologies Ltd) and account to HMRC for that VAT. The retailer will charge VAT on each of the computers sold to individual customers. Each computer is sold for £1,200, plus VAT to consumers (ie £240 VAT is paid by the customer to the retailer). Ignoring the Capital Goods Scheme (see **17.15**), the retailer will be entitled to deduct its VAT input cost of £200,000 from the total VAT output tax it charges to and receives from customers.

Example 17.2

Global Internet Services Ltd, a UK supplier, provides an internet access service to UK business subscribers. The annual subscription is £10,000 and the gross turnover is £5 million. This form of supply will be subject to UK VAT at the standard rate. Global Internet Services Ltd will charge VAT and it should be able to set off its VAT costs (input tax) incurred in making the supply against the output tax due on its internet access services. Any business subscriber will also be able to set off the VAT costs incurred on the supply received from Global Internet Services Ltd if it is using the supply for business purposes in making a taxable (ie standard rated or zero rated) supply.

Example 17.3

Search Engine Services Ltd, a UK supplier, provides banner advertisements for UK businesses on its search engine website. Gross turnover is £1 million. This service will be subject to UK VAT at the standard rate, and it should be able to set off its VAT costs (input tax) incurred in making the supply against the output tax on its banner advertisement services. Any business paying for banner advertisement will also be able to set off the VAT costs incurred on the supply received from Search Engine Services Ltd if it is using the supply for business purposes in making a taxable (ie standard-rated or zero-rated) supply.

17.4.2   What is the nature of the supply?

It is always important to identify the nature of the supply which is being made in order to determine the correct VAT treatment. The nature of what is being supplied can normally be determined by referring to the contract between the supplier and consumer. Typically, a written contract

---

[46]   See *Customs and Excise Commissioners v Oliver* [1980] STC 73, at 74, where Griffiths J said '"supply" is a word of the "widest import"'.

[47]   VATA 1994, s 5(2)(a).

will determine all the rights and obligations that arise between the parties in relation to a supply of goods and/or services.[48] However, it is also possible that the nature of the rights and obligations between the parties will be determined by their conduct (ie by what is done and said) to the extent that the written contract does not cover all the supplies made between the parties.[49] In this regard, it is always important to ensure that any form of supply is properly and comprehensively referred to in the contract in order to create certainty of VAT treatment. Helpful guidance on how a UK court will construe a contract is provided in a case involving the supply of hotel accommodation through a website, in which the issue arose as to whether the person operating the website was acting as agent of the hotel operators (whose accommodation was booked via the website), *Secret Hotels2 Ltd v Revenue and Customs Commissioners*.[50] The Upper Tier Tribunal provided the following guidance on how contracts should be construed:[51]

> 'When construing a written agreement, the court has regard to all of the provisions of the contract. The court construes the agreement against the relevant background. The material which is admissible in relation to that background is everything which a reasonable man would regard as relevant and which would have affected the way in which a reasonable man would have understood the language used in the document: *Investors Compensation Scheme Ltd v West Bromwich B.S.* [1998] 1 WLR 896 at 912–913. The relevant material is restricted to the material which would have been available to the parties. At the risk of stating the obvious, this last proposition means that the court cannot be influenced, when construing a written agreement, by material which would not have been available to the parties when they entered into that agreement.
>
> The court may also be assisted by considering the commercial purpose of the agreement. In some cases, the ordinary literal meaning of the language used will be in accordance with the apparent commercial purpose of the agreement. If the ordinary meaning of the language appears to convey a meaning which does not make reasonable commercial sense, then a court will look more critically at the wording to see if the ordinary meaning is really what the parties must be taken to have intended. In a case where the ordinary meaning of the language is in serious conflict with commercial sense, then the court may conclude that the language has not been well chosen and may choose a possible meaning (even though it would not be the most likely meaning of the language in other circumstances) which fits better with commercial sense.
>
> In some cases, the parties purport to state the legal effect of their agreement. They may, for example, state that the agreement is a licence in relation to land and not a tenancy. They may do this even where there is no question of

---

[48] See *A1 Lofts Ltd v HMRC (and related appeal)* [2010] UKFTT 581, [2009] EWHC 2694.

[49] See *A1 Lofts Ltd v HMRC (and related appeal)* [2010] UKFTT 581, [2009] EWHC 2694.

[50] [2011] UKUT 308.

[51] [2011] UKUT 308, at [88]–[90].

the agreement being a sham. They may act in this way through a misunderstanding of what is involved in the legal concept to which they refer or for other reasons. Notwithstanding this, the court will examine the substance of the agreement to determine its legal effect: see, for example, *Street v Mountford* [1985] AC 809. This will often produce the result that the court finds the parties have correctly described the legal effect of the agreement but in other cases the court will determine that the description used by the parties is incorrect and is overridden by the substance of what they have otherwise agreed.'

As discussed above, it is necessary to consider what has been agreed in the contract between the supplier and customer to identify the nature of a supply. However, the law allows consideration to be given to other factors, particularly in identifying the *chain* of a supply. In this regard, the recipient of a supply of a service is normally the person who instructed the supplier, and who is liable to pay for the service provided the payer obtains or receives a business benefit from the service in return for the payment.[52] But the ECJ has formulated an approach whereby the chain of supply is determined by the 'economic reality' of the arrangements, and not solely by the contractual arrangements and a payment analysis.[53] The nature of a supply for VAT purposes is not therefore always determined solely by the contract between the parties; the substance of the arrangements can affect the VAT analysis. The approach here is likely to be to consider the nature of the overall arrangements as well as of the supply, the identity of the parties, who pays for the supply and/or incurs the commercial risk associated with the supply.

17.4.3   Is the supply a single or multiple supply?

A supplier may make a combination of supplies which comprise elements that if provided separately will be subject to different VAT treatment. For example, a trader may supply printed material which is zero-rated and certain printing or tuition services that are standard-rated. The supplier may wish to argue that where bundled supplies are made there is in fact one principal supply, and that the ancillary supplies should be taxed in accordance with the VAT characterisation of the principal supply. This may be because, for example, the principal supply is zero-rated. It is a

---

[52]   See *C&E Commrs v Redrow Group plc* [1999] STC 161. See more recently *HMRC v Airtours Holidays Transport Ltd* [2011] STC 239.

[53]   *HMRC v Loyalty Management Ltd; Baxi Group Ltd v HMRC (Joined ECJ Cases C-53/09 and C-55/09)* [2010] STC 2651, at para 39 of the ECJ's judgment. However, in *Secret Hotels2 Ltd v Revenue and Customs Commissioners* [2011] UKUT 308, at [112] Morgan J commented in relation to the *Loyalty Management Ltd* case that: 'There is, no doubt, scope for argument as to how … [it is] … to be interpreted and applied. But, whatever its meaning, I do not think that an approach which uses a contractual analysis to determine the identity of the supplier of hotel accommodation and which results in that supplier, rather than someone else, bearing the liability to account for VAT, in any way lacks economic reality. It is quite possible in a case like the present for the relevant parties to adopt different legal structures to produce similar (but not identical) economic results.'

question of law as to whether bundled supplies for VAT characterisation purposes represent either a single supply or multiple supplies.[54]

In *Card Protection Plan v C & E Comrs*[55] the ECJ considered whether a transaction which comprised several elements should be treated as a single supply with a single VAT liability, or as two or more distinct supplies to be assessed to VAT on a separate basis. The ECJ ruled as to how to determine whether there are single or multiple supplies as follows:[56]

'In this respect, taking into account, first, that it follows from art 2(1) of the Sixth Directive[57] that every supply of a service must normally be regarded as distinct and independent and second, that a supply which comprises a single service from an economic point of view should not be artificially split, so as not to distort the functioning of the VAT system, the essential features of the transaction must be ascertained in order to determine whether the taxable person is supplying the customer, being a typical customer, with several distinct principal services or with a single service.

There is a single supply in particular in cases where one or more elements are to be regarded as constituting the principal service, whilst one or more elements are to be regarded, by contrast, as ancillary services which share the tax treatment of the principal service. A service must be regarded as ancillary to a principal service if it does not constitute for customers an aim in itself, but a means of better enjoying the principal service supplied.' (emphasis added)

The UK test for single and multiple supplies has been described in the following way in *C&E Comrs v Wellington Private Hospital Ltd*:[58]

'The proper inquiry is whether one element of the transaction is so dominated by another element as to lose any separate identity as a supply for fiscal purposes, leaving the latter, the dominant element of the transaction, as the only supply. If the elements of the transaction are not in this relationship with each other, each remains as a supply in its own right with its own separate fiscal consequences.'

If the elements of a transaction are so closely linked from an economic perspective so as to constitute a single indivisible supply, then the relevant transaction will be a single supply.[59]

How should these principles be applied? The following factors are important (including as set out above in *Card Protection Plan*):[60]

---

[54] See *British Airways plc v C&E Comrs* [1990] STC 643, at 646, CA.
[55] Case C-349/96 [1999] STC 270, ECJ decision applied by the House of Lords [2001] STC 174. HMRC's view of the *Card Protection Plan* case is expressed in VAT Information Sheet 2/01 (July 2001).
[56] At paras 29–30 of the ECJ's judgment.
[57] Replaced by the VAT Directive, as noted above.
[58] [1997] STC 445, at 462.
[59] See *Levob Verzekeringen BV, OV Bank NV v Staatssecretaris van Financiën* (Case C-41/04) [2006] STC 766, ECJ.
[60] Case C-349/96 [1999] STC 270, at paras 29–31 of the ECJ decision.

- every supply must normally be regarded as distinct and independent;

- a supply which comprises a single service from an economic point of view should not be artificially split, so as not to distort the functioning of the VAT system;

- the essential features of the transaction must be ascertained in order to determine whether the taxable person is supplying the customer, being a typical consumer, with several distinct principal supplies or with a single supply;

- there is a single supply in particular in cases where one or more elements are to be regarded as constituting the principal supply, whilst one or more elements are to be regarded, by contrast, as ancillary, incidental or integral components that share the tax treatment of the principal supply. HMRC's example of an overall single supply with incidental or integral elements is that of an instructions booklet provided with new electronic equipment – the booklet naturally accompanies the equipment. A supply must be regarded as ancillary to a principal supply if it does not constitute for customers an aim in itself, but a means of better enjoying the principal supply supplied;

- the fact that a single price is charged for the supply is not decisive if, in reality, distinct supplies take place – however, if the supply provided to customers consists of several elements for a single price, the single price may suggest that there is a single supply;

- if circumstances indicate that customers intended to purchase two distinct supplies, then it is necessary to identify the part of the single price which relates to the separate supplies;

- where services are supplied in consideration of specific and separately priced aspects as indicated on an invoice or otherwise, this may lead to the inference that there are multiple supplies, but this is not conclusive. As an example of a multiple supply, HMRC's guidance refers to when goods are packaged together such as a book with an accompanying audio tape, which may be used independently and requires particular equipment for its use;[61] and

- where the recipient seeks an integrated service, then this may lead to the conclusion that there is a single supply.[62]

---

[61] See *Levob Verzekeringen BV, OV Bank NV v Staatssecretaris van Financiën* (Case C-41/04) [2006] STC 766, at para 25.

[62] Ibid. For further guidance on single and multiple supplies, see HMRC's staff VAT manual, 'Supply and Consideration' located at www.hmrc.gov.uk/manuals/vatscmanual/Index.htm in particular at page VATSC80000. HMRC provides examples and indicators of single and multiple supplies from page VATSC82700.

Other factors can include whether elements of a transaction are advertised as a package and whether different components are provided or available separately.

17.4.4   What is the predominant nature of the supply?

Once the nature of the supplies have been identified, including as to whether there are single or multiple supplies, it is then necessary to categorise the supply to determine its VAT liability, including whether it is within any relevant VAT exemption (for the exemptions see **17.17**), particularly if there is a single supply. In this regard, the question focuses on what is 'the single or core supply', 'the essential feature of the scheme or its dominant purpose' or its 'main objective'.[63] From a commercial perspective, it is necessary to determine the nature of a transaction by reference to taking into account all of the facts and circumstances, and the objectives and perception of the customer.

17.5   WHAT IS CONSIDERATION?

VAT is charged on consideration for the supply of goods or services.[64] A direct link must exist between the consideration provided and a supply.[65] If there is no link then VAT cannot be charged on a supply. It can be argued that everything therefore depends upon the contract under which the supply is provided. In addition, if a link is established, the VAT charge applies only to consideration that relates to a particular supply. Consideration is not defined under either VATA 1994 or the VAT Directive. Some guidance is provided in the VAT Directive, which provides that the taxable amount, ie the consideration, is 'everything which constitutes consideration obtained or to be obtained by the supplier, in return for the supply, from the customer or a third party, including subsidies directly linked to the price of the supply'.[66] This has been interpreted as meaning that consideration includes not only money or cash amounts but also includes the monetary value of goods and/or services received in exchange for a supply.[67] Some further guidance is provided by the UK courts. In *Trafalgar Tours Ltd v C & E Comrs* the judge commented:[68]

---

[63]   See *Customs and Excise Commissioners v Electronic Data Systems Ltd* [2003] STC 688, at para 130.

[64]   VATA 1994, s 2(1); VAT Directive, Art 2(1).

[65]   See e g *Naturally Yours Cosmetics Ltd v Customs and Excise Commissioners* [1988] STC 879, at para 12. For further details relating to this case see note 75 below.

[66]   VAT Directive, Art 73.

[67]   See again, e g *Naturally Yours Cosmetics Ltd v Customs and Excise Commissioners* [1988] STC 879 mentioned at note 65 above, followed in *Empire Stores Ltd v Customs and Excise Commissioners* [1994] STC 623.

[68]   [1990] STC 127, at 135.

'Having regard to art 11(A)(1)(a) of the Sixth Directive,[69] we are therefore, subject to one important qualification, prepared to accept that the expression "consideration" in s 10(2) of the 1983 Act[70] means everything which the supplier has received or is to receive from the purchaser, the customer or a third party for the relevant supplies. The one important qualification is this. The concept of receipt for this purpose is not to be confined to mere physical receipt; anything which is received by persons for and on behalf of the supplier must be treated for this purpose as received by the supplier himself.'

Example 17.1

Harriet ('the subscriber') pays £5 each month plus £1.50 for each day's use of an internet access service. The internet access agreement provides that in consideration for this payment each month the subscriber has the right to use the service which:

> '... consists of computing and information services and software, information and other content provided by the internet access provider, as well as access to services, software, information and other content provided by third parties.'

In the context of this licence agreement it is clear that all the services specifically mentioned are directly referable to the consideration of £5 per month, plus £1.50 for each day the subscriber uses the service.

17.6   WHAT IS THE VALUE OF THE CONSIDERATION?

As noted above, normally anything done other than for consideration is not subject to a VAT charge, because it is not capable of being a supply.[71] However, there are some cases whereby a VAT charge arises even if there is no consideration. For example, where a person disposes of goods that form part of the assets of its business free of charge, this is nonetheless treated as a supply of goods.[72]

Supplies are usually made in return for a consideration wholly in money. Under the general rule,[73] the value of the supply made for cash consideration for UK VAT purposes is that part of the payment which, when added to the VAT itself, gives a total amount and that total amount will be equal to the 'consideration' for the supply. The VAT element of a VAT-inclusive figure is calculated by multiplying the consideration by a VAT fraction depending on the rate of VAT (the fraction is 1/6 in respect of the 20% UK VAT rate (2011)).

---

[69]   Now the VAT Directive, Art 73.
[70]   VATA 1994, s 19(2).
[71]   VATA 1994, s 5(2); VAT Directive, Art 2(1). See **17.4**.
[72]   VATA 1994, Sch 4, para 5(1); VAT Directive, Art 74. See further at **17.7.2** and **17.7.3**.
[73]   VATA 1994, s 19(2).

In assessing the value of consideration other than money, the VAT Directive makes no reference to objective criteria. In such circumstances, it will be necessary for the supply to be capable of being expressed in monetary terms in order to determine the money-equivalent value of the consideration. As held by the ECJ,[74] the value test is based on subjective criteria, because the VAT charge is imposed on the consideration actually received in exchange for the supply. It is therefore necessary to examine what is agreed upon between the parties, for example, by reference to the contract, to determine the value of the transaction.[75] Where an exchange takes place, the value of the supply is determined and calculated by the value of the consideration provided by the other party. In other words, it is necessary to ascertain the value assigned to the supply by the parties. For example, if there is a supply of services in exchange for goods, the value of the consideration for the services is the cost of the goods, because

---

[74] See *Staatssecretaris van Financien v Cooperative Aardappelenbewaarplaats GA* (Case 154/80) [1981] ECR 445.

[75] The case of *Naturally Yours Cosmetics Ltd* (Case 230/87) [1988] STC 879, ECJ involved a company, 'NYC', that carried on business as a wholesaler of cosmetic products for resale by retailers ('beauty consultants'), who approached friends and acquaintances ('hostesses') for the purpose of organising private parties at which NYC's products were offered for sale. The supply chain involved the beauty consultants buying products from NYC at wholesale prices and selling them at the parties for a recommended retail price. The difference between those two prices constituted the profit made by the beauty consultants. The beauty consultants were exempt from collecting VAT since their turnover fell short of the threshold fixed by the UK for VAT registration as a taxable person. The beauty consultants would reward the hostesses for organising the parties by gifting them one of the products on sale at the party. When a pot of cream was used for that purpose, NYC supplied it to the beauty consultant for £1.50, materially below its normal wholesale price of £10.14. HMRC sought to assess VAT on the basis of the normal wholesale price of £10.14 for each pot of cream, including those intended to be used as gifts. NYC argued that the taxable amount should be the price of £1.50 actually paid by the beauty consultant for the pots of cream to be used as gifts. The ECJ examined the agreement between the supplier and an individual beauty consultant. Under the agreement, a pot of cream would be supplied to the beauty consultant at £1.50, on condition that the beauty consultant arranged for a party to be held (via a party hostess). In the event of no party being arranged, the pot of cream had to be either returned or paid for at its normal wholesale price. The ECJ reiterated that the basis of assessment for a service is everything which makes up the consideration for the service; there must therefore be a direct link between the service provided and the consideration received if the supply of a service is to be taxable (at para 11). The question therefore was whether there was a direct link between the pots of cream supplied for a price materially lower than the normal price and the value of the service provided by the beauty consultant. On the facts, the parties had reduced the wholesale price of the pot of cream by a specific amount in exchange for the supply of a service by the beauty consultant, which consisted in applying the pots of cream in procuring, for the parties' mutual benefit, hostesses to arrange parties for the sale of NYC's beauty products, ie by offering the pots of cream to hostesses as gifts or inducements/rewards. Accordingly, in those circumstances, the ECJ considered it possible to ascertain the monetary value which the two parties to the contract attributed to that service from the beauty consultant and thus the taxable amount for VAT purposes for each pot of cream (see at para 18), such monetary value being equal to the difference between the cost price actually paid for the pots and the normal wholesale price. The ECJ therefore decided that the sum of the value of the supply of services by the beauty consultant and the payment of £1.50 constituted the consideration for a pot of cream.

that represents what the recipient of the services was prepared to pay. The point is illustrated by *Empire Stores Ltd v Customs and Excise Commissioners*,[76] where the ECJ held that the consideration on an exchange must be ascertained in the following way:[77]

> 'Where that value is not a sum of money agreed between the parties, it must, in order to be subjective, be the value which the recipient of the services constituting the consideration for the supply of goods attributes to the services which he is seeking to obtain and must correspond to the amount which he is prepared to spend for that purpose. Where, as here, the supply of goods is involved, that value can only be the price which the supplier has paid for the article which he is supplying without extra charge in consideration of the services in question.'

The *Empire Stores* case is a useful illustration of how VAT can be charged on the exchange of goods for services, or services for services, in the context of e-commerce. First consider the facts of this case before turning to an example of e-commerce business. In the *Empire Stores* case a retailer sold merchandise through a catalogue. In order to acquire new clientele it operated various schemes. Under one scheme, a 'self-introduction scheme', a person would provide personal information about themselves, including the implicit right to use the information to check creditworthiness. The customer list could then be sold by the catalogue retailer. The information provided therefore had economic value. Additionally, the retailer received the real advantage that if a person introduced themselves to the catalogue that the person would make purchases. Once the information was provided and accepted (ie after a credit check) a 'free' gift would be sent to the person providing the information (eg a household item such as a toaster, a kettle or an iron – these were not items in the Empire Stores catalogue so they did not have a normal retail price). Under a second scheme, the 'introduce-a-friend scheme', Empire Stores offered an article to established customers who recommended one of their friends as a potential customer. The article was supplied once the new customer had completed a form, had been approved by the retailer and had made a first payment relating to an order. Under each scheme, Empire Stores accounted for VAT in respect of the articles on the basis of their cost price. The UK tax authority argued that the VAT treatment should be the tax-exclusive cost price plus 50%, being the tax authority's estimate of the prices which Empire Stores would have charged for the articles if they had been offered in its sales catalogue.

The issue in this case was whether VAT had to be charged, and if so what the taxable amount was for VAT purposes. In essence the retailer undertook to provide goods in exchange for the supply of information. The gift was intended as the quid pro quo for an advantage provided to

---

[76] [1994] STC 623.
[77] [1994] STC 623, at para 19.

the retailer by a person introducing themselves as a customer or another potential customer, and not in return for the purchase by that customer of goods offered in the retailer's sales catalogue. In the ECJ's judgment in *Empire Stores* there was a direct link between the provision of the introduction of a customer because it had an economic value for the retailer. The value in this case had a subjective value, because the retailer was prepared to give an article for which it had paid the cost price. The ECJ's conclusions were as follows, as to the nature of the supplies, and the value of those supplies for VAT purposes (as previously illustrated above):[78]

> 'The link between the supply of the article without extra charge and the introduction of a potential customer must be regarded as direct, since if the service is not provided no article is due from or supplied without extra charge by Empire Stores.
>
> Moreover, since the services provided to Empire Stores are remunerated by the supply of goods the value of the services can unquestionably be expressed in monetary terms.
>
> As for the determination of that value, which is the substance of the section question, the court held in *Naturally Yours Cosmetics* [1988] STC 879 at 894, [1988] ECR 6365 at 6390, at para. 16, that the consideration taken as the taxable amount in respect of a supply of goods is a subjective value, since the taxable amount is the consideration actually received and not a value estimated according to objective criteria.
>
> Where that value is not a sum of money agreed between the parties, it must, in order to be subjective, be the value which the recipient of the services constituting the consideration for the supply of goods attributes to the services which he is seeking to obtain and must correspond to the amount which he is prepared to spend for that purpose. Where, as here, the supply of goods is involved, that value can only be the price which the supplier has paid for the article which he is supplying without extra charge in consideration of the services in question.'

Example 17.5

A high street catalogue retailer provides an electronic version of its catalogue through an internet site to anyone who accesses the site. The retailer provides access free of charge to consumers. However, every person who accesses the site for the first time is required to register and complete an extensive questionnaire. The data is then used by the retailer and sold to other retailers. In exchange for the provision of the data the catalogue retailer provides each new registering consumer with a 'free good' from a select range of goods which are not available in its main catalogue.

The issue from a VAT perspective is whether there is consideration for VAT purposes. The scheme is based on the retail scheme referred to in the *Empire*

---

[78]   [1994] STC 623, at para 111.

Stores case (as discussed above). There is a supply subject to VAT, but what is the value of the consideration? The value must be capable of being expressed monetarily. It is clear that the information provided by each new registering consumer has economic value because it enables the catalogue retailer to generate revenue by onward sale of the information to other retailers. On the basis of *Empire Stores* the value of the consideration is the cost of supplying the 'free good'.

17.7   WHAT IS A SUPPLY OF GOODS?

The meaning of a supply of goods has received consideration by the courts.[79] It is important to make a distinction between the physical article and the property rights that exist within the article. For example, a person who owns tangible property, such as computer hardware, is entitled to sell or lease that article, etc. These rights of ownership are the property in the tangible property. Against this background it must be remembered that (absent special rules) a VAT charge only generally arises where:[80]

- the goods are transferred by sale;

- possession of goods is transferred under an agreement for the sale of the goods; or

- possession of goods is transferred under agreements which expressly contemplate that the property will also pass at some time in the future (but not later than when the goods are fully paid for).

An agreement that transfers property in goods is a supply of goods. There does not necessarily have to be an instantaneous physical transfer of goods to the purchaser for a supply of goods to take place. All that is required is the transfer of the whole property in the goods. It is possible for a supply of goods to be achieved through e-commerce by a contract being concluded by the seller and purchaser (see Chapter 4).

> *Example 17.6*
>
> UK Merchandising Ltd carries on a trade in the sale of products that are a spin-off from a television series and films. The site is accessed by people

---

[79] In the ECJ decision, known as the *Theotrue* case, the following explanation of what is a supply of goods is given ([1983] VATTR 88, at 92): '"Supply" for such purposes in relation to goods requires the transfer of goods from one taxable person to another, either immediately or at a future date, and implies the existence of the goods at such time of transfer. That, we consider, is inherent in the definition of "supply" given by Mr Justice Griffiths in the case of *Commissioners of Customs and Excise v JRB Oliver* in which he stated "supply" is the passing of possession in goods pursuant to an agreement whereunder the supplier agrees to part with and the recipient agrees to take possession. By "possession" is meant in this context control over the goods, in the sense of having the immediate facility for their use. This may or may not involve the physical removal of the goods.'

[80] VATA 1994, Sch 4, para 1(2). See also VAT Directive, Art 14.

throughout the world, who place orders for novelty merchandise. Orders placed by UK individuals for the acquisition of merchandise will be subject to UK VAT on the basis that there is a sale of goods in the UK. This is because the order is essentially a basic transaction for the acquisition of tangible products to be delivered via conventional means, albeit that the sale is facilitated by the internet. However, not all transactions will be subject to VAT at the standard rate. If the supply is classified as a zero-rated supply the UK consumer will pay no VAT since the rate for such a supply is nil. For instance, articles designed as clothing or footwear for young children that are not suitable for older persons are zero-rated.[81]

Example 17.7

Emily lives in the UK and she places an online order for the purchase of music CDs from a UK supplier. The total cost for these supplies is £75. The place of supply is in the UK and the amount of VAT to be paid is 20% on the consideration of £75. Emily also places an online order for the purchase of books to be delivered to her home address. This supply is within the scope of the UK's zero-rating rules with the result that the supply has no VAT cost for the customer. However, due to it being a zero-rated supply the supplier has a right to recover its VAT costs associated with making the supply.

The VAT Directive refers to a supply of goods as meaning 'the transfer of the right to dispose of tangible property as owner'.[82] In addition, according to the VAT Directive, the following are also treated as a supply of goods: (a) the actual handing over of goods under a contract for the hire of goods for a certain period, or for the sale of goods on deferred terms, which provides that in the normal course of events ownership is to pass at the latest upon payment of the final instalment; and (b) the transfer of goods pursuant to a contract under which commission is payable on purchase or sale.[83] The following are also treated as a supply of goods: (a) the supply of any form of power, heat, refrigeration or ventilation; and (b) the grant, assignment or surrender of a major interest in land.[84]

17.7.1 Software

Can normalised 'off-the-shelf' software (e g usually sold via the media of a DVD) that is transferred electronically be classified as a supply of goods? A 'good' is not defined in VATA 1994. While the VAT Directive provides that the supply of goods means the transfer of the right to dispose of 'tangible property' as owner,[85] it does not define 'tangible property'. However, in the UK the concept of goods is defined in the Sale of Goods Act 1979 as including 'all personal chattels other than things in

---

[81] VATA 1994, Sch 8, Group 16, Item 1.
[82] VAT Directive, Art 14(1).
[83] VAT Directive, Art 14(2).
[84] VATA 1994, Sch 4, paras 3–4. The definition of a 'major interest' is defined in VATA 1994, s 96(1).
[85] VAT Directive, Art 14(1).

action or money'.[86] It is clear from this definition that there must be an element of tangible existence, such as a device like a CD-ROM or DVD upon which the software is recorded. Accordingly, an item of 'off-the-shelf' software which is delivered to a purchaser in a tangible format, such as a CD-ROM or DVD, can be a supply of goods. This is explored further in Chapter 21. In contrast, software products which are customised (i e bespoke or specific) and reside on a tangible carrier medium can be treated as a supply of services, and any software sold through the medium of e-commerce and installed directly onto the purchaser's computer hard disk via a digital download will be regarded as a supply of services.[87] HMRC should recognise the supply and delivery of normalised computer software via a digital download as a supply of services.[88] The VAT implications of supplying computer software through the medium of the internet are examined in more detail in Chapter 22 (Services Supplied Electronically).

17.7.2   Goods forming part of the assets of a business

Where goods form part of the assets of a business and these are transferred or disposed of under the direction of the person carrying on the business, this action is deemed to be a supply of goods, irrespective of the fact that there is no consideration.[89]

17.7.3   Gifts and samples

The disposal of goods forming part of the assets of a business free of charge will not be treated as a supply of goods if it is a business gift,[90] or one of several business gifts, to the same person in the same year, costing less than £50 (2011),[91] or if it is the provision to a person, for no consideration, of a sample of goods[92] distributed either by the taxable person or by a third party.[93]

---

[86]   Sale of Goods Act 1979, s 61.

[87]   See HMRC Notice 702 *Imports* (April 2010), paras 7.1–7.6 and note 95 below.

[88]   HMRC Notice 741A *Place of Supply of Services* (January 2010) and Notice 701/10 *Zero Rating of Books etc* (December 2011), at para 2.

[89]   VATA 1994, Sch 4, para 5(1).

[90]   For this purpose 'business gift' means a gift of goods that is made in the course or furtherance of the business in question: VATA 1994, Sch 4, para 5(2ZA).

[91]   VATA 1994, Sch 4, para 5(2)(a). For this purpose 'cost', in relation to a gift of goods, means the cost to the donor of acquiring or, as the case may be, producing the goods: VATA 1994, Sch 4, para 5(2ZA).

[92]   VATA 1994, Sch 4, para 5(2)(b). There is no longer a restriction in the UK which used to prevent VAT relief applying where more than one sample was given and those other samples were identical or did not differ in any material respect from the first sample (i e the rules only allowed one sample to be supplied to one person free of VAT). This restriction (in VATA 1994, Sch 4, para 5(3)) was removed by the Finance (No 3) Act 2011 with effect from 19 July 2011. This follows the ECJ's decision (and taxpayer's victory) in the case of *EMI Group Ltd v HMRC* (Case C-581/08) [2010] All ER (D) 06 (Oct) on 30 September 2010. See further in HMRC Brief 51/10.

[93]   HMRC states on its website at www.hmrc.gov.uk (2011) in relation to samples: 'If you

Example 17.8

Computer Graphic Designs Ltd, a UK supplier, issues a CD-ROM containing its graphic package, which retails for £85. The CD-ROM is attached free of charge on computer magazines. Access to the graphics package on the CD-ROM is limited to a 30-day trial period. After this time the computer program is locked and cannot be accessed (and only one licence is granted per person to use the software). In these circumstances the graphics program is issued as a sample in the furtherance of business, as a promotion of the company's product. Any subsequent unlocking of the software, after payment of a sum, would represent a supply and consequentially be subject to VAT. By engaging the magazine (based in the UK) to distribute the CD-ROM, Computer Graphics Design Ltd will be charged UK VAT for the services provided by the distributor.

17.8   WHAT IS A SUPPLY OF SERVICES?

Anything which is not a supply of goods but is done for consideration is a supply of services.[94] Accordingly, as indicated in **17.7.1** above, the supply of software provided electronically as an e-commerce transaction in the form of digital content will be treated as a supply of services (eg music downloads and book downloads onto portable reading devices).[95] Further, the granting, assignment or surrender of any right (such as copyright), if done for consideration, is treated as a supply of services.[96] The VAT Directive provides that a supply of services may consist in one of the following transactions: (a) the assignment of intangible property, whether or not the subject of a document establishing title, and (b) the obligation to refrain from an act, or to tolerate an act or situation.[97]

---

give free samples of your goods to another person or business you don't have to charge VAT as long as you give them for marketing purposes. Your samples must be given to promote sales by demonstrating the product and provided in quantities consistent with that purpose. So, for example, you would not have to charge VAT on a small glass of wine given to a customer to try in a restaurant, whereas a full bottle would amount to more than marketing – because of the quantity involved – and you would have to charge VAT. You would also have to charge VAT where you provide something from a discontinued range, as there is no product to promote.' Again, see further in HMRC Brief 51/10.

[94]   VATA 1994, s 5(2)(b). See also VAT Directive, Art 24(1).
[95]   The EU Commission agreed that supplies of digital products must be classified as services even if such products would, if delivered in their tangible form, be treated as goods for VAT purposes. See Communication from the Commission to the Council, the European Parliament and the Economic and Social Committee 'Electronic Commerce and Indirect Taxation' COM (1998) 374 final, Section V, Guideline 2. Digital products represent content which is transferred and delivered electronically via an electronic network, eg the internet. For example, the transfer and delivery via the internet in digital form of 'off-the-shelf' software, films, books, newspapers and games represents the supply of a digital product. See Chapters 21 and 22.
[96]   VATA 1994, s 5(2)(b). See also VAT Directive, Art 24(1).
[97]   VAT Directive, Art 25.

In addition, in some circumstances, a supply, although involving goods, will be classified as supply of services. For example, Sch 4 to VATA 1994 provides that while the transfer of the whole property in goods is a supply of goods, the transfer of any undivided share of a property, or the transfer of the possession of goods is a supply of services.[98]

17.9 WHO IS A TAXABLE PERSON?

A taxable person is required to charge VAT in accordance with VATA 1994, and to account for it to HMRC. The existence of a taxable person is key for a VAT charge being identified. As discussed previously in this chapter, VAT is charged on all supplies of goods and services (including anything treated as being goods or services) made in the UK *by a taxable person* for consideration as part of the economic activities of that person, unless the supplies are exempt. There is therefore a duty to account for VAT on any supply within the scope of the tax if a transaction is made by a taxable person (including both those registered for VAT and any person who should be registered).

17.9.1 VATA 1994

A taxable person is defined in the UK as a person who is, or is required to be, registered under VATA 1994.[99] A person who makes taxable supplies is required to register for the purposes of VAT where the value of those supplies is in excess of £73,000 (2011)[100] to the year ending for any month.[101] A taxable supply is a supply of goods or services made in the UK other than an exempt supply.[102] An obligation also exists to register at any time where the person has reasonable grounds for believing that the value of supplies will exceed £73,000 within a following 30-day period.[103] A person is not, however, obliged to register where HMRC is satisfied that the value of supplies will not exceed £71,000 in a period of one year beginning at the time at which that person would become liable to be registered.[104] If a person is not already UK VAT registered and they receive supplies of services which are subject to the reverse charge procedure (see at **17.12**), the value of those supplies must be added to the value of the person's other taxable supplies in determining whether they should be registered for UK VAT. If such a person does not make taxable

---

[98] VATA 1994, Sch 4, paras 1–3. This is, however, subject to the rules relating to the transfer of the possession of goods under an agreement for the sale of goods, which is treated as a supply of goods rather than services. See **17.7**.

[99] VATA 1994, s 3(1), Schs 1–3.

[100] Refer to HMRC's website to confirm current registration thresholds: www.hmrc.gov.uk.

[101] VATA 1994, Sch 1, para 1(1)(a). Liability must be notified to the Commissioners within 30 days of the end of the month in which the liability arises (para 5(1)).

[102] VATA 1994, s 4(2).

[103] VATA 1994, Sch 1, para 1(1)(b). Liability must be notified to the Commissioners before the end of the 30-day period by reference to which the liability arises (para 6(1)).

[104] VATA 1994, Sch 1, para 1(3).

supplies, they can still be a taxable person if the value of their 'imported' services exceeds the above VAT registration limit.[105]

A person can cease to be registered under VATA 1994 only in specified circumstances: (a) a person ceases to be liable to register where HMRC is satisfied that the person has ceased to make taxable supplies[106] or (b) there is no obligation to remain registered if the conditions specified above obliging a person to register are no longer satisfied.[107] In addition, a person is entitled to deregistration from VAT where HMRC can be satisfied that the value of his taxable supplies will not exceed £71,000 within one year.[108]

A person who is not obliged to register under VATA 1994 may nonetheless seek voluntary registration even if the value of his supplies does not exceed the VAT registration threshold. This can occur where a person satisfies HMRC that he will make taxable supplies, or alternatively that the person is carrying on a business and intends to make taxable supplies in the course of furtherance of business.[109] In these circumstances, HMRC will register the person from the date on which the request is made or from such earlier date as may be agreed.[110] A person may want to register voluntarily so that VAT incurred in making taxable supplies can be reclaimed.

A person may also register where supplies are made outside the UK, provided that the supply would be a taxable supply if made in the UK.[111] For example, the export of goods outside the EU may be a taxable supply.[112] The rate of tax for such supplies can be nil, which would make it a zero-rated supply, but such supply would still be a taxable supply – see **17.16**. Registering in such circumstances would be advantageous because it enables any input VAT to be reclaimed.

Conversely, an exemption from registration is available where HMRC is satisfied, and thinks it appropriate, that the person concerned makes or intends to make taxable supplies which are solely zero-rated. For example, an e-commerce trader who specialises in the sale of children's clothes

---

[105] VATA 1994, s 8(1), Sch 1.
[106] VATA 1994, Sch 1, para 3(a).
[107] VATA 1994, Sch 1, para (3)(b).
[108] VATA 1994, Sch 1, para 4(1). A person will not, however, be deregistered if the reason the value of their supplies will not exceed the £71,000 limit is because the person will cease making taxable supplies or their supplies will be suspended for a period of 30 days or more (para 4(2)).
[109] VATA 1994, Sch 1, para 9.
[110] VATA 1994, Sch 1, para 9.
[111] VATA 1994, Sch 1, para 10.
[112] VATA 1994, s 30(6).

could claim this exemption.[113] An obligation then exists to inform the Commissioners, within 30 days, of any material change in the nature of those supplies.[114]

A special registration scheme applies for non-EU established taxable persons supplying electronic services to non-taxable persons, and this is explored in Chapter 22 (Services Supplied Electronically) in relation to its operation in the UK.

17.9.2   VAT Directive

In contrast with VATA 1994, which uses the concept of 'taxable person', the VAT Directive is not based on financial turnover thresholds and not all Member States have VAT registration thresholds, unlike the UK. By Art 9(1) of the VAT Directive, a 'taxable person' is defined as meaning 'any person who independently carries out in any place any economic activity ... whatever the purpose or results of that activity'. An economic activity is defined as 'any activity of producers, traders or persons supplying services ...'.[115] A person who carries on an economic activity under a contract of employment does not carry on the activity independently.[116]

Any state, regional or local authority governed by public law is not, unless otherwise provided for, a taxable person in respect of activities carried on by it as a public authority. This prohibition applies even where the public authority collects fees, contributions or payments in respect of those activities or transactions.[117] A public authority is, however, treated as a taxable person where it would lead to significant distortions of competition.[118] Where any of the following activities are carried on by a body governed by public law it is treated as a taxable person in respect of the activities, provided it is not carried out on such a small scale as to be negligible:[119]

- telecommunication services;

- supply of new goods manufactured for sale;

- running of trade fairs and exhibitions;

- activities of commercial publicity bodies;

---

[113] VATA 1994, Sch 1, para 14(1).
[114] VATA 1994, Sch 1, para 14(2).
[115] VAT Directive, Art 9(1).
[116] VAT Directive, Art 10.
[117] VAT Directive, Art 13(1).
[118] VAT Directive, Art 13(1).
[119] VAT Directive, Art 13(1). For the purposes of this book only the activities relevant to IT and internet transactions are listed.

- activities of travel agencies;

- transactions (other than those specified in Art 132(1)(q)) of radio and television bodies.[120]

17.10 WHERE IS THE PLACE OF SUPPLY OF GOODS OR SERVICES?

The place of supply is determined by reference to a number of specific rules. For VAT purposes, the country where a supply is deemed to be made is called the 'place of supply' and is the place where it is liable to VAT, if any. There are various place of supply rules applicable to services of different kinds. These rules are necessary to ensure that VAT, where payable, is paid only in the correct country and to avoid the possibility of supplies being taxed more than once or not at all. Where the place of supply of a service is in another Member State, that supply is outside the scope of UK VAT and is liable to the VAT rules in that other Member State. If the place of supply of a service is outside the EU, that supply is described as outside the scope of EU VAT altogether and is therefore not liable to VAT in any Member State. Table 17.2 summarises the UK's place of supply rules for both goods and services (see **17.10.2**).[121] For goods, the place of taxation is broadly determined by where the goods are located when supplied, and on how the supply is made, such as whether the goods will be physically moved (removed) from or to the UK, where such movement begins or ends and the identity of the customer (whether private or business).

For services, 1 January 2010 saw the implementation of the EU's so-called Place of Supply of Services Directive,[122] which resulted in substantial changes to the place of supply of services rules in the VAT Directive. Amongst these changes was a new basic rule (the 'general rule'), but this general rule does not take precedence – it is subject to a number of overriding exceptions (see Table 17.2 at **17.10.2**). For this reason, it is important always to look first at the exceptions, and only if none apply should the general rule be used. The guidance on the rules for services included in Table 17.2 is written in relation to the rules effective from 1 January 2010 and referred to in HMRC's VAT Notice 741A. Further changes have recently come into effect in 2011 (services supplied where performed) and more are due to come into effect in 2013 (long-term hire of means of transport) and 2015 (broadcasting, telecommunications, and

---

[120] VAT Directive, Art 132 relates to the exemption of specific activities in the public interest. The relevant paragraph in Art 132 exempts 'activities of public radio and television bodies other than those of a commercial nature'.

[121] The nature of the VAT rules is such that it is important to examine the scope of any charging and/or deeming provisions and reliefs to determine the extent of their application.

[122] Council Directive 2008/8/EC amending Directive 2006/112/EC (the VAT Directive) as regards the place of supply of services, OJ L 44/11, 20/2/2008 pp 11–22.

electronically supplied services). The position in respect of electronically provided services is considered in further detail in Chapter 22. In the context of e-commerce and e-infrastructure activities, the place of supply rules are extremely important since they determine where and in what circumstances VAT is chargeable.

17.10.1 The territorial extent of the UK for VAT purposes

Where a supply takes place outside of the UK, a UK VAT charge cannot be imposed upon the supply.[123] In other words, for a UK VAT charge to arise the supply must be made in the UK. VATA 1994 defines the UK as including the territorial sea of the UK.[124] Greater light is thrown on the matter by the Interpretation Act 1978, which provides that the UK comprises England, Scotland, Wales and Northern Ireland.[125] For VAT purposes, the Isle of Man is essentially treated as part of the UK unless otherwise indicated.[126] In the context of e-infrastructure, the Channel Islands do not form part of the UK. At the time of publication VAT is not charged in the Channel Islands.

17.10.2 Summary of the place of supply rules for VAT purposes

As noted above, the place of supply rules for UK VAT purposes are summarised in Table 17.2, together with some references to the VAT Directive, as applied by the UK's VAT rules, and to the EU Implementing Regulation, to assist in the interpretation or application of these rules. As clarified in the EU Implementing Regulation,[127] in applying these rules to services only the circumstances existing at the time of the chargeable event[128] will be taken into account. Any subsequent changes to the use of the service received will not affect the determination of the place of supply (unless there is an abusive practice[129] in respect of those supplies). A summary of the place of supply rules for services is also provided in the form of a flow chart diagram in Figure 17.1.

---

[123] VATA 1994, s 4(1).

[124] VATA 1994, s 96(11).

[125] Interpretation Act 1978, ss 5 and 22(1) and Sch 1.

[126] See Value Added Tax (Isle of Man) Order 1982, SI 1982/1067 and Value Added Tax (Isle of Man) (No 2) Order 1982, SI 1982/1068.

[127] See EU Implementing Regulation, Art 25.

[128] 'Chargeable event' is defined in the VAT Directive, Art 62 as the occurrence by virtue of which the legal conditions necessary for VAT to become chargeable are fulfilled.

[129] This is a general principle of EU law developed by the ECJ and confirmed as applicable to VAT in *Halifax plc v C&E Commrs (a joint case covering other, related appeals)* (Case C–255/02) [2006] ECR I-1609, [2006] STC 919, broadly, to prevent acts which have as their essential purpose the obtaining of a tax advantage contrary to VAT laws by artificial means.

Figure 17.1: Summary of place of supply of services rules

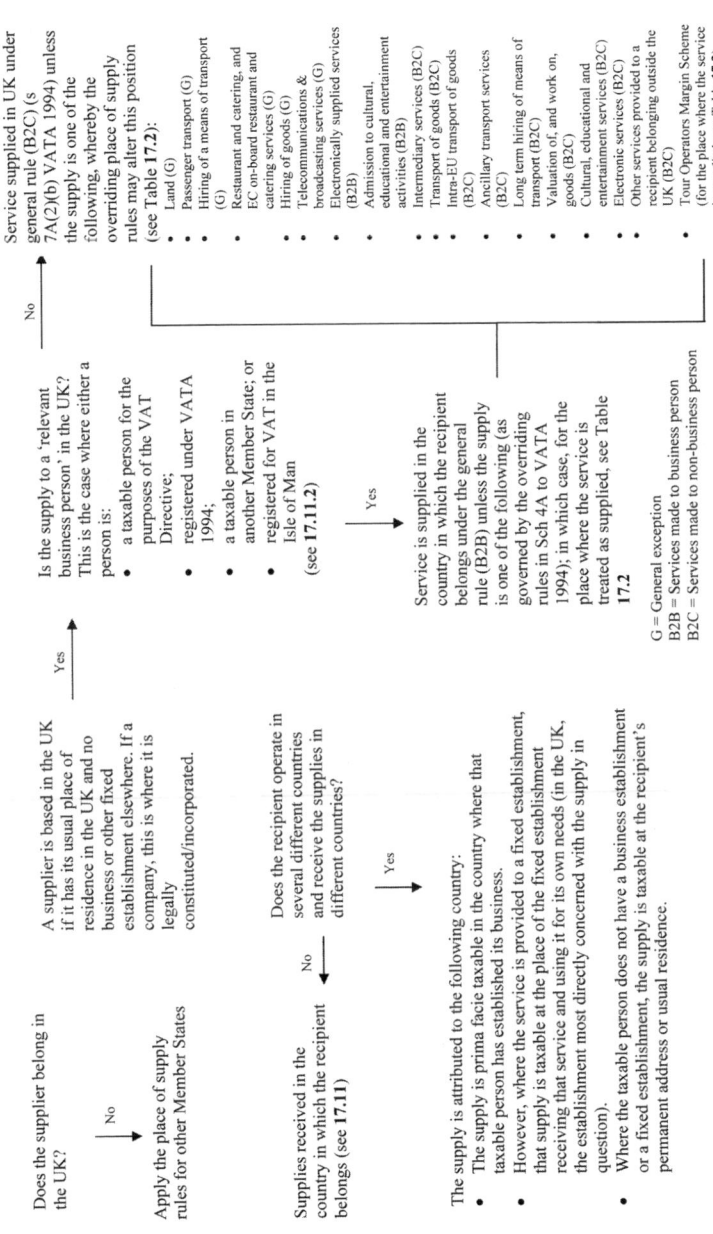

Table 17.2: Place of supply rules for goods and services – VATA 1994

Type of supply	Place of supply	Reference (VATA 1994)
Goods		
Goods not removed from the UK that are in the UK when supplied.	Goods supplied in the UK.	s 7(2) (VAT Directive, Arts 31 and 32)
Goods not removed to the UK that are outside the UK when supplied.	Goods supplied outside the UK.	s 7(2) (VAT Directive, Arts 31 and 32)
Goods installed or assembled at a place in the UK to which they are removed.	Goods supplied in the UK.	s 7(3)(a) (VAT Directive, Art 36)
Goods installed or assembled outside the UK at a place to which they are removed.	Goods supplied outside the UK.	s 7(3)(b) (VAT Directive, Art 36)
A supply involving the removal of goods to the UK by or under the directions of the person who supplies them; the supply is a transaction in pursuance of which the goods are acquired in the UK from another Member State by a person who is not a taxable person; the supplier is liable to be registered under VATA 1994; and the supply is neither a supply of goods consisting in a new means of transport nor anything which is treated as a supply of goods by virtue of being a deemed supply of assets from a business or transfer of own goods (whether for consideration or not).	Goods supplied in the UK. This place of supply rule applies unless any of the preceding rules apply. The place of supply rules for goods are hierarchical.	s 7(4) (VAT Directive, Arts 33 and 34)

A supply of goods that does not consist of a new means of transport, where the supply involves the removal of goods, by or under the directions of the person who supplies them, from the UK to another Member State; the person who makes the supply is taxable in another Member State; and the provisions of the law of that Member State corresponding, in relation to that Member State, to the rules referred to in the row above (for s 7(4) regarding supplies to non-taxable customers) make that person liable to VAT on the supply in that Member State.	Goods supplied outside the UK. This place of supply rule applies unless any of the preceding rules apply. This rule does not however apply where the VAT liability of the person in the other Member State depends on the exercise by any person of an option (to tax in the Member State of destination whatever the value of supplies) in the UK, under specific rules which treats supplies as being made outside the UK.	s 7(5) (VAT Directive, Arts 33 and 34)
A supply of goods, where the supply involves the goods being imported into the UK from somewhere outside the EU by or under the directions of the person who supplies them. Where, or to whom, the goods are delivered in the UK following importation does not affect the position.	Goods supplied in the UK. Again, this place of supply rule applies unless any of the preceding rules apply. Effectively, under this rule the place of supply is determined by who acts as the importer. So, if the supplier imports the goods into the UK, the supply to the UK customer is treated as taking place in the UK and the supplier may be liable to register for VAT in the UK. However, if the UK customer imports the goods, the supply is treated under s 7(7)(b) (see below) as taking place outside the UK. See also later in Chapter 19.	s 7(6) (VAT Directive, Art 32)

Goods removed from the UK without also involving their previous removal to the UK, e g goods removed from the UK to another Member State (other than supplies to private/non-taxable customers under s 7(5) above), and an export of goods from the UK to outside the EU.	Goods supplied in the UK. However, the VAT liability should be zero-rated – see further at Chapters 18 and 20. The supplier would need to complete an EC Sales List (see further below in relation to B2B services) for supplies of goods to a VAT registered business in another Member State.	s 7(7)(a). See also s 30(8). (VAT Directive, Art 32)
Goods removed to the UK from another Member State (other than supplies to private/non-taxable customers under s 7(4) above), or imported from outside the EU to the UK where the UK customer (rather than the supplier) is the person responsible for the importation.	Goods supplied outside the UK.	s 7(7)(b) (VAT Directive, Art 32)
Services		
General rules		
Business to Consumer (B2C)		
Supply of services by a supplier who belongs in the UK to a private individual, charity, government department or other body that has no business activities (excluding services supplied to a recipient who is a 'relevant business person').	Service supplied in the country in which the supplier belongs (unless overriding place of supply rules apply in Schedule 4A to VATA: see following summary). UK VAT will be due where the supplier belongs in the UK, irrespective of where the customer belongs.	s 7A(2) (b). See **17.11** for details relating to where a person 'belongs'. (Art 44 VAT Directive)

HMRC Notice 741A (January 2010), para 3.7

Where a customer has several establishments it is necessary to identify at which of the establishments the customer receives the supplies to determine whether VAT is chargeable. It is necessary to establish the facts, and consider at which establishment the services are used, and which establishment gives the supplier instructions. Further factors include obvious use of services at an establishment and delivery of 'products', eg. mastertape, to a particular establishment.

Business to Business (B2B)		
Supply of services to a 'relevant business person' by a UK supplier (the supply must not be received for a wholly private purpose).	Service supplied in the country in which the recipient/customer belongs (unless overriding place of supply rules apply in Sch 4A to VATA 1994: see following summary).	s 7A(2)(a) See **22.4** for details relating to where a person 'belongs'.
	If the customer is in the UK then UK VAT is due.	(Art 45 VAT Directive)
	If the customer is outside the UK then the supply is outside the scope of UK VAT; if the customer is outside the EU then there will be no VAT (again, subject to any exceptions in VATA 1994, Sch 4A).	
	If the customer belongs in another Member State (and is VAT registered), no UK VAT will be due but the supply will be subject to any local VAT at either the standard or reduced rate in that Member State under the reverse charge, i e accountable by the customer. In addition, the supplier may need to complete and submit an EC Sales List, which, (from 1 January 2010), must now be completed by suppliers for supplies of taxable services subject to the reverse charge in the customer's Member State. See HMRC's Notice 725 *The Single Market* (February 2011) for further details on EC Sales Lists, particularly at Section 17 of that notice.	

| | Information provided on EC Sales Lists is used by the UK and Member States to ensure VAT has been correctly accounted for. | |

HMRC Notice 741A (January 2010), para 2.7

- • Supplier should obtain commercial evidence that the customer belongs outside the UK, and does not receive the supply for a wholly private purpose;

- • VAT registration numbers are generally the best evidence that the supply is not received for a wholly private purpose and should be requested. Alternative types of evidence include other commercial documents indicating the nature of the customer's activities, such as certificates from fiscal authorities and business letterheads.

General exceptions to place of supply of services rules		Sch 4A (Arts 46–59 VAT Directive)
Land		
Services relating to land, including (a) the provision in a hotel, inn, boarding house or similar establishment of sleeping accommodation or of accommodation in rooms which are provided in conjunction with sleeping accommodation or for the supply of catering and (b) services such as are supplied by estate agents, auctioneers, architects, surveyors, engineers and others involved in matters relating to land.	Supply treated as made in the country in which the land is situated.	Sch 4A, para 1.

HMRC Notice 741A (January 2010), para 6.4/6.5 (Examples of supplies within/outside the heading)

- • Within: Legal Services such as conveyancing, the supply of warehouse space

- • Outside: Advice or information relating to land prices or property markets (since the information does not relate to specific sites); provision of a recorded studio where technicians are included as part of the supply (these are treated as engineering services)

Passenger transport		
A supply of services consisting of the transportation of passengers (or of any luggage or motor vehicles accompanying passengers).	Made in the country in which the transportation takes place, and, in a case where it takes place in more than one country, in proportion to the distances covered in each. There are special rules for passenger transport which leaves and re-enters a country, which can treat the transportation as taking place wholly in that country.	Sch 4A, para 2
Hiring of means of transport		
A supply consisting of the short-term[130] hiring of a means of transport. NB: 'Means of transport' includes vehicles, whether motorised or not, and other equipment and devices designed to transport persons or objects from one place to another, which might be pulled, drawn or pushed by vehicles and which are normally designed to be used and actually capable of being used for transport. The means of transport includes, in particular, the following vehicles:	Made in the country in which the means of transport is actually put at the disposal of the person by whom it is hired (this treatment applies for both B2B and B2C supplies); but (a) if the hiring of a means of transport would otherwise be treated as being made in the UK, and the services are to any extent effectively used and enjoyed in a country which is not a Member State, then the supply is to be treated to that extent as being made in that country and (b) where a supply consists of the hiring of a means of transport which would otherwise be treated as made in a country which is not a Member State, and the services are to any extent effectively used and enjoyed in the UK the supply is to be treated to that extent as made in the UK. This additional rule is known as the 'use and enjoyment' rule – see further below and in Chapter 22.	Sch 4A, para 3 (EU Implementing Regulation, Arts 38–40)

---

[130] For this purpose, 'short-term' hiring means transport which is hired for a continuous period not exceeding (a) if the means of transport is a vessel, 90 days and (b) otherwise, 30 days. Any hire beyond this point is a long-term hire of the means of transport.

(a) land vehicles, such as cars, motor cycles, bicycles, tricycles and caravans; (b) trailers and semi-trailers; (c) railway wagons; (d) vessels; (e) aircraft; (f) vehicles specifically designed for the transport of sick or injured persons; (g) agricultural tractors and other agricultural vehicles; (h) mechanically or electronically propelled invalid carriages. But vehicles which are permanently immobilised and containers will not be considered to be means of transport. (EU Implementing Regulation, Art 38)	NB: The place where the means of transport is put at the disposal of the customer is the place where the customer or a third party acting on his behalf takes physical possession of it.	

HMRC Notice 741A (January 2010), para 7 (Examples of supplies of means of transport within/outside the heading)

- Within: Ships, boats, yachts, barges, aircraft, cars, trucks, lorries, motorcycles, cycles, touring caravans and trailers, railway wagons

- Outside: Freight containers, static caravans, racing cars (where the provision of the car forms part of a supply of sporting activities)

- The hire of a means of transport does not include transport–related supplies which include the services of a driver, pilot, operator or crew; the place of supply of which depends on the nature of those services supplied.

Hiring of goods		
A supply of services consisting of the hiring of any goods other than a means of transport which would otherwise be treated as made in the UK, and the services are to any extent effectively used and enjoyed in a country which is not a Member State.	Subject to the use and enjoyment rule. Therefore, the supply is made in the non-EU country to the extent it is effectively used and enjoyed in that country.	Sch 4A, para 7(1)
A supply of services consisting of the hiring of any goods other than a means of transport which would otherwise be treated as made in a country which is not a Member State, and the services are to any extent effectively used and enjoyed in the UK.	Subject to the use and enjoyment rule. Therefore, the supply takes place in the UK to the extent it is effectively used and enjoyed in the UK during the hiring period.	Sch 4A, para 7(2)

HMRC Notice 741(A) (January 2010), para 16.4/16.6.1

- Effective use and enjoyment takes place where the hired goods are used (in practice this will be where the goods are physically located) irrespective of contract, payment or beneficial interest.

- Example: A company belonging in Switzerland hires fax machines from a supplier in the US. The fax machines are partly used and enjoyed at the Swiss company's London branch. The place of supply is the UK to the extent that the machines are used at the London branch. This is because the goods are used and enjoyed in the UK and the place of supply would otherwise have been outside the EC.

Telecommunications and broadcasting services		
A supply of services consisting of the provision of: (a) telecommunications services, or (b) radio or television broadcasting services. For this purpose, 'telecommunications services' means services relating to the transmission, emission or reception of signals, writing, images and sounds or information of any nature by wire, radio, optical or other electromagnetic systems, including (a) the related transfer or assignment of the right to use capacity for such transmission, emission or reception and (b) the provision of access to global information networks.	Covered by the general rules described above (until January 2015 – see Note below), but subject to the use and enjoyment rule. Therefore, where (a) the supply of services would otherwise be treated as made in the UK and (b) the services are to any extent effectively used and enjoyed in a country which is not a Member State, the supply is to be treated to that extent as made in that country. Where (a) the supply of services would otherwise be treated as made in a country which is not a Member State, and (b) the services are to any extent effectively used and enjoyed the UK, the supply is to be treated to that extent as made in the UK. However, from 1 January 2015 (without prejudice to the use and enjoyment rule), a B2C supply of these services is not subject to VAT if the supplier demonstrates that the place of supply is outside the EU in accordance with the EU Implementing Regulation (Art 3).	Sch 4A, para 8

Note:

From 1 January 2015, B2C supplies of these services will move from the current general rule (supplier establishment) to where the customer is established, has their permanent address, or usually resides, and the special registration scheme discussed in Chapter 22, which is available to non-EU suppliers in respect of electronically supplied services to EU private consumers, will be extended to both EU and non-EU businesses, and widened to include telecommunications and broadcasting services, called the 'One Stop Shop' by the EU. To review the EU's progress on these further changes, refer to the EU Commission's current press releases/communications and draft proposals on amending the VAT Directive and the EU Implementing Regulation, available at or within the following links:

http://europa.eu/rapid/pressReleasesAction.do?reference=IP/11/1508&101mat–HTML&aged=0&language=en&guiLanguage=en: Press release IP/11/1508, 6 December 2011

http://ec.europa.eu/taxation_customs/taxation/vat/key_documents/communications/index_en.htm: COM (2011) 851: Communication from the Commission to the European Parliament, the Council and the European Economic and Social Committee on the future of VAT – Towards a simpler, more robust and efficient VAT system tailored to the single market

http://europa.eu/rapid/pressReleasesAction.do?reference=IP/12/17&format=HTML&aged=0&language=EN&guiLanguage=en: Press Release IP/12/17, 13/01/2012: Taxation: Developing the One Stop Shop for cross border VAT compliance

http://ec.europa.eu/taxation_customs/taxation/vat/key_documents/legislation_proposed/index_en.htm: COM (2012) 2: Proposal for a Council Regulation amending Implementing Regulation (EU) No 282/2011 as regards the special schemes for non-established taxable persons supplying telecommunication services, broadcasting services or electronic services to non-taxable persons

Homepage of Commissioner Algirdas Šemeta, EU Commissioner for Taxation and Customs Union, Audit and Anti-fraud and Audit: http://ec.europa.eu/commission_2010-2014/semeta/index_en.htm

---

HMRC Notice 741A (January 2010), para 16

- The additional rules [ie use and enjoyment] for letting on hire of goods (see above), telecommunications services and radio and television broadcasting services apply in either of the following situations:

    – the place of supply would be the UK under another rule (because the supplier or customer belongs in the UK) but the service are effectively used and enjoyed outside the EC; or

    – the place of supply would be outside the EC under another section (because the supplier or customer belongs outside the EC) but the services are effectively used and enjoyed in the UK.

  In these circumstances, the place of supply is where their effective use and enjoyment takes place. Where this is the UK, the services are subject to UK VAT.

- It does not always matter where the letting on hire of goods, telecommunications services and radio and television broadcasting services are effectively used and enjoyed. It only matters in the situations described above. The use and enjoyment provisions apply where the EC position would otherwise be distortive. Consequently, they do not apply where:

    – the place of supply is the UK (because either the supplier or the customer belongs in the UK) and the service was effectively used and enjoyed in another Member State; or

    – the place or supply is another Member State (because either the supplier or the customer belongs there) but the supply is effectively used and enjoyed in the UK.

- Effective use and enjoyment takes place where the customer actually consumes telecommunications services and radio and television broadcasting services (in practice this will be where the services are physically used) irrespective of contract, payment or beneficial interest (para 16.7)

- Examples for telecommunications services (para. 16.7.1)

  - A private individual whose usual place of residence is in the UK rents a telephone line for his holiday home in Florida from a UK supplier. The services are actually used and enjoyed in Florida. The place of supply is outside the EC because effective use and enjoyment takes place outside the EC and the services would otherwise be supplied in the UK.

  - A UK resident rents a telephone line for his elderly mother's house in Australia. He receives and pays the bills from his UK provider. The services are actually used and enjoyed in Australia by his mother. The place of supply is outside the EC because effective use and enjoyment takes place outside the EC and the services would otherwise be supplied in the UK.

  - The parents of a student travelling in the Far East accept a reverse charge call to their UK home from their daughter. The accepted call forms part of the service from their local provider and is actually used and enjoyed at the UK family home. The place of supply is the UK because the services are not effectively used and enjoyed outside the EC.

  - A business traveller makes a reservation at a Hong Kong hotel from his London office using a toll free number. The telecommunications services are supplied to, and used by, the Hong Kong hotel. The place of supply is outside the EC because the services are not effectively used and enjoyed in the UK.

- How do the extra rules apply to travellers? (para. 16.7.2)

  - Telecommunications services are subject to UK VAT when used in the UK by non-EC visitors. Examples include public pay-phones, fax shop services and charges for calls made from hotel rooms. However, elements of telecommunications services used in the UK are ignored if they are:

    - simply an incidental part of an established telephone contract or account held by a customer who belongs outside the EC

    - used by a non-EC temporary visitor, and

    - HMRC is satisfied that these conditions are not being abused.

  If a UK resident uses telecommunications services outside the EC under such an account with a UK provider, those services will be outside the scope of UK VAT, provided that evidence is retained to substantiate the element of use and enjoyment that occurs outside the EC.

- Do I have to apply different rules if I supply the electronically supplied services as well as telecommunications services or radio and television broadcasting services? (para. 16.8)

  HMRC recognises that in certain situations, the place of supply would be the same whether the rules for telecommunications services and radio and television broadcasting services, or those for electronically supplied services were applied. This is because most non-business customers use and enjoy services in the same country in which they belong.

- Accounting procedures for non-UK suppliers of the letting on hire of goods (including means of transport), telecommunications services and radio and television broadcasting services used and enjoyed in the UK (para. 16.10)

  If you are a supplier who does not belong in the UK and your customer is registered for UK VAT, your customer is responsible for accounting for any VAT due on the supply under the reverse charge procedure. [see **17.12**]

Value Added Tax: European Union Trade

If you are a supplier who does not belong in the UK, and your customer is not registered for UK VAT, you, as the supplier, are responsible for accounting for any VAT due on your supply where the place of supply is the UK. If you are not already registered in the UK, you may be liable to register.

If you are a supplier who does not belong in the EC, you are required to register and account for UK VAT if you supply B2C services that are used and enjoyed in the UK, subject to the normal rules.

- Accounting procedures for UK VAT registered recipients of services of the letting on hire of goods (other than means of transport), telecommunications services and radio and television broadcasting services from a non-EC supplier where the place of supply is the UK (para. 16.11)

If you are a UK VAT registered recipient of these services and:

  – you belong outside the EC for the purposes of receiving the supply

  – you use and enjoy the services in the UK, and

  – your supplier belongs outside the UK

you are required to account for UK VAT using the reverse charge procedure.

- Accounting procedures for UK VAT registered recipients of services of hired means of transport from a non-EC supplier where the place of supply is the UK (para. 16.12)

If you are a UK VAT registered recipient of these services, you are required to account for the reverse charge where your supplier belongs outside the EC.

- How do I account for VAT on the letting on hire of goods, telecommunications services and radio and television broadcasting services that are only partly liable to UK VAT because of the use and enjoyment provisions? (para. 16.13)

You are only required to account for UK VAT to the extent that the place of supply of services is the UK. Therefore you should seek to identify the location where the services are actually used.

HMRC will normally accept any records or documentation that demonstrates any division in the provision of services but, where such records do not exist, you should make a fair and reasonable assessment.

There is no prescribed method for determining the extent to which services are used in the UK. You may adopt whatever method is available to you that produces a fair and reasonable reflection of services that are liable to UK VAT.... Evidence of how the apportionment has been made should be retained and made available on request.

- Liability to register in other Member States (para. 16.14)

If you supply the letting on hire of any goods, telecommunications services or radio and television broadcasting services where the place of supply would be outside the EC, and the services are effectively used and enjoyed by your customer in another Member State, you may be liable to register for VAT in that Member State.

Exceptions to place of supply of services relating to supplies made to a relevant business person (B2B).		
Electronically supplied services Provision of electronically supplied services to a relevant business person. Examples of such services: • website supply, web-hosting and distance maintenance of programmes and equipment; • the supply of software and the updating of software; • the supply of images, text and information, and the making available of databases; • the supply of music, films and games (including games of chance and gambling games); • the supply of political, cultural, artistic, sporting, scientific, educational or entertainment broadcasts (including broadcasts of events); and • the supply of distance teaching.	Covered by the B2B general rule so the place of supply is where the business customer belongs, but this is subject to the use and enjoyment rule. Therefore, if there is a supply of services consisting of the provision of electronically supplied services to a relevant business person which would otherwise be treated as made in the UK, but the services are to any extent effectively used and enjoyed in a country which is not a Member State, then the supply is to be treated to that extent as made in that country. If there is a supply of services consisting of the provision of electronically supplied services to a relevant business person which would otherwise be treated as made in a country which is not a Member State, but the services are to any extent effectively used and enjoyed in the UK, then the supply is to be treated to that extent as made in the UK.	Sch 4A, para 9
NB: Where the supplier of a service and the supplier's customer communicate via e-mail, this does not of itself mean that the service provided is an electronically supplied service.	NB: The use and enjoyment rule does not apply in the UK to B2C supplies of these services. See more fully in Chapter 22, Table 22.1 at **22.3.2**, and at **22.7**.	
Note: See generally in Chapter 22.		

Admission to cultural, educational and entertainment activities		
Supply of the following services to a relevant business person: (a) services in respect of admission to cultural, artistic, sporting, scientific, educational, entertainment or similar events (including fairs and exhibitions); and (b) ancillary services relating to admission to such events.	A supply to a relevant business person of these services is to be treated as made in the country in which the events in question actually take place.	Sch 4A, para 9A (as of January 2011) EU Implementing Regulation, Arts 32–33

Note:

(1) Services in respect of admission to cultural, artistic, sporting, scientific, educational, entertainment or similar events include the supply of services of which the essential characteristics are the granting of the right of admission to an event in exchange for a ticket or payment, including payment in the form of a subscription, a season ticket or a periodic fee. In particular, this includes:

(a)   the right of admission to shows, theatrical performances, circus performances, fairs, amusement parks, concerts, exhibitions and other similar cultural events;

(b)   the right of admission to sporting events such as matches or competitions;

(c)   the right of admission to educational and scientific events such as conferences and seminars.

(EU Implementing Regulation, Art 32)

(2) The ancillary services referred to includes services which are directly related to admission to cultural, artistic, sporting, scientific, educational, entertainment or similar events and which are supplied separately for a consideration to a person attending an event. Such ancillary services include in particular the use of cloakrooms or sanitary facilities but shall not include mere intermediary services relating to the sale of tickets.

(EU Implementing Regulation, Art 33)

Exceptions relating to supplies not made to a relevant business person (B2C)		
Intermediaries		
A supply to a person who is not a relevant business person consisting of the making of arrangements for a supply by or to another person or of any other activity intended to facilitate the making of such a supply. This also covers the services of intermediaries acting in the name and on behalf of the recipient of the service procured, and the services performed by intermediaries acting in the name and on behalf of the provider of the services procured.	Made in the same country as the (underlying) supply to which it relates. Most B2B intermediary services are subject to the general B2B rule and are supplied where the recipient belongs, (ie, subject to any specific exceptions such as land-related services).	Sch 4A, para 10 (EU Implementing Regulation, Arts 30–31)

Note:

Services supplied by intermediaries acting in the name and on behalf of another person consisting of the intermediation in the provision of accommodation in the hotel sector or in sectors having a similar function shall fall within the scope of:

(a)   Art 44 of the VAT Directive if supplied to a taxable person (ie B2B, so the place of supply is treated as being the place where the taxable person has established its business, or to their fixed establishment located in another place (where applicable), or failing this, the place where the taxable person who receives the services has its permanent address or usually resides);

(b)   Art 46 of the VAT Directive if supplied to a non-taxable person (so that the place of supply is the place where the underlying transaction is supplied).

(EU Implementing Regulation, Art 31)

HMRC Notice 741A (January 2010), para 12.1

A person is an intermediary if that person acts as a third party in arranging, or facilitating, the making of supplies. An intermediary arranges supplies between two other parties, a supplier and the supplier's customer. The intermediary may be referred to as a broker, buying or selling agent, commissionaires or agent acting in their own name (undisclosed agent). The intermediary's customer is the person to whom that person supplies its intermediary services (ie supplier and/or recipient).

Transport of goods: general		
A supply of services to a person who is not a relevant business person consisting of the transportation of goods (but not Intra-Community transport of goods).	Made in the country in which the transportation takes place, and (in a case where it takes place in more than one country) in proportion to the distances covered in each. B2B supplies of these services are subject to the general rule and supplied where the recipient belongs.	Sch 4A, para 11
Intra-Community transport of goods		
A supply of services to a person who is not a relevant business person consisting of the transportation of goods which begins in one Member State and ends in another.	Made in the Member State in which the transportation begins.	Sch 4A, para 12
Ancillary transport services		
A supply to a person who is not a relevant business person of ancillary transport services. 'Ancillary transport services' means loading, unloading handling and similar activities.	Made where the services are physically performed. B2B supplies remains subject to the general rule.	Sch 4A, para 13

Long-term hiring of means of transport		
A supply to a person who is not a relevant business person ('the recipient') of services consisting of the long-term hiring of a means of transport.	Made in the country in which the recipient belongs, unless the hire is a long-term hire of a pleasure boat.	Sch 4A, para 13A (with effect in relation to supplies made on or after 1 January 2013)
The hiring of a means of transport is 'long term' if it is not short term (see above).	A supply to a person who is not a relevant business person ('the recipient') of services consisting of the long-term hiring of a pleasure boat which is actually put at the disposal of the recipient at the supplier's business establishment, or some other fixed establishment of the supplier, is to be treated as made in the country where the pleasure boat is actually put at the disposal of the recipient.	
	B2B supplies of long-term hiring of a means of transport remain subject to the general rule for B2B supplies and supplied where the recipient/customer belongs. However, the long-term hire of a means of transport is also subject to use and enjoyment rule, where the supply is B2B or B2C.	
	In addition, from 1 January 2013 (without prejudice to the use and enjoyment rule), the supply of B2C long-term hiring of a means of transport is not subject to VAT if the supplier demonstrates that the place of supply is outside the EU in accordance with the EU Implementing Regulation (Art 3).	

Valuation of, or work carried out, on goods		
A supply to a person who is not a relevant business person of services consisting of the valuation of, or carrying out of work on, goods	Made where the services are physically performed. For this rule, the goods must constitute tangible, moveable property (eg, computer hardware), so this excludes permanently installed goods and fixtures. See generally HMRC Notice 741A, Section 8. B2B supplies remain subject to the general rule.	Sch 4A, para 14
Cultural, educational and entertainment activities etc		
Supply of the following services to a person who is not a relevant business person: (a) services relating to cultural, artistic, sporting, scientific, educational, entertainment or similar events (including fairs and exhibitions); and (b) ancillary services relating to such activities, including services of organisers of such activities.	A supply of these services is to be treated as made in the country in which the activities concerned actually take place. (Such services supplied to relevant business persons are subject to the general rule for B2B supplies noted above, unless the B2B exception rule for admission and services ancillary to admission in Sch 4A, para 9A is applicable, see earlier.)	Sch 4A, para 14A (as of January 2011)
Electronic services		
A supply consisting of the provision by a person who belongs in a country which is not a Member State (other than the Isle of Man) of electronically supplied services (see below for meaning) to a person ('the recipient') who: (a) is not a relevant business person and (b) belongs in a Member State.	Made in the country in which the recipient belongs. However, from 1 January 2015 (without prejudice to the use and enjoyment rule where applicable), the supply is not subject to VAT if the supplier demonstrates that the place of supply is outside the EU in accordance with the EU Implementing Regulation (Art 3).	Sch 4A, para 15 (EU Implementing Regulation, Art 24(2))

	Where supplied to a non-taxable person who is established in more than one country or has his permanent address in one country and his usual residence in another, priority is to be given to the place that best ensures taxation at the place of actual consumption when determining the place of supply of those services.	
	See further above and in Chapter 22 at **22.2.2**, and in Table 22.1, in reference to changes being introduced in 2015 for the place of supply of cross border B2C supplies of telecommunications, broadcasting and electronically supplied services.	
Other services provided to a recipient belonging outside EC		
A supply consisting of the provision to a person ('the recipient') who: (a) is not a relevant business person and (b) belongs in a country which is not a Member State (other than the Isle of Man),of the following services: (a) transfers and assignments of copyright, patents, licences, trademarks and similar rights; (b) the acceptance of any obligation to refrain from pursuing or exercising (in whole or in part) any business activity or any rights within paragraph (a); (c) advertising services; (d) services of consultants, engineers, consultancy bureaux, lawyers, accountants, and similar services, data processing and provision of information, other than any services relating to land;	Made in the country in which the recipient belongs. However, as noted earlier, the B2C services listed at (h), (i) and (j) are subject to the UK's use and enjoyment provisions – see also HMRC Notice 741A, para 14.6. Without prejudice to the use and enjoyment rule (where applicable), the supply is not subject to VAT if the supplier demonstrates that the place of supply is outside the EU in accordance with the EU Implementing Regulation (Art 3).	Sch 4A, para 16

(e)	banking, financial and insurance services (including reinsurance), other than the provision of safe deposit facilities;	See further above and in Chapter 22, in reference to changes being introduced in 2015 for the place of supply of cross border B2C supplies of telecommunications, broadcasting and electronically supplied services.
(f)	the provision of access to, or transmission or distribution through:	
	(i) a natural gas system situated within the territory of a Member State or any network connected to such a system;	
	(ii) an electricity system; or	
	(iii) a network through which heat or cooling is supplied,	
	and the provision of other directly linked services;	
(g)	the supply of staff;	
(h)	the letting on hire of goods other than means of transport;	
(i)	telecommunication services (until January 2015);	
(j)	radio and television broadcasting services (until January 2015); and	
(k)	electronically supplied services (until January 2015) (again, see Chapter 22 for further details).	

HMRC Notice 741A (January 2010), para 15 (examples of services within and outside above headings (a) to (j); examples for (k) are given in Chapter 22)

- The common feature of services covered in this section is that their place of performance can be indeterminate or variable and they are easily undertaken in a different place to where a supplier has established a business. They are often intangible in nature.

(a) transfers and assignments of copyright, patents, licences, trademarks and similar rights:

- Within: granting of a licence to use computer software, transfer of permission to use a logo, granting of a right by a photographer for a photograph to be published in a magazine article (including material which is downloaded to the customer)

(b) the acceptance of any obligation to refrain from pursuing or exercising (in whole or in part) any business activity or any rights within paragraph (a)

- Within: Agreement by the owner of a trademark to refrain from using it

(c) advertising services

　　　　　　　– Within: All services of publicizing another person's name or products with a view to encouraging their sale. It includes supplies of advertising services in the established media: eg, radio or television advertising time; of the right to place an advertisement on a hoarding; or of advertising space in any publication. It also covers newer promotional methods such as an entry in a telephone directory or advertising space in any electronic location (eg, website advertising). The heading applies to everything provided as part of an advertising campaign, even where elements of the campaign would have fallen under other place of supply rules had they been supplied in isolation.

(d)　　services of consultants, engineers, consultancy bureaux, lawyers, accountants, and similar services, data processing and provision of information, other than any services relating to land

　　　　　　　– Within: research and development, market research, production of customized ('bespoke' or 'specific') computer software, excluding digitally downloaded software, as well as the services of adapting existing packages (some 'off-the-shelf' software packages are treated as supplies of goods); software maintenance involving upgrades, advice, and resolving any problems (the place of performance is not relevant as solutions may be provided by telephone conversations, remote links or attending a mainframe site; (However a contract for simply maintaining computer hardware relates to work on goods [see Section 8 of HMRC's Notice 741A and above in relation to the place of supply rules for work carried out on goods]); a contract for maintaining computer hardware is a work on goods); services of engineers/technicians within the entertainment industry (covering editors/sound engineers) producing an edit master from which copies can be made as well as those who exercise artistic control or influence over material.

　　　　　　　– What is 'data processing?' (para 15.5.10/11)

　　　　　　　　　　- Data processing is the application of programmed instructions on existing data which results in the production of required information.

　　　　　　　　　　- **Examples of exclusions: services which include an element of data processing (where just required for a contract to be completed), simple re-formatting where there is no change to the meaning of the content.**

　　　　　　　– What is the 'provision of information?' (para 15.5.12)

　　　　　　　　　　- HMRC considers that it covers the supplying of knowledge of any type and in any form. Information includes facts, data, figures and other material. Examples include: tourist information, weather forecasts, information supplied by a private enquiry agent, telephone helpdesk services (such as for computer software), satellite, navigational and location services, and provision of online information.

　　　　　　　　　　- Examples of exclusions from provision of information: the delivery or transmission of another person's information by whatever means (for electronic delivery see Chapter 22); information relating to specific land or property.

(e)　　banking, financial and insurance services (including reinsurance), other than the provision of safe deposit facilities

　　　　　　　– Examples (para 15.6.2)

　　　　　　　　　　- Granting of loans

　　　　　　　　　　- The provision of insurance or reinsurance

　　　　　　　　　　- Supply of financial futures and financial options

(h)　　the letting on hire of goods other than means of transport

       –   Examples (para 15.9.2)

         -   Hire of mobile telephone handsets (but not the supply of telecommunications services); hire of freight containers; hire of computer and office equipment

(i)   telecommunication services (para 15.10)

       –   Telecommunications services means services relating to the transmission, emission or reception of signals, writing, images and sounds or information of any nature by wire, radio, optical or other electromagnetic systems, including: (a) the related transfer or assignment of the right to use capacity for such transmission, emission or reception, and (b) the provision of access to global information networks

       –   Heading includes the sending or receiving of material by electronic or similar communications systems. This may be via cable, fibre optics, radio waves, microwaves, satellite, or copper wire and covers telephony (systems for transmission of speech and other sounds) and telegraphy (systems for providing distant reproduction of written, printed or pictorial matter) as well as the right to use such facilities

       –   If a person supplies the 'content' of a transmission, it is necessary to identify the actual nature of the services provided. For example, a weather forecasting service where weather charts are faxed to the customer is a supply of delivered information and not transmission

       –   Examples of telecommunications services

         -   Telephone calls, calls delivered by cellular phones, paging, the transmission element of Electronic Data Interchange, teleconferencing and call-back services

         -   Switching, completion of another provider's calls, the provision of leased lines and circuits or global networks

         -   Telex, facsimile, multi-messaging

         -   Email and access to the Internet

         -   Satellite transmission services, covering transponder rental/hire and both space segments and earth segments, which includes uplinks and downlinks via land earth stations, coastal stations, outside broadcasting units, or similar

         –   Transmission or delivery of another person's material by electronic means

       –   Examples of services that are not telecommunications services

         -   Supplies of information ordered and delivered through the Internet

         -   Travel information accessed by telephone

         -   Granting copyright to use transmitted material

         -   Processing of data

         -   Broadcasting to subscribers

       –   Do Internet services constitute telecommunications?

         -   Access to the Internet and World Wide Web, the provision of email addresses and chatline facilities are telecommunications services. If you supply basic access to the Internet, even if related software, some information and customer support facilities are included, HMRC treat the supply as being of telecommunications services

- *However*: (a) if a person supplies a package of Internet services where the emphasis is on content rather than communication, the supply is not of pure telecommunications services. The place of supply of such a package depends on the nature of the services provided, or (b) if a person supplies services separately or services which are simply delivered to a customer by electronic transmission, the place of supply depends on the nature of the services provided

(j)   radio and television broadcasting services

– Examples: subscription for satellite or cable television

– Examples outside heading: service of transmitting another person's material by electronic means

(k)   electronically supplied services (see chapter 22).

Special Scheme for Travel Operators		
The Tour Operators Margin Scheme (TOMS) is a special scheme for businesses that buy in and resell travel, accommodation and certain other services as a principal or undisclosed agent (ie acting in your own name). TOMS applies to travel agents and tour operators, and also to traders who are not travel agents or tour operators within the normal meaning of those terms but who carry out identical transactions comparable to those of a tour operator or travel agent but in the context of another activity, such as that of hotelier (the *Howden Court Hotel* case[131]).	TOMS enables VAT to be accounted for on travel supplies without businesses having to register and account for tax in each Member State where the services and goods are enjoyed. Accordingly, the place of supply rules are altered so that all of the services provided by a tour operator are treated as a single composite supply, which takes place where the supplier belongs.	VATA 1994, s 53 and Sch 8, Group 8, item 12 Value Added Tax (Tour Operators) Order 1987, SI 1987/ 1806, as amended.
TOMS does not apply to: • supplies arranged as a disclosed agent/intermediary and where commission is readily identifiable; • in-house or agency supplies a supplier makes which are not packaged/supplied with margin scheme supplies;	TOMS means that a supplier cannot reclaim any UK or EC VAT charged on the travel services and goods that are bought-in and re-supplied – the tax on such goods or services is accounted for in the relevant Member State by the providers of those services (ie hotels, airlines).	See in particular HMRC's Tour Operators Margin Scheme Notice 709/5 (November 2009). Sections 8–13 of this notice are stated to have the force of law.

---

[131] Case C-308/96 [1998] ECR I-06229, ECJ. See also *Finanzamt Heidelberg v ISt internationale Sprach- und Studienreisen GmbH* (Case C-200/04) [2006] STC 52, ECJ.

• supplies made to business customers for subsequent resale by them; or • supplies that are incidental to other supplies. If acting as a tour operator then the person must account for VAT using TOMS. The following are margin scheme supplies: accommodation, passenger transport, hire of a means of transport, trips or excursions, services of tour guides, use of special lounges at airports.	The tour operator will only account for VAT on the margin to which TOMS applies. The margin is the difference between the amount the supplier receives from customers (including any amounts paid on behalf of customers by third parties) and the amount which the supplier pays to its suppliers.	

Note: The place of supply rules also make specific provision for restaurant and catering services and EU on-board restaurant and catering services.[132]

Example 17.9

Dr Smith operates a legal practice in the Cayman Islands. He is happy to provide advice to both professional and lay clients in the UK via video-conferencing and e-mail, etc. A UK-based firm of solicitors requires clarification on trust law in the Cayman Islands. A video conference is held, and the fee payable to Dr Smith is the sterling equivalent of £30,000. Dr Smith is e-mailed by John and Rita, who want to retire to the Cayman Islands. They seek his advice on the legal requirements to gain residence. The advice costs the sterling equivalent of £1,000.

Dr Smith, as supplier of the services, belongs outside the UK and the EU. He is not under any obligation to charge and account for VAT to any EU tax authority. However, the UK-based firm of solicitors will be required to account for UK VAT because it receives Dr Smith's service for business purposes. John and Rita are not business customers, and accordingly the place of supply is deemed to be where the supplier belongs (in this case, the Cayman Islands).

Example 17.10

Thomas lives in the UK and he places an online order for the purchase of kitchen equipment from a UK supplier. The supplier will also gift-wrap the equipment. The total cost for these supplies (including postage and

---

[132] See VATA 1994, Sch 4A, paras 5 and 6. (Broadly, the place of supply is where the services are physically carried out, or the point of departure if supplied on intra-EU passenger transport.)

packaging) is £150. The place of supply is in the UK and the amount of VAT to be paid is 20% on the consideration of £150.

Example 17.11

Helga lives in Germany and she places an online order for the purchase of kitchen equipment from a UK supplier, to be received in Germany. The UK supplier makes annual supplies of less than £10,000 to Germany. The supplier will also gift-wrap the equipment. The total cost for these supplies (including postage and packaging) is £160. The place of supply is initially the UK, and the amount of VAT to be paid is 20% on the consideration of £160. Since the place of supply is in the UK, the UK supplier is obliged to collect UK VAT on goods dispatched to another EU country. However, if the value of the supplies by the UK supplier exceeded certain thresholds under the distance selling rules (see Chapter 18), in Germany in this example, the place of supply would shift and move to Germany and the UK supplier would be liable to register for VAT in Germany and charge German VAT (rather than UK VAT) in accordance with the rules of Germany, to where the goods are supplied and delivered.

Example 17.12

Sam lives in the US and he places an online order for the purchase of kitchen equipment from a UK supplier to the US. The supplier will also gift-wrap the equipment. The total cost for these supplies (including postage and packaging) is £170. The place of supply is outside the UK and the EU, and the amount of VAT to be paid is nil since the supplies are outside the scope of VAT (see Chapter 20 on exports). However, under the rules of the country to which the goods are supplied, there may also be import or customs fees to be paid once the goods arrive in that country.

Example 17.13

Amsterdam BV is a company located and VAT-registered in The Netherlands. Amsterdam BV places an online order for the purchase of commercial equipment from a UK supplier and the equipment is dispatched or transported from the UK to The Netherlands. The total cost for these supplies (including postage and packaging) is £5,000. The place of supply of the intra-EU supply from the UK is the UK but there is an acquisition in The Netherlands since the supply is made to a VAT-registered business in another Member State and the equipment has been moved there. Therefore, the place of taxation/acquisition is The Netherlands so nil UK VAT should be due (zero-rated) and VAT will instead be accounted for in The Netherlands at the rate that would have applied had it been a domestic supply there (because of the rules relating to acquisition VAT on intra-EU supplies between VAT registered suppliers: see Chapter 18 for further details). Certain evidence will need to be obtained and kept in these circumstances by the UK supplier to ensure that no UK VAT is charged.

17.11 DETERMINING WHERE A SUPPLIER OR RECIPIENT BELONGS FOR THE PURPOSES OF A SUPPLY OF SERVICES

17.11.1 Introduction

Under the general rules for services as summarised in Table 17.2 above, a service is treated as supplied in the UK if the supplier 'belongs' in the UK, unless the person to whom the supply is made is a 'relevant business person', in which case the service is supplied in the country in which the recipient belongs.[133] Whether a supplier belongs in the UK is determined under VATA 1994,[134] but this has to be construed in accordance with the EU Implementing Regulation (see further below).

Briefly, a supplier is based in the UK if it has its 'usual place of residence' in the UK and no 'business establishment' or other 'fixed establishment' elsewhere; where the supplier is a company, the 'usual place of residence' is where it is legally constituted (ie the country where it is incorporated).[135]

While VATA 1994 refers to the place of belonging, the VAT Directive refers to the place of establishment. Under the VAT Directive, the place of supply of services to a taxable person is the place where that person has established its business.[136] However, if the services are provided to a fixed establishment of the taxable person that is located in a place other than the place where the business is established, the place of supply is the place where that fixed establishment is located.[137] In the absence of such place of establishment or fixed establishment, the place of supply of services is the place where the taxable person who receives such services has his permanent address or usually resides.[138]

The VAT Directive also provides the general EU rule for the place of supply of services to a non-taxable person. In this regard, the place of supply of services to a non-taxable person is the place where the supplier has established his business.[139] However, if those services are provided from a fixed establishment of a supplier located in a place other than the place where he has established his business, the place of supply of those services is to be treated as the place where that fixed establishment is located.[140] In the absence of such place of establishment or fixed

---

[133] VATA 1994, s 7A.
[134] VATA 1994, s 9.
[135] VATA 1994, s 9.
[136] VAT Directive, Art 44.
[137] VAT Directive, Art 44.
[138] VAT Directive, Art 44.
[139] VAT Directive, Art 45.
[140] VAT Directive, Art 45.

establishment, the place of supply of services will be the place where the supplier has his permanent address or usually resides.[141]

17.11.2　Relevant business person

As noted above, if the recipient of services is a relevant business person then the place of supply is where the recipient belongs (unless overriding place of supply rules apply in Sch 4A to VATA 1994, again, which are summarised in Table 17.2 at **17.10.2**).[142]

A person is treated as a 'relevant business person' for UK VAT purposes if that person is:[143]

(a)　a taxable person within the meaning of Art of 9 of the VAT Directive, (as mentioned at **17.9.2** this means, broadly, any person who independently carries out in any place any economic activity,[144] whatever the purpose or results of that activity);

(b)　registered under VATA 1994;

(c)　identified as a taxable person under the law of another Member State; or

(d)　registered under an Act of Tynwald[145] for the purposes of any tax imposed under that Act which corresponds to VAT,

and the services are received by the person otherwise than wholly for private purposes.

---

[141]　VAT Directive, Art 45.

[142]　VATA 1994, s 7A(5).

[143]　VATA 1994, s 7A(4).

[144]　In HMRC's guidance in V1-6 (Business/Non-Business) it is acknowledged that neither UK nor EC legislation has provided an exhaustive statutory definition or test for determining if an activity is in business and so the meaning of 'business' and 'economic activity' has emerged from case-law. In considering the application of the case-law 'business test' referred to in V1-6 (Section 2), the following indicators are relevant: (a) Is the activity a serious undertaking earnestly pursued? (b) Is the activity an occupation or function that is actively pursued with reasonable or recognisable continuity? (c) Does the activity have a certain measure of substance in terms of the quarterly or annual value of taxable supplies made (bearing in mind that exempt supplies can also be business)? (d) Is the activity conducted in a regular manner and on sound and recognised business principles? (e) Is the activity predominately concerned with the making of taxable supplies for a consideration? (f) Are the taxable supplies that are being made of a kind which, subject to differences of detail, are commonly made by those who seek to profit from them? If a sufficient number of these criteria are satisfied, then an activity can be held to be a business (see V1-6). Further, HMRC looks for objective evidence of a person's 'business' status and there are a number of factors that HMRC will consider in testing for objective evidence of an 'intention to trade', including: (a) entering into contracts, (b) soliciting customers and (c) advertising.

[145]　The laws of the Isle of Man.

The evidential circumstances in which a person can be considered to be a taxable person are considered below.

It is also important to remember that the place of where a 'relevant business person' is treated as belonging for the purposes of VATA 1994 must be construed in accordance with the EU Implementing Regulation, as this clarifies certain aspects of the VAT Directive, with the objective of ensuring a more uniform application of VAT rules within the EU and is, as indicated earlier at **17.2**, 'directly applicable' in the EU.

For the purposes of the UK's place of supply rules, under VATA 1994 a 'relevant business person' is treated as belonging in a 'relevant country', which means (a) if the person has a business establishment or some other fixed place of establishment, in a country (and none in any other country), that country; or (b) if the person has a business establishment, or some other fixed establishment or establishments, in more than one country, the country in which the relevant establishment[146] is located; or (c) if none of the foregoing apply, the country in which the person's usual place of residence is located.[147] The concept of fixed establishment is discussed below.

In some circumstances, supplies are deemed to take place in the UK due to the fact that they represent a supply of services provided to, and consumed by, a relevant business person in the UK but who may not belong in the UK, under the so-called additional 'use and enjoyment' rules as mentioned in Table **17.2**.[148] The type of supplies which are within this category include telecommunication services and electronically supplied services.[149]

A taxable person or a non-taxable legal person deemed to be a taxable person who receives services exclusively for private use (including use by staff) will always be treated as a non-taxable person.[150] A supplier is entitled to consider that the services are for the customer's business use if, for that transaction, the customer has communicated his individual VAT identification number (this is subject to any information to the contrary) – see **17.11.6**.[151] However, where the same service is intended for both private use, including use by the customer's staff, and business use, the supply of that service will be covered exclusively as a supply to a taxable person, provided there is no abusive practice.

---

[146] A 'relevant establishment' in the UK means whichever of the person's establishments is most directly concerned with the supply: VATA 1994, s 9(4). See note 167 below.

[147] VATA 1994, s 9(3).

[148] See Chapter 22 at **22.7** for further details in relation to electronically supplied services.

[149] Eg under VATA 1994, Sch 4A, paras 8(3), (4) and 9(1), (2).

[150] EU Implementing Regulation, Art 19.

[151] EU Implementing Regulation, Art 19.

17.11.3   Relevant business person: business establishment

Under the EU Implementing Regulation the place where the business of a taxable person is established is the place where the functions of the business's central administration are carried out.[152] The following matters must be taken into account in determining this location:[153]

- the place where essential decisions concerning the general management of the business are taken;

- the place where the registered office of the business is located; and

- the place where management meets.

Where these criteria do not allow the place of establishment of a business to be determined with certainty, the place where essential decisions concerning the general management of the business are taken will take precedence.[154] However, the mere presence of a postal address may not be taken to be the place of establishment of a business of a taxable person.[155]

17.11.4   Relevant business person: fixed establishment

The EU Implementing Regulation provides[156] that in the context of the place of supply rules for services to a taxable person, a 'fixed establishment' means any establishment, other than the place of establishment of a business (referred to above), characterised by a sufficient degree of permanence and a suitable structure in terms of human and technical resources to enable it to receive and use the services

---

[152] EU Implementing Regulation, Art 10(1).

[153] EU Implementing Regulation, Art 10(2).

[154] EU Implementing Regulation, Art 10(2).

[155] EU Implementing Regulation, Art 10(3). For UK VAT purposes and in reference to ECJ case-law (*Planzer Luxembourg Sarl* (Case C-73/06) OJ 2007 C199/10), HMRC states that the: 'determination of a company's place of business requires a series of factors to be taken into consideration, foremost amongst which are its registered office, the place of its central administration, the place where its directors meet and the place, usually identical, where the general policy of that company is determined. Other factors, such as the place of residence of the main directors, the place where general meetings are held, the place where administrative and accounting documents are kept, and the place where the company's financial, and particularly banking, transactions mainly take place, may also need to be taken into account. This fits in with our long held interpretation of business establishment as meaning the principal place of business of a supplier, being a single place which is usually the head office, headquarters, or "seat" of the business from which the business is run.' See HMRC *Place of Supply Services Manual* page VATPOSS04400, at www.hmrc.gov.uk.

[156] EU Implementing Regulation, Art 11. See also the ECJ's decision in *Gunter Berkholz* (Case C-168/84) [1985] ECR 2251, ECJ. Useful guidance in relation to UK VAT principles on fixed establishments is further provided by HMRC in its staff VAT manual, 'Place of Supply of Services', at www.hmrc.gov.uk/manuals/vatpossmanual/index.htm.

supplied to it for its own needs. Based on EU case-law, a fixed establishment can also include a branch or agency provided it satisfies the rules to be regarded as such an establishment.[157]

In the context of e-commerce, a website itself should not constitute a fixed establishment as it does not give rise to any physical property or presence. However, could a server constitute a 'fixed establishment'? This particular issue is discussed further in Chapter 22, at **22.5.2**. In the UK, HMRC's manuals have expressly stated that 'the mere presence of a server does not constitute either a business/fixed establishment or a usual place of residence'.[158] It may, however, be the case that personnel need to be employed to carry out occasional, non-remote maintenance of the server, for example, in relation to a data centre or hosting facility, in which case there may be a possibility of creating a 'fixed establishment' because there will then be more than just 'facilities' (the UK data centre) in the UK for conducting its business. The question here would depend on whether the presence of, for example, programming employees in the UK is 'necessary'[159] for the business carried on through the UK server/data centre. The resources 'necessary' would depend on the type of services provided through the UK data centre. It is not, however, necessary for all human and technical resources to be employed by the business itself, for

---

[157]   See eg the ECJ case of *DFDS A/S* (Case C-260/95) OJ 1997 ECR I-1005. As stated by HMRC in its *Place of Supply of Services Manual* in reference in the *DFDS A/S* case (at VATPOSS04700, see www.hmrc.gov.uk); 'the key test for agency, so far as the place of belonging rules are concerned, is one of independence. An agency cannot operate independently of its principal. In deciding independence, what matters is the reality, function and substance, and not any mere label or legal form. One should therefore have particular regard for the actual arrangements which exist between the prima facie agency and its principal, rather than any mere wording in contracts. Where there is no independence, agencies may include: a subsidiary acting for its parent principal; a company acting for its associated principal; and a company acting for an unrelated principal. A non-UK company can operate through a branch or agency as either a supplier or a recipient of services. Any charge for its services made by a branch or agency in the UK to its non-UK parent or principal is itself regarded as supplied in the UK, since such services are used most directly at the UK establishment created by the agency itself.'

[158]   The quotation is from the old Customs & Excise Manual V1-37 *Internet Selling Control Note*. However, there is similar discussion at www.hmrc.gov.uk/manuals/international/INTM266100.htm, in the International manual.

[159]   In one UK VAT Tribunal case (*RAL (Channel Islands) Ltd v The Commissioners of Customs and Excise* (2002) VAT Decision 17914), it was held that amusement arcade machines from which the taxpayer (a Channel Islands company) provided gaming services to customers through the machines were fixed establishments, as there were staff employed on a permanent basis to perform a number of tasks essential to the gaming machine supplies. This case in particular has indicated that the activity by staff of regularly maintaining a machine could constitute an essential and necessary technical resource. The tribunal also held, however, that it did not consider that all inputs (ie costs) are 'resources necessary for the provision' of gaming services to customers. For example, refreshments and advertising were inducements to play the games rather than resources necessary for playing. This case was referred to the ECJ posing a number of questions on place of supply and it was eventually concluded that the supplies were of entertainment so that the place of supply of the gaming services was where performed, and not under the rules concerning the fixed establishment.

example, they can be outsourced from third parties, and there is no prescribed way in which the minimum permanent presence and resources are provided, the concept being economic rather than legal.

17.11.5 Non-business person

Under VATA 1994, a person who is not a relevant business person is treated as belonging in the country in which the person's usual place of residence is located.[160] As mentioned above, the 'usual place of residence' for a body corporate is treated as being the place where it is legally constituted.[161] In the case of an individual receiving supplies in a private capacity, the individual's 'usual place of residence' will typically be where the individual is resident for tax purposes, namely where they have set up their family home and are in full time employment. However, again it is necessary to construe VATA 1994 in accordance with the EU Implementing Regulation, which provides that the place where a natural person 'usually resides', whether or not a taxable person, is the place where that natural person usually lives as a result of personal and occupational ties.[162] Where the occupational ties are in a country different from that of the personal ties, or where no occupational ties exist, the place of usual residence is determined by personal ties that show close links between the natural person and the place where he is living.[163]

17.11.6 Determining the status of the customer: whether a taxable person

Under the EU Implementing Regulation, a supplier may regard a customer established within the EU as a taxable person (subject to any information to the contrary):[164]

(a) where the customer has communicated his individual VAT identification number to him, and the supplier obtains confirmation of the validity of that identification number and of the associated name and address;

(b) where the customer has not yet received an individual VAT identification number, but informs the supplier that he has applied for it and the supplier obtains any other proof which demonstrates that the customer is a taxable person or a non-taxable legal person required to be identified for VAT purposes and carries out a reasonable level of verification of the accuracy of the information provided by the customer, by normal commercial security measures such as those relating to identity or payment checks.

---

[160] VATA 1994, s 9(5). See also HMRC Notice 741, para 3.5 and examples at 3.5.1.
[161] VATA 1994, s 9(6).
[162] Implementing Regulation, Art 13.
[163] Implementing Regulation, Art 13.
[164] Implementing Regulation, Art 18(1).

Under the EU Implementing Regulation, a supplier may regard a customer established within the EU as a non-taxable person (subject to any information to the contrary) when he can demonstrate that the customer has not communicated his individual VAT identification number to him.[165]

A supplier may regard a customer established[166] outside the EU as a taxable person (again, subject to any information to the contrary):

(a) if he obtains from the customer a certificate issued by the customer's competent tax authorities as confirmation that the customer is engaged in economic activities in order to enable him to obtain a refund of VAT under Council Directive 86/560/EEC (arrangements for the refund of value added tax to taxable persons not established in Community territory);

(b) where the customer does not possess that certificate, if the supplier has the VAT number, or a similar number attributed to the customer by the country of establishment and used to identify businesses or any other proof which demonstrates that the customer is a taxable person, and if the supplier carries out a reasonable level of verification of the accuracy of the information provided by the customer, by normal commercial security measures such as those relating to identity or payment checks.

17.11.7 Taxable person located in multiple countries with a fixed establishment: determining location of the supply

The following EU VAT principles[167] apply to determine in which country a supply is taxable where a taxable person is established in more than one country:[168]

---

[165] Implementing Regulation, Art 18(2).

[166] Implementing Regulation, Art 18(3).

[167] For UK VAT purposes, and as noted in note 146 above, when a supplier has establishments in different countries, the place of belonging under VATA 1994 is determined by reference to the establishment 'most directly concerned' with the supply. HMRC acknowledges in its VAT manual, 'Place of supply of services' (at www.hmrc.gov.uk/manuals/vatpossmanual/VATPOSS05100.htm) that the 'most directly concerned' test is not expressly provided for in EU VAT law, but it considers that the case of *DFDS A/S* (Case C-260/95) [1997] ECR I-1005, confirmed its view that it is consistent with the purpose of VAT Directive. HMRC also states: 'In the case of Gunter Berkholz ECJ 168/84 the ECJ considered the meaning of the equivalent terms in the Sixth Directive – the place where the supplier has established his business or has a fixed establishment from which the service is supplied. The trader in this case operated gaming machines on ferry boats plying between Germany and Denmark, and had their main place of business at an office in Hamburg. The machines were maintained intermittently on the ships by their staff but there were no permanent staff on board. The appellant argued that supplies were made on the ferry boats as a fixed establishment. The Court stated that the purpose of Art 9 of the Sixth Directive [now Arts 44 and 44 of the VAT Directive] was to avoid conflicts of jurisdiction between

- the supply is taxable in the country where that taxable person has established his business (ie the head office is the preferred establishment, unless that leads to an inappropriate or irrational result for tax purposes);

- where the service is provided to a fixed establishment of the taxable person located in a place other than that where the customer has established his business, that supply is taxable at the place of the fixed establishment receiving that service and using it for its own needs;

- where the taxable person does not have a business establishment or a fixed establishment, the supply is taxable at his permanent address or usual residence.

The following EU VAT principles[169] are applied to determine the identity of the fixed establishment to which a service is supplied:[170]

- the supplier is required to examine the nature and use of the service provided to the taxable person;

Member States which might result in double taxation or non-taxation. Thus a supplier belonged where the business was established unless that led to an irrational result for tax purposes, or created conflict with another Member State. It was possible in principle for a fixed establishment to exist on a ship, but only if that establishment was of a certain minimum size, with both the human and technical resources necessary for the provision of the services permanently present there, and if it was not appropriate to regard the services as supplied where the supplier had its main business establishment. Neither of these conditions had been fulfilled in this case, so the services were supplied at Berkholz's main office in Hamburg. In DFDS A/S (ECJ C-260/95), a case concerning the Tour Operators' Margin Scheme and the interpretation of the relevant legal provisions on establishment in what was Art 26 of then Sixth Directive and Art 5 of the Value Added Tax (Tour Operators) Order 1987, SI 1987/1806, the Court concluded that where services have been provided by a tour operator from a fixed establishment in a Member State other than that where the business is established, the services are taxable in the Member State where that fixed establishment is located. Together, these two cases provide authority for approaching the test as follows: the businesses' headquarters or main seat is a primary point of reference; another establishment only becomes relevant if reference to the headquarters of the business produces an inappropriate or irrational result for tax purposes or creates conflict with another Member State; alternative establishments may only be considered if they are of a certain minimum size and both the human and technical resources necessary for the provision of the particular services are permanently present; and the actual economic situation, (economic substance and reality as opposed to the contractual provisions) can be taken into account in determining the point of reference for tax purposes. There is some further discussion on the above cases in Chapter 22.

[168] Implementing Regulation, Art 21.

[169] For UK VAT principles/purposes, again see further at HMRC's Place of supply of services VAT manual, in particular at www.hmrc.gov.uk/manuals/vatpossmanual/VATPOSS05000.htm, 'Place of supply of services: Establishment making or receiving the supply. See also HMRC Notice 741A (January 2010), in particular at paras 3.6 and 3.7 and section 19, considered in Chapter 22, at Table 22.1 (and **22.5.3**).

[170] Implementing Regulation, Art 22.

- where the nature and use of the service provided do not enable the supplier to identify the fixed establishment to which the service is provided, the supplier, in identifying that fixed establishment, is required to pay particular attention to whether:

  - the contract;
  - the order form; and
  - the VAT identification number attributed by the Member State of the customer and communicated to the supplier by the customer,

  identify the fixed establishment as the customer of the service, and whether the fixed establishment is the entity paying for the service.

Where the customer's fixed establishment to which the service is provided cannot be determined in accordance with the above principles or where services are supplied to a taxable person under a contract covering one or more services used in an unidentifiable and non-quantifiable manner (eg under a global contract whereby a business could enter into a contract for a single supply of consultancy services to analyse the global set-up and e-commerce practices at the head office and overseas branches), the supplier is entitled to consider that the services have been supplied at the place where the customer has established its business.[171] HMRC should regard services under a global contract with a clear direct benefit to the business as a whole, including a number of establishments, as supplied to the main business establishment. However, this approach should be distinguished from a global framework agreement which sets the terms for a number of individual supplies. In the UK, HMRC considers that it is important to look at those individual transactions which, as separate supplies, will have separate VAT consequences. In this respect, HMRC's example is that of a head office customer which enters into a framework agreement with a supplier pursuant to which its individual branches would draw up and purchase work from local branches of the supplier. According to HMRC, the supplier's services will be viewed as supplied to the customer's branches even if the head office dictates the terms and receives an indirect benefit. HMRC's general approach in relation to multiple fixed establishments is considered in more detail in Chapter 22, at **22.5.3**.

There are also further EU VAT rules on who accounts for VAT where a taxable person has a fixed establishment. These are that where a taxable person (the supplier) has a fixed establishment in the territory of a Member State where VAT is due, the supplier is treated as a taxable person who is not established within that Member State when it makes a taxable supply in that Member State and any such fixed establishment of the supplier 'does not intervene in that supply'.[172] In other words, VAT is

---

[171] Implementing Regulation, Art 22.
[172] VAT Directive, Art 192a. In the application of this Article, a fixed establishment of a taxable person will only be taken into consideration when it is characterised by a

not due from a supplier's fixed establishment located within the same Member State as its customer, unless that establishment intervenes in the supply. However, where a taxable person has established its place of business within the territory of the Member State where the VAT is due, this does not apply, irrespective of whether or not that place of business intervenes in the supply of goods or services which are made in that Member State.[173]

17.12   REVERSE CHARGE

Where services are received by a relevant business person in the UK from a supplier who belongs outside the UK, the identity of the person who is required to account for VAT is altered for certain services.[174] Normally, it is the supplier who is required to account for any VAT due on the supply, but this is reversed by virtue of the reverse charge procedure, and accordingly, it will be the business recipient who must account for the VAT due. This procedure is also known as the tax shift. A UK business recipient will usually incur the costs of a supply of services from abroad for its own business purposes, so that it can make onward supplies to its consumers. VAT will be imposed on these supplies to the end consumer, if they are taxable supplies. The reverse charge is therefore a simplification measure designed to avoid overseas suppliers needing to register for VAT purposes in a Member State when it is possible for the customer (eg a VAT-registered customer) to account for the VAT on a supply. The procedure does not apply to supplies of services where both the supplier and recipient belong in the UK. In addition, the procedure currently only applies insofar as a customer receives the supply for a business purpose (and evidence such as the customer's VAT registration number would need to be obtained by the supplier too, although it extends to organisations

---

sufficient degree of permanence and a suitable structure in terms of human and technical resources to enable it to make the supply of goods or services in which it intervenes: EU Implementing Regulation, Art 53(1). Where a taxable person has a fixed establishment within the territory of the EU where the VAT is due, that establishment shall be considered as not intervening in the supply of goods or services, unless the technical and human resources of that fixed establishment are used by that person for transactions inherent in the fulfilment of the taxable supply of those goods or services made within that Member State, before or during this fulfilment: Art 53(2). Where the resources of the fixed establishment are only used for administrative support tasks such as accounting, invoicing and collection of debt-claims, they shall not be regarded as being used for the fulfilment of the supply of goods or services: Art 53(2). However, if an invoice is issued under the VAT identification number attributed by the Member State of the fixed establishment, that fixed establishment shall be regarded as having intervened in the supply of goods or services made in that Member State unless there is proof to the contrary: Art 53(2). In the UK, HMRC states that the UK position is that the establishment making the supply is the one most closely connected to it. Therefore, minimal involvement in making the supply will not be viewed as 'intervening' for UK VAT purposes. HMRC believes that the overall UK legislation (which does not explicitly cover 'intervening'), together with interpretation, achieves the right result.

173   Implementing Regulation, Art 54.
174   VATA 1994, s 8. See further at para 18 of HMRC's Notice 741A *Place of Supply of Services* (January 2010).

involved in both business and non-business activities, even if a service is received in connection with the non-business activity).[175]

Under the reverse charge rules a relevant business person is required to account for VAT on such service supplies as if there were a supply of the services by the recipient in the UK in the course or furtherance of a business carried on by the recipient, and that supply were a taxable supply (a deemed supply).[176] This is designed to prevent distortion of trade, otherwise businesses could acquire tax-free benefits by obtaining services from abroad. Accordingly, instead of being charged VAT by the supplier, the UK business recipient would credit (increase) his VAT account with the necessary output tax as if the recipient had supplied the services in the UK for the purposes of VAT (the deemed supply), and at the same time in the same VAT return, debit (deduct) his VAT account with the input tax to which he is entitled under the normal rules if he can relate this input VAT to taxable supplies. The practical result of this is that the recipient continues to be entitled to claim credit for input tax, although input tax of the supplier cannot be attributed to the aforementioned deemed supply made by it (which would give full input tax credit), but only to the actual use to which the service was put by the recipient.[177] If the recipient can attribute the input tax to taxable supplies that he makes, he can reclaim it via his VAT returns so that the reverse charge transaction has no net cost to him. If he cannot, the effect is to make the recipient pay VAT on the supply at the applicable UK VAT rate, ie as if he had received the supply from a UK supplier instead of the non-UK supplier. This will affect businesses which are not entitled to recover VAT fully, such as partly exempt businesses, where VAT costs are only recoverable to the extent of their partial exemption recovery method (see also **17.15**).[178]

The reverse charge applies if:[179]

(a) the recipient is a relevant business person who belongs in the UK, and the place of supply of the services is inside the UK, ie under the general B2B rule: see Table 17.2 at **17.10.2**; or

---

[175] Supplies need to be received wholly for private purposes to be treated as a business-to-non-business supply – VATA 1994, s 7A(4). HMRC's examples are as follows (Notice 741A, para 18.10.1): 'A UK charity with business and non-business activities receives a supply of legal services from a French business in relation to its non-business activities (B2B general rule service). The place of supply is the UK and the UK charity must account for VAT under the reverse charge', and 'a UK business receives customised software from a USA business (B2B general rule service). The place of supply is the UK and the UK business must account for VAT under the reverse charge'.

[176] VATA 1994, s 8(1).

[177] VATA 1994, s 8(1)(b), (3).

[178] See generally HMRC's Notice 706 *Partial Exemption* (June 2011). A review of the partial exemption rules is outside the scope of this book.

[179] VATA 1994, s 8(2).

(b) the supply of the services is one to which any paragraph of Part 1 or 2 of Sch 4A to VATA 1994 applies ('relevant services': see **17.13**), the place of supply of those services is the UK and the recipient is registered as a taxable person under VATA 1994.

The value of services received in the UK from abroad is deemed to be exclusive of VAT, so the value of the transaction on which VAT must be calculated and accounted for under the reverse charge is the full value of the supply.

> *Example 17.14*
>
> Supplies are received from abroad costing £10,000. Output and input VAT on the supplies that are deemed to be made and received by the recipient is (£10,000 x 20%) = £2,000. The UK recipient has incurred VAT of £5,000 (including the input VAT attributable to the supply received from abroad) in making supplies in the course of its business. The company also receives output VAT of £5,000 on taxable supplies made to its customers. When accounting for VAT to HMRC, the company will therefore be entitled to deduct input VAT of £5,000.

The reverse charge does not apply to services of a description in VATA 1994, Sch 9 (Exemptions) – see **17.17**.

Overseas non-UK suppliers, whose customers account for VAT under the reverse charge procedure, may be able to reclaim VAT incurred in the UK on eg, purchases and services used in the UK for business purposes, where certain conditions are met.[180]

17.13   RELEVANT SERVICES

The services in respect of which the reverse charge also operates are as follows (see Table 17.2 at **17.10.2** for a summary: these are the services referred to under the general exceptions, and exceptions relating to supplies made to a relevant business person):[181]

(a) services relating to land and property;

(b) passenger transport;

(c) hiring of means of transport;

(d) restaurant and catering services, EC on-board restaurant and catering services;

---

[180] See generally HMRC Notice 723A *Refunds of VAT in the European Community for EC and non-EC businesses* (October 2011) and see HMRC Notice 741A, paras 18.9, 20.20 and 20.34.

[181] VATA 1994, s 8(2).

(e)　hiring of goods;

(f)　telecommunication and broadcasting services;

(g)　electronically supplied services; and

(h)　admission to cultural, educational and entertainment services.

17.14　TIME OF SUPPLY

When a taxable supply is made the obligation to charge VAT arises.[182] The time of supply is governed by specific rules in VATA 1994. Table 17.3 provides a summary of the principal rules.

Table 17.3: Time of supply

Type of supply	Time of supply	VATA 1994
Services		
(1)　Supply of services.	When performed.	s 6(3)
VAT invoice[183] *(goods or services)*		
(2)　Time of supply has not been established above, but a VAT invoice is issued.	Time invoice issued.	s 6(4)

---

[182]　VATA 1994, s 4(1).

[183]　A 'VAT invoice' is one which complies with VATA 1994, Sch 11, para 2A: VATA 1994, s 6(15) and VAT Regulations 1995, SI 1995/2518. In essence, a VAT invoice must give such particulars as may be prescribed of the supply, the supplier and the person supplied; and such indication as may be prescribed of whether VAT is chargeable on the supply under VATA 1994 or the law of another Member State. However, there are ongoing EU developments on VAT invoices, including on electronic invoicing, such as the adoption of Council Directive 2010/45/EU of 13 July 2010, to be applied by Member States as from 1 January 2013, amending the VAT Directive as regards the rules on invoicing to promote the uptake of e-invoicing and further simplify invoicing rules. For example, for cross-border supplies of general B2B services, and for dispatches of goods between EU businesses (see Chapter 20), a harmonised time limit for issuing invoices is being introduced, requiring an invoice to be issued by the 15th day of the month following the time of the relevant chargeable event. Broadly, the result of this is that VAT will become chargeable (from 1 January 2013) on the issue of the invoice, or on expiry of that time limit if no invoice has been issued by that time (see the proposed amendment to the VAT Directive, Art 222). A further review of these developments is outside the scope of this book but they can be reviewed / followed at: http://ec.europa.eu/taxation_customs/taxation/vat/traders/invoicing_rules/index_en.htm.

Type of supply	Time of supply	VATA 1994
(3) Supplier receives payment in respect of supply before time of supply established above.	Time payment received.	s 6(4)
(4) If within 14 days after the time identified in (1) above, the person making the supply issues a VAT invoice in respect of that supply of goods or services.	Time invoice issued.	s 6(5) An election can be made to displace this provision. A longer period may be imposed (s 6(6)).
Reverse charge services received from outside the UK		
(5) Such services (excluding those supplied for a period for a consideration the whole or part of which is determined or payable periodically or from time to time).	Treated as made when the services are performed.	Vat Regs 1995,[184] reg 82
(6) Such services that are supplied for a period for a consideration the whole or part of which is determined or payable periodically or from time to time.	Treated as separately and successively made at the end of the periods in respect of which payments are made or invoices issued, and to the extent covered by the relevant payment or invoice.	VAT Regs 1995, reg 82(4)
(7) When in the case of a service to which (5) applies, a payment is made in respect of the supply before the time specified in (5).	Treated as made at the time the payment is made.	VAT Regs 1995, reg 82(5)

---

[184] SI 1995/2518.

Type of supply	Time of supply	VATA 1994
(8) Where in the case of services to which (6) applies, and either (a) a payment is made at a time that is earlier than the end of the period to which it relates or (b) a payment is made which is not made in respect of any identified period.	Treated as made at the time the payment is made.	VAT Regs 1995, reg 82(5)
(9) Where a payment is made in respect of services in respect of which a period as described in (7) above has ended on or before that date.	Treated as made at the time the payment is made.	VAT Regs 1995, reg 82(5)
(10) Where a payment is made in respect of services and the recipient has received the benefit of on or before that date.	Treated as made at the time the payment is made.	VAT Regs 1995, reg 82(5)
(11) Where the supply of services to which (7) applies (a) commences before 1 January and continues after 31 December of any year, and during that year no invoice is issued that has effect for the purposes of (7) above and no payment is made in respect of that supply.	Services supplied during that year are treated as being supplied on the 31 December of that year to the extent that the recipient has received the benefit of them.	VAT Regs 1995, reg 82(6)
Continuous supplies of services		
(12) Where services are supplied for a period for a consideration the whole or part of which is determined or payable periodically or from time to time.	Treated as separately and successively supplied at the earlier of the following times: (a) each time that a payment in respect of the supplies is received by the supplier; or (b) each time that the supplier issues a VAT invoice relating to the supplies.	VAT Regs 1995, reg 90

Type of supply	Time of supply	VATA 1994
(13) Where separate and successive supplies of services as referred to in (12) are made under an agreement which provides for successive payments, and the supplier at or about the beginning of any period not exceeding one year, issues a VAT invoice containing the following particulars: (a) the dates on which payments under the agreement are to become due in the period; (b) the amount payable (excluding VAT) on each due date; and (c) the rate of VAT in force at the time of issue of the VAT invoice and the amount of VAT chargeable in accordance with that rate on each of such payments.	Treated as separately and successively supplied each time that a payment in respect of them becomes due or is received by the supplier, whichever is the earlier.	VAT Regs 1995, reg 90

Provision is made for the time of supply of various goods and services which are deemed to be treated as such supplies, for example, the transfer of assets that form part of a business, whether transferred for consideration or not.[185]

17.15   INPUT AND OUTPUT TAX

A taxable person is required to account for and pay UK VAT in respect of all taxable supplies made by it in the course or furtherance of business, and in respect of the acquisition of any goods from other Member States.[186] A taxable supply is a supply that is not an exempt supply.[187] In accounting for VAT to the tax authorities, a taxable person is entitled to credit for the VAT incurred by it (known as 'input tax') upon supplies attributable to enable the taxable person to make supplies to its own customers. The input tax is credited against the VAT charged and received

---

[185]   See generally VATA 1994, s 8(11)–(14) and at **17.7.2**. See also the Value Added Tax Regulations 1995, SI 1995/2518, Part XI.

[186]   VATA 1994, s 25(1). The VAT charge in relation to the acquisition of goods from another Member State is discussed in Chapter 18.

[187]   VATA 1994, s 4(2). The nature of exempt supplies is considered below.

by the taxable person on the onward supplies made to its customers (known as 'output tax').[188] Input tax is defined under VATA 1994 as VAT incurred on the supply of any goods or services used or to be used for the purpose of any business carried on by a taxable person.[189] Accordingly, the nature of the input tax which can be recovered by a taxable person is VAT incurred which is related to:[190]

- taxable supplies;

- supplies made outside the UK which would be taxable if they were made in the UK; or

- supplies of exempt insurance services and certain exempt financial services (or supplies made outside the UK which would have been such exempt supplies if they had been made in the UK), where such supplies: (a) are made to a person who belongs outside the EU, or (b) are directly linked to the export of goods to a place outside the EU, or (c) consist of the making of arrangements for such supplies.

In contrast, output tax means VAT on supplies or acquisitions made by a taxable person.[191]

Example 17.15

> Internet Services Ltd provides internet access to its subscribers. In the appropriate accounting period for VAT purposes, it is paid subscriptions totalling £100,000. The aggregate VAT charged and collected from subscribers is £20,000. The company incurs VAT in the course of providing internet access to its subscribers of £5,000. The amount payable to HMRC is therefore £15,000 (£20,000 minus £5,000).

Where the input tax exceeds the amount of output tax the taxable person is entitled to a refund of the excess.[192] This situation may arise due to the fact that the taxable person receives no VAT because supplies to customers are zero-rated, or due to the taxable person having incurred excessive input tax costs.

The ECJ has emphasised that the deduction mechanism for input VAT is 'intended to relieve the trader entirely of the burden of the VAT payable or paid in the course of all his economic activities'.[193] The right to deduct and recover input VAT is a fundamental principle underlying the common system of VAT, and, in principle, may not be limited with the consequence

---

[188] VATA 1994, s 25(2).

[189] VATA 1994, s 24(1). See also s 26.

[190] VATA 1994, s 24(1).

[191] VATA 1994, s 24(2).

[192] VATA 1994, s 25(3).

[193] See *Revenue and Customs Commissioners v RBS Deutschland Holdings GmbH* (Case C-277/09) [2010] All ER (D) 273 (Dec) at para 38 of the ECJ's judgment.

that a taxable person is entitled to deduct VAT imposed on goods and services acquired for taxable activities.[194] However, it is also fundamental to the deduction of input VAT that the cost has been incurred for the purposes of a business, and specifically a business of the taxpayer concerned.

Accordingly, the recovery of input VAT is available only to the extent that it relates to taxable supplies, or to certain other supplies specified in the VAT regulations. Some businesses (such as banks) make exempt supplies (see 17.17) that are not taxable, but may also make taxable supplies. In these circumstances, such a business is subject to partial exemption, and there are particular arrangements for recovering the correct amount of input VAT attributable to the taxable supplies of such a business.[195]

There are also some forms of input VAT which are blocked from recovery, such as input VAT on motor cars, which is covered by the Value Added Tax (Input Tax) Order 1992.[196] This broadly denies relief for all VAT on the purchase, but not the leasing, of a car; so as to block 100% of the VAT paid on purchased cars, and 50% of the input VAT on all cars leased . A review of the scope of the input VAT block provisions is beyond the scope of this book.

Furthermore, the recovery of input VAT may also require adjustment under what is known as the 'capital goods scheme'. Adjustments are made under the scheme to reflect taxable use of capital items during a certain 'adjustment period', as it is possible for items to be used for wholly exempt purposes and then for taxable purposes during ownership. For example, a property which is let out as an exempt supply and then converted into a taxable supply by the supplier exercising an option to tax. If, during such adjustment period, there is any change in the proportion of taxable use of the item, including a future sale of the item, then an adjustment is made to the input VAT recovery amount as initially recovered (if any) to reflect this change. For the scheme to apply a person does not have to be carrying on partly exempt or non-business activities for it to be relevant. The scheme is of no application however where assets (ie, stock) are purchased by a taxable person for the purposes of resale. Under UK law, the capital goods scheme is governed by Part XV of the Value Added Tax Regulations 1995 (SI 1995/2518).[197] The scheme does

[194] See generally *Abbey National v Customs & Excise Commissioners* [2001] ECR I-1361, para 24; *Investrand v Staatssecretaris van Financiën* [2007] ECR I-1315, para 22; and *NCC Construction Danmark A/S v Skatteministeriet* [2009] ECR I-10567, para 27. The right of VAT recovery may, however, be subject to the ECJ's 'abuse of rights' doctrine – referred to very briefly above at note 129 above – as transposed into national VAT regimes, and see also the *RBS* case mentioned above at note 193 above.

[195] As mentioned in note 178 above, a review of the partial exemption rules is beyond the scope of this book. Again, see generally HMRC Notice *706 Partial Exemption* (June 2011).

[196] SI 1992/3222.

[197] The Regulations in their current form apply to input VAT incurred by a taxable person

not apply to all capital assets, only to (as at 2011): (1) computers and individual items of computer equipment of a value of not less than £50,000 (the reference to computer means a single item of equipment and not a complete network);[198] (2) an aircraft, a ship, boat or other vessel of a value of not less than £50,000; and (3) land; (4) buildings (or parts of a building); and (5) civil engineering works (or part of a civil engineering work) (eg, works on roads, bridges, installation of pipes for connection to mains services), each, in the case of (3), (4) and (5), with a value of not less than £250,000. A review of the application of the capital goods scheme is beyond the scope of this book.[199]

17.16   ZERO-RATED SUPPLIES

Where a supply is classified as zero-rated for the purposes of VAT, it is a taxable supply, but the rate of VAT is set at zero, as opposed to the standard rate of 20% (2011).[200] Zero-rated supplies in the UK are specified in Sch 8 to VATA 1994.[201] A summary of relevant zero-rated supplies for the purposes of e-commerce activities is set out below.[202] This includes some of the specific items referred to in the zero-rating provisions; but others, which are less likely to be relevant to e-commerce, are either omitted or only the specific group is referred to.

Group 1 – Food

(1)   Food of a kind used for human consumption.

(2)   Animal feeding stuffs.

(3)   Seeds or other means of propagation of plants comprised in (1) or (2) above.

(4)   Live animals of a kind generally used as, or yielding or producing, food for human consumption.

Excepted items:

---

on goods imported or acquired by, or goods or services supplied to, that taxable person on or after 1 January 2011. Transitional rules apply to expenditure incurred before this date.

[198]   HMRC has stated that computer software and computerised equipment such as a phone exchange are not included (HMRC Notice 706/2 *Capital Goods Scheme* (October 2011), para 3.1).

[199]   See generally HMRC Notice 706/2 *Capital Goods Scheme* (October 2011).

[200]   VATA 1994, s 30(1).

[201]   VATA 1994, s 30(2).

[202]   The scope of any relief or exemption will be strictly construed, and it is particularly important to take appropriate advice as to whether zero-rating or an exemption applies in VATA 1994, Sch 8 or 9.

(1)   Ice cream, ice cream lollies, frozen yoghurt, water ices and similar frozen products, and prepared mixes and powders for making such products.

(2)   Confectionery, not including cakes or biscuits other than biscuits wholly or partly covered with chocolate or some other product similar in taste and appearance.

(3)   Beverages chargeable with any duty of excise specifically charged on spirits, beer, wine or made-wine and preparations thereof.

(4)   Other beverages (including fruit juices and bottled waters) and syrups, concentrates, essences, powders, crystal or other products for the preparation of beverages.

(5)   Any of the following when packaged for human consumption without further preparation, namely potato crisps, potato sticks, potato puffs, and similar products made from potato, or from potato flour, or from potato starch, and savoury food products obtained by the swelling of cereals or cereal products, and salted or roasted nuts other than nuts in shell.

(6)   Pet foods, canned, packaged or prepared; packaged foods (not being pet foods) for birds other than poultry or game, and biscuits and meal for cats and dogs.

...

(11) Goods described in items (1), (2) and (3) of the general items which are canned, bottled, packaged or prepared for use in the domestic brewing of any beer, domestic making of any cider or perry, domestic production of any wine or made-wine.

Items overriding the exceptions:

(1)   Yoghurt unsuitable for immediate consumption when frozen.

(2)   Drained cherries.

(3)   Candied peels.

(4)   Tea, mate, herbal teas and similar products, and preparations and extracts thereof.

(5)   Cocoa, coffee and chicory and other toasted coffee substitutes, and preparations and extracts thereof.

(6)   Milk and preparations and extracts thereof.

...

(11) Preparations and extracts of meat, yeast or egg.

Group 3 – Books, etc

(1) Books, booklets, brochures, pamphlets and leaflets.

(2) Newspapers, journals and periodicals.

(3) Children's picture books and paining books.

(4) Music (printed, duplicated or manuscript).

(5) Maps, charts and topographical plans.

(6) Covers, cases and other articles supplied with items (1) to (5) and not separately accounted for.

Group 4 – Talking books for the blind and handicapped

Group 7 – International services

(1) The supply of services of work carried out on goods which, for that purpose, have been obtained or acquired in, or imported into, any of the Member States and which are intended to be, and in fact are, subsequently exported to a place outside the Member States: (a) by or on behalf of the supplier; or (b) where the recipient of the services belongs in a place outside the Member States, by or on behalf of the recipient.

(2) The supply of services consisting of the making of arrangements for: (a) the export of any goods to a place outside the Member States; (b) a supply of services of the description specified in item (1) of this group; or (c) any supply of services which is made outside the Member States.

Group 8 – Transport

(1) The supply, repair or maintenance of a qualifying ship or the modification or conversion of any such ship provided that when so modified or converted it will remain a qualifying ship.

(2) The supply, repair or maintenance of a qualifying aircraft or the modification or conversion of any such aircraft provided that when so modified or converted it will remain a qualifying aircraft.

(2A)   The supply of parts and equipment, of a kind ordinarily installed or incorporated in, and to be installed, or incorporated in:

    (a)   the propulsion, navigation or communication systems; or
    (b)   the general structure,
of a qualifying ship or, as the case may be, aircraft.

(2B)   The supply of life jackets, life rafts, smoke hoods and similar safety equipment for use in a qualifying ship or, as the case may be, aircraft
    [...]

(4)   Transport of passengers:

    (a)   in any vehicle, ship or aircraft designed or adapted to carry not less than 10 passengers;
    (b)   by a universal service provider;
    (c)   on any scheduled flight; or
    (d)   from a place within to a place outside the UK or vice versa, to the extent that those services are supplied in the UK.

(5)   The transport of goods from a place within to a place outside the Member States or vice versa, to the extent that those services are supplied within the UK.

(6)   Any services provided for:

    (a)   the handling of ships or aircraft in a port, customs and excise airport or outside the United Kingdom; or
    (b)   the handling or storage:

        (i)   in a port;
        (ii)   on land adjacent to a port;
        (iii) in a customs and excise airport; or
        (iv)   in a transit shed,
    of goods carried in a ship or aircraft.

(6A)   Air navigation services.

(7)   Pilotage services.

(8)   Salvage or towage services.

(9)   Any services supplied for or in connection with the surveying of any ship or aircraft or the classification of any ship or aircraft for the purposes of any register.

(10) The making of arrangements for:

(a) the supply of, or of space in, any ship or aircraft;
(b) the supply of any service included in items 1 and 2, 3 to 9 and 11; or
(c) the supply of any goods of a description falling within items 2A or 2B, or paragraph (d) of item 3.

(11) The supply:

(a) of services consisting of:

(i) the handling or storage of goods at, or their transport to or from, a place at which they are to be exported to or have been imported from a place outside the Member States; or
(ii) the handling or storage of such goods in connection with such transport; or

(b) to a person who receives the supply for the purpose of a business carried on by him and who belongs outside the UK, of services of a description specified in paragraph (a) of item 6, item 6A, item 9 or paragraph (a) of item 10 of this group.

(12) The supply of a designated travel service to be enjoyed outside the EC, to the extent to which the supply is so enjoyed.

(13) Intra-Community transport services supplied in connection with the transport of goods to or from the Azores or Madeira or between those places, to the extent that the services are treated as supplied in the United Kingdom.

Notes:

(A1) In this group:

(a) a 'qualifying ship' is any ship of a gross tonnage of not less than 15 tons which is neither designed nor adapted for use for recreation or pleasure; and
(b) a 'qualifying aircraft' is any aircraft which:

(i) is used by an airline operating for reward chiefly on international routes; or
(ii) is used by a State institution and meets the condition in Note (B1).

(B1) The condition is that the aircraft:

(a) is of a weight of not less than 8,000 kg; and
(b) is neither designed nor adapted for use for recreation or pleasure.

(C1)   In Note (A1)(b):

'airline' means an undertaking which provides services for the carriage by air of passengers or cargo (or both);

'State institution' has the same meaning as in Part B of Annex X to Council Directive 2006/112/EC on the common system of value added tax (transactions which Member States may continue to exempt).

(1)   In items 1 and 2 the supply of a qualifying ship or, as the case may be, aircraft includes the supply of services under a charter of that ship or aircraft except where the services supplied under such a charter consist wholly of any one or more of the following:

(a)   transport of passengers;
(b)   accommodation;
(c)   entertainment;
(d)   education,
being services wholly performed in the UK.

(2)   Items 1, 2, 2A, 2B and 3 include the letting on hire of the goods specified in the items.

(4A)   Item 4 does not include the transport of passengers:

(a)   in any vehicle to, from or within:

(i)   a place of entertainment, recreation or amusement; or
(ii)   a place of cultural, scientific, historical or similar interest, by the person, or a person connected with him, who supplies a right of admission to, or a right to use facilities at, such a place;
(b)   in any motor vehicle between a car park (or land adjacent thereto) and an airport passenger terminal (or land adjacent thereto) by the person, or a person connected with him, who supplies facilities for the parking of vehicles in that car park; or
(c)   in an aircraft where the flight is advertised or held out to be for the purpose of:

(i)   providing entertainment, recreation or amusement; or
(ii)   the experience of flying, or the experience of flying in that particular aircraft,
and not primarily for the purpose of transporting passengers from one place to another.

(4C)   In Note (4A)(b) 'motor vehicle' means a mechanically propelled vehicle intended or adapted for use on the roads.

(4D)   Item 4(a) includes the transport of passengers in a vehicle:

    (a)   which is designed, or substantially and permanently adapted, for the safe carriage of a person in a wheelchair or two or more such persons; and

    (b)   which, if it were not so designed or adapted, would be capable of carrying no less than 10 persons.

(4E)   'Universal service provider' means a person who provides a universal postal service (within the meaning of the Postal Services Act 2000), or part of such a service, in the UK.

(5)   Item 6 does not include the letting on hire of goods.

(7)   Except for the purposes of item 11, paragraph (a) of item 6, item 6A, item 9 and paragraph (a) of item 10 only include supplies of services where the ships or aircraft referred to in those paragraphs are qualifying ships or, as the case may be, aircraft.

(8)   'Designated travel service' has the same meaning as in the Value Added Tax (Tour Operators) Order 1987.[203]

(9)   'Intra-Community transport services' means:

    (a)   the intra-Community transport of goods within the meaning of the Value Added Tax (Place of Supply of Services) Order 1992;[204]

    (b)   ancillary transport services within the meaning of the Value Added Tax (Place of Supply of Services) Order 1992 which are provided in connection with the intra-Community transport of goods; or

    (c)   the making of arrangements for the supply by or to another person of a supply within (a) or (b) above or any other activity which is intended to facilitate the making of such a supply,

and, for the purpose of this Note only, the Azores and Madeira shall each be treated as a separate Member State.

Group 12 – Drugs, medicines, aids for the handicapped etc

Group 13 – Imports, exports etc

(1)   The supply before the delivery of an entry (within the meaning of reg 5 of the Customs Controls on Importation of Goods

---

[203]   SI 1987/1806.
[204]   SI 1992/3121.

Regulations 1991[205]) under an agreement requiring the purchaser to make such entry of goods imported from a place outside the Member States.

[...]

(3)   The supply to an overseas authority, overseas body or overseas trader of jigs, patterns, templates, dies, punches and similar machine tools used in the UK solely for the manufacture of goods for export to places outside the Member States.

Group 16 – Clothing and footwear

(1)   Articles designed as clothing or footwear for young children and not suitable for older persons.

(2)   The supply to a person for use otherwise than by employees of his of protective boots and helmets for industrial use.

(3)   Protective helmets for wear by a person driving or riding a motor bicycle or riding a pedal cycle.

Notes:

(1)   'Clothing' includes hats and other headgear.

(2)   Item 1 does not include articles of clothing made wholly or partly of fur skin, except:

    (a)   headgear;
    (b)   gloves;
    (c)   buttons, belts and buckles;
    (d)   any garment merely trimmed with fur skin unless the trimming has an area greater than one-fifth of the area of the outside material or, in the case of a new garment, represents a cost to the manufacturer greater than the cost to him of the other components.

(3)   'Fur skin' means any skin with fur, hair or wool attached except:

(a)   rabbit skin;

(b)   woolled sheep or lamb skin; and

(c)   the skin, if neither tanned nor dressed, of bovine cattle (including buffalo), equine animals, goats or kids (other than Yemen, Mongolian and Tibetan goats or kids), swine (including peccary), chamois, gazelles, deer or dogs.

---

[205] SI 1991/2724.

17.17 EXEMPT SUPPLIES

Where a supply is classified as exempt, no VAT is charged on the supply.[206] As already highlighted in the chapter, VAT is only charged on a taxable supply, which does not include an exempt supply. Accordingly, there is no right to deduct VAT that has been incurred on supplies purchased by a taxable person for the purposes of making its own exempt supplies. Exempt supplies in the UK are specified in Sch 9 to VATA 1994.[207] A summary of relevant supplies classified as exempt for the purposes of e-commerce activities is set out below. This includes some of the specific items referred to in the exemption provisions, but others which are less likely to be relevant to e-commerce are either omitted or only the specific group is referred to below.

Group 2 – Insurance

(1)   Insurance transactions and reinsurance transactions.

(4)   The provision by an insurance broker or insurance agent of any of the services of an insurance intermediary in a case in which those services:

(a)   are related (whether or not a contract of insurance or reinsurance is finally concluded) to an insurance transaction or a reinsurance transaction; and

(b)   are provided by that broker or agent in the course of his acting in an intermediary capacity.

Group 4 – Betting, gaming and lotteries

(1)   The provision of facilities for the placing of bets or for the playing of any games of chance for a prize.

(2)   The granting of a right to take part in a lottery.

Item 1 within Group 4 does not include, among other things, the provision of anything which is a gaming machine for the purposes of s 23 of VATA 1994.[208]

Group 5 – Finance

(1)   The issue, transfer or receipt of, or any dealing with money, any security for money or any note or order for the payment of money.

---

[206]   VATA 1994, s 4(2).

[207]   VATA 1994, s 31(1).

[208]   VATA 1994, Sch 9, Group 4, Note (1)(d). Section 23(4) defines a 'gaming machine' as a 'machine which is designed or adapted for use by individuals to gamble (whether or not it can also be used for other purposes)'.

(2)   The making or any advance or the granting of any credit.

(3)   The provision of the facility of instalment credit finance in a hire-purchase, conditional sale or credit sale agreement for which facility a separate charge is made and disclosed to the recipient of the supply of goods.

(5)   The provision of intermediary services in relation to any transaction comprised in item 1, 2, 3 … (whether or not any such transaction is finally concluded by a person acting in an intermediary capacity).

(6)   The issue, transfer or receipt of, or any dealing with, any security or secondary security being:

   (a)   shares, stocks, bonds, notes (other than promissory notes), debentures, debenture stock or shares in an oil royalty;
   (b)   any document relating to money, in any currency, which has been deposited with the issuer or some other person, being a document which recognises an obligation to pay a stated amount to bearer or to order, with or without interest, and being a document by the delivery of which, with or without endorsement, the right to receive that stated amount, with or without interest, is transferable;
   (c)   any bill, note or other obligation of the Treasury or of a government in any part of the world, being a document by the delivery of which, with or without endorsement, title is transferable, and not being an obligation which is or has been legal tender in any part of the world;
   (d)   any letter of allotment or rights, any warrant conferring an option to acquire a security included in this item, any renounceable or scrip certificates, rights coupons, coupons representing dividends or interest on such a security, bond mandates or other documents conferring or containing evidence of title to or rights in respect of such a security; or
   (e)   units or other documents conferring rights under any trust established for the purpose, or having the effect of providing, for persons having funds available for investment, facilities for the participation by them as beneficiaries under the trust, in any profits or income arising from the acquisition, holding, management or disposal of any property whatsoever.

(8)   The operation of any current, deposit or savings account.

Group 6 – Education

(1)   The provision by an eligible body of:

   (a)   education;

(b)   research supplied to an eligible body;

(c)   vocational training.

(2)   The supply of private tuition, in a subject ordinarily taught in a school or university, by an individual teacher acting independently of an employer.

...

(4)   The supply of any goods or services (other than examination services) which are closely related to a supply of a description falling within item 1 (the principal supply) by or to the eligible body making the principal supply provided:

(a)   the goods or services are for the direct use of the pupil, student or trainee (as the case may be) receiving the principal supply; and

(b)   where the supply is to the eligible body making the principal supply, it is made by another eligible body.

...

(6)   Provision of facilities by:

(a)   a youth club or an association of youth clubs to its members; or

(b)   an association of youth clubs to members of a youth club which is a member of that association.

A club is a youth club under VATA 1994 if, among other things, it is established to promote the social, physical, educational or spiritual development of its members.

17.18   OVERSEAS TRADERS SUPPLYING UK NON-TAXABLE PERSONS: REGISTERING FOR VAT

Although an overseas e-commerce supplier may have no physical trading presence within the country in which the recipient is located (eg the UK) for the purposes of a direct tax charge, such as corporation tax, it may nonetheless be subject to VAT laws. The ingredients of the VAT tax charge can be satisfied without the existence of any physical office within the UK. If, for example, goods are treated as supplied in the UK and the relevant registration thresholds are met, the overseas supplier will be required to register for VAT in the UK.

The term 'distance sales' within the EU describes the situation where a supply of goods is made by a taxable person in a Member State to a consumer who is not a taxable person for the purposes of VAT in another

Member State. In other words, a non-taxable person is an individual or company who is not required to account for VAT (ie a person who is not VAT registered).

Where a taxable person in another Member State makes a supply of goods to a non-taxable person in the UK the supply is treated as taking place in the UK under the distance sales rules (briefly summarised in Table 17.2 at **17.10.2** in relation to goods) where:[209]

- the supply of goods involves their removal to the UK by or under the directions of the person who supplies them (ie an EU trader);

- the supply is a transaction under which the goods are acquired in the UK from another EU Member State by a person who is not a taxable person;

- the supplier (ie the EU trader) is liable to be registered under Sch 2 to VATA 1994 (value of supplies exceeds £70,000, the UK's distance selling threshold (2011)), or would be so liable to be registered if such person were not already registered under Sch 1 (see earlier discussion in this chapter); and

- the supply is not a supply of goods consisting in a new means of transport.

Broadly therefore, traders in other EU Member States will be required to register for UK VAT purposes where their 'distance sales' supplies to UK non-taxable persons exceed £70,000 (2011) in the relevant calendar year from 1 January. Once this threshold is met, the place of supply of goods becomes the UK as a result of the rules outlined above. Until this threshold is met the non-UK, but EU, trader will continue to charge local EU VAT on the supply according to the rate prevailing in their own country (ie country of origin). Accordingly, EU traders must pay close attention to the volume of supplies to other Member States because when the relevant thresholds are met, they will be required to register and account for VAT in another Member State (ie country of destination) as a result of these distance selling rules. These rules are considered further in Chapter 18.

Example 17.16

Z SA operates an internet trading site in Spain and sells goods via this medium. Isabelle, based in the UK, places an order via the internet site for the supply of goods. Z SA has a gross turnover of £100,000 in respect of internet-derived trade from the UK. In these circumstances the Spanish trader would be liable to be registered as a taxable person under Sch 2 to

---

[209] VATA 1994, s 7(4).

VATA 1994, as supplies of this nature would be deemed to take place in the UK with the result that UK VAT must be accounted for by Z SA to HMRC.

An importer may also be treated as a taxable person, and accordingly be required to register for VAT (see **17.9**).

17.19   VAT REPRESENTATIVE

An overseas supplier is unlikely to have any physical representation in the country to which it makes supplies via e-commerce. However, it is clear that a person who makes supplies to the UK is required to register once a specific threshold is met. HMRC has the power to order, or an overseas supplier can request, the appointment of a person within the UK as that person's VAT representative for UK purposes.[210] Broadly, once appointed, the representative becomes responsible for its principal's VAT responsibilities in the UK. Effectively the representative must ensure the principal discharges its VAT liabilities and compliance obligations under VATA 1994. Where a UK representative fails in discharging these obligations, the representative will be held jointly and severally liable with the principal.

17.20   AGENCY: COMMERCIAL INTERMEDIARIES

The range of commercial intermediaries that are capable of being used in a supply chain for the provision of goods and/or services is discussed in Chapter 3. The issue that arises in using an agent is how the relationship between the principal, agent and third party customer is to be treated for VAT purposes. An agent may be acting on either a disclosed or undisclosed basis for a principal in connection with the supply of goods or services. From a UK VAT perspective, this arrangement will result in the principal being required to account for UK VAT on a supply in either case, though in different ways (the following discussion assumes the UK principal has registered for VAT and, as such, has a VAT identification number).

Where a person acts as an agent it is important to ensure that the arrangement is properly drafted so that the person is only treated as an agent. Otherwise there is a risk that the agent could be treated as the principal, with the consequence that it has the associated VAT liabilities of being treated as making the supplies to customers.

17.20.1 Disclosed agent

If an agent acts on a disclosed basis for a principal (ie acting in the name of and on behalf of the principal) in making a supply of taxable goods and/or services to a customer, the VAT consequences are:

- The principal will account for UK VAT (at the applicable rate) on the full sale price to the third party customer, assuming the place of supply is in the UK. The VAT is accounted for in the principal's VAT return, as determined by the time of the supply to the third party customer.

- The agent will issue the VAT invoice to the third party customer, and the invoice should reflect the principal's UK VAT identification number. The agent, in issuing the invoice, should reflect on the invoice that the principal is the supplier.

- If a supply is zero-rated for UK VAT purposes, either as an intra-EU supply or as an export from the EU, then the agent should obtain and hold appropriate evidence to support such VAT treatment.

- The agent will separately invoice the principal for its commission. If the principal does not belong in the UK or does not have a fixed establishment in the UK for VAT purposes, then UK VAT should not apply to the agent's invoice to the principal. If UK VAT is charged on any commission paid to the agent, then the principal should recover it through its UK VAT return.

17.20.2 Undisclosed agent (acting in own name)

If an agent acts on an undisclosed basis for a principal, in making a supply of taxable goods and/or services to a third party customer, the VAT consequences are based on the fact that the arrangement is essentially treated as a two-stage sale for UK VAT purposes. In other words, there is a supply from the principal to agent, and a supply from agent to the third party customer. The VAT consequences are:[211]

- The principal should account for UK VAT on the supply to the agent, at a price net of the agent's commission. The UK VAT should be accounted for in the principal's VAT return relating to the time of the supply to the third party customer. The principal should provide a VAT invoice to its agent.

---

[211] VATA 1994, s 47.

- The agent should account for UK VAT (at the applicable rate) on the supply to the third party customer. The agent should also provide a VAT invoice showing its own VAT identification number to the third party customer.

- The agent should pay the amount owing to its principal, including any UK VAT.

- The agent should recover any UK VAT on the invoice from the principal as a credit (ie as input VAT), through its VAT return.

- The agent must hold evidence to support its VAT treatment of supplies.

Special rules apply where an agent acts for a non-taxable person in respect of imports of goods from outside the EU, or acquisitions from another EU Member State, as in these circumstances, onward supplies of such goods are treated, as appropriate, as imported/acquired by, and then supplied by, the agent.[212]

Example 17.17[213]

Holidays Ltd, a UK-based business, operates a website through which it markets hotel accommodation. The website features several thousand resort hotels, villas and apartments in a broad range of destinations throughout the world. Approximately 95% of hotel sales made via Holidays Ltd's website are to travel agents acting on behalf of individual holidaymakers. The remaining 5% of sales are made directly to individual holidaymakers.

The question that arises is who makes the supply of hotel accommodation via Holidays Ltd's website, either directly or indirectly to holidaymakers. If Holidays Ltd is acting as agent in the supply of services to the hotel operators then the supply of hotel accommodation will be by the relevant hotel operator. For VAT purposes there is a difference in treatment. If Holidays Ltd acts as principal then it will be required to account for VAT under the Tour Operators Margin Scheme[214] (TOMS), but if Holidays Ltd acts as agent then the supplies are treated as taking place in the jurisdiction in which the hotel belongs. Specifically if the hotel accommodation is supplied by the hotel operator, and not by Holidays Ltd, to the holidaymaker, then Holidays Ltd is not liable to account for VAT on that supply. Holidays Ltd will have supplied agency services to the hotel operator and will be liable to account for VAT on that supply or to arrange for that VAT to be paid by its principal, the hotel operator.

---

[212] VATA 1994, s 47(1). See Chapter 19, at **19.8**.

[213] Similar facts in this example arose in *Secret Hotels2 Ltd v Revenue and Customs Commissioners* [2011] UKUT 308, at 316, discussed **17.4.2**.

[214] See Table 17.2 at **17.10.2** (under the heading Special Scheme for Travel Operators).

In determining the VAT treatment of the arrangement it is necessary to ask who is the person making the supply to the holidaymaker? To answer this, it is helpful to consider the contract entered into by the holidaymaker for the supply of hotel accommodation.

Holidays Ltd's terms and conditions of contract with holidaymakers include the following:

- Holidays Ltd acts as agent on behalf of each of the hotels for which it offers accommodation.

- By making a reservation on the website you enter into a contract with the hotel company itself rather than with Holidays Ltd, and you are responsible for paying the hotel.

- Holidays Ltd acts as agent only for each of the hotels to provide you with information on the hotels and an on-line reservation service.

- Holidays Ltd provides an online reservation service, and as such it passes your reservation details to the hotel of your choice.

- Holidays Ltd uses its website service to provide to you information concerning the price and availability of hotels, together with a range of other information to assist in making a hotel reservation.

- Any reservations you make on the Holidays Ltd website are made directly with the company whose hotel services you are booking.

- Holidays Ltd acts as a booking agent on behalf of all the hotels, apartments and villas featured on our website and your contract will be made with these accommodation providers.

- Holidays Ltd has no liability for any of the accommodation arrangements.

Holidays Ltd's terms and conditions of contract with travel agents include the following:

- Holidays Ltd is entitled to a 10% commission plus value added tax of the amount relating to items arranged through or by the travel agent.

- Holidays Ltd appoints the travel agent as a nonexclusive agent for the retail sale of the accommodation arrangements.

- In consideration of the marketing provided by the travel agents Holidays Ltd will share with the travel agent the commission it receives from the hotel operator.

- The travel agent will promote and use its best endeavours to increase sales of the accommodation arrangements (offered via the Holidays Ltd website) to existing and potential customers through all means, including but not limited to teletext, the internet and direct marketing activity.

- Each of Holidays Ltd and the travel agent are acting in the capacity of selling agents and will not be responsible for accounting for Value Added Taxation on the value of products sold to customers.

Holidays Ltd's terms and conditions of contract with hotel operators include the following:

- The hotel operator is principal and Holidays Ltd is its agent.

- The principal will supply to Holidays Ltd advertising material including website address, CDs, slides, brochures and marketing video tapes relating to the accommodation.

- The principal will provide all accommodation, property, resort or surroundings and services, amenities and/or facilities to the customer.

- The principal will ensure that all customer accommodation requests, options and reservations taken by Holidays Ltd are honoured by the principal, and if appropriate the principal will supply replacement accommodation to the customer.

- The principal on behalf of itself, its employees, agents and subcontractors accepts liability and agrees fully to indemnify Holidays Ltd in respect of all losses, damages, liabilities, expenses and demands of whatever nature which Holidays Ltd may suffer or incur directly or indirectly as a result of any breach by the principal of any term or condition of this contract.

- Holidays Ltd is entitled to receive a commission from the principal, which will be calculated as any sum charged to a customer by Holidays Ltd which is over and above the prices set out in an agreed fee rate.

- The contract between the parties does not operate so as to create a partnership or joint venture.

For VAT purposes the supply of hotel accommodation is a standard rated supply (Arts 135(1)(1) and 135(2)(a) of the VAT Directive). This is an exception to the general rule that the leasing or letting of immovable property is an exempt supply for VAT.

The place of supply of services connected with immovable property is the place where the property is situated (VAT (Place of Supply of Services) Order 1992, Art 5, now VATA 1994, Sch 4A, Part 1, para 1). In other words, the supply of hotel accommodation is treated as being made where the hotel is located. Under this rule a UK company offering holiday accommodation (as principal) in another Member State is liable to pay VAT in that other Member State, and would therefore need to be registered there for VAT. The normal rule is displaced by the application of a special scheme for travel operators which provides for them to account for VAT on their margin within their own state of establishment (Arts 306–310 of the VAT Directive provides for TOMS). A supplier of services within TOMS cannot reclaim any UK or EU VAT charged on the travel services and goods the supplier buys in and re-supplies, but only accounts for VAT on the margin (ie the difference between the amount received from customers and that paid to suppliers).

Holidays Ltd should be treated as agent of the hotel operators with the result that the hotel accommodation is supplied by the hotel operator, and not by Holidays Ltd. Accordingly, Holidays Ltd is not liable to account for VAT on that supply. Holidays Ltd will have supplied agency services to the hotel operator and it will be liable to account for VAT on that supply or to arrange for that VAT to be paid by its principal, the hotel operator.

The nature of the contract for the provision of hotel accommodation is between the hotel operator and the holidaymaker. It does not matter whether the holidaymaker contracts are made as a result of a direct contact with Holidays Ltd or by means of indirect contact with Holidays Ltd through a travel agent. Furthermore, Holidays Ltd has express authority to enter into contracts on behalf of the hotel operator to provide hotel accommodation to holidaymakers.

17.21   VAT IN CONTRACTS

For contracts where VAT has to be dealt with in connection with agency supplies, the contract should deal with the following matters:

- Expressly state whether the agreed price for the supply includes or excludes VAT.

- Specify the requirements about the issue of VAT invoices, particularly if an agent is acting as disclosed agent for the principal.

- Wherever a disclosed or undisclosed agency is used, the principal will require information and payment on a timely basis from its agent in order to file its quarterly UK VAT return. Such matters should be reflected in the agreement between the principal and agent.

17.22   OVERVIEW OF THE UK VAT FRAMEWORK

Table 17.4 provides an overview of the VAT framework.

Table 17.4: Overview of the UK's VAT framework

Rule 1 VAT charge	Rule 2 Taxable person	Rule 3 Taxable supply	Rule 4 Supply
VAT must be charged on the supply of goods or services in the UK.	A person who is, or is required to be registered under VATA 1994.	This is a supply of goods or services made in the UK, other than an exempt supply.	A supply is defined in the Act as including 'all forms of supply, but not anything done otherwise than for consideration'.
VATA 1994, s 1	VATA 1994, s 3(1)	VATA 1994, s 4(2)	VATA 1994, s 5(2)(a)
VAT must be charged at the rate of 20% unless otherwise specified.	A person is liable to be registered, in general terms, if taxable supplies are in excess of £73,000 (2011).		
VATA 1994, s 2(1)	VATA 1994, Sch 1		
The supply, to be subject to VAT must possess the following characteristics: (1) be a taxable supply; (2) by a taxable person; (3) in the course or furtherance of any business; (4) carried on by the person in (3).	In appropriate circumstances a person who is not liable to be registered can voluntarily seek to become registered. To do this, the person must satisfy the Commissioners that: (1) it makes taxable supplies; (2) is carrying on a business and intends to make such supplies in the course or furtherance of that business.		
VATA 1994, s 4(1)	VATA 1994, Sch 1, para 9		

Rule 5 Classification as goods or services	Rule 6 Time of supply	Rule 7 Place of supply of services	Rule 8 Reverse charge/Tax shift
Anything which is not a supply of goods, but is done for consideration is a supply of services.	See Table 17.3 at **17.14** for a summary of the principal rules.	A supply of services is treated as taking place where: (1) the supplier belongs; (2) unless the supply is to a relevant business person in which case it takes place where the recipient belongs.	The reverse charge applies if: (a) the recipient is a relevant business person who belongs in the UK, and the place of supply of the services is inside the UK, or (b) the supply of the services is one to which any paragraph of Part 1 or 2 of Sch 4A to VATA 1994 applies, and the recipient is registered as a taxable person.
VATA 1994, s 5(2)(b)		See Table 17.2 at **17.10.2** for a summary of the principal rules. VATA 1994, s 7A	VATA 1994, s 8
The granting, assignment or surrender of any right, if done for consideration is a supply of services. VATA 1994, s 5(2)(b)			

Rule 9 Right to credit input tax against output tax	Rule 10 Zero-rating	Rule 11 Exempt supplies	Definitions
A taxable person is required in respect of supplies made to account for and pay VAT in respect of those supplies.	Where a taxable person supplies goods or services, that would otherwise be charged to VAT on the supply but which are zero-rated no VAT is chargeable on the supply.	Where a person makes an exempt supply no VAT is charged on the supply, and there is no right to claim input tax which is attributable to the making of that supply.	'Business' includes any trade, profession or vocation.
VATA 1994, s 25(1)	VATA 1994, s 30(1)	VATA 1994, s 31	VATA 1994, s 94(1)

The person who is required to account for VAT on supplies, is entitled to credit for input tax which is then deducted from any output tax that is due on supplies made.	However the supply is still treated as a taxable supply with the result that the supplier is entitled to credit for his input tax. The rate of VAT on these supplies is nil.		The Act provides that 'the disposition of a business as a going concern, or of its assets or liabilities (whether or not in connection with its reorganisation or winding up), is a supply made in the course or furtherance of that business'.
VATA 1994, s 25(1)	VATA 1994, s 30(1)		VATA 1994, s 94(6)
Input tax is VAT which is attributable to supplies made in the course or furtherance of business which are:	Zero-rated supplies are classified in VATA 1994, Sch 8.		'Input tax' means: VAT on the supply to a taxable person of any goods or services used or to be used for the purpose of any business carried on or to be carried on by him.
(a) taxable supplies;			VATA 1994, s 24(1)
(b) supplies outside the UK which would be taxable supplies if made in the UK;			'Output tax' means vat on supplies which a taxable person makes.
(c) such other supplies outside the UK and such exempt supplies as the Treasury may by order specify.			VATA 1994, s 24(2)
VATA 1994, s 26(2)			

CHAPTER 18

INTRA-EU TRADE: GOODS

18.1 INTRODUCTION

VAT is payable on the 'acquisition' of goods in the UK from another Member State of the EU,[1] and is charged at the same rates as would have applied to a UK domestic supply of such goods acquired by a business from another business in the UK. In other words, acquisitions will be subject to VAT at the standard rate of 20% (2011),[2] the reduced rate of 5% (2011)[3] or the rate of 0% ('zero rate').[4] It is also possible for a supply from another Member State to be exempt, but such a supply will not be a taxable acquisition.[5]

Acquisition VAT is accounted for by the business customer who makes the acquisition via the normal VAT return for the period in which the acquisition occurs. The UK VAT legislation states that VAT on an acquisition from another Member State is usually only payable by a person who is a taxable person (ie required to be VAT registered in the UK)[6] where there is a taxable acquisition made in the UK (otherwise than

---

[1]   The countries which comprise the VAT territory of the EU are: Austria, Belgium, Bulgaria, Cyprus, Czech Republic, Denmark (excluding Busingen and the Isle of Heligoland), Greece, Hungary, the Republic of Ireland, Italy (except the communes of Livigno and Camione d'Italia and the Italian waters of Lake Lugano), Latvia, Lithuania, Luxembourg, Malta, The Netherlands, Poland, Portugal (including the Azores and Madeira), Romania, Slovakia, Slovenia, Spain (including the Balearic Islands but excluding Ceuta and Melilla), Sweden and the United Kingdom (including the Isle of Man). Territories of some of the foregoing are not within the VAT territory of the EU, and accordingly supplies of goods from these territories will be treated as imports. The territories are: Andorra, the Åland Islands (Finland), the Channel Islands (Jersey, Guernsey, Sark) and Gibraltar, the Canary Islands (Spain), the overseas departments of France (Guadeloupe, Martinique, Reunion and French Guiana) and Mount Athos (Greece). To check on any alterations in the extent of the VAT territory see www.hmrc.gov.uk.

[2]   VATA 1994, s 1.

[3]   VATA 1994, s 29A, Sch 7A.

[4]   VATA 1994, s 30(1), Sch 8.

[5]   VATA 1994, s 10(2), s 31, Sch 9.

[6]   See Chapter 17 for details.

in pursuance of a taxable supply).[7] The main exceptions to the requirement for there to be a taxable person in order for 'acquisition VAT' to be imposed are where:

(1)   certain non-business users (eg clubs, associations, companies) make 'relevant acquisitions' of goods from the EU which exceed the UK's annual VAT registration threshold[8] (£73,000 (2011)) for acquisitions, even though the goods were not necessarily acquired by way of business – the broad effect of this is to make the non-business user liable to register for VAT purposes and consequently account for VAT on those acquisitions (see **18.4**);

(2)   the goods acquired are subject to a duty of excise;[9] or

(3)   the goods consist of a new means of transport.[10]

The fact that a UK business recipient of goods is generally required to pay UK VAT on the acquisition of goods from another Member State does not mean that a UK non-business private individual avoids the payment of VAT on acquiring goods from the EU. Where goods are supplied by a taxable person to a recipient in another EU country who is not a taxable person then the EU supplier will either charge VAT under the rules of its country of origin, with the result that a UK non-business recipient of goods will pay VAT of the EU country from which the supply is made; or, if the value of those supplies reaches a specified threshold in the Member State of the recipient, (such as the UK), it will be necessary for the supplier to register for and charge VAT under the rules of the country of the recipient (these are known as the 'distance selling' rules). These rules are examined at **18.5** and **18.6**.

Broadly, supplies made to a UK taxable person by another taxable person located in another EU Member State should be zero-rated in that other EU Member State as 'dispatches' to the UK; and the position is the same for a UK supplier of goods to a taxable person located in another Member State (see Chapter 20).[11] The zero-rating should enable the supplier in the country of origin to claim back the VAT incurred by it in

---

[7]   VATA 1999, s 10(1)(c), ie a supply which already takes place in the UK as defined under the UK's domestic place of supply rules for goods. See eg for installed or assembled goods as summarised in Table 17.2 in Chapter 17 at **17.10.2**, where the initial removal of components to the UK of goods which require installation or assembly in the UK will be treated as a taxable supply in the UK. However, most intra-EU movements to the UK of goods will be as a result of a supply by an EU supplier that takes place outside the UK – normally in the Member State of departure.

[8]   VATA 1994, s 10(2), (3), Sch 3, para 1.

[9]   VATA 1994, s 10(1)(c).

[10]   VATA 1994, s 10(1)(c). See generally HMRC's Notice 728 *New Means of Transport* (September 2008).

[11]   VATA 1994, s 30(8) and Value Added Tax Regulations 1995, SI 1995/2518, reg 134, derived from the VAT Directive, Art 138(1). See generally HMRC's Notice 725 *The Single Market* (February 2011), and in particular, ss 4–8 of that notice, and HMRC's

acquiring the goods up until the supply. The recipient of the goods who is a taxable person in the other EU Member State, such as the UK, will then be liable to account for UK VAT on the acquisition, at the rate applicable to the supply.

The primary purpose of this chapter is to illustrate the main fabric of the UK's VAT acquisition rules in connection with business to business (B2B) supplies, and to provide some illustrations of how they might operate in the context of e-commerce activities.

18.2 ACQUISITIONS: BUSINESS ACQUISITIONS BY A UK SUPPLIER

VAT is charged on a taxable acquisition from another Member State of the EU of goods received *in* the UK by a UK VAT registered business.[12] The person making the acquisition is liable to account for the VAT, which becomes due at the time of the acquisition.[13] VAT is applied by reference to the *value* of the acquisition at the time of the acquisition.[14] The VAT is accounted for on the acquirer's VAT return covering the period in which the acquisition occurs. The VAT incurred as a result of the acquisition rules should then qualify as input tax on the same VAT return, which can be set off (subject to the normal rules) against appropriate business supplies upon which output tax is received.[15]

Where a UK taxable person acts as an intermediate supplier, the original supply from another Member State to the UK trader and the supply by the UK trader to the final customer may be disregarded.[16]

18.2.1 Overview: acquisition rules

The basic rules of UK VAT on acquisitions are summarised below.

Rule 1: Pre-conditions to a VAT charge on an acquisition

UK VAT is charged on an acquisition from another EU Member State where the following conditions are all satisfied:[17]

VAT Single Market Manual, available at www.hmrc.gov.uk/manuals/vatsmanual/index.htm, on HMRC's interpretation of the VAT rules on acquisitions and dispatches.

[12] VATA 1994, s 1(1)(b). The main EU law provisions on acquisitions are set out in the VAT Directive, Arts 2(1)(b), 20, 40–41, 68–69 and 200.

[13] VATA 1994, s 1(3).

[14] VATA 1994, s 2(1)(b).

[15] VATA 1994, s 24(1)(b). For the meaning and nature of the concepts of 'input' and 'output' tax, see Chapter 17. See also, however, note 50 below, as to certain circumstances when acquisition VAT is not reclaimable as input tax.

[16] VATA 1994, s 14(6).

[17] VATA 1994, s 10(1).

(1)   there is a taxable acquisition of goods,

(2)   which takes place in the UK;

(3)   the acquisition is otherwise than in pursuance of a taxable supply;[18]
      and

(4)   either (i) the person who makes the acquisition is a taxable person,
      (ii) the goods are subject to a duty of excise[19] or (iii) consist of a new
      means of transport.

Rule 2: Taxable acquisition

VAT only applies to a taxable acquisition. A taxable acquisition occurs
where:[20]

(1)   it is not an exempt acquisition;[21] and

(2)   the goods are acquired in the course or furtherance of:

    (i)   any business carried on by any person; or
    (ii)   any activities carried on otherwise than by way of business by
        any body corporate or by any club, association, organisation,
        or other unincorporated body;

(3)   it is the person who carries on that business or, as the case may be,
      those activities which acquires the goods; and

(4)   the supplier:

    (i)   is taxable in another Member State at the time of the
        transaction in pursuance of which the goods are acquired;[22]
        and
    (ii)   in participating in that transaction, acts in the course or
        furtherance of a business carried on by it; or

---

[18]   VATA 1994 defines a taxable supply as 'a supply of goods … made in the United
       Kingdom other than an exempt supply' (s 4(2)). See also note 7 above and Chapter 17,
       Table 17.2 at **17.10.2** – as stated, an acquisition of goods by a UK VAT-registered person
       from another Member State will not normally be a supply of goods made in the UK as
       the place of supply will be the other Member State.
[19]   Excise duty is a tax on alcohol, petrol and tobacco.
[20]   VATA 1994, s 10(3).
[21]   VATA 1994 provides that the acquisition of goods from another EU Member State is an
       exempt acquisition if the goods are acquired in pursuance of an exempt supply (s 31(1)).
[22]   Broadly, VATA 1994 provides that references to a person being taxable in another
       Member State means a person who is a taxable person for the purposes of VAT in that
       Member State (s 92(2)(a)). Broadly therefore, acquisition VAT will not be due in the UK
       if the supplier in the other Member State is not VAT registered.

(5)   if only (1) above is satisfied, the goods consist of a new means of transport.

Example 18.1

X Ltd, a UK-based business, which is VAT registered, places an order for 20,000 widgets from France via an e-commerce system with a French-based company called Paris SA. The French company is a taxable person for the purposes of French VAT law. The widgets are acquired by X Ltd for the purposes of a business carried on by it and arrive in the UK. In this situation X Ltd will be required to account for UK acquisition VAT at the standard rate of 20% (2011) on the widgets, since the supply is a taxable acquisition from another Member State of the EU. The UK VAT incurred by X Ltd qualifies as input VAT, which can be offset against output VAT from the taxable supplies made by it.

Rule 3: *Acquisition of goods from another Member State*

For the acquisition VAT rules to apply it is necessary for a taxable person to make an acquisition of goods from another Member State. In other words, there must be the acquisition of goods from another Member State of the EU under a transaction in relation to which the following conditions are satisfied:[23]

(1)   the transaction is a supply of goods (including anything treated for the purposes of VATA 1994 as a supply of goods); and

(2)   the transaction involves the removal of goods from another Member State (though not necessarily to the UK – see Rule 5 below).

The fact that the removal of the goods from another Member State is under the direction of either the supplier or the person acquiring them (or any other person) is irrelevant.[24] Under special rules, a transaction may also be deemed to involve an acquisition of goods even if there is no change in the person having 'property' in the goods[25] (ie a physical transfer by a trader of their own goods which form part of their business assets from one Member State to another Member State – a review of these 'transfer of own goods' rules is, however, beyond the scope of this

---

[23]   VATA 1994, s 11(1).
[24]   VATA 1994, s 11(2). In other words, the removal of the goods can be organised by the supplier, purchaser or someone else acting on either's behalf. Consequently, a UK purchaser who collects goods from their supplier in another Member State is still liable to account for acquisition VAT in the UK. See HMRC's *VAT Single Market Manual* at VATSM3345.
[25]   VATA 1994, s 11(3), and VAT Directive, Art 17. See also VATA 1994, Sch 4, para 6; Value Added Tax (Removal of Goods) Order 1992, SI 1992/3111; and HMRC Notice 725, Section 9.

book). Conversely, certain other transactions are deemed as a matter of law not to amount to the acquisition of goods from another Member State.[26]

Rule 4: Time of acquisition

VAT arising on an acquisition of goods from another Member State becomes due at the *time of acquisition*.[27] Unless otherwise provided for under VATA 1994, where goods are acquired from another Member State, the acquisition is treated as taking place on whichever is the earlier of the following:[28]

(a) the fifteenth day of the month following that in which the event occurs, which, in relation to that acquisition, is the first relevant event for the purposes of taxing the acquisition (the 'event' for the purposes of taxing the acquisition is the first removal of the goods);[29] and

(b) the day of the issue, in respect of the transaction in pursuance of which the goods are acquired, of an invoice which is a tax invoice under the law of the Member State.[30] The invoice may be issued by either the supplier or the customer, but in either case the invoice must be issued under the provisions of the law of the Member State where the goods were supplied.[31]

Special rules apply for determining the time of acquisition of warehoused goods,[32] water, gas, power, heat, ventilation and refrigeration.[33] In essence where such supplies are acquired from another Member State and the whole (or part) of any consideration is payable periodically (or from time to time) then the goods are treated as separately and successively acquired on each occasion that an invoice is issued.[34]

Example 18.2

X Ltd, a UK-based company, orders the delivery of 100 computers from a Spanish-based company called Y SA. The order is placed by using e-commerce. The goods are ordered on 5 June, the date on which an invoice

[26] See Value Added Tax (Treatment of Transactions) (No 2) Order 1992, SI 1992/3132; and Value Added Tax (Special Provisions) Order 1995, SI 1995/1268, reg 7. The 1992 Order relates to the supply of gold to a central bank of a Member State; and the 1995 Order to VAT paid on supplies which are to be accounted for, and paid, in another Member State in accordance with a profit margin scheme.
[27] VATA 1994, s 1(3).
[28] VATA 1994, s 12(1).
[29] VATA 1994, s 12(2).
[30] See Value Added Tax Regulations 1995, SI 1995/2518, reg 83.
[31] See Value Added Tax Regulations 1995, SI 1995/2518, reg 83.
[32] See VATA 1994, ss 18 and 18B.
[33] See Value Added Tax Regulations 1995, SI 1995/2518, reg 87.
[34] See Value Added Tax Regulations 1995, SI 1995/2518, reg 87.

is raised, and they are removed from Spain in transit to the UK on 12 June. Since an invoice is issued on 5 June, this is the date which is regarded under VATA 1994 as the time of acquisition for UK VAT purposes (due to the invoice being issued prior to the fifteenth day of the month following the date of the goods being removed from Spain to the UK).

Suspending the time of acquisition

There are two broad categories of scheme that exist under VATA 1994, which permit the suspension of the time of acquisition for VAT purposes. These are:

(1)   goods subject to a tax warehousing regime (applying to goods subject to excise duty);[35] and

(2)   goods subject to a fiscal warehousing regime.[36]

The purpose of these schemes is to suspend the time of acquisition for the purposes of charging VAT. Effectively, when goods pass into a warehousing regime the goods are deemed to be supplied outside of the UK (so no UK VAT is due at that stage) until the goods leave the warehouse. These schemes may operate in the context of e-commerce. Fiscal warehousing is discussed below. HMRC has published Notice 702/8 (January 2011) on Fiscal warehousing, which provides a detailed account of the current position.[37] HMRC has also issued Notice 702/10 (October 2009) in relation to Tax warehousing.[38]

Effect of fiscal warehousing

As noted above, an acquisition of goods that falls within the ambit of the fiscal warehouse scheme is deemed to take place outside the UK whilst the goods are subject to the scheme.[39] Where goods are no longer subject to the scheme and an acquisition of those goods is treated as taking place in the UK, the acquisition is treated as taking place when the goods are removed from the fiscal warehousing scheme.[40] VAT, together with any excise duty, must be paid at the time the goods are removed from the fiscal warehouse.[41] The VAT is the liability of the person who removes the

---

[35]   VATA 1994, s 18(2), (3).
[36]   VATA 1994, s 18A.
[37]   Available at www.hmrc.gov.uk.
[38]   Available at www.hmrc.gov.uk.
[39]   VATA 1994, s 18B(3).
[40]   VATA 1994, s 18B(4).
[41]   VATA 1994, s 18D(2).

goods.[42] If excise duty is also payable, then the person who is required to pay that duty is liable.[43] The timing of payment can be modified by VAT regulations.[44]

Fiscal warehousing also applies to a supply of goods (ie from a taxable person in the UK), as opposed to an acquisition from another Member State.[45] The rules are similar but are not considered specifically in this book.

Conditions for application of effect of fiscal warehouse scheme

The effect of the fiscal warehouse scheme operates where:[46]

- there is an acquisition of goods from another Member State;

- the goods acquired are 'eligible goods';

- either:

   (a) the acquisition takes place while the goods are subject to a fiscal warehousing regime; or
   (b) after the acquisition but before the supply, if any, of those goods which next occurs, the acquirer causes the goods to be placed in a fiscal warehousing regime; and

- the person making the acquisition, not later than the time of the acquisition, prepares and keeps a certificate that the goods are subject to a fiscal warehousing regime.

'Eligible goods' include those within Sch 5A to VATA 1994 upon which import duties have been paid or deferred.[47] The goods within Sch 5A are mainly primary resources, such as tin, copper, zinc, nickel, aluminium, lead, indium, cereals, oil seeds, olives, grains and seeds, tea, coffee (not roasted), raw sugar, rubber, wool, chemicals in bulk, mineral oils, potatoes and vegetable oils (but not chemically modified).

Rule 5: Place of acquisition

Under Rule 1, UK VAT only applies to the acquisition of goods *in* the UK from another Member State of the EU. VATA 1994 provides the following rules for determining the place of acquisition.

---

[42]   VATA 1994, s 18D(2).
[43]   VATA 1994, s 18D(2).
[44]   VATA 1994, s 18D(3).
[45]   VATA 1994, s 18B(2).
[46]   VATA 1994, s 18B(1).
[47]   VATA 1994, s 18B(6).

(1) Goods are treated as acquired in the UK (subject to any other provision):[48]

    (a) if the goods are acquired under a transaction which involves their removal to the UK, and

    (b) does not involve their removal from the UK; and

    (c) the goods shall otherwise be treated as acquired outside the UK.

(2) Goods are treated as acquired in the UK where:[49]

    (a) they are acquired by a person who, for the purposes of their acquisition, makes use of a number assigned to that person for the purposes of UK VAT (ie even if the goods do not arrive in the UK);

    (b) however, (a) shall not require any goods to be treated as acquired in the UK where it is established, in accordance with regulations made by the Commissioners, that VAT:

        (i) has been paid in another Member State on the acquisition of those goods; and

        (ii) the VAT fell to be paid by virtue of provisions of the law of that Member State corresponding to the provisions, referred to in (1) above, made under UK law. In other words, VAT falls to be paid because goods are removed to that Member State.[50]

---

[48] VATA 1994, s 13(2).

[49] VATA 1994, s 13(3), (4). See the VAT Directive, Arts 40–41. Broadly, under these rules, an acquirer can be liable to account for VAT on the same delivery of goods in more than one Member State where the Member State of final arrival of the goods (after transportation/departure) differs from the Member State of identification, ie where the acquirer is VAT registered. VAT may need to be paid in the Member State of arrival followed by an adjustment of the VAT paid/accounted for in the Member State of registration. See also further below at note 50 in relation to HMRC's view on how these rules operate in the UK.

[50] On the place of acquisition, HMRC states (in its *VAT Single Market Manual* at VATSM3350) as follows:

'The Court of Justice of the European Union [ECJ] confirmed in Facet Holding BV (C-539/08) that acquisition VAT accounted for under these arrangements cannot be reclaimed as input tax ... [the reference to arrangements are to the use of an eg UK VAT registration number to secure a zero-rated supply in the Member State of departure, otherwise known as the 'fall-back' arrangements set out in Art 41 of the VAT Directive] ... The Court considered two similar cases. In each, supplies of computer goods were sourced from Member States other than the Netherlands and sent direct to customers located elsewhere in the EU. Dutch VAT registration numbers were used to secure zero-rating of the intra-EU supplies.

The ECJ held that there could be no right to deduct acquisition VAT in the Netherlands, where it fell due under the fallback arrangements, as the goods did not actually enter the Member State. In arriving at its decision the Court noted that, if there were a right to deduct in these circumstances, it could jeopardise the operation of the normal rules, as it would remove the incentive for the acquisition to be taxed in the Member State of arrival. The decision provided a welcome clarification of what was previously an

(3)   For warehoused goods, the place of acquisition is altered in various circumstances where goods are transferred within a warehoused scheme permitted under VATA 1994 (see Rule 4, above). Relevant schemes are:

   (a)   the warehousing regime;[51] and
   (b)   fiscal warehousing.[52]

Example 18.3

X (UK) Ltd orders 100,000 tyres via a form of e-commerce from a German company, Y AG. The tyres are to be delivered in France. Under the normal rules, the place of acquisition is France. However, on making the order X (UK) Ltd makes use of its UK VAT registration number. In these circumstances there is an acquisition in the UK, unless X (UK) Ltd can show that it has paid VAT in France, as the country to which the goods were sent. If X (UK) Ltd can show it has subsequently accounted for acquisition VAT in France, it will be entitled to a refund of tax paid in the UK.

18.3   VALUE OF GOODS

VAT is applied to the *value* of the goods at the time of acquisition.[53] The value of goods acquired from another Member State is taken to be the value of the transaction under which the goods are acquired (in other words, what was paid as consideration for the goods, including any payment to cover the supplier's costs of packing, transport or insurance).[54] If the transaction is for a consideration in money then its

---

uncertain position.

In 1997 Customs & Excise [HMRC] agreed to arrangements under which a UK VAT-registered business could account for acquisition VAT in the UK on a yacht purchased from a supplier in another Member State without the yacht arriving in the UK. This was announced in Business Brief 12/97, which also permitted input tax deduction, subject to the normal rules. Following the ECJ decision, the agreement was withdrawn from 1 June 2011. However, as a transitional measure, where a UK VAT-registered business had entered into a contract for the purchase of a yacht before 1 June 2011, and had intended to adopt the procedure as agreed in Business Brief 12/97, that business could continue to rely on those arrangements (including recovery of the acquisition VAT as input tax, subject to the normal rules). But this was subject to their holding satisfactory evidence of the contract and the date that it was agreed.

Other than that, the only basis on which the UK VAT may now be adjusted is where it can be demonstrated that acquisition VAT has been accounted for in the Member State of arrival. This can arise because accounting for acquisition tax under the fall-back arrangements does not extinguish a liability to account for the acquisition in the Member State to which the goods are sent. So, section 13(4) [VATA 1994] provides for a refund if it can be shown that the tax has been, or is subsequently, accounted for in the Member State of destination of the goods ...'

51   VATA 1994, s 18.
52   VATA 1994, s 18A.
53   VATA 1994, s 2(1)(b).
54   VATA 1994, s 20(1). Special rules apply to goods acquired from another Member State otherwise than under a taxable supply: VATA 1994, s 20(2). See also HMRC Notice 725, section 8 (Tax value of acquisitions), such as at para 8.4, which covers the tax value of

value is taken to be such amount as is equal to the consideration.[55] If the consideration does not consist wholly of money (eg, the supply is in return for payment in goods or services) then its value is the monetary equivalent of the consideration, calculated by reference to the price, excluding VAT, which would have been paid if the consideration were monetary.[56]

18.4 NON-TAXABLE PERSONS AND ACQUISITIONS

It was noted at **18.1** that generally, a person who is not VAT registered, and who is not a taxable person, is not liable to pay UK VAT on the acquisition of goods from another EU Member State. However, there are two exceptions which are treated as acquisitions regardless of the status of the acquirer, where:

(1)   goods are acquired that are subject to excise duty; or

(2)   a new means for transport is acquired.[57]

However, as indicated at **18.1**, another exception exists to the general rule, which must be borne in mind. Certain non-taxable persons (companies, clubs, public bodies, charities, institutions, certain individuals (according to HMRC, if they are not acting in a purely personal capacity), organisations, but excluding private individuals) may be required to pay UK VAT on acquisitions where 'relevant acquisitions' are made and received by them, as a result of an activity carried on by them (otherwise than by way of business), meaning that such persons can be required to register for UK VAT on the strength of their acquisitions alone. VATA 1994 provides that, if at the end of any month in a calendar year from 1 January, acquisitions exceed £73,000 (2011), that person is liable to register as a taxable person.[58] HMRC must be notified within 30 days of the end of the month in which the threshold is met.[59] A person is also placed under an obligation to register where there are reasonable grounds for believing that the person will make relevant acquisitions which shall exceed £73,000 (2011) within 30 days.[60] Such a person must notify HMRC before the end of that 30-day period.[61]

---

acquisitions where the consideration involves payment of a discounted amount or includes offers of conditional discounts, and where there is no consideration (in which case, the value is stated by HMRC to be the cost of purchasing the goods in question at the time of acquistion).

[55]   VATA 1994, s 20(3).
[56]   VATA 1994, s 20(4). For further analysis of the position on non-monetary consideration see Chapter 17.
[57]   See VATA 1994, s 10(1)(c). See HMRC Notice 728 *New Means of Transport* (September 2008)
[58]   VATA 1994, s 10(3)(a)(ii) and Sch 3, para 1(1).
[59]   VATA 1994, Sch 3, para 3(1)(a).
[60]   VATA 1994, Sch 3, para 1(2).
[61]   VATA 1994, Sch 3, para 3(1)(b).

Example 18.4

On a regular basis, X Ltd, a UK-based company, acquires electrical components from Z Gmbh, a company based in Germany. The placing of the order, delivery and payment is facilitated by an e-commerce system. X Ltd is currently not registered under VATA 1994 because it is not a taxable person. X Ltd places orders on a monthly basis. The last order placed was in mid-August. The management become aware on 31 August that it will make an acquisition of £75,000-worth of electrical components within 15 days. X Ltd must notify HMRC by 30 September of its liability to be UK VAT registered

A person who is not a taxable person may also seek voluntary registration where that person satisfies HMRC that relevant acquisitions are being made.[62] In these circumstances, HMRC will register the person with effect from the day on which the request is made, or from such earlier date as is agreed.[63] Provisions similar to those that apply where a person is required to register in respect of UK supplies also apply where acquisitions create a liability or entitlement to register as a taxable person. For example, there is a duty to notify when a person ceases to be registrable, there are provisions for the cancellation of registration, and an exemption from registration in respect of the acquisition of zero-rated items.[64]

18.5   DISTANCE SALES OF GOODS BY TRADERS FROM OTHER MEMBER STATES TO UK NON-TAXABLE PERSONS

Where a supply of goods is made which triggers the distance sales rules, a supplier is required to register for VAT in another country of the EU, and charge VAT on taxable supplies. The term 'distance sales' within the EU describes the situation where, for example, a supply of goods is made by a taxable person from another Member State to a consumer in the UK, who is not a taxable person for the purposes of VAT, where the supplier is responsible for delivery of the goods. A non-taxable person includes an individual or company who is not required to account for VAT under VATA 1994 (ie not VAT registrable). As noted by HMRC in Notice 725 on the Single Market, the most common examples of 'distance sales' are goods supplied by mail order or ordered over the internet.

The basic rules on distance selling in VATA 1994 provide that, where a taxable person in another Member State makes a supply of goods to a non-taxable person in the UK, the supply is treated as taking place in the UK when the following apply (without these distance selling rules, the place of supply would be the Member State of departure):[65]

---

[62]   VATA 1994, Sch 3, para 4(1).
[63]   VATA 1994, Sch 3, para 4(2).
[64]   VATA 1994, Sch 3, paras 5, 6 and 8.
[65]   VATA 1994, s 7(4), derived from VAT Directive, Arts 33 and 34. According to HMRC

- the supply of goods involves their removal to the UK by or under the directions of the person who supplies them (ie an EU taxable person);

- the supply is a transaction under which the goods are acquired in the UK from another Member State by a person who is not a taxable person (eg a private individual);

- the supplier (ie the EU taxable person) is liable to be registered under Sch 2 to VATA 1994 (value of supplies exceed £70,000 (2011) – see below), or would be so liable to be registered if that person were not already registered under the normal rules for registration in respect of UK taxable supplies under Sch 1 to VATA 1994; and

- the supply is not a supply of goods consisting in a new means of transport, nor anything which is treated as a supply for the purposes of VATA 1994 due to goods forming part of the assets of a business being transferred.[66]

Broadly, as a result of the above rules, traders in other Member States will be required to register for UK VAT where their 'relevant supplies' exceed £70,000 (2011) in a calendar year.[67] A 'relevant supply' is defined as being a supply which:[68]

- involves the removal of goods to the UK by or under the directions of the person making the supply (ie the trader in another Member State);

- *does not* involve the installation or assembly of the goods at a place in the UK;

(at www.hmrc.gov.uk/manuals/vatposgmanual/vatposg3510.htm), the rationale for these rules is as follows: 'The [distance selling] rules are intended to combat distortion of trade and unfair competition by transferring the place of supply to the Member State in which the customer receives the goods. Without this, cross-border supplies to private individuals would be subject to VAT in the Member State of dispatch as a domestic supply. With the variations in VAT rates between Member States this could encourage businesses selling mainly to private individuals (for example mail order companies) to relocate their businesses to Member States with the lowest rates of domestic VAT. New means of transport are excluded from these arrangements. Consequently the place of supply for intra-EC supplies of new motor vehicles, boats and aircraft remains the Member State of despatch, regardless of the status of the customer. Nevertheless, special arrangements apply for taxation in the Member State of arrival and you can find further details about this in the manual covering new means of transport and Notice 728 (New means of transport). Distance selling is also covered in the manuals covering the Single Market and registration, and Notices 700/1 (Should I be registered for VAT?) and 725 (the Single Market).'

[66] VATA 1994, s 7(4): transfers within Sch 4, para 5(1) and 6. See also Chapter 17.
[67] VATA 1994, Sch 2, para 1(1). The threshold does not apply to goods subject to excise duty.
[68] VATA 1994, Sch 2, para 10.

- is a transaction under which goods are acquired in the UK from another Member State by a person who is not a taxable person (ie a person who is not UK VAT registered);

- in the course or furtherance of a business is carried on by the supplier; and

- is neither an exempt supply nor a supply of goods subject to a duty of excise, nor a new means of transport, nor the supply of assets forming part of the business.

Once the £70,000 threshold is met the place of supply of goods is treated as being in the UK pursuant to the rules outlined above. Until this threshold is met, the non-UK, but EU trader, will continue to charge VAT on the supply according to the rate prevailing in their own country (ie country of origin), although a trader can also opt to register and account for VAT in the UK even though its 'distance sales' are below the threshold. In any event, EU traders must pay close attention to the volume of supplies to other Member States for the purposes of ensuring compliance with their registration obligations in those other Member States under these rules, since where the relevant thresholds are met, this will result in VAT having to be accounted for in another Member State (ie country of destination).

Example 18.5

Z SA, based in Spain, operates an internet trading site and sells goods via e-commerce. Isabelle, based in the UK, places an order via the internet site for the supply of goods. Z SA has a gross turnover of £100,000 in respect of internet sales derived trade from the UK. In these circumstances the Spanish trader is liable to be registered as a taxable person under VATA 1994, Sch 2, since supplies of this nature would be deemed to take place in the UK with the result that UK VAT must be accounted for by Z SA.

18.6   DISTANCE SALES OF GOODS FROM THE UK TO ANOTHER MEMBER STATE TO NON-TAXABLE PERSONS

Broadly, where a UK taxable person makes supplies of goods[69] to a non-taxable person in another Member State the place of supply will *not* be the UK in the following circumstances (without this rule, the place of supply would be the UK as the place of departure):[70]

---

[69]   But excluding for this purpose a new means of transport: VATA 1994, s 7(5). See HMRC Notice 728.

[70]   VATA 1994, s 7(5), derived from Arts 33 and 34 of the VAT Directive. See HMRC Notice 725, at para 6.4. If a UK supplier makes distance sales of excise goods to another Member State, the supplier will be required to register and account for VAT in that Member State, irrespective of the value involved (HMRC Notice 725, para 6.7).

- the supply of goods involves the removal of the goods, by or under the direction of the person who supplies them (ie by the UK supplier) to another Member State; and

- the person who makes the supply is taxable in another Member State (ie the UK supplier has exceeded the relevant distance selling threshold and is subject to VAT registration in the country the goods are supplied to under rules comparable to those where a supplier in another Member State makes distance sales to a non-taxable person in the UK (ie under Sch 2 to VATA 1994: see discussion at **18.5**), or alternatively, they have opted to register and account for VAT in that other Member State).

Where the place of supply moves outside of the UK under the above rules, the place of supply will effectively be the EU country to which the goods are dispatched (although the UK's rules do not explicitly prescribe the alternative place of supply). In other words, the UK supplier will be required to account for VAT under the rules of the other country to which the goods are transferred and not those of the UK. If the UK supplier is not responsible for the removal of the goods from the UK, or is not yet taxable in the other Member State, the place of supply will continue to be the UK.[71] Effectively, until a UK supplier meets the relevant distance selling threshold in a Member State for registration (or has otherwise opted for registration) in that other Member State, UK VAT will continue to be charged.

Example 18.6

UK Goods Ltd makes a supply of goods to Zorro, who is a non-taxable person resident in Spain. The value of the goods is £500, and UK Goods Ltd is responsible for the delivery of the goods to Spain. Supplies to Spain do not exceed more than £5,000 each year. UK Goods Ltd is not liable to pay Spanish VAT. UK Goods Ltd is not required to account for Spanish VAT, because it does not make supplies which render it liable to Spanish VAT under the distance selling rules. However, the supply may be subject to UK VAT. This is because UK Goods Ltd is a taxable person and the place of supply will be deemed to be the UK under the UK's domestic rules (see Table 17.2 in Chapter 17 at **17.10.2**).

Each Member State will apply distance selling thresholds before registration is required subject to the limits set by the EU (as of 2011, the distance selling thresholds which can be set by Member States are either €35,000 or €100,000 (approx £70,000 in GBP equivalent). Accordingly, it is necessary to check these VAT registration thresholds in order to ensure compliance with VAT laws where supplies are made to a Member State.

---

[71] VATA 1994, s 7(7)(a).

Each Member State is responsible for setting its own threshold, which is set in its own currency. The level of thresholds is given on either the website of the European Commission,[72] or of the relevant tax authority.

---

[72]   http://ec.europa.eu/.

CHAPTER 19

IMPORTS: NON-EU TRADE IN GOODS

19.1 INTRODUCTION

VAT is charged on the importation of goods from countries that do not form part of the EU.[1] For example, goods imported from the US or the Channel Islands under a transaction entered into via e-commerce will be subject to import VAT (subject to any applicable import relief). Import VAT is charged on the importation of goods,[2] and is charged and payable as if it were a customs duty.[3] The rate of tax which currently applies to imported goods is the standard rate of 20% (2011), the reduced rate of 5% (2011)[4] or the rate of 0% ('zero-rate').[5]

Goods entering the UK from another Member State and supplied to business recipients are treated as acquisitions for VAT purposes, and subject to a different VAT regime from that applicable to the importation of goods from outside the EU.[6] VAT is however chargeable upon both types of transaction.[7] The VAT liability incurred on the importation of

---

[1] The countries which comprise the VAT territory of the EU are: Austria, Belgium, Bulgaria, Cyprus, Czech Republic, Denmark (excluding Busingen and the Isle of Heligoland), Greece, Hungary, the Republic of Ireland, Italy (except the communes of Livigno and Camione d'Italia and the Italian waters of Lake Lugano), Latvia, Lithuania, Luxembourg, Malta, The Netherlands, Poland, Portugal (including the Azores and Madeira), Romania, Slovakia, Slovenia, Spain (including the Balearic Islands but excluding Ceuta and Melilla), Sweden and the United Kingdom (including the Isle of Man). Territories of some of the foregoing are not within the VAT territory of the EU, and accordingly supplies of goods from these territories will be treated as imports. The territories are: Andorra, the Åland Islands (Finland), the Channel Islands (Jersey, Guernsey, Sark) and Gibraltar, the Canary Islands (Spain), the overseas departments of France (Guadeloupe, Martinique, Reunion and French Guiana) and Mount Athos (Greece). To check on any alterations in the extent of the VAT territory see www.hmrc.gov.uk, and Value Added Tax Regulations 1995, SI 1995/2518, regs 136–139. Goods removed from the Isle of Man to the UK are not treated as an importation provided that any VAT due has been accounted for in the Isle of Man, or if there has been relief from VAT in the Isle of Man, then the conditions for relief have not been broken: Value Added Tax (Isle of Man) Order 1982, SI 1982/1067, reg 3.
[2] VATA 1994, s 1(1)(c).
[3] VATA 1994, s 1(4).
[4] VATA 1994, s 29A, Sch 7A.
[5] VATA 1994, s 30(3), Sch 8.
[6] See Chapter 18.
[7] VATA 1994, s 1(1).

goods is placed upon the importer. Where goods are acquired from another Member State the VAT liability is imposed upon the person acquiring the goods.[8]

E-commerce by its very nature facilitates international trade with the UK. The activities of overseas traders may result in the importation of goods to the UK either to non-business consumers or to business consumers who use the import for onward supply to UK consumers or specific export markets. The effect of import VAT is that it may be imposed upon overseas traders, who will be required to account for it to HMRC. The following example illustrates how e-commerce may result in import VAT issues arising.

Example 19.1

> Alpha Ltd, a UK company, places an order via an e-commerce trading site for the purchase of 100 computers manufactured and sold by Beta Inc, a company based in the US. Under the terms of the contract of sale, the purchaser agrees to pay all import duties and other taxes arising from the importation of goods. Additionally, the effect of the contract of sale is to transfer ownership in the goods as soon as dispatched from the US distribution centre. In these circumstances Alpha Ltd is the importer for the purposes of VAT. Because Alpha Ltd is registered for VAT purposes, the import VAT can be reclaimed as input VAT against the output VAT received on supplies made by Alpha Ltd to UK consumers who purchase the imported computers.

Some suppliers have established themselves outside the EU in order to enable private customers within the EU to purchase goods in circumstances where no import VAT is payable. For example, a supplier carrying on its business in Jersey will not be required to charge VAT on supplies to UK customers. This is because Jersey is not a Member State of the EU, and it does not charge VAT on goods purchased in Jersey. As discussed in this chapter, import VAT is a liability of the importer (see **19.2.1** and **19.3**), which under the terms and conditions of sale, will usually be the customer. However, there is a special relief that exempts personal imports of low value goods (not exceeding £15) from import VAT into the UK (ie from Jersey). This relief is known as 'low value consignment relief', which could be used when the Jersey supplier sent such low value goods (eg, CDs, DVDs, video games, PC consumables, etc) from Jersey to the UK (see also **19.5.10**). To the extent the value of the goods did not qualify for the low-value exemption from import VAT, the customer (as importer) would be liable for import VAT at the time of importation. However, the UK Government considers that the low value consignment relief has been exploited by businesses based in the Channel Islands. The low value consignment relief has therefore been withdrawn completely for goods imported to the UK from the Channel Islands, with

---

[8]   VATA, s 1(3).

effect from 1 April 2012. However, the relief remains available for goods imported from other non-EU countries.[9]

19.2 IMPORTS

As set out in VATA 1994, VAT is charged on the importation of goods from a place outside the EU,[10] and is charged and payable in relation to the importation of such goods as if it were a customs duty.[11] VAT is applied to the *value* of the goods at the time of importation (see **19.4**).[12] The VAT incurred as a result of the importation rules qualifies as input tax, which can be set off against appropriate supplies upon which output tax is received.[13] Any goods arriving in the UK from outside the EU by post must also have a customs declaration fixed to the package, which will have been completed by the supplier. A declaration should show the following information relating to the goods: (a) their description, (b) their value and (c) whether the goods are gifts, commercial or personal items.

Import VAT is collected by HMRC. Goods imported for business purposes are normally declared to HMRC using Form C88, Single Administration Document[14] (known as SAD), which can be submitted electronically if authorised to do so (via Direct Trader Input).[15] Some sellers who supply goods from outside the EU have arrangements with the UK whereby any import VAT that is due on the supply is paid to the supplier at the time the order is made by a UK non-business customer. The supplier will then pay the amount of import VAT to their postal authority, which in turn will pay that amount to HMRC. Only certain suppliers are authorised to do this, and they will have a special number, which is shown on the customs declaration (which will say 'Import VAT pre-paid').[16]

VATA 1994 is the legal authority for the application of UK VAT to imports. The legislation also provides that the provisions of the Customs and Excise Management Act 1979 (CEMA 1979) have effect in relation to customs duties on the importation of goods into the UK; and any EU legislation relating to Community customs duties on goods entering into the Community are to apply to any VAT chargeable on the importation of

---

[9]   Draft legislation is to be included in the Finance Bill 2012.
[10] VATA 1994, s 1(1)(c).
[11] VATA 1994, s 1(4).
[12] VATA 1994, s 2(1)(c).
[13] VATA 1994, s 24(1)(c). For the meaning and nature of the concepts of 'input' and 'output' tax, see Chapter 17.
[14] This is also used for postal imports of goods where their value exceeds £2,000. Goods with a value of less than £2,000 are the subject of either Form CN22 or CN23 (see **19.6**).
[15] HMRC's view of the law and practice on the import of goods is provided in Notice 702 *Imports* (April 2010) and Notice 501 *A Brief Guide to Import Procedures* (April 2010). See also HMRC Notice 199 *Imported Goods: Customs procedures and Customs debt* (April 2010), Section 7.
[16] See **19.6** for further details.

goods from places outside the Member States as they apply in relation to any such customs duty or excise, or Community customs duties.[17] The application of customs duty to goods is beyond the scope of this book.

19.2.1 Overview: UK import rules

The basic rules of UK VAT on importations are summarised below.

Rule 1: Pre-conditions to a VAT charge on an import

UK VAT is charged on the importation of goods into the UK from a place outside the Member States.[18] Goods are imported from a place outside the Member States where all of the following conditions are met:[19]

(1)   the goods having been removed from a place outside the Member States enter the territory of the Community;

(2)   they enter that territory by being removed to the UK or are removed to the UK after entering that territory (of the Community); and

(3)   the circumstances are such that it is on their removal to the UK or subsequently while they are in the UK that any Community customs debt in respect of duty on their entry into the territory of the Community would be incurred.

Goods will not be treated as imported for the purposes of VAT at any time before a Community customs debt in respect of duty on their entry into the territory of the Community would be incurred.[20]

The conditions are subject to any rules to the contrary in the customs enactments.[21] A failure to comply with provisions of EU and UK customs laws could result in prosecution, a fine, and any goods in respect of which an offence has been committed may be seized by HMRC as liable to forfeiture.

Rule 2: Importer to pay duty

The obligation to pay import duty is upon the importer.[22] No imported goods can be removed or delivered on importation until the importer has paid any duty chargeable, ie VAT.[23] The duty must be paid at the time of

---

[17]   VATA 1994, s 16.
[18]   VATA 1994, s 1.
[19]   VATA 1994, s 15(1).
[20]   VATA 1994, s 15(2).
[21]   VATA 1994, s 15(3). See VATA 1994, s 16 and HMRC Notice 199, Section 10.
[22]   CEMA 1979, s 43(1).
[23]   CEMA 1979, s 43(1).

'making the entry' (ie when the goods make entry into the UK).[24] However, it is possible for an importer to apply to delay payment until a later prescribed payment day under the Duty Deferment Scheme.[25] Evidence of payment of import VAT is an import VAT certificate (known as Form C79).

Rule 3: Time of importation

The time of importation is critical, because this normally equates with when import VAT is due on goods.[26] In other words, the time of importation is generally the time of 'making the entry' of goods. Unless goods are placed into an approved customs arrangement (eg a 'free zone') then VAT is due and payable at the time of importation (though payment may be deferred under the duty deferrment arrangements noted above).[27]

The time of importation of goods is summarised in Table 19.1.[28]

Table 19.1: Time of importation

Method of entry	Time of entry
Sea	When ship comes within limits of port.
Air	When aircraft lands in UK or goods unloaded in UK (whichever is earlier).
Land	When the goods are brought across the boundary into Northern Ireland.

Where goods from a country outside the EU are placed directly into storage arrangements known as customs warehousing, the time of importation is suspended with the result that the payment of the import VAT is suspended.[29] Further, any excise duty, where applicable, on non-Community goods will not become due until the goods leave the customs warehousing procedure. The principal schemes that suspend the obligations to pay VAT in one way or another are as follows:[30]

---

[24] CEMA 1979, s 43(1).
[25] CEMA 1979, s 45; Customs Duties (Deferred Payment) Regulations 1976, SI 1976/1223. See generally HMRC Notice 101 *Deferring Duty, VAT and Other Charges* (March 2009).
[26] VATA 1994, s 1(1); CEMA 1979, s 43. See HMRC Notice 702 *Imports* (April 2010), para 4.1.
[27] VATA 1994, s 17. A 'free zone' is an area in the UK which is designated by the Treasury: see CEMA 1979, s 100A.
[28] The rules are provided by s 5 of CEMA 1979.
[29] The customs warehousing regime is provided for by Council Regulation 2913/92/EEC and Commission Regulation 2454/93/EC, both of which contain the EU's principal customs legislation, known as the Community Customs Code and implementing provisions. See: http://ec.europa.eu/taxation_customs/customs/procedural_aspects/general/community_code/index_en.htm.
[30] For a full list of the Customs arrangements which suspend the obligation to pay import VAT, see HMRC Notice 702/9 *Import Customs Procedures* (November 2005).

(1)   goods subject to a customs warehousing scheme;[31] and

(2)   goods subject to a free zone.[32]

Rule 4: Recovery of import VAT

When a person incurs import VAT on goods, the extent to which VAT can be reclaimed depends upon the person's status under VATA 1994. If a person is registered for VAT purposes, ie where turnover exceeds £73,000 in a year (2011), such a person is usually entitled to claim input tax incurred in making taxable supplies in the course of that person's business.[33] That input tax is offset against output tax on those taxable supplies. Any excess of input tax is credited to the person concerned.[34] For the purposes of UK law, VAT incurred on imports qualifies as input tax for an importer, provided the goods have been imported for the purposes of the importer's business.[35] An input VAT claim would normally need to be made on the VAT return for the accounting period during which the importation took place, supported by the normal evidence of payment of import VAT (ie the import VAT certificate (Form C79)). In contrast, in the case of persons who are not VAT registered and who import for business purposes, while the same import procedures for entry of goods and payment or deferment of VAT will apply to them as for VAT-registered persons, they will not generally be entitled to reclaim the import VAT amount as input tax and would not receive an import VAT certificate. In addition, in the case of, for example, a shipping or freight agent who is simply responsible for the shipping/clearance of the goods on importation and does not act for the importer in respect of an onward supply, he will not be entitled to reclaim as input tax the VAT amount which they may pay or defer on an importer's behalf. This is because the goods have not been imported for the purposes of their business; only the importer would be entitled to recover such VAT. The recovery of such amount by such an agent would need to be agreed with the importer as part of their own commercial arrangements (although special rules can apply in favour of the agent to allow recovery from HMRC in certain specific cases, such as where the importer has gone into liquidation, where the necessary conditions are met).[36] See **19.7** for a short summary of UK VAT registration requirements affecting overseas suppliers. The circumstances in which a person is required to register as a

---

[31]   CEMA 1979, s 46. See generally Regulation 2503/88/EEC; Regulation 2561/90/EEC; and Excise Warehousing (etc) Regulations 1988, SI 1988/809.
[32]   See VATA 1994, s 17 and Free Zone Regulations 1991, SI 1991/2727.
[33]   VATA 1994, s 26(1), (2). See HMRC Notice 702, para 6.1.
[34]   VATA, s 25(2).
[35]   VATA, s 24(1)(c).
[36]   See HMRC Notice 702, paras 2.3, 2.4 and 6.1, and para 2.5, which covers the rules/conditions applicable in respect of a shipping or forwarding agent's ability to recover import VAT from HMRC in place of the importer.

taxable person, or is entitled to voluntary registration (as well as the concepts of 'input tax' and 'output tax'), are considered further in Chapter 17.

Example 19.2

X Ltd, a UK-based company, incurs import VAT on goods used to make taxable supplies in the UK. The goods are ordered by X Ltd through use of e-commerce. In the first quarter of 2011 the company incurs import VAT of £70,000 and makes taxable supplies to UK consumers worth £100,000. VAT at the standard rate of 20% (2011) means that X Ltd receives output tax of £20,000 from UK consumers. X Ltd should therefore be entitled to set £70,000 of input tax against the £20,000 of output tax and to obtain a credit of £50,000 from HMRC.

19.3   IMPORTER: THE MEANING

CEMA 1979 defines an 'importer' as:[37]

'... in relation to any goods at any time between their importation and the time when they are delivered out of charge, includes any owner or other person for the time being possessed of or beneficially interested in the goods ...'

As explained above, any import duty is the liability of the importer. The importer may be the seller or buyer based on this definition. If title to the goods passes to a UK buyer prior to importation the liability to account for import duty will be upon the buyer as the importer. In these circumstances the non-UK seller will not be responsible for any import duty, and there will be no question of such a person being required to be VAT registered in the UK in the absence of any other supplies. It is to be noted from the definition that an importer does not actually need to be the owner of the goods.

19.4   VALUE OF IMPORTED GOODS

Import VAT is applied to the *value* of the goods at the time of importation.[38] The value of imported goods for VAT purposes is determined by the applicable customs duties rules (irrespective of whether or not the goods in question are subject to any duties).[39] However, the

---

[37]   CEMA 1979, s 1(1).
[38]   VATA 1994, s 2(1)(c).
[39]   See HMRC Notice 252 *Valuation of Imported goods for Customs purposes, VAT and Trade Statistics* (June 2009).

value of the goods must also be taken to include the following matters (to the extent not already included under the applicable customs duties rules):[40]

- all taxes, duties and other charges levied either outside or, by reason of importation, within the UK (except VAT);

- all incidental expenses, such as commission, packing, transport and insurance costs, up to the goods' first destination in the UK;[41] and

- if at the time of the importation of the goods from a place outside the Member States a further destination for the goods is known, and that destination is within the UK or another Member State, all such incidental expenses insofar as they result from the transport of the goods to that other destination.

If a discount has been given this will reduce the value of the goods in circumstances where goods are imported from outside the Member States for a monetary consideration, the terms on which those goods are imported allow a discount for prompt payment of the price, and the terms do not include provision for payment of that price by instalments.[42]

19.5   RELIEF FROM IMPORT VAT

In some cases, no import VAT is payable on goods imported from a country that is not a Member State of the EU. The circumstances in which no import VAT is payable are set out below.

19.5.1   Zero-rated imports

Where goods are within the zero-rating classification and are imported into the UK from a place outside the EU, no import VAT is charged.[43] The nature of the zero-rating classifications is examined in Chapter 17. Table 19.2 summarises the groupings for which zero-rating is granted, insofar as considered relevant to e-commerce activities. It must be remembered that there are many exceptions to these classifications. For example, while 'food' appears under Group 1 as zero-rated, there are many exceptions for certain food items, the supply of which are standard-rated and upon which import VAT would be payable.

---

[40]   VATA 1994, s 21(2). Special provisions apply to commission and premiums in respect of works of art, antiques and collectors' items: VATA 1994, s 21(2A).

[41]   This is the place indicated on the consignment note or any other document by means of which the goods are imported into the UK, or, in the absence of such documentation, the place of the first transfer of cargo in the UK: VATA 1995, s 21(2).

[42]   VATA 1994, s 21(3).

[43]   VATA 1994, s 30(3).

Table 19.2: Summary of zero-rated goods

Zero-rated goods	Excepted items from group (illustrative examples)
Food used for human consumption.	Confectionery, beverages subject to excise duty.
Books, brochures, newspapers, children's picture books.	Plans, drawings for industrial, architectural, engineering and commercial purposes.

Goods temporarily imported for removal to another EU Member State, and which are to be the subject of a zero-rated supply, are not subject to UK import VAT where the necessary conditions as imposed by HMRC are met.[44]

19.5.2 Goods produced by the United Nations and other UN organisations

No import VAT is payable in respect of certain imported goods produced by the United Nations or by other UN organisations.[45] The purpose of import is not relevant to this relief. The goods subject to relief are specified in Sch 1 to the Value Added Tax (Imported Goods) Relief Order 1984. The goods subject to relief include:

- holograms for laser projection;

- multimedia kits;

- materials for programmed instruction, including materials in kit form, with the corresponding printed materials;

- films of an educational, scientific or cultural character; and

- newsreels (with or without soundtrack).

19.5.3 Capital goods and equipment on transfer of activities from abroad

No import VAT is payable in respect of capital goods and equipment which are imported by a person into the UK for the purposes of a business which he has ceased to carry on abroad, but which he is to carry

---

[44] See Value Added Tax Regulations 1995, SI 1995/2518, reg 123. See generally HMRC Notice 702/7 *Import VAT relief for goods supplied onward to another country in the EC* (April 2010).

[45] Value Added Tax (Imported Goods) Relief Order 1984, SI 1984/746, art 4.

on in the UK.[46] It is a condition of relief that the business will be used to make exclusively taxable supplies, and that the imported capital goods and equipment were used in the business carried on abroad for at least 12 months before cessation of the business.

19.5.4 Goods used for promotion of a trade

Certain types of goods distributed for the purposes of promotion of a trade are not subject to import VAT.[47] This is an important area of relief because many e-commerce traders will provide free goods, such as samples, as a way of soliciting trade. For example, an overseas trader could offer to send samples to all people providing details via the trader's internet business site.

The import relief classifications given in the context of trade promotion are summarised in Table 19.3.

Table 19.3: Trade promotion

Item no	Scope
1	Articles of no intrinsic commercial value sent free of charge by suppliers of goods and services for the sole purpose of advertising.
2	Samples of negligible value of a kind and in quantities capable of being used solely for soliciting orders for goods of the same kind.
3	Printed advertising matter, including catalogues, price lists, directions for use and brochures, which relates to goods for sale or hire by a person established outside the UK, or to transport, commercial insurance or banking services offered by a person established in a third country, and which clearly displays the name of the person by whom the goods or services are offered. Unless in the case of printed matter intended for distribution free of charge and relating to either goods for sale or hire, this item does not apply to (a) any consignment containing two or more copies of different documents; (b) any consignment containing two or more copies of the same document, unless the total gross weight of such consignment does not exceed one kg; or (c) any goods which are the subject of grouped consignments from the same consignor to the same consignee.
4	Goods to be distributed free of charge at an event, as small representative samples,[48] for use or commercial consumption by the public.
5	Goods imported solely for the purpose of being demonstrated at an event.

---

[46] Value Added Tax (Imported Goods) Relief Order 1984, SI 1984/746, art 5, Sch 2, Group 1.

[47] Value Added Tax (Imported Goods) Relief Order 1984, SI 1984/746, art 5, Group 3.

[48] The term 'representative samples' means goods which are '(a) imported free of charge or obtained at such event from goods imported in bulk, (b) identifiable as advertising

Item no	Scope
6	Goods imported solely for the purpose of being used in the demonstration of any machine or apparatus displayed at an event.
7	Paints, varnishes, wallpaper and other materials of low value to be used in the building, fitting-out and decoration of a temporary stand at an event.
8	Catalogues, prospectuses, price lists, advertising posters, calendars (whether or not illustrated), unframed photographs and other printed matter or articles advertising goods displayed at an event, supplied without charge for the purpose of distribution free of charge to the pubic at such an event.

Items 4 to 8 relate to the distribution of goods for the purposes of an 'event'. The term 'event' is defined under the import relief regulations as meaning, among other things:

'(a) any trade, industrial, agricultural or craft exhibition, fair or similar show or display, not being an exhibition, fair, show or display organised for private purposes in a shop or on business premises with a view to the sale of the goods displayed; ...'[49]

19.5.5 Goods for testing

No import VAT is applied to goods imported 'for the purposes of examination, analysis or testing to determine their composition, quality or other technical characteristics, to provide information or for industrial or commercial research'.[50]

19.5.6 Printed material

Various forms of printed material imported from outside the EU are given relief from import VAT. Materials considered relevant in the context of e-commerce/general internet-based business activity that are given relief include:[51]

- printed forms, labels, tickets and similar documents sent to travel agents in the UK by transport and tourist undertakings abroad;

samples of low value, (c) not easily marketable and, where appropriate, packaged in quantities which are less than the lowest quantity of the same goods as marketed, and (d) intended to be consumed at such event, where the goods comprise foodstuffs or beverages not packaged as described in paragraph (c) above': Value Added Tax (Imported Goods) Relief Order 1984, SI 1984/746, art 5, Sch 2, Group 3, Note 4.

[49] Value Added Tax (Imported Goods) Relief Order 1984, SI 1984/746, art 5, Sch 2, Group 3.

[50] Value Added Tax (Imported Goods) Relief Order 1984, SI 1984/746, art 5, Sch 2, Group 4.

[51] Value Added Tax (Imported Goods) Relief Order 1984, SI 1984/746, art 5, Sch 2, Group 7.

Value Added Tax: European Union Trade

- documents sent for the purpose of free distribution to encourage persons to visit foreign countries, and particularly to attend cultural, tourist, sporting, religious, trade or professional meetings or events; and

- foreign hotel lists and yearbooks published by or on behalf of official tourist agencies and timetables for foreign transport services, for free distribution.

19.5.7   Material in connection with intellectual property rights

To obtain the protection of intellectual property laws under a national system such as the UK of technical knowledge, or commercial marketing symbols, documentary material must sometimes by submitted to the relevant registry. Material imported for the purpose of being submitted to bodies competent to deal with protection of copyright or industrial or commercial patent rights is not subject to import VAT.[52]

19.5.8   Information carriers

No import VAT is payable in relation to recorded media, such as punched cards, sound recordings and microfilm, that are sent free of charge for the purposes of transmission of information.[53]

19.5.9   Goods as gifts

No import VAT is payable in respect of goods sent on an occasional basis as gifts in token of friendship or goodwill between bodies, public authorities or groups carrying on activity in the public interest. This relief does not include goods which are alcoholic beverages or tobacco products.[54]

19.5.10   Goods of limited value

No import VAT is payable in respect of any consignment of goods (other than alcoholic beverages, tobacco products, perfumes and toilet waters) not exceeding £15 (2011) in value.[55] However, as mentioned at **19.1**, the UK Government considers that the low value consignment relief has been

---

[52]   Value Added Tax (Imported Goods) Relief Order 1984, SI 1984/746, art 5, Sch 2, Group 8, item 1.

[53]   Value Added Tax (Imported Goods) Relief Order 1984, SI 1984/746, art 5, Sch 2, Group 8, item 4.

[54]   Value Added Tax (Imported Goods) Relief Order 1984, SI 1984/746, art 5, Sch 2, Group 8, item 7.

[55]   Value Added Tax (Imported Goods) Relief Order 1984, SI 1984/746, art 5, Sch 2, Group 8, item 8. The Government announced its intention in March 2011 to explore options with the European Commission to limit the scope of the relief so that it cannot be exploited for any purpose for which it was not intended.

exploited by businesses based in the Channel Islands for the purposes of selling, on an increasingly large scale, low value goods to UK consumers VAT free. The low value consignment relief has therefore been withdrawn completely for goods imported from the Channel Islands, with effect from 1 April 2012. However, the relief currently remains available for goods imported from other non-EU countries.[56]

Example 19.3

Alpha Ltd, a non-EU, non-Channel Islands tax resident company, operates an independent retail business from Country X in relation to the supply of various goods. Alpha Ltd uses the e-commerce platform of Beta Ltd (a UK tax resident company) to sell its goods to customers in the UK. Alpha Ltd's terms and conditions of sale provide, among other things, that:

- Beta Ltd acts as disclosed agent of Alpha Ltd;

- any order placed for goods via Beta Ltd's e-commerce platform results in an e-mail being sent by Beta Ltd on behalf of Alpha Ltd confirming receipt of the order (including details of the order);

- an order placed over the e-commerce platform represents an offer by the customer to purchase goods from Alpha Ltd;

- an order is accepted by Alpha Ltd when the company sends the customer an e-mail confirming that the goods have been dispatched to the customer;

- goods are dispatched from Country X to the customer;

- delivery rates for goods are as shown on Beta Ltd's e-commerce platform;

- all ownership, title and risk relating to the goods passes to the customer at the time when the goods are dispatched from Alpha Ltd's premises;

- where the delivery address for the goods is outside Country X, the customer (as addressee) will be the importer of the goods into their country; and

- the importer must comply with all laws of the country to which the goods are delivered, including paying any import duties and taxes (import VAT) relating to the goods.

---

[56] Draft legislation is to be included in the Finance Bill 2012. See www.hmrc.gov.uk/tiin/tiin874.pdf and HMRC's announcement at www.hmrc.gov.uk/news/removal-lvcr.htm, in which it was reported that 75% of all international parcel post to the UK from outside the EU is estimated to originate in the Channel Islands.

Chloe places an order via the e-commerce platform of Beta Ltd, which acts as agent for Alpha Ltd. The order placed with Alpha Ltd relates to the purchase of DVDs worth less than £15 for personal use. Chloe receives e-mail confirmation of the order and notice of dispatch of the goods in accordance with the terms and conditions referred to above. Alpha Ltd is under no obligation to charge UK VAT since it is established outside the EU. Under the terms and conditions of the supply Chloe is the importer of the goods. However, under current UK law, since the value of the goods is less than £15 she should qualify for exemption from import VAT.

19.5.11   Gifts between individuals

Gifts of any nature, such as computer software, between individuals not in excess of £40 in value (2011) imported from a country outside the EU are not subject to import VAT.[57] The relief only applies to a consignment of goods of a non-commercial character. Broadly, this is a consignment of goods for no consideration, between individuals, intended solely for personal use by the recipient or his family, and not for any commercial purpose. The appropriate Customs declaration will also need to be completed correctly. The relief will only be available in relation to gifts of an occasional nature,[58] for example, items sent for a birthday, anniversary or religious holiday.

> *Example 19.4*
>
> Brian Rhodes sends a parcel containing a computer software program to John Rhodes, his cousin, who lives in the UK. The software program is a gift for John's son. In these circumstances no import VAT is payable unless the value of the computer software is in excess of £40 (2011).

However, ordering goods over the internet which are to be delivered to another person will not count as a gift under current HMRC practice,[59] although HMRC will allow the relief to apply to one package containing gifts for several people, with the consequence that the VAT import gift allowance of £40 (2011) applies to each gift individually provided that it is separately wrapped, addressed and listed on the customs declaration.[60]

19.6   POSTAL IMPORTATION OF GOODS

Many goods purchased through e-commerce, such as DVDs, computer software and books, will be despatched via the postal system. Under the Postal Packets (Revenue and Customs) Regulations 2011[61] and the Postal

---

[57] Value Added Tax (Small Non-Commercial Consignments) Relief Order 1986, SI 1986/939, art 3.
[58] Value Added Tax (Small Non-Commercial Consignments) Relief Order 1986, SI 1986/939, art 4.
[59] See www.hmrc.gov.uk/customs/post/buying.htm (2011).
[60] See www.hmrc.gov.uk/customs/post/buying.htm (2011).
[61] SI 2011/3036.

Services Act 2000, all 'foreign postal packets' posted from the UK to outside the EU or posted from outside the EU into the UK must be accompanied by a customs declaration.[62] 'Foreign postal packet' means:[63]

> '... any postal packet either posted in the United Kingdom and sent to a place outside the United Kingdom, or posted in a place outside the United Kingdom and sent to a place within the United Kingdom, or in transit through the United Kingdom to a place outside the United Kingdom.'

Postal packet means:[64]

> '... a letter, parcel, packet or other article transmissible by post.'

The customs declaration will either be a CN22 or CN23, as appropriate. The declaration must state the nature, quantity and value of the goods contained within the parcel.[65]

In relation to packages arriving from outside the EU,[66] customs officers may send a notice to the addressee requiring entry to be made of the goods or a full and accurate account to be delivered to the officer.[67] In relation to any foreign postal packet, a customs officer may require the proper officer of the postal operator to produce and open the packet for examination.[68] The Regulations permit an appropriate officer of the postal operator to demand payment of any duty on delivering a postal packet.[69] Any payment received is then transferred by the postal operator to HMRC.[70] When a demand for payment is not met, the postal operator, with the agreement of HMRC, can dispose of the goods contained in the packet in any way it sees fit.[71]

19.7 OVERSEAS TRADERS: REGISTERING FOR VAT

Although an overseas e-commerce supplier may have no physical trading presence within the country in which the recipient is located (eg the UK) for the purposes of a direct tax charge, such as corporation tax, it may be subject to VAT laws. The ingredients of the VAT tax charge can be satisfied without the existence of any physical office within the UK or if appropriate, another Member State. If goods are treated as imported into

---

[62] Postal Packets (Revenue and Customs) Regulations 2011, SI 2011/3036, reg 17.
[63] Postal Services Act 2000, s 105(3).
[64] Postal Services Act 2000, s 125(1).
[65] Postal Packets (Revenue and Customs) Regulations 2011, SI 2011/3036, reg 18.
[66] Postal services within the EU are governed by Council Regulation 2913/92/EEC, OJ L 302, 19/10/1992 p 1.
[67] Postal Packets (Revenue and Customs) Regulations 2011, SI 2011/3036, reg 22(1).
[68] Postal Packets (Revenue and Customs) Regulations 2011, SI 2011/3036, reg 21.
[69] Postal Service Act 2000, s 105(3).
[70] Postal Packets (Revenue and Customs) Regulations 2011, SI 2011/3036, reg 23(1).
[71] Postal Packets (Revenue and Customs) Regulations 2011, SI 2011/3036, reg 23(2).

the UK and the relevant registration thresholds are met in relation to taxable supplies in the UK, the non-EU overseas supplier will be required to register for VAT in the UK.[72]

Where goods are imported into the UK under the directions of an overseas supplier and supplied to a UK customer, the place of that subsequent supply is treated as the UK. Specifically, VATA 1994 provides that where the supply of goods involves them being imported from a place outside the EU and the person who supplies them is the person by whom, or under whose directions, they are so imported, the place of supply is the UK.[73] The effect of this is that where the supplier acts as the importer, it may be liable to register for VAT in the UK in respect of its onward supply, even though a supply of goods involving their movement to the UK from outside the UK is normally treated under UK VAT rules as taking place outside the UK (in the place of departure).[74] These place of supply rules should be noted carefully since the place of supply is only in the UK in respect of goods removed from a country outside the EU where *the supplier* and *not the customer* directs the importation of the goods (see also Chapter 17, Table 17.2 at **17.10.2**).

Example 19.5

> Britannia Ltd places an order via the internet for the supply of £50,000-worth of goods from a trader, US Inc, based in the US. US Inc arranges for the importation of the goods into the UK. In these circumstances the place of supply of the goods is the UK because the supplier (ie US Inc) is the person who arranges (ie directs) their importation.

An overseas supplier who makes taxable supplies that are treated as being made in the UK will be required to register for UK VAT as a non-established taxable person where the relevant thresholds are met. A taxable person is defined as a person who is, or is required to be, registered under the VATA 1994.[75] A person who makes taxable supplies is required to register for the purposes of VAT where those supplies are in excess of £73,000 (2011)[76] to the year ending for any month.[77] An obligation also exists to register where the person has reasonable grounds

---

[72] VATA 1994, s 3(1), Sch 1. See also HMRC Notice 700/1 *Should I be registered for VAT?* (April 2010), at Section 8 in relation to 'non-established taxable persons', ie persons with no business establishment, incorporation or usual residence in the UK. There is, however, no need for a non-EU overseas supplier to register if the only UK supplies they make are supplies of general business-to-business services, ie, imported services in respect of which their business customer is liable to account for UK VAT under the 'reverse charge' procedure – see further in Chapter 17 at **17.12**.

[73] VATA 1994, s 7(6).

[74] VATA 1994, s 7(7)(b).

[75] VATA 1994, s 3(1), Schs 1–3A. See also note 72 above and Chapter 17 on establishments.

[76] Refer to HMRC's website to confirm current registration thresholds: www.hmrc.gov.uk.

[77] VATA 1994, Sch 1, para 1(1)(a). Liability must be notified to the Commissioners within 30 days of the end of the month in which the liability arises (para 5(1)).

for believing that the value of supplies will exceed £73,000 within a following 30-day period.[78] A person is not obliged to register where HMRC is satisfied that the value of supplies will not exceed £71,000 in a period of one year beginning at the time at which that person would become liable to be registered.[79]

A person can cease to be registered under VATA 1994 only in specified circumstances: (a) a person ceases to be liable to register where HMRC is satisfied that the person has ceased to make taxable supplies[80] or (b) there is no obligation to remain registered where the conditions specified above obliging a person to register are no longer satisfied.[81] A person is entitled to deregistration where HMRC can be satisfied that the value of taxable supplies will not exceed £71,000 (2011) within one year.[82]

A non-established overseas supplier who is not obliged to register under VATA 1994 may nonetheless seek voluntary registration. A person may want to register so that input VAT incurred in making taxable supplies can be reclaimed (see also **19.2.1**). This can occur where a person satisfies HMRC that he will make taxable supplies, or alternatively that the person is carrying on a business and intends to make taxable supplies in the course of furtherance of business.[83] In these circumstances, HMRC will register the person from the date on which the request is made or from such earlier date as may be agreed.[84]

Broadly, an overseas supplier with no business establishment in the UK (see Chapter 17) has three options in relation to registering for UK VAT voluntarily (and/or when it is required to be registered), namely (a) to appoint a tax/VAT representative to deal with its UK VAT affairs,[85] (b) to appoint an agent to deal with its UK VAT affairs (HMRC cannot hold contractual agents responsible for the supplier's VAT debts) or (c) to deal with the VAT obligations itself. Where an overseas supplier registers for VAT it will need to comply with the same obligations that are imposed on a UK VAT registered supplier.

---

[78] VATA 1994, Sch 1, para 1(1)(b). Liability must be notified to the Commissioners before the end of the 30-day period by reference to which the liability arises (para 6(1)).

[79] VATA 1994, Sch 1, para 1(3).

[80] VATA 1994, Sch 1, para 3(a).

[81] VATA 1994, Sch 1, para 3(b).

[82] VATA 1994, Sch 1, para 4(1). A person will not, however, be deregistered if the reason the value of their supplies will not exceed the £71,000 limit is because the person will cease making taxable supplies or their supplies will be suspended for a period of 30 days or more.

[83] VATA 1994, Sch 1, para 9.

[84] VATA 1994, Sch 1, para 9.

[85] VATA 1994, s 48. However, such a representative becomes jointly and severally liable for the discharge of its principal's compliance with and discharge of any VAT debts, obligations and liabilities. See Chapter 17 at **17.19** and also HMRC Notice 700/1, Section 10. HMRC can in certain circumstances insist or direct a non-established taxable person to appoint a tax representative (para 10.3).

19.8   OVERSEAS TRADERS: GOODS IMPORTED BY A UK AGENT

Where goods are imported for onward supply into the UK and the value of any other supplies in the UK does not exceed UK registration thresholds (as referred to above), a non-UK trader can appoint an agent, who is VAT registered and resident in the UK, for the purposes of importing on its behalf and supplying the non-UK trader's goods to UK consumers. Under this arrangement, the non-UK trader can avoid the need to be registered for VAT in the UK,[86] However, for the arrangement to work the agent must issue tax invoices for the supplies of the goods. Additionally, the services of the agent for the non-UK trader may be subject to VAT at the standard rate (20%: 2011) if the supply of the services is treated as made in the UK and not where the non-UK trader belongs (the place of supply rules are generally examined in Chapter 17).

Pursuant to the above arrangement, the agent will be treated as the principal importer and supplier and will be required to enter goods into the UK as the importer and pay any relevant VAT. However, the agent (in contrast to a mere shipping or freight agent discussed earlier) should be able to reclaim any such import VAT as input tax, and set it off against the VAT received on the further supply of the goods by the agent to the UK consumer (as invoiced by the agent and in respect of which the agent has charged and accounted for UK VAT).

---

[86]   VATA 1994, s 47 and HMRC Notice 702 *Imports* (April 2010), para 2.7.

CHAPTER 20

EXPORTS AND DISPATCHES: NON-EU AND EU TRADE IN GOODS

20.1   INTRODUCTION

The movement of goods from the UK has VAT consequences where they are either physically transferred to another country outside the Member States of the EU,[1] or to another country within the EU.

For VAT purposes, the main effect of exporting goods is that the supply is usually treated as zero-rated where made to a person outside the EU and the benefit of such treatment is that a trader registered for VAT purposes should qualify to deduct all of its input tax incurred in making that taxable supply. When goods are exported they are 'consumed' outside the EU, and accordingly no VAT should be imposed on such goods. It will be recalled from Chapter 17 that VAT is solely a tax levied on goods and services consumed within the EU.

Where goods are physically transferred from a Member State to a taxable person in another Member State the terminology used in the VAT rules is of a 'removal' or 'dispatch' instead of an 'export'. The term 'export' is now used for VAT purposes for goods leaving the EU to outside the EU. As for exports, dispatches of goods to another Member State can also be zero-rated in the Member State of dispatch where certain conditions are met (see **20.3**).

---

[1]   The countries which comprise the VAT territory of the EU are: Austria, Belgium, Bulgaria, Cyprus, Czech Republic, Denmark (excluding Busingen and the Isle of Heligoland), Greece, Hungary, the Republic of Ireland, Italy (except the communes of Livigno and Camione d'Italia and the Italian waters of Lake Lugano), Latvia, Lithuania, Luxembourg, Malta, The Netherlands, Poland, Portugal (including the Azores and Madeira), Romania, Slovakia, Slovenia, Spain (including the Balearic Islands but excluding Ceuta and Melilla), Sweden and the United Kingdom (including the Isle of Man). Territories of some of the foregoing are not within the VAT territory of the EU. The territories are: Andorra, the Åland Islands (Finland), the Channel Islands (Jersey, Guernsey, Sark) and Gibraltar, the Canary Islands (Spain), the overseas departments of France (Guadeloupe, Martinique, Reunion and French Guiana) and Mount Athos (Greece). To check on any alterations in the extent of the VAT territory see www.hmrc.gov.uk and Value Added Tax Regulations 1995, SI 1995/2518, regs 136–139.

Where goods are supplied between Member States to a recipient who is not a taxable person in a Member State then the supplier will either charge and account for VAT under the rules of its country of origin, or, if the value of supplies reach a specified threshold in the recipient's Member State then it will be necessary to charge and account for VAT under the rules of that country (these are known as the 'distance selling' rules). These rules are examined in Chapter 18.

The purpose of this chapter is to very briefly examine the basic VAT rules on the export and dispatch of goods from the UK.

20.2   NON-EU: ZERO-RATING OF EXPORT GOODS

Where HMRC is satisfied that goods supplied by a person are exported to a place outside the EU the supply will be zero-rated.[2] Broadly, zero-rating treatment will apply where the following conditions are met:[3]

> '(a)   Goods intended for export to a place outside the member States of the EU have been supplied, otherwise than to a taxable person, to:
>   (i)   a person not UK resident;
>   (ii)   a trader who has no business establishment in the UK from which taxable supplies are made; or
>   (iii) an overseas authority; and
> (b)   The goods are exported to a place outside the Member States of the EU.'

Zero-rating is also available where the goods have been shipped for use as stores on a voyage or flight to an eventual destination outside the UK, or as merchandise for retail sale to people carried on such a voyage or flight.[4]

To obtain zero-rating a trader will need to satisfy HMRC that goods have in fact been exported from the UK within certain time limits and obtain evidence of export within those limits (generally 3 months from the time of supply), see HMRC Notice 703.[5] The evidence necessary to satisfy HMRC that an export has occurred is explained in Notice 703. The evidence may be provided either by way of official or commercial transport documents. The type of official document which may be provided is a Single Administrative Document (SAD) endorsed by Customs at the point of exit from the EU.[6] Alternatively, for example, in

---

[2]   VATA 1994, s 30(6), implementing the VAT Directive, arts 131 and 146(1)(a), (b) and (e).
[3]   Value Added Tax Regulations 1995, SI 1995/2518, reg 129(1).
[4]   VATA 1994, s 30(6).
[5]   *VAT: Export of Goods from the United Kingdom* (August 2006). See, in particular, Section 3 which covers conditions and time-limits for zero-rating and where paras 3.3, 3.4 and 3.5 are stated by HMRC to have the force of law, and Section 6 of this notice on proof of export. See also HMRC's VAT manual, Export of Goods from the United Kingdom, at www.hmrc.gov.uk/manuals/vexpmanual/VEXP10000.htm, for instance, at page VEXP30400 – Conditions for zero-rating: evidence of export.
[6]   *VAT: Export of Goods from the United Kingdom* (August 2006), section 6.2.

the context of air or sea freight, production of the authenticated air waybill or of the shipped bill of lading is appropriate evidence to support a claim for zero-rating.[7]

Example 20.1

X Ltd, a UK-based internet trader that is registered for VAT, sells goods via e-commerce. Barbara, who is a citizen of the US, places an order via X Ltd's website from her home state of California. The cost of the goods is £150, which she pays for by credit card. X Ltd dispatches the goods via air freight.

X Ltd will be able to satisfy HMRC that the goods have been exported because it will be in possession of the air waybill. Since the supply is zero-rated it will be able to reclaim the input tax attributable to the supply to Barbara.

Export treatment only applies to goods. HMRC considers that any software transmitted by telephone or by any other type of data network (ie internet supplies) will not qualify for zero-rating as an export of goods.[8] This is because the supply of such electronic data is regarded as a supply of services. However, the export of standard ('normalised') computer software packages is regarded by HMRC as a supply of goods (this is discussed further in Chapter 21), which may be zero-rated on export from the EU. The 'export' of services out of the EU should be treated as occurring outside the UK, and not subject to VAT so that the recipient of either physical or downloaded software should be in the same position (this aspect is examined in Chapter 22).

20.3 ZERO-RATING OF GOODS REMOVED FROM THE UK TO THE EU

The removal of goods from the UK and acquired in another Member State of the EU is zero-rated where certain conditions are met.[9] The rules apply where there is both a removal of the goods from the UK and their acquisition in another Member State by a taxable person who is liable to pay VAT on the acquisition in the other Member State, in accordance with the rules in that Member State which correspond to the obligation of a person in the UK to pay acquisition VAT. Specifically, the UK's Value Added Tax Regulations 1995[10] provide that where HMRC is satisfied that:

(1) a supply of goods by a taxable person involves their removal from the UK;

---

[7]   *VAT: Export of Goods from the United Kingdom* (August 2006), section 6.3.

[8]   *VAT: Export of Goods from the United Kingdom* (August 2006), section 4.5.

[9]   VATA 1994, s 30(8), (10). See also the VAT Directive, art 138(1) which provides the legal basis under EU law for the exemption (called zero-rating in the UK) of goods supplied for removal from a Member State (eg, the UK) to a taxable person in another Member State.

[10] SI 1995/2518, reg 134.

(2)　　the supply is to a person taxable in another Member State;

(3)　　the goods are removed to another Member State;

(4)　　the goods are not taxed by reference to the profit margin scheme provided for under VATA 1994, s 50A[11] (the effect of which is to charge VAT on a profit margin),

then the supply, subject to such other conditions as HMRC may impose, shall be zero rated.[12] For example (as is similar for exports of goods from the UK to outside the EU), HMRC states that the goods must be removed from the UK and valid evidence of such removal of the goods to the other Member State must be obtained within certain time limits (broadly, within 3 months from the time of supply) after which, if not met, UK VAT could then become chargeable.[13] The effect of zero-rating is that a UK taxable person should be able to obtain a full refund of input tax incurred in making the supply (subject to normal rules).

Example 20.2

Alpha Ltd (a UK VAT registered company) operates an independent retail business from the UK and operates an e-commerce platform. A company carrying on business in The Netherlands, which is VAT registered in that country, orders goods from Alpha Ltd. The goods are acquired by the Dutch company for the purposes of its business. Since the Dutch company is registered in The Netherlands for VAT and acquires the goods for business purposes, Alpha Ltd is not required to charge UK VAT. Instead, the Dutch company will account for Dutch VAT on the acquisition. For the supply to be treated in this way, it is necessary that:

---

[11]　Section 50A applies to supplies of works of art, antiques, collectors' items, supplies of motor vehicles, supplies of second-hand goods and any supply of goods through a person who acts as an agent (but in that person's own name) in relation to the supply. See VAT (Special Provisions) Order 1995, SI 1995/1268, reg 12.

[12]　Value Added Tax Regulations 1995, SI 1995/2518, reg 134. See also HMRC's Notice 725 *The Single Market* (February 2011) at Section 4, in particular, para 4.3.

[13]　VATA 1994, s 30(8), (10), and HMRC Notice 725, Section 4, in particular, para 4.4, which is stated to have the force of law, and para 4.6. However, the validity of the imposition of time limit constraints in relation to the VAT rules on intra-EU dispatches has been called into question in the ECJ case of *X v Skatteverket*, Case C-84/09 [2010] All ER (D) 42; [2011] STC 189. As regards HMRC's power in VATA 1994, s 30(10), this can apply in cases where goods are discovered in the UK after the alleged export/shipment removal date or where the conditions for zero-rating have not been met, and there can be two main consequences – the goods will be liable to forfeiture and HMRC will be permitted to demand payment of output VAT which would have been chargeable but for the zero-rating, from the person to whom the goods were supplied or any person found in possession of the goods in the UK. However, any such VAT due can be waived by HMRC in their discretion and HMRC also state that the occasions on which this power would be used should be rare/exceptional, for example, where the relevant person is implicated in the incorrect treatment and did not act in good faith.

- Alpha Ltd obtains evidence from the customer that it is in business in The Netherlands, which is achieved by Alpha Ltd obtaining the Dutch company's VAT number and country of VAT registration;

- the goods are sent or transported from the UK to The Netherlands and arrive in the Netherlands;

- Alpha Ltd issues a VAT sales invoice to the Dutch company (the invoice must reflect the Dutch company's VAT number);

- the VAT invoice description should be annotated to indicate that the sale is a zero-rated dispatch of goods, for example: 'Supply subject to EU Acquisition VAT';

- Alpha Ltd obtains and keeps valid commercial evidence that the goods have left the UK.

If the Dutch company does not give the required evidence to show it is in business for VAT purposes the supplies may be subject to UK VAT. However, this may also be caught under distance selling rules if Alpha Ltd is subject to these in The Netherlands (see earlier in Chapter 18 at **18.6**).

Example 20.3

Y Ltd, a UK-based internet trader, registered for VAT, sells goods via the internet. Vania, who is a citizen of Italy, places an order via Y's website from her home city of Naples. Vania carries on business in Italy and the goods are acquired for the purposes of her business. The cost of the goods is £450, which she pays for by credit card. Y Ltd dispatches the goods via air freight. Vania is liable to pay acquisition VAT in Italy since she is a taxable person. Accordingly, the supply can be zero-rated for UK purposes. For this reason Y Ltd should be entitled to reclaim the input tax incurred upon this supply.

Example 20.4

X Ltd, a UK based company registered for VAT purposes, incurs input tax of £50,000 on components that are subsequently supplied by X Ltd to Z Gmbh, based in Germany, which is subject to German VAT and registered for German VAT purposes. Since the components are supplied to another Member State of the EU, and to a taxable person, the supply will be zero-rated. As a consequence X Ltd should be entitled to recover the input tax of £50,000 attributable to the supply made to Z Gmbh.

CHAPTER 21

COMPUTER SOFTWARE: VAT ASPECTS

21.1   SOFTWARE: WHAT IS IT?

The nature of computer software was discussed in Chapter 10. To recap, software (otherwise known as a program) represents the instructions which causes IT hardware to operate in a particular way, such as displaying and moving images from a game on a television or computer screen in response to motion sensors in a hand held device. Computer software and data (information used for processing by the software) is stored on a physical piece of IT. For example, information/data may be stored on a CD or DVD as a series of 'etches' created by a laser. Where these physical carriers are produced on a mass-market basis, the plastic carrier will have been stamped by a metal master disc, which creates the necessary mould on the disc (which is then coated with protective layers). The disc may be capable of only being read by a device, or it may be possible for data on the disc to be recorded and then altered. The physical carrier costs very little to manufacture. Software may be stored on a variety of physical carriers such as computer hard drives, external hard drives, memory sticks etc.

The value of the software resides in the information/instructions, and the intellectual property rights which protect the owner from unlawful copying. The type of intellectual property rights that exist in software is varied (this aspect is considered in **21.1.1**).

The purpose of this chapter is to provide an overview of the VAT categorisation aspects relating to the exploitation of computer software. In dealing with the taxation of software it is necessary to identify the constituent elements of the software, and how it is classified for the purposes of VAT. For example, if software is classified as goods it will be subject to VAT as a supply of goods; whilst software classified as services will be subject to VAT as a supply of services. The difference is of critical importance because the application of VAT differs for goods and services, as explored in Chapters 17 to 20. To recap, the nature and scope of VAT is examined in Chapter 17, and Chapters 18 to 20 deal with specific aspects of VAT relating to the supply of goods (namely Chapter 18: intra-EU trade; Chapter 19: non-EU trade; Chapter 20: exports and dispatches). Finally Chapter 22 examines in more detail (principally from a UK VAT perspective) the VAT implications of computer software which is supplied electronically through the medium of the internet, ie digitised products, which are classified as services by the VAT legislation.

21.1.1 Intellectual property

As discussed in Chapter 10, the value of software from a development and manufacturing perspective lies in the proprietary rights, which can be used to prohibit the reproduction of the software by competitors. Computer software is essentially pure information/instructions recorded on a physical device as a series of 0s and 1s (ie as a binary code). In itself, this information is not subject to a proprietary right.[1]

Computer software is, however, protected by copyright to the extent that it is a literary work.[2] This is the primary form of intellectual property right by which computer software is exploited. Copyright will also exist in a computer database.[3] Payment for use of software or a database will involve the grant of a licence to the end-user, although a licence can also be granted where use of a computer program is made available without consideration.

Patent rights cannot be granted in respect of computer programs to the extent the application relates to such subject-matter 'as such'.[4] It has proved difficult for inventions with a computer program to qualify for patent right protection.[5]

21.1.2 Multimedia products

Multimedia products comprise computer software, which produces multiple types of media, such as text, images and sound on a television or monitor. The intellectual property rights that exist in this type of media are potentially very wide. For discussion on this aspect see Chapter 10.

21.1.3 Off-the-shelf software/standardised software

For discussion on the nature of this software see **10.1.3**.

---

1   *Boardman v Phipps* [1967] 2 AC 46, at 128, HL; *Oxford v Moss* (1978) 68 Cr App R 193.
2   CDPA 1988, s 3(1)(b).
3   CDPA 1988, s 3(1)(b). CDPA 1988, s 3A defines a 'database' as: '(1) ... a collection of independent works, data or other materials which – (a) are arranged in a systematic or methodical way, and (b) are individually accessible by electronic or other means. (2) For the purposes of this Part a literary work consisting of a database is original if, and only if, by reason of the selection or arrangement of the contents of the database the database constitutes the author's own intellectual creation.'
4   Patents Act 1977, s 1(2).
5   See *Merril Lynch's Application* [1989] RPC 561; *Gale's Application* [1991] RPC 305; *Fujitsu's Application* [1991] RPC 305.

For tax purposes it is important to identify the nature of what has been supplied. Where software is downloaded directly over the internet the end-user has paid consideration for a licence to use the software; and where off-the-shelf software is acquired the supply could be categorised as two things, namely payment for the device upon which the software is stored and for the licence to use the computer software. The fact that payment can be categorised in this way raises the question of how the purchase of this type of software is to be classified for VAT purposes. As first discussed briefly in Chapter 17, at **17.7.1**, and in the next section of this chapter, software downloaded directly onto a computer is a supply of services for VAT, whilst the purchase of a device storing such off-the-shelf software (such as a DVD) is a supply of goods for VAT.

21.1.4   Specific software

Specific software is computer software that is custom-made by a computer developer for a specific client. It is characterised by the fact that it is not mass-produced and is not readily available to the general public. Again, procuring the services of a person to develop this type of software raises the issue of whether the contract is one for the supply of goods, or for the supply of services (discussed further below at **21.2**).

21.1.5   Internet downloaded software

Software downloaded over the internet (eg from a retailer's website) is computer software which a consumer obtains by an electronic download via the telecommunication or electronic network. Software available for download can be acquired either from retailers for payment of a fee or, sometimes, free of charge from software developers. The characterisation of this type of software is that its acquisition lacks any type of physical existence. The consumer acquires software that is transferred as a binary code from the retailer's computer network and installed directly onto the recipient's hard disk in their computer. This type of supply is of services. The basis of this treatment is derived from EU VAT policy. In order to seek to provide legal certainty and simplicity for e-commerce in the EU VAT regime, it was agreed as a key EU VAT policy, that supplies of digitised products must be classified as services, even if such products which, if delivered in their tangible form, would be treated as goods for VAT purposes.[6]

21.1.6   Software incorporated on hardware

Hardware such as a microprocessor, graphics card or a hard drive in a computer are supplied with pre-encoded software. When the hardware is

---

[6]   See Communication from the Commission to the Council, the European Parliament and the Economic and Social Committee 'Electronic Commerce and Indirect Taxation' COM (1998) 374 final, Section V, Guideline 2. See also Chapter 22.

purchased the consumer acquires not only the device, but also a licence for use of the software encoded on the device. These classifications have different tax consequences.

21.2   VALUE ADDED TAX

To recall from Chapter 17, VAT is a tax charge based on the supply of goods or services for consideration, and this is generally regardless of the means of communication or commercial method made to effect a transaction. VAT is a common tax imposed in the territory of the EU.[7] The scope of the charge to VAT has been cast widely to include numerous forms of consumption by a consumer made for consideration. Examples of the types of e-commerce and e-infrastructure activities to which VAT can apply is given in Chapter 17, at **17.1**, all of which can have VAT consequences for the supplier and/or consumer, including:

(1)   a copyright licence permitting the use of a search engine database by a mirror-site in another country;

(2)   sale of computer software 'off-the-shelf';

(3)   sale of computer software devised specifically for a business ('bespoke software');

(4)   sale of micro-processors and other forms of IT equipment;

(5)   sale of computer software through the medium of an internet transaction; and

(6)   purchase of computer hardware, with pre-installed computer software, licensed for use by the end-user.

The application of VAT law in the area of e-commerce and e-infrastructure activities such as those listed above falls to be mainly

---

[7]   The countries which comprise the VAT territory of the EU are: Austria, Belgium, Bulgaria, Cyprus, Czech Republic, Denmark (excluding Busingen and the Isle of Heligoland), Greece, Hungary, the Republic of Ireland, Italy (except the communes of Livigno and Camioned'Italia and the Italian waters of Lake Lugano), Latvia, Lithuania, Luxembourg, Malta, The Netherlands, Poland, Portugal (including the Azores and Madeira), Romania, Slovakia, Slovenia, Spain (including the Balearic Islands but excluding Ceuta and Melilla), Sweden and the United Kingdom (including the Isle of Man). Territories of some of the foregoing are not within the VAT territory of the EU, and accordingly supplies of goods from these territories will be treated as imports. The territories are: Andorra, the Åland Islands (Finland), the Channel Islands (Jersey, Guernsey, Sark), the Canary Islands (Spain), the overseas departments of France (Guadeloupe, Martinique, Reunion and French Guiana) and Mount Athos (Greece). To check on any alterations in the extent of the VAT territory, see www.hmrc.gov.uk, and Value Added Tax Regulations 1995, SI 1995/2518, regs 136–139. Gibraltar is not part of the EU.

determined by the general framework of VAT created under EU laws and as implemented by national VAT legislation such as the UK's VATA 1994. This is covered more fully in Chapter 17.

However, it is worth reiterating here that e-commerce transactions broadly comprise two distinct categories for VAT purposes in respect of computer software, namely (a) the supply of physical goods ordered via e-commerce which are delivered either to businesses or private consumers and (b) the supply of services, such as computer software delivered via a direct download. In relation to supplies of physical goods, the nature of IT and e-commerce should not create any unusual issues, since goods must be delivered by conventional methods, and accordingly the tax authorities will continue to be able to collect VAT, for example, on goods imported from outside the EU at the time of importation, and the distance selling arrangements within the EU will continue to apply (eg to mail order sales within the EU) (see Chapters 17 to 19).

21.2.1 The charge to UK VAT

As covered further in Chapter 17, a UK VAT charge will arise in the following circumstances, where there is:[8]

- a supply of goods or services;

- the place of supply of which is in the UK;

- the supply is a taxable supply;

- made by a taxable person;

- in the course or furtherance of business[9] carried on by the supplier; and

- a supply is not otherwise an exempt supply.

Where VAT applies to a supply there are, for the purposes of e-commerce and e-infrastructure businesses, two main types of VAT rate. A VAT charge of 20% (2011) applies on standard rated supplies,[10] while the charge is nil for zero-rated supplies.[11] Certain supplies are subject to a 5% (2011) rate of tax, which relate to limited classes of goods and services.[12]

---

[8]   VATA 1994, s 4.
[9]   A business is defined in VATA 1994 as including any 'trade, profession or vocation' (s 94(1)). The comments made in relation to a trade in the context of corporation tax are equally valid in determining whether a trade is carried on for the purposes of VAT.
[10] VATA 1994, s 2(1).
[11] VATA 1994, s 30 and Sch 8.
[12] VATA 1994, s 29A, Sch 7A (such as contraceptive products, women's sanitary products, domestic fuel, installation of energy-saving materials).

The taxable person who charges VAT on supplies made by it to a consumer is required to account for that amount to HMRC.[13] In accounting for VAT to HMRC the taxable person is entitled to subtract the amount of VAT incurred by it in making those supplies, known as 'input tax' against the VAT that has been received from the end consumer (known as 'output tax').[14] The right of set-off only exists where a person makes taxable supplies. Where a person makes wholly exempt supplies there is no right of set-off.[15]

Although VAT is generally charged at a standard rate of 20% (2011) in respect of computer software supplies, a distinction must nonetheless be made between the supply of goods and services. This is an important distinction to make because, as mentioned earlier, and as is clear from Chapter 17, different rules apply to goods versus services in determining when and where a supply is deemed to take place in the UK. The purpose of the next section is to concentrate on the classification issues that arise particularly in respect of computer software.

21.2.2   Classifying software: goods or services?

For the purposes of determining whether a supply of software is one of goods or services HMRC classifies it into the following for UK VAT purposes:[16]

(1)   'normalised' ('off-the-shelf') software; and

(2)   'specific' (custom-made or bespoke) software.

Where normalised software is supplied, this is said to be a supply of goods where supplied as part of a device (ie DVD),[17] whilst if transferred over a satellite, telephone or anything which is an internet-based delivery it will be treated as a supply of services.[18] In contrast, specific software is classified as a supply of services where it relates to items of software made to customers' special requirements, either as unique programs or adaptations from standard programs.[19]

21.2.3   Normalised or specific software

In ascertaining how software is to be classified for VAT purposes, it is necessary to go a step further than just analysing the physical carrier and the information borne. The next step is to determine whether the software

---

[13]   VATA 1994, s 25(1).
[14]   VATA 1994, s 25(2).
[15]   VATA 1994, s 4(2).
[16]   HMRC Notice 702 *Imports* (April 2010), para 7.
[17]   HMRC Notice 702 *Imports* (April 2010), para 7.2.
[18]   HMRC Notice 702 *Imports* (April 2010), para 7.6.
[19]   HMRC Notice 702 *Imports* (April 2010), para 7.4.

is normalised or specific. The following paragraphs explain, by reference to HMRC practice for UK VAT purposes, how the distinction is to be made, and the consequences which flow from it.

Normalised software

Normalised software is defined by HMRC as mass-produced items which are freely available to customers, for example, personal or home computer software and games packages, which are usable by them independently after installation and limited training in a standard form to carry out the same applications or functions.[20] This definition also includes any accompanying support material, such as instruction manuals,[21] as HMRC goes on to comment that normalised software will usually comprise a coherent set of programs and support material and often include the service of installation, training and maintenance.[22] Furthermore, in the view of HMRC, the definition includes software that are 'standard packages' but are adjusted in some way at the supplier's instigation,[23] for example, to include security features, sophisticated password programs etc.

VAT treatment of normalised software

UK supply of goods

The supply of software transferred electronically and not in a tangible form cannot be classified as a supply of goods for VAT purposes (see **21.1.5**). However, where normalised (off-the-shelf) software is delivered, otherwise than via electronic means such as the internet, the supply may be treated by HMRC as a supply of goods (see generally Chapter 17 for the circumstances in which the VAT charge arises, and Chapter 18 for the VAT charge which applies on the acquisition of goods from another Member State of the EU by a UK business recipient). The supply of normalised (off-the-shelf) software transferred electronically cannot be classified as a supply of goods for VAT purposes. A 'good' is not defined in VATA 1994. Council Directive 2006/112/EC (the VAT Directive) provides that the supply of goods shall mean the transfer of the right to dispose of 'tangible property' as owner;[24] but the Directive does not define 'tangible property'. However, the concept of goods in the UK is defined in the Sale of Goods Act 1979 as including 'all personal chattels other than things in action or money'.[25] It is clear from this definition that there must be an element of tangible existence, such as a device like a CD-ROM or DVD upon which the software is recorded. Accordingly, an

---

[20]   HMRC Notice 702 *Imports* (April 2010), para 7.2.
[21]   HMRC Notice 702 *Imports* (April 2010), para 7.2.
[22]   HMRC Notice 702 *Imports* (April 2010), para 7.2.
[23]   HMRC Notice 702 *Imports* (April 2010), para 7.2.
[24]   Council Directive 2006/112/EC on the common system of value added tax, OJ L 347, 28/11/2006 p 1 (VAT Directive), Art 14(1).
[25]   Sale of Goods Act 1979, s 61.

item of software which is delivered to a purchaser in a tangible format, such as a CD-ROM or DVD, will be treated as a supply of goods on the basis of not being separately identifiable between the carrier medium (goods) and the data/instructions (services). In contrast, as discussed earlier, any software sold through the medium of e-commerce and which is installed directly onto the purchaser's computer hard disk via a direct download will be regarded as a supply of services. HMRC should therefore recognise the supply and delivery of normalised (off-the-shelf) computer software via a digital download as a supply of services.[26]

Non-EU: import of goods

Where normalised software is delivered from outside the EU, otherwise than via electronic means such as the internet, the supply will be treated as an importation of goods (see generally Chapter 19 for the circumstances in which the VAT charge arises on imports from outside the EU). Broadly, VAT is paid on the importation of the goods and charged on the customs value of the imported item, for example, the total value of the carrier medium and the data and instructions (the software) on it.[27]

Export: supplies outside EU

Since normalised software is treated as a supply of goods, this will mean that supplies to countries outside the EU will typically be zero-rated.[28] The supplier will in these circumstances be entitled to recover the input VAT incurred on the components in making the export. For the treatment of exports, see Chapter 20.

Electronically delivered normalised computer software

As previously noted, since software sold through the medium of e-commerce and installed directly onto the purchaser's computer hard drive via a direct digital download will be regarded as a supply of services, HMRC should recognise the supply and delivery of normalised computer software via a digital download as a supply of services and not of goods.[29] For example, HMRC Notices 702 and 703, which respectively cover the importation and exportation of computer software, specifically state that the transmission of information and software by satellite, telephone, telex, or other data network etc is regarded as a supply of services.[30] Chapter 22 considers the VAT aspects relating to the supply of electronically delivered services.

---

[26] HMRC Notice 741A *Place of Supply of Services* (January 2010).
[27] VATA 1994, s 21, but as adjusted as required under the EU's Community Customs code. (See HMRC Notice 702 *Imports* (April 2010), para 7.5.
[28] VATA 1994, s 30.
[29] HMRC Notice 741A *Place of Supply of Services* (January 2010).
[30] HMRC Notice 702 *Imports* (April 2010), para. 7.6.

Specific software

HMRC considers that 'specific' software are items made on the specific instructions of a customer, for example, creation of unique programs or the adaptation of standards programs.[31] Notice 702 also provides that the following are specific programs:[32]

- inter-company information data and accounts;

- enhancements and updates of existing 'specific' programs; and

- enhancements and updates of existing 'normalised' programs supplied under contractual obligation to customers who have bought the original program.

This type of software is wholly different from 'normalised' software because it is not mass-produced and is not readily available to the general consumer. The type of software with which we are concerned here is that customised to a particular business activity, such as control of robotic arms for the mass production and installation of motor components.

For the purposes of applying the VAT legislation, HMRC takes the view that specific software involves the supply of both goods (ie the physical carrier) and services (ie the information). However, because the major element of the supply is of services, ie the work of a developer, VAT is charged on the basis of a supply of services (including in respect of the carrier medium).[33] In addition, HMRC specifically states in Notice 703, dealing with the export of goods from the UK, that supplies of specific items of software tailored to the individual requirements of a company are regarded as supplies of services.

See generally Chapter 17 for the circumstances in which the VAT charge arises on a supply of services.

Tax treatment of specific software

Anything which is not a supply of goods, but is done for consideration, is a supply of services, and as summarised in **21.2.1**, UK VAT will be charged if there is a taxable supply made by a taxable person in the UK in the course or furtherance of business.[34]

Meanwhile, the VAT Directive provides that a supply of services may consist in one of the following transactions: (a) the assignment of

---

[31]   HMRC Notice 702 *Imports* (April 2010), para 7.4.
[32]   HMRC Notice 702 *Imports* (April 2010), para 7.4.
[33]   HMRC Notice 702 *Imports* (April 2010), para 7.5.
[34]   VATA 1994, ss 4, 5(2)(b). See also VAT Directive, Art 24(1).

intangible property, whether or not the subject of a document establishing title and (b) the obligation to refrain from an act, or to tolerate an act or situation.[35]

Bearing the above in mind, in connection with the supply of specific software, or 'import' of such software (in this context, meaning the purchase by an EU-based recipient of such software from a non-EU supplier), since the major element of the supply is the work performed by software developers, VAT will be charged on the basis of a supply or 'import' of services. Further, the granting, assignment or surrender of any right (such as copyright in a computer program), if done for consideration, is deemed to be a supply of services for UK VAT purposes.[36]

Accordingly, an 'import' or supply of such software to the UK will not be subject to UK import VAT, which only applies to goods. Instead, the total amount of the value of both the software and carrier medium may be treated as the consideration for the supply of services, which would be taxed accordingly in the UK, or other Member State which has the proper jurisdiction to tax such services. This would be determined in accordance with the place of supply rules applicable to those services. The place of supply will depend on matters such as the business status of the recipient of the services and the location and relevant establishments of the supplier/customer, since, as highlighted in Chapter 17, the place of supply rules have general default rules for business to (non-taxable/private) customer (B2C) and business to business (B2B) supplies. On the other hand, it will also be recalled from Chapter 17 that there are specific rules and exceptions which can override the default provisions,[37] including for electronically supplied services – see Chapter 22, under which concepts such as the business status of the customer are particularly important in deciding on the place of supply.

Where, however, the place of supply is the UK, UK VAT will be due or accountable to HMRC on a supply of the specific software. For example, under the general rules for services, a UK supplier would be liable to account for UK VAT on such supplies to non-business customers based in the EU, whereas, in the case of a non-UK supplier supplying the specific software to a UK VAT-registered business customer, that UK business would account for the UK VAT under the 'reverse charge' procedure.

For ease of reference, a short summary of the UK's general default place of supply rules for services and those particular to electronically supplied services is given in Table 21.1, while the rest of this chapter will briefly

---

[35]   VAT Directive, Art 25.
[36]   VATA 1994, s 5(2)(b). See also VAT Directive, Art 24(1).
[37]   The nature of the VAT place of supply rules is such that it is important to examine the scope of any charging and/or deeming provisions, and reliefs to determine the extent of their application.

recall from Chapter 17 the basic rules on determining where a supplier or recipient may belong for the purposes of a supply of services and on the 'reverse charge' procedure.

Table 21.1: Place of supply rules for services

Services	Place of supply	VATA 1994
General rules		
Supply of services by a supplier who belongs in the UK,[38] other than services supplied to a recipient who is a 'relevant business person'.[39]	Service supplied in the country in which the supplier belongs (unless overriding place of supply rules apply in VATA 1994, Sch 4A,[40] which includes electronically supplied services: see Table 17.2 in Chapter 17 at **17.10.2** and below in relation to electronically supplied services). UK VAT will be due where the supplier belongs in the UK under this rule, irrespective of where the customer belongs.	s 7A(2)(b)
Supply of services to a 'relevant business person' by a UK supplier.	Service supplied in the country in which the recipient belongs (unless overriding place of supply rules apply in VATA 1994, Sch 4A, which includes electronically supplied services: see Table 17.2 in Chapter 17 at **17.10.2** and below in relation to electronically supplied services). UK VAT will be due if the customer belongs in the UK. If the customer is outside the UK then the supply is outside the scope of UK VAT; if the customer belongs outside the EU, then there will be no VAT (again, subject to any exceptions in VATA 1994, Sch 4A)	s 7A(2)(a)

---

[38] Whether a supplier belongs in the UK is determined under VATA 1994, s 9. A supplier is based in the UK if it has its usual place of residence in the UK; and this means where the supplier is a company, the place where it is legally constituted (ie the country where it is incorporated).

[39] VATA 1994, s 7A(4). See **21.2.4** for the definition of a 'relevant business person'.

[40] VATA 1994, s 7A(5).

Services	Place of supply	VATA 1994
	If the customer belongs in another Member State (and is VAT registered), no UK VAT will be due but the supply will be subject to any local VAT at either the standard or reduced rate in that Member State under the reverse charge, ie accountable by the customer. In addition, the supplier may need to complete and submit an EC Sales List, which must now be completed by suppliers for supplies of taxable services subject to the reverse charge in the customer's Member State. See HMRC's Notice 725 *The Single Market* (February 2011) for further details on EC Sales Lists, particularly at Section 17 of that notice.	
Exceptions to place of supply of services relating to supplies made to a relevant business person.		See generally Chapter 22.
Provision of electronically supplied services to a relevant business person. Examples of such services: <ul><li>website supply, web-hosting and distance maintenance of programmes and equipment;</li><li>the supply of software and the updating of software;</li><li>the supply of images, text and information, and the making available of databases;</li><li>the supply of music, films and games (including games of chance and gambling games);</li><li>the supply of political, cultural, artistic, sporting, scientific, educational or entertainment broadcasts (including broadcasts of events); and</li><li>the supply of distance teaching.</li></ul>	Covered by the B2B general rule so the place of supply is where the business customer belongs, but this is subject to the 'use and enjoyment' rule. Therefore, if there is a supply of services consisting of the provision of electronically supplied services to a relevant business person which would otherwise be treated as made in the UK, but the services are to any extent effectively used and enjoyed in a country which is not a Member State, then the supply is to be treated to that extent as made in that country. If there is a supply of services consisting of the provision of electronically supplied services to a relevant business person which would otherwise be treated as made in a country which is not a Member State, but the services are to any extent effectively used and enjoyed in the UK, then the supply is to be treated to that extent as made in the UK. NB: The use and enjoyment rule does not apply in the UK to B2C supplies of these services.	Sch 4A, para 9

Services	Place of supply	VATA 1994
NB: Where the supplier of a service and the supplier's customer communicate via e-mail, this does not of itself mean that the service provided is an electronically supplied service.	See more fully in Chapter 22, Table 22.1 at **22.3.2** and at **22.7**.	
Exceptions relating to supplies not made to relevant business person		
Electronic services		
A supply consisting of the provision by a person who belongs in a country which is not a Member State (other than the Isle of Man) of electronically supplied services (see above for meaning) to a person ('the recipient') who: (a) is not a relevant business person, and (b) belongs in a Member State.	Made in the country in which the recipient belongs. Where supplied to a non-taxable person who is established in more than one country or has his permanent address in one country and his usual residence in another, priority is to be given to the place that best ensures taxation at the place of actual consumption when determining the place of supply of these services. See further in Chapters 17 and 22, including with regard to changes being introduced in 2015 for the place of supply of cross-border B2C supplies of telecommunications, broadcasting and electronically supplied services.	Sch 4A, para 15
Other services provided to a recipient belonging outside EC		
A supply consisting of the provision to a person ('the recipient') who: (a) is not a relevant business person, and (b) belongs in a country which is not a Member State (other than the Isle of Man), of the following services (this list does not include all of those services listed in Sch 4A, para 16 – see Chapter 17): (a) transfers and assignments of copyright, patents, licences, trademarks and similar rights;	Made in the country in which the recipient belongs. See further in Chapters 17 and 22, including with regard to changes being introduced in 2015 for the place of supply of cross border B2C supplies of telecommunications, broadcasting and electronically supplied services.	Sch 4A, para 16

Services	Place of supply	VATA 1994
(b) the acceptance of any obligation to refrain from pursuing or exercising (in whole or in part) any business activity or any rights within paragraph (a);		
(c) services of consultants, engineers, consultancy bureaux, lawyers, accountants, and similar services, data processing and provision of information, other than any services relating to land;		
(d) electronically supplied services (until January 2015) – see above for meaning and further in Chapter 22.		

HMRC Notice 741A Place of Supply of Services (January 2010) para 15, contains some comments in the examples of services within the above headings relevant to computer software supplies. For example:

(*a*) For transfers and assignments of copyright, patents, licences, trademarks and similar rights: (para 15.2.2)

   – Services within this heading include: granting of a licence to use computer software, transfer of permission to use a logo, granting of a right by a photographer for a photograph to be published in a magazine article (including material which is downloaded to the customer)

(*b*) For the acceptance of any obligation to refrain from pursuing or exercising (in whole or in part) any business activity or any rights within paragraph (*a*)

   – Services within this heading: Agreement by the owner of a trademark to refrain from using it.

(*c*) For services of consultants, engineers, consultancy bureaux, lawyers, accountants, and similar services, data processing and provision of information, other than any services relating to land (para 15.5.2)

   – Services within this heading: research and development, market research, production of customized ('bespoke' or 'specific') computer software, excluding digitally downloaded software, as well as the services of adapting existing packages (though it is acknowledged that some 'off-the-shelf' software packages are treated as supplies of goods); and software maintenance involving upgrades, advice, and resolving any problems (the place of performance is not relevant as solutions may be provided by telephone conversations, remote links or attending a mainframe site; (However a contract for simply maintaining computer hardware relates to work on goods [see Section 8 of HMRC's Notice 741A and Table 17.2 in Chapter 17 in relation to the place of supply rules for work carried out on goods]); also included are services of engineers/technicians within the entertainment industry (covering editors/sound engineers) producing an edit master from which copies can be made as well as those who exercise artistic control or influence over material (para 15.5.4).

   – What is the 'provision of information?' (para 15.5.12)

Services	Place of supply	VATA 1994
– HMRC considers that it covers the supplying of knowledge of any type and in any form. Information includes facts, data, figures and other material. Examples include: tourist information, weather forecasts, information supplied by a private enquiry agent, telephone helpdesk services (such as for computer software), satellite, navigational and location services, and provision of online information. – Examples of exclusions from provision of information: the delivery or transmission of another person's information by whatever means (including electronic delivery, again, see Chapter 22).		

21.2.4 Determining where a supplier and recipient belongs for the purposes of a supply of services

For certain types of services, including under the general default rules summarised in Table 21.1, the place where a supplier or recipient belongs will determine where services are supplied and who accounts for any VAT due. The place of belonging of either the supplier or the customer will not, however, affect the place of supply of services such as land-related services (supplied where the land is located) or those services which are supplied 'where performed' (see Chapter 17, at Table 17.2).

To recap from Table 21.1, under the general rules, a service is treated as supplied in the UK if the supplier belongs in the UK, unless the person to whom the supply is made is a 'relevant business person', in which case the service is supplied in the country in which the recipient belongs[41] (unless overriding place of supply rules apply in Sch 4A to VATA 1994 (see generally Chapter 17).[42] Whether a supplier or recipient belongs in the UK is determined under VATA 1994.[43]

In VATA 1994, a person is treated as a 'relevant business person' if that person:[44]

(a) is a taxable person within the meaning of Art 9 of the VAT Directive;

(b) is registered under VATA 1994;

(c) is identified as a taxable person under the law of another Member State; or

(d) is registered under an Act of Tynwald[45] for the purposes of any tax imposed under that Act which corresponds to VAT,

---

[41] VATA 1994, s 7A.
[42] VATA 1994, s 7A(5).
[43] VATA 1994, s 9.
[44] VATA 1994, s 7A(4).
[45] The laws of the Isle of Man.

V Value Added Tax: European Union Trade

and the services are received by the person otherwise than wholly for private purposes.

For the purposes of the place of supply of services rules, a supplier or 'relevant business person' is treated as belonging in a 'relevant country', which means the country identified in accordance with the following rules: (a) if the person has a business establishment, or some other fixed place of establishment, in a country (eg the UK) (and none in any other country), that country (ie the UK); or (b) if the person has a business establishment (eg in the UK), or some other fixed establishment or establishments, in more than one country, the country in which the 'relevant establishment'[46] is located – this means whichever of the person's establishments is most 'directly concerned' with the supply (the concepts of establishment and the 'directly concerned' test are discussed in detail in Chapter 22 (see Chapter 22, at **22.5.2** and **22.5.3**), or (c) if none of the foregoing apply, the country in which the person's 'usual place of residence' is located.[47] A person who is not a relevant business person is also treated as belonging in the country in which that person's usual place of residence is located.[48] The 'usual place of residence' for a body corporate is treated as being the place where it is legally constituted.[49]

Finally, in some circumstances, supplies are deemed to take place in the UK due to the fact that they represent a supply of services provided to, and consumed by, a relevant business person in the UK but who may not belong in the UK, under the so-called 'use and enjoyment' rules mentioned in Table 21.1. Broadly, this extra rule allows Member States to deal with place of supply situations for certain services where the EU VAT position would otherwise be distortive as a result of considering only where the supplier and the customer belongs. The types of supplies which are within this category include electronically-supplied services.[50] Further issues relating to determining the location of a supplier and recipient and the application of the 'use and enjoyment' rules are considered more fully in Chapters 17 and 22.

21.2.5   Reverse charge

The reverse charge operates in respect of several kinds of services,[51] including electronically supplied services. Where services are received by a relevant business person from a supplier who belongs outside the UK, the identity of the person who is required to account for VAT is altered.[52] Normally, it is the supplier who is required to account for any VAT due on

---

[46]   VATA 1994, s 9(4).
[47]   VATA 1994, s 9(3).
[48]   VATA 1994, s 9(5).
[49]   VATA 1994, s 9(6).
[50]   VATA 1994, Sch 4A, para 9.
[51]   See Chapter 17 at **17.12**.
[52]   VATA 1994, s 8.

the supply, but this is reversed by virtue of the reverse charge procedure, and, accordingly, it will be the business recipient who must account for the VAT due. This procedure is also known as the tax shift. A UK business recipient will usually incur the costs of a supply of services from abroad for its own business purposes, so that it can make onward supplies to its consumers. VAT will be imposed on these supplies to the end consumer if they are taxable supplies. The reverse charge is therefore a simplification measure designed to avoid overseas suppliers needing to register for VAT purposes in a Member State when it is possible for the customer (eg a VAT-registered customer) to account for the VAT on a supply. The procedure does not apply to supplies of services where both the supplier and the recipient belong in the UK. In addition, the procedure currently only applies insofar as a customer receives the supply for a business purpose.[53]

Under the reverse charge rules a relevant business person is required to account for VAT on such service supplies as if there were a supply of the services by the recipient in the UK in the course or furtherance of a business carried on by the recipient and that supply were a taxable supply (a deemed supply).[54] This is designed to prevent distortion of trade, as otherwise businesses could acquire tax-free benefits by obtaining services from abroad. Accordingly, instead of being charged VAT by the supplier, the UK business recipient would credit (increase) its VAT account with the necessary output tax as if the recipient had supplied the services in the UK for the purposes of VAT (the deemed supply), and at the same time in the same VAT return, debit (deduct) its VAT account with the input tax to which it is entitled under the normal rules if it can relate this input VAT to taxable supplies. The practical result of this is that the recipient continues to be entitled to claim credit for input tax (although the input tax cannot be attributed to the aforementioned deemed supply made by it (which would give full input tax credit), but only to the actual use to which the service was put by the recipient.[55]

The reverse charge applies if:[56]

(a)   the recipient is a relevant business person who belongs in the UK and the place of supply of the services is inside the UK, ie under the general B2B rule – see Table 21.1; or

(b)   the supply of the services is one to which any paragraph of Part 1 or 2 of Sch 4A to VATA 1994 applies ('relevant services') and the recipient is registered as a taxable person. In this regard, the services

---

[53]   Supplies need to be received wholly for private purposes to be treated as a business-to-non business supply: VATA 1994, s 7A(4).
[54]   VATA 1994, s 8(1).
[55]   VATA 1994, s 8(1)(b), (3).
[56]   VATA 1994, s 8(2).

(Right margin:) **Value Added Tax: European Union Trade**

in respect of which the reverse charge operates in the context of specific software delivered over the internet are electronically supplied services.[57]

In HMRC Notice 741A *Place of Supply of Services* (January 2010), HMRC specifically gives an example on how the reverse charge would apply to a supply of 'customised' (ie bespoke or specific) computer software under the B2B general rule, where a person belongs in the UK and receives such service from a non-UK supplier (Notice 741A, para 18.10.1):

> '... a UK business receives customised software from a USA business (B2B general rule service). The place of supply is the UK and the UK business must account for VAT under the reverse charge.'

The application of the reverse charge is considered more fully in Chapter 17 at **17.12**.

---

[57] VATA 1994, s 8(2).

CHAPTER 22

SERVICES SUPPLIED ELECTRONICALLY

22.1 INTRODUCTION

It will be recalled from Chapter 17, which examines the general nature of the charge to VAT, that the scope of the charge to VAT has been cast widely to include numerous forms of consumption by a consumer made for a consideration. VAT is therefore capable of being applied in many areas of e-commerce and several examples were given in Chapter 17, at **17.1**, as having the potential to fall within the VAT legislation. Meanwhile, Chapters 18 to 20 have covered the scope of VAT in relation to supplies of goods within the EU, imports from countries outside the EU and exports to countries outside the EU.

Certain VAT aspects relating to supplies of computer software delivered in eg, a tangible format, were discussed in Chapter 21. The purpose of this chapter is to examine in more detail (principally from a UK VAT perspective) the VAT place of supply rules and consequences of services supplied electronically, such as internet commerce, ie digitised products supplied via the medium of the internet (eg computer software downloaded online) in pursuance of an internet contract. Additionally, parts of this chapter will recap some of the key aspects covered in Chapter 17, such as registration, fixed establishments and the reverse charge.

As discussed in Chapter 17 and 21, a supply of digitised products is a supply of services rather than goods, and the UK subscribes to this approach. This means that the place of supply rules in relation to the supply of these services would determine which country (if any) has the jurisdiction to charge VAT on such products.

However, electronically supplied services provided on a cross-border basis raise particular issues for VAT purposes. For example, a non-EU supplier can be required to register as a taxable person for VAT as the place of supply of these services is treated as being made where the recipient belongs, even in the absence of an establishment in the EU (see **22.4.2**). Or if a supplier belongs in the UK or outside the UK (eg another EU Member State), the supply of such services, if treated as having its place of supply in the UK, may result in that person being required to register for VAT as a taxable person in the UK (see **22.2.1** for registration requirements). In this context, the VAT place of supply rules relevant to electronically supplied services are especially important, and are described in this chapter at **22.3**. These place of supply rules have general default rules for business to (non-taxable/private) customer (B2C) and business to business (B2B) supplies, but there are specific rules which override the default provisions, including for electronically supplied services, set out later in this chapter. It is therefore always important first to identify the exact nature of the services in order to determine whether there is a specific rule which applies regarding the place of supply.

Services that are supplied electronically may take many different forms, and the substance of the supply may not necessarily be treated as an electronic supply of services for VAT purposes. In each case it is necessary to identify precisely what is being supplied, by whom and to whom in order to determine the appropriate VAT treatment.

Examples of services that are recognised (and defined) as being supplied electronically are:[1]

- website supply, web-hosting and distance maintenance of programs and equipment;

- the supply of software and the updating of software;

- the supply of images, text and information, and the making available of databases;

- the supply of music, films and games (including games of chance and gambling games);

- the supply of political, cultural, artistic, sporting, scientific, educational and entertainment broadcasts (including broadcasts of events); and

- the supply of distance teaching.

However, where the supplier of a service and that person's customer communicate via e-mail, that does not of itself mean the service performed is an electronically supplied service.

Accordingly, some services will not be treated as being supplied electronically although the contract for the supply is entered into via the medium of e-commerce (eg the sale of physical goods delivered by

---

[1] Value Added Tax Act 1994 (VATA 1994), Sch 4A, Part 2, paras 9 and 15 and Council Implementing Regulation 282/2011/EU laying down implementing measures for Directive 2006/112/EC (the VAT Directive) on the common system of value added tax (recast), OJ L77/1, 15/03/2011 pp 1–22 (the EU Implementing Regulation).

conventional means). In addition, the supply of some electronic services will not benefit from the same VAT treatment as their physical counterparts. For example, all supplies of downloaded publications are treated as a supply of services and not of goods. The zero-rating of books (printed matter) therefore does not apply to digital products[2] because the zero-rating treatment is for goods and not services. Therefore, for current UK VAT purposes, there can be a difference between the VAT treatment of a conventional sale of goods and its equivalent transaction on or via the internet. This is not only relevant to the rate of VAT charged, but can also give rise to further additional issues, ie that by defining digitised products as services and not goods, differing channels of delivery can result in different tax rates and discrimination. To illustrate this point, in *Forexia (UK) Ltd*,[3] the tribunal upheld a decision that the publication and distribution of a regular news digest communicated to customers by fax or e-mail or by accessing the website was a supply of services (the provision of information) which was standard rated when supplied in the UK. In contrast, it was recognised that a supply of a book or other written material (such as a leaflet or newspaper/periodical) was treated as a supply of goods which, if supplied in the UK, was zero-rated. The tribunal reached its decision with the 'greatest reluctance' and gave reasons for its reluctance, including that its decision offended the principle of neutrality (between e-commerce and traditional commerce) and produced a distortion of competition. Conversely, the EU Commission has in the past sought to justify the differential treatment, on the basis that the supply of digitised information services is not necessarily the direct equivalent of the traditional or hard copy product, which, it was argued, can produce a 'fundamentally different' product to the point where the tax treatment should be different.

However, it is important to note that in a recent report of the Commission (December 2011) issued following the outcome of its public consultation and EU discussions on the future of the EU VAT regime generally, it has expressly acknowledged that 'the issue of equal treatment for products which are available in both traditional and online formats provoked considerable reactions in the public consultation. Those

---

[2] See para 15.12.4 of HMRC's Notice 741A *Place of Supply of Services* (January 2010) and HMRC Notice 701/10 *Zero Rating of Books etc* (December 2011) Section 2. See also Chapter 17 on zero-rated supplies, at **17.16**.

[3] VAT and Duties Tribunal Decision No 16041, 22 April 1999. The Tribunal stated that: 'it is accepted that if delivery is by letter post, courier, or even by hand, the supply is zero-rated. However, the Commissioners contend that when the supply is by fax or e-mail or via the website – methods used by the vast majority of the Appellant's customers because of the need for speed in the dissemination of financial information of this nature – what is being supplied is not a leaflet or periodical but information which the recipient then uses his own equipment and paper to transform into a leaflet or periodical ... with the greatest reluctance, we are forced to the conclusion that the Commissioners' contention is correct in law. Exemptions and zero-ratings must be strictly construed; taking Group 3 [of Sch 8 (Books, etc)] as a whole, it clearly refers to goods. What the Appellant is supplying, in the case of the disputed supplies, is information, presumably in the form of electrical impulses.'

issues need to be addressed', and that, as a priority area for future work towards a more VAT-efficient regime, a review of the current VAT rates structure is required (to be launched in 2012) which review should be based on certain guiding principles including as follows: 'similar goods and services should be subject to the same VAT rate and progress in technology should be taken into account in this respect, so that the challenge of convergence between the on-line and physical environment is addressed'. Therefore, this is a topic area which is likely to change across Member States, including the UK, in the future. For example, it has already been reported that some Member States have announced new reduced VAT rates applicable for electronic books from 2012 as for paper books (a reduced rate of 7% has been introduced in France and 3% in Luxembourg).[4]

Another important question in this area is the extent to which the supply of tangible computer software ordered via the internet can be classified as the supply of goods and/or services, and this is explored further in Chapter 21.

22.2 INGREDIENTS OF THE UK VAT CHARGE: A SUMMARY

The key to the application of the tax charge in the UK is s 4 of VATA 1994. By this section, a UK VAT charge will apply in the following circumstances:

- a supply of goods or services;

- the place of supply of which is in the UK;

- the supply is a taxable supply;

- made by a taxable person;

---

[4] COM(2011) 851 final, Brussels, 6.12.2011, 'Communication from the Commission to the European Parliament, the Council and the European Economic And Social Committee on the future of VAT, towards a simpler, more robust and efficient VAT system tailored to the single market'. One of the previous FAQs on the EU Commission's website (at http://ec.europa.eu/taxation_customs/taxation/vat/how_vat_works/e-services/article_1610_en.htm) has been: 'Will the Directive ensure neutrality between traditional and electronic media?' The answer given is: 'Yes. The standard rate of VAT also applies to the vast majority of content supplied via traditional media – music, software, video, etc – so there will be no issue of discrimination compared with electronic media which under the Directive is taxable at the standard rate in all Member States. Current VAT legislation permits reduced rates of tax (or in some cases a zero rate) on printed material. Books, newspapers and periodicals are amongst the most common items to which Member States apply reduced rates. But it is by no means clear that digital information services are the direct equivalent of traditional printed products – even where the content is similar, the additional functionality (eg search facilities, hyperlinks, archives) increasingly associated with electronic content produces a fundamentally different product . . .'

- in the course of furtherance of business[5] carried on by the supplier; and

- the supply is not otherwise an exempt supply.

The rate of UK VAT depends upon how the transactions, known as supplies, are classified. A transaction can be classified in one of three ways. Those designated as standard-rated are subject to a tax of 20% (2011)[6] of the value of the supply. Some supplies are classified as exempt,[7] or zero-rated, which effectively means that the rate of VAT is nil from the perspective of the ultimate consumer,[8] or reduced-rated (5%), this relating to a limited class of goods and services which are unlikely to be very relevant to e-commerce.[9] If the supply is classified as exempt the supplier will not be in a position to recover its own VAT costs incurred in making that supply.[10] Electronically supplied services supplied in a Member State will normally be taxable at the standard rate in accordance with Arts 97–98(2) of the VAT Directive[11] (formerly Art 12(3)(a) of the Sixth VAT Directive[12]), unless an exempting provision in a Member State applies. For example, when considering the supply of gambling, if the supply in the traditional manner is exempt in a Member State, it would also be exempt even if it constituted a supply of an electronically supplied service. This treatment does not, however, apply where a comparable supply is made in the traditional manner and is either zero-rated or reduced-rated, as discussed above. Therefore, particular care should be taken where a service includes both electronic and other elements. Such composite transactions would generally need to be considered on a case-by-case basis (See Chapter 17).

The taxable person who is the supplier and who charges VAT on supplies made by him, known as output tax, is normally required to account for that VAT amount to HMRC.[13] In accounting for this amount, the taxable person is entitled to subtract the amount of VAT incurred by him in making those supplies, known as input tax.[14] The right of set-off exists only where a taxable person makes taxable supplies (including zero-rated

---

[5]   A business is defined in VATA 1994 as including any 'trade, profession or vocation' (s 94(1)). The comments made in relation to a trade in the context of corporation tax are equally valid in determining whether a trade is carried on for the purposes of VAT.

[6]   VATA 1994, s 2.

[7]   VATA 1994, s 31 and Sch 9.

[8]   See Chapter 17.

[9]   VATA 1994, s 29A, Sch 7A (such as, contraceptive products, women's sanitary products, domestic fuel, installation of energy-saving materials).

[10]   VATA 1994, s 30 and Sch 8.

[11]   Council Directive 2006/112/EC on the common system of value added tax, OJ L 347, 28/11/2006 p 1. See also HMRC Notice 741A *Place of Supply of Services* (January 2010), para 17.1.

[12]   77/388/EEC of 17 May 1977, OJ L 145 13/6/1977, p1.

[13]   VATA 1994, s 25(1).

[14]   VATA 1994, s 25(2).

supplies). (As mentioned above, where a person makes wholly exempt supplies there is no right of set-off.[15])

22.2.1   Who is a taxable person?

As discussed in Chapter 17, VAT is chargeable on supplies of goods and services (including anything treated as being goods and services) made in the UK *by a taxable person* for consideration as part of the economic activities of that person, unless the supplies are exempt. There is therefore a duty to account for VAT on any supply within the scope of the tax if a transaction is made by a taxable person (including both those registered for VAT and any person who should be registered).

A taxable person is defined as a person who is, or is required to be, registered under the Act.[16] A person who makes taxable supplies is required to register for the purposes of VAT, where the value of those supplies are in excess of £73,000 (2011)[17] to the year ending for any month.[18] An obligation also exists to register where the person has reasonable grounds for believing that the value of supplies will exceed £73,000 within the next 30 days.[19] A person is not obliged to register where HMRC is satisfied that the value of supplies will not exceed £71,000 in a period of one year beginning at the time at which that person would become liable to be registered.[20] If a person is not already UK VAT registered and they receive supplies of certain services which are subject to the reverse charge procedure (see at **22.6**), the value of those supplies must be added to the value of the person's other taxable supplies in determining whether they should be registered for UK VAT. If such a person does not make taxable supplies, he can still be a taxable person if the value of his 'imported' services exceeds the above VAT registration limit.[21] A person can cease to be registered under VATA 1994 only in specified circumstances and a person who is not obliged to register under VATA 1994 may nonetheless seek voluntary registration – these aspects are covered in Chapter 17 at **17.9.1**. In addition, as mentioned in Chapter 17,[22] a special registration scheme applies for non-EU established taxable persons supplying electronic services to non-taxable persons. This is explored in the following section in relation to its operation in the UK.

---

[15]   VATA 1994, s 4(2).
[16]   VATA 1994, s 3(1), Schs 1–3.
[17]   Refer to HMRC's website to confirm current registration thresholds: www.hmrc.gov.uk.
[18]   VATA 1994, Sch 1, para 1(1)(a). Liability must be notified to the Commissioners within 30 days of the end of the month in which the liability arises (para 5(1)).
[19]   VATA 1994, Sch 1, para 1(1)(b). Liability must be notified to the Commissioners before the end of the 30 day period by reference to which the liability arises (para 6(1)).
[20]   VATA 1994, Sch 1, para 1(3).
[21]   VATA 1994, s 8(1), Sch 1.
[22]   At **17.9.1**.

22.2.2 Overseas traders supplying UK non-taxable persons: registering for VAT

Introduction

Although an overseas e-commerce supplier may have no physical trading presence within the country in which the recipient is located (ie the UK) for the purposes of a direct tax charge, such as corporation tax, it may nonetheless be subject to VAT laws. The ingredients of the VAT tax charge can be satisfied without the existence of any physical office within the UK. If goods and/or services are treated as supplied in the UK and the relevant registration thresholds are met, an overseas supplier will be required to register for VAT in the UK.

Before June 2003, the VAT treatment of supplies of services between businesses delivered via the internet was determined by the actual nature of the services, rather than by their means of delivery. The result was that it was necessary to determine the precise nature of the service provided in order to decide on the appropriate place of supply rules and the Member State (if any) that had the jurisdiction to levy the VAT. Under this treatment, a non-EU trader who made a supply of electronic services, for example, website design or hosting, was not required to charge and account for VAT to any tax authority within the EU. This was because under the former Sixth VAT Directive[23] the place of supply for those services was deemed to be supplied where the supplier belonged under the general rule, which for non-EU traders was outside the EU. Pursuant to that same general rule, however, an EU operator was required to charge VAT at the applicable rate in their Member State on such supplies, irrespective of the customer's location, even if located outside the EU. In addition, at that stage, the supply of certain other services, including from such a non-EU trader, was only subject to VAT if the recipient of the supply received it for business purposes (ie where that supply was within a previous, specific category of the reverse charge mechanism, in which event, the overseas trader would not need to register and account for the VAT due).[24] By contrast, a non-business recipient of such supplies from a non-EU trader was not required to pay VAT in respect of such supplies.

This resulted in non-EU traders obtaining a competitive advantage over EU traders in respect of their supplies to non-business recipients, since EU traders were required to charge EU VAT in their local jurisdiction on the same kinds of supplies.

With the rapid increase in the levels of supplies of services over the internet from outside the EU to EU customers, this distortion of

---

[23] Directive 77/388/EEC, Art 9.1 (now recast (and repealed) as a result of the adoption of the VAT Directive).

[24] VATA 1994, Sch 5 (now repealed with effect from 1 January 2010). See further for the current rules at **22.6** on the reverse charge.

competition between non-EU and EU traders raised concerns about the effects of the place of supply of services rules on competition and the internal market within Europe.

Eventually, it was considered that the rules for taxing such services consumed within the EU and for preventing the distortion of competition were inadequate, and that action needed to be taken to ensure that such services where consumed by customers established in the EU were taxed in the EU and not taxed if consumed outside the EU. To this end, it was decided that, in order to re-establish a balance of competition between EU and non-EU suppliers, radio and television broadcasting services and electronically supplied services provided from non-EU businesses to persons established in the EU or from the EU to recipients established in non-EU countries should be taxed where the recipient of the services is established, ie at the place of consumption.

Accordingly, the VAT position for telecommunications, broadcasting and electronically supplied services changed with effect from 1 July 2003 by virtue of Council Directive 2002/38/EC.[25] Amendments were made to rectify the weakness of the VAT rules in respect of those services supplied from outside the EU, ie digital products supplied online and, for example, pay-per-view radio and television broadcasting, by the imposition of a general obligation on non-EU overseas suppliers to register and charge VAT. However, there would continue to be no obligation to register in respect of B2B supplies because of the operation of the reverse charge mechanism (see further at **22.6**).

These changes were initially a temporary measure but were made permanent as a result of Council Directive 2008/8/EC.[26] In addition, it is important to note that from 1 January 2015, the latter Directive also provides that VAT on telecommunications, radio and television broadcasting and electronically-supplied services rendered by a supplier (whether EU or non-EU) to non-taxable customers also established within the EU will be charged in the Member State where the customer belongs/is established or usually resides. This will particularly impact intra-EU B2C supplies, which are still subject to the general rule of where the supplier belongs – some further details of which are set out at Table 22.1 at **22.3.2**). An example is given by the EU Commission on how the new rules will work from 2015, as follows: 'When webhosting is supplied to a private customer living in Lisbon, Portuguese VAT must be charged irrespective of whether the supplier is established in Portugal, in another Member State or outside the EU.'[27]

---

[25] 7 May 2002, amending temporarily Directive 77/388/EEC as regards the value added tax arrangements applicable to radio and television broadcasting services and certain electronically supplied services.

[26] 12 February 2008, amending Directive 2006/112/EC (the VAT Directive) as regards the place of supply of services.

[27] To review and follow the EU's latest proposals, please refer to the summary for

In implementing the above EU VAT rules, the UK's place of supply rules in respect of electronically supplied services (until 2015) (see **22.3**) now operate to cause such services supplied to UK based private customers to be treated as being supplied in the UK where the supplier is located outside the EU, resulting in an obligation to register in the UK as a taxable person where the relevant thresholds are met (see earlier discussion at **22.2.1**). However, in order to avoid multiple EU VAT registrations for non-EU suppliers, since they may be required to register under the normal rules in every Member State in which they make these supplies, they may instead request a single VAT registration that is effective throughout the whole of the EU under the so-called 'special scheme' or 'one-stop-shop'. This scheme is available to non-EU traders irrespective of the value of their supplies, as there is no threshold for registration under the special scheme.

By way of an overview the special scheme is offered to provide a simplified means for non-EU businesses supplying electronically supplied services to EU non-business customers of registering and accounting electronically for EU VAT. The scheme works by giving eligible non-EU businesses the option of registering electronically in a single Member State of their choice and accounting for VAT on their sales of electronically supplied services to all EC non-business consumers on a single quarterly electronic VAT declaration, which provides details of VAT due in each Member State. This is submitted with payment to the tax administration in the Member State of registration, which then distributes the VAT to the Member States where the services are consumed. The law in the UK on the special scheme is in VATA 1994, Sch 3B. The conditions to be satisfied as set out in Sch 3B are considered in the next section.

How can a non-EU trader register as a taxable person under one UK registration for electronically supplied services to non-business customers?

A person may request registration for VAT purposes in the UK (which would then be effective throughout the EU in respect of 'qualifying supplies') if the five conditions mentioned below are met; and if met then HMRC must permit registration.[28] Upon registration, a supplier is given a registration number (which is notified electronically).[29] The effect of registration is that a supplier must pay VAT in respect of qualifying supplies. If the supply is treated as made in the UK, the amount is the

---

telecommunications services in Table 17.2 in Chapter 17 at **17.10.2** for relevant resources/links, and, for example, see: http://ec.europa.eu/taxation_customs/taxation/vat/how_vat_works/e-services/index_en.htm; and http://ec.europa.eu/taxation_customs/taxation/vat/how_vat_works/vat_on_services/index_en.htm. See also Council Regulation 143/2008/EC of 12 February 2008, concerning the inclusion of these B2C services from 2015 in the 'one stop shop'/special registration scheme.

[28] VATA 1994, Sch 3B, para 4. See also HMRC's Notice 741A *Place of Supply of Services* (January 2010), Section 20.

[29] VATA 1994, Sch 3B, para 6.

amount of VAT that would have been charged on the supply under VATA 1994 if the person had been registered under the VAT rules when the supply was made.[30] However, if the supply is treated as made in another EU Member State under the place of supply rules, then the amount of VAT due is the amount of VAT that would have been charged on the supply in accordance with the law of that Member State if the person had been treated as a taxable person in that Member State when the supply was made.[31]

HMRC provides an example[32] as follows. 'a USA business registers for the Special Scheme in the UK. Its customers are located in the UK, Italy and Spain. The USA business charges UK VAT to its UK customers, Italian VAT to its Italian customers and Spanish VAT to its Spanish customers. The business enters the VAT for each country on the appropriate line of the electronic declaration. It sends the declaration electronically with payment to HMRC, who retain the UK VAT and pass on the Italian VAT to the Italian authorities and the Spanish VAT to the Spanish authorities.'

For purposes of registration, 'qualifying supplies' refers to a supply of 'electronically supplied services' (ie those defined at **22.1** – further details are set out in Table 22.1 at **22.3.2**) to a person who (a) belongs in the UK or another EU Member State and (b) receives those services otherwise than for the purposes of a business carried on by that person (ie B2C supplies).[33] HMRC states that a non-EU supplier can use the special scheme for B2C supplies to consumers in the EU even if they also make B2B supplies, but they are not entitled to use the special scheme for those B2B supplies. This should not generally be problematic, however, since, as noted earlier, the non-EU supplier should not be required to charge and account for VAT on B2B cross-border supplies of electronically supplied services supplied in the EU because their business customers will account for the VAT due in their Member State under the reverse charge procedure.[34]

The five conditions for registration are:[35]

- Condition 1: the person makes or intends to may 'qualifying supplies' in the course of business carried on by that person.

- Condition 2: the person has neither a business establishment nor a fixed establishment (see **22.5**) in the UK or in another Member State in relation to any supply of goods or services.

---

[30] VATA 1994, Sch 3B, para 10(3).
[31] VATA 1994, Sch 3B, para 10(4).
[32] In HMRC's Notice 741A *Place of Supply of Services* (January 2010), para 20.3.1.
[33] VATA 1994, Sch 3B, para 3.
[34] See further at **22.6**.
[35] VATA 1994, Sch 3B, para 2.

- Condition 3: the person is not (a) registered under VATA 1994, (b) identified for the purposes of VAT in accordance with the law of another Member State or (c) registered under an Act of Tynwald[36] for the purposes of any tax imposed by or under an Act of Tynwald which corresponds to VAT.

- Condition 4: the person (a) is not required to be registered or indentified as mentioned in Condition 3 or (b) is required to be so registered or identified, but solely by virtue of the fact that he makes or intends to make qualifying supplies.

- Condition 5: the person is not identified under any provision of the law of another Member State which corresponds to the registration which is permitted under UK law in respect of qualifying supplies (ie which implements the VAT Directive).[37]

Information requirements for registration

The request for registration must contain information on the following matters, which must be made by electronic means:[38]

- the name of the person making the request;

- the person's postal address;

- the person's electronic address (including any websites);

- the person's number (if any) that has been allocated by the tax authorities in the country in which the person belongs; and

- the date on which the person began, or intends to begin, making qualifying supplies.

In addition the person must include a statement to the effect that the person is not (a) registered under VATA 1994, (b) identified for the purposes of VAT in accordance with the law of another Member State or (c) registered under an Act of Tynwald for the purposes of any tax imposed by or under an Act of Tynwald which corresponds to VAT.[39]

A supplier must notify HMRC of any changes in the information that has been provided, or any cessation in making qualifying supplies, or if any of

---

[36] The laws of the Isle of Man.
[37] See Arts 359–369.
[38] VATA 1994, Sch 3B, para 4(3) and (5).
[39] VATA 1994, Sch 3B, para 4(4).

Conditions 2 to 5 cease to be met.[40] Notification must be made within 30 days of the date of the change of particulars or of the cessation.[41]

Cancellation of registration

HMRC must cancel a supplier's registration if that person ceases to make, or has the intention of ceasing to make, qualifying supplies.[42] Cancellation will also occur where a supplier ceases to meet any of Conditions 2 to 5, or where a supplier has persistently failed to comply with that person's obligations under the VAT rules.[43]

Obligations and rights on registration

Once a supplier is registered under the special scheme, that person is liable to pay VAT if (a) a qualifying supply is made and (b) that person is registered under VATA 1994 (due to making supplies of electronic services) when the supply is made.[44] There is an obligation on the supplier to submit a special accounting return to HMRC for each reporting period.[45] The reporting period is each quarter for the period of which a person is registered under the VAT rules (due to making a supply of electronic services). The special accounting return must contain the following information:[46]

- the person's registration number;

- the total value of qualifying supplies treated as made in each Member State;

- the rate of VAT applicable to the supplies (ie whether that applying in the UK or another Member State); and

- the total amount of VAT payable by the supplier in respect of the supplies for that period. This amount must be paid at the same time as the return is submitted.[47]

The return must also specify the total amount of VAT which the supplier is liable to pay in connection with all qualifying supplies.[48] The

---

40 VATA 1994, Sch 3B, para 7.
41 VATA 1994, Sch 3B, para 7.
42 VATA 1994, Sch 3B, para 8.
43 VATA 1994, Sch 3B, para 8.
44 VATA 1994, Sch 3B, para 10(1).
45 VATA 1994, Sch 3B, para 11(1).
46 VATA 1994, Sch 3B, para 11(3), (4). The return specifies the amounts in sterling, and any conversion is at rates published by the European Central Bank for the last day of the reporting period or, if there is no such rate for that day, then the rate for the next day: VATA 1994,Sch 3B, para 12(2).
47 VATA 1994, Sch 3B, para 13.
48 VATA 1994, Sch 3B, para 11(4).

accounting return must be submitted within the period of 20 days after the last day of the reporting period to which it relates.[49] All records must be retained to enable the tax authorities for the Member State in which a qualifying supply is treated as made to determine whether any return is correct.[50] These records must be available for the tax authorities to inspect if they so request (they must be made available electronically, and be retained for 10 years beginning with 1 January following the date on which the transaction was entered into by the supplier).[51]

A supplier who is registered under this special scheme is entitled to a refund of UK VAT charged on goods imported by such person into the UK, and on supplies made to such person in the UK in connection with the making by that person of qualifying supplies whilst a participant of the special scheme, provided that the VAT was paid under the terms of the EC 13th VAT Directive (of 17 November 1986 (86/560/EEC), which concerns arrangements for VAT refunds to taxable persons established outside the EU).[52]

Deregistration

A supplier who is already registered as a taxable person under Sch 1 to VATA 1994 may apply to cancel the registration under that Schedule, where the supplier shows that it intends to apply for registration under Sch 3B to VATA 1994 (supply of electronic services) or under any similar provision of another Member State.[53]

22.2.3 VAT Representative

An overseas supplier is unlikely to have any physical representation in the country to which it makes supplies electronically. However, it is clear that a person who makes supplies to the UK is required to register once a specific VAT registration threshold is met (see earlier discussion in Chapter 17 at **17.9.1** and also at **22.2.1**). Furthermore, HMRC has the power to order, or an overseas supplier can request, the appointment of a person within the UK as that person's VAT representative for UK purposes – although, this power is not available to HMRC where a person is registered under Sch 3B to VATA 1994 (see discussion at **22.2.2**).[54]

Broadly, once appointed the representative becomes responsible for its principal's VAT responsibilities in the UK. Effectively the representative

[49] VATA 1994, Sch 3B, para 12(3).
[50] VATA 1994, Sch 3B, para 14(2).
[51] VATA 1994, Sch 3B, para 14(3)–(5).
[52] VATA 1994, Sch 3B, para 22. As stated by HMRC, VAT refund claims cannot be made via the special scheme itself but can be made on form VAT 65A. See generally HMRC Notice 723A *Refunds of VAT in the European Community for EC and non-EC businesses* (October 2011), and see HMRC Notice 741A, paras 20.20 and 20.34.
[53] VATA 1994, Sch 3B, para 18.
[54] VATA 1994, Sch 3B, para 19.

must ensure the principal discharges its VAT liabilities and compliance obligations under VATA 1994. Where a UK representative fails in discharging these obligations, the representative will be held jointly and severally liable with the principal.

22.3 WHERE IS THE PLACE OF SUPPLY OF ELECTRONICALLY SUPPLIED SERVICES?

It was noted in Chapter 17 that in the context of e-commerce and e-infrastructure activities the place of supply rules are extremely important. This is because the cost of using technology for the purposes of providing goods and/or services is low. It is now relatively easy to send large portions of data across continents through the use of submarine lines or via a satellite network.

As discussed in Chapter 17, the place of supply is determined by reference to a number of specific rules. Table 22.1 at **22.3.2** summarises the place of supply rules relevant for electronically supplied services for UK VAT purposes.

As for other services summarised in Chapter 17, in applying the rules to electronically supplied services, only the circumstances existing at the time of the chargeable event will be taken into account. Any subsequent changes to the use of the service received will not affect the determination of the place of supply (unless there is an abusive practice in relation to the supply).[55] Further guidance to help suppliers in deciding the place of supply of electronically supplied services from a UK VAT perspective is also provided in the form of decision tables[56] in Tables 22.2 to 22.4 at **22.3.3**.

22.3.1 The territorial extent of the UK for VAT purposes

To recap from Chapter 17, where a supply takes place outside of the UK, a UK VAT charge cannot be imposed upon the supply.[57] In other words, for a UK VAT charge to arise the supply must be made in the UK. VATA 1994 defines the UK as including the territorial sea of the UK (which is the waters within 12 nautical miles of the coastline).[58]

Greater light on the territorial extent of the UK is thrown on the matter by the Interpretation Act 1978, which provides that the UK comprises England, Scotland, Wales and Northern Ireland.[59] For VAT purposes, the

---

[55] See EU Implementing Regulation, Art 25. See also note 129 in Chapter 17, at **17.10.2**.
[56] See HMRC's Notice 741A *Place of Supply of Services* (January 2010), para 23.
[57] VATA 1994, s 4(1).
[58] VATA 1994, s 96(11).
[59] Interpretation Act 1978, ss 5 and 22(1), Sch 1.

Isle of Man is deemed to be part of the UK unless otherwise indicated.[60]
By contrast the Channel Islands do not form part of the UK. At the time
of publication, VAT is not charged in the Channel Islands.

22.3.2 Place of supply rules for electronically supplied services

Table 22.1: Summary of place of supply rules for electronically supplied services – VATA 1994

Type of supply	Place of supply	Reference (VATA 1994)
Services		
General rules		
Business to consumer (B2C)		
Supply of services by a supplier who belongs in the UK to a private individual, charity, government department or other body that has no business activities (excluding services supplied to a recipient who is a 'relevant business person').[61]	Service supplied in the country in which the supplier belongs (unless overriding place of supply rules apply in Sch 4A to VATA, which includes electronically supplied services: see Table 17.2 in Chapter 17 and below).[62]	s 7A(2) (b). See **22.4** for details on where a person 'belongs'.
	UK VAT will be due where the supplier belongs in the UK, irrespective of where the customer belongs	(Art 44 VAT Directive)

HMRC Notice 741A (January 2010), para 3.7

Where a customer has several establishments it is necessary to identify at which of the establishments the customer receives the supplies to determine whether VAT is chargeable. It is necessary to establish the facts, and consider at which establishment the services are used, and which establishment gives the supplier instructions.

---

[60] See Value Added Tax (Isle of Man) Order 1982, SI 1982/1067 and Value Added Tax (Isle of Man) (No 2) Order 1982, SI 1982/1068.

[61] VATA 1994, s 7A(4): See later in this chapter at 22.4.3 and 22.4.4 for the definition of a 'relevant business person'.

[62] VATA 1994, s 7A(5).

Type of supply	Place of supply	Reference (VATA 1994)
Business to business (B2B)		
Supply of services to a 'relevant business person'[63] by a UK supplier (the supply must not be received for a wholly private purpose).	Service supplied in the country in which the recipient/customer belongs (unless overriding place of supply rules apply in Sch 4A to VATA 1994, which includes electronically supplied services. See Table 17.2 in Chapter 17 and below).[64]	s 7A(2)(a). See **22.4** for details on where a person 'belongs'.
	If the customer is in the UK then UK VAT is due.	(Art 45 VAT Directive)
	If the customer is outside the UK then the supply is outside the scope of UK VAT; if the customer is outside the EU then there will be no VAT (again, subject to any exceptions in VATA 1994, Sch 4A).	
	If the customer belongs in another Member State (and is VAT registered) and the supply is subject to local VAT in that Member State under the reverse charge at either the standard or reduced rate then the supplier may need to complete and submit an EC Sales List, which must now be completed by suppliers for supplies of taxable services subject to the reverse charge in the customer's Member State. See HMRC's Notice 725 The Single Market (February 2011) for further details, particularly at Section 17 of the notice.	

HMRC Notice 741A (January 2010), para 2.7

- Supplier should obtain commercial evidence that the customer belongs outside the UK, and does not receive the supply for a wholly private purpose;

- VAT registration numbers are generally the best evidence that the supply is not received for wholly private purposes and should be requested. Alternative types of evidence include other commercial documents indicating the nature of the customer's activities, such as certificates from fiscal authorities and business letterheads.[63]

Telecommunication and broadcasting services		

---

[63]   See above.

[64]   VATA 1994, s 7A(5).

Type of supply	Place of supply	Reference (VATA 1994)
(NB, further details are provided in Chapter 17 (Table 17.2) in relation to telecommunications and broadcasting services and in para 16.7.1 of HMRC's Notice 741A.		
A supply of services consisting of the provision of: (a) telecommunication services, or (b) radio or television broadcasting services.	Covered by the general rules described above (until January 2015, where the general rule will change for B2C supplies of these services), but subject to the use and enjoyment rule. Therefore where (a) the supply of services would otherwise be treated as made in the UK and (b) the services are to any extent effectively used and enjoyed in a country which is not a Member State, the supply is to be treated to that extent as made in that country.	Sch 4A, para 8
For this purpose, 'telecommunication services' means services relating to the transmission, emission or reception of signals, writing, images and sounds or information of any nature by wire, radio, optical or other electromagnetic systems, including (a) the related transfer or assignment of the right to use capacity for such transmission, emission or reception and (b) the provision of access to global information networks.	Where (a) the supply of services would otherwise be treated as made in a country which is not a Member State, and (b) the services are to any extent effectively used and enjoyed in the UK, the supply is to be treated to that extent as made in the UK. However, from 1 January 2015 (without prejudice to the use and enjoyment rule), a B2C supply of these services is not subject to VAT if the supplier demonstrates that the place of supply is outside the EU in accordance with the EU Implementing Regulation (Art 3).	
Exceptions to place of supply of services relating to supplies made to a relevant business person.	See further in Chapter 17, Table 17.2 in reference to changes being introduced in 2015 for the place of supply of cross border B2C supplies of these services.	
Electronically supplied services		
Provision of electronically supplied services to a relevant business person.	Covered by the B2B general rule so the place of supply is where the business customer belongs, but this is subject to the use and enjoyment rule.	Sch 4A, para 9

Value Added Tax: European Union Trade

Type of supply	Place of supply	Reference (VATA 1994)
Examples of such services. • website supply, web-hosting and distance maintenance of programmes and equipment; • the supply of software and the updating of software; • the supply of images, text and information, and the making available of databases; • the supply of music, films and games (including games of chance and gambling games); • the supply of political, cultural, artistic, sporting, scientific, educational or entertainment broadcasts (including broadcasts of events); and • the supply of distance teaching. NB: Where the supplier of a service and the supplier's customer communicate via e-mail, this does not of itself mean that the service provided is an electronically supplied service.	Therefore, if there is a supply of services consisting of the provision of electronically supplied services to a relevant business person which would otherwise be treated as made in the UK, but the services are to any extent effectively used and enjoyed in a country which is not a Member State, then the supply is to be treated to that extent as made in that country. If there is a supply of services consisting of the provision of electronically supplied services to a relevant business person which would otherwise be treated as made in a country which is not a Member State, but the services are to any extent effectively used and enjoyed in the UK, then the supply is to be treated to that extent as made in the UK. NB. The use and enjoyment rule does not apply in the UK to B2C supplies of these services (see 17.6). See 17.2.2 and further in Chapter 17, Table 17.2, in reference to changes being introduced in 2015 for the place of supply of cross border B2C supplies of these services.	Art 58 VAT Directive

Note:

Under the EU Implementing Regulation which is expressly stated to be 'directly applicable' throughout the EU in respect of the VAT Directive (see Chapter 17, at 17.2), the concept of 'electronically supplied services' is required to include services which are delivered over the internet or an electronic network and the nature of which renders their supply essentially automated and involving minimal human intervention, and impossible to ensure in the absence of information technology.

In particular, the concept includes all of the following matters (those not included are referred to later):

(a) the supply of digitised products generally, including software and changes to or upgrades of software;

(b) services providing or supporting a business or personal presence on an electronic network such as a website or a webpage;

(c) services automatically generated from a computer via the internet or an electronic network, in response to specific data input by the recipient;

Type of supply	Place of supply	Reference (VATA 1994)

(d) the transfer for consideration of the right to put goods or services up for sale on an Internet site operating as an online market on which potential buyers make their bids by an automated procedure and on which the parties are notified of a sale by electronic mail automatically generated from a computer;

(e) Internet service packages of information in which the telecommunications component forms an ancillary and subordinate part (ie packages going beyond mere internet access and including other elements such as content pages giving access to news, weather or travel reports, playgrounds, website hosting, access to online debates etc);

(f) the services listed:

    (1) Point (1) of Annex II to Directive 2006/112/EC (website supply, web-hosting, distance maintenance of programs and equipment):

        (a) website hosting and webpage hosting;

        (b) automated, online and distance maintenance of programs;

        (c) remote systems administration;

        (d) online data warehousing where specific data is stored and retrieved electronically;

        (e) online supply of on-demand disc space.

    (2) Point (2) of Annex II to Directive 2006/112/EC (supply of software and updating thereof):

        (a) accessing or downloading software (including procurement/accountancy programs and anti-virus software) plus updates;

        (b) software to block banner adverts showing, otherwise known as Bannerblockers;

        (c) download drivers, such as software that interfaces computers with peripheral equipment (such as printers);

        (d) online automated installation of filters on websites;

        (e) online automated installation of firewalls.

    (3) Point (3) of Annex II to Directive 2006/112/EC (supply of images, text and information and making available of databases):

        (a) accessing or downloading desktop themes;

        (b) accessing or downloading photographic or pictorial images or screensavers;

        (c) the digitised content of books and other electronic publications;

        (d) subscription to online newspapers and journals;

        (e) weblogs and website statistics;

        (f) online news, traffic information and weather reports;

        (g) online information generated automatically by software from specific data input by the customer, such as legal and financial data (in particular such data as continually updated stock market data, in real time);

        (h) the provision of advertising space including banner ads on a website/web page;

        (i) use of search engines and Internet directories.

Type of supply	Place of supply	Reference (VATA 1994)

(4)   Point (4) of Annex II to Directive 2006/112/EC (supply of music, films and games of chance and gambling games, and of political, cultural, artistic, sporting, scientific and entertainment broadcasts and events):

     (a)   accessing or downloading of music on to computers and mobile phones;

     (b)   accessing or downloading of jingles, excerpts, ringtones, or other sounds;

     (c)   accessing or downloading of films;

     (d)   downloading of games on to computers and mobile phones;

     (e)   accessing automated online games which are dependent on the internet, or other similar electronic networks, where players are geographically remote from one another.

(5)   Point (5) of Annex II to Directive 2006/112/EC (supply of distance learning):

     (a)   automated distance teaching dependent on the internet or similar electronic network to function and the supply of which requires limited or no human intervention, including virtual classrooms, except where the Internet or similar electronic network is used as a tool simply for communication between the teacher and student;

     (b)   workbooks completed by pupils online and marked automatically, without human intervention.

In particular, the concept excludes all of the following matters:

(a)   radio and television broadcasting services;

(b)   telecommunications services;

(c)   goods, where the order and processing is done electronically;

(d)   CD-ROMs, floppy disks and similar tangible media;

(e)   printed matter, such as books, newsletters, newspapers or journals;

(f)   CD-ROMs and audio cassettes;

(g)   video cassettes and DVDs;

(h)   games on a CD-ROM;

(i)   services of professionals such as lawyers and financial consultants, who advise clients by e-mail;

(j)   teaching services, where the course content is delivered by a teacher over the internet or an electronic network (namely via a remote link);

(k)   offline physical repair services of computer equipment;

(l)   offline data warehousing services;

(m)   advertising services, in particular as in newspapers, on posters and on television;

(n)   telephone helpdesk services;

(o)   teaching services purely involving correspondence courses, such as postal courses;

(p)   conventional auctioneers' services reliant on direct human intervention, irrespective of how bids are made;

(q)   telephone services with a video component, otherwise known as videophone services;

(r)   access to the internet and world wide web;

Type of supply	Place of supply	Reference (VATA 1994)
(s) telephone services provided through the internet.		
Exceptions relating to supplies not made to a relevant business person		
Electronic services		
A supply consisting of the provision by a person who belongs in a country which is not a Member State (other than the Isle of Man) of electronically supplied services (see above for meaning) to a person ('the recipient') who: (a) is not a relevant business person and (b) belongs in a Member State.	Made in the country in which the recipient belongs. However, from 1 January 2015 (without prejudice to the use and enjoyment rule where applicable), the supply is not subject to VAT if the supplier demonstrates that the place of supply is outside the EU in accordance with the EU Implementing Regulation (Art 3). Where supplied to a non-taxable person who is established in more than one country or has his permanent address in one country and his usual residence in another, priority is to be given to the place that best ensures taxation at the place of actual consumption when determining the place of supply of those services. See further in Chapter 17, Table 17.2 with regard to changes being introduced in 2015 for the place of supply of cross border B2C supplies of telecommunications, broadcasting and electronically supplied services.	Sch 4A, para 15 EU Implementing Regulation, Art 24(2)
Other services provided to a recipient belonging outside EC		
A supply consisting of the provision to a person ('the recipient') who: (a) is not a relevant business person and (b) belongs in a country which is not a Member State (other than the Isle of Man),of the following services:	Made in the country in which the recipient belongs. Without prejudice to the use and enjoyment rule (if applicable), the supply is not subject to VAT if the supplier demonstrates that the place of supply is outside the EU in accordance with the EU Implementing Regulation (Art 3).	Sch 4A, para 16

V Value Added Tax: European Union Trade

Type of supply	Place of supply	Reference (VATA 1994)
(a) transfers and assignments of copyright, patents, licences, trademarks and similar rights;		
(b) the acceptance of any obligation to refrain from pursuing or exercising (in whole or in part) any business activity or any rights within paragraph (a)¹		
(c) advertising services;		
(d) services of consultants, engineers, consultancy bureaux, lawyers, accountants, and similar services, data processing and provision of information, other than any services relating to land;		
(e) banking, financial and insurance services (including reinsurance), other than the provision of safe deposit facilities;		
(f) the provision of access to, or transmission or distribution through: (i) a natural gas system situated within the territory of a Member State or any network connected to such a system; (ii) an electricity system; or (iii) a network through which heat or cooling is supplied, and the provision of other directly linked services;		
(g) the supply of staff;		
(h) the letting on hire of goods other than means of transport;		
(i) telecommunication services (until January 2015);		
(j) radio and television broadcasting services (until January 2015); and		
(k) electronically supplied services (until January 2015).		

HMRC Notice 741A (January 2010), paras 17 and 19

- When do the additional rules for electronically supplied services apply?

Type of supply	Place of supply	Reference (VATA 1994)

The additional rules for electronically supplied services apply only where there is a B2B supply in either of the following situations:

- the place of supply would be the UK (because the supplier or the customer belongs in the UK) but the services are effectively used and enjoyed outside the EC, or

- the place of supply would be outside the EC (because the supplier or the customer belongs outside the EC), but the services are effectively used and enjoyed in the UK.

In these circumstances, the place of supply of the electronically supplied services is where their effective use and enjoyment takes place. Where this is the UK, the services are subject to UK VAT.

- What do I need to know to decide whether these rules apply?

You need to know:

- where the supplier and customer belong, and

- the place where the services are effectively used and enjoyed.

- Does it always matter where electronically supplied services are effectively used and enjoyed?

It does not always matter where electronically supplied services are effectively used and enjoyed. It only matters in the situations described above. The use and enjoyment provisions apply where the EC position would otherwise be distortive. Consequently, they do not apply in any situation where:

- B2C supplies of electronically supplied services are made. This is because most consumers are considered to use and enjoy the services in the same country in which they belong,

- the place of supply is the UK (because either the supplier or the customer belongs in the UK) and the service was effectively used and enjoyed in another Member State, or

- the place of supply is in another Member State (because either the supplier or the customer belongs there) but the supply is effectively used and enjoyed in the UK.

- What does effective use and enjoyment of electronically supplied services mean?

Effective use and enjoyment takes place where the customer actually consumes the electronically supplied services irrespective of contract, payment or beneficial interest.

- Examples for electronically supplied services

- A UK business purchases digitised software from an Irish supplier for use only in its branch in the Channel Islands. Although the supply is received in the UK where the business belongs, it is used outside the EC and is outside the scope of UK (and EC) VAT.

- A USA business purchases web-hosting services for its international business, including its UK branch. Although the supply is received in the USA, to the extent that it is used in the UK, it is subject to UK VAT.

- A UK charity which undertakes both business and non-business activities purchases downloaded information from another UK business for use in both its UK headquarters and its Canadian branch. Although the supply is received in the UK, to the extent it is used in Canada it is outside the scope of UK VAT. UK VAT is only due to the extent of use by the UK headquarters.

Type of supply	Place of supply	Reference (VATA 1994)

- Do I have to apply different rules if I supply telecommunications services or radio and television broadcasting services as well as electronically supplied services?

  HMRC recognises that in certain situations, the place of supply would be the same whether the rules for telecommunications services and radio and television broadcasting services, or those for electronically supplied services were applied. This is because most customers receiving B2C supplies use and enjoy services in the same country in which they belong.

  Consequently, if you are:

  – a UK business which supplies electronically supplied services your services are B2C supplies, and

  – your existing accounting systems are set up to tax supplies where they are effectively used and enjoyed,

  you may, exceptionally, opt to apply the use and enjoyment rules to your supplies of electronically supplied services.

  This is a simplification measure which prevents the need for businesses to adjust their systems. However, HMRC will not allow this simplification to be used in any case where we consider it leads to abuse.

- Non-UK supplier supplying a customer registered for UK VAT

- If you are a supplier who does not belong in the UK and you make B2B supplies to a customer belonging in the UK who is registered for UK VAT, your customer is responsible for accounting for any VAT due on the supply under the reverse charge procedure.

- Non-UK supplier supplying a customer not registered for UK VAT

- If you are a supplier who does not belong in the UK, and you make B2B supplies but your customer is not registered for UK VAT, you, as the supplier, are responsible for accounting for any VAT due on your supply where the place of supply is the UK. If you are not already registered in the UK, you may be liable to register.

- If you are a non-EC supplier of electronically supplied services providing B2C services to in the EC, you may be potentially required to register and account for VAT in every Member State where you supply your services (according to the rules which apply in the various Member States). However, to relieve this burden, a simplified special scheme permits you to register electronically in the Member State of your choice and account for EC VAT on an electronic VAT return.

- Accounting procedures for UK VAT registered recipients receiving electronically supplied services from a non-EC supplier where the place of supply is the UK

- If you are a UK VAT registered recipient receiving a B2B supply and:

  – you belong outside the EC for the purposes of receiving the supply

  – you use and enjoy the services in the UK, and

  – your supplier belongs outside the UK,

  you are required to account for VAT using the reverse charge procedure.

- How do I account for VAT on electronically supplied services that are only partly liable to UK VAT because of the use and enjoyment provisions?

  You are only required to account for UK VAT to the extent that the place of supply of services is the UK. Therefore you should seek to identify the location where the services are actually used.

Type of supply	Place of supply	Reference (VATA 1994)

HMRC will normally accept any records or documentation that demonstrates the extent to which services are used and enjoyed in the UK but, where such records do not exist, you should make a fair and reasonable assessment.

There is no prescribed method for determining the extent to which services are used in the UK. You may adopt whatever method is available to you that produces a fair and reasonable reflection of services that are liable to UK VAT. If you are in doubt you should contact our Helpline. Evidence of how the apportionment has been made should be retained to be made available on request.

- Liability to register in other Member States

If you supply B2B electronically supplied services where the place of supply would be outside the EC, and the services are effectively used and enjoyed by your customer in another Member State, you may be liable to register for VAT in that Member State.

- How do I verify my customer's business status? (para. 19.2)

If you make B2B supplies within the EC the evidence required at the time of the transaction would normally be the customer's VAT registration number and country identification code prefix. The number must conform to the format for the registered person's Member State.

Under normal trading practices you will often know your business customers. Therefore, in such cases, you will not need to routinely check all VAT numbers quoted, provided that the numbers conform to the correct country format.

However, where a relationship has not been established with a business customer the VAT number should be checked when:

- the VAT involved exceeds £500 on a single transaction, or

- the cumulative VAT on transactions for electronically supplied services to a single customer in a VAT quarter exceeds £500.

Similarly, if you supply downloaded music, games, films and so on of a kind normally supplied to a private consumer, you would not expect a VAT number to be quoted in such circumstances. However, where a VAT number is quoted in what is clearly a supply to a private consumer the use of that number should be challenged.

Full verification should be undertaken in all cases where you have any reason to believe that a VAT number quoted by a customer is false or is being used incorrectly.

If a customer claims to be in business but not to be VAT registered then alternative evidence should be obtained to support the claim. This can be in the form of other reasonable commercial evidence or records that should normally be available. Examples include contracts, business letterheads, a commercial website address, publicity material, certificates from fiscal authorities. A digital certificate from a reputable organisation can also be used for this purpose.

The VAT Information Exchange System (VIES) can support your decision-making process by providing an online verification system. The system can be accessed using the HMRC website, go to Businesses & Corporations and select the link to the EU VAT registration checker, or go direct to the Europa website.

You may also contact our Helpline to verify names and addresses as well as dates of registration and deregistration where appropriate.

Other Member States may have similar systems by which it is possible to check the validity of VAT registration numbers.

Value Added Tax: European Union Trade

V

Type of supply	Place of supply	Reference (VATA 1994)

If any of the above checks fail to confirm that your customer is in business or if there remains any doubt about the use of a VAT registration number, VAT should be charged as appropriate on all supplies to that customer including supplies that have already been made.

Any VAT that has been charged in error may be credited under the normal rules.

- How do I identify my customer's country of residence? (para. 19.3)

Under normal trading practices you will often know your business customers and where they are located. However, this is less likely to be the case with B2C supplies and with lower value transactions to business customers. As technology cannot determine with certainty the place where such customers belong, self-declaration by the customer combined with a reasonable level of verification will be acceptable.

It is likely that you already have established procedures in place to identify and verify the country where your customer belongs. HMRC will rely as much as possible on those practices to ensure you are not burdened with unnecessary requirements. If the method you use is not included in the list of examples in the following paragraph, you are advised to contact HMRC.

Customer self-declaration will be acceptable (without prior approval from HMRC) in respect of electronically supplied services, where one or other of the following practices is followed:

(a) Use of your customer's postal address provided you have used it to send (for example) goods, catalogues, samples, CD-Roms, invoices, correspondence without these items having been returned, undelivered. (However, alternative means will have to be used if mail is returned undelivered.)

(b) Acceptance of payment by credit/debit card where you compare the customer's home address with the billing address, but then rely on satisfactory alternative evidence if the match is unsuccessful.

(c) Acceptance of payment by credit/debit card and, using proprietary software, you compare the customer's country of residence with the location of the issuing bank but then rely on satisfactory alternative evidence if the match is unsuccessful.

(d) Use of geo-location or proprietary software to verify where your customer belongs but then rely on satisfactory alternative evidence if the match fails.

(e) Use of systems that are configured to identify where the service is used and enjoyed (for example telecommunications suppliers). HMRC will accept the arrangement as a proxy for identifying the country where the customer belongs.

If you use one or other of the above methods, you will need to demonstrate that HMRC's requirements have been met. For example, you may be asked to show how your system processes the relevant information.

What if the information provided by customers is found to be incorrect? (para. 19.4)

Where verification has been undertaken and the details provided were believed to be correct at that time, but subsequently the customer is found to have made a false declaration, HMRC will not seek to recover VAT from you, the supplier, where it was not charged to the customer. This does not apply if there was reasonable information at the time of the sale to indicate that the customer's information was incorrect. HMRC's treatment of such cases will be subject to periodic review.

HMRC Notice 741A (January 2010), paras 15.10–15.12 relating to electronically supplied services

Type of supply	Place of supply	Reference (VATA 1994)

[See Chapter 17, Table 17.2, for examples of the kinds of services which are covered by the services listed in (a) to (j) above under the heading 'Other services provided to a recipient belonging outside EC'.]

(a) Examples of telecommunication services (para 15.10) are given in further detail in Chapter 17 at Table 17.2. However, in the context of electronically supplied services, it is helpful to reiterate here that in answer to the question whether internet services constitute telecommunication services, HMRC states as follows:

'Access to the Internet and World Wide Web, the provision of email addresses and chatline facilities are telecommunications services. If you supply basic access to the Internet, even if related software, some information and customer support facilities are included, HMRC treat the supply as being of telecommunications services. *However*: (a) if a person supplies a package of Internet services where the emphasis is on content rather than communication, the supply is not of pure telecommunications services. The place of supply of such a package depends on the nature of the services provided, or (b) if a person supplies services separately or services which are simply delivered to a customer by electronic transmission, the place of supply depends on the nature of the services provided.'

(b) electronically supplied services (see above for definition)

– This heading covers a service: (a) delivered over the Internet or an electronic network (in other words is reliant on the Internet or similar network for its provision) and (b) where the nature of the particular service means it is heavily dependent on information technology for its supply. In other words the service is essentially automated, involving minimal human intervention and in the absence of information technology does not have viability

– In general the use of the Internet or other electronic networks by parties to communicate with respect to transactions or to facilitate trading does not, any more than the use of a telephone or fax, affect the VAT treatment. For example, when parties simply use the internet to convey information in the course of a business transaction (eg e-mail), this does not change the nature of that transaction. This differs from a supply that is completely dependent on the internet in order to be carried out (eg searching and retrieving information from a database with no human intervention).

– Examples of electronically supplied services:

- website supply or web-hosting services;

- distance maintenance of programs and equipment;

- supplies of software and updating thereof;

- supplies of images, text and information and making available of databases;

- supply of music, films and games, including games of chance and gambling games and of political, cultural, artistic, sporting, scientific, educational or entertainment broadcasts of events;

- supply of distance teaching.

– Examples of exclusions from electronically supplied services:

- supplies of goods, where the order and processing is done electronically;

- supplies of CD-Roms, games on a CD-Rom, floppy disks and similar tangible media;

- supplies of printed matter, such as books, newsletters, newspapers or journals;

Type of supply	Place of supply	Reference (VATA 1994)
supplies of CDs, audio cassettes, videos cassettes, DVDs; - services of lawyers and financial consultants and so on, who advise clients through e-mail; - teaching services, where the course content is delivered by a teacher over the internet or an electronic network (in other words, via a remote link); - offline physical repair services of computer equipment; offline data warehousing services· - advertising services, in particular as in newspapers, on posters and on television; - telephone helpdesk services; - teaching services purely involving correspondence courses, such as postal courses; - conventional auctioneers' services reliant on direct human intervention, irrespective of how bids are made; - telephone services with a video component, otherwise known as videophone services; - internet and worldwide web access services; - telephone services provided through the internet.		

22.3.3 UK VAT position of electronically supplied services – further guidance

Further guidance to help suppliers determine the UK VAT position of electronically supplied services is given in Tables 22.2 to 22.4, sourced from HMRC's Notice 741A.

HMRC Notice 741A, para 23

Table 22.2: Examples where the supplier belongs in the UK

Customer belongs	General UK VAT position **	Additional rules: use and enjoyment provisions
In the UK and receives the services for business purposes.	Services are supplied in the UK and the supplier accounts for any UK VAT due.	Services used and enjoyed outside the EU are outside the scope of UK (and EU) VAT.
In the UK and receives the services for non-business purposes.	Services are supplied in the UK and the supplier accounts for any UK VAT due.	Do not apply.
In another Member State and receives the services for business purposes.	Services are supplied outside the scope of UK VAT and the customer accounts for any VAT due (by applying the reverse charge).	Do not apply.

In another Member State and receives the services for non-business purposes.	Services are supplied in the UK and the supplier accounts for any UK VAT due.	Do not apply.
Outside the EU and receives the services for business purposes	(If the services are not used and enjoyed in the EU), the services are supplied outside the EU and are outside the scope of UK (and EU) VAT.	Services used and enjoyed in the UK are supplied in the UK and the supplier accounts for any UK VAT due. Services used and enjoyed in another Member State are outside the scope of UK VAT but may be within the scope of VAT in the Member State where they are used and enjoyed. Check with Member State.
Outside the EU and receives the services for non-business purposes	Services are supplied outside the EU and are outside the scope of UK (and EU) VAT.	Do not apply.

Table 22.3: Examples where the supplier belongs in another Member State

Customer belongs	General UK VAT position **	Additional rules: use and enjoyment provisions
In the UK and receives the services for business purposes.	Services are supplied in the UK and the customer accounts for UK VAT by applying the reverse charge.	Services used and enjoyed outside the EU are outside the scope of UK (and EU) VAT.
In the UK and receives the services for non-business purposes.	Services are supplied in the supplier's Member State and the supplier accounts for any VAT due.	Do not apply.
In another Member State.	Services are outside the scope of UK VAT.	Do not apply.

Value Added Tax: European Union Trade

Outside the EU and receives the services for business purposes	(If the services are not used and enjoyed in the EU), the services are supplied outside the EU and are outside the scope of UK (and EU) VAT.	Services used and enjoyed in the UK are supplied in the UK. Supplier accounts for any UK VAT due unless the customer provides a UK VAT registration number and accounts for UK VAT using the reverse charge. Services used and enjoyed in another Member State are outside the scope of UK VAT but may be within the scope of VAT in the Member State where they are used and enjoyed. Check with Member State.
Outside the EU and receives the services for non-business purposes	Services are supplied outside the EU and are outside the scope of UK (and EU) VAT.	Do not apply.

Table 22.4: Examples where the supplier belongs outside the EU

Customer belongs	General UK VAT position **	Additional rules: use and enjoyment provisions
In the UK and receives the services for business purposes.	Services are supplied in the UK and the customer accounts for any UK VAT by applying the reverse charge.	Services used and enjoyed outside the EU are outside the scope of UK (and EU) VAT.
In the UK and receives the services for non-business purposes.	Services are supplied in the UK. Supplier should account for UK VAT (the supplier may opt to use the special registration scheme where the relevant conditions are met.).	Do not apply.
In another Member State.	Services are supplied in the other Member State and are outside the scope of UK VAT.	Do not apply.

Outside the EU and receives the services for business purposes	Services are supplied outside the EU and are outside the scope of UK (and EU) VAT.	Services used and enjoyed in the UK are supplied in the UK. Supplier accounts for any UK VAT due unless the customer provides a UK VAT registration number and accounts for UK VAT using the reverse charge. Services used and enjoyed in another Member State are outside the scope of UK VAT but may be within the scope of VAT in the Member State where they are used and enjoyed. Check with Member State.
Outside the EU and receives the services for non-business purposes	Services are supplied outside the EU and are outside the scope of UK (and EU) VAT.	Do not apply.

** means, for all three tables, column two is the correct VAT treatment unless the additional rules shown in the last/third column apply.

22.4 DETERMINING WHERE A SUPPLIER AND RECIPIENT BELONGS FOR THE PURPOSES OF A SUPPLY OF SERVICES

22.4.1 Introduction

Under the general rules summarised in Table 22.1,[65] a service is treated as supplied in the UK if the supplier belongs in the UK, unless the person to whom the supply is made is a 'relevant business person', in which case the service is supplied in the country in which the recipient belongs. Whether a supplier or recipient belongs in the UK is determined under VATA 1994,[66] but it is also important to remember that this also has to be construed in accordance with the EU Implementing Regulation, as this clarifies certain aspects of the VAT Directive with the objective of ensuring a more uniform application of VAT rules within the EU and is 'directly applicable' in the EU. If either a supplier or recipient of services has an establishment in more than one country then each establishment has to be considered separately, since such a person is regarded for UK VAT purposes as belonging in the country where the establishment most directly concerned with the particular supply is located.

---

[65] VATA 1994, s 7A
[66] VATA 1994, s 9.

22.4.2 Supplier and relevant business person: where such a person belongs

Briefly, a supplier is based in the UK if it has its usual place of residence in the UK and no 'business establishment' or other 'fixed establishment' elsewhere; where the supplier is a company, the 'usual place of residence' is where it is legally constituted (ie the country where it is incorporated).

As summarised in Table 22.1, if the recipient of the services is a relevant business person then the UK will not be regarded as the place of supply, and instead the services will be supplied where the recipient belongs (unless overriding place of supply rules apply in Sch 4A to VATA 1994).[67]

While VATA 1994 refers to the place of belonging, the VAT Directive refers to the place of establishment. Under the VAT Directive, the place of supply of services to a taxable person is the place where that person has established his business.[68] However, if the services are provided to a fixed establishment of the taxable person that is located in a place other than the place where the business is established, the place of supply is the place where that fixed establishment is located.[69] In the absence of such place of establishment or fixed establishment, the place of supply of services is the place where the taxable person who receives such services has its permanent address or usually resides.[70]

The VAT Directive also provides the general EU rule for the place of supply of services to a non-taxable person. In this regard, the place of supply of services to a non-taxable person is the place where the supplier has established his business.[71] However, if those services are provided from a fixed establishment of a supplier located in a place other than the place where he has established his business, the place of supply of those services is to be treated as the place where that fixed establishment is located.[72] In the absence, of such place of establishment or fixed establishment, the place of supply of services will be the place where the supplier has his permanent address or usually resides.[73]

22.4.3 Relevant business person

UK legislation provides that a person is treated as a 'relevant business person' if that person:[74]

---

[67] VATA 1994, s 7A(5).
[68] VAT Directive, Art 44.
[69] VAT Directive, Art 44.
[70] VAT Directive, Art 44.
[71] VAT Directive, Art 45.
[72] VAT Directive, Art 45.
[73] VAT Directive, Art 45.
[74] VATA 1994, s 7A(4). See also Chapter 17 at **17.11.2** and note 144 therein.

(a) is a taxable person within the meaning of Art 9 of the VAT Directive (as mentioned in Chapter 17 at **17.9.2**, this means, broadly, any person who, independently, carries out in any place any economic activity, whatever the purpose or results of that activity);

(b) is registered under VATA 1994;

(c) is identified as a taxable person under the law of another Member State; or

(d) is registered under an Act of Tynwald[75] for the purposes of any tax imposed under that Act which corresponds to VAT,

and the services are received by the person otherwise than wholly for private purposes.

The evidential circumstances in which a person can be considered to be a taxable person are considered below.

22.4.4 Supplier and relevant business person: identifying the relevant country of belonging

For the purposes of the UK's place of supply rules, under VATA 1994, a supplier or relevant business person is treated as belonging in a 'relevant country', which means the country identified in accordance with the following rules:[76]

(a) if the person has a business establishment, or some other fixed place of establishment, in a country (eg the UK) (and none in any other country), that country (ie the UK);

(b) if the person has a business establishment (eg in the UK), or some other fixed establishment or establishments, in more than one country, the country in which the relevant establishment is located (eg the establishment most directly concerned with the supply);[77] or

(c) if none of the above apply, the country in which the person's usual place of residence is located.[78] For this purpose, the 'usual place of residence' for a body corporate is (as previously mentioned) treated as being the place where it is legally constituted.[79]

---

[75] The laws of the Isle of Man.

[76] VATA 1994, s 9(3).

[77] This means whichever of the person's establishments is most directly concerned with the supply: VATA 1994, s 9(4).

[78] VATA 1994, s 9(3).

[79] VATA 1994, s 9(6).

In some circumstances, supplies are deemed to take place in the UK due to the fact that they represent a supply of services provided to, and consumed by, a relevant business person in the UK but who may not belong in the UK, under the so-called additional 'use and enjoyment' rules referred to in Table 22.1,[80] which indicates that the types of supplies which are within this category include telecommunication services and electronically supplied services. This extra rule is discussed generally at **22.7**.

22.4.5   Not a relevant business person

A taxable person, or a non-taxable legal person deemed to be a taxable person, who receives services exclusively for private use, including use by staff, will always be treated as a non-taxable person.[81] A supplier is entitled to consider that the services are for the customer's business use if, for that transaction, the customer has communicated his individual VAT identification number (this is subject to any information to the contrary).[82] However, where one service is intended for both private use, including use by the customer's staff, and business use, the supply of that service shall be covered exclusively as a supply to a taxable person, provided there is no abusive practice.

22.4.6   Relevant business person: business establishment

Under the EU Implementing Regulation the place where the business of a taxable person is established is the place where the functions of the business's central administration are carried out.[83] To determine this location the following matters must be into account:[84]

- the place where essential decisions concerning the general management of the business are taken;

- the place where the registered office of the business is located; and

- the place where management meets.

Where the above criteria do not allow the place of establishment of a business to be determined with certainty, the place where essential decisions concerning the general management of the business are taken

---

[80]   Eg under VATA 1994, Sch 4A, paras 8(3), (4) and 9(1), (2).
[81]   EU Implementing Regulation, Art 19.
[82]   EU Implementing Regulation, Art 19.
[83]   EU Implementing Regulation, Art 10(1).
[84]   EU Implementing Regulation, Art 10(2).

will take precedence.[85] However, the mere presence of a postal address may not be taken to be the place of establishment of a business of a taxable person.[86]

22.4.7 Relevant business person: fixed establishment

The EU Implementing Regulation[87] provides that in the context of the place of supply rules for services to a taxable person, a 'fixed establishment' means any establishment, other than the place of establishment of a business (referred to above), characterised by a sufficient degree of permanence and a suitable structure in terms of human and technical resources to enable it to receive and use the services supplied to it for its own needs. Based on EU case-law, a fixed establishment can also include a branch or agency, provided it satisfies the rules to be regarded as such an establishment.[88]

22.4.8 Non-business person

Under VATA 1994, a person who is not a relevant business person (eg an individual consumer) is treated as belonging in the country in which that person's usual place of residence is located.[89] Meanwhile, it was noted earlier that the 'usual place of residence' for a body corporate is treated as being the place where it is legally constituted[90] (ie incorporated). In the case of an individual receiving supplies in a private capacity, according to HMRC, the individual's 'usual place of residence' will typically be where

---

[85] EU Implementing Regulation, Art 10(2).

[86] EU Implementing Regulation, Art 10(3).

[87] EU Implementing Regulation, Art 11. See also the ECJ's decision in *Gunter Berkholz v Finanzamt Hamburg* (Case C-168/84) [1985] ECR 2251, discussed further below. Useful guidance in relation to UK VAT principles on fixed establishments is further provided by HMRC in its staff manual, 'Place of Supply of Services', at www.hmrc.gov.uk/manuals/vatpossmanual/index.htm.

[88] Eg, the ECJ case of *DFDS A/S* (C-260/95). As set out in note 157 in Chapter 17 at **17.11.4**, HMRC states in its Place of Supply of Services Manual in reference in the DFDS A/S case, (at page VATPOSS04700, located at www.hmrc.gov.uk); 'the key test for agency, so far as the place of belonging rules are concerned, is one of independence. An agency cannot operate independently of its principal. In deciding independence, what matters is the reality, function and substance, and not any mere label or legal form. One should therefore have particular regard for the actual arrangements which exist between the prima facie agency and its principal, rather than any mere wording in contracts. Where there is no independence, agencies may include: a subsidiary acting for its parent principal; a company acting for its associated principal; and a company acting for an unrelated principal. A non-UK company can operate through a branch or agency as either a supplier or a recipient of services. Any charge for its services made by a branch or agency in the UK to its non-UK parent or principal is itself regarded as supplied in the UK, since such services are used most directly at the UK establishment created by the agency itself'. For further details on the DFDS A/S case, see note 109 below.

[89] VATA 1994, s 9(5). See HMRC's Notice 741A, para 3.5 and HMRC's examples at para 3.5.1.

[90] VATA 1994, s 9(6). See **22.4.4**.

the individual is resident for tax purposes, namely where that person has their family home and is in full-time employment.

However, it is again necessary to construe VATA 1994 in accordance with the EU Implementing Regulation, which provides that the place where a natural person 'usually resides', whether or not a taxable person, is the place where that natural person usually lives as a result of personal and occupational ties.[91] Where the occupational ties are in a country different from that of the personal ties, or where no occupational ties exist, the place of usual residence is determined by personal ties which show close links between the natural person and a place where he is living.[92]

22.4.9 Determining the status of the customer: whether a taxable person

Under the EU Implementing Regulation, a supplier may regard a customer established within the EU as a taxable person (subject to any information to the contrary):[93]

(a) where the customer has communicated his individual VAT identification number to him, and the supplier obtains confirmation of the validity of that identification number and of the associated name and address; or

(b) where the customer has not yet received an individual VAT identification number, but informs the supplier that he has applied for it and the supplier obtains any other proof which demonstrates that the customer is a taxable person or a non-taxable legal person required to be identified for VAT purposes and carries out a reasonable level of verification of the accuracy of the information provided by the customer, by normal commercial security measures such as those relating to identity or payment checks.

Under the EU Implementing Regulation, a supplier may regard a customer established within the EU as a non-taxable person (subject to any information to the contrary) when he can demonstrate that the customer has not communicated his individual VAT identification number to him.[94]

A supplier may regard a customer established outside the EU as a taxable person (again, subject to any information to the contrary):[95]

---

[91] EU Implementing Regulation, Art 13.
[92] EU Implementing Regulation, Art 13.
[93] EU Implementing Regulation, Art 18(1).
[94] EU Implementing Regulation, Art 18(2).
[95] EU Implementing Regulation, Art 18(3).

(a)   if he obtains from the customer a certificate issued by the customer's competent tax authorities as confirmation that the customer is engaged in economic activities in order to enable him to obtain a refund of VAT under Council Directive 86/560/EEC (Arrangements for the refund of value added tax to taxable persons not established in Community territory); or

(b)   where the customer does not possess that certificate, if the supplier has the VAT number, or a similar number attributed to the customer by the country of establishment and used to identify businesses or any other proof which demonstrates that the customer is a taxable person and if the supplier carries out a reasonable level of verification of the accuracy of the information provided by the customer, by normal commercial security measures such as those relating to identity or payment checks.

22.4.10   Taxable person located in multiple countries with a fixed establishment: determining location of the supply

The following EU VAT principles apply to determine in which country a supply is taxable where a taxable person is established in more than one country:[96]

- the supply is taxable in the country where that taxable person has established his business (ie the head office is the preferred establishment, unless that leads to an inappropriate or irrational result for tax purposes – see later below at **22.5.2**).

- where the service is provided to a fixed establishment of the taxable person located in a place other than that where the customer has established his business, that supply is taxable at the place of the fixed establishment receiving that service and using it for its own needs; and

- where the taxable person does not have a business establishment or a fixed establishment, the supply is taxable at his permanent address or usual residence.

The following EU VAT principles are applied to determine the identity of the fixed establishment to which a service is supplied:[97]

---

[96]   EU Implementing Regulation, Art 21.

[97]   EU Implementing Regulation, Art 22. For UK VAT principles/purposes, again see further at HMRC's Place of supply of services manual, in particular at www.hmrc.gov.uk/manuals/vatpossmanual/VATPOSS05000.htm, 'Place of supply of services: Establishment making or receiving the supply'. See also HMRC Notice 741A (January 2010), in particular at paras 3.6 and 3.7 and Section 19, considered earlier at Table 22.1, (and at **22.5.3**).

- the supplier is required to examine the nature and use of the service provided to the taxable person;

- where the nature and use of the service provided do not enable the supplier to identify the fixed establishment to which the service is provided, the supplier, in identifying that fixed establishment, is required to pay particular attention to whether:

  - the contract;
  - the order form; and
  - the VAT identification number attributed by the Member State of the customer and communicated to the supplier by the customer,

  identify the fixed establishment as the customer of the service, and whether the fixed establishment is the entity paying for the service (see further at **22.5.2**).

Where the customer's fixed establishment to which the service is provided cannot be determined in accordance with the above principles or where services are supplied to a taxable person under a contract covering one or more services used in an unidentifiable and non-quantifiable manner, for example, under a global contract whereby a business could enter into a contract for a single supply of consultancy services to analyse the global set-up and e-commerce practices at the head office and overseas branches, the supplier is entitled to consider that the services have been supplied at the place where the customer has established its business.[98] HMRC should regard services under a global contract with a clear, direct benefit to the business as a whole, including a number of establishments, as supplied to the main business establishment. However, this approach should be distinguished from a global framework agreement which sets the terms for a number of individual supplies. In the UK, HMRC considers that it is important to look at those individual transactions which, as separate supplies, will have separate VAT consequences. In this respect, HMRC's example is that of a head office customer which enters into a framework agreement with a supplier pursuant to which its individual branches would draw up and purchase work from local branches of the supplier. According to HMRC, the supplier's services will be viewed as supplied to the customer's branches even if the head office dictates the terms and receives an indirect benefit. HMRC's general approach in relation to multiple fixed establishments is considered in further detail below, at **22.5.3**.

There are also further EU VAT rules on who accounts for VAT where a taxable person has a fixed establishment. These are that where a taxable person (the supplier) has a fixed establishment in the territory of a Member State where VAT is due, then the supplier is treated as a taxable person who is not established within that Member State when it makes a

---

[98]   EU Implementing Regulation, Art 22.

taxable supply in that Member State and any such fixed establishment of the supplier 'does not intervene in that supply'.[99] In other words, VAT is not due from a supplier's fixed establishment located within the same Member State as their customer, unless that establishment intervenes in the supply. However, where a taxable person has established its place of business within the territory of the Member State where the VAT is due, the above does not apply irrespective of whether or not that place of business intervenes in the supply of goods or services which are made in that Member State.[100]

22.5 ESTABLISHMENTS

22.5.1 Business establishment

According to HMRC, the business establishment for a person is the principal place of business for that person, and is regarded as being the head office, headquarters or 'seat' from which the business is operated.[101] There can only be once such place, such as an office, showroom or factory.[102] A more detailed overview on the meaning and related VAT legislation in respect of the terms 'business establishment' and 'fixed establishment' is provided in Chapter 17 at **17.11.3** and **17.11.4**. However, the next section provides further discussion on the meaning of a 'fixed establishment' in the context of a server through which electronically supplied services may be remotely provided, and from multiple establishments.

---

[99] VAT Directive, Art 192a. In the application of this Article, a fixed establishment of a taxable person will only be taken into consideration when it is characterised by a sufficient degree of permanence and a suitable structure in terms of human and technical resources to enable it to make the supply of goods or services in which it intervenes: EU Implementing Regulation, Art 53(1). Where a taxable person has a fixed establishment within the territory of the EU where the VAT is due, that establishment shall be considered as not intervening in the supply of goods or services, unless the technical and human resources of that fixed establishment are used by that person for transactions inherent in the fulfilment of the taxable supply of those goods or services made within that Member State, before or during this fulfilment: Art 53(2). Where the resources of the fixed establishment are only used for administrative support tasks such as accounting, invoicing and collection of debt-claims, they are not regarded as being used for the fulfilment of the supply of goods or services: Art 53(2). However, if an invoice is issued under the VAT identification number attributed by the Member State of the fixed establishment, that fixed establishment shall be regarded as having intervened in the supply of goods or services made in that Member State unless there is proof to the contrary: Art 53(2). In the UK, HMRC states that the UK position is that the establishment making the supply is the one most closely connected to it. Therefore, minimal involvement in making the supply will not be viewed as 'intervening' for UK VAT purposes. HMRC believes that the overall UK legislation, (which does not explicitly cover 'intervening'), together with interpretation, achieves the right result.

[100] EU Implementing Regulation, Art 54.

[101] HMRC Notice 741A *Place of Supply of Services* (January 2010), para 3.3. See HMRC examples at para 3.3.1.

[102] HMRC Notice 741A, para 3.3.

22.5.2 Fixed establishment

Overview

As discussed above, a fixed establishment is relevant where a supply is made. It is clear from the VAT legislation that a fixed establishment is capable of bearing a different meaning from a business establishment. The concept of fixed establishment is interpreted by HMRC as:[103]

> ' an ʀstablishment other than the business establishment, which the technical and human resources necessary for providing or receiving services permanently present. A business may have several fixed establishments, which may include a branch of a business or an agency.
>
> If you have a temporary presence of human and technical resources, this does not create a fixed establishment in the UK. For example, an overseas television company sending staff and equipment to the UK to film for a week does not constitute a fixed establishment in the UK.'

The concept of a business establishment (referred to under VATA 1994) and the place where the supplier has established a business (referred to under the VAT Directive) effectively means the registered place of business of the enterprise supplying the services (this is the interpretation placed on the phrase in the Sixth VAT Directive (now the VAT Directive) by the Advocate General in *Berkholz*) (see below).[104]

> *Example 22.1*
>
> Gaming Ltd, a company incorporated in the Cayman Islands, sets up a branch in the UK which has staff and offices in the UK. The UK office provides services. In these circumstances the Cayman Islands represents the business establishment and the UK branch is a fixed establishment.

Can computer equipment constitute a fixed establishment?

As noted in Chapter 17, at **17.11.4**, the important question for the purposes of place of supply of services is whether an automated computer server can amount to a fixed establishment. In the UK, HMRC's manuals have expressly stated in the past that 'the mere presence of a server does not constitute either a business/fixed establishment or a usual place of residence'. It may, however, be the case that personnel need to be employed to carry out occasional, non-remote maintenance of the server, for example, in relation to a data centre or hosting facility. In this context, the concept of fixed establishment has received consideration at the highest levels within the EU. In the case of *Gunter Berkholz v*

---

[103] HMRC Notice 741A, para 3.4. See HMRC examples at para 3.4.1.
[104] *Gunter Berkholz v Finanzamt Hamburg* (Case C-168/84) [1985] ECR 2251.

Finanzamt Hamburg,[105] gaming machines were installed on ferries operating between Denmark and Germany. The tax authority in Germany sought to apply VAT on the gaming machines. The owner operator of the gaming machines employed individuals to maintain, repair and replace the machines and collect money from them at regular intervals, which was done on board the vessels, but the operator did not maintain a permanent staff on board the vessels. In 1980 the operation of these machines earned the owner 346,702.20 DEM. Turnover tax was assessed on the whole amount. Two questions arose. First, whether the gaming machines were fixed establishments for the purposes of determining the place of supply of services and, second, how to determine the place of supply where the principal place of business of the supplier and any fixed establishment do not coincide.

As to the first question, the Advocate General in his Opinion said that the term 'fixed':

'... is synonymous with "permanent" and is the opposite of "uncertain" or "occasional". But this is not sufficient. A business, particularly if it supplies services extending over a period of time, requires a minimum kind of organisation. However, there is no organisation, ie an orderly system of human and material resources, which does not involve division of labour. Therefore the person supplying the services must have material resources or employees to help him in operating and administering the services.'

He went on to say:

'With this, the court making the references has the interpretation which it was seeking: the fixed establishment within the meaning of Article 9(1) can perfectly well be an installation (such as a gaming machine), but subject to the proviso that it is installed permanently in a certain place and requires the use of human resources for its management.'

As to the second question, the Advocate General said that in the absence of specific rules in the legislation he would propose adopting the general principle whereby VAT is levied at the place of consumption. In this case, it would be the place of the fixed establishment, ie the gaming machines.

When the case went before the panel of the ECJ it was recognised that (the former) Art 9 of the Sixth VAT Directive (now Arts 44 and 45 of the VAT Directive) refers to a number of different concepts that can be used to pinpoint the place of supply of services. The ECJ said that the main reference for determining the place of supply is the supplier's place of business. However, the existence of another establishment that is connected with a particular service is only relevant where that establishment has a sufficient minimum strength in the form of 'the

---

[105] [1985] 2 CMLR 667, ECJ. Please also refer to note 167 in Chapter 17 in relation to HMRC's review and comments on this case and on the DFDS A/S case referred to later in this section (see note 109).

permanent presence of both the human and technical resources necessary'
for supplying specific services.[106] Applying this principle to the
installation of gaming machines on a ferry, the ECJ said.

> 'It does not appear that the installation on board a sea-going ship of gaming
> machines, which are maintained intermittently, is capable of constituting
> such an establishment, especially if tax may appropriately be charged at the
> place where the operator of the machines has his permanent business
> establishment.'

The ECJ said that in reading Art 9 the preferred point for determining the
place of supply of services was the supplier's place of business, except
where this point would 'not lead to a rational result for tax purposes or
results in a conflict with another Member State'. The ECJ also used the
phrase that a qualifying fixed establishment may be used as the point for
determining the place of supply where it would not be 'appropriate to
deem those services to have been provided at the place where the supplier
has established his business'.

In the decision *Customs and Excise Commissioners v DFDS A/S* the
Advocate General (A La Pergola) summarised the approach, as stated in
Berkholz, between the place of business and a fixed establishment in the
following way:[107]

> 'With regard to the connection between the two points of reference, the
> court went on to make it clear that an order of precedence must be
> observed. Specifically, it is only if "the reference to a place where the
> supplier has established his business does not lead to a rational result for tax
> purposes or creates a conflict with another Member State" that account
> must be taken of another establishment from which the services are supplied
> (see *Berkholz* (at 2263, para 17)). In short, the place where the supplier has
> established his business must be seen as the "primary point of reference" (see
> *Berkholz* (at 2263, para 17)).'

How are we to decide which place of supply is to be preferred?

(1)   In the decision of *Customs and Excise Commissioners v DFDS A/S*
      the Advocate General said that the place of taxation must coincide
      with that at which the service is supplied to the consumer. He said,

---

[106]   *Faaborg-Gelting Linien A/S v Finanzamt Flensburg* [1996] STC 774 the ECJ, referring to
        Berkholz, explained, in the context of the choice between the different concepts of place
        of business and fixed establishment other than the place where the supplier has
        established his business, that services cannot be deemed to be supplied at an
        establishment other than the place where the supplier has established his business unless
        that establishment is of a certain minimum size and both the human and technical
        resources necessary for the provision of particular services are permanently present
        (para 17).

[107]   *Customs and Excise Commissioners v DFDS A/S* [1997] STC 384 (Case C-260/95); see
        also the ECJ judgment at paras 19 and 20.

'the VAT system must be applied in a manner as far as possible in harmony with the actual economic situation'.[108]

(2)   The place of supply as between the business establishment or a fixed establishment should be that which leads to a rational result for the purposes of taxation. In *Customs and Excise Commissioners v DFDS A/S*[109] the ECJ accepted the UK's view that for a rational result to be achieved it is necessary to take account of the actual place where the service is supplied. In that case, it was where travel tours were marketed (para 22 of the ECJ decision). Where a business establishment and fixed establishment exist it is likely that the latter will be chosen as the place of supply because, as the ECJ observed in *Customs and Excise Commissioners v DFDS A/S*:[110]

> 'Systematic reliance on the place where the supplier has established his business could in fact lead to distortions of competition, in that it might encourage undertakings trading in one member state to establish their business, in order to avoid taxation, in another member state which has availed itself of the possibility of maintaining the VAT exemption for the services in question.'

This statement was made against the context of VAT and travel services. However, the same is true in respect of internet business. A strict adherence to the place of business (or business establishment) might encourage services to be located outside Europe creating fixed establishments which facilitate trade within Europe.[111]

---

[108]   Ibid, para 32.

[109]   In HMRC's VAT staff manual, 'Place of Supply of Services', Belonging: Business carried on through an agency, located at http://www.hmrc.gov.uk/manuals/vatpossmanual/vatposs04700.htm, HMRC summarises the DFDS A/S case as follows: 'the Court [ECJ] considered whether DFDS A/S, a Danish tour operator, had a fixed establishment in the UK through the agency of its wholly owned subsidiary, DFDS Ltd. DFDS A/S had no premises or staff of its own in the UK. The resources needed to make the supplies of services belonged to the UK company. In deciding this case, the Court asked whether the UK agency was independent of the Danish company. The Court was influenced by both ownership and contractual obligations. The UK company was found to be wholly owned by the Danish company and had various contractual obligations imposed upon it by the Danish parent. In particular, it had to seek prior approval from the parent regarding its management, for example appointment of senior staff, conclusion of major contracts, appointment of advertising and public relations agents, any work it wished to perform for other transport companies, and no discretion in setting prices. This showed that it acted as a mere auxiliary organ of its parent and it was therefore a fixed establishment of the Danish company.'

[110]   *Customs and Excise Commissioners v DFDS A/S* [1997] STC 384, para 23.

[111]   Pending the place of supply B2C changes coming into effect in 2015 for telecoms, broadcasting and electronically supplied services, it is worth noting that HMRC has stated as follows: '… in the meantime some suppliers may attempt to put in place structures that purport to move the place of supply to a Member State with a more favourable VAT rate. In May 2009 HMRC published a Revenue and Customs Brief (58/09) about this. It is reproduced below. Readers are warned that 'we will carefully scrutinise any structure or scheme under which services supplied to UK customers, using UK resources, are claimed to be made from a Member State with a lower rate of VAT

From the case-law a number of influences can be drawn as to the impact of VAT on internet business transactions:

(1)   installed hardware such as a computer server can theoretically constitute a fixed establishment;

(2)   computer hardware will only constitute a fixed establishment where the necessary human and technical resources for supplying the services accompany the establishment; and

(3)   computer hardware which constitutes a fixed establishment will only be used for determining the place of supply of services where it is more appropriate than choosing the supplier's place of business.

22.5.3   Multiple establishments

It is possible for a supplier to have more than one establishment and this may cause potential difficulties in identifying the place of supply of services. Although the VAT legislation contains no rules on multiple establishments, HMRC adopts the following approach:[112]

...'

'**Revenue & Customs Brief 58/09 – VAT: Relocation of telecommunication service providers, Internet service providers and broadcasters.**
This Revenue & Customs Brief is of interest to all businesses within the telecommunications, Internet service provision and broadcasting sectors who claim to have moved or may consider moving the place of supply of their services from the UK to another Member State. The purpose of this Brief is to explain HM Revenue & Customs (HMRC) concerns and intended response and to encourage you to discuss these arrangements with your Customer Relationship Manager or the alternative contact given below. HMRC are aware that some businesses within the telecommunications, Internet service provision and broadcasting sectors have implemented arrangements that claim to move the place of supply of their services from the UK to another Member State in order to take advantage of more favourable VAT rates. The place of supply of telecommunications, Internet service provision and broadcasting services when provided to non-business customers in the EU is the place where the supplier is established [position changing in 2015]. Some suppliers to the UK market claim to have reorganised their businesses so that the place of supply is no longer in the UK but another Member State. HMRC accepts that businesses have the freedom to choose where to locate and to enjoy any resultant benefits. However, HMRC will carefully examine all such arrangements. Where HMRC considers that there are sufficient human and technical resources in the UK to form a fixed establishment from which the services are supplied, or where the entity purporting to make the supplies does not have a sufficient presence in the other Member State to be established there, HMRC will mount a robust challenge.'

[112]   HMRC Notice 741A *Place of Supply of Services* (January 2010), paras 3.6 and 3.7, and also see HMRC's examples of where a supplier and a recipient has more than one establishment, at para 3.6.1. Similarly, according to HMRC's staff guidance mentioned at note 109 above (at page VATPOSS05400, located at www.hmrc.gov.uk) on the 'directly concerned' test, there is no clear and exhaustive test but the following factors would be relevant in determining if services are most directly concerned with a UK fixed establishment compared with, and as an alternative to, the business establishment/head

'If, as either supplier or the recipient of services, you have establishments in more than one country, the supplies you make from, or receive at, each establishment have to be looked at separately. For each supply of services, you are regarded as belonging in the country where the establishment most directly connected with that supply is located.

To decide which establishment is most directly connected with the supply, you should consider all the facts, including:

- for suppliers, from which establishment the services are actually provided
- for recipients, at which establishment the services are actually consumed, effectively used or enjoyed
- which establishments appear on the contracts, correspondence and invoices
- where the directors of others who entered into the contracts are permanently based, and
- at which establishment decisions are taken and controls are exercised over the performance of the contracts.

Normally it is the establishment actually providing or receiving the supply of services which is the establishment most directly connected with the supply, even if the contractual position is different.'

As mentioned above, in *Berkholz* the ECJ indicated that a fixed establishment should be used for the purposes of determining the place of supply where it is practical (and not irrational) to do so: for example, where there would otherwise be a conflict of rules between Member States.

Example 22.2

An overseas company, incorporated in the Cayman Islands, contracts with non-business customers in the UK to provide information. The services are

office:
- how are the particular services provided?
- what is the significance of the activities carried out at each establishment in contributing to the services provided?
- where are the necessary human and technical resources (for example database, technical equipment, office equipment, telephones, and so on) for actually providing the services permanently based?
- which establishment appears on the relevant contracts, correspondence and invoices?
- where are the directors or other personnel who entered into the contract permanently based?
- where are decisions taken and controls exercised over the performance of the contracts?
- does reference to the preferred establishment lead to a more appropriate or rational result for tax purposes? Examples of evidence to support any decision on the establishment which is most 'directly concerned' with a supply are provided by HMRC at page VATPOSS05500, including telephone bills, fax printouts etc ... demonstrating the extent of day-to-day contact with a particular establishment, invoices, office rental payments, company minutes and reports, and witness statements of staff of businesses involved in the supply chain and staff performance agreements, which may be indicative of the substance and reality of work performed at a particular establishment.

provided and invoiced by its UK branch. Customers' day-to-day contact is with the UK branch and they pay the UK branch. The services are supplied from the UK branch, which is a fixed establishment

A UK incorporated company contracts to supply advertising services to a business recipient. The customer has a business establishment in Portugal and a fixed establishment in the UK (represented by a branch). Day-to-day contact on routine matters is between the supplier and UK branch. However, the Portuguese establishment takes all artistic and other decisions relating to the advertising. The supplies are received in Portugal.

22.6   REVERSE CHARGE

The reverse charge operates in respect of several kinds of services,[113] including electronically supplied services. Where services are received by a relevant business person from a supplier who belongs outside the UK, the identity of the person who is required to account for VAT is altered.[114] Normally, it is the supplier who is required to account for any VAT due on the supply, but this is reversed by virtue of the reverse charge procedure, and, accordingly, it will be the business recipient who must account for the VAT due. This procedure is also known as the tax shift. A UK business recipient will usually incur the costs of a supply of services from abroad for its own business purposes, so that it can make onward supplies to its customers. VAT will be imposed on these supplies to the end consumer, if they are taxable supplies. The reverse charge is therefore a simplification measure designed to avoid overseas suppliers needing to register for VAT purposes in a Member State when it is possible for the customer (eg a VAT-registered customer) to account for the VAT on a supply. The procedure does not apply to supplies of services where both the supplier and the recipient belong in the UK. In addition, the procedure currently only applies insofar as a customer receives the supply for a business purpose (and evidence such as the customer's VAT registration number would need to be obtained by the supplier too, although it extends to organisations involved in both business and non-business activities, even if a service is received in connection with the non-business activity.[115]

Under the reverse charge rules a relevant business person is required to account for VAT on such service supplies as if there were a supply of the services by the recipient in the UK in the course or furtherance of a

---

[113]   See Chapter 17 at **17.12**.

[114]   VATA 1994, s 8.

[115]   Supplies need to be received wholly for private purposes to be treated as a business-to-non business supply: VATA 1994, s 7A(4). HMRC's examples are as follows (Notice 741A, para 18.10.1): 'A UK charity with business and non-business activities receives a supply of legal services from a French business in relation to its non-business activities (B2B general rule service). The place of supply is the UK and the UK charity must account for VAT under the reverse charge', and 'a UK business receives customised software from a USA business (B2B general rule service). The place of supply is the UK and the UK business must account for VAT under the reverse charge'.

business carried on by the recipient, and that supply were a taxable supply (a deemed supply).[116] This is designed to prevent distortion of trade, otherwise businesses could acquire tax-free benefits by obtaining services from abroad. Accordingly, instead of being charged VAT by the supplier, the UK business recipient would credit (increase) its VAT account with the necessary output tax as if the recipient had supplied the services in the UK for the purposes of VAT (the deemed supply), and at the same time in the same VAT return, debit (deduct) its VAT account with the input tax to which it is entitled under the normal rules if it can relate this input VAT to taxable supplies. The practical result of this is that the recipient continues to be entitled to claim credit for input tax (although the input tax cannot be attributed to the aforementioned deemed supply made by it (which would give full input tax credit), but only to the actual use to which the service was put by the recipient.[117] If the recipient can attribute the input tax to taxable supplies that they make, the recipient can reclaim it via its VAT returns so that the reverse charge transaction has no net cost to it. If it cannot, the effect is to make the recipient pay VAT on the supply at the applicable UK VAT rate, ie as if it had received the supply from a UK supplier instead of the non-UK supplier. This will affect businesses that are not entitled to recover VAT fully, such as partly exempt businesses, where VAT costs are only recoverable to the extent of their partial exemption recovery method.[118]

The reverse charge applies if:[119]

(a) the recipient is a relevant business person who belongs in the UK, and the place of supply of the services is inside the UK, ie under the general B2B rule (see Tables 17.2 and 22.1); or

(b) the supply of the services is one to which any paragraph of Part 1 or 2 of Sch 4A to VATA 1994 applies (see generally Chapter 17), the place of supply of those services is the UK, and the recipient is registered as a taxable person under VATA 1994.

The value of services received in the UK from abroad is deemed to be exclusive of VAT, so the value of the transaction on which VAT must be calculated and accounted for under the reverse charge is the full value of the supply.

The reverse charge does not apply to services of a description in Sch 9 to VATA 1994 (Exemptions): see Chapter 17, at **17.17**.

---

[116] VATA 1994, s 8(1).

[117] VATA 1994, s 8(1)(b), (3).

[118] See generally HMRC's Notice 706 *Partial Exemption* (June 2011) and Chapter 17, at **17.15**. A review of the partial exemption rules is outside the scope of this book.

[119] VATA 1994, s 8(2).

Overseas suppliers, whose customers account for VAT under the reverse charge procedure may be able to reclaim VAT incurred in the UK where certain conditions are met.[120]

22.7 USE AND ENJOYMENT: ELECTRONICALLY SUPPLIED SERVICES

Table 17.2 in Chapter 17 and Table 22.1 at **22.3.2**, refer to the 'use and enjoyment' principle.

Broadly, this extra rule allows Member States to deal with place of supply situations for certain services where the EU VAT position would otherwise be distortive as a result of considering only where the supplier and the customer belong. For example, it would be distortive for supplies such as telecommunications services that are actually consumed outside the EU to be subject to UK VAT. Equally, it would be distortive for there to be no EU VAT on such services where they are consumed in the UK.

This rule applies in the UK to telecommunications services, radio and broadcasting services, electronically supplied services (the latter for business customers only), hired goods and hired means of transport. This rule may be applied on a more extensive basis in different Member States, since the VAT Directive[121] provides that Member States may, if they choose, apply the use and enjoyment provisions to general rule services as well as to, for example, intangible services supplied from the EU to non-taxable persons outside the EU (but excluding, until 2015, electronically supplied services provided from the EU to such non-taxable persons[122]). This could lead to inconsistency between Member States in respect of the application of this rule, in terms of scope and interpretation.

To recall from Table 22.1, the 'use and enjoyment' provisions are applied for UK VAT purposes as follows:

(1) where the services would otherwise be treated as supplied in the UK (because the supplier or customer belongs there), they will not be treated as supplied in the UK (and UK VAT will not therefore be charged) to the extent that the effective use and enjoyment of the services takes place outside the EU; and

---

[120] See generally HMRC Notice 723A *Refunds of VAT in the European Community for EC and non-EC businesses* (October 2011) and see HMRC Notice 741A, paras 18.9, 20.20 and 20.34.

[121] Art 59a.

[122] From 2015, Member States may choose to apply the use and enjoyment rule to electronically supplied services rendered to non-taxable persons – VAT Directive, Article 59a, as amended from 2015 pursuant to the provisions of Council Directive 2008/8/EC.

(2)   where the services would otherwise be treated as supplied in a place outside the EU (because the supplier or customer belongs outside the EU), they shall be treated as supplied in the UK (and UK VAT will therefore be charged) to the extent that the effective use and enjoyment of the services takes place in the UK,

and, in respect of electronically supplied services, the above rules only apply where the services are received by a person for the purposes of a business carried on by him.

As further summarised in Table 22.1 (at **22.3.2**), for electronically supplied services, part of the rationale for why the use and enjoyment provisions do not apply in any situation where the customer is a non-business customer is because most non-business/private customers are considered to use and enjoy the services in the same country in which they belong, though it has also been noted that it would be very difficult to apply this principle to private consumers receiving such services (due to the mobility of the act of downloading from the internet, for instance).

It is also clarified in HMRC's guidance, for UK VAT purposes, that the place of effective use and enjoyment is only a consideration when certain services made by a UK provider are consumed outside the EU or those services when supplied by a non-EU provider are consumed in the UK. When services are provided by an EU supplier and consumed in the UK, or provided by a UK supplier and consumed in another EU country, this extra rule will not apply.

The term 'effective use and enjoyment' is not expressly defined in VAT legislation. However, as set out in Table 22.1, HMRC states that the 'use and enjoyment' takes place where a service is consumed (irrespective of contract, payment or beneficial interest). This should normally be at the final stage of supply (in particular, services supplied electronically). However, the question of measuring or quantifying use and enjoyment can be difficult, particularly where only part of a supply is consumed in the UK, and even more so in relation to branches/offices of an international entity. There are no prescribed methods of apportionment when supplies are used and enjoyed outside the EU as well as in the UK – the level of use and enjoyment will depend upon the exact circumstances surrounding the particular supplies. It is therefore important to identify where the customer is physically using the service and where the benefit is felt.

HMRC has, however, said it will adopt a pragmatic and systematic approach in order to reach a mutually agreeable solution with the supplier and avoid disputes. Invariably, the approach adopted will have as its basis factual data available, such as measured usage, internal company management records showing inter-company recharges, percentage business transactions at the specific location, proportion of relevant equipment and number of sites (assuming equal use at such sites, which may be reasonable in the absence of information to the contrary). Traders should be invited to suggest a workable method of quantifying use on a reasonable assessment basis, and should retain any records or documentation that demonstrates any division or apportionment in the provision of such services.

HMRC's example in this respect looks at the position relating to UK branches. A UK VAT-registered branch of an international company that is using electronically supplied services which were previously supplied to its US headquarters by a US provider may be required to account for UK VAT, to the extent that the services are used and enjoyed in the UK, by applying the reverse charge at the time the US provider is paid. HMRC recognises that branches may not always know at the relevant point in time the exact amount which relates to its use and enjoyment in the UK (or may even be unaware that a payment has been made). In these circumstances, HMRC will accept agreed provisional figures to be corrected at such time as actual figures become available.[123]

22.8   TIME OF SUPPLY

When a taxable supply is made the obligation to charge VAT arises.[124] The time of supply is governed by specific rules in VATA 1994. See the summary of the principal rules provided in Table 17.3 in Chapter 17.

---

[123]   HMRC VAT Information Sheet 01/03.
[124]   VATA 1994, s 4(1).

PART VI

CASE STUDY

VI Case Study

CHAPTER 23

CASE STUDY: JUST-EAT INTERNET BUSINESS

23.1 JUST-EAT

JUST EAT

www.just-eat.com

Case Study

VI

What is Just-Eat?

Just-Eat enables customers to order food which is delivered straight to the doorstep, from either a PC or a variety of smartphone devices. The choice of restaurants on Just-Eat ranges all the way from high-end luxury food to the local pizza-house, offering something for any taste or time schedule.

The future is online? We're already there

The internet is a regular part of everyday life and soon using the phone to call your local take-away restaurant will be a thing of the past. Here's why millions of people are making the switch to online ordering:

Choice

Users are not limited to one single offering; they can pick their favourite restaurant and cuisine type among thousands of outlets.

Convenience

All menus are online and are constantly updated with the latest offers. Furthermore the Just-Eat menu template allows users to compare prices and find the best solution to their culinary needs.

Service

The combination of 2-way 'Just-Connect technology' (JCT) with industry-leading customer service (online via order support and chat, offline via the phone) ensures that orders are processed efficiently and customers are always up-to-date about their order status. Customer care offers reliability and a constant point of contact between restaurants and consumers.

Speed, comfort and reliability

Avoid phone queues and annoying misunderstandings by ordering online. Orders are printed within 3 seconds from pressing the 'order button' at the restaurant's end, avoiding confusion on both sides. Furthermore, JCT allows users to see if the order has been accepted by the restaurant and the expected delivery time.

I own a delivery restaurant. Why should I join Just-Eat?

Using Just-Eat as their online ordering partner enables restaurants to focus on what they do best: cooking great food.

Increase your orders

Just-Eat restaurant partners see their revenue increase between 15 and 25% a year, on average.

Just-Eat marketing

Just-Eat spends significant sums on marketing to make sure that when consumers want take-away, they know to log on to Just-Eat. Just-Eat advertise online, on mobile, in trade and on TV to make sure local consumers know that they can find restaurants online.

Your business, online

In choosing Just-Eat as their online ordering partner, restaurants avoid the massive set-up costs and hassle of building a transactional website.

JCT box: industry-leading technology

JCT allows instant 2-way communication with the customer. Restaurants receive and confirm orders while keeping the phone line completely free. The box does not even need an internet connection or a dedicated phone line! It works wirelessly and only needs electricity.

Customer care

As a Just-Eat partner restaurant, a business will be managed by one of a dedicated team of account managers who will help the restaurant make the most of Just-Eat. A customer care centre is also ready to answer all questions and conducts thorough checks to avoid fraudulent orders being placed.

How does the Just-Eat business operate?

When a customer visits the Just-Eat (JE) website, they enter their postcode, and all of the available Delivery Restaurants (DRs) on the JE estate that deliver to that customer's postcode are listed. The DRs can be sorted by cuisine type, restaurant name, ratings (as given by customers based on earlier orders) or the date they joined JE.

When the list of DRs first appears, up to four of the DRs listed at the top are sponsored and clearly labelled as separate to the core search results – ie the DRs pay a premium to be at the top of the list. This is called TopPlacement.

After choosing a restaurant, the customer selects items from the menu and orders online. Returning customers can log in and re-order their saved favourite meals in one click, or select from their saved favourite restaurants.

The customer can pay in cash to the delivery driver or by credit card through the JE website. The cost of the food should never be more expensive than if a customer had rung the DR directly. This is embedded in the Terms & Conditions (T&Cs) of JE's contracts with the DRs. A copy of the T&Cs is included at the end of this case study.

When the order is made, the restaurant is notified through JE's bespoke JCT terminal. When a DR joins the JE Network it pays JE for the provision of a JCT box and then pays to connect and install the box. A JCT box looks like this:

It is a chip & pin-sized terminal that allows the DRs to accept orders and confirm delivery times so website users have immediate confirmation of their orders in real time. It prints the order for the DR so that the food can be prepared and eliminates the need for laptops/fax machines in the restaurant. It does not need an internet, wireless or fixed telephone connection; it only needs to be plugged in and within GPRS network range. The order is printed on standard till roll.

Below is a summary of the transaction flow between a customer, a DR and JE. The T&Cs cement JE's position as an agent in the transactions, rather than a principal. This is also important for tax purposes. JE does not issue VAT receipts to the customers as it is an agent and its relationship is with the DR. When JE invoices the DRs it includes VAT on the services supplied. If a customer requests a VAT receipt, JE directs them to the DR.

Below is a summary of the flow of funds between the parties. For simplicity, we will assume two £10 orders are made (one paid by cash and the other by credit card), and the commission rate is 10%. The commission is charged by JE to the DRs for all orders generated through the JE website (whether settled by cash or Credit Card (CC)). It is based on the gross order value (GOV)

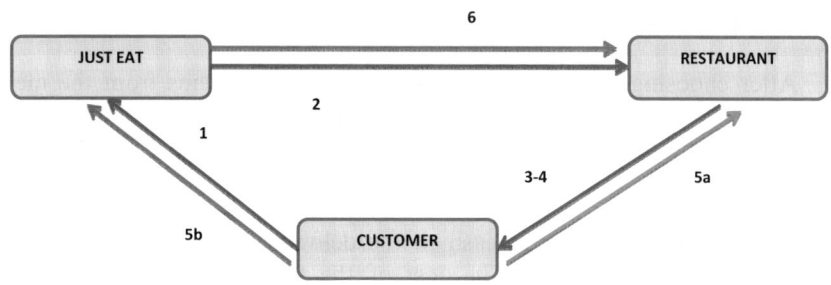

Key:

1. Customer orders food through JE website.
2. DR is notified of order via JCT terminal.
3. DR confirms order on its JCT box to customer (via website) in real time.
4. DR delivers food to hungry customer.
5a. Customer pays £10 in cash to DR's delivery driver upon delivery, or
5b. Customer pays £10 on a credit card through the JE website at time of order.
6. Twice a month JE remits funds collected through CC on transactions made through the website to the DRs, less any amounts owed (in this example, £8 would be remitted to the DR as JE is owed 10% x £20 for the cash and CC order but received £10 for the CC order).

Below we have used an actual invoice as an example, so that the amounts shown below can be agreed to amounts invoiced to the restaurant. A redacted copy of an actual invoice is given at **23.2**.

This is the first invoice the restaurant received after joining JE. On its first invoice, it was charged for the JCT box, installation and connection fee. The total of these was £599. These are one-off payments made to join the network. A refund of the JCT box is made to the DR if it chooses to leave the JE network. The amount refunded depends on the length of time the DR was with JE and the return of the JCT terminal.

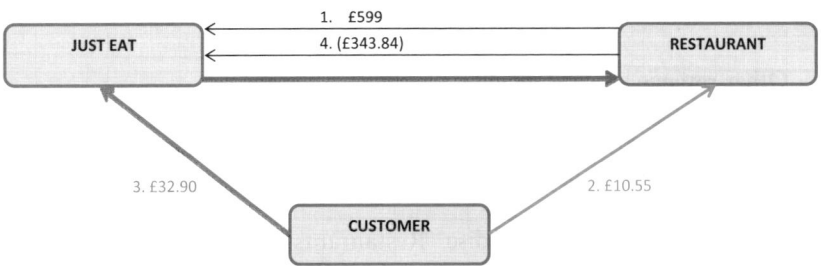

Key:

1. Restaurant pays Just Eat JCT box deposit, installation and connection fee. Total is £599.
2. One customer placed a cash order through website for £10.55. This is paid to the DR upon delivery.
3. Customers placed two CC orders through website for a total cost of £32.90. These are paid directly to JE.
4. JE sends an invoice to the DR twice a month for:
    a. Commission – charged on every order (11% in this instance). The total commission charged was £4.78 (11% x (10.55 + 32.90)).
    b. Administration fee – 50p is charged to the DRs for every CC order processed. Total fee charged was £1 (50p x 2 orders paid by credit/debit card).
    c. The total of the commission and administration fee (£5.78), plus VAT is netted-off against the £32.90 collected and returned to the restaurant. However, as this is the first invoice raised since joining the network, the restaurant also owes JE the £599 plus VAT. £349 of this was paid up front, with the remainder still showing as outstanding at the time of invoicing. Thus, the DR still owes JE £69.80, plus £250 (plus VAT) for the connection fee. These balances will be deducted against future receipts. Therefore, this invoice shows:
        • the £32.90 JE owes the DR for credit card receipts collected;
        • less the £6.94 (£5.78 plus VAT) commission and administration fee;
        • less the £300 connection fee (£250 plus VAT);
        • less the £69.80 remaining from the (£349 plus VAT) that was not collected upon installation;
        • resulting in a balance the DR owes JE of £343.84 – which is the balance on the invoice. This is shown in brackets above because, in practice, JE just deducts this balance from future receipts, rather than asking the DR to settle the amount in cash. It usually takes 4 months for the amount to be fully settled.

VI Case Study

- If this was an invoice from an established restaurant, it would show JE returning £25.96 to the DR after netting off the £5.78 plus VAT.

Other revenue streams include:

- TopPlacement. As mentioned above, DRs can pay to be top of the listings by postcode.

- JE branded merchandise. Restaurants can purchase menu cards, pizza boxes, bags etc that carry the JE logo. The economies of scale mean that JE can secure a very competitive price with printers for menu cards for our DR partners. JE does not typically take a commission for these services, but the DRs can make considerable savings on the menu cards purchased.

- Some restaurants charge a credit card fee to the end customer. This is usually 50p (not to be confused with the administration fee, which is also 50p). This is included in the GOV, so JE's commission is charged on this fee, but the majority is passed back to the DR.

- Where changes are required to the online menus, a charge is made to the DR. The charge depends on the scale of the changes, which can vary from a few items to a complete menu rewrite.

However, the commission stream usually accounts for more than 70% of all revenues.

Where does Just-Eat operate its business?

JE currently operate in 13 countries. This growth has been achieved by launching new operations based on the established JE model (eg Spain, Ireland, Norway) or by partnering with existing operations (eg Brazil, Switzerland, India). Most countries adopt the JE brand. In Switzerland, the company acquired was known as eat.ch, so the 'Just' was not added. In Brazil, RestauranteWeb was already a well-known business, so its brand was retained, likewise in France with Alloresto.

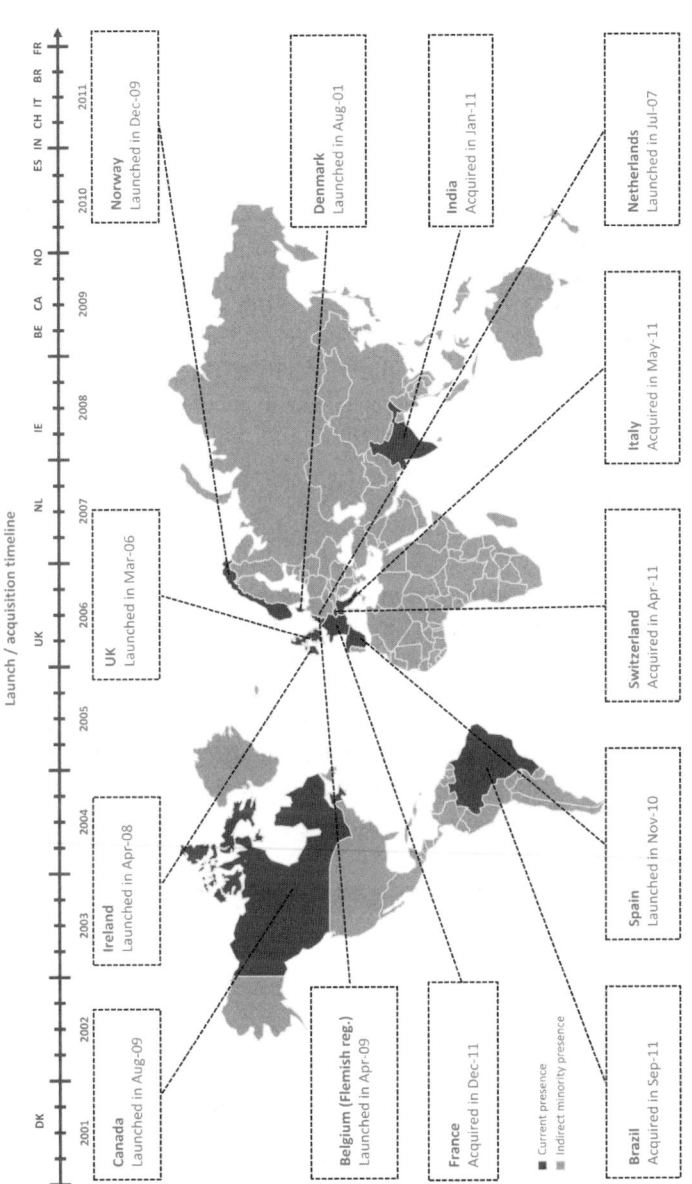

Launch / acquisition timeline

Norway — Launched in Dec-09
Denmark — Launched in Aug-01
India — Acquired in Jan-11
Netherlands — Launched in Jul-07
Italy — Acquired in May-11
UK — Launched in Mar-06
Switzerland — Acquired in Apr-11
Ireland — Launched in Apr-08
Spain — Launched in Nov-10
Canada — Launched in Aug-09
Belgium (Flemish reg.) — Launched in Apr-09
France — Acquired in Dec-11
Brazil — Acquired in Sep-11

■ Current presence
■ Indirect minority presence

Marketing

JE's marketing is split between online and offline. The online focus is on search engine optimisation (SEO) – making sure that JE appears top of search results when key words are entered into a search engine. A considerable part of the marketing budget is spent on pay per click (PPC). This is where the JE website link appears as a sponsored result at the top of the list of search results when key words are entered into a search engine. Over time, the spend on PPC should fall as the countries become more established, for two reasons. First, JE's SEO should improve such that JE is top of a results page without having to pay to be there and, secondly, customers start typing in the JE website directly, rather than using a search engine. Marketing via social media is increasingly becoming a major channel for JE to acquire and build brand advocate – specifically by utilising enhanced features of Facebook and twitter. This, alongside JE's CRM programme, is a key tactic in increasing reorder rates.

The offline focus is on ensuring that all of the restaurants on the JE network are branded – ie JE stickers in the window, JE banners, JE menu cards etc. JE can also supply branded paper bags, pizza boxes and t-shirts for subsidised prices. Once the JE operation is more established in a country JE also undertakes TV and other traditional brand-focused advertising. Two characters were devised for the JE brand – Belly and Brain – and the 30-second commercials tend to air in the early evenings, when people are deciding what to do for dinner.

23.2   EXAMPLE INVOICE TO RESTAURANT

JUST EAT

Invoice No.	Just-Eat.co.uk Ltd
Customer:	Imperial Place 4 Maxwell Road Borehamwood WD6 1JN Pho.: 0844 243 7777 Fax: 0845 299 1026 E-mail: account@justeat.co.uk VAT No. GB 945 7192 91

Invoice date:
For Period: 01 – 15 August

You owe Just-Eat	Amount
1 x Connection Fee Subscription	£250.00

1 x JCT Deposit	£174.00
1 x JCT Install	£175.00
1 x Administration fee	£1.00
1 x Commission to Just-Eat	£4.78

	Subtotal	£604.78
	+ 20% vat	£120.96
	Invoice total incl. VAT	**£725.74** *

Account Summary

01-08	Outstanding amount	£0.00
10-08	JCT Pymt 503946 21304	£349.00
15-08	Payment (card) 202207	£32.90
15-08	Invoice 350673	£-725.74 *

Account Balance: **£-343.84**

should pay £343.84 on account: sort code: acc. no: last paydate:

23/08   NOTICE: If amount not paid before last paydate there will be charged a fee on £10 + vat. (interests on non payed amount are 1.5% / month.)

If you have any questions to this invoice please call us on tel. 0844 243 7777 or write to us at info@just-eat.co.uk

Period: 01-08 – 15-08

Your orders for this period

Restaurant id:

specification for invoice no.:

Order No.	Date	Payment method	Type	Amount
12192794	10-08	Cash	Delivery	£10.55
12225518	12-08	Credit-Debit Card	Delivery	£15.35 }
12294147	14-08	Credit-Debit Card	Delivery	£17.55
			Total Sales:	**£43.45**

Total Sales: Cash **= £10.55**

Total Sales: Credit-Debit Card **= £32.90**

This period you rejected 0 orders. The Total amount rejected: £0.00

23.3 RESTAURANT AGREEMENT

JUST EAT

Part 1

BETWEEN

Just-Eat.co.uk Ltd.
Imperial Place 4
Maxwell Road
Borehamwood WD6 1JN

Tel: 0844 243 7777   Fax: 0845 299 1026   E-mail: info@just-eat.co.uk

(hereafter designated 'JE')

AND

NAME OF PREMISES ....   VAT NO ....

which is a [COMPANY],   TEL NO ....
[PARTNERSHIP], or [INDIVIDUAL] of .

ADDRESS ....   CITY/POSTCODE ....

(hereafter referred to as 'The Restaurant')

OWNER(S) ....

A contract for the Restaurant's use of Just-Connect technology ('JCT') has been concluded as of the date below. It consists of this Part 1 and Part 2, together forming the 'Restaurant Agreement'.

1.   THE SERVICE

JE, primarily via its internet website [www.just-eat.co.uk] [and affiliated websites] and the JCT, shall enable customers to order take-away food and drinks for delivery from the Restaurant (the 'Service').

2.   THE PRODUCT

The Restaurant has chosen the products below to enable the Restaurant to use the Service:

[ ] JCT Equipment Provision & Installation   £349.00 (plus VAT)

Delivery and Installation paid by: Cash [ ]; Electronic card payment [ ]; Other [ ]. TICK accordingly

[ ] Connection Fee   £250.00 (plus VAT)

Paid by: Cash [ ]; Electronic card payment [ ]; Deduction from forthcoming card orders [ ]. TICK accordingly

[ ] JCT Warranty for years 2 and 3   £49.99 (plus VAT)

(without which there may be further charges for replacing JCT boxes)

(collectively the 'Products')

3.   **PAYMENT AND TIME OF DELIVERY**

Commission rate is 11% (plus VAT) of the total gross order value of each order ('Gross Order Value') from a customer using the Service. Administration fee of £0.50 (plus VAT) will be charged to the Restaurant and included within the Gross Order Values for customers paying online. Delivery and installation of the JCT will take place at a mutually agreed time between JE and the Restaurant, and can only be carried out once payment in full has been made by the Restaurant. Please agree the terms of payment with your Account Manager, who will advise accordingly. **For customers that pay for the Service online, a charge of £0.50 will be added to their order and included in the Gross Order Value charged to the customer by the Restaurant. JE will include this additional charge in the Gross Order value on the Twice Monthly Statement and should be included on any receipt issued by the Restaurant to the customer. Please speak to your Account Manager if you do not wish to charge your customers this £0.50 online charge.**

4.   **TERM**
This Restaurant Agreement shall continue for a **minimum of 12 month**s from the first date below, subject to JE's rights to terminate as stated in Part 2. After this minimum term, the Restaurant must give one month's notice to terminate this agreement, which must be in writing. **The JCT remains the property of JE at all times.** If you wish to cancel, the JCT must be returned in a clean and good working condition. **Please note JE payments are made twice per month and no monies will be paid, nor online representation of the Restaurant on the Website until all relevant documentation has been received by JE from the Restaurant.** Please speak to your Account Manager who will advise accordingly.

5.   **CHANGES TO OWNERSHIP OF RESTAURANT (Note that a charge will be applied for any changes to ownership)**
JE must be notified of any changes in ownership of the Restaurant as soon as possible. Failure to notify JE may result in monies being paid to an incorrect account which JE cannot take responsibility for. Unless a 'Changes to Ownership' form has been signed by JE and the Restaurant, no rights or obligations of either party under this

Restaurant Agreement will change. Please speak to your Account Manager who will advise accordingly.

6.   CANCELLATIONS AND REFUNDS

Once JE has received a valid written cancellation notice in accordance with this Restaurant Agreement, the Restaurant will be sent a letter from JE confirming the termination of account and final payment details, and a BACS payment for any outstanding monies owing to the Restaurant, or, a request to pay any outstanding balance owing to JE.

7.   ADDITIONAL TERMS AND CONDITIONS

The terms and conditions set out in Part 2 form part of this Restaurant Agreement. The terms of this Restaurant Agreement may not be deviated from unless through written agreement between JE and the Restaurant. The Restaurant shall keep the content of this Restaurant Agreement confidential at all times. **JE reserves the right to change the prices for the Service by giving the Restaurant one month's advance notice.**

8.   SIGNATURE

The Restaurant hereby confirms that it has received and accepts the terms and conditions of Part 1 and Part 2 (General Terms and Conditions) of this Restaurant Agreement. This Restaurant Agreement is signed in two identical parts – JE will have one and the Restaurant the other.

DATE .... Signed on behalf of JE ....

Signed by Restaurant Owner   Signed by Restaurant Owner (if joint owner)

....

Name (print) .... Name (print) ....

Part 2

THE TERMS AND CONDITIONS OF THIS PART 2 SHALL BE INCORPORATED INTO PART 1 OF THIS RESTAURANT AGREEMENT AND THE DEFINITIONS IN PART 1 SHALL BE INCORPORATED IN THIS PART 2, TOGETHER FORMING ONE AGREEMENT.

1.   THE PURPOSE

1.1   The parties to Part 1 agree to co-operate in receiving online orders through www.just-eat.co.uk, JE's (as defined in Part 1) internet portal, of Just-Eat.co.uk Ltd (hereinafter, designated 'the Website').

2. RESTAURANT SERVICES

2.1 The Restaurant undertakes to receive, process and deliver the customers' orders as placed via the Website, fax, phone, e-mail or JCT (hereafter the 'Order') using the best care, skill and diligence in accordance with best practice in the Restaurant's industry, profession or trade. The Restaurant's preparation, processing and delivery must correspond to what is stated in the Order and the Restaurant warrants that such activities shall be without error. It shall be the Restaurant's responsibility to provide an official receipt (and VAT receipt if appropriate) to the customer, if requested.

2.2 **On-line ordering**: When the Restaurant delivers the prepared Order, the Restaurant must check that the Order number given by the customer corresponds with the Order number received by the Restaurant from JE. The Restaurant undertakes to request identification from the customer in the form of the signed credit card used and check that the credit card conforms with the receipt data for the Order, acting always in accordance with JE's data protection policy (which is available via the Website) prior to the delivery of the prepared Order.

2.3 **On-line ordering**: When choosing the Product (defined in Part 1), the Restaurant commits itself to receive and maintain the JCT (as defined in Part 1) using the best skill and care required to receive the Orders. Furthermore, the Restaurant undertakes to establish and maintain the necessary signal (GPRS) including but not limited to installing the JCT in the Restaurant in such a way that the Orders received will be processed instantly.

2.4 **Marketing**: The Restaurant undertakes to market www.just-eat.co.uk and the Website continuously in its establishment by means of menus, stickers or other relevant advertising material in accordance with guidelines provided by JE.

2.5 **Checking information**: The Restaurant undertakes to check daily that the information contained in menus (including prices) and other advertising material that it has provided to JE or that the Restaurant is using is correct and in accordance with all applicable laws, including but not limited to allergy information such as whether certain foods contain nuts and corresponds exactly to the information that is used on the Website and other promotional materials that JE is using and report immediately to JE any errors and changes required to such menus, the Website or advertising materials. **The Restaurant remains solely responsible for the information contained on the Website that relates to its business, including but not limited to: menus, pricing logos and/or profile.**

VI Case Study

2.6 **Menus**: Subject always to the provision of the Payments clause below, JE will update and/or change the contents of the information about the Restaurant within 7 working days of receiving a written request from the Restaurant to correct errors or changes to such menus and information. The Restaurant agrees that the menu price must be the same price on the Website as they are in hard copy versions used by the Restaurant.

2.7 **Compliance**: The Restaurant undertakes to obtain and at all times maintain all necessary licences and consents to comply at all times with all relevant and applicable laws and regulations in force. Also the Restaurant will comply with all applicable laws and regulations (including, without limitation, observing all health and safety and data protection laws, rules and regulations) that apply in the Restaurant's receipt, processing, preparation and delivery of the Orders.

2.8 The Restaurant shall at all times comply with the Website terms and conditions of JE (available on the Website), and in particular (but not limited to) comply with all security obligations regarding customer information, data protection provisions and guidelines, for receipt, processing and delivery of Orders. The terms and conditions available on the Website are hereby incorporated into this Restaurant Agreement.

In the event of any conflict between this Restaurant Agreement and any terms and conditions set out on the Website, the terms of this Restaurant Agreement shall comply to the extent of such conflict.

2.9 The Restaurant undertakes to refer positively to JE in relation to any publicity regarding the Orders and the Service in accordance with guidelines provided by JE.

2.10 **Connection**: Within 14 days of the Restaurant's payment having cleared in JE's bank account for the Service (as defined in Part 1) and JE having received complete and correct information from the Restaurant, JE undertakes to set up the Restaurant's profile, menu and logo on the Website.

2.11 The Restaurant undertakes either to meet the customer's or JE's demand for a redelivery, or give the customer a proportionate price reduction if requested.

2.12 **WHERE A CUSTOMER DEMANDS A REDELIVERY, CANCELS THE ORDER, OR DEMANDS A PROPORTIONATE PRICE REDUCTION WHICH IS AGREED TO BY A RESTAURANT AND/ OR JE, THIS SHALL NOT AFFECT THE AMOUNT OF THE TRANSACTION FEE THAT JE RECEIVES**

**FOR HAVING PROCURED THE ORDER. THE TRANS-
ACTION FEE IS THEREFORE BASED ON THE PRICE OF
THE FAULTLESS ORDER.**

2.13 **Allergy information**: The Restaurant must immediately give and
constantly update JE with details of any allergy information in
relation to the dishes that the Restaurant prepares, including but not
limited to which dishes contain nuts. It shall be the Restaurant's sole
responsibility to provide this information and check that the Website
contains the correct information regarding allergies and the
Restaurant's food. **THE RESTAURANT, AND NOT JE, SHALL
ALWAYS BE RESPONSIBLE FOR THE ACCURACY OF THE
CONTENT OF THE MENUS.**

2.14 **JCT Warranty**: If the Restaurant has chosen the JCT warranty
option in the Product (as set out in Part 1) then JE, **for the period of
cover chosen in Part 1**, at no further cost to the Restaurant, shall
repair any faults in the JCT (or replace the JCT) due to faults in
materials, workmanship and construction. This excludes batteries
contained within the JCT. **THIS WARRANTY WILL NOT COVER
AND JE WILL NOT BE LIABLE OR RESPONSIBLE FOR
PRODUCTS (INCLUDING BUT NOT LIMITED TO THE JCT)
WHICH IN JE's SOLE OPINION HAVE BEEN SUBJECT TO
MISUSE, ALTERATION, ACCIDENT OR FOR REPAIRS NOT
PERFORMED BY JE. IN ALL CASES JE's OBLIGATIONS
ARE LIMITED TO REPAIR OR REPLACEMENT OF THE JCT,
AT JE's OPTION AND THIS SHALL BE THE RESTAURANT'S
SOLE AND EXCLUSIVE REMEDY IN RESPECT OF ANY
FAULTS IN THE JCT. THIS WARRANTY SHALL ONLY
APPLY IF THE RESTAURANT CHOOSES TO PURCHASE
THE JCT WARRANTY OPTION AS SET OUT IN PART 1.**

2.15 **The Restaurant shall be charged £175 (excluding VAT) for
replacement of any JCT which has been misused, altered, or repaired
by a non JE person. In any event the JCT shall be replaced after 3
years at a cost to the Restaurant of £175 (excluding VAT).**

3. **PRICES AND PAYMENT**

3.1 Twice per month JE shall provide a statement of outstanding
accounts between the Restaurant and JE ('Twice-monthly Statement'). This statement shall include at least:

   (i)   Relevant credit card and online charge payments received by JE
for Orders;

   (ii) Details of relevant Orders paid by cash to the Restaurant;

   (iii) The transaction fees that are due to JE according to the Gross
Order Values, Section 3 (Payment and Time of Delivery) of

Part 1, administration fee, and any other services provided to Restaurant from JE ('Transaction Fees').

(iv)   Details of Orders which JE is aware that the customer has paid the Restaurant directly.

3.2   If the Restaurant has any monies owed to JE according to the Twice-monthly Statement, JE will aim to invoice the Restaurant, on providing the Twice-monthly Statement or deduct it from any monies owed by the Restaurant to JE. If the Restaurant is owed any monies from JE based on the Twice-monthly Statement, JE will transfer this amount, to the Restaurant after JE's receipt of a correct invoice.

3.3   Any payment under this Restaurant Agreement shall be due and payable within 7 days of the date of invoice, whichever of the parties is invoiced.

3.4   In case of any overdue payments JE is entitled either to set off the outstanding accounts against the next Twice-monthly Statement, the sums received from credit card Orders for the Restaurant, or calculate 1.5% interest per month as from the relevant invoice date until the amount is credited to JE's bank account. The Restaurant shall pay to JE any costs in connection with the settling or recovering of an overdue payment.

3.5   The Restaurant is not entitled to withhold payments or balance by way of set-off against any alleged claim or shortcoming in the Service rendered by JE without prior written permission from JE.

3.6   If the Restaurant disagrees with the Twice-monthly Statement issued by JE, the Restaurant must notify JE of its disagreement within 14 days of the delivery of the statement to the Restaurant. If the Restaurant fails to notify JE of any such disagreement within 14 days, the Fortnightly Statement shall be deemed to be accepted by the Restaurant.

3.7   **Changes**: Changes to the Restaurant's menu used on the Website do have a cost; such cost will be notified to and payable by the Restaurant, dependent on the extent of the changes.

4.   REMOVAL OF RESTAURANTS

4.1   If, in JE's sole opinion, the Restaurant ignores relevant and applicable laws and regulations relating to the Service, and/or JE's guidelines on levels of service required of the Restaurant including but not limited to:

- being repeatedly impolite to customers who have made Orders;

- repeatedly providing incorrect food or drink for the Orders; and/or
- repeatedly providing late and/or poor food delivery services.

JE shall be entitled to remove the Restaurant's name, menu and logo, from the Website without liability to the Restaurant. The Restaurant is not thereby entitled to any refund of any connection fee already paid.

4.2 JE reserves the right to inspect the Restaurant's premises on 24 hours notice.

5. JE'S OBLIGATIONS

5.1 JE intends to make the Website available and functional for customers for 24 hours of the day but is under no liability to do so. JE shall not be responsible for any lack of availability or applicability of the Website or the Service caused by adverse weather conditions, technical problems including but not limited to problems due to suppliers of the Website's design, technology, hosting and any credit card service providers.

5.2 JE is entitled to interrupt the access to the Website at any time and without notice in order to maintain and update the Website. In connection therewith, JE shall use reasonable endeavours to ensure that such interruption is as brief as possible and if possible takes place at a time when the number of Orders is at a minimum.

5.3 It is JE's intention that the Website complies with the relevant and applicable laws and regulations at any given time, including the laws relating to treatment of personal data. SHOULD JE GIVE THE RESTAURANT DIRECT ACCESS TO MAKING CHANGES ON THE WEBSITE, THE RESTAURANT SHALL BE SOLELY RESPONSIBLE FOR ANY SUCH CHANGES AND SHALL FULLY INDEMNIFY JE FOR ANY LOSSES, DAMAGES CLAIMS, OR ORDERS MADE AGAINST OR INCURRED BY JE DUE TO ANY ACTS OR OMISSIONS OF THE RESTAU-RANT.

6. LIABILITY AND LIMITATION OF LIABILITY

6.1 NOTHING IN THIS RESTAURANT AGREEMENT SHALL LIMIT OR EXCLUDE EITHER JE'S OR THE RESTAURANT'S LIABILITY FOR:

6.1.1 DEATH OR PERSONAL INJURY CAUSED BY ITS NEGLI-GENCE, OR THE NEGLIGENCE OF ITS EMPLOYEES, AGENTS OR SUBCONTRACTORS;

VI Case Study

6.1.2 FRAUD OR FRAUDULENT MISREPRESENTATION;

6.1.3 BREACH OF THE TERMS IMPLIED BY SECTION 2 OF THE SUPPLY OF GOODS AND SERVICES ACT 1982 (TITLE AND QUIET POSSESSION); OR

6.1.4 ANY OTHER LIABILITY THAT CANNOT BE LIMITED OR EXCLUDED UNDER APPLICABLE LAW.

6.1.5 SUBJECT TO CLAUSE 6.1·

6.1.6 JE SHALL NOT BE LIABLE TO THE RESTAURANT, WHETHER IN CONTRACT, TORT (INCLUDING NEGLIGENCE), BREACH OF STATUTORY DUTY, OR OTHERWISE, FOR ANY LOSS OF PROFIT, OR FOR ANY INDIRECT OR CONSEQUENTIAL LOSS ARISING UNDER OR IN CONNECTION WITH THIS RESTAURANT AGREEMENT.

6.1.7 FURTHERMORE, JE IS NOT LIABLE FOR FAULTS, BREAKDOWNS OR OTHER INTERRUPTIONS TO SERVICES DUE TO ACTIONS TAKEN DUE TO TECHNICAL, MAINTENANCE, OR OPERATIONAL CAUSES, OR IMPOSED BY RELEVANT AND COMPETENT AUTHORITIES.

6.2 **IF A CUSTOMER PAYS FOR AN ORDER BY CREDIT CARD, AND THE PAYMENT IS WITHHELD DUE TO FAULTS OF THE RESTAURANT'S DELIVERY, OR DUE TO MISUSE OF THE CREDIT CARD, THE RESTAURANT IS NOT ENTITLED TO PAYMENT FROM JE.**

6.3 The Restaurant shall fully indemnify JE and keep JE indemnified against any claim (and all related costs) made against JE by a customer or any third party in connection with the Restaurant's failure to deliver, imperfect delivery of the placed Order or the Restaurant's failure to comply with this Restaurant Agreement, security regulations, health and safety regulation and/or any applicable laws, rules and regulations in force at the relevant time.

6.4 The Restaurant shall accept and shall not object to being included by JE in any manner to any third party notice or otherwise in any proceedings instituted against JE, relating to the Restaurant's services or its conduct in connection with this Restaurant Agreement.

6.5 **SUBJECT TO CLAUSES 6.1 AND 6.2, JE'S TOTAL LIABILITY TO THE RESTAURANT IN RESPECT OF ALL OTHER LOSSES ARISING UNDER OR IN CONNECTION WITH THIS RESTAURANT AGREEMENT, WHETHER IN CONTRACT,**

TORT (INCLUDING NEGLIGENCE), BREACH OF STATU-
TORY DUTY, OR OTHERWISE, INCLUDING LOSSES
CAUSED BY JE'S REPUDIATORY BREACH OR A DELIBER-
ATE BREACH OF THE RESTAURANT AGREEMENT BY JE,
ITS EMPLOYEES, AGENTS OR SUBCONTRACTORS SHALL
NOT EXCEED THE AMOUNT OF TRANSACTIONS FEES
PAID TO JE BY THE RESTAURANT ACCORDING TO THIS
RESTAURANT AGREEMENT REGARDING ORDERS IN THE
12 MONTHS PRIOR TO THE DATE THAT THE LIABILITY
AROSE.

6.6 EXCEPT AS EXPRESSLY SET OUT IN THIS RESTAURANT
AGREEMENT, ALL WARRANTIES, CONDITIONS AND
OTHER TERMS IMPLIED BY STATUTE OR COMMON LAW
ARE, TO THE FULLEST EXTENT PERMITTED BY LAW,
EXCLUDED.

6.7 THIS CLAUSE 6 SHALL SURVIVE TERMINATION OF THE
RESTAURANT AGREEMENT.

6.8 FORCE MAJEURE

6.8.1   JE shall not be liable to the Restaurant as a result of any delay or
failure to perform its obligations under this Agreement as a result of
a Force Majeure Event. A 'Force Majeure Event' means an event
beyond the reasonable control of JE including but not limited to
strikes, lock-outs or other industrial disputes (whether involving the
workforce of JE or any other party), failure of a utility service or
transport network, act of God, war, riot, civil commotion, malicious
damage, compliance with any law or governmental order, rule,
regulation or direction, accident, breakdown of plant or machinery,
fire, flood, storm or default of suppliers or subcontractors, import
and export restrictions, faults, breakdowns or other operational
interruptions.

6.8.2   If the Force Majeure Event prevents JE from providing the Service
for more than one week, JE may, without limiting its other rights or
remedies, terminate this Agreement immediately by giving written
notice to the Restaurant.

7.   INTELLECTUAL PROPERTY RIGHTS

7.1   All Intellectual Property Rights in or arising out of or in connection
with the Services or the Website shall be owned by JE and nothing in
this Restaurant Agreement shall constitute a transfer of those
Intellectual Property Rights to the Restaurant.

7.2 The Restaurant confirms irrevocably to JE that the Restaurant's name, menu, logo and other material do not violate, infringe or conflict with Intellectual Property Rights of any third party. **'Intellectual Property Rights'** means: all patents, rights to inventions, utility models, copyright and related rights, trademarks, service marks, trade, business and domain names, rights in trade dress or get-up, rights in goodwill or to sue for passing off, unfair competition rights, rights in designs, rights in computer software, database right, topography rights, moral rights, rights in confidential information (including know-how and trade secrets) and any other intellectual property rights, in each case whether registered or unregistered and including all applications for and renewals or extensions of such rights, and all similar or equivalent rights or forms of protection in any part of the world.

7.3 If a third party makes a claim against JE for the violation of the third party's Intellectual Property Rights relating to the Restaurant's name, menu, logo and/or other material, the Restaurant shall fully indemnify and keep JE indemnified against any claim of any nature and all costs resulting there from.

8. EXCLUSIVITY CLAUSE

8.1 For the duration of this Restaurant Agreement and for a period of 12 months after its expiry or termination, the Restaurant agrees that it shall not have any direct or indirect financial interest or involvement in any establishments that carries out Competing Activities to JE within the United Kingdom. Furthermore, within the period specified herein, the Restaurant shall not be a member of any other association or cooperate in any way with any third party which carries out Competing Activities to JE. 'Competing Activities' means a third party or association wholly or partly having the same purpose and/or performing or providing the same or similar services as JE is providing to the Restaurant under this Restaurant Agreement.

8.2 If JE believes that the Restaurant is in breach of Clause 8.1, JE reserves the right to remove the Restaurant's name, menu and logo from the Website without notice.

9. TERM AND TERMINATION

9.1 This Restaurant Agreement comes into force when signed by both parties and is valid until such time as this Restaurant Agreement is terminated in accordance with its provisions.

9.2 Without prejudice to its other rights and remedies, JE may terminate this Restaurant Agreement immediately by giving written notice to the Restaurant without further liability to the Restaurant.

9.3 The Restaurant may only terminate this Restaurant Agreement by one month's prior written notice after expiry of 12 months from the commencement of this Restaurant Agreement.

9.4 Payments made for the leasing of the JCT and any connection fees by the Restaurant are non-refundable.

9.5 Without limiting its other rights or remedies, JE shall have the right to suspend provision of the Services under this Restaurant Agreement or any other contract between the Restaurant and JE if the Restaurant materially breaches any of its obligations under this Restaurant Agreement, which are not remedied within 5 days' of JE sending notice to the Restaurant, including but not limited to if the Restaurant fails to pay any amount due under this Restaurant Agreement on the due date for payment.

9.6 The rights and obligations of the parties under this Restaurant Agreement which are intended to continue beyond the termination or expiry of this Restaurant Agreement (including those under this Clause 9 and Clauses 6, 7, 8, 13, 14 and 15) shall survive the termination or expiry of this Restaurant Agreement.

10. SERIOUS BREACH OF OBLIGATIONS

10.1 In the event of repeated incidents of default by the Restaurant and complaints from customers about the Restaurant, JE shall be entitled to determine in its sole discretion, whether or not such breaches can be remedied.

10.2 Without limiting its other rights or remedies, JE reserves the right to remove the Restaurant's name, menu and logo from the Website without notice and without further liability to the Restaurant.

11. AMENDMENTS

11.1 Upon one months' prior written notice, JE may amend the terms of this Restaurant Agreement. The Restaurant shall be notified of such amendments either by fax, e-mail or in writing. Unless the Restaurant responds to such notification within 2 weeks objecting to the amendments or terminates this Restaurant Agreement in accordance with Clause 9.3, such amendments shall henceforth be construed as forming part of this Restaurant Agreement and accepted by the Restaurant.

VI Case Study

11.2 If there are any conflicts between Part 1 and Part 2 of this Restaurant Agreement, then this Part 2 shall prevail, in respect of such conflict.

12. ASSIGNMENT

12.1 JE shall be entitled to assign its rights and obligations under this Restaurant Agreement to any third party.

12.2 The Restaurant may only assign, transfer, charge, subcontract or deal in any other manner with all or any of its rights or obligations under the Restaurant Agreement to a third party with the express prior written consent from JE.

12.3 The Restaurant shall procure that immediately on assignment that any third party assignee assumes the legal obligations and duties of the Restaurant and such assignee is liable for any claim made against Restaurant before the date of such assignment. The Restaurant that assigns its rights and obligations is released from liability only when all or any claims made before the date of such assignment are paid. The Restaurant shall procure that any assignee of this Restaurant Agreement shall enter into a Restaurant Agreement directly with JE.

13. CONFIDENTIALITY

13.1 The content of this Restaurant Agreement and any information concerning the other party is to be treated as confidential and shall not be disclosed unless such information is generally accessible to the public. However, JE is entitled to use the Restaurant's name as a reference.

14. INVALIDITY CLAUSE

14.1 If any of the terms or conditions of this Restaurant Agreement are declared wholly or partly invalid, the remainder of this Restaurant Agreement shall remain in full force and effect and any wholly or partly invalid terms or conditions may be replaced by valid terms or conditions agreed between the parties, so as to maintain the relationship between the parties in similar manner as if the terms or conditions had not been declared invalid.

15. GOVERNING LAW AND JURISDICTION

15.1 This Restaurant Agreement and any dispute or claim arising out or in connection with this Restaurant Agreement or its subject matter or formation (including any dispute or claim relating to non-contractual obligations) shall be governed by and construed in accordance with English law.

15.2 The parties agree to submit any dispute arising in connection with this Restaurant Agreement to the exclusive jurisdiction of the courts of England and Wales (including any dispute or claim relating to non-contractual obligations).

APPENDIX A

DOMAIN NAMES

Note: You should check the appropriate domain name registry for any change in registration requirements. The information provided below does not extend to all jurisdictions throughout the world.

GENERIC TOP LEVEL DOMAIN NAMES
(gTLDs)

gTLD	Residency requirements	Registry details
.com / .info / .name / .net / .org	No residency requirements	http://www.internic.net
.coop	Only cooperatives, cooperative service organizations and wholly owned subsidiaries of cooperatives will be eligible to use the .coop domain name.	http://www.internic.net
.aero	a member of the aviation community.	http://www. information.aero/

CODE TOP LEVEL DOMAINS
(ccTLDs)

Country	ccTLD	Residency requirements
Ascension Island	.ac	No residency requirements
Andorra	.ad	Residency requirements
Anguilla	.ai	No residency requirements

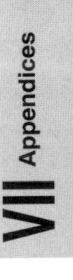

VII Appendices

Country	ccTLD	Residency requirements
Antigua and Berbuda	.ag	No residency requirements
American Samoa	.as	No residency requirements
Austria	.at	No residency requirements
Australia	.au	No residency requirements
Aruba	.aw	Residency requirements
Barbados	.bb	Residency requirements
Belgium	.be	No residency requirements
Bulgaria	.bg	Residency requirements
Burundi	.bi	No residency requirements
Bermuda	.bm	Residency requirements
Bahamas	.bs	No residency requirements
Canada	.ca	Residency requirements
Switzerland	.ch	No residency requirements
Chile	.cl	No residency requirements but must have domestic rep
China	.cn .cn.com	Residency requirements
Christmas Island	.cx	No residency requirements
Cyprus	.cy	Residency requirements
Czech Republic	.cz	No residency requirements
Germany	.de	Residency requirements for administrative contact
Denmark	.dk	No residency requirements
Dominican Republic	.do	No residency requirements
Ecuador	.ec	No residency requirements

Country	ccTLD	Residency requirements
Estonia	.ee	Residency requirements (need to name representative in Estonia as their administrative contact)
Egypt	.eg	No residency requirements
Eritrea	.er	Residency requirements
Spain	.es	No residency requirements
Finland	.fi	Residency requirements
Fiji	.fj	No residency requirements
Faroe Islands	.fo	Residency requirements
France	.fr	Residency requirements
Guernsey	.gg	No residency requirements
Gibraltar	.gi	Residency requirements
Greenland	.gl	No residency requirements
Gambia	.gm	Residency requirements
Guinea	.gn	Residency requirements
Greece	.gr	No residency requirements
South Georgia and the South Sandwich Islands	.gs	No residency requirements
Hong Kong	.hk	No residency requirements (individuals send fax copy of passport; companies need registration number)
Hungary	.hu	Residency requirements
Ireland	.ie	Residency requirements
Israel	.il	No residency requirements
Isle of Man	.im	No residency requirements
India	.in	No residency requirements
Iran	.ir	Residency requirements

VII Appendices

Country	ccTLD	Residency requirements
Iceland	.is	No residency requirements
Italy	.it	Any EU member citizen or EU member registered company
Jersey	.je	No residency requirements
Japan	.jp	No residency requirements (need a local presence)
Cayman Islands	.ky	Residency requirements
Saint Lucia	.lc	No residency requirements
Liechtenstein	.li	No residency requirements
Sri Lanka	.lk	Residency requirements
Liberia	.lr	Residency requirements
Luxembourg	.lu	No residency requirements
Monaco	.mc	Residency requirements
Montserrat	.ms	No residency requirements
Malta	.mt	No residency requirements
Malaysia	.my	Residency requirements
Namibia	.na	No residency requirements
Norfolk Islands	.nf	No residency requirements
The Netherlands	.nl	Residency requirements
Norway	.no	Residency requirements
New Zealand	.nz	No residency requirements
Peru	.pe	No residency requirements
Papua New Guinea	.pg	Residency requirements
Philippines	.ph	No residency requirements
Pakistan	.pk	No residency requirements
Poland	.pl	No residency requirements

Country	ccTLD	Residency requirements
Pitcairn	.pn	No residency requirements
Portugal	.pt	No residency requirements
Romania	.ro	No residency requirements
Russian Federation	.ru	No residency requirements
Saudi Arabia	.sa	Residency requirements
Sweden	.se	No residency requirements
Singapore	.sg	Residency requirements
St Helena	.sh	No residency requirements
Slovenia	.si	No residency requirements
Slovakia	.sk	Residency requirements
San Marino	.sm	No residency requirements
Sao Tome and Principe	.st	No residency requirements
Swaziland	.sz	Residency requirements
The Turks and Caicos Islands	.tc	No residency requirements
French Southern Territories	.tf	No residency requirements
Thailand	.th	Residency requirements
Tajikistan	.tj	No residency requirements
Tokelau	.tk	No residency requirements
Turkmenistan	.tm	Residency requirements
Tonga	.to	No residency requirements
Turkey	.tr	Residency requirements
Trinidad and Tobago	.tt	No residency requirements
Taiwan	.tw	No residency requirements

VII Appendices

Country	ccTLD	Residency requirements
Tanzania	.tz	Residency requirements
United Kingdom	.uk .co.uk .plc.uk .ltd.uk	No residency requirements No residency requirements A UK public limited co only A UK limited co only
United States	.us	Residency requirements
British Virgin Islands	.vg	No residency requirements
US Virgin Islands	.vi	Residency requirements
Vanuatu	.vu	No residency requirements
Samoa	.ws	No residency requirements
South Africa	.za	No residency requirements

APPENDIX B

JORDANS COMPANY FORMATION CHECKLIST: OCTOBER 2009

Your Jordans company formation checklist

Provided by Jordans Ltd

www.jordans.co.uk

Forming your company with your officers and shareholders is easy. There are no forms to complete or sign – you provide the information and we send it electronically to Companies House. Use this simple checklist to make sure you have all the details you need before you begin.

Company name

Full company name to include Limited or Ltd (use our free namechecking facility to ensure that your chosen name is available).

Domain Name

It makes sense to register your domain name at the same time so it's worth considering at this stage what you would like this to be. Registering your domain at the same time as your company makes you more likely to secure the name of your choice and means your business is internet-ready from the outset. Checking your domain name is also free.

Registered office

The address of the company's registered office to include postcode.

Statement of capital

For the purposes of your Jordans formation, this will be produced automatically based on the shareholding information you provide together with our standard share provision detail.

Officers

Details of each of the directors, company secretary (optional) and shareholders

Your company must have at least one director who is a natural person over 16 years of age. You cannot form a company with only a corporate director in office i.e. with another company acting as the only director.

Directors

For each individual director you will need:

- Full forename(s)

- Surname

- Any former name(s) used for business purposes, including maiden names/s

- Full service address including town, county and postcode (for the public record)

- Usual residential address (protected information)

- Country/state of residence

- Date of birth

- Nationality

- Occupation

- The number of shares, if any, the director is to have in the company

- Security items (choose any 3, see below)

Choose any 3 of the following security items. This information allows for electronic filing at Companies House without the need for any paper forms or live signatures. The information provided will not appear anywhere on the public record:

Town of birth (first 3 letters)	Passport number (last 3 digits)
Telephone number (last 3 digits)	Mother's maiden name (first 3 letters)
Eye colour (first 3 letters)	Father's first name (first 3 letters)
National insurance number (last 3 digits)	

For a corporate director you will need:

- Corporate/firm name

- Registered/principal office address

- For an EEA* company, details of the register where the company file is kept (including state) and its registration number in that register

- For a non-EEA* company, details of the legal form of the corporate body or firm and the law by which it is governed; and, if applicable, the register in which it is entered (including the state) and its registration number in that register

- The name of the person who has the authority to sign documents on behalf of the corporate officer

- Security items for the signatory (chose any 3 as before)

Secretary

Note you do not have to appoint a secretary, but if you choose to do so you will need:

- Full forename/s

- Surname

- Any former name/s used for business purposes, including maiden names/s

- Full service address including town, county and postcode

- The number of shares, if any, the secretary is to have in the company

- Security items (chose any 3 as before)

If another company is to act as secretary, you will need:

- Corporate/firm name

- Registered/principal office address

- For an EEA* company, details of the register where the company file is kept (including state) and its registration number in that register

- For a non-EEA* company, details of the legal form of the corporate body or firm and the law by which it is governed; and, if applicable,

VII Appendices

the register in which it is entered (including the state) and its registration number in that register

- The name of the person who has the authority to sign documents on behalf of the corporate officer

- Security items for the signatory (choose any 3, see below)

If the company secretary is also a Director this information can be provided in one transaction.

Shareholder

A shareholder may also be a director or secretary in which case the information can then be provided in one transaction.

For a shareholder who is not a director or secretary you will need:

- Full forename(s)

- Surname

- Full address including town, county and postcode

- The number of shares the shareholder is to have in the company

- Security items (chose any 3 as before)

If you have any further questions about forming a new company, please contact us on (0117) 918 1391 or by email at companyformation@jordans.co.uk

* EEA – European Economic Area comprises countries in the EU plus Iceland, Liechtenstein and Norway.

Jordans Limited
21 St Thomas Street Bristol BS1 6JS
T: +44 (0) 117 923 0600 E: info@jordans.co.uk DX: 78161 Bristol
W: www.jordans.co.uk

APPENDIX C

ELECTRONIC COMMERCE: TAX STATUS OF WEB SITES AND SERVERS (HMRC)

84/2000

11 April 2000

The UK today set out its views on the tax status of web sites and servers.

Speaking at a conference in Lisbon, the Director of the Inland Revenue's International Division, Gabs Makhlouf, said:

'The OECD has been reviewing with the business community the long term future of the "permanent establishment" concept – the threshold in the OECD's model tax treaty below which a country will not tax on non-residents carrying on a business in that country. This is crucial work. And it is important that it is carried out with due consideration, and in partnership between representatives of Government and business.

"Permanent establishment" is a long standing concept. It is tried and tested. And it is widely supported. As yet, we do not know enough about how e-commerce will develop for anyone to make reasoned decisions on whether or not to move away from it. But now is clearly the time for the debate to begin.

In the meantime, early decisions are needed on the status of web sites and servers under the existing rules of permanent establishment. Businesses need to know where they stand in order to make investment decisions and calculate their tax liabilities.

A particularly important policy objective is that the outcome is a practical one. One that works in the real world as well in the heads of lawyers. Governments and businesses need an outcome that allows e-commerce to flourish, that keeps down compliance costs, and that is enforceable.

In the UK we take the view that a web site of itself is not a permanent establishment. And we take the view that a server is insufficient of itself to constitute a permanent establishment of a business that is conducting e-commerce through a web site on the server. We take that view that regardless of whether the server is owned, rented or otherwise at the disposal of the business.'

NOTES FOR EDITORS

1. The Government's goal is for the UK to be the best environment in the world in which to trade electronically by 2002.

2. The Inland Revenue and Customs and Excise published on 26 November 1999 a comprehensive review of the tax issues concerning e-commerce ('Electronic Commerce: The UK's Taxation Agenda'). Chapter 8 highlighted a number of outstanding issues to do with the application of international tax rules to e-commerce, including the application of the permanent establishment concept in double taxation treaties.

3. Under the OECD's model tax treaty, a non-resident business is only taxable in a foreign country to the extent that it is carrying on business there through a permanent establishment. A permanent establishment is defined as being 'a fixed place of business through which the business of an enterprise is wholly or partly carried on'.

4. The OECD published a 2nd draft of a consultation note clarifying the position on the status of web sites and servers. It concerns the legal interpretation of the existing Article 5 of the model treaty and records that there are differing views among OECD member countries on whether a server may be a permanent establishment. It is available on the OECD's web site at: http://www.oecd.org/daf/fa/treaties/art5rev_3March.pdf.

HMRC'S CURRENT STATEMENT ON WEBSITES

HMRC's current statement on websites and servers is in its International Tax Manual, which states:

> **'INTM266100 – Non-residents trading in the UK: Treaty permanent establishment: fixed place of business permanent establishment: e-commerce**
>
> **E-commerce, E-tailers, servers and internet trading**
>
> The development of e-commerce places a strain on the traditional definition of a PE in cases where the computer equipment is positioned in one territory whilst the enterprise has no personnel active in the business in that territory. The UK does not concur with other OECD Member States on whether a server of itself can constitute a fixed place of business permanent establishment. Accordingly the UK has made an observation to that effect in the commentary to the Model Treaty Article 5(1).

In the UK, we take the view that a server either alone or together with web sites could not as such constitute a PE of a business that is conducting e-commerce through a web site on the server. We take that view regardless of whether the server is owned, rented or otherwise at the disposal of the business.

Other OECD Member States take the view that a server, as distinct from mere web sites (which cannot fulfil the geographic situs condition) could constitute a PE where the equipment is in fact fixed, i.e. that in fact it is not moved and is located at a specific location for a sufficient duration to indeed become fixed ...'

VII Appendices

APPENDIX D

TAX TREATY CHARACTERISATION ISSUES ARISING FROM E-COMMERCE (OECD)

REPORT TO WORKING PARTY NO. 1 OF THE OECD COMMITTEE ON FISCAL AFFAIRS

1 February 2001

By the Technical Advisory Group on Treaty Characterisation of Electronic Commerce Payments

1. INTRODUCTION

1.   The Technical Advisory Group (TAG) on Treaty Characterisation Issues arising from Ecommerce was set up by the OECD Committee on Fiscal Affairs in January 1999 with the general mandate "to examine the characterisation of various types of electronic commerce payments under tax conventions with a view to providing the necessary clarifications in the Commentary."[1]

2.   The TAG met four times on 22-24 September 1999, 17-18 February 2000, 3-4 July 2000 and 7-8 November 2000. During its first two meetings, it identified a number of typical e-commerce transactions and analysed the various treaty characterisation issues that could arise from these. The result of that work was a document which described 26 categories of transactions together with the analysis and preliminary conclusions of the Group. That document was released for comments on 24 March 2000.

3.   At its meeting of 3-4 July, the TAG continued its work on the basis of these comments. This allowed the TAG to narrow down areas of disagreement between its members, to revise its list of transactions and to draft some general conclusions on treaty characterisation issues. The results of that work were included in a document which was released for comments on 1 September 2000. That document described the various treaty characterisation issues that were identified by the Group and presented the views of the Group concerning these issues; it also included

---

[1]   The detailed mandate and the composition of the TAG appear in Annex 3.

a revised analysis of the various categories of typical e-commerce transactions identified in the previous draft.

4.   After further analysis, and having regard to the comments received, the Group, at its last meeting, was able to reach a consensus and to finalise this report to the Working Party.

5.   This report is divided as follows:

–   section 2 includes the overall recommendation that the TAG makes to Working Party No. 1;

–   section 3 constitutes the main part of the report and includes a description of the various treaty characterisation issues identified by the Group, together with the conclusions of the Group on how to address each such issue and, where appropriate, suggestions for changes to the Commentaries on the Model Tax Convention;

–   annex 1 reproduces all the suggestions for changes to the Commentaries on the Model Tax Convention which are found throughout section 3;

–   annex 2 is a revised version of the document first released on 24 March, which now includes the Group's analysis of 28 categories of typical e-commerce transactions;[2]

–   annex 3 reproduces the mandate given to the Group by the OECD Committee on Fiscal Affairs and includes the list of persons who participated in its meetings.

2.   RECOMMENDATION TO WORKING PARTY NO. 1

6.   During its work, the Group has examined characterisation issues that are relevant to the OECD Model Tax Convention as currently drafted and also some issues that relate to alternative treaty provisions not found in the Model Tax Convention. Its recommendation covers both sets of issues.

7.   The TAG recommends to Working Party No. 1 to issue a document clarifying, along the lines of section 3 of this report, how the various tax treaty characterisation issues arising from e-commerce should be solved. In doing so, and since the mandate of the TAG invited it to

---

[2]   The Group did not attempt to cover all categories of current and future e-commerce transactions. Instead, it sought to identify the principles to be applied in analysing the various treaty characterisation issues so that they can be applied to the existing and emerging transactions as required.

examine these characterisation issues "with a view to providing the necessary clarifications in the Commentary", the Working Party is invited to take account of the suggestions for changes to the Commentary of the OECD Model Tax Convention which are included in this report (these suggestions are all reproduced in Annex 1). The Working Party is also invited to take account of the conclusions of this report concerning various provisions which are not part of the OECD Model Tax Convention but are found in some bilateral conventions.

3. TREATY CHARACTERISATION ISSUES ARISING FROM E-COMMERCE TRANSACTIONS

8. This section describes the various treaty characterisation issues that were identified by the Group in the course of its work and presents the views of the Group concerning these issues.

9. Throughout its work, the Group has assumed that all payments made in connection with the typical e-commerce transactions that it identified were received in the course of carrying on a business, whether or not the payers were themselves carrying on business. It follows that all these payments are capable of falling within Article 7 of the OECD Model Tax Convention, which deals with business profits. Some payments, however, may be taken out of Article 7 by the rule of paragraph 7 of Article 7, which gives priority to any other Article that expressly deals with the specific type of income concerned. One such Article is Article 12, dealing with royalties. On the basis of its analysis, the Group does not consider that any of the payments that it has examined fall within Article 21, which deals with other income.

Business profits and royalties

10. The definition of royalties currently found in paragraph 2 of Article 12 of the OECD Model Tax Convention reads as follows:

> "The term 'royalties' as used in this Article means payments of any kind received as a consideration for the use of, or the right to use, any copyright of literary, artistic or scientific work including cinematograph films, any patent, trade mark, design or model, plan, secret formula or process, or for information concerning industrial, commercial or scientific experience."

11. In the 1977 Double Taxation Convention, that definition also included "payments [...] for the use, or the right to use, industrial, commercial or scientific equipment" and some bilateral conventions still include this previous definition of royalties.

12. This section analyses classification issues arising from the possible application of various elements of these two definitions to

payments made in e-commerce transactions. It also examines classification issues arising from alternative treaty provisions which deal with the
provision of services or technical fees.

Business profits and payments for the use of, or the right to use, a copyright

Analysis and conclusions

13,   The Group found that one of the most important characterisation issues arising from e-commerce was the distinction between business
profits and the part of the treaty definition of "royalties" that deals with
payments for the use of, or the right to use, a copyright. Whilst differing
views were originally expressed within the Group as regards this issue (as
reflected in the March and September 2000 drafts for comments), further
discussion in light of the comments received allowed the Group to reach
the unanimous conclusions below. These are fully consistent with the
views, which the Group has unanimously endorsed, that are expressed in
paragraphs 14 to 14.2 of the Commentary on Article 12 as regards
software payments.

14.   Since the definition of royalties applies to "payments for" any of
the various items listed in that definition, the Group has concluded that,
in any given transaction, the main question to be addressed is the
identification of the consideration for the payment. Under the relevant
legislation of some countries, transactions which permit the customer to
electronically download computer programs or other digital content may
give rise to use of copyright by the customer, *e.g.* because a right to make
one or more copies of the digital content is granted under the contract.
Where the essential consideration is for something other than the use of,
or right to use, rights in the copyright (such as to acquire other types of
contractual rights, data or services), and the use of copyright is limited to
such rights as are required to enable downloading, storage and operation
on the customer's computer, network or other storage, performance or
display device, such use of copyright should be disregarded in the analysis
of the character of the payment for treaty purposes. This would be the
case, for instance, where a payment is made by a person for the
downloading and the operation of a copy of a computer program. Whilst
electronic downloading of the program may or may not constitute the use
of a copyright by the user (as opposed to by the provider) depending on
the relevant copyright law and contractual arrangements, the essential
consideration for the payment is not that possible use of a copyright.

15.   In the case of transactions that permit the customer to
electronically download digital products (such as software, images, sounds
or text), the payment is made to acquire data transmitted in the form of a
digital signal for the own use or enjoyment of the acquiror.[3] This

---

3   The same result would apply regardless of whether the payment was made as regards the

constitutes the essential consideration for the payment. To the extent that the act of copying the digital signal onto the customer's hard disk or other non-temporary media (including transfers to other storage, performance or display devices) constitutes the use of a copyright by the customer under the relevant law and contractual arrangements, this is merely an incidental part of the process of capturing and storing the digital signal. This incidental part is not important for classification purposes because it does not correspond to the essential consideration for the payment (*i.e.*, to acquire data transmitted in the form of a digital signal), which is the determining factor for the purposes of the treaty definition of royalties.

Suggested changes to the Commentary

16.   Based on the following, the Group suggests that the following changes be made to the Commentary on Article 12 of the OECD Model Tax Convention:

> *Add the following paragraphs 17.1 to 17.4 immediately after paragraph 17 of the Commentary on Article 12:*

> 17.1   The principles expressed above as regards software payments are also applicable as regards transactions concerning other types of digital products such as images, sounds or text. The development of electronic commerce has multiplied the number of such transactions. In deciding whether or not payments arising in these transactions constitute royalties, the main question to be addressed is the identification of the consideration for the payment.

> 17.2   Under the relevant legislation of some countries, transactions which permit the customer to electronically download digital products may give rise to use of copyright by the customer, e.g. because a right to make one or more copies of the digital content is granted under the contract. Where the essential consideration is for something other than for the use of, or right to use, rights in the copyright (such as to acquire other types of contractual rights, data or services), and the use of copyright is limited to such rights as are required to enable downloading, storage and operation on the customer's computer, network or other storage, performance or display device, such use of copyright should be disregarded in the analysis of the character of the payment for purposes of applying the definition of "royalties".

> 17.3   This is the case for transactions that permit the customer (which may be an enterprise) to electronically download digital products (such as software, images, sounds or text) for that customer's own use or enjoyment. In these transactions, the payment is made to acquire data transmitted in the form of a digital signal for the acquiror's own use or enjoyment. This constitutes the essential consideration for the payment, which therefore does not constitute royalties but falls within Article 7 or Article 13, as the case

downloading of one specific product or in the form of a subscription fee for the right to access a web site where that digital product may be downloaded.

may be. To the extent that the act of copying the digital signal onto the customer's hard disk or other non-temporary media constitutes the use of a copyright by the customer under the relevant law and contractual arrangements, this is merely an incidental part of the process of capturing and storing the digital signal. This incidental part is not important for classification purposes because it does not correspond to the essential consideration for the payment (i.e., to acquire data transmitted in the form of a digital signal), which is the determining factor for the purposes of the definition of royalties. There also would be no basis to classify such transactions as "royalties" if, under the relevant law and contractual arrangements, the creation of a copy is regarded as a use of copyright by the provider rather than by the customer.

17.4   By contrast, transactions where the essential consideration for the payment is the granting of the right to use a copyright in a digital product that is electronically downloaded for that purpose will give rise to royalties. This would be the case, for example, of a book publisher who would pay to acquire the right to reproduce a copyrighted picture that it would electronically download for the purposes of including it on the cover of a book that it is producing. In this transaction, the essential consideration for the payment is the acquisition of rights to use the copyright in the digital product, i.e. the right to reproduce and distribute the picture, and not merely for the acquisition of the digital content."

Business profits and payments for know-how

Analysis and conclusions

17.   Whilst e-commerce transactions resulting in know-how payments are relatively rare, In some transactions, it is necessary to distinguish whether the consideration for a payment is the provision of services or the provision of know-how (*i.e.* information concerning industrial, commercial or scientific experience).

18.   The Group noted that paragraph 11 of the Commentary on Article 12 refers to the following key elements to identify transactions for the provision of know-how:

–   according to the ANBPPI *[Association des Bureaux pour la Protection de la Propriété Industrielle]*, know-how is "undivulged technical information that is necessary for the industrial reproduction of a product or process, directly and under the same conditions; inasmuch as it is derived from experience, know-how represents what a manufacturer cannot know from mere examination of the product and mere knowledge of the progress of technique";

–   "In the know-how contract, one of the parties agrees to impart to the other, so that he can use them for his own account, his special knowledge and experience which remain unrevealed to the public";

- in the know-how contract "the grantor is not required to play any part himself in the application of the formula . . . and . . . does not guarantee the results thereof";

- the provision of know-how must be distinguished from the "provision of services, in which one of the parties undertakes to use the customary skills of his calling to execute work himself for the other party".

19.   The paragraph also includes the following examples of payments which should not be considered to be received as consideration for the provision of know-how but rather, for the provision of services:

- payments obtained as consideration for after-sales service,

- payments for services rendered by a seller to the purchaser under a guarantee,

- payments for pure technical assistance, and

- payments for an opinion given by an engineer, an advocate or an accountant

20.   Applying these criteria and examples to e-commerce transactions, the Group agrees that, for instance, online advice, communications with technicians and using the trouble-shooting database, would clearly involve actual services being performed on demand rather than the provision of know-how.

21.   The Group recognises that the distinction between payments for services rendered and payments for the supply of know-how may sometimes raise practical difficulties. It considers that the following criteria, developed in a ruling by the Australian Tax Office, may be useful in that respect.

- under a contract for the supply of know-how:

    (a) a "product" (*i.e.* knowledge, information, technique, formula, skills, process, plan, etc.) which has already been created or developed or is already in existence is transferred;
    (b) the product which is the subject of the contract is transferred for use by the buyer (*i.e.* it is supplied); and
    (c) except in the case of a disposition where the seller divests himself completely of any further interest in the product, the property in the product remains with the seller. All that is obtained by the buyer is the right to use the product. Subject to the terms of the contract, the seller retains the right to use the product himself and to transfer it to others.

– by contrast, in a contract involving the performance of services:

(d) the contractor undertakes to perform services which will result in the creation, development or the bringing into existence of a product (which may or may not be know-how);

(e) in the course of developing a product, the contractor would apply existing knowledge, skill and expertise – there is not a transfer (*i.e.* supply) of know-how from the contractor to the buyer as such but a use by the contractor of his knowledge for his own purposes; and

(f) the product created as a result of the services belongs to the buyer for him to use without having to obtain any further rights in respect of the product. However, in the course of rendering services the contractor would, in most cases, also produce as a byproduct a work (*e.g.* plan, design, specification, report, etc., – which could contain knowledge, etc. not otherwise known to the buyer and which may or may not be protected by patents, etc..) in which copyright would subsist. Unless specifically agreed otherwise, the contractor is the owner of such copyright and the buyer or any other person is, by law, precluded from using the property in which the copyright subsists for any purpose other than the purpose for which it was originally designed without first obtaining the approval of the contractor. This would not alter the nature of the contract which would remain one for the performance of services.

– another very important factor is the incidence of cost, *i.e.*, both the level and the nature of the expenditure incurred by the seller:

(g) in most cases involving the supply of know-how which is already in existence there would appear to be very little more which needs to be done by the supplier other than to copy existing material [...] On the other hand, a contract for the performance of services would, in the majority of cases, involve a very much greater level of expenditure.

(h) a contract for the performance of services would, depending on the nature of the services to be rendered, involve the contractor in such items of expenditure as salaries and wages to employees engaged in researching, designing, testing, drawing and other associated activities, payments to sub-contractors for the performance of similar services, etc.

– these factors all point to the one main distinctive feature of know-how – that it is an asset and, as such, it is something which is already in existence and is not something brought into being in pursuance of the particular contract.[4]

---

[4] The wording of the preceding criteria corresponds, with some adaptations, to paragraphs 28 to 33 of the Australian Tax Office's Taxation Ruling IT 2660, "Income

22.   The Group also considers that the following excerpt of the "software regulations", which U.S. IRS and Treasury issued in 1998 regarding the characterisation of income from cross-border transactions involving computer programs, provides useful criteria to distinguish payments for services and payments for know-how as regards e-commerce transactions related to computer programs. Those regulations deal with the distinction between the provision of services (for the development or modification of the computer program) and the provision of know-how (relating to computer programming techniques) in the following words:

> "Provision of services. The determination of whether a transaction involving a newly developed or modified computer program is treated as either the provision of services or another transaction described [above] is based on all the facts and circumstances of the transaction, including, as appropriate, the intent of the parties (as evidenced by their agreement and conduct) as to which party is to own the copyright rights in the computer program and how the risks of loss are allocated between the parties.
>
> Provision of know-how. The provision of information with respect to a computer program will be treated as the provision of know-how ... only if the information is
>
> (1) Information relating to computer programming techniques;
>
> (2) Furnished under conditions preventing unauthorised disclosure, specifically contracted for between the parties; and
>
> (3) Considered property subject to trade secret protection."
>
> Example ...
>
> (i) Facts. Corp A, a U.S. corporation, and Corp I, a Country Z corporation, agree that a development engineer employed by Corp A will travel to Country Z to provide know-how relating to certain techniques not generally known to computer programmers, which will enable Corp I to more efficiently create computer programs. These techniques represent the product of experience gained by Corp A from working on many computer programming projects, and are furnished to Corp I under nondisclosure conditions. Such information is property subject to trade secret protection.
>
> (ii) Analysis. This transaction contains the elements of know-how specified [above]. Therefore, this transaction will be treated as the provision of know-how."

Suggested changes to the Commentary

23.   The Group considers that it would be useful to provide greater guidance in the Commentary, on the basis of the above criteria and

---

Tax: Definition of Royalties" available at http://law.ato.gov.au/atolaw/view.htm?basic=know-how&&docid=ITR/IT2660/NAT/ATO/00001.

factors, on the distinction to be made between payments for the provision of know-how and payments for the provisions of services. It therefore suggests that the following changes be made to the Commentary on Article 12 of the OECD Model Tax Convention:

Replace paragraph 11 of the Commentary on Article 12 by the following paragraphs 11 to 11.5 (additions to the existing text of paragraph 11 appear in bold italics):

"11   In classifying as royalties payments received as consideration for information concerning industrial, commercial or scientific experience, paragraph 2 alludes to the concept of "know-how". Various specialist bodies and authors have formulated definitions of know-how which do not differ intrinsically. One such definition, given by the *"Association des Bureaux pour la Protection de la Propriété Industrielle"* (ANBPPI), states that 'know-how is all the undivulged technical information, whether capable of being patented or not, that is necessary for the industrial reproduction of a product or process, directly and under the same conditions; inasmuch as it is derived from experience, know-how represents what a manufacturer cannot know from mere examination of the product and mere knowledge of the progress of technique'.

11.1   In the know-how contract, one of the parties agrees to impart to the other, so that he can use them for his own account, his special knowledge and experience which remain unrevealed to the public. It is recognised that the grantor is not required to play any part himself in the application of the formulas granted to the licensee and that he does not guarantee the result thereof.

11.2   This type of contract thus differs from contracts for the provision of services, in which one of the parties undertakes to use the customary skills of his calling to execute work himself for the other party. *Payments made under the latter contracts generally fall under Article 7.*

11.3   The need to distinguish these two types of payments, i.e. payments for the supply of knowhow and payments for the provision of services, sometimes gives rise to practical difficulties. The following criteria are relevant for the purpose of making that distinction:
- *Contracts for the supply of know-how concern information that already exists or concern the supply of information after its development or creation and include provisions concerning the confidentiality of that information.*
- *In the case of contracts for the provision of services, the supplier undertakes to perform services which may require the use, by that supplier, of special knowledge, skill and expertise but not the transfer of such special knowledge, skill or expertise to the other party.*
- *In most cases involving the supply of know-how, there would generally be very little more which needs to be done by the supplier under the contract other than to supply existing information or reproduce existing material. On the other hand, a contract for the performance of services would, in the majority of cases, involve a very much greater level of expenditure by the supplier in order to perform his contractual obligations. For instance,*

the supplier, depending on the nature of the services to be rendered, may have to incur salaries and wages for employees engaged in researching, designing, testing, drawing and other associated activities or payments to subcontractors for the performance of similar services.

- *In the particular case of a contract involving the provision, by the supplier, of information concerning computer programming, as a general rule the payment will only be considered to be made in consideration for the provision of such information so as to constitute know-how where it is made to acquire information constituting ideas and principles underlying the program, such as logic, algorithms or programming languages or techniques, where this information is provided under the condition that the customer not disclose it without authorisation and where it is subject to any available trade secret protection.*

11.4 Examples of payments which should therefore not be considered to be received as consideration for the provision of know-how but, rather, for the provision of services, include:
- payments obtained as consideration for after-sales service,
- payments for services rendered by a seller to the purchaser under a guarantee,
- payments for pure technical assistance,
- payments for an opinion given by an engineer, an advocate or an accountant, and
- *payments for advice provided electronically, for electronic communications with technicians or for accessing, through computer networks, a trouble-shooting database.*

11.5 In business practice, contracts are encountered which cover both know-how and the provision of technical assistance. One example, amongst others, of contracts of this kind is that of franchising, where the franchisor imparts his knowledge and experience to the franchisee and, in addition, provides him with varied technical assistance, which, in certain cases, is backed up with financial assistance and the supply of goods. The appropriate course to take with a mixed contract is, in principle, to break down, on the basis of the information contained in the contract or by means of a reasonable apportionment, the whole amount of the stipulated consideration according to the various parts of what is being provided under the contract, and then to apply to each part of it so determined the taxation treatment proper thereto. If, however, one part of what is being provided constitutes by far the principal purpose of the contract and the other parts stipulated therein are only of an ancillary and largely unimportant character, then it seems possible to apply to the whole amount of the consideration the treatment applicable to the principal part." *[paragraph 49 below includes suggested changes to this last sentence]*

Business profits and payments for the use of, or the right to use, industrial, commercial or scientific equipment

Analysis and conclusions

24. As already mentioned, a number of bilateral conventions include a definition of royalties that covers "payments for the use of, or the right

to use, industrial, commercial or scientific equipment" even though these words are no longer found in the definition of the current OECD Model Tax Convention.[5]

a)   Digital products

25.   The Group examined a few transactions where the issue could arise whether the words "payments for the use of, or the right to use, industrial, commercial or scientific equipment" covered payments for time-limited use of a digital product (*e.g.* category 5 dealing with limited duration software and other digital information licenses).

26.   The members of the Group all agreed that payments for such use of digital products cannot be considered as payments "for the use of, or the right to use, industrial, commercial or scientific equipment" on the basis of one or more of the following reasons:

–   because digital products cannot be considered as "equipment", either because the word "equipment" can only apply to a tangible product (and the fact that the digital product is provided on a tangible medium would not change the fact that the object of the transaction is the acquisition of rights to use the digital content rather than rights to use the tangible medium) or because the word "equipment", in the context of the definition of royalties, applies to property that is intended to be an accessory in an industrial, commercial or scientific process and could not therefore apply to property, such as a music or video CD, that is used in and for itself;

–   because such products cannot be viewed as "industrial, commercial or scientific", at least when provided to the private consumer. Based on the nature of these products or the purpose of videos cannot be considered as "industrial, commercial or scientific"; or

–   because the payments involved in that type of transaction generally cannot be considered to be "for the use, or the right to use" the product since these words do not apply to a payment made to definitively acquire a property designed to have a short useful life, which is the case for most of these products, *e.g.* where someone acquires a video game CD that is programmed to become unusable after a certain period of time.

---

[5]   Paragraph 9 of the Commentary on Article 12 indicates that these words were deleted from the definition of royalties in order "to exclude income from ... leasing [of such equipment] from the definition of royalties and, consequently, to remove it from the application of Article 12 in order to make sure that it would fall under the rules for the taxation of business profits..."

b) Computer equipment

27.   The Group also examined a few transactions where it could be argued that tangible computer equipment (hardware) was being used by a customer so as to allow the relevant payment to be characterised as "payments for the use of, or the right to use, industrial, commercial or scientific equipment" (see categories 7, 8, 9, 11 and 13 in annex 2).

28.   The Group examined various factors used to distinguish rental from service contracts for purposes of section 7701(e) of the U.S. Internal Revenue Code and found these factors to be useful for purposes of determining whether payments are for "the use of, or the right to use, industrial, commercial or scientific equipment". Once adapted to the transactions examined by the Group, these factors, which indicate a lease rather than the provision of services, can be formulated as follows:

(a)   the customer is in physical possession of the property,

(b)   the customer controls the property,

(c)   the customer has a significant economic or possessory interest in the property,

(d)   the provider does not bear any risk of substantially diminished receipts or substantially increased expenditures if there is nonperformance under the contract,

(e)   the provider does not use the property concurrently to provide significant services to entities unrelated to the service recipient, and

(f)   the total payment does not substantially exceed the rental value of the computer equipment for the contract period.

29.   This is a non-exclusive list of factors, and some of these factors may not be relevant in particular cases. All relevant facts bearing on the substance of the transaction should be taken into account when determining whether the agreement is a service contract or a lease.

30.   Applying these factors to application service provider transactions, the Group concluded that these should generally give rise to services income as opposed to rental payments. In a typical transaction, the service provider uses the software to provide services to customers, maintains the software as needed, owns the equipment on which the software is loaded, provides access to many customers to the same equipment, and has the right to update and replace the software at will. The customer may not have possession or control over the software or the

equipment, will access the software concurrently with other customers, and may pay a fee based on the volume of transactions processed by the software.

31.   Likewise, data warehousing transactions should be treated as services transactions. The vendor uses computer equipment to provide data warehousing services to customers, owns and maintains the equipment on which the data is stored, provides access to many customers to the same equipment, and has the right to remove and replace equipment at will. The customer will not have possession or control over the equipment and will utilise the equipment concurrently with other customers.

Provision of services

Analysis and conclusions

32.   Whilst the OECD Model Tax Convention does not deal separately with payments for the provision of services, the distinction between these payments and payments made as consideration for the acquisition of property is relevant for certain bilateral conventions as well as for some domestic tax law purposes. The Group therefore considered it useful to discuss the distinction between the provision of services and transactions resulting in the acquisition of property, noting that the preceding subsection already dealt with the particular question of the distinction between a rental of property and the provision of services.

33.   The basic distinction between, on the one hand, a transaction resulting in the acquisition of property and, on the other hand, a transaction in services is whether the consideration for the payment is the acquisition of property from the provider. In this regard, a transaction resulting in the acquisition of property should be understood to include a transaction where a digital product (such as a copy of electronic data, a software program, digitised music or video images, and other forms of digital information and content), whether provided on a tangible medium or in the form of a digital signal, is acquired by a customer.

34.   Generally speaking, if the customer owns the relevant property after the transaction, but the property was not acquired from the provider, then the transaction should be treated as a services transaction. For example, if one party engages another party to create an item of property that the first party will own from the moment of its creation, then no property will have been acquired by the first party from the other and the transaction should be characterised as the provision of services.

35.   The Group recognised, however, that if one party acquires property from another party, the transaction should nonetheless be characterised as a services transaction to the extent that the predominant

nature of the transaction is the provision of services and the acquisition of property is merely ancillary. This would be the case, for example, where the relevant property itself has little intrinsic value and the provider creates value through the exercise of its particular talents and skills to create a unique result for the acquiror. Online consulting or other professional services is an example of an electronic commerce transaction that typically results in services income. In these transactions, the customer usually does not acquire any form of property from the other party. If the customer does acquire property, such as a report, it most likely will have been created specifically for him and arguably was owned by the customer from the moment of its creation. If, however, the customer acquires a valuable report or other property that was not created specifically for that customer, then the transaction could give rise to income from the sale of property. For example, the sale of the same investment report or other high-value proprietary information to many customers should be treated as a sale of property rather than a service. Even if the customer obtained the report electronically by downloading it from a database of reports maintained on the vendor's server, the essential consideration would still be to acquire data transmitted in the form of a digital signal for the own use or enjoyment of the acquiror rather than to obtain a service.

Technical fees

Analysis and conclusions

36.   The Group discussed how various e-commerce payments would be treated under alternative treaty provisions that allow source taxation of "technical fees".

37.   Whilst these provisions may be drafted differently, they often include the following definition:

> "The term 'technical fees' as used in this Article means payments of any kind to any person, other than to an employee of the person making the payments, in consideration for any service of a technical, managerial or consultancy nature."

38.   Alternative formulations of provisions dealing with technical fees typically limit the application of these provisions to some categories of services that could fall within the scope of the definition above.[6] For these reasons, the Group decided to restrict its analysis to that definition so as to try to clarify the limits of application of these provisions. In doing so, the Group examined separately the three different types of services referred to in the definition, *i.e.* technical services, managerial services and consultancy services.

---

[6]   See, for example, the provision of the India-United States tax convention dealing with "included services".

Technical services

39.   For the Group, services are of technical nature when special skills or knowledge related to a technical field are required for the provision of such services. Whilst techniques related to applied science or craftsmanship would generally correspond to such special skills or knowledge, the provision of knowledge acquired in fields such as arts or human sciences would not. As an illustration, whilst the provisions of engineering services would be of a technical nature, the services of a psychologist would not.

40.   The fact that technology is used in providing a service is not indicative of whether the service is of a technical nature. Similarly, the delivery of a service via technological means does not make the service technical. This is especially important in the e-commerce environment as the technology underlying the internet is often used to provide services that are not, themselves, technical (*e.g.* offering on-line gambling services through the internet).

41.   In that respect, it is crucial to determine at what point the special skill or knowledge is used. Special skill or knowledge may be used in developing or creating inputs to a service business. The fee for the provision of a service will not be a technical fee, however, unless that special skill or knowledge is required when the service is provided to the customer. For example, special skill or knowledge will be required to develop software and data used in a computer game that would subsequently be used in carrying on the business of allowing consumers to play this game on the internet for a fee. Similarly, special skill or knowledge is used to create a troubleshooting database that customers will pay to access over the Internet. In these examples, however, the relevant special skill or knowledge is not used when providing the service for which the fee is paid, *i.e.* allowing the consumer to play the computer game or consult the troubleshooting database.

42.   Many categories of e-commerce transactions similarly involve the provision of the use of, or access to, data and software (see, for example, categories 7, 8, 9, 11, 13, 15, 16, 20 and 21 in annex 2). The service of making such data and software, or functionality of that data or software, available for a fee is not, however, a service of a technical nature. The fact that the development of the necessary data and software might itself require substantial technical skills is irrelevant as the service provided to the client is not the development of that data and software (which may well be done by someone other than the supplier) but rather the service of making the data and software available to that client. For example, the mere provision of access to a troubleshooting database would not require more than having available such a database and the necessary software to access it. A payment relating to the provision of such access would not, therefore, relate to a service of a technical nature.

Managerial services

43.   The Group considers that services of a managerial nature are services rendered in performing management functions. The Group did not attempt to give a definition of management for that purpose but noted that this term should receive its normal business meaning. Thus, it would involve functions related to how a business is run as opposed to functions involved in carrying on that business. As an illustration, whilst the functions of hiring and training commercial agents would relate to management, the functions performed by these agents (*i.e.* selling) would not.

44.   The comments in paragraphs 40 to 42 above are also relevant for the purposes of distinguishing managerial services from the service of making data and software (even if related to management), or functionality of that data or software, available for a fee. The fact that this data and software could be used by the customer in performing management functions or that the development of the necessary data and software, and the management of the business of providing it to customers, might itself require substantial management expertise is irrelevant as the service provided to the client is neither managing the client's business, managing the supplier's business nor developing that data and software (which may well be done by someone other than the supplier) but rather making the software and data available to that client. The mere provision of access to such data and software does not require more than having available such a database and the necessary software. A payment relating to the provision of such access would not, therefore, relate to a service of a managerial nature.

Consultancy services

45.   For the Group, "consultancy services" refer to services constituting in the provision of advice by someone, such as a professional, who has special qualifications allowing him to do so. It was recognised that this type of services overlapped the categories of technical and managerial services to the extent that the latter types of services could well be provided by a consultant.

Mixed payments

Analysis and conclusions

46.   The Group identified a number of e-commerce transactions where the consideration of the payment could be considered to cover various elements (*e.g.* the software maintenance transactions described in category 12). It noted the principles for dealing with mixed contracts which are set out in paragraph 11 of the Commentary on Article 12.

47.   It also noted, however, that the last sentence of the paragraph provides that "it seems possible to apply to the whole amount of the consideration the treatment applicable to the principal part" where "the other parts [...] are only of an ancillary and largely unimportant character". The Group considers that it would be more practical, as well as more consistent with the conclusions put forward in the recently approved changes to the Commentary on Article 12, to provide that, in such circumstances, the treatment applicable to the principal part should generally be applied to the whole consideration.

48.   Some members of the Group took the view that, in most e-commerce transactions, the treaty classification applicable to the predominant element of the payment involved should be applied to the whole of that payment. These members noted that where as a commercial matter the transaction is regarded as a single transaction, an obligation to break down the payments involved in these transactions would impose an unreasonable compliance burden on taxpayers, especially for consumer transactions that involve relatively small amounts of money. Whilst the Group invited comments on that issue, no such comments were received. The conclusion was therefore that only the change suggested in the preceding paragraph should be recommended by the Group.

Suggested changes to the Commentary.

49.   Based on the following, the Group suggests that the following changes be made to the Commentary on Article 12 of the OECD Model Tax Convention:

> *Replace the last sentence of paragraph 11 of the Commentary on Article 12 by the following (changes to the existing text appear in strike-through and bold italics):*
>
> "If, however, one part of what is being provided constitutes by far the principal purpose of the contract and the other parts stipulated therein are only of an ancillary and largely unimportant character, **then the treatment applicable to the principal part should generally be applied to the whole amount of the consideration.** then it seems possible to apply to the whole amount of the consideration the treatment applicable to the principal part."

ANNEX 1
SUGGESTIONS FOR CHANGES TO THE COMMENTARY TO THE OECD MODEL TAX CONVENTION

*[Changes to the existing text of the Commentary appear in **bold italics** for additions and for deletions]*

1.   Replace paragraph 11 of the Commentary on Article 12 by the following paragraphs 11 to 11.5:

> *Replace the last sentence of paragraph 11 of the Commentary on Article 12 by the following (changes to the existing text appear in strike-through and bold italics):*

> "11.   In classifying as royalties payments received as consideration for information concerning industrial, commercial or scientific experience, paragraph 2 alludes to the concept of "know-how". Various specialist bodies and authors have formulated definitions of know-how which do not differ intrinsically. One such definition, given by the *"Association des Bureaux pour la Protection de la Propriété Industrielle"* (ANBPPI), states that 'know-how is all the undivulged technical information, whether capable of being patented or not, that is necessary for the industrial reproduction of a product or process, directly and under the same conditions; inasmuch as it is derived from experience, know-how represents what a manufacturer cannot know from mere examination of the product and mere knowledge of the progress of technique.

> *11.1*   In the know-how contract, one of the parties agrees to impart to the other, so that he can use them for his own account, his special knowledge and experience which remain unrevealed to the public. It is recognised that the grantor is not required to play any part himself in the application of the formulas granted to the licensee and that he does not guarantee the result thereof.

> *11.2*   This type of contract thus differs from contracts for the provision of services, in which one of the parties undertakes to use the customary skills of his calling to execute work himself for the other party. *Payments made under the latter contracts generally fall under Article 7.*

> *11.3   The need to distinguish these two types of payments, i.e. payments for the supply of know-how and payments for the provision of services, sometimes gives rise to practical difficulties. The following criteria are relevant for the purpose of making that distinction:*
> – *Contracts for the supply of know-how concern information that already exists or concern the supply of information after its development or creation and include provisions concerning the confidentiality of that information.*
> – *In the case of contracts for the provision of services, the supplier undertakes to perform services which may require the use, by that*

> *supplier, of special knowledge, skill and expertise but not the transfer of*
> *such special knowledge, skill or expertise to the other party.*
> – *In most cases involving the supply of know-how, there would generally be*
> *very little more which needs to be done by the supplier under the contract*
> *other than to supply existing information or reproduce existing material.*
> *On the other hand, a contract for the performance of services would, in*
> *the majority of cases, involve a very much greater level of expenditure by*
> *the supplier in order to perform his contractual obligations. For instance,*
> *the supplier, depending on the nature of the services to be rendered, may*
> *have to incur salaries and wages for employees engaged in researching,*
> *designing, testing, drawing and other associated activities or payments to*
> *subcontractors for the performance of similar services.*
> – *In the particular case of a contract involving the provision, by the*
> *supplier, of information concerning computer programming, as a general*
> *rule the payment will only be considered to be made in consideration for*
> *the provision of such information so as to constitute know-how where it*
> *is made to acquire information constituting ideas and principles*
> *underlying the program, such as logic, algorithms or programming*
> *languages or techniques, where this information is provided under the*
> *condition that the customer not disclose it without authorisation and*
> *where it is subject to any available trade secret protection.*

11.4　　Examples of payments which should therefore not be considered to
be received as consideration for the provision of know-how but, rather, for the
provision of services, include:
– payments obtained as consideration for after-sales service,
– payments for services rendered by a seller to the purchaser under a
　guarantee,
– payments for pure technical assistance,
– payments for an opinion given by an engineer, an advocate or an
　accountant, and
– *payments for advice provided electronically, for electronic communica-*
　tions with technicians or for accessing, through computer networks, a
　trouble-shooting database.

11.5　　In business practice, contracts are encountered which cover both
know-how and the provision of technical assistance. One example, amongst
others, of contracts of this kind is that of franchising, where the franchisor
imparts his knowledge and experience to the franchisee and, in addition,
provides him with varied technical assistance, which, in certain cases, is
backed up with financial assistance and the supply of goods. The
appropriate course to take with a mixed contract is, in principle, to break
down, on the basis of the information contained in the contract or by means
of a reasonable apportionment, the whole amount of the stipulated
consideration according to the various parts of what is being provided under
the contract, and then to apply to each part of it so determined the taxation
treatment proper thereto. If, however, one part of what is being provided
constitutes by far the principal purpose of the contract and the other parts
stipulated therein are only of an ancillary and largely unimportant
character, *then the treatment applicable to the principal part should generally*

be applied to the whole amount of the consideration. then it seems possible to apply to the whole amount of the consideration the treatment applicable to the principal part. *"*

2.   Add the following paragraphs 17.1 to 17.4 immediately after paragraph 17 of the Commentary on Article 12:

"17.1   The principles expressed above as regards software payments are also applicable as regards transactions concerning other types of digital products such as images, sounds or text. The development of electronic commerce has multiplied the number of such transactions. In deciding whether or not payments arising in these transactions constitute royalties, the main question to be addressed is the identification of the consideration for the payment.

17.2   Under the relevant legislation of some countries, transactions which permit the customer to electronically download digital products may give rise to use of copyright by the customer, e.g. because a right to make one or more copies of the digital content is granted under the contract. Where the essential consideration is for something other than for the use of, or right to use, rights in the copyright (such as to acquire other types of contractual rights, data or services), and the use of copyright is limited to such rights as are required to enable downloading, storage and operation on the customer's computer, network or other storage, performance or display device, such use of copyright should be disregarded in the analysis of the character of the payment for purposes of applying the definition of "royalties".

17.3   This is the case for transactions that permit the customer (which may be an enterprise) to electronically download digital products (such as software, images, sounds or text) for that customer's own use or enjoyment. In these transactions, the payment is made to acquire data transmitted in the form of a digital signal for the acquiror's own use or enjoyment. This constitutes the essential consideration for the payment, which therefore does not constitute royalties but falls within Article 7 or Article 13, as the case may be. To the extent that the act of copying the digital signal onto the customer's hard disk or other non-temporary media constitutes the use of a copyright by the customer under the relevant law and contractual arrangements, this is merely an incidental part of the process of capturing and storing the digital signal. This incidental part is not important for classification purposes because it does not correspond to the essential consideration for the payment (i.e. to acquire data transmitted in the form of a digital signal), which is the determining factor for the purposes of the definition of royalties. There also would be no basis to classify such transactions as "royalties" if, under the relevant law and contractual arrangements, the creation of a copy is regarded as a use of copyright by the provider rather than by the customer.

17.4   By contrast, transactions where the essential consideration for the payment is the granting of the right to use a copyright in a digital product that is electronically downloaded for that purpose will give rise to royalties.. This would be the case, for example, of a book publisher who would pay to acquire the right to reproduce a copyrighted picture that it would electronically download for the purposes of including it on the cover of a book that it is

VII **Appendices**

producing. In this transaction, the essential consideration for the payment is the acquisition of rights to use the copyright in the digital product, i.e. the right to reproduce and distribute the picture, and not merely for the acquisition of the digital content."

ANNEX 2
ANALYSIS OF VARIOUS CATEGORIES OF TYPICAL E-COMMERCE TRANSACTIONS

1.   This annex is an updated version of the draft released by the TAG on 24 March 2000 and first revised on 1 September 2000. This last version reflects the conclusions reached by the Group on the various characterisation issues identified in section 2 of the report.

Category 1:   Electronic order processing of tangible products

Definition

> The customer selects an item from an online catalogue of tangible goods and orders the item electronically directly from a commercial provider. There is no separate charge to the customer for using the online catalogue. The product is physically delivered to the customer by a common carrier.

Analysis and conclusions

2.   Whilst the Group considers that category of transaction as a useful starting point, it does not see it as raising any treaty characterisation issue. In this type of transaction, the payment made by the customer constitutes consideration that clearly falls within Article 7 (Business Profits) rather than Article 12 (Royalties), because it does not involve a use of copyright.

Category 2:   Electronic ordering and downloading of digital products

Definition

> The customer selects an item from an online catalogue of software or other digital products and orders the product electronically directly from a commercial provider. There is no separate charge to the customer for using the online catalogue. The digital product is downloaded onto the customer's hard disk or other non-temporary media.

Analysis and conclusions

3.   The Group found that this category of transaction raised the fundamental characterisation issue discussed in paragraphs 13 to 15 of

section 3 above, *i.e.* the distinction between business profits and the part of the treaty definition of "royalties" dealing with payments for the use of, or the right to use, a copyright. It concluded that in the case of transactions that permit the customer to electronically download digitised products (such as software, images, sounds or text) for the customer's own use or enjoyment, the payment is made to acquire data transmitted in the form of a digital signal. Since this constitutes the essential consideration for the payment, that payment cannot be considered as royalties as a payment made for the use or the right to use a copyright so as to constitute a royalty. To the extent that the act of copying the digital signal onto the customer's hard disk or other non-temporary media (including transfers to other storage, performance or display devices) constitutes the use of a copyright under the relevant law and contractual arrangements, this is merely an incidental part of the process of capturing and storing the digital signal. This incidental part is not important for classification purposes because it does not correspond to the essential consideration for the payment (*i.e.* to acquire data transmitted in the form of a digital signal), which is the determining factor for the purposes of the treaty definition of royalties.

Category 3:   Electronic ordering and downloading of digital products for purposes of commercial exploitation of the copyright

Definition

> *The customer selects an item from an online catalogue of software or other digital products and orders the product electronically directly from a commercial provider. There is no separate charge to the customer for using the online catalogue. The digital product is downloaded into the customer's hard disk or other non-temporary media. The customer acquires the right to commercially exploit the copyright in the digital product (e.g. a book publisher acquires a copyrighted picture to be included on the cover of a book that it is producing).*

Analysis and conclusions

4.   The Group considered it useful to refer to this category of transaction in order to illustrate a case where all its members agree that the payment qualifies as a royalty. Indeed, in that case, the payment is made as consideration for the right to use the copyright in the digital product. In the example given, that use takes the form of the reproduction and sale, for commercial purpose, of the copyrighted picture.

VII Appendices

Category 4: Updates and add-ons

Definition

> The provider of software or other digital product agrees to provide the customer with updates and add-ons to the digital product. There is no agreement to produce updates or add-ons specifically for a given customer.

Analysis and conclusions

5. The Group agrees that this category of transaction should be treated

- like the transactions described in category 1 above if the updates and adds-on are delivered on a tangible medium;

- like the transactions described in category 2 above if the updates and adds-on are delivered electronically.

6. Since both categories 1 and 2 would give rise to payments falling under Article 7, payments made by the customer in this category of transaction should therefore be treated similarly.

Category 5: Limited duration software and other digital information licenses

Definition

> The customer receives the right to use software or other digital products for a period of time that is less than the useful life of the product. The product is either downloaded electronically or delivered on a tangible medium such as a CD. All copies of the digital product are deleted or become unusable upon termination of the license.

Analysis and conclusions

7. The Group unanimously concluded that, under the OECD Model as currently worded, that transaction should be treated exactly as transactions falling under categories 1 or 2 so that the payment to the commercial provider of the limited duration digital product would fall under Article 7 (Business Profits).

8. Also, if a particular convention includes a definition of royalties that covers "payments for the use of, or the right to use, industrial, commercial or scientific equipment", the Group concluded that such payments cannot be considered as payments "for the use of, or the right to use, industrial, commercial or scientific equipment" for the reasons set out in paragraphs 25 and 26 of section 3 above.

Category 6: Single-use software or other digital product

Definition

> *The customer receives the right to use software or other digital products one time. The product may be either downloaded or used remotely (e.g. use of software stored on a remote server). The customer does not receive the right to make copies of the digital product other than as required to use the digital product for its intended use.*

Analysis and conclusions

9. Whilst some members view this type of transaction as contracts for services and others view them as being similar to the transactions referred to in categories 2 and 5, the Group unanimously agreed that payments made in these transactions fall under Article 7 as business profits.

Category 7: Application Hosting – Separate License

Definition

> *A user has a perpetual license to use a software product. The user enters into a contract with a host entity whereby the host entity loads the software copy on servers owned and operated by the host. The host provides technical support to protect against failures of the system. The user can access, execute and operate the software application remotely. The application is executed either at a customer's computer after it is downloaded into RAM or remotely on the host's server. This type of arrangement could apply, for example, for financial management, inventory control, human resource management or other enterprise resource management software applications.*

Analysis and conclusions

10. The Group agrees that, under the current wording of the OECD Model, this type of transaction gives rise to business profits falling under Article 7.

11. Where, however, a particular convention includes a definition of royalties that covers "payments for the use of, or the right to use, industrial, commercial or scientific equipment", the issue arises whether these words can be applied to all or part of the payments arising from these transactions.

12. As discussed in paragraphs 27 to 31 of section 3 above, the Group concluded that these transactions should generally give rise to services income as opposed to rental payments. In a typical transaction, the vendor uses computer equipment to provide data warehousing services to

customers, owns and maintains the equipment on which the data is stored, provides access to many customers to the same equipment, and has the right to remove and replace equipment at will. The customer will not have possession or control over the equipment and will utilise the equipment concurrently with other customers.

13.   The Group also discussed whether payments arising in this type of transaction could be treated as payments for services of a "technical nature" under alternative treaty provisions that allow source taxation of "technical fees". To the extent that main service being provided is merely that of storing the data and software of customers, this service is akin to mere warehousing and the performance of that function does not require the direct exercise of any special technical skill or knowledge.

Category 8:   Application Hosting – Bundled Contract

Definition

> *For a single, bundled fee, the user enters into a contract whereby the provider, who is also the copyright owner, allows access to one or more software applications, hosts the software applications on a server owned and operated by the host, and provides technical support for the hardware and software. The user can access, execute and operate the software application remotely. The application is executed either at a customer's computer after it is downloaded into RAM or remotely on the host's server. The contract is renewable annually for an additional fee.*

Analysis and conclusions

14.   The Group agrees that, under the current wording of the OECD Model, there would be no need to separate the payment described in this example as all of it would constitute business profits falling under Article 7.

15.   Pursuant to the existing paragraph 11 of the Commentary on Article 12, however, the need to separate the payment into various components could arise when applying bilateral conventions that include the alternative provisions referred to in the previous category (see paragraphs 46 to 49 of section 3 above). This would be the case to the extent that part of the payment relates to the provision of technical support for the software that would constitute services of a technical nature. In that case, that part would be treated differently from the parts relating to allowing access to one or more software applications and hosting such software applications as such functions do not require the application of special skills or knowledge (they essentially require owning the relevant equipment and software rights that are made available).

Category 9: Application Service Provider ("ASP")

Definition

> *The provider obtains a license to use a software application in the provider's business of being an application service provider. The provider makes available to the customer access to a software application hosted on computer servers owned and operated by the provider. The software automates a particular back-office business function for the customer. For example, the software might automate sourcing, ordering, payment, and delivery of goods or services used in the customer's business, such as office supplies or travel arrangements. The provider does not provide the goods or services. It merely provides the customer with the means to automate and manage its interaction with third-party providers of these goods and services. The customer has no right to copy the software or to use the software other than on the provider's server, and does not have possession or control of a software copy.*

Analysis and conclusions

16.   As regards the payment made by the customer, the Group agrees that the issues arising are similar to those discussed under the preceding category.

Category 10: ASP License Fees

Definition

> *In the example above, the ASP pays the provider of the software application a fee which is a percentage of the revenue collected from customers. The contract is for a one year term.*

Analysis and conclusions

17.   The Group agrees that this type of transaction, being essentially for the provision of a software product to be used in the business of the transferee, falls within Article 7. The Group acknowledged that the fact that the ASP's customer will have access to the software copy hosted on servers owned and operated by the provider may technically involve the ASP displaying to the customers some copyrighted information (*e.g.* forms for data input). The Group agreed, however, that if providing such access constituted the use of a copyright right by the ASP (for example a display or other right), such use of copyright would be such a minimal part of the consideration for the payment made by the ASP to the software provider that it should not be relevant for the treaty characterisation of that payment.

Category 11:   Web site hosting

Definition

The provider offers space on its server to host web sites. The provider obtains no rights in the copyrights created by the developer of the web site content. The owner of the copyrighted material on the site may remotely manipulate the site, including modifying the content on the site. The provider is compensated by a fee based on the passage of time.

Analysis and conclusions

18.   The Group agrees that, under the current wording of the OECD Model, this type of transaction gives rise to business profits falling under Article 7. The Group also notes that where a particular convention includes a definition of royalties that covers "payments for the use of, or the right to use, industrial, commercial or scientific equipment" or alternative treaty provisions that allow source taxation of "technical fees", this type of transaction would not give rise to these two types of income under the circumstances and for the reasons presented under category 7, which deals with application hosting.

Category 12:   Software maintenance

Definition

Software maintenance contracts typically bundle software updates together with technical support. A single annual fee is charged for both updates and technical support. In most cases, the principal object of the contract is the software updates.

Analysis and conclusions

19.   The Group concluded that the remarks expressed in paragraphs 46 to 48 of section 3 above as regards mixed contracts, which refer to the principles set out in paragraph 11 of the Commentary on Article 12, apply to such transactions. Where, under those principles, part of the payment is regarded to be for the provision of technical support, the issues described in category 14 below as regards alternative treaty provisions that allow source taxation of "technical fees" will arise.

Category 13:   Data warehousing

Definition

The customer stores its computer data on computer servers owned and operated by the provider. The customer can access, upload, retrieve and manipulate data remotely. No software is licensed to the customer under this transaction. An example would be a retailer who stores its inventory records on the provider's hardware and persons on the customer's order desk remotely access this information to allow them to determine whether orders could be filled from current stock.

Analysis and conclusions

20.   The Group agrees that, under the current wording of the OECD Model, this type of transaction gives rise to business profits falling under Article 7. The Group also notes that where a particular convention includes a definition of royalties that covers "payments for the use of, or the right to use, industrial, commercial or scientific equipment" or alternative treaty provisions that allow source taxation of "technical fees", this type of transaction would not give rise to these two types of income under the circumstances and for the reasons presented under category 7, which deals with application hosting.

Category 14:   Customer support over a computer network

Definition

The provider provides the customer with online technical support, including installation advice and trouble-shooting information. This support can take the form of online technical documentation, a trouble-shooting database, and communications (e.g. by e-mail) with human technicians.

Analysis and conclusions

21.   The Group agreed that, based on this description and under the wording of the OECD Model Convention, the payment arising in this type of transaction would fall within Article 7. In reaching its conclusion, the Group discussed the extent to which the payment could be considered as a payment for "information concerning industrial, commercial or scientific experience" (know-how) so as to constitute royalties.

22.   Based on paragraphs 17 to 23 of section 3 above and, in particular, the factors listed in paragraphs 18 and 19, the Group agrees that online advice, communications with technicians and using the trouble-shooting database, would clearly involve actual services being performed on demand rather than the provision of know-how.

23.   Whilst the provision of technical documentation could, depending on the circumstances, constitute the provision of know-how, this would require that the information be "undivulged technical information" as described in paragraph 11 of the Commentary on Article 12. Also, as mentioned in the same paragraph, know-how "is necessary for the industrial reproduction of a product or process". To the extent that know-how must be technical information relating to industrial

reproduction of a product or process, the Group considers that information that merely relates to the operation or use of products as opposed to their development or production would not fall under the definition of know-how.

24.   The Group notes that the remarks in paragraphs 46 to 48 of section 3 above, which deal with mixed contracts, would be relevant if the contract were considered to cover the provision of both services and know-how.

25.   The Group finally discussed how the payment arising in this type of transaction would be treated under alternative treaty provisions that allow source taxation of "technical fees".

26.   Whilst the provision of online advice through communications with technicians may require the application of special skill and knowledge and might therefore constitute services of a technical nature, the mere provision of access to a troubleshooting database would not require more than having available such a database and the necessary software to access it. The part of the payment relating to the provision of such access would not, therefore, relate to a service of a technical nature.

Category 15:   Data retrieval

Definition

> *The provider makes a repository of information available for customers to search and retrieve. The principal value to customers is the ability to search and extract a specific item of data from amongst a vast collection of widely available data.*

Analysis and conclusions

27.   All members of the Group consider that the payment arising from this type of transaction would fall under Article 7. Some of them reach that conclusion because, given that the principal value of such a database would be the ability to search and extract the documents, these members view the contract as a contract for services. Others consider that, in this transaction, the customer pays in order to ultimately obtain the data that he will search for. They therefore view the transaction as being similar to those described in category 2 and will accordingly treat the payment as business profits.

28.   The Group also addressed the issue of whether these could be considered as services "of a technical nature" under the alternative provisions on technical fees previously referred to. The Group agreed that providing a client with the use of search and retrieval software and with access to a database does not involve the exercise of special skill or

knowledge when the software and database is delivered to the client. The fact that the development of the necessary software and database would itself require substantial technical skills was found to be irrelevant as the service provided to the client was not the development of the software and database (which may well be done by someone other than the supplier) but rather making the completed software and database available to that client.

Category 16: Delivery of exclusive or other high-value data

Definition

> *As in the previous example, the provider makes a repository of information available to customers. In this case, however, the data is of greater value to the customer than the means of finding and retrieving it. The provider adds significant value in terms of content (e.g. by adding analysis of raw data) but the resulting product is not prepared for a specific customer and no obligation to keep its contents confidential is imposed on customers. Examples of such products might include special industry or investment reports. Such reports are either sent electronically to subscribers or are made available for purchase and download from an online catalogue or index.*

Analysis and conclusions

29.   The Group agrees that these transactions involve the same characterisation issues as those described in the previous category. It therefore believes that the payment arising from this type of transaction would fall under Article 7 and is not a technical fee for the same reason.

Category 17: Advertising

Definition

> *Advertisers pay to have their advertisements disseminated to users of a given web site. So-called "banner ads" are small graphic images embedded in a web page, which when clicked by the user will load the web page specified by the advertiser. Advertising rates are most commonly specified in terms of a cost per thousand "impressions" (number of times the ad is displayed to a user), though rates might also be based on the number of "click-throughs" (number of times the ad is clicked by a user).*

Analysis and conclusions

30.   All members of the Group agreed that the payments arising from these transactions would constitute business profits falling under Article 7 rather than royalties, even under alternative definitions of royalties that cover payments "for the use, or the right to use, industrial, commercial or scientific equipment".

VII Appendices

Category 18:   Electronic access to professional advice (*e.g.* consultancy)

Definition

> *A consultant, lawyer, doctor or other professional service provider advises customers through email, video conferencing, or other remote means of communication.*

Analysis and conclusions

31.   Again, all members of the Group agreed that the payments arising from these transactions would constitute business profits falling under Article 7 rather than royalties. As already stated, the provision of on-demand advice is a service and not the supply of know-how.

32.   As these transactions involve the provision of technical, managerial or consultancy services, the Group also addressed the issue of whether these could be considered as services "of a technical nature" under the alternative provisions on technical fees that have been previously referred to. The Group concluded that to the extent that the services were rendered by someone acting as a consultant, they would constitute services of a consultancy nature so as to fall within the definition quoted in paragraph 37 of section 3.

Category 19:   Technical information

Definition

> *The customer is provided with undivulged technical information concerning a product or process (e.g. narrative description and diagrams of a secret manufacturing process).*

Analysis and conclusions

33.   The Group agrees that payments arising from this category of transactions constitute royalties as they are made for the supply of know-how, *i.e.* "for information concerning industrial, commercial or scientific experience."

Category 20:   Information delivery

Definition

> *The provider electronically delivers data to subscribers periodically in accordance with their personal preferences. The principal value to customers is*

the convenience of receiving widely available information in a custom-packaged format tailored to their specific needs.

Analysis and conclusions

34.   The Group agrees that this type of transaction raises basically the same issues as those described under category 15 above. The members of the Group therefore consider that the payments arising from these transactions constitute business profits falling under Article 7 and are not technical fees for the same reason.

Category 21:   Access to an interactive web site

Definition

> *The provider makes available to subscribers a web site featuring digital content, including information, music, video, games, and activities (whether or not developed or owned by the provider). Subscribers pay a fixed periodic fee for access to the site. The principal value of the site to subscribers is interacting with the site while online as opposed to getting a product or services from the site.*

Analysis and conclusions

35.   The Group agrees that the subscription fee paid in this type of transactions would constitute a payment for services. As that payment is mainly for the interaction with the site for purposes of the personal enjoyment of the user and not for the provision of any service of a technical, managerial or consultancy nature, it would not, under the previously quoted definition of "technical fees", fall under the alternative provisions covering these types of payments. The Group also agreed any payment to the owner of the copyright in the digital content that would be made by the provider for the right to display that content to its subscribers would constitute royalties.

Category 22:   Online shopping portals

Definition

> *A web site operator hosts electronic catalogues of multiple merchants on its computer servers. Users of the web site can select products from these catalogues and place orders online. The web site operator has no contractual relationship with shoppers. It merely transmits orders to the merchants, who are responsible for accepting and fulfilling orders. The merchants pay the web site operator a commission equal to a percentage of the orders placed through the site.*

VII Appendices

Analysis and conclusions

36.   The Group agrees that these payments are revenues from advertising or similar services that constitute business profits falling under Article 7.

Category 23:   Online auctions

Definition

> *The provider displays many items for purchase by auction. The user purchases the items directly from the owner of the items, rather than from the enterprise operating the site. The vendor compensates the provider with a percentage of the sales price or a flat fee.*

Analysis and conclusions

37.   The Group agrees that these payments are revenues similar to those of an auction house and constitute business profits falling under Article 7.

Category 24:   Sales referral programs

Definition

> *An online provider pays a sales commission to the operator of a web site that refers sales leads to the provider. The web site operator will list one or more of the provider's products on the operator's web site. If a user clicks on one of these products, the user will retrieve a web page from the provider's site from which the product can be purchased. When the link on the operator's web page is used, the provider can identify the source of the sales lead and will pay the operator a percentage commission if the user buys the product.*

Analysis and conclusions

38.   The Group agrees that these payments constitute business profits falling under Article 7.

Category 25:   Content acquisition transactions

Definition

> *A web site operator pays various content providers for news stories, information, and other online content in order to attract users to the site. Alternatively, the web site operator might hire a content provider to create new content specifically for the web site.*

Analysis and conclusions

39.   The Group agrees that the two alternatives described above need to be distinguished. Where the site operator pays a content provider for the right to display copyrighted material, the payment would fall under the definition of royalties to the extent that the public display of the content constitutes a right covered by the copyright of the owner of the content. Where, however, the operator pays for the creation of new content and, as a result of the relevant contractual arrangements, becomes the owner of the copyright in the content so created, the payment cannot be for royalties and falls under Article 7.

Category 26:   Streamed (real time) web based broadcasting

Definition

> *The user accesses a content database of copyrighted audio and/or visual material. The broadcaster receives subscription or advertising revenues.*

Analysis and conclusions

40.   The Group agrees that the subscription or advertising fees that would be received in these transactions would constitute business profits falling under Article 7.

Category 27:   Carriage fees

Definition

> *A content provider pays a particular web site or network operator in order to have its content displayed by the web site or network operator.*

Analysis and conclusions

41.   The Group agrees that in that type of transactions, the web site or network operator is providing a commercial service for a fee and its income should be characterised as business profits under Article 7. In these transactions, unlike in those described in category 25, it is the owner of the copyrighted material who makes the payment, which makes it clear that Article 12 is not applicable.

VII Appendices

Category 28:   Subscription to a web site allowing the downloading of digital products

Definition

> *The provider makes available to subscribers a web site featuring copyrighted digital content (e.g. music). Subscribers pay a fixed periodic fee for access to the site. Unlike category 21, the principal value of the site to subscribers is the possibility to download these digital products.*

Analysis and conclusions

42.   The Group agrees that the subscription fee paid in this type of transaction would fall under Article 7. As explained in paragraph 3 above, transactions that permit the customer to electronically download digitised products (*i.e.* music in this case) for the customer's own use or enjoyment do not give rise to royalties. The Group also agreed that this category of transaction is closer to category 2 than to category 21 since the essential consideration for the payment is not the temporary interaction with the site but, rather, the acquisition of the music data transmitted in the form of a digital signal.

ANNEX 3
MANDATE AND COMPOSITION OF THE TAG

[The following is the mandate that the TAG received by the Committee on Fiscal Affairs]

General mandate

The general mandate for the TAG on Treaty Characterisation of Electronic Commerce Payments is as follows:

> "To examine the characterisation of various types of electronic commerce payments under tax conventions with a view to providing the necessary clarifications in the Commentary."

Specific mandate

The work of the TAG on Treaty Characterisation of Electronic Commerce Payments will involve primarily, but not exclusively, a consideration of the application of the definition of royalties in the context of electronic commerce.

It has already been decided to seek comments from interested parties on how the principles that underlie the proposed changes to the Commentary on software payments may be relevant in considering how that definition applies in the case of electronic commerce transactions involving digitised contents. The first responsibility of the TAG will therefore be to examine these comments and to make appropriate suggestions.

In the course of its work, the TAG will be invited to examine and provide comments on the distinction that can be drawn between various types of payments in determining whether a particular electronic commerce payment, *e.g.* a payment made for electronically searching a computer database and downloading a document from it, is made for the sale or lease of property, for the provision of a service or as a royalty. In particular:

a) the TAG is invited to identify different types of electronic commerce transactions and the particular characteristics of such transactions which might enable distinctions to be drawn between payments for services and income from sales or leasing of property;

b) the TAG is invited to identify characteristics of electronic commerce transactions which might enable distinctions to be drawn between business profits and royalties and, in particular, the circumstances, if any, in which electronic commerce payments may be considered to be payments for use of copyright or use of know-how;

c) the TAG is invited to comment on whether there are reasons for preferring one characterisation to another;

d) the TAG is invited to identify the circumstances in which electronic commerce transactions can be considered to give rise to payments for industrial, commercial or scientific equipment.

Composition of the TAG

The following persons have participated in the activities of the TAG and have attended one or more of its meetings: It should be noted that this report reflects the personal views of the TAG participants at the time it was prepared. These views should not, therefore, be attributed to any government, business or organisation for which these participants work.

AUSTRALIA

Ms. Ariane Pickering *(Co-Chair of the TAG)*
Australian Taxation Office

Ms. HK Holdaway
Australian Taxation Office

CHILE

Ms. Liselott Kana *(Co-Chair of the TAG)*
Ministry of Finance

CHINA

VII Appendices

Mr. Wang Yukang
Ministry of Finance

GERMANY

Mr. Helmut Krabbe
Federal Ministry of Finance

Mr. Martin Kreienbaum
Federal Ministry of Finance

INDIA

Mr. Vijay Mathur
Ministry of Finance

ISRAEL

Mr. Yehoshua Sherman
Israel Income Tax and Property
Tax Commission
*(Mr. Sherman left the Israel
Income Tax and Property Tax
Commission before the report was
completed)*

Ms. Frida Israeli
Israel Income Tax and Property
Tax Commission

Mr. Yuval Cohen
Israel Income Tax and Property
Tax Commission

JAPAN

Mr. Hiroyuki Iguchi
Ministry of Finance

Mr. Isao Watanabe
Ministry of Finance

Mr. Akihiko Yoshida
Ministry of Finance

Mr. Katsumi Shinagawa
Ministry of Finance

NORWAY

Mr. Gjert Melsom
Ministry of Finance

UNITED KINGDOM

Mr. Mike Waters
Inland Revenue

UNITED STATES

Mr. Michael Mundaca
Department of Treasury

BUSINESS

Mr. Gary Sprague *(Co-Chair of
the TAG)*
Baker & McKenzie
United States

Mr. Frank Steimel
SIEMENS
Germany

Mr. Yasushi Ogasawara
NTT Data
Japan

Mr. M. Onodera
NTT Data
Japan

Mr. David Fuller
REED ELSEVIER plc
United Kingdom

Mr. Charles Fontaine
REED ELSEVIER Inc.
United States

Ms. Anne Buettner	Mr. Mark Williams
WALT DISNEY Co.	WALT DISNEY Co.
United States	United States

Ms. Carol Felepchuk
IBM Canada Ltd.
Canada

Mr. Mark E. Nebergall
SOFTEC
United States

While representatives of the Government of Israel participated in the work of the Group, these representatives wish to indicate that they do not necessarily support some of the conclusions reached by the Group, especially as regards the meaning of the words "payments for the use, or the right to use, industrial, commercial or scientific equipment".

APPENDIX E

ATTRIBUTION OF PROFIT TO A PERMANENT ESTABLISHMENT INVOLVED IN ELECTRONIC COMMERCE TRANSACTIONS (OECD)

A DISCUSSION PAPER FROM THE TECHNICAL ADVISORY GROUP ON MONITORING THE APPLICATION OF EXISTING TREATY NORMS FOR THE TAXATION OF BUSINESS PROFITS

February 2001

DRAFT FOR PUBLIC COMMENT

Deadline: 30 June 2001

Foreword

1.   To date, much attention has been focused on the question of in what circumstances do electronic commerce activities, especially the operation of a server in a particular jurisdiction, lead to the recognition of the existence of permanent establishment in that jurisdiction (the threshold question) under Article 5 of the OECD Model Tax Convention. Indeed, the Committee on Fiscal Affairs has recently published a Report adding to the existing Model Commentary on Article 5 to clarify the application of the provisions of the Article in respect of web sites and servers. The clarification will be incorporated in the next update of the Model Tax Convention.

2.   Now that the threshold question has been settled, at least in respect of the application of the existing rules, attention turns naturally to what profits can be attributed to e-commerce activities that have passed the threshold of Article 5 so that a permanent establishment is held to exist. The allocation of the taxing rights between the jurisdiction of the enterprise and the jurisdiction of the permanent establishment are determined under Article 7 of the OECD Model Tax Convention. This discussion paper is a first attempt at exploring the interpretation and application of Article 7 to a PE carrying on retail e-commerce activities ("e-tailing").

3.   The discussion paper has been produced by the Technical Advisory Group on Monitoring the Application of Existing Treaty Norms for the Taxation of Business Profits ("Business Profits TAG"). This group was set up to assist in implementing the Ottawa Framework Conditions with a mandate to examine how the current tax treaty rules for the taxation of business profits apply in the context of electronic commerce and to consider proposals for alternative rules. This paper is a discussion draft only and does not represent a consensus view of the government or business members of the Business Profits TAG. However, the intention of releasing the discussion paper is to stimulate debate on how to attribute profit to a permanent establishment in an e-commerce context. This should assist in the ultimate development of an internationally agreed consensus on the interpretation and application of Article 7 amongst business, OECD Member and non-member Governments.

4.   Accordingly, ***comments on this discussion paper are invited, and indeed, positively encouraged by 30 June 2001***. Areas where comments would be particularly welcome are referred to directly in the text. Comments can be posted on the public EDG (http://appli1.oecd.org/daf/ taxandel.nsf (to register for the EDG, if you are not already a member, please see: http://www.oecd.org/daf) or e-mailed to Jeffrey Owens, Head of Fiscal Affairs (daffa.contact@oecd.org) and copied to John Neighbour, Head of Transfer Pricing and Financial Transactions Unit (john.neighbour@oecd.org).

Executive summary

5.   This discussion paper from the Technical Advisory Group on Monitoring the Application of Existing Treaty Norms for the Taxation of Business Profits ("Business Profits TAG") provides a detailed analysis of the transfer pricing issues arising in attributing profit to a permanent establishment involved in electronic commerce activities, in the context of an enterprise engaged in the retail distribution of entertainment products ("e-tailing"). The paper provides an overview of the current treaty rules for attributing profit to a permanent establishment under Article 7 of the OECD Model Tax Convention. It also refers to the on-going work of the Committee on Fiscal Affairs in this area, which is attempting to develop a common interpretation of Article 7 that is in accordance with the articulation of the arm's length principle found in the Transfer Pricing Guidelines, and foreshadows some of issues raised in the context of this review in the *Discussion Draft on the Attribution of Profits to Permanent Establishments*[1], a discussion paper issued on 8 February 2001 by the Committee on Fiscal Affairs (CFA). That document looks at issues relating to the attribution of profits to permanent establishments in

---

[1]   See http://www.oecd.org/daf for a link to the *Discussion Draft on the Attribution of Profits to Permanent Establishments*, posted 8 February 2001.

general and is not confined to permanent establishments in the e-commerce sector ("CFA general discussion draft").

6.   This paper illustrates the various steps of the analysis that are required to attribute profit to a permanent establishment, in the context of a specific example of an enterprise distributing products over the internet through a web site hosted on a server situated in a permanent establishment in another country. Four different variations of the example are developed and analysed. The first variation is the extreme case of a stand-alone computer server performing automated functions (in particular, online processing of transactions and transmission of digitised products) without the presence of personnel in the permanent establishment. The second variation examines the case of multiple servers performing identical tasks. The third variation assumes the presence of personnel in the permanent establishment to provide online services and maintain the server. The last variation assumes that the development of the hardware and software used by the permanent establishment was entirely performed in the permanent establishment.

7.   The paper provides an analysis of the likely outcome of the application of the arm's length principle to the four examples and identifies some issues arising under the current interpretation of Article 7 that may prevent, in certain circumstances, a profit attribution to the permanent establishment that is fully consistent with the arm's length principle. These issues are developed more fully in the CFA general discussion draft.

8.   In summary, it is found that the under the arm's length principle, the amount of profit to be attributed to the permanent establishment will be related to the nature of the functions that it performs (taking into account the assets used and risks assumed). Given the importance of intangible assets in the earning of profits from e-commerce activities, it is also be essential to determine which part of the enterprise economically "owns" or has created the intangible assets used by the permanent establishment. In the context of the stand-alone computer server (and the multiple server variation), the functional and factual analysis is likely to show that the permanent establishment is performing only routine functions and is reliant on other parts of the enterprise to provide the intangible assets necessary for it to perform most, if not all, of those functions. Accordingly, the activities of the permanent establishment are very unlikely to warrant it being attributed with a substantial share of the profit associated with the distribution activities of the enterprise conducted through the server. Further, it is suggested that the nature of this type of server-permanent establishment, especially its lack of personnel, is likely to mean that tasks performed by the server would likely be conducted under a "contract service provider" arrangement that would leave all substantial assets and risks with the head office and attribute to the permanent establishment the profits associated with the

VII Appendices

physical operation of the computer server. Under an alternative interpretation of the arrangement, whereby the permanent establishment is considered to be instead an "independent service provider", the conclusion would be similar, given the need for the permanent establishment to recognise, in computing profit, the arm's length value of the tangible and intangible property that it uses and that were contributed to it by other parts of the enterprise.

9.   Where personnel are present in the permanent establishment to perform maintenance and online services tasks, the quantum of the profit attributable to the permanent establishment would be commensurate with what independent service providers would be expected to earn in a similar situation. Finally, the last variation (in-house development of server and web site) is likely to produce a more substantial attribution of profit to the permanent establishment, as it assumes sufficient development risks to be considered as the economic owner of the intangible property developed to operate the server and the web site and, therefore, is entitled to the profit associated with the exploitation of such property.

10.   This discussion paper is limited to an analysis of an "e-tailing" situation. The implications for Article 7 of the transfer pricing issues raised by other business models could warrant further work. The paper is also limited to an analysis of transfer pricing issues and does not address issues of compliance or other administrative aspects. Finally, the paper is meant to provide a technical analysis of current rules under the OECD Model Tax Convention, and does not offer a policy evaluation of the effectiveness or appropriateness of the rules. These issues are currently being examined by the Business Profits TAG.

11.   Views are invited on the analysis contained in this discussion paper and on areas where further work could be undertaken by the Business Profits TAG (please see the Foreword for details of where to send comments).

Introduction

12.   The purpose of this discussion paper is to examine the issues surrounding the attribution of profit to a permanent establishment involved in electronic commerce transactions. In particular, the discussion paper provides a detailed analysis of the steps required to attribute, in accordance with the arm's length principle, profit to a permanent establishment that would be considered to exist under Article 5 of the OECD Model Tax Convention[2] as a result of the use by an enterprise of a stand-alone computer server in a foreign jurisdiction in the course of processing online retail transactions. The assumption that the operation of a computer server by an enterprise in a country can give rise to a

---

[2]   *Model Tax Convention on Income and on Capital*, OECD Committee on Fiscal Affairs, Paris.

permanent establishment in that country is based on the conclusions reached by Working Party No. 1 on Tax Conventions and Related Questions and, in particular, on the recently released additions it has proposed to the Commentary to the Model Tax Convention. The scope of this paper is limited to a technical interpretation and application of the arm's length principle to such a permanent establishment. The wider policy issue of whether the current provisions of the OECD Model Tax Convention regarding the taxation of permanent establishments are the most appropriate to deal with the issues presented by the development of electronic commerce is not discussed in this note and is another item on the work programme of the Technical Advisory Group on Monitoring the Application of Existing Treaty Norms for the Taxation of Business Profits ("Business Profits TAG").

13.   The starting point for the analysis contained in this discussion paper is the current Commentary to the Business Profits Article (Article 7) of the OECD Model Tax Convention. However, the analysis also takes into account the preliminary results of a review currently on-going within the Committee on Fiscal Affairs, whose aim is to test and develop an interpretation of Article 7 that is more consistent with the interpretation of the arm's length principle in the Associated Enterprise Article (Article 9) and that takes into account the important evolution contained in the revised 1995 Transfer Pricing Guidelines.[3] The preliminary results of the review, conducted on the basis of a "working hypothesis" that does not bind OECD Member countries, can be found in *Discussion Draft on the Attribution of Profits to Permanent Establishments*, released by the CFA on 8 February 2001. That document ("CFA general discussion draft") looks at issues relating to the attribution of profits to permanent establishments in general and is not confined to permanent establishments in the e-commerce sector.

14.   The next section outlines the principles that are relevant in attributing profit to permanent establishments in general. The third section begins with a detailed example of a commercial retail operation relying on a stand-alone computer server to host its web site and process online transactions with customers. Then, a detailed analysis of the application of the arm's length principle is performed on the basis of the parameters of the example, setting out the steps that must be followed in order to attribute profit to such a permanent establishment. Considerable analysis is devoted to this first scenario. Three additional variations on the basic example are then examined in order to show how different fact patterns affect the analysis. The second variation assumes the existence of several servers in as many foreign jurisdictions performing identical tasks. The third variation assumes the presence of technical personnel in the

---

[3]   *Transfer Pricing Guidelines for Multinational Enterprises and Tax Administrations*, OECD Committee on Fiscal Affairs, Paris.

permanent establishment. The last variation illustrates the attribution of profit when hardware and software used in the business are developed within the permanent establishment.

15. Several other variations could have been considered. Likewise, it is recognised that electronic commerce can occur under other forms of business models. The example examined in this discussion paper illustrates a so-called "e-tailing" operation. Other models include "B2B" (business-to-business transactions), the auction model (whereby a virtual bidding forum for purchasers and suppliers is provided) and web hosting. The principles applied in this discussion paper with regard to "e-tailing" could equally apply to other forms of e-commerce but would need to be adapted to the particular factual situation.

16. This discussion paper does not consider issues of compliance by taxpayers and administration by tax authorities that may be raised in the context of the example examined in the third section. These issues are to be considered as part of the wider policy analysis currently conducted by the Business Profits TAG.

General principles for attributing profit to a permanent establishment

17. The purpose of this section is to provide an overview of the rules governing the attribution of profits to permanent establishments under Article 7 of the OECD Model Tax Convention, including the latest developments on the interpretation and application of Article 7, as reflected in the CFA general discussion draft released on 8 February 2001. The description of the rules and latest developments in this section will serve as a starting point for a more thorough analysis, in the next section, of their possible application to various forms of permanent establishments involved in electronic commerce activities. Some of the challenges that may be faced in attributing profit to a permanent establishment in an electronic commerce environment are already apparent in this part. Readers are referred to the CFA general discussion draft for a more detailed analysis of the issues and explanation of the background to the review of Article 7. In brief, the CFA has noted that there is currently not a consensus amongst the OECD Member countries as to the correct interpretation of Article 7. This lack of a common interpretation of Article 7 can lead to double, or less than single taxation. The development of global trading of financial products and of electronic commerce has helped to focus attention on this unsatisfactory situation and on the need to establish a consensus position regarding the interpretation and practical application of Article 7.

18. As a first step in establishing a consensus position, a working hypothesis (WH) has been developed as to the *preferred* approach for attributing profit to a permanent establishment under Article 7. The WH

has been tested by considering how it would apply in practice to attribute profit both to permanent establishments in general and, in particular, to permanent establishments of businesses operating in the financial sector, where trading through a permanent establishment is widespread. The CFA has released a general discussion draft that contains the results of testing the application of the WH to permanent establishments in general (Part I) and to permanent establishments of banking enterprises (Part II).

19.   The analysis in this discussion paper is based on the WH and how it might be applied to attribute profit to a permanent establishment of an e-tailer. Differences between the results of applying the WH and of applying the existing interpretation of Article 7 are identified and discussed. It should be noted that the use of the WH in this discussion paper should not be interpreted as implying support for the adoption of the WH by any of the business or government representatives on the Business Profits TAG.

20. The rest of this section provides more detail on the existing interpretation of the first three paragraphs of Article 7 and on how the WH might apply to those paragraphs.

Article 7(1) – Calculating profit to be allocated to a permanent establishment

21.   Article 7 of the OECD Model Tax Convention sets out the rules for allocating profits to a permanent establishment. Article 7(1) provides that only so much of the "profits of an enterprise" as are attributable to a permanent establishment in a country may be taxed in that country. The Commentary to this paragraph confirms that the profits attributable to a permanent establishment do not include profits that an enterprise may derive otherwise than through the permanent establishment. This limits the taxing rights of a host country so that profits of a non-resident enterprise that are not attributable to the permanent establishment cannot be subject to tax, for example under the "force of attraction" principle.

22.   The OECD Model Commentary provides little additional guidance concerning how the term "profits of an enterprise" is to be interpreted; in particular, whether the profits attributable to the permanent establishment are limited by the profits of the entire enterprise. Historically, there has been a lack of consensus amongst countries on how far to take the "distinct and separate enterprise" approach of Article 7(2). Some countries put more weight on treating a permanent establishment as far as possible as if it were a separate enterprise, the "separate enterprise" approach, while others put greater weight on the fact that the permanent establishment is only a part of a single legal entity, the "single entity" approach. Between these two polar approaches, several nuances are also possible.

VII Appendices

23.　　　In order to attain its goal of achieving an international consensus on the interpretation and practical application of Article 7, the WH adopts a single interpretation (the "functionally separate entity" approach). This approach requires that the profits to be attributed to a permanent establishment are the profits that it would have earned at arm's length as if it were a separate enterprise performing the same functions under the same or similar conditions, determined by applying the arm's length principle of Article 7(2). The phrase "profits of an enterprise" in Article 7(1) should not therefore be interpreted as affecting the determination of the quantum of profits that can be attributed to the permanent establishment but rather as limiting the profits to "only so much of them as is attributable to that permanent establishment" and in particular as providing specific confirmation that "the right to tax does not extend to profits that the enterprise may derive from that State otherwise then through the permanent establishment" (*i.e.* there should be no "force of attraction" principle).

UN Model Convention

24.　　　A number of bilateral tax treaties adopt features of the UN Model Convention. Article 7 of the UN Model Convention generally follows the principles of the corresponding Article of the OECD Model Tax Convention with respect to the attribution of profit to a permanent establishment. However, there are differences between the two models. The major difference between the two models is that the UN Model extends source country taxing rights beyond the strict attribution of profit to a permanent establishment and grants a host country the right to tax profits attributable to sales made by the non-resident enterprise in the country's territory "of goods or merchandise of the same or similar kind as those sold through that permanent establishment". This is the so-called "limited force of attraction" principle. This paper does not examine the implications of the application of this principle to electronic commerce transactions. Instead, it is written on the assumption that the arm's length principle is the most appropriate principle to apply when attributing profit to a permanent establishment in the contexts of both electronic and traditional commerce.

Article 7(2) of the OECD Model Tax Convention

25.　　　Paragraph 2 of Article 7 states the arm's length principle in the context of permanent establishments, and is the key paragraph for attributing profits to a permanent establishment. It states that the profits to be attributed to a permanent establishment are those that it would have made if it had been a separate enterprise engaged in the same or similar activities, under the same or similar conditions, dealing with other parts of the enterprise wholly independently.

26. The Commentary confirms that Article 7(2) is to be considered a statement of the arm's length principle of Article 9 in the context of permanent establishments. The OECD Transfer Pricing Guidelines ("the Guidelines") contain detailed guidance on how to apply the arm's length principle under Article 9 in the context of associated enterprises. The WH is based on the premise that the guidance on the application of the arm's length principle of Article 9 given by the Guidelines should be applied to the attribution of profit to a permanent establishment using the arm's length principle under Article 7(2). However, this guidance has to be applied by analogy rather than directly as it is based on evaluating *transactions* between associated enterprises, rather than *dealings* within the same enterprise.

27. The preferred interpretation of Article 7 (2) under the WH is that a two-step analysis is required: first, a functional and factual analysis, in order to appropriately hypothesise the permanent establishment and the remainder of the enterprise (or a segment or segments thereof) as if they were associated enterprises, each undertaking functions, using assets, and assuming risks; second, an analysis of the Guidelines relevant to applying the arm's length principle to the hypothesised enterprises so undertaking functions, using assets, and assuming risks. Each of these steps is discussed below.

First step: Determining the characteristics and functions of the hypothesised distinct and separate enterprise

28. Following, by analogy, the approach adopted in the Guidelines, the technique of functional analysis can be used to determine what economically significant activities are undertaken by the enterprise as a whole. The functional analysis must go on to determine which of the identified activities of the enterprise are associated with the permanent establishment, and to what extent.

29. The functional analysis must also take into account the assets used and risks assumed by the permanent establishment. As regards assets, the working hypothesis is to undertake a functional analysis that takes into account "assets *used*" (emphasis added), with no reference to legal ownership. The facts and circumstances must be examined in order to determine the extent to which the assets of the enterprise are used in the business activity carried on by the permanent establishment. To the extent that assets are used in the business activity carried on by the permanent establishment, the use of those assets should be taken into account in rewarding the functions performed by the permanent establishment. Assets of the enterprise that are not used by the permanent establishment should not be taken into account for the purposes of attributing profits to it.

30.   Following the analysis of assets, the working hypothesis is to treat the permanent establishment as assuming certain risks, even though legally it is the enterprise as a whole that assumes those risks. Indeed, the permanent establishment should be considered as assuming any risks inherent in, or created by, the permanent establishment's own functions (*i.e.* for the purpose of the permanent establishment), and any risks that relate directly to those activities. The division of risks assumed and functions performed by the head office and the permanent establishment respectively may be set out in writing, in the same manner as risks and functions may be documented contractually between separate legal entities. However, in the absence of contractual terms between the permanent establishment and the rest of the enterprise of which it is a part, determining what assumption of risks should be attributed to the permanent establishment will have to be highly fact specific. Following, by analogy, paragraph 1.28 of the Guidelines, the division of risks and responsibilities within the enterprise will have to be "deduced from their [the parties] conduct and the economic principles that govern relationships between independent enterprises." This deduction may be aided by examining internal practices of the enterprise (*e.g.* compensation arrangements), by making a comparison with what similar independent enterprises would do and by examining any internal data or documentation purporting to show how that attribution of risks has been made.

31.   In summary, to the extent that risks are found to have been assumed by the enterprise as a result of a function performed by the permanent establishment, the assumption of those risks should be taken into account when attributing profit to the performance of that function by the permanent establishment. If risks are found not to have been assumed by the enterprise as a result of a function performed by the permanent establishment, the assumption of those risks should not be taken into account for the purposes of attributing profits to the permanent establishment. It should be noted that this discussion of risk only relates to the assumption of risks, inherent in, or created by, the performance of a function.

Second step: Determining the profits of the hypothesised distinct and separate enterprise based upon a comparability analysis

32.   The WH provides for the choice and application of methods described in the Guidelines to be applicable when determining the profits to be attributed to a permanent establishment based upon its functions performed (taking into account assets used and risks assumed). The permanent establishment should obtain an arm's length return for its functions, taking into account the assets used and risks assumed, in the same manner as would a comparable independent enterprise.

33.   A functional analysis of the permanent establishment will already have been accomplished in the process of constructing the hypothesised "distinct and separate" enterprise under the first step of the analysis. Additionally, the working hypothesis is to undertake a comparison of *dealings* between the permanent establishment and the enterprise of which it is a part, with *transactions* between independent enterprises. This comparison is to be made by following, by analogy, the comparability analysis described in the Guidelines. By analogy with the Guidelines, comparability in the permanent establishment context means either that there are no differences materially affecting the measure used to attribute profit to the permanent establishment, or that reasonably accurate adjustments can be made to eliminate the material effects of such differences.

34.   An important question is whether inter-branch dealings have taken place and so should be recognised for the purposes of attributing profit. In the associated enterprise situation it will usually be self-evident that a transaction has occurred, *e.g.* the transaction will have legal consequences other than for tax purposes. However, a dealing within a single legal entity is not something which is self-evident but is a construct, the existence of which is often inferred solely for the purpose of determining an arm's length attribution of profit. Consequently, it will be necessary at the outset to determine whether any dealing exists before deciding whether the dealing, as found, should be used as the basis for the analysis used to determine an arm's length attribution of profit.

35.   Under the WH, a "dealing" will be recognised, for the purpose of attributing profit, where it relates to a real and identifiable event (*e.g.* the physical transfer of stock in trade, the provision of services, the use of an intangible asset, a change in which part of the enterprise is using a capital asset, the transfer of a financial asset, etc.). A functional analysis should be used to determine whether such an event has occurred and should be taken into account as an inter-branch dealing of economic significance. This will require the determination of whether there has been any economically significant transfer of risks, responsibilities and benefits as a result of the "dealing". In transactions between independent enterprises, the determination of the transfer of risks, responsibilities and benefits would normally require an analysis of the contractual terms of the transaction, following the guidance on contractual terms found in paragraphs 1.28 and 1.29 of the Guidelines. This guidance should be applied by analogy in the permanent establishment context.

36.   Once the above threshold has been passed and a dealing recognised as existing, the WH applies, by analogy, the guidance at 1.36-1.41 of the Guidelines. The guidance is applied not to transactions but to the dealings between the permanent establishment and the other parts of the enterprise. So the examination of a dealing should be based on the *dealing* actually undertaken by the *permanent establishment and the*

other part of the enterprise as it has been structured by them, using the methods applied by the taxpayer insofar as these are consistent with the methods described in Chapters II and III of the Guidelines. Except in the two circumstances outlined at paragraph 1.37, tax administrations should apply the guidance in paragraph 1.36 when attributing profit to a permanent establishment and so "should not disregard the actual *dealings* or substitute other *dealings* for them."

37.   Where the permanent establishment has dealings with other parts of the enterprise, those dealings are an important factor to be considered and will affect the attribution of profits to the extent that the dealings are relevant to the functions performed by the permanent establishment and the other parts of the enterprise, taking into account assets used and risks assumed. Such inter-branch dealings should have the same effect on the attribution of profits between the permanent establishment and other parts of the enterprise, as would comparable transactions between independent enterprises. However, the inter-branch dealings are postulated *solely* for the purpose of attributing the appropriate amount of profit to the permanent establishment.

38.   The comparability analysis might determine that there has been a provision of goods, services or assets, etc. between one part of the enterprise and another, that is comparable to a provision of goods, services or assets, etc. between independent enterprises. Accordingly, the part of the enterprise making such a "provision" should receive the return which an independent enterprise would have received for making a comparable "provision" in a transaction at arm's length. Another outcome of the comparability analysis might be that the permanent establishment and the other part of the enterprise dealing with it are found to be acting, under all the facts and circumstances, in a comparable manner to economic co-participants in an activity corresponding theoretically to a cost contribution arrangement (CCA). If the permanent establishment and the rest of the enterprise are found to be economic co-participants in such an activity, then the dealings would result in the attribution of profits in a manner similar to transactions between associated enterprises in a CCA. The comparability analysis may result in other outcomes and these should be equally susceptible to analysis, by analogy, with the guidance contained in the Guidelines.

Article 7 (3) of the OECD Model Tax Convention

39.   Historically, some countries interpreted Article 7(3) as mandating an allocation of costs (without any profit element). However, most Member countries, including those that interpret Article 7(3) as *requiring* modifications to the arm's length principle, believe that it would be preferable if Article 7(3) did not result in modifications to the arm's length principle of Article 7(2). Accordingly, the working hypothesis is that the role of Article 7(3) should be just to ensure that the expenses

associated with a permanent establishment's activity are not disallowed for inappropriate reasons, in particular, because the expense is incurred outside the permanent establishment's jurisdiction, or is not incurred exclusively for the permanent establishment.

Special considerations in attributing profit to a permanent establishment in an electronic commerce environment

Server creates a permanent establishment

40.   This section is developed on the basis of a hypothetical example with a basic scenario and a number of variations. The example focuses only on the computer server as a tool to support a retail distribution function. It is assumed, under the proposed additions to the Commentary to Article 5 of the Model Tax Convention, that the server constitutes a permanent establishment of the enterprise so that the jurisdiction of the permanent establishment has a right to tax the profits of the non-resident enterprise attributable to that permanent establishment.

Variation 1: Single server

41.   Starco Inc., a hypothetical corporation resident in country A, is an online distributor of music and video products worldwide. Starco purchases the right to distribute music and full-length movies from producers in several countries and makes various types of products available at the retail level to consumers over the World Wide Web through its well-known web site.

42.   Starco's web site, much like a catalogue, displays the entire range of Starco's products and allows visitors to purchase its products on line. Consumers have the choice to order a physical copy of the product they wish to purchase (available on various supports, such as CD, DVD, VHS cassettes, etc.) or to download a digitised version of the product on line from its server to the consumer's computer, once the payment is confirmed. Most of Starco's products are available in digitised form.

43.   Starco hosts its web site on a single server in country B. The server was installed toward the end of 1998 and has been operational since 1 January 1999, the beginning of Starco's financial year. The web site became well-known as a result of an aggressive worldwide publicity campaign conducted by Starco prior to and around the time it was launched. No personnel attended the server throughout the 1999 financial year and the server performed as expected. The server is a powerful computer fitted with software programmed to:

i)   Display the various pages of Starco's web site.

ii)   Process orders placed by customers for the purchase of physical products.

iii)   Process orders placed by customers for the purchase of digitised products.

iv)   Hold a digitised copy of all available products.

v)   Transmit digitised products on line to the computer of customers.

44.   Here is how a typical transaction takes place:

i)   The customer considers the list of products available on the web site and selects the products that he/she wishes to purchase and the mode of delivery – physical support or digitised transmission.

ii)   The customer fills in an order form with all the required information, and provides a credit card number as the means of payment for the products to be purchased.

iii)   The customer sends the order on line.

iv)   The customer receives, on line, within two minutes, confirmation that his/her order has been received and that the credit card company has accepted the transaction. Where a physical product was ordered, the message includes an estimate of the delay before delivery by mail. Where a digitised product was ordered, downloading of the product may commence after the customer received the purchase confirmation. Where technical problems occur, the consumer may contact Starco either via a toll-free telephone number or e-mail.

45.   Here is how the server operates in the course of this typical transaction:

i)   The order is received by the server in country B. The server is programmed to contact by phone the credit card company of the customer in order to secure immediately payment for the product purchased. Once the transaction is accepted by the credit card company, payment is made by it to a Starco bank account in country A. Where the payment is made as directed, the server moves on to the next step. If the payment is, for whatever reason, not authorised, notice is sent to the customer that the transaction cannot be completed.

ii)   The next step depends on the form of the product ordered. If a physical product was ordered, the server sends a notice to the customer informing him/her of the delay before the product is delivered by mail. At the same time, a message is sent to the computer of Starco's central warehouse in country A, requesting that the products selected by the customer be delivered at the address provided in the order. In most occasions, the products to be delivered can be drawn directly from the warehouse's extensive inventory. However, it may also be required, in order to fulfil the customer's order, to purchase products from its suppliers.

iii) If a digitised product was ordered, the server provides permission to the customer to download a copy of the product immediately. Downloading entails sending on line a copy of digitised product ordered, which sits in a digitised format on the server. The customer may perform the downloading once. When the downloading is successfully completed, the server sends notice that the transaction is completed. If the downloading is interrupted before completion, the customer may resume downloading until it is successfully completed. The server provides a menu of troubleshooting options to handle the most common problems encountered by customers during the downloading process.

46.   On the basis of the interpretation of Article 5 recently issued by the Committee on Fiscal Affairs, it is assumed, under the fact pattern described above, that Starco's server in country B constitutes, for tax purposes, a permanent establishment of Starco.

General considerations

47.   The analysis below is concerned with attributing profit to the permanent establishment for the 1999 financial year. The attribution of profit to a permanent establishment begins with a functional analysis, which establishes the role of the permanent establishment in the enterprise and informs the next step, which requires one to hypothesise the attributes of the permanent establishment as a separate and distinct enterprise as well as the nature of the "dealings" between the permanent establishment and the rest of the enterprise, in order to apply the appropriate transfer pricing method to attribute profit to the permanent establishment.

First step: Determining the conditions of the hypothesised distinct and separate enterprise

Functions performed
48.   The functional analysis will show that the permanent establishment performs the following functions autonomously:

– The establishment of an internet connection between the server and any person with a computer, a modem and an internet browser

through an interface created by the joint operation of the permanent
establishment's hardware and software, the web site;

–   Presentation of Starco, of Starco's products, of instructions for
    visitors to enter into a commercial transaction with Starco, of phone
    numbers to handle any inquiries about products or about online
    transactions;

–   Processing of orders submitted by customers on line, immediate
    validation of payments provided by customers with credit card
    companies, immediate approval or refusal of orders on line,
    processing of instructions to Starco for the subsequent physical
    delivery of products, performance of online transmission of
    digitised products, provision of online trouble-shooting.

Assets used

49.   The functional and factual analysis will show that the permanent
establishment requires assets, in the form of both hardware and software
to undertake the above functions. The permanent establishment of Starco
in country B consists of both hardware and software located in an office
space rented by Starco. The hardware, a physical asset, is a powerful
computer with the latest communication devices capable of handling a
large volume of traffic. The software, which is intangible property either
acquired or developed by Starco,[4] consists of the sums of all the programs
required to ensure that: (i) the computer can be operational
autonomously; (ii) the computer can be linked via communication lines
with one or more Starco's computers in other locations, including Starco's
head office and warehouse in country A; (iii) the computer can be linked
via modem lines (or similar means of communication) with any person
seeking to access Starco's web site; (iv) the computer can maintain
Starco's web site and (v) the computer can perform operations relating to
the processing of commercial transactions with customers, including
seeking and obtaining authorisation from the financial institution for the
payment to be made. "Software", therefore, is given a wide meaning in the
following discussion and is not limited to commercial software widely
available on the market (for example, a computer's operating system), but
encompasses the product resulting from the development work necessary
for the creation and all aspects of the operation of Starco's web site. Such
development work is specific to the needs of Starco and results in the
creation of "custom" software. The cost of such development work

---

4   Software is, for the purpose of this note, referred to as "intangible" property,
    notwithstanding the broader issue of how it is characterised under the Model Tax
    Convention or domestic law. While the software may or may not be intellectual property
    of the enterprise (depending, for example, on whether the software was acquired on the
    market or developed by the enterprise), this paper avoids making the distinction. Of
    course, such a distinction can potentially be material to the determination of the arm's
    length compensation associated with a transaction involving such property.

(whether incurred internally or under contract with outside experts) is expected to represent the bulk of the cost of the software installed in the permanent establishment.

50.   Hardware and software do not, on their own, ensure that commercial activities occur on a web site. The permanent establishment also makes use of Starco's other intangible assets. The most obvious of these assets is the marketing intangible associated with the enterprise. The main component of this intangible is the enterprise's own brand name, which will attract potential customers on the web site and, therefore, result in commercial transactions occurring through the permanent establishment. Another intangible (an "e-commerce marketing intangible") may be directly related to the operation of the web site. For example, is it laid out clearly, is it fun to use, does it carry interviews with "hot" groups or musicians, does it manage the purchases of its supplies and process customer orders quickly and efficiently. Both these intangibles are directly relevant to the success of a commercial web site.

51.   It is not sufficient, for purposes of attributing profit to Starco's permanent establishment, to determine which intangible assets are used by it. One needs to determine which part of the enterprise is entitled to the benefits associated with the use of the intangibles by the permanent establishment. The reward associated with an intangible property does not necessarily accrue to the part of the enterprise making use of it, but rather to the part of the enterprise that developed or otherwise contributed the intangible.

Risks assumed

52.   Having determined the functions performed and assets (including intangible property) "used" by the permanent establishment, one also needs to determine the risks assumed respectively by the permanent establishment and the rest of the enterprise.

53.   Legally, these risks are borne by the enterprise as a whole. The challenge, for the purpose of attributing profit to the permanent establishment, is to determine which risks, if any, should be attributed to the permanent establishment as opposed to the rest of Starco. Under the WH, the functional and factual analysis will determine the extent to which the permanent establishment should be considered to assume any risks inherent in or created by its own functions or that relate directly to those functions. The rest of this sub-section looks at the various types of risk inherent in the business of Starco.

Credit risk

54.   The extent of the credit risk assumed by Starco will depend on how transactions are processed. In the vast majority of cases, payment will likely be made with a credit card. Where Starco seeks some form of corroboration (*e.g.* a confirmation number) from the issuer of the credit

VII Appendices

card before proceeding with the transaction, payment for the transaction will be effectively guaranteed. In such cases, credit risk is probably negligible. However, where such validation is not performed systematically, for example where single payments to Starco are of a low monetary value, Starco would assume the credit risk in respect of these transactions.

55.   Under the WH, the associated credit risk would be treated as assumed by the part of the enterprise carrying out the function leading to the creation of that risk. This raises the question of which part of Starco carries out that function. Is it the permanent establishment because it accepts the customer's order or is it the head office because it has provided the software that enables the permanent establishment to accept that order? In short, can risk be assumed by the actions of a computer or is human intervention required? The WH links the assumption of risk with the carrying out of functions and so would be indifferent to whether the function leading to the assumption of risk was carried out with, or without, human intervention. Views on this issue would be particularly welcome.

Market risks

56.   The cost of holding physical inventory depends on the nature of the arrangements between Starco and its suppliers. If the arrangements allow Starco to return unsold inventory after a given period of time, then the market risk is mostly borne by Starco's suppliers – Starco's share of the risk would be commensurate with the transactions costs that may be involved in returning unsold inventory. If no such possibility exists, all of the market risk is borne by Starco. The extent of this market risk, in turn, depends on the nature of the consideration paid by Starco for the intangible property element of the products it acquires from suppliers. Let us assume that for both digital and physical products, a payment is made to suppliers each time a product is purchased by a customer. Market risks include the transactional costs associated with the possibility of having to replace a defective product – the cost of the defective product itself would not ordinarily be borne by Starco as arrangements with suppliers may provide for the replacement of such products at no charge.

57.   In the case of digitised products, the cost of the physical support is irrelevant. The server is able to provide a digitised version of each product, and to transfer that product to the customer each time a transaction is entered into with a customer on line.

58.   Therefore, under a per-unit payment arrangement, Starco's market risk is limited to the cost of the physical support of the products acquired from suppliers, since royalties are payable only when products are sold on the retail market. The cost of the marginal physical support is infinitesimal in the case of digitised products (assuming that the business is successful). Therefore, the risk borne by Starco of having to replace a defective digitised product amounts to the extra royalty that may become

payable (depending on the nature of the arrangement with Starco's suppliers) when the customer is allowed to download again the product.

59.   Conversely, Starco's credit risk is the sum of both the cost of the physical support and the payment made in connection with the delivery of a product for which the proceeds of transactions may later prove to be non-existent where the customer made a fraudulent use of a credit card or where there was no corroboration of the transaction by the credit card company. In the case of a digitised transmission, the cost is limited to the royalty payable by Starco.

Technological risks

60.   The foregoing also has implications for determining which part of the enterprise bears the technological risks associated with the operation of the server in country B. Two broad categories of technological risks can be distinguished. The first category encompasses risks that directly affect the volume of business of the enterprises, for example, where the malfunctioning of the hardware or software in the server results in the loss of business for the permanent establishment. The second category includes other risks that result from the performance of routine automated functions, for example, where the server is used by hackers to spread defamatory material about one of the artists featured on the site, or where a customer's credit card number is obtained from the site and used fraudulently. Arguably, the activities of the permanent establishment create this second category of risks and so the permanent establishment should be treated as assuming this category of risk.

61.   For the permanent establishment to be considered to solely assume the first category of risk, the economic position of the head office should be unaffected by the realisation of the risks – for example, as in the case where perishable goods are transferred to a permanent establishment and the permanent establishment assumes the entire inventory risk. It is arguable that this is not the case for Starco's permanent establishment, as loss of business by the permanent establishment due to the permanent establishment's own making is, in fact, a revenue loss for the head office, given the nature of the "inventory" held by the permanent establishment – digitised products on a hard drive are not "inventory" and the permanent establishment does not have any inventory of physical products. On the other hand, it may be argued that functions of the permanent establishment are such that it does expose the enterprise to at least limited market risk – if it fails then the enterprise may forego current revenues and, possibly, because of the premium put on instant availability of the latest fashionable releases, future customers. Because the permanent establishment is the source of such risk, it may be appropriate to allocate limited market risk to the permanent establishment. In other circumstances, where the permanent establishment is able, for example

VII Appendices

through sophisticated software,[5] to perform a function comparable to that of a full function distributor, the sharing of risk may be different.

Implications of the functional analysis

62.   In order to appropriately hypothesise the permanent establishment as a distinct and separate enterprise, for example as the equivalent of a retail outlet or a service provider, it is necessary to consider the result of the functional and factual analysis and to perform a comparison with the functions usually associated with such enterprises, including the division of risks inherent to such functions. The functions ordinarily associated with a retail outlet include: decision-making regarding the ordering of inventory and the level of inventory to be held; negotiations regarding terms with suppliers; decisions on product pricing, marketing and promotion; establishing contacts with customers; concluding contracts with customers; the physical distribution of goods; credit control, including decisions on credit arrangements for customers; the management of incoming funds; accounting functions such as cash flow control. A functional analysis must include determining the extent to which these functions are carried out in Starco's permanent establishment.

63.   It is likely that a functional analysis of Starco will reveal that the head office in country A and not the permanent establishment in country B carries out many of these functions exclusively. The lack of human or artificial intelligence in the permanent establishment precludes any ability to bargain, make key decisions or carry out many of these elements of a normal sales or distribution function. There are also likely to be conceptual difficulties in regarding digital information on the permanent establishment's server as "inventory", which could be the implied conclusion if the permanent establishment was considered to be akin to an independent retail outlet. Therefore, while the permanent establishment can be considered to carry out routine (autonomous) aspects of a sales function, it cannot be regarded as having all the attributes of a conventional retail outlet nor to carry out the various functions that give rise to the substantive market and credit risks. As a result, it would not be consistent with the factual and functional analysis to assume that the permanent establishment has notionally "acquired" digital inventory from the head office. The same conclusion could be reached for the market risks associated with the sale of physical products. They clearly arise from, and are associated with, the functions carried out by Starco's head office. The factual and functional analysis would show that the permanent establishment could not be considered to notionally hold title to physical products sold through its server. Indeed, the sales functions of the permanent establishment do not include the actual handling of physical

---

[5]   One could imagine a situation where the server PE had software that researched the latest consumer trends, ordered material from suppliers based on that research and on the basis of the lowest possible cost. The question arises as to whether, in such a situation, the functional and factual analysis could show that the permanent establishment was actually assuming some market risk.

products obtained from suppliers and shipped to purchasers (the actual shipping is performed by the head office), which is a core function of most conventional retail outlets. The situation is less clear-cut with credit and technological risks, as these appear to be more associated with the routine functions of accepting and handling customer transactions that are performed by the permanent establishment.

64.   The foregoing suggests that, in the context of this example, the permanent establishment's functions are closer to that of a service provider.

65.   However, within such a characterisation, more than one type of arrangement is possible, essentially depending on the sharing of risk between the service provider and the beneficiary of such services. The issue is whether the permanent establishment can be said to bear the full technological risk associated with the operation of its server. In a similar arrangement between arm's length parties, the purchaser of the service would not be expected to reward a service supplier incapable, for a given period of time, of providing the service, which it undertook to provide. On the other hand, the provider of the service would not be expected to fully compensate the purchaser for lost transactions.

66.   One possibility is to that the permanent establishment is acting as the equivalent of an independent service provider. Under this model, the permanent establishment is considered to have acquired at arm's length prices the hardware and software necessary for the provision of services and, crucially, it assumes the risks usually associated with the operation of such an enterprise.

67.   However, it is also possible that the permanent establishment is acting like a "contract service provider". Under this model, Starco's head office is considered to retain control ("economic ownership") of all the property (tangible and intangible) transferred to the permanent establishment. This means that the risks associated with the use of such assets are also considered to remain with the head office. The only risk for the permanent establishment is that it might not be compensated adequately for the services that it has performed.

68.   Between independent enterprises, an analysis of the contractual terms would assist considerably in determining how the responsibilities, risks and benefits of a service arrangement are to be divided between the parties and consequently whether the arrangement is that of a contract service provider or as an independent service provider. As noted in the section regarding Article 7(2) above, the WH applies the guidance on this matter in the Guidelines (paragraph 1.28) by analogy and by reference to the conduct of the parties and the economic principles that govern relationships between independent enterprises. Following the guidance in

VII Appendices

the WH should enable a determination to be made as to whether the permanent establishment is acting as a contract service provider or as an independent service provider.

Conclusions

69.   The result of the functional and factual analysis, and in particular the determination of risks assumed by the permanent establishment, will determine the true nature of the operations of the permanent establishment. For a permanent establishment carrying out retailing activities the analysis may reveal that the permanent establishment is performing functions, using assets and assuming risks akin to those performed by a retail outlet, *i.e.* the purchasing and distributing of products for a profit. Or it may reveal that the functions performed, assets used and risks assumed by the permanent establishment are similar to those of a service provider, providing services[6] for and on behalf another part of the enterprise

70.   However, it would appear that under the fact pattern of this example, the factual and functional analysis is unlikely to show that the permanent establishment is performing many of the functions, or assuming many of the risks, of an independent retail outlet. The lack of personnel at the permanent establishment under this fact pattern makes it hard to envisage the permanent establishment assuming anything but the most routine risks that are directly related to the automated functions it performs. The functions it performs are more akin to sales support functions or to back office functions in a global trading business. The "service provider" model is therefore likely to be the most useful tool for analysing this type of server-permanent establishment and for finding comparables under the second step of the analysis described below. In the case of Starco, the limited functionality of the permanent establishment means one could credibly characterise the arrangement as one similar to that of a "contract service provider", whereby the permanent establishment is mandated to provide services to the head office using tangible and intangible property provided by, and remaining under the control and responsibility of, the head office.

71.   On the basis of these findings, the proper attributes of the permanent establishment and the nature of the "dealings" that it is assumed to have with the rest of the enterprise can be established for purposes of applying the principles of Article 7 of the Model Tax Convention.

---

6   The "service provider" model should not be confused with the approach that consists of treating transactions in digitised products as "services" for purposes of value added taxes. This model is only meant to imply that the revenues of the permanent establishment are in the form of a fee for services performed for the benefit of the head office. The issue of the characterisation of transactions in digitised products occurring between Starco and customers is not relevant to the issue of the attribution of income to the permanent establishment and, therefore, is not considered further in this discussion paper.

Second step: Determining the profits of the hypothesised distinct and separate enterprise

72.   Because the permanent establishment of Starco in country B does not have a distinct legal personality, transactions entered into by a customer on its web site hosted on its server in country B are legally entered into with all of Starco. However, the legal aspect of the transaction is of little relevance to the task of attributing profit to the permanent establishment. The question to be answered is what profit the permanent establishment would earn, in similar circumstances, if it were dealing at arm's length with the rest of Starco, under the relevant business model. Because of the lack of legal personality of the permanent establishment, it cannot enter into legally enforceable transactions with the rest of Starco, because an enterprise cannot transact with itself. However, in order to provide an answer to the above question, one is required to establish whether "dealings" occurred between the permanent establishment and the rest of the enterprise and to determine the true nature of such "dealings", in order to be able to apply the arm's length principle, as if a transaction had occurred between two distinct and separate enterprises.

73.   The response to the above question will differ according to whether the relevant dealings of the permanent establishment can best be compared to transactions undertaken by a "retail outlet", an "independent service provider" or a "contract service provider". In the case of the particular fact pattern examined in this note, the analysis of the previous section suggested that the functions performed, assets used and risks assumed by the permanent establishment were unlikely to be comparable to those of a "retail outlet", although the conclusion may differ in different circumstances. The rest of the section will therefore focus on comparing the dealings undertaken by the permanent establishment with the two variants of the "service provider" model.

"Contract service provider" model
74.   Under this model, a functional and comparability analysis is likely to find that there have been few dealings between the permanent establishment and the head office. In the pre-commercial exploitation phase, property (hardware and software) was transferred from the head office to the permanent establishment. As noted in the section regarding Article 7(2) above, a dealing will be recognised where it results in an economically significant transfer of risks and responsibilities between the parties. Any such transfer would, in the absence of contractual terms, have to be deduced from the conduct of the parties and the economic principles that govern relationships between independent enterprises. Once again, the limited nature of the functions that can be performed by the permanent establishment due to its lack of personnel, leads to the provisional conclusion that the analysis is unlikely to show the head office as notionally disposing of such property for tax purposes but rather as

retaining control and "economic ownership" of such valuable property. Therefore, it is not considered that a "dealing" is likely to have taken place between both parts of the enterprise at that time. During the commercial exploitation stage, the permanent establishment performs services for the benefit of Starco and, therefore, the functional and comparability analysis is thought likely to characterise dealings as a notional service contract between the head office and the permanent establishment, where the head office retains most of the responsibilities, risks and benefits of the service arrangement. Such an arrangement gives rise to a dealing in respect of which an arm's length consideration must be established.

"Independent service provider" model
75.   Under this model, the functional and comparability analyses are likely to recognise a number of dealings that take place between the different parts of the enterprise.

76.   As under the previously examined model, a transfer of tangible and intangible assets occurred prior to the commercial exploitation phase of the web site hosted in the permanent establishment. Where the permanent establishment is considered to perform functions, use assets and assume risks in a manner comparable to a full service provider, these transfers give rise to "dealings", in that the permanent establishment is considered to notionally acquire assets, or the right to use assets, as the case may be, much like would be the case if the permanent establishment were an independent enterprise. In a conventional situation where such transfers occur, the permanent establishment would compute its profit so as to recognise an arm's length compensation for the head office in consideration for the provision of such property. This is so because the head office originally acquired the hardware and the digitised products and developed the software contributed to the permanent establishment and arm's length parties would seek remuneration for the transfer of such property.

77.   The next paragraphs consider closely the particular issues arising from the transfer to the permanent establishment of each category of property.

Software
78.   A question may arise as to the exact nature of the right acquired by the permanent establishment when software was transferred to it from the head office. The functional and factual analysis is unlikely to show that the head office has relinquished any significant rights associated with the software, other than the right to use the software, given the limited capacity of a permanent establishment that lacks personnel. The enterprise is likely to make continuing use of the software in head office, in other permanent establishments or in subsidiaries it controls. Moreover, the permanent establishment has clearly not acquired the right to resell or modify the software, given the nature of the activity of the

permanent establishment (and *a fortiori* because of the lack of human or artificial intelligence at the location of the permanent establishment). Therefore, the appropriate analysis of the nature of this dealing is to consider that the permanent establishment has notionally acquired a right to use the software. In computing its profit, the permanent establishment would consequently deduct an amount that represents what arm's length parties would pay for the acquisition of such a right.

Marketing intangibles

79.   A question arises as to whether a similar analysis should apply in the case of the marketing intangible (for example, the brand name) used on the web site hosted on the permanent establishment's server. Whereas it would be appropriate to assume that the permanent establishment had acquired the notional right to use Starco's marketing intangible if it had been viewed as the equivalent of a retail outlet, it is not apparent that such an assumption remains suitable where the permanent establishment is considered to be the equivalent of a provider of services to the rest of Starco. This is because it is arguably the head office that is considered to exploit the marketing intangible – comparable independent service providers would not need to acquire a marketing intangible for purposes of providing services to Starco, and Starco would not need to cede the right to use it if it dealt with an arm's length service provider. Moreover, it is not clear how the service provider could exploit or benefit from the marketing intangible. Should a dealing be recognised, an independent enterprise utilising a marketing intangible (or benefiting from other organisational expertise) developed by another enterprise would, under the arm's length principle, be expected to compensate the latter for the use of such an intangible and, therefore, an arm's length charge in an equivalent amount should be deducted in computing the profit of the permanent establishment. Views on the appropriate treatment of marketing intangible in the context of this example and more generally are welcome.

80.   A subsidiary issue, assuming the existence of a dealing for marketing intangibles, is whether the activities of permanent establishment could ever be such as to increase the value of a marketing intangible provided by the head office and, therefore, entitle the permanent establishment to some of the profits associated with the use of such an intangible (to the same extent observed between associated enterprises). Views are invited on this issue, in particular in the context of this example.

81.   A question also arises as to which part of the enterprise would be the economic owner of any e-commerce marketing intangible", related to the web site. Similar issues might arise for other marketing intangibles: for example where the permanent establishment collects customer information, does it mean that the permanent establishment is treated as the economic "owner" of the resulting marketing intangible, a customer list? If the permanent establishment is treated as the sole economic "owner" of

VII Appendices

these intangibles then no dealings need to be recognised in relation to them, unless other parts of the enterprise start to exploit them.

82.   Similar issues arise in relation to digitised products on the permanent establishment's server. If such property is considered to remain under the economic ownership of the head office (as would likely be the case for a service provider), there would be no dealings to take into account.

Application of Article 7 in the case of intangible property

83.   The above discussion suggests that where the existence of dealings in respect of software, marketing intangible or other intangibles needs to be recognised, consideration for such dealings needs to be determined under the arm's length principle. However, Article 7 of the Model Tax Convention does not presently permit such an outcome with respect to software and marketing intangible. While the Commentary clearly mandates a mark-up in accordance with the arm's length principle where stock in trade is being transferred from one part of an enterprise to another, such is not the case with regard to other types of property, in particular intangibles. There is no explicit authority in the current Commentary to assess the transfer of economic value (other than for inventory) from the head office to the permanent establishment at market value under the arm's length principle. Consider the current Model Tax Convention Commentary on intangible property:

> "In the case of intangible rights, the rules concerning the relations between enterprises of the same group (e.g. payments of royalties or cost sharing arrangements) cannot be applied in respect of the relation between parts of the same enterprise. Indeed, it may be extremely difficult to allocate "ownership" of the intangible right solely to one part of the enterprise and to argue that this part of the enterprise should receive royalties from the other parts as if it were an independent enterprise. Since there is only one legal entity it is not possible to allocate legal ownership to any particular part of the enterprise and in practical terms it will often be difficult to allocate the costs of creation exclusively to one part of the enterprise. It may therefore be preferable for the costs of creation of intangible rights to be regarded as attributable to all parts of the enterprise which will make use of them and as incurred on behalf of the various parts of the enterprise to which they are relevant accordingly. In such circumstances, it would be appropriate to allocate the actual costs of the creation of such intangible rights between the various parts of the enterprise without any mark-up for profit or royalty."[7]

84.   This implies that such transfers are valued at cost. In our example, this produces a somewhat perverse result, as it amounts to treating the new permanent establishment as the effective economic "owner" of the software and of other relevant intangibles that were

---

[7]   Paragraph 17.4 of the Commentary to the OECD Model Tax Convention.

created before it came into existence. In that sense, the permanent establishment is getting a "free ride" on the back of the efforts and expertise of the head office.

85.   The problem with this approach is that the market value of software or of other intangibles may not bear much relation to the cost of creating it. This is a particular problem with intellectual property such as software, which is based fairly directly on ideas and that does not necessarily require the presence of a large infrastructure to create. Also the original cost may have been depreciated before the permanent establishment came into existence so that there are no costs of the enterprise to attribute to the permanent establishment.

86.   The undesirable consequences of the rather outdated approach of the current Commentary can be seen by supposing that Starco sets up an identical server performing identical functions in Country Z but that it forms a subsidiary to own and operate the server. If the market value of the intangible is substantially greater than the costs of creating it, then the subsidiary in Country Z will, under the arm's length principle, have to pay far more to Starco for the continuing right to use the intangible than the permanent establishment in Country B will have to pay in order to reimburse Starco for its share of the historical costs of creating that intangible. Of course, the situation would be the reverse if the market value of the intangible was less than the historical costs of creating it.

87.   In either case, a different tax result is obtained simply by virtue of whether the same economic function is performed through a subsidiary or through a permanent establishment. This does not seem sensible tax policy and points to a limitation to the current Commentary to Article 7. While it is true that such a situation is not unique to electronic commerce, such differences of result between a permanent establishment and a subsidiary are likely to be greater and more frequent in the e-commerce context because of the prevalence of intangibles, especially those based on ideas. These issues are discussed in greater detail in the CFA general discussion draft, and the Committee on Fiscal Affairs is actively considering the issues relating to the attribution of profit to permanent establishments. Views from the public are invited on these important issues.

88.   Finally, the allocation of costs (for example pursuant to a cost contribution arrangement) may, indeed, be appropriate where the permanent establishment is in existence at the time of the development of the intangible and the enterprise intends to have the permanent establishment make use of the intangible, when and if developed.

Hardware
89.   Finally, the facts and circumstances (including any internal documentation) regarding the transfer of the hardware to the permanent

establishment must be examined in order to determine the character of such a transfer ("dealing") and especially the division of the risks and responsibilities of ownership between the parties. Under the WH, the determination must be made by making a full examination of the facts and circumstances surrounding the change in use, including the subsequent conduct of the parties and any relevant documentation. The intent of the enterprise in effecting this change of use, as documented and as corroborated by its conduct, will be relevant in determining the nature of the dealing. Once the full facts and circumstances have been established, the nature of the inter-branch dealing (sale, lease or licence) would be determined by reference to the nature of comparable transactions between independent enterprises. In this context, it may be relevant to establish whether the enterprise itself owns the assets, leases it or rents it from an independent supplier and to know what independent parties would do in similar circumstances. While the documentation of the arrangement will assist in the determination, if the conduct of the parties is inconsistent with this documentation, consideration must be given to the actual conduct of the permanent establishment and the rest of the enterprise in order to establish the true nature of the arrangement. One result of this examination could be to characterise the transfer as a lease arrangement between the head office and the permanent establishment, in which case a notional arm's length lease payment would be deductible in computing the profit of the permanent establishment. Another possible result would be to characterise the dealing as an outright sale, *i.e.* that the head office has disposed of the hardware and that the permanent establishment has acquired it at its fair market value. In such a case, capital cost allowance in accordance with the depreciation system of country B would be deducted in computing the permanent establishment's profit. The issue of how to account for the transfer of tangible property between two parts of a single enterprise is discussed in details in Part I of the CFA general discussion draft, in which the wider issue of attribution of profit to permanent establishments is examined. The question here is whether the above guidance has much relevance to a fact pattern such as this, given the lack of personnel of the permanent establishment, so making any analysis of the intention of the parties is only relevant from the head office perspective.

90.   In the commercial exploitation stage, a dealing assumed to take place under the "independent service provider" model between the permanent establishment and the head office in the form of a service contract notionally concluded between both parties, whereby the permanent establishment is considered to have performed functions on behalf, and for the benefit of the head office. These include hosting a web site, handling transactions with customers and channelling proceeds of transactions to Starco. The value of the fee payable pursuant to this notional contract is to be determined under the arm's length principle.

91.   Therefore, under the "independent service provider" model, the setting up of a server by Starco in country B can be characterised as an initial provision of tangible and intangible property to the permanent establishment in order to enable the permanent establishment to provide a service to the rest of the enterprise. Having established the attributes of the permanent establishment and the nature of its "dealings" with the rest of the enterprise, one can now apply a traditional transfer pricing analysis on such "dealings" in order to determine the arm's length compensation for each dealing. This will determine the quantum of profit attributable to the permanent establishment.

Application of transfer pricing methods

"Contract service provider" model
92.   Under this model, the only arm's length charge to be determined relates to the provision of services to the head office. Remuneration between independent enterprises for such services would take the form of a fee, which reflects the value of the functions performed by it and the relatively riskless nature of the arrangement from its point of view.

93.   The starting point for the analysis would be to examine if there were comparable transactions undertaken by arm's length contract service providers such that a comparable uncontrolled price (CUP) could be applied. The transactions would have to be comparable in terms of the functions performed, assets used and risks (indeed lack of risks) assumed. Views on the likely availability of CUPs are welcome. Where the CUP method cannot be applied reliably, it may be possible to apply a cost plus method to determine an arm's length reward for such a permanent establishment. The costs to be taken into account would be the direct and indirect costs incurred in the permanent establishment in the course of providing the service (rent, insurance, electricity, communication lines, etc.), but would not take into account any capital costs associated with tangible and intangible assets, on the basis that the head office is assumed to retain economic "ownership" of such property. An arm's length profit margin could be found by considering the mark up charged in similar arrangements entered into by independent enterprises. Other transfer pricing methods found in the Guidelines may also be applied where the comparability standard in Chapter 1 can be satisfied.

"Independent service provider" model
94.   In this model, arm's length charges must be established for "dealings" assumed to take place between the permanent establishment and the rest of the enterprise before and during the commercial exploitation stage. Dealings for the former include the provision of the hardware and of intangible property in the form of software by the head office to the permanent establishment.

95.   Application of the arm's length principle requires one to find comparable products and services traded in comparable transactions between independent parties, or at least comparable functions performed by independent parties.

96.   Finding a CUP for both the hardware and the software (to the extent authorised under the Model Tax Convention, as discussed previously) may be possible. However, establishing the arm's length compensation for the transfer of the right to use the software may not be a straightforward exercise, because of the difficulty of finding products that are sufficiently comparable. Where no exact CUP can be found, one could attempt to find the arm's length price for software used for comparable functions.

97.   The costs of the permanent establishment are not limited to the arm's length charge to be recognised in consideration for the use of both tangible and intangible property. Expenses are incurred in the permanent establishment in the form of payment for the use of the premises, the cost of electricity and communication lines, the payment of insurance premiums, etc. Unlike conventional situations, such payments are not actually made out of actual revenue earned by the permanent establishment but are presumably paid by the head office. An argument can be had over whether these costs are the costs of the permanent establishment or costs of the head office incurred for the purpose of the permanent establishment, which must be recognised, pursuant to Article 7(3) of the Model Tax Convention, in computing the permanent establishment's profits. In practice, this is an issue of little consequence since, in either case, such cost should reduce the taxable profit of the permanent establishment.

98.   During the commercial exploitation stage, one must establish an arm's length compensation for the service provided to the head office by the permanent establishment. It may be that independent enterprises, making use of similar hardware and software are in the business of providing similar web hosting services to other enterprises. If such comparable enterprises can be found, a CUP for a similar type of transaction would be the best estimation of an arm's length price. If a CUP is not available, a cost-plus charge for the provision of similar services would be appropriate. Internet service suppliers would be an obvious source of either CUP or comparable gross margins for similar service arrangements, provided adjustments are made to take into account any differences between the services provided by an internet service provider and the permanent establishment. Care would also need to be exercised to ensure that the cost base from which the gross margin is derived is similar to that used for the permanent establishment. Unlike the determination made in the "contract service provider" model, the cost base to be used for purposes of applying the cost plus method would take

into account the notional expenses associated with the transfer to and use by the permanent establishment of the tangible and intangible property contributed by the head office.

99.   The use of a profit method, especially a transaction net margin method (TNMM), should not be overlooked where it is not possible to apply traditional transaction methods reliably. A net margin analysis over costs may be possible.

100.   The above analysis of the "independent service provider" model shows that one needs to posit several intra-company dealings that raise complex valuation issues under the arm's length principle. Furthermore, the arm's length character of such estimates is in doubt under the current interpretation of Article 7. This suggests that this model may not represent the most appropriate or practical model to apply to the fact pattern provided in this section.[8] However, it is not denied that it may be appropriate in different circumstances.

Conclusion

101.   While it is difficult, in abstract, to determine how significant the quantum of profit attributed to Starco's permanent establishment would be, a number of observations can be offered.

102.   Under the "independent service provider" model, the profit margin of the permanent establishment is computed as the difference between the arm's length compensation that can be charged on the market for the service provided to the head office and the arm's length charge that must be recognised for the use of the tangible and intangible property contributed by the head office. Such a calculation is not necessarily indicative of the profit margin that would be earned by an independent enterprise whose business is to provide such services to third parties, given that such an enterprise would likely own the hardware and develop the software itself (see Variation 4). The profit margin of such an independent enterprise would be mostly attributable to the value added associated with the development of software and the renting of either the hardware or of space on a server. It is probably fair to say that the profit

---

[8]   The reader may be left wondering why so much of the analysis is devoted to approaches that may not prove to be practical or appropriate in the circumstances. There are two answers to this question: first, this paper is meant to illustrate the thought process that takes place while performing a functional and factual analysis where the outcome cannot necessarily be anticipated at the outset. Second, whereas the discussion in this note is based on a specific and simple example and, consequently, could allow one to perform precise analysis leading to specific conclusions, reliance on such a specific example is also, by definition, limiting in nature, because one cannot necessarily infer that the analysis and conclusions are of general application. This is why it is useful to identify in this paper the different directions that may be adopted in the course of performing a functional and factual analysis when the fact pattern is different and more complex.

accruing to a typical internet service provider would exceed the profit accruing to the permanent establishment in this variation of the example. An internet service provider will typically host the software developed or acquired by its customer but use its own software (which it has developed or acquired itself) in order to provide a portal into the internet. In this variation of the example, the head office has provided the permanent establishment with all software, including that needed to establish a portal into the internet.

103.   Ultimately, the profit generated by the permanent establishment comes from two main sources. The first source stems from the on-going operation of a package of hardware and software that makes up the server and supports a web site. If the compensation for the transfer of this package from the head office to the permanent establishment were done on arm's length terms, substantially all of the profit associated with the exploitation of such assets would effectively accrue to the head office. The second source relates to the exploitation of marketing intangibles, including "e-commerce marketing intangibles". Again, substantially all of the profits associated with the exploitation of such assets would accrue to the head office provided that the intangibles are "owned" by the head office. This would appear to be the case for marketing intangibles such as the brand but may be less clear cut for "e-commerce marketing intangibles" which are more closely related to the operations of the web site.

104.   This outcome is explicitly achieved under the "contract service provider" model, whereby the profit of the permanent establishment will likely be determined by reference to a cost plus calculation performed on the basis of the direct operating costs incurred in the permanent establishment. Therefore, the computation of the compensation attributable to the permanent establishment specifically ignores the value of the tangible and intangible property used by it, which de facto attributes the reward for such property to the head office.[9]

---

[9]   The server-permanent establishment is peculiar as, unlike more conventional situations, both types of property are not used as input in a human process creating value added – the mere autonomous operation of both types of property creates the value added. For example, where a manufacturing intangible developed by an enterprise is contributed to either a permanent establishment or a subsidiary of the enterprise for commercial exploitation, the resulting value created by the manufacturing function using the intangible is the sum of the value added attributable to the pure manufacturing function and the value added associated with the exploitation of the intangible. Manufacturing absent the intangible would not create the same value and the value could only be extracted by the intangible where it is used in a manufacturing function. In the case of the computer server, the exploitation of the combination of the hardware and software is essentially a passive function, in that no other significant factors of productions need be involved. A possible exception is the use of the information gathering function to create marketing intangibles such as customer lists and e-commerce marketing intangibles. The value of these intangibles will depend respectively on the nature of the information obtained and the operation of the web site. Both of these are a function of the complexity of the relevant software.

105.   Therefore, for this example, the application of the functional and factual analyses described in the guidance on the arm's length principle of Article 9 found in the Guidelines would, in all likelihood, leave the permanent establishment with a quantum of profit that is insignificant relative to either the value of transactions processed through the permanent establishment or the arm's length cost of securing the use of the hardware and software required to ensure the continuous operation of the server without human intervention. An independent enterprise providing the same software and hardware to the permanent establishment would insist on an arm's length reward for the exploitation of both types of property. Under this fact pattern, the permanent establishment is only performing low-level automated functions that make up only a small proportion of the functions necessary to act as a full function retail outlet/distributor or as a full function service provider. The level of profit earned is likely to be commensurately low and be very significantly less than that earned by full function retail outlet/distributors or full function service providers.

106.   Given these observations, the question to be answered is whether the existing international tax policy rules for taxing business profits (Articles 7 and 9 of the OECD Model Tax Convention) allow this result. The guidance on the application of that Article found in the Guidelines applies the arm's length principle of Article 9 without restriction and in a manner based on economic reality. However, although Article 7 contains a provision similar to the arm's length principle of Article 9 [Article 7(2)], the Model Commentary appears to restrict the application of that principle in a number of ways (see previous remarks on the transfer of software and marketing intangible). More details on this issue can be found in the CFA general discussion draft released on 8 February 2001. Views on this issue are welcome.

107.   The prohibition of a deduction in computing the profits of the permanent establishment for an amount equivalent to the market value for using software or intangible property developed by the head office, if mandated under the current interpretation of Article 7, would lead to an over-attribution of profit to the permanent establishment, where the market value exceeds the allocation of costs related to the intangible property in accordance with the current interpretation of Article 7. When undertaking a comparability analysis with transactions between independent enterprises (CUP method), the permanent establishment would be treated as having the right to use the software and the marketing intangible and so the arm's length price would have to reflect the use of such property. Similarly, when making a comparison with gross margins earned by independent enterprises (cost plus or resale price methods), the arm's length gross margin earned by the permanent establishment would reflect the use of the intangible.

VII Appendices

108.   However, it would seem to follow from the above prohibition that, although the permanent establishment would obtain the same price or gross margin as the independents (based on use of the software and marketing intangible), it would be able to earn a higher net profit as it would not have to recognise, in computing its profit for tax purposes, the full market value for using such property (assuming that the market value is greater than historic costs of developing it). In such cases, the permanent establishment would be a "free-rider" as it would be rewarded for functions and activities it had not carried out and that it could never have carried out given its lack of either human or artificial intelligence. In cases where the market value of the intangible is lower than historic costs of developing it, the permanent establishment would earn less profit due to factors outside its control (inefficiency of the head office R&D function).

109.   Another issue that arises is whether the above problems occur when, in last resort situations, profit methods are used such that a net, rather than a gross margin are compared. The comparable net margin will have been computed by deducting operating expenses (including any payments made for the use of intangible property) from the gross margins. To be consistent with the current interpretation of Article 7, would it be necessary to add back any payments for the use of intangible property to arrive at the comparable net margin?

110.   In conclusion, it is questionable whether, under the "independent service provider" model, the current rules for Article 7 are capable of producing a result that leads to an attribution of profit that is fully consistent with the arm's length principle as articulated in the Guidelines (when applied to permanent establishments by analogy). To the extent that they are not, results would differ depending on whether the particular economic function is carried out through a subsidiary or though a permanent establishment. Arguably, such a result is not desirable on tax policy grounds and so the Model Commentary on Article 7 would need to be changed. As described in the section above on Article 7(2) above, a preferable approach might be to apply the arm's length principle of Article 7 in a manner as similar as possible to the guidance on the application of the arm's length principle of Article 9 found in the Guidelines. Views are invited on this important issue in the context of a permanent establishment undertaking e-commerce activities.

Variation 2: Multiple servers

111.   The facts are the same as in the previous example, except for the following modifications:

112.   Starco's web page is hosted on four different servers located in country B (Americas), country C (Western Europe), country D (Eastern Europe and Asia) and Country E (Southern Hemisphere). When a person

attempts to connect to Starco's web site, the person is connected to a given server according to a predetermined procedure, programmed on and managed by the server located in country B, that takes into account the geographical proximity of the person and the traffic on each server. Once a connection has been established between a would-be customer and a given server, all aspects of the transactions are performed on the same server.[10]

113.   The benefits, from Starco's point of view, of relying on multiple servers include: speeding up the customer's access to, and interaction with, the web site; providing extra security for both the enterprise and its clients; and reducing the risks associated with technology breakdowns.

114.   The main relevant difference, from a tax point of view, between this example and the previous example is that the functions that were performed exclusively by Starco's server in country B are now duplicated by several servers. However, the range of functions performed by any one server in respect of a transaction (from the time that the prospective customer establishes communication with Starco's web site until the customer receives delivery of products) remains the same. But the volume of transactions will now be shared among servers in different countries. The existence of several servers performing identical functions contributes to reducing the risks associated with the operation of any given server.

115.   The principles developed in the previous section on Variation 1 remain applicable to this example, although the administrative and compliance issues may be more difficult. The "contract service provider" model, under which profit will likely be attributed to the permanent establishment on the basis of the cost plus method, may be the model that best suits the facts and circumstances. Alternatively, the "independent service provider" model may be contemplated. The functional and factual analysis would determine whether and to what extent the *de facto* pooling of risks among several servers would affect the quantum of reward attributable to each permanent establishment. Of course, the more difficult transfer pricing issues occurring between the head office and the permanent establishment under this model, such as the determination of the proper charge for the right to use the software and marketing intangible, would be increased four-fold.

116.   This example assumes that all the steps of commercial transactions are performed by a single server, once the particular server has been selected. Therefore, no transfer pricing issue arises in connection with "dealings" between two or more server because no such "dealings"

---

[10] Another variation, where different aspects of a transaction are performed by different servers, could also be examined. However, such an assumption raises the threshold issue of whether performance of certain activities and not others would still qualify any of the particular servers as a permanent establishments under Article 5 of the Model Tax Convention.

take place. On the other hand, if one had assumed that the billing of the transaction took place in a server while electronic delivery of a digitised product occurred from another server, one would have had to consider how to allocate the remuneration associated with each step among the different permanent establishments.

Server is part of an existing permanent establishment

117.   Two variations from the initial example are examined briefly where personnel are present in the permanent establishment in country B and are involved in attending the operation of the server. In the first variation, the personnel have installed hardware specified by the head office and software created by the head office in country A. In the second variation, all of the programming and software development is assumed to have taken place within the permanent establishment in country B and on-going improvements to the web site are performed in the permanent establishment.

Variation 3: Technical support staff in permanent establishment

118.   The facts relating to Starco's operations and the characteristics of the server in country B are the same as in the first variation. However, personnel are present in country B to perform the following tasks: ensure the maintenance of the server, perform repairs to the hardware and address any problems affecting the operation of the web site. The personnel are also responsible for handling trouble-shooting with customers or web site visitors worldwide experiencing difficulties with the web site, in particular in connection with online transactions. Finally, the personnel provide after-sales services and support to customers. Interactions with customers or would-be customers either occur on line or, exceptionally, on the telephone.

General considerations

119.   This example moves away from the extreme situation where a combination of tangible and intangible assets can, on their own, constitute a permanent establishment and presents a situation more commonly found in commercial arrangements. One peculiarity remains: contacts between the permanent establishment and customers remain virtual, as they occur on line, as opposed to face-to-face. However, this is not a critical consideration in the following analysis.

Functional analysis and conditions of the hypothesised distinct and separate enterprise

120.   The presence of personnel in the permanent establishment to maintain the continuous operation of the server and to provide technical support to online customers changes the nature of the functions

performed by the respective parts of the enterprise and adds additional functions to the existing routine automated functions already performed by the permanent establishment. Whereas the additional functions were performed by personnel situated in Starco's head office in previous examples, they are now functions performed within the permanent establishment.

121.   A functional and factual analysis would also reveal that personnel in the permanent establishment are required to make use of both tangible assets (for example, computers) and intangible assets (for example, software) over and above those required by the perm anent establishment posited in Variation 1 in order to provide technical services to customers. In both cases, such assets will either have been provided by the enterprise or acquired by personnel of the permanent establishment from third parties. Depending on the nature of the arrangement between the head office and the permanent establishment, the existence of "dealings" between the head office and the permanent establishment may need to be recognised in order to account for the use of the assets of the enterprise by the permanent establishment.

122.   An important consideration to take into account is that the services provided by personnel of the permanent establishment to customers are not separately charged to them. The cost of the provision of services by Starco is internalised in the prices it charges customers for its products. Therefore, any incremental provision of services does not directly increase Starco's revenue – although it may indirectly contribute to increase its market share by gaining a reputation as an efficient e-business because of the service support originating from the permanent establishment and thereby lead to the creation of an e-commerce marketing intangible.

123.   Likewise, the incremental provision of services does not increase Starco's costs, since personnel are basically on stand-by, available at any time to deal with customer's queries.

124.   Given the nature of the operation of the permanent establishment, and in the light of the analysis of the situation described in the previous section on Variation 1, it is unlikely that the functional and comparability analyses would characterise the permanent establishment as undertaking functions, using assets and assuming risks comparable to those of a "retail outlet". Therefore, the following focuses on the two variants of the "service provider" model as being the most likely outcomes of the functional and comparability analyses. Views on whether the retail outlet is an unlikely outcome are particularly invited.

125.   Under this model, the functions performed by the server remain a service provided by the permanent establishment to the rest of the enterprise. The additional functions, the provision of services to Starco's

customers, represent services either provided to the rest of the enterprise or provided to third parties on behalf of the enterprise. The permanent establishment cannot be said to bear significant risk from the provision of such services (except the small risk arising from the fact that the extra arm's length remuneration received for performing additional services may not cover the extra costs of performing those services). As under the previous model, the head office bears the full market risk associated with the possible loss of business due to a failure to help would-be customers. The revenues of the permanent establishment associated with the provision of online services to customers would not be a function of the outcome of performing particular services, but would be structured as a fee for the continuous availability of the service.

126.   As under the first two examples, the functional and factual analysis could reveal that the nature of the arrangement is one similar to that of a "contract service provider". In such cases, the only dealing that needs to be taken into account is the remuneration of the permanent establishment for the services it provides to, and on behalf of, the rest of the enterprise. However, the same analysis could also reveal that the permanent establishment is better characterised as an "independent service provider", fully equipped to provide the services sought by Starco and seeking to cover both capital and operating costs and earn a profit. In such cases, as explained earlier, dealings would need to be recognised with respect to the transfer of tangible and intangible property to the permanent establishment, as well as for the provision of services by it. Comments on the above conclusions would be welcome.

Application of transfer pricing methods

127.   This portion of the analysis is similar to that found in the previous section on Variation 1. However, under this version of the "contract service provider" model, the remuneration for the permanent establishment would be more substantial than under the first two variations, owing to the additional functions performed within the permanent establishment. Where a cost plus method is applied, the cost base by reference to which a cost plus calculation would be performed would reflect the additional direct and indirect costs incurred in the permanent establishment (principally employee compensation). Similarly, the applicable arm's length margin would reflect the different nature and functions of the permanent establishment.

128.   Under the "independent service provider" model, a CUP, if available, would be the best estimation of an arm's length price and should first be sought, assuming that one can determine the market price for services of an identical nature (or of a sufficiently similar nature to allow for adjustments to make it sufficiently comparable) provided on the market by independent suppliers. Where a CUP is not available, a service fee determined on a cost plus basis, based on the gross mark-up

associated with the provision of similar services, would be appropriate. Alternatively, the application of TNMM could be considered if it does not prove possible to apply with sufficient reliability one of the traditional transaction methods. The permanent establishment would also, under this model, be attributed a more significant quantum of profit than under the first two variations, given the additional functions performed therein.

Variation 4: Web site fully developed in permanent establishment

129.   The facts relating to Starco's operations and the characteristics of the server in country B are the same as in Variation 1. However, the history of the creation of the web site differs. It is assumed that the server was set up in 1997 and that personnel in country B performed throughout 1997 and 1998 further developments to the software, gradually upgrading the configuration of the web site to its present form. Significant development costs were incurred during that time within the permanent establishment in country B.

GENERAL CONSIDERATIONS

130.   There is a fundamental difference between this example and the previous ones. In the previous examples, the earnings associated with the development of the software required to create an operational server and a web site in a remote location were clearly attributable to Starco's head office, where all development efforts took place and development costs were incurred.

131.   This example assumes (arguably somewhat unrealistically) that the full development efforts and costs toward the development of the server and the web site were expended in country B, for purposes of subsequently exploiting the server and hosting the web site so developed.[11] Consequently, under the WH the permanent establishment is treated as the economic "owner" of the intangibles. It should be noted that the WH looks to a number of factors, not just where the developments took place, in order to determine which part of the enterprise is the economic "owner" of an intangible. See the CFA general discussion draft for further details. The determination of the economic "owner" of the intangible property impacts significantly on the allocation of earnings attributable to the creation of such property within the enterprise under the arm's length principle.

VII Appendices

---

[11]   In other words, the development was undertaken with the intention of providing a long-term benefit for the PE itself and was not developed on behalf of, or for the benefit of, other parts of Starco.

FUNCTIONAL ANALYSIS AND CONDITIONS OF THE HYPOTHESISED DISTINCT
AND SEPARATE ENTERPRISE

132.　　　Unlike the previous example, tangible and intangible assets
(except for the marketing intangible) are not transferred from the head
office to the permanent establishment. Starco sets up a completely new
operation in country B (presumably because of favourable external
factors such as proximity of similar businesses, the presence of a
fully-trained work force or attractive tax incentives) and capitalises it with
the financial resources required to develop the hardware and software
necessary to launch and operate a commercial web site for the benefit of
Starco.

133.　　　A functional and factual analysis is likely to reveal that the
permanent establishment is in the business of providing services related to
Starco's e-tailing activities. The activities and functions that the
permanent establishment carries out in the commercial exploitation phase
are unchanged in comparison with Variation 3. The key difference is that
the permanent establishment can be considered, for tax purposes, to
utilise software over which it has economic ownership in order to carry
out those functions and this situation should be reflected in the
attribution of profit.

134.　　　The development phase leading to the creation of a web site
entails the development of intangible property, akin to a research and
development project. Following the guidance in the section on
Article 7(2), on determining the divisions of responsibilities, risk and
benefits of a transaction in the absence of contractual terms, the financial
risk associated with this development of the software was incurred in the
permanent establishment. Because the permanent establishment is
considered to be the economic "owner" of the web site, it follows that the
economic benefit derived from the commercial exploitation of the web
site should accrue to the permanent establishment. That is, the permanent
establishment would be considered, under the separate enterprise fiction
required by Article 7 of the Model Tax Convention, to be the economic
owner of the software that supports the web site. This can be contrasted
to the example in Variation 1 where the permanent establishment could
not be considered to be the economic owner of these intangibles. In that
example, the profit margin of the permanent establishment was computed
either on a cost plus basis or as the difference between (a) the arm's length
compensation for the service provided to the head office and (b) the arm's
length charge payable for the use of the tangible and intangible property
contributed by the head office. In the present variation of the example, the
latter element would be nil (no dealings would need to be taken into
account) or at least much reduced so that the compensation to the
permanent establishment comprise (a), net of the costs of development of
the software incurred by the permanent establishment.

135.   The permanent establishment can be seen to derive profit from the exploitation of tangible and intangible property that it notionally "owns", in an economic sense. Unlike the issue raised in the discussion under Variation 1 regarding the internal transfer of software, there is no doubt that this framework of analysis is consistent with Article 7 and its current interpretation found in the OECD Model Commentary. Therefore, the profit of the permanent establishment should be the reward that a separate independent entity exploiting the same "package" of assets would be expected to earn. However, similar problems with Article 7 would arise where the permanent establishment makes its intangible property available to other parts of Starco, for example where new server/web sites are set up in other jurisdictions.

136.   A situation in between those described under Variation 1 and this section, whereby some of the development work towards the creation of, say, software, would be undertaken at head office and some subsequent development would take place within the permanent establishment, could also be imagined. The basic analysis developed in both sections would remain applicable: an appropriate proportion of the profit directly associated with the commercial exploitation of that software would be attributed to the head office and another would be attributable to the permanent establishment. The appropriate proportion would reflect the relative value of the contribution made by the permanent establishment and by the head office towards the development of the software.

APPLICATION OF TRANSFER PRICING METHODS

137.   The best estimate of the profit to be attributed to the permanent establishment would be obtained from the service fee that similar operations conducted by independent enterprises would charge for a similar service (a CUP). It may be possible, for this purpose, to find operations with similar characteristics, or with a sufficient degree of comparability to permit relevant adjustments to be made. It is useful to compare this with the service typically provided by an internet service provider. In this variation it is probably fair to say that the reward to the permanent establishment would exceed that expected to be earned by a typical internet service provider. The latter will typically host the software developed or acquired by its customer but use its own software (which it has developed or acquired itself) in order to provide a portal into the internet. In this variation the permanent establishment does more than this: it develops the software that the "customer" has on its server as well as provides a portal into the internet. Nevertheless, an internet service provider may provide a reasonable comparable in this case provided that sufficiently reliable adjustments can be made to compensate for functional differences.

138.   Where a CUP for the service fee is not available, other transfer pricing methods authorised by the Guidelines would have to be applied.

These may include profit methods that require the difficult task of arriving at an arm's length valuation of the return on the intangible property used in Starco's business.

Conclusions

139.   This discussion paper has provided a detailed analysis of the issues surrounding the attribution of profit to different types of permanent establishments involved in the "e-tailing" business of an enterprise. It is recognised that electronic commerce is not limited to "e-tailing" and that other types of business models ("B2B", auctioning) exist. It would have been beyond the scope of this discussion paper to analyse the tax implications of all types of business models. However, the general principles developed in this paper, in particular in the case where the permanent establishment operates autonomously without the presence of personnel, is capable of application to other business models. However, these principles may need to be adapted to the particular factual situation.

140.   The foregoing analysis, intended to determine how, and to what extent, one would attribute profit to a permanent establishment involved, with or without the assistance of personnel, in electronic commerce activities, has resulted in the following provisional findings based on the WH:

–   Where, as in Variations 1 and 2, a permanent establishment consists only of a server supporting a web site through which commercial transactions and transmission of digitised products take place, the bulk of the benefit generated by the permanent establishment derives from the exploitation of hardware and software used by the permanent establishment and from marketing intangibles. Under a "contract service provider" arrangement, economic ownership and most risks associated with the property and the marketing intangibles is likely to remain with the head office. Under an "independent service provider" arrangement, where the head office transferred such a package of assets to the permanent establishment, an arm's length charge in consideration for such transfer would attribute substantially all of the profits directly associated with such a package to the head office, thereby leaving comparatively little profit to the permanent establishment, in relation to the value of the commercial activities carried on through it. The computer server in the permanent establishment is only performing low-level automated support functions that make up only a small proportion of the functions necessary to act as a full function retail outlet/distributor or as a full function service provider. The level of profit earned is likely to be commensurately low and be very significantly less than that earned by full function retail outlet/distributors or full function service providers. However, issues do arise as to whether some of the return related to the use of "e-commerce marketing intangibles" and the assumption of credit risk and technology risks, would be attributed to the permanent establishment on the basis that they are related to the operation of the web site itself and to the functions performed by the permanent establishment.

– Where, as in Variation 3, personnel are present in the permanent establishment to ensure the continuous operation of the web site and provide technical support to customers and would-be customers, the permanent establishment should be expected to be attributed the profit associated with such service functions, in accordance with the arm's length principle. However, the profit directly associated with the exploitation of the hardware and software created by the enterprise and from marketing intangibles would continue to be largely attributed to the head office, as under the previous examples.

– Finally, where, as in Variation 4, the hardware and software is entirely developed and constructed by personnel of the permanent establishment such that the permanent establishment is treated as the economic owner of the intangible property, the profit directly associated with the commercial operation of such assets is attributable, under the principles of Article 7 and the arm's length principle, to the permanent establishment. Where the software is developed partially by head office and partially by the permanent establishment, the relevant proportion, determined under the arm's length principle, of the profit directly associated with the commercial exploitation of that software is attributable to the permanent establishment. Such a proportion would reflect the relative value of the contribution made by the permanent establishment and by the head office.

141.   The analysis of the first variation has demonstrated the difficulty of developing a factual and functional analysis in the extreme case where a computer server is considered to constitute a permanent establishment and to apply the arm's length principle. In particular, it can be difficult to determine which part of the enterprise should be treated as the economic "owner" of "e-commerce marketing intangibles" that are related to the operations of the web site itself. It may also be difficult to apply the arm's length principle to "dealings" involving the transfer of intangible property between two parts of an enterprise, as valuation for this type of property, in particular finding suitable comparable transactions, can be challenging. Further, one of the key, and most difficult determination that has to be made in the permanent establishment context relates to the assumption of risks and the allocation of risks assumed by the enterprise as a whole to its various parts. The approach generally taken under the WH is to apply the approach taken for associated enterprises, *i.e.* the concept of contractual terms, by analogy to the relationships between, say, the permanent establishment and head office. This requires an analysis of the conduct of the parties

and of the economic relationships that generally govern the relationships between independent enterprises. Where the permanent establishment lacks personnel, it is difficult to apply this approach. One possibility might be to say that it is not really possible for the permanent establishment to assume risks except those that arise as a direct result of the functions it performs. For example, where the permanent establishment accepts and settles customer transactions, it could be viewed as assuming the credit risk associated with such transactions.

142.   Issues similar to those described in this discussion paper would arise in the situation where the server is owned and operated by a subsidiary of Starco, such that the paradigm moves from Article 7 to Article 9 of the OECD Model Tax Convention. Indeed, the conclusions reached above are based more on an analysis of the arm's length principle of Article 9 (as elaborated by the Guidelines) than on the Commentary to Article 7. The conclusions may therefore not always be consistent with the current interpretation of Article 7 of the Model Tax Convention.

143.   However, as already noted, the current interpretation of Article 7 does not appear to produce a result that is consistent with the arm's length principle as developed in the Guidelines where "dealings" involving intangible property must be taken into account in attributing profit to the permanent establishment. Further, the result will differ depending on whether the particular economic function is carried out through a subsidiary or though a permanent establishment. Such a result is not desirable on tax policy grounds and may require the Model Commentary on Article 7 to be changed. A preferable approach would be to apply the arm's length principle of Article 7 in a manner as similar as possible to the guidance on the application of the arm's length principle of Article 9 found in the Guidelines. The extent to which this approach is desirable and, if so, how it might best be achieved, is under active consideration by the Committee on Fiscal Affairs.

144.   This discussion paper does not pretend to offer the definitive answer to the question of the attribution of profit to the type of permanent establishments examined therein. The purpose of this draft discussion paper is to elicit a discussion of the relevant issues and to invite interested parties to share their views on this important subject for consideration by the Business Profit TAG and by the Committee on Fiscal Affairs.

APPENDIX F

EXTRACT FROM HMRC BUSINESS INCOME MANUAL

BIM35800 – CAPITAL/REVENUE DIVIDE – COMPUTER SOFTWARE: CONTENTS

This chapter explains the treatment of expenditure on computer software in the context of the capital/revenue divide and covers the following:

BIM35801	Purchased on or after 10 March 1992 – developed in-house after 31 December 1996
BIM35805	Purchased before 10 March 1992
BIM35810	Treatment on or after 10 March 1992
BIM35815	General considerations

BIM35801 – CAPITAL/REVENUE DIVIDE – COMPUTER SOFTWARE: PURCHASED ON OR AFTER 10 MARCH 1992 – DEVELOPED IN-HOUSE AFTER 31 DECEMBER 1996

Availability of capital allowances

Following the enactment of CAA90/S67A (now CAA01/S71), capital allowances became available for capital expenditure on "a right to use or otherwise deal with" computer software for the purposes of the trade. For guidance on computer software expenditure before 10 March 1992 see BIM35805 and for expenditure on or after that date see BIM35810 – BIM35815.

The main changes of emphasis on or after 10 March 1992 are that:

1. for expenditure on computer software licences on or after 10 March 1992 on which capital allowances will be available you should give more critical consideration to whether lump sums paid out for the licences are in law capital expenditure,

2.   where a single payment is made to purchase computer hardware plus a licence to use the accompanying software we now take the view that the expenditure should be apportioned except where that exercise will not have significant tax consequences.

In some cases the treatment of expenditure on software will have been agreed under the practice set out in BIM35805. For agreements in relation to expenditure before 10 March 1992 you may continue to allow deductions in the accounts that arise in consequence. But for expenditure incurred on or after 10 March 1992, you should refer to the guidance in BIM35810 onwards.

In-house software development costs

For in-house computer software expenditure, see BIM35820 to BIM35865. The guidance therein should normally be applied to expenditure incurred after 31 December 1996. It may also be convenient to agree the treatment of earlier expenditure by reference to the guidance. But where its application would lead to treatment of software development expenditure that is inconsistent with a previously agreed approach, you need not insist on applying it to expenditure incurred in 1996 or earlier. Nor need the guidance be applied to post-1996 expenditure in relation to a project the treatment of which was agreed in 1996 or earlier.

For a reference to legislation which from 1 April 2002 may require the accounting entries in respect of in-house software development costs to be followed in computations of income for CT, even if they are of a capital nature see, however, BIM35501.

BIM35805 – CAPITAL/REVENUE DIVIDE – COMPUTER SOFTWARE: PURCHASED BEFORE 10 MARCH 1992

Capital expenditure qualifies for capital allowances: revenue expenditure allowed as incurred

Expenditure on computer software incurred before 10 March 1992 should normally be dealt with as set out in the paragraphs below. If in any particular case you do not consider that this provides a reasonable result, guidance should be sought from CT&VAT (Technical).

Software acquired with associated hardware or acquired separately – capital or revenue expenditure?

When software is acquired along with the associated hardware (and the expenditure on acquisition of the system is capital expenditure) you should normally accept that the system as a whole qualifies for capital allowances as plant. But when software is acquired separately, you should consider whether the expenditure is revenue or capital. If the expected life of the software is sufficiently short for the expenditure to be regarded as revenue, the timing of the deduction for tax purposes will normally follow correct accounting principles (see BIM31090 onwards). Whether or not the cost of software can be regarded as revenue expenditure will depend on the circumstances of individual cases, but an expected life of two years or less may be taken as a broad guideline for treating the expenditure as revenue.

Capital expenditure

If the expenditure is capital, it will usually be regarded as qualifying for capital allowances as plant, provided that the software is sufficiently durable to satisfy the "permanent employment in the trade" test to be regarded as plant. It will satisfy that test if it has an expected life of more than two years. Alternatively, if the expenditure has been amortised in the accounts over a period related to the expected life of the software, this treatment should normally be followed for tax purposes.

Payments for licence to use software

Regular payments for a licence to use software will normally be revenue expenditure, allowable as they are incurred. A lump sum payment for a licence will not, however, necessarily be capital. You should consider the terms of the agreement and the expected life of the software. Because the software will not belong to the licensee, capital allowances are not available for this type of expenditure.

BIM35810 – CAPITAL/REVENUE DIVIDE – COMPUTER SOFTWARE: TREATMENT ON OR AFTER 10 MARCH 1992

Tax Bulletin 9F

Computer software expenditure on or after 10 March 1992 should be dealt with along the lines of the article in TB9F (November 1993), which is reproduced below.

Text of TB9F

Software acquired under licence

This is the way that nearly all off-the-shelf software is acquired nowadays. The treatment of expenditure of this nature depends on the form the consideration for the licence takes.

Regular payments akin to a rental

Payments of this kind are revenue. The timing of deductions is governed by correct accounting practice which normally requires the rentals to be spread over the useful life of the software in accordance with the fundamental accruals concept in SSAP2 (see BIM31030). What is correct accounting practice is ultimately a question of law but the courts are heavily influenced by current generally acceptable practice.

Lump sum

The first question to be asked here is whether the licence is a capital asset in the trade of the licensee. In broad terms a licence is a capital asset if it has a sufficiently enduring nature. This approach has to be applied by reference to the function of the licensed software in the context of the licensee's trade. Very often the expectation will be that the software will function as a tool of the trade for a period of several years. On the other hand, the benefit to be obtained by the licensee in question may be sufficiently transitory to stamp the payment as revenue even though the licence granted is for an indefinite period.

No simple rule of thumb covering every business situation can be successfully devised but, in any event, where software is expected to have a useful economic life of less than two years Inspectors will accept that the expenditure is revenue. In these circumstances the timing of the deduction will depend on the correct accounting treatment in the same way as it does for regular payments.

Where the licensed software functions as a capital asset of the licensee's trade capital allowances on plant and machinery will be due under CAA01/S71. This will be the case whether or not the software comes in a corporeal medium (such as on "floppy discs") separate from the licensee's computer hardware. A short life asset election may be made where appropriate. Computer software is not defined for capital allowances purposes and therefore has its normal meaning which is wide and covers both programs and data (for example books stored in digital form).

Equipment acquired as a package

Often computer hardware and the licence to use software are purchased as a package for a single payment. In these circumstances the expenditure between hardware and software should be apportioned. Capital allowances under the ordinary plant and machinery rules will be due on the expenditure attributable to the hardware. The treatment of the balance of the expenditure, attributable to the software licence, will depend on the considerations described above. Where, however, both the hardware and software are acquired on capital account and the expenditure all goes into the general machinery and plant "pool", apportionment will not in practice be necessary.

Software owned outright

Most widely marketed software is licensed to users and not sold to them outright. But some, particularly larger, concerns may develop their own software. The treatment of expenditure on software acquired outright follows the same principles as those governing the treatment of licensed software. In particular, where the expenditure concerned (including salaries of in-house computer professionals) is capital or revenue again depends on the economic function of the software in the trade in question as it does for licences acquired for lump sums.

BIM35815 – CAPITAL/REVENUE DIVIDE – COMPUTER SOFTWARE: GENERAL CONSIDERATIONS

Do not contend that software with less than a two year life is capital

Unless you can show that periodical payments are instalments of a capital sum (see below for what constitutes capital expenditure in this context) such payments are deductible. The timing of relief follows generally acceptable accounting practice whereby expenditure is charged against profits in accordance with the accruals concept in FRS18 over the shorter of the useful life of the asset or the term of the licence (see BIM31030). The central role of accountancy in timing matters was re-affirmed by the Court Of Appeal in *Gallagher v Jones* [1993] 66TC77 – (see BIM35201).

You are most likely to encounter difficulties where the payment profile under a licence is front-end loaded and it is argued that, for tax at least, the expenditure should not be spread over the shorter of the useful life of the software or the length of the licence.

TB9F (now in BIM35810) explained that the treatment of a single payment for a software licence as capital expenditure or revenue depends on the rôle in economic terms that the software plays in the business concerned. Lord Wilberforce's judgement in *Strick v Regent Oil Co Ltd* [1965] 43TC1 (on page 55C – see BIM35560) is authority for this approach.

Lump sum payments for licences

On this view it would be wrong to place too great an emphasis on the intangible nature of software (as a set of instructions in digital form and therefore as intellectual property). What the software achieves for the

VII Appendices

business concerned should be the central consideration. For most businesses (apart of course from those dealing in items of this kind) the software functions as a tool of the trade in the same way as the computer hardware itself. Neither can function without the other.

It follows from Lord Wilberforce's approach that decided cases involving expenditure on the acquisition of legal rights (such as *Bolam v Regent Oil Co Ltd* [1956] 37TC56) – see BIM35555) are of very limited relevance. Rather, a lump sum payment for a licence can reasonably be viewed as analogous to a premium for a lease of a tangible capital asset like land. Such a payment is itself capital on the authority of *MacTaggart v B & E Strump* [1925] 10TC17 – see BIM43265 and BIM35005 for discussion of the distinction between capital and revenue generally.

You should not contend that software with an expected useful life of less than two years is capital. But you should not accept that a particular piece of software has such a limited life solely because updates appear at frequent intervals. The issue is whether the business concerned in fact trades up to the new versions at intervals, which are short enough to give a particular version only a transitory value to that business.

In selecting for challenge cases where expenditure is charged immediately to revenue, you should bear in mind that the advantage obtained is wholly one of timing.

Software owned outright

The treatment of expenditure on software owned outright (often developed in-house) follows that on licences. In the case of software developed in-house the fact that the expenditure may take the form of such recurring items as salaries paid to computer programmers does not stop it from being capital. In *McVeigh v Arthur Sanderson & Sons Ltd* [1968] 45TC273 it was clear that part of the salaries of staff engaged in producing wallpaper and fabric designs was attributable to the capital cost of the physical piece of plant (the printing etc blocks). These staff costs are broadly comparable with the salaries of staff producing software. Where the nature of the advantage obtained by the expenditure makes it borderline, the recurring nature of the expenditure may tip the balance towards revenue treatment – see Lord Wilberforce's comments in *Strick v Regent Oil Co Ltd* [1965] 43TC1 on page 56C (see BIM35560).

In the normal way the ordinary recurring expenditure of a concern's computer services department will not be capital unless some major new project can be identified. Expenditure on salaries etc of staff engaged on making changes to computer systems, which can at most be viewed as piecemeal improvements, is unlikely to be capital.

The treatment of expenditure in a trader's accounts as capital or revenue is only of marginal relevance to the tax treatment. But, where the expenditure is revenue, the accounting treatment is central to the timing of relief – see regular payments for licences above. In particular where expenditure has been capitalised under SSAP13 ("Accounting for Research and Development") the contention that a deduction should be given in the tax computation for expenditure as it is incurred should be resisted. Instead you should argue that the Case I deduction should be equal to the charge for the amortised expenditure in the trader's accounts.

VII Appendices

APPENDIX G

DEFINITION OF MICRO, SMALL AND MEDIUM-SIZED ENTERPRISES ADOPTED BY THE EUROPEAN COMMISSION

Commission Recommendation 2003/361/EC of 6 May 2003 concerning the definition of micro, small and medium-sized enterprises, OJ L124/39, 20/5/2003

ANNEX

Title I
Definition of micro, small and medium-sized enterprises adopted by the Commission

Article 1

Enterprise

> An enterprise is considered to be any entity engaged in an economic activity, irrespective of its legal form. This includes, in particular, self-employed persons and family businesses engaged in craft or other activities, and partnerships or associations regularly engaged in an economic activity.

Article 2

Staff headcount and financial ceilings determining enterprise categories

> 1.   The category of micro, small and medium-sized enterprises (SMEs) is made up of enterprises which employ fewer than 250 persons and which have an annual turnover not exceeding EUR 50 million, and/or an annual balance sheet total not exceeding EUR 43 million.

> 2.   Within the SME category, a small enterprise is defined as an enterprise which employs fewer than 50 persons and whose annual turnover and/or annual balance sheet total does not exceed EUR 10 million.

> 3.   Within the SME category, a microenterprise is defined as an enterprise which employs fewer than 10 persons and whose annual turnover and/or annual balance sheet total does not exceed EUR 2 million.

Article 3

Types of enterprise taken into consideration in calculating staff numbers and financial amounts

1. An 'autonomous enterprise' is any enterprise which is not classified as a partner enterprise within the meaning of paragraph 2 or as a linked enterprise within the meaning of paragraph 3.

2. 'Partner enterprises' are all enterprises which are not classified as linked enterprises within the meaning of paragraph 3 and between which there is the following relationship: an enterprise (upstream enterprise) holds, either solely or jointly with one or more linked enterprises within the meaning of paragraph 3, 25 % or more of the capital or voting rights of another enterprise (downstream enterprise).

However, an enterprise may be ranked as autonomous, and thus as not having any partner enterprises, even if this 25 % threshold is reached or exceeded by the following investors, provided that those investors are not linked, within the meaning of paragraph 3, either individually or jointly to the enterprise in question:

(a)   public investment corporations, venture capital companies, individuals or groups of individuals with a regular venture capital investment activity who invest equity capital in unquoted businesses ('business angels'), provided the total investment of those business angels in the same enterprise is less than EUR 1,250,000;

(b)   universities or non-profit research centres;

(c)   institutional investors, including regional development funds;

(d)   autonomous local authorities with an annual budget of less than EUR 10 million and fewer than 5,000 inhabitants.

3. 'Linked enterprises' are enterprises which have any of the following relationships with each other:

(a)   an enterprise has a majority of the shareholders' or members' voting rights in another enterprise;

(b)   an enterprise has the right to appoint or remove a majority of the members of the administrative, management or supervisory body of another enterprise;

(c)   an enterprise has the right to exercise a dominant influence over another enterprise pursuant to a contract entered into with that enterprise or to a provision in its memorandum or articles of association;

(d)   an enterprise, which is a shareholder in or member of another enterprise, controls alone, pursuant to an agreement with other shareholders in or members of that enterprise, a majority of shareholders' or members' voting rights in that enterprise.

There is a presumption that no dominant influence exists if the investors listed in the second subparagraph of paragraph 2 are not involving themselves directly or indirectly in the management of the enterprise in question, without prejudice to their rights as stakeholders.

Enterprises having any of the relationships described in the first subparagraph through one or more other enterprises, or any one of the investors mentioned in paragraph 2, are also considered to be linked.

Enterprises which have one or other of such relationships through a natural person or group of natural persons acting jointly are also considered linked enterprises if they engage in their activity or in part of their activity in the same relevant market or in adjacent markets.

An 'adjacent market' is considered to be the market for a product or service situated directly upstream or downstream of the relevant market.

4. Except in the cases set out in paragraph 2, second subparagraph, an enterprise cannot be considered an SME if 25 % or more of the capital or voting rights are directly or indirectly controlled, jointly or individually, by one or more public bodies.

5. Enterprises may make a declaration of status as an autonomous enterprise, partner enterprise or linked enterprise, including the data regarding the ceilings set out in Article 2. The declaration may be made even if the capital is spread in such a way that it is not possible to determine exactly by whom it is held, in which case the enterprise may declare in good faith that it can legitimately presume that it is not owned as to 25 % or more by one enterprise or jointly by enterprises linked to one another. Such declarations are made without prejudice to the checks and investigations provided for by national or Community rules.

Article 4

Data used for the staff headcount and the financial amounts and reference period

1. The data to apply to the headcount of staff and the financial amounts are those relating to the latest approved accounting period and calculated on an annual basis. They are taken into account from the date of closure of the accounts. The amount selected for the turnover is calculated excluding value added tax (VAT) and other indirect taxes.

2. Where, at the date of closure of the accounts, an enterprise finds that, on an annual basis, it has exceeded or fallen below the headcount or financial ceilings stated in Article 2, this will not result in the loss or acquisition of the status of medium-sized, small or microenterprise unless those ceilings are exceeded over two consecutive accounting periods.

3. In the case of newly established enterprises whose accounts have not yet been approved, the data to apply is to be derived from a bona fide estimate made in the course of the financial year.

Article 5

Staff headcount

The headcount corresponds to the number of annual work units (AWU), i.e. the number of persons who worked fulltime within the enterprise in question or on its behalf during the entire reference year under consideration. The work of persons who have not worked the full year, the work of those who have worked part-time, regardless of duration, and the work of seasonal workers are counted as fractions of AWU. The staff consists of:

(a)   employees;

(b)   persons working for the enterprise being subordinated to it and deemed to be employees under national law;

(c)   owner-managers;

(d)   partners engaging in a regular activity in the enterprise and benefiting from financial advantages from the enterprise.

Apprentices or students engaged in vocational training with an apprenticeship or vocational training contract are not included as staff. The duration of maternity or parental leaves is not counted.

Article 6

Establishing the data of an enterprise

1. In the case of an autonomous enterprise, the data, including the number of staff, are determined exclusively on the basis of the accounts of that enterprise.

2. The data, including the headcount, of an enterprise having partner enterprises or linked enterprises are determined on the basis of the accounts and other data of the enterprise or, where they exist, the consolidated accounts of the enterprise, or the consolidated accounts in which the enterprise is included through consolidation.

To the data referred to in the first subparagraph are added the data of any partner enterprise of the enterprise in question situated immediately upstream or downstream from it. Aggregation is proportional to the percentage interest in the capital or voting rights (whichever is greater). In the case of cross-holdings, the greater percentage applies.

To the data referred to in the first and second subparagraph is added 100 % of the data of any enterprise, which is linked directly or indirectly to the enterprise in question, where the data were not already included through consolidation in the accounts.

3.   For the application of paragraph 2, the data of the partner enterprises of the enterprise in question are derived from their accounts and their other data, consolidated if they exist. To these is added 100 % of the data of enterprises which are linked to these partner enterprises, unless their accounts data are already included through consolidation.

For the application of the same paragraph 2, the data of the enterprises which are linked to the enterprise in question are to be derived from their accounts and their other data, consolidated if they exist. To these is added, pro rata, the data of any possible partner enterprise of that linked enterprise, situated immediately upstream or downstream from it, unless it has already been included in the consolidated accounts with a percentage at least proportional to the percentage identified under the second subparagraph of paragraph 2.

4.   Where in the consolidated accounts no staff data appear for a given enterprise, staff figures are calculated by aggregating proportionally the data from its partner enterprises and by adding the data from the enterprises to which the enterprise in question is linked.

Title II
Sundry provisions

Article 7

Statistics

The Commission will take the necessary measures to present the statistics that it produces in accordance with the following size-classes of enterprises:

(a)   0 to 1 person;

(b)   2 to 9 persons;

(c)   10 to 49 persons;

(d)   50 to 249 persons.

Article 8

References

1.   Any Community legislation or any Community programme to be amended or adopted and in which the term 'SME', 'microenterprise', 'small enterprise' or 'medium-sized enterprise', or any other similar term occurs, should refer to the definition contained in this Recommendation.

2.   As a transitional measure, current Community programmes using the SME definition in Recommendation 96/280/EC will continue to be implemented for the benefit of the enterprises which were considered SMEs when these programmes were adopted. Legally binding commitments entered into by the Commission on the basis of such programmes will remain unaffected.

Without prejudice to the first subparagraph, any amendment of the SME definition within the programmes can be made only by adopting the definition contained in this Recommendation in accordance with paragraph 1.

Article 9

Revision

On the basis of a review of the application of the definition contained in this Recommendation, to be drawn up by 31 March 2006, and taking account of any amendments to Article 1 of Directive 83/349/EEC on the definition of linked enterprises within the meaning of that Directive, the Commission will, if necessary, adapt the definition contained in this Recommendation, and in particular the ceilings for turnover and the balance-sheet total in order to take account of experience and economic developments in the Community.

APPENDIX H

MANAGEMENT GUIDELINES PROTOCOL

In managing a company from a non-UK country, the guidelines outlined below should be followed in relation to UK-based activities. Failure to follow these principles could result in the company potentially being treated as tax resident in the UK rather than in its country of incorporation for UK corporation tax purposes and/or trading from a permanent establishment in the UK, as well as treating its supplies as being made from a UK establishment for VAT purposes. Separate advice should be taken in any other jurisdiction in which the company is operating.

(1) Ideally there should be no UK tax resident directors on the board of directors of the non-resident company but, as that may be impractical, extra care should be taken to ensure that it can be shown that no discussions concerning the management and control of the company's business matters take place involving UK resident directors whilst in the UK, for example, there should be no e-mails or letters going to or from UK directors discussing such matters other than anything which is clearly advice for the board to consider at a duly held board meeting outside the UK.

(2) All key business decisions should be made in the country of incorporation of the company: in a board meeting if it is a strategic decision and by a local non-UK director if it does not need separate board approval. Where there is a UK resident director, care must be taken to ensure that there is no way that he can be regarded as the directing mind making all the decisions in the UK or giving instructions prior to meetings which are then merely executed at a formal board meeting in the country of incorporation of the company. This is particularly relevant where a UK resident director is also the principal shareholder.

(3) Board packs/agendas and other papers should emanate from a local non-UK director, who should also call the meeting. No UK tax resident director should chair a board meeting of the non-resident company, by telephone or otherwise.

(4) Board meetings should be held only in the country of incorporation of the non-resident company, and the majority, if not all, of the

non-resident company's directors should be physically present at such meetings. The majority of attendees must not consist of UK tax resident directors. Minority UK-based attendance by conference call or electronic link from the UK should be acceptable provided that the majority of directors are in the country of incorporation of the company and/or there are more directors physically present in the country of incorporation than are dialling in from any other country. UK-based directors should, however, attend in person as many meetings in the country of incorporation of the company as possible, and if the decision-making powers of the UK-based directors are greater or have more significant influence over a decision to be made than other directors, then it would be preferable for the UK-based directors to be physically present in the non-resident company's country of incorporation.

(5) Board meetings should actually consider issues and not rubber-stamp decisions already made. In particular, the board must give genuine consideration to the proposals put forward by the shareholders of the non-resident company and not merely pass them automatically. This means that strategic documents must be subject to prior review and approval by the board. The constitutional documents of the non-resident company should be drafted so that decisions of the non-resident company can only be made at board meetings and those decisions should be by majority. The board should oversee the implementation of any proposals concerning the non-resident company's business.

(6) Care must be taken that there is no person 'usurping' the board of directors of the non-resident company, such that the board cannot be said to control the company. No director should be exercising a degree of control to be able to bind the non-resident company outside of its country of incorporation, without any local director involvement. This can occur if one director exercises the highest level of control of the company alone, which could result in the tax authorities regarding that person as managing the company. Directors who are resident of the country in which the company is incorporated must be involved in more than administrative activities/matters.

(7) Board meetings should be properly minuted. The minutes should record that the board would not countenance an action that was improper and not in the best interests of the non-resident company.

(8) Day-to-day company activities should take place in the country of incorporation of the company, for example, issuing payment directions to banks, completing paperwork.

(9)   All contracts, commercial agreements, investment agreements and corporate documents/resolutions to be entered into by the non-resident company should be approved by the board or local director (if appropriate) and signed in the country of incorporation of the company.

(10) Officers should not enter into or sign contracts for the non-resident company or hold themselves out as contracting for the non-resident company while in the UK, nor should they hold themselves out as if they were a local office/agent of the non-resident company in the UK (or in other jurisdictions).

(11) A clear and complete document trail should be kept in the country of incorporation of the company: constitutional documents of the non-resident company, complete set of board/company minutes and other internal correspondence, complete set of documents circulated before each board meeting, copy evidence of any advice and/or reports sought by directors in arriving at board decisions, a proper record of travel schedules to the country in which the company is incorporated, who attended board meetings, e-tickets and boarding cards of every director who attended board meetings; a record of texts and e-mails passing between directors of the non-resident company relating to company/business matters; telephone bills, fax printouts etc; invoices and payments for office rental in the country of incorporation of the company; job descriptions, employment contracts of local employees and performance agreements (indicative both of the substance and reality of work performed in the country of incorporation of the company); any contract(s) entered into by the non-resident company; and any contracts(s) signed between the non-resident company and its UK and non-UK establishments.

(12) When considering alternatives to a non-resident company's head office as the establishment most directly concerned with the non-resident company's supplies for UK VAT purposes, the UK authorities state that the following factors will be relevant:

- How are the particular services provided?
- What is the significance of the activities carried out at each establishment in contributing to the services provided?
- Where are the necessary human and technical resources (eg database, technical equipment, office equipment, telephones and so on) for providing the services permanently based?
- Which establishment appears on the relevant contracts, correspondence and invoices?
- Where are the directors or other personnel who entered into the contracts permanently based?

VII Appendices

- Where are decisions taken and controls exercised over the performance of the contracts?

Most/all of the above factors should point to the country of incorporation of the company.

(13) To ensure that the non-resident company's place of belonging does not shift to the UK for UK VAT purposes, the company would need to ensure, for example, that:

- employees of the UK establishment (and any directors based in the UK) do not become a point of contact for customers;
- no payments are taken into/from a UK bank account;
- importantly, as mentioned above, any decisions relating to contracts/terms and conditions continue to be made in the country of incorporation of the company and executed or concluded in the country of incorporation;
- employees of the UK establishment do not undertake any sales activity in the UK or conclude/negotiate terms (eg pricing) with third parties or enter into any contractual relations with third parties;
- preferably, the servers are located outside the UK. The non-resident company should seek to identify where the leased servers are located, and if the server is located elsewhere, the non-resident company should take specific advice as to whether the server(s) could constitute a taxable presence.

(14) The company's address should appear on all business cards, e-mail signatures, correspondence, letterheads, invoices and contracts. Any terms and conditions should refer to the non-resident company in its country of incorporation as operating any website.

(15) Payments collected and sent to hosts should go through a Swiss bank account.

(16) Changes or decisions concerning the terms and conditions of the website or, for example, pricing of the commission should be: (a) documented; and (b) dealt with/made while in the country of incorporation of the company, as evidence that the source of control and decision-making is in the country of incorporation of the company.

This is clearly not an exhaustive list. The *correct mindset* is: all actions or decisions should be taken in the country of incorporation of the company unless advised otherwise in exceptional circumstances. The *incorrect mindset* is: all decisions or actions shall be taken wherever the directors want unless they are advised to take them where the company is incorporated. It should be borne in mind that ideally all decisions relating to management and control should be taken by the company's board at board meetings in the country of incorporation of the company, at which all directors participate by attending in person. The further one moves away from this, the greater the risk of challenge from the tax authorities.

APPENDIX I

USEFUL INTERNET SITES FOR E-COMMERCE

INTERNATIONAL ORGANISATIONS

OECD: www.oecd.org

International Chamber of Commerce: www.iccwbo.org

International Monetary Fund: www.imf.org

International Fiscal Association: www.ifa.nl/

World Intellectual Property Organization: www.wipo.int

World Trade Organization: www.wto.org

EUROPE

European Union: http://europa.eu

European Commission: http://ec.europa.eu

European Parliament: www.europarl.europa.eu

European Court of Justice (case-law): http://curia.europa.eu

UNITED KINGDOM

Department for Business Innovation & Skills: www.bis.gov.uk

UK Government Directory: www.direct.gov.uk

Parliament: www.parliament.uk

Legislation: www.legislation.gov.uk

HMRC: www.hmrc.gov.uk

HM Treasury: www.hm-treasury.gov.uk

Institute for Fiscal Studies: www.ifs.org.uk

AUSTRALIA

Australian Tax Office: www.ato.gov.au

Australian Treasury: www.treasury.gov.au

Taxation Institute of Australia: www.taxinstitute.com.au

BELGIUM

Ministry of Finance: http://minfin.fgov.be

CANADA

Canadian Revenue: www.rc.gc.ca

Department of Finance: www.fin.gc.ca

DENMARK

Ministry of Finance: uk.fm.dk

IRELAND

Revenue Service: www.revenue.ie

THE NETHERLANDS

Ministry of Finance: www.minfin.nl

NEW ZEALAND

Revenue service: www.ird.govt.nz

SOUTH AFRICA

Revenue service: www.sars.gov.za

UNITED STATES

Internal Revenue Service: www.irs.gov

Department of the Treasury: www.ustreas.gov

White House: www.whitehouse.gov

VII Appendices

INDEX

References are to paragraph numbers.